PMP®

Project Management Professional Exam

Study Guide

Seventh Edition

PMP®
Project Management Professional Exam
Study Guide
Seventh Edition

Kim Heldman

SYBEX®
A Wiley Brand

Senior Acquisitions Editor: Jeff Kellum
Development Editor: Sara Barry
Technical Editors: Vanina Mangano and Brett Feddersen
Production Editor: Rebecca Anderson
Copy Editor: Elizabeth Welch
Editorial Manager: Pete Gaughan
Production Manager: Tim Tate
Vice President and Executive Group Publisher: Richard Swadley
Vice President and Publisher: Neil Edde
Media Project Manager 1: Laura Moss-Hollister
Media Associate Producer: Doug Kuhn
Media Quality Assurance: Shawn Patrick
Book Designers: Judy Fung and Bill Gibson
Proofreader: Sarah Kaikini, Word One New York
Indexer: Robert Swanson
Project Coordinator, Cover: Katherine Crocker

Cover Designer: Ryan Sneed

Cover Image: © Jeremy Woodhouse / Getty Images

Dear Reader,

Thank you for choosing *PMP: Project Management Professional Exam Study Guide, Seventh Edition*. This book is part of a family of premium-quality Sybex books, all of which are written by outstanding authors who combine practical experience with a gift for teaching.

Sybex was founded in 1976. More than 30 years later, we're still committed to producing consistently exceptional books. With each of our titles, we're working hard to set a new standard for the industry. From the paper we print on, to the authors we work with, our goal is to bring you the best books available.

I hope you see all that reflected in these pages. I'd be very interested to hear your comments and get your feedback on how we're doing. Feel free to let me know what you think about this or any other Sybex book by sending me an email at nedde@wiley.com. If you think you've found a technical error in this book, please visit http://sybex.custhelp.com. Customer feedback is critical to our efforts at Sybex.

Best regards,

Neil Edde
Vice President and Publisher
Sybex, an Imprint of Wiley

To BB, my forever love
—Kimmie

Acknowledgments

Thank you for buying *PMP®: Project Management Professional Exam Study Guide, Seventh Edition* to help you study and prepare for the PMP® exam. Thousands of readers worldwide have used previous editions of this book to help them study for and pass the exam. Because of their success and their recommendations to friends and coworkers, we've been able to keep this study guide up-to-date to match the changes made in *A Guide to the Project Management Body of Knowledge (PMBOK® Guide), Fifth Edition*.

I would also like to thank the countless instructors who use my book in their PMP® prep classes. Over the past few months, I've heard from many of you wondering when this edition would be available. Thank you for your continued interest in using the *Study Guide* in your classes. A big thanks goes to all the PMI® chapters who use this book in their classes as well.

A huge thank-you goes to Neil Edde, vice president and publisher at Sybex, for giving me the opportunity to revise and update this edition. Neil took a chance way back when on the first edition of this book. I can't thank him enough for having the foresight at that time to believe in this little-known exam.

This book clearly fits the definition of a project, and the team at Sybex is one of the best project teams you'll ever find. I appreciate all the hard work and dedication everyone on the team put into producing this book. A special thanks goes to Jeff Kellum, acquisitions editor. Jeff and I have worked on several editions of this book together, and I appreciate his diligence and insightful ideas for updates to the book over the years. It's always a pleasure to work with Jeff.

Next, I'd like to thank Sara Barry, development editor, for her diligent work in helping me make this edition the best it can be. She has a very keen eye and her recommendations were always spot on and helped clarify the concepts. A big thanks also goes to Rebecca Anderson, production editor, for all her help on the book. It was great to work with her. And thanks also to Liz Welch, copyeditor, for all her help.

There were many folks involved behind the scenes who also deserve my thanks, including proofreader Sarah Kaikini and indexer Robert Swanson.

Next, I'd like to thank Vanina Mangano, technical editor, for her wealth of suggestions and ideas for new topics I should add to the text. It is always a pleasure to work with Vanina. She is a true professional. Vanina is an instructor and consultant in project management. I highly recommend Vanina's classes and videos if you're looking for additional study materials for the exam.

I have a special heartfelt thanks for Brett Feddersen, who served as the final technical editor on the book. I have had the great pleasure of working with Brett at the State of Colorado in the past and have delighted in our friendship and in watching him stretch and grow professionally while dealing with the many challenges that came his way. If you are ever in need of the best leader or project manager in the world, Brett is your man.

Last, but always the first on my list, is my best friend for a couple of decades and counting, BB. I love you and I would never have accomplished what I have to date without your love and support. You're the best! And I'd be remiss if I didn't also thank Jason and Leah, Noelle, Amanda, and of course the two best granddaughters on the planet, Kate and Juliette, for their support and understanding.

About the Author

Kim Heldman, MBA, PMP® is a Business Relationship Manager for the Regional Transportation District in Denver, CO. Kim is responsible for overseeing technology projects and services related to the Finance and Administration area. She manages and oversees projects with IT components ranging from small in scope and budget to multimillion dollar, multiyear projects. She has over 23 years of experience in information technology project management. Kim has served in a senior leadership role for over 15 years and is regarded as a strategic visionary with an innate ability to collaborate with diverse groups and organizations, instill hope, improve morale, and lead her teams in achieving goals they never thought possible.

In addition to her project management experience, Kim has experience managing enterprise resource planning systems, application development, web development, network operations, infrastructure, security, and customer service teams.

Kim wrote the first edition of *PMP®: Project Management Professional Study Guide*, published by Sybex, in 2002. Since then, thousands of people worldwide have used the *Study Guide* in preparation for the PMP® exam. Kim is also the author of *Project Management JumpStart, Third Edition* and *Project Manager's Spotlight on Risk Management* and coauthor of *CompTIA Project+, Second Edition*. Kim has also published several articles and is currently working on a leadership book.

Most of the Real World Scenarios in the *Study Guide* are based on Kim's real-life experiences. The names and circumstances have been changed to protect the innocent.

Kim continues to write on project management best practices and leadership topics, and she speaks frequently at conferences and events. You can contact Kim at Kim.Heldman@comcast.net. She personally answers all her email.

Contents at a Glance

Contents

Introduction

This book was designed for anyone thinking of taking the Project Management Professional (PMP®) exam sponsored by the Project Management Institute (PMI®). This certification is growing in popularity and demand in all areas of business. PMI® has experienced explosive growth in membership over the last few years, and more and more organizations are recognizing the importance of project management certification.

> Although this book is written primarily for those of you taking the PMP® exam, you can also use this book to study for the Certified Associate in Project Management (CAPM®) exam. The exams are similar in style, and the information covered in this book will help you with either exam.

This book has been updated to reflect the latest edition of *A Guide to the Project Management Body of Knowledge (PMBOK® Guide), Fifth Edition*. It assumes you have knowledge of general project management practices, although not necessarily specific to the *PMBOK® Guide*. It's written so that you can skim through areas you are already familiar with, picking up the specific *PMBOK® Guide* terminology where needed to pass the exam. You'll find that the project management processes and techniques discussed in this book are defined in such a way that you'll recognize tasks you've always done and be able to identify them with the *PMBOK® Guide* process names or methodologies.

PMI® offers the most recognized certification in the field of project management, and this book deals exclusively with its procedures and methods. Project management consists of many methods, each with its own terminology, tools, and procedures. If you're familiar with another organized project management methodology, don't assume you already know the *PMBOK® Guide* processes. I strongly recommend that you learn all of the processes—their key inputs, tools and techniques, and outputs. Take the time to memorize the key terms found at the end of every chapter as well. Sometimes just understanding the definition of a term will help you answer a question. It might be that you've always done that particular task or used the methodology described but called it by another name. Know the name of each process and its primary purpose.

> The process names, inputs, tools and techniques, outputs, and descriptions of the project management process groups and related materials and figures in this chapter are based on content from *A Guide to the Project Management Body of Knowledge (PMBOK® Guide), Fifth Edition* (Sybex, 2010).

What Is the PMP® Certification?

PMI® is the leader and the most widely recognized organization in terms of promoting project management best practices. PMI® strives to maintain and endorse standards and ethics in this field and offers publications, training, seminars, chapters, special interest groups, and colleges to further the project management discipline.

PMI® was founded in 1969 and first started offering the PMP® certification exam in 1984. PMI® is accredited as an American National Standards Institute (ANSI) standards developer and also has the distinction of being the first organization to have its certification program attain International Organization for Standardization (ISO) 9001 recognition.

PMI® boasts a worldwide membership of more than 650,000, with members from 185 countries. Local PMI® chapters meet regularly and allow project managers to exchange information and learn about new tools and techniques of project management or new ways to use established techniques. I encourage you to join a local chapter and get to know other professionals in your field.

Why Become PMP® Certified?

The following benefits are associated with becoming PMP® certified:

- It demonstrates proof of professional achievement.
- It increases your marketability.
- It provides greater opportunity for advancement in your field.
- It raises customer confidence in you and in your company's services.

Demonstrates Proof of Professional Achievement

PMP® certification is a rigorous process that documents your achievements in the field of project management. The exam tests your knowledge of the disciplined approaches, methodologies, and project management practices as described in the *PMBOK® Guide*.

You are required to have several years of experience in project management before sitting for the exam, as well as 35 hours of formal project management education. Your certification assures employers and customers that you are well grounded in project management practices and disciplines. It shows that you have the hands-on experience and a mastery of the processes and disciplines to manage projects effectively and motivate teams to produce successful results.

Increases Your Marketability

Many industries are realizing the importance of project management and its role in the organization. They are also seeing that simply proclaiming a head technician to be a "project manager" does not make it so. Project management, just like engineering, information technology, and a host of other trades, has its own specific qualifications and skills. Certification tells potential employers that you have the skills, experience, and knowledge to drive successful projects and ultimately improve the company's bottom line.

A certification will always make you stand out above the competition. If you're a PMP® credential holder and you're competing against a project manager without certification, chances are you'll come out as the top pick. As a hiring manager, all other things being equal, I will usually opt for the candidate who has certification over the candidate who doesn't have it. Certification tells potential employers you have gone the extra mile. You've spent time studying techniques and methods as well as employing them in practice. It shows dedication to your own professional growth and enhancement and to adhering to and advancing professional standards.

Provides Opportunity for Advancement

PMP® certification displays your willingness to pursue growth in your professional career and shows that you're not afraid of a little hard work to get what you want. Potential employers will interpret your pursuit of this certification as a high-energy, success-driven, can-do attitude on your part. They'll see that you're likely to display these same characteristics on the job, which will help make the company successful. Your certification displays a success-oriented, motivated attitude that will open up opportunities for future career advancements in your current field as well as in new areas you might want to explore.

Raises Customer Confidence

Just as the PMP® certification assures employers that you've got the background and experience to handle project management, it assures customers that they have a competent, experienced project manager at the helm. Certification will help your organization sell customers on your ability to manage their projects. Customers, like potential employers, want the reassurance that those working for them have the knowledge and skills necessary to carry out the duties of the position and that professionalism and personal integrity are of utmost importance. Individuals who hold these ideals will translate their ethics and professionalism to their work. This enhances the trust customers will have in you, which in turn will give you the ability to influence them on important project issues.

How to Become PMP® Certified

You need to fulfill several requirements in order to sit for the PMP® exam. PMI® has detailed the certification process quite extensively at its website. Go to www.pmi.org, and click the Certification tab to get the latest information on certification procedures and requirements.

As of this writing, you are required to fill out an application to sit for the PMP® exam. You can submit this application online at the PMI®'s website. You also need to document 35 hours of formal project management education. This might include college classes, seminars, workshops, and training sessions. Be prepared to list the class titles, location, date, and content.

In addition to filling out the application and documenting your formal project management training, there is one set of criteria you'll need to meet to sit for the exam. The criteria in this set fall into two categories. You need to meet the requirements for only one of these categories:

- Category 1 is for those who have a baccalaureate degree. You'll need to provide proof, via transcripts, of your degree with your application. In addition, you'll need to complete verification forms—found at the PMI® website—that show 4,500 hours of project management experience that spans a minimum of three years.

- Category 2 is for those who do not have a baccalaureate degree but do hold a high school diploma or equivalent. You'll need to complete verification forms documenting 7,500 hours of project management experience that spans a minimum of five years.

As of this writing, the exam fee is $405 for PMI® members in good standing and $555 for non-PMI® members. Testing is conducted at Prometric testing centers. You can find a center near you on the Prometric center website, but you will not be able to schedule your exam until your application is approved by PMI®. You have one year from the time PMI® receives and approves your completed application to take the exam. You'll need to bring two forms of identification, such as a driver's license, with you to the Prometric testing center on the test day. You will not be allowed to take anything with you into the testing room and will be provided with a locker to store your personal belongings. You will be given a calculator, pencils, and scrap paper. You will turn in all scrap paper, including the notes and squiggles you've jotted during the test, to the center upon completion of the exam.

The exam is scored immediately, so you will know whether you've passed at the conclusion of the test. You're given four hours to complete the exam, which consists of 200 randomly generated questions. Only 175 of the 200 questions are scored. Twenty-five of the 200 questions are "pretest" questions that will appear randomly throughout the exam. These 25 questions are used by PMI® to determine statistical information and to determine whether they can or should be used on future exams. You will receive a score of Proficient, Moderately Proficient, or Below Proficient for each exam domain, as well as a Pass or Fail score. Because PMI® uses psychometric analysis to determine whether you have passed the exam, a passing score is not published. The questions on the exam cover the five process groups and professional responsibility. You'll answer questions on:

- Initiating
- Planning
- Executing
- Monitoring and Controlling
- Closing
- Professional Responsibility

NOTE Questions pertaining to professional responsibility on the exam will be intermixed with questions for all the process groups. You won't see a section or set of questions devoted solely to professional responsibility, but you will need to understand all of the concepts in this area. I've devoted a good portion of the last chapter of this book to discussing professional responsibility topics.

All unanswered questions are scored as wrong answers, so it benefits you to guess at an answer if you're stumped on a question.

After you've received your certification, you'll be required to earn 60 professional development units (PDUs) every three years to maintain certification. Approximately one hour of structured learning translates to one PDU. The PMI® website details what activities constitute a PDU, how many PDUs each activity earns, and how to register your PDUs with PMI® to maintain your certification. As an example, attendance at a local chapter meeting earns one PDU.

How to Become CAPM® Certified

If you find you don't have quite enough experience or education to sit for the PMP® exam, you should consider sitting for the Certified Associate in Project Management (CAPM®) exam. The CAPM® exam is structured like the PMP® exam, only the content of the exam focuses solely on the *PMBOK® Guide*. CAPM® candidates typically work in a supporting role with a project manager or as a subproject manager. Like the PMP®, CAPM® has two categories of requirements; each category requires applicants to have a secondary diploma, such as a high school diploma or global equivalent:

- Category 1 is for applicants who have a minimum of 1,500 hours of project management experience.

- Category 2 is for applicants who have obtained at least 23 hours of formal education in project management (contact hours).

As of this writing, the CAPM® exam fee is $225 for PMI® members and $300 for non-PMI® members.

A sample CAPM® exam is included on the book's website. If you're sitting for the CAPM® exam, I encourage you to answer all of the end-of-chapter questions and take the bonus exams in addition to the sample CAPM® exam. You'll get a much broader sense of the types of questions and the topics you'll encounter on the actual exam by using all of the sample questions provided in this book and on the website.

Who Should Buy This Book?

If you are serious about passing the PMP® exam (or the CAPM® exam for that matter), you should buy this book and use it to study for the exam. This book is unique in that it walks you through the project processes from beginning to end, just as projects are performed in practice. When you read this book, you will benefit by learning specific *PMBOK® Guide* processes and techniques coupled with real-life scenarios that describe how project managers in different situations handle problems and the various issues all project managers are bound to encounter during their careers. This study guide describes in detail the exam objective topics in each chapter and has attempted to cover all of the important project management concepts.

How to Use This Book and Its Website

We've included several testing features, both in the book and on the companion website, www.sybex.com/go/pmpsg7e. Following this introduction is an assessment test that you can use to check your readiness for the actual exam. Take this test before you start reading the book. It will help you identify the areas you may need to brush up on. The answers to the assessment test appear after the last question of the test. Each answer includes an explanation and a note telling you in which chapter this material appears.

An Exam Essentials section appears at the end of every chapter to highlight the topics you'll most likely find on the exam and help you focus on the most important material covered in the chapter so that you'll have a solid understanding of those concepts. However, it isn't possible to predict what questions will be covered on your particular exam, so be sure to study everything in the chapter.

> Like the exam itself, this *Study Guide* is organized in terms of process groups and the natural sequence of events a project goes through in its life cycle. This is in contrast to other study guides, where material is organized by Knowledge Area (Human Resource Management, Communications Management, and so on); such organization can make mapping the processes in each Knowledge Area to process groups confusing when you're studying for the exam.

Review questions are also provided at the end of every chapter. You can use them to gauge your understanding of the subject matter before reading the chapter and to point out the areas in which you need to concentrate your study time. As you finish each chapter, answer the review questions and then check to see whether your answers are right—the correct answers appear on the pages following the last question. You can go back to reread the section that deals with each question you got wrong to ensure that you answer the question correctly the next time you are tested on the material. If you can answer at least 80 percent of the review questions correctly, you can probably feel comfortable moving on to the next chapter. If you can't answer that many correctly, reread the chapter, or the section that seems to be giving you trouble, and try the questions again. You'll also find more than 200 flashcard questions on the website for on-the-go review.

Don't rely on studying the review questions exclusively as your study method. The questions you'll see on the exam will be different from the questions presented in the book. There are 200 randomly generated questions on the PMP® exam and 150 on the CAPM®, so it isn't possible to cover every potential exam question in the Review Questions section of each chapter. Make sure you understand the concepts behind the material presented in each chapter and memorize all the formulas as well.

In addition to the assessment test and the review questions, you'll find bonus exams on the website. Take these practice exams just as if you were actually taking the exam (that is, without any reference material). When you have finished the first exam, move on to the next exam to solidify your test-taking skills. If you get more than 85 percent of the answers correct, you're ready to take the real exam.

The website also contains an audio file that you can download to your favorite MP3 player to hear a recap of the key elements covered in each chapter.

Finally, you will notice various Real World Scenario sidebars throughout each chapter. They are designed to give you insight into how the various processes and topic areas apply to real-world situations.

The Exam Objectives

Behind every certification exam, you can be sure to find exam objectives—the broad topics in which the exam developers want to ensure your competency. The PMP® exam objectives are listed at the beginning of every chapter in this book.

Exam objectives are subject to change at any time without prior notice and at PMI®'s sole discretion. Please visit the Certification page of PMI®'s website, www.pmi.org, for the most current listing of exam objectives.

How to Contact the Author

I welcome your feedback about this book or about books you'd like to see from me in the future. You can reach me at Kim.Heldman@comcast.net. For more information about my work, please visit my website at KimHeldman.com.

Sybex strives to keep you supplied with the latest tools and information you need for your work. Please check the website at www.sybex.com/go/pmpsg7e, where we'll post additional content and updates that supplement this book if the need arises.

PMP®: Project Management Professional Exam Study Guide, 7th Edition

Exam Objectives

Objective	Chapter
Performance Domain I: Initiating the Project	
Perform project assessment based on available information and meetings with the sponsor, customer, and other subject matter experts, in order to evaluate the feasibility of new products or services within the given assumptions and/or constraints.	2
Define the high-level scope of the project based on business and compliance requirements in order to meet the customer's project expectations.	2
Perform key stakeholder analysis using brainstorming, interviewing, and other data-gathering techniques in order to ensure expectation alignment and gain support for the project.	2
Identify and document high-level risks, assumptions, and constraints based on current environment, historical data, and/or expert judgment in order to identify project limitations and propose an implementation approach.	2
Develop Project Charter by further gathering and analyzing stakeholder requirements in order to document project scope, milestones, and deliverables.	2
Obtain approval of the project charter from the sponsor and customer (if required) in order to formalize the authority assigned to the project manager and gain commitment and acceptance for the project.	2

Objective	Chapter
Create a stakeholder management plan to document needs, interests, and impacts of stakeholders.	5
Present the project plan to the key stakeholders (if required), in order to obtain approval to execute the project.	7
Conduct a kickoff meeting with all key stakeholders, in order to announce the start of the project, communicate the project milestones, and share other relevant information.	2

Performance Domain III: Executing the Project

Objective	Chapter
Obtain and manage project resources, both internal and external to the organization, by following the procurement plan in order to ensure successful project execution.	9
Execute the tasks as defined in the project plan in order to achieve the project deliverables within budget and schedule.	8, 9
Implement the quality management plan, using the appropriate tools and techniques, in order to ensure that work is being performed according to required quality standards.	9
Implement approved changes according to the change management plan, in order to meet project requirements.	10
Implement approved actions (e.g., workarounds) by following the risk management plan in order to minimize the impact of the risks on the project.	9
Use effective communication tools and techniques to convey project information and properly gather, document, and store project information.	9
Continue to engage stakeholders on the project, manage their expectations, manage and engage them in issues, and communicate project information.	9
Maximize team performance through leading, mentoring, training, and motivating team members.	8

Performance Domain IV: Monitoring and Controlling the Project

Objective	Chapter
Measure project performance using appropriate tools and techniques in order to identify and quantify any variances, perform approved corrective actions, and communicate with relevant stakeholders.	10
Manage changes to the project scope, schedule, and costs by updating the project plan and communicating approved changes to the team in order to ensure that revised project goals are met.	10

Objective	Chapter
Ensure that project deliverables conform to the quality standards established in the quality management plan.	11
Prepare and communicate earned value measurements and forecasts.	11
Update the risk register and risk response plan by identifying any new risks, assessing old risks, and determining and implementing appropriate response strategies in order to manage the impact of risks on the project.	11
Assess corrective actions on the issue register and determine next steps for unresolved issues by using appropriate tools and techniques in order to minimize the impact on project schedule, cost, and resources.	10, 11
Communicate project status to stakeholders for their feedback, in order to ensure the project aligns with business needs.	5, 8, 11
Control stakeholder engagement by managing expectations, informing stakeholders of project issues, and obtaining feedback.	5
Performance Domain V: Closing the Project	
Obtain final acceptance of the project.	12
Transfer the ownership of deliverables to the organization.	12
Prepare administrative closure and index and file project records.	12
Distribute the final project report including all project closure–related information to all stakeholders.	12
Document lessons learned and update the organization's knowledge base.	12
Archive project documents.	12
Measure customer satisfaction at the end of the project.	12

Exam objectives are subject to change at any time without prior notice and at PMI®'s sole discretion. Please visit PMI®'s website (www.pmi.org) for the most current listing of exam objectives.

Assessment Test

1. The project sponsor has approached you with a dilemma. At the annual stockholders meeting, the CEO announced that the project you're managing will be completed by the end of this year. The problem is that this is six months prior to the scheduled completion date. It's too late to go back and correct her mistake, and now stockholders expect implementation by the announced date. You must speed up the delivery date of this project. Your primary constraint before this occurred was the budget. Choose the best action from the options listed to speed up the project.

    A. Hire more resources to get the work completed faster.

    B. Ask for more money so that you can contract out one of the phases you had planned to do with in-house resources.

    C. Utilize negotiation and influencing skills to convince the project sponsor to speak with the CEO and make a correction to her announcement.

    D. Examine the project management plan to see whether there are any phases that can be fast-tracked, and then revise the project management plan to reflect the compression of the schedule.

2. These types of dependencies can create arbitrary total float values and limit your scheduling options.

    A. Discretionary

    B. External

    C. Mandatory

    D. Hard logic

3. Project managers spend what percentage of their time communicating?

    A. 90

    B. 85

    C. 75

    D. 50

4. Which of the following is not another term for inspections?

    A. Reviews

    B. Assessment

    C. Walk-throughs

    D. Audits

5. The primary function of the Closing processes is to perform which of the following?

    A. Formalize lessons learned and distribute this information to project participants.

    B. Perform audits to verify the project results against the project requirements.

    C. Assure project records accurately reflect the final specifications of the product.

    D. Perform postimplementation audits to document project successes and failures.

6. During your project meeting, a problem was discussed, and a resolution to the problem was reached. During the meeting, the participants started wondering why they thought the problem was such a big issue. Sometime after the meeting, you received an email from one of the meeting participants saying they've changed their mind about the solution reached in the meeting and need to resurface the problem. The solution reached during the initial project meeting is a result of which of the following conflict resolution techniques?

    A. Collaborate

    B. Force

    C. Smooth

    D. Storm

7. What are decision models?

    A. Project selection criteria

    B. Project selection methods

    C. Project selection committees

    D. Project resource and budget selection methods

8. You've been assigned as a project manager on a research and development project for a new dental procedure. You're working in the Project Scope Management Knowledge Area. What is the purpose of the scope management plan?

    A. The scope management plan describes and documents a scope baseline to help make future project decisions.

    B. The scope management plan decomposes project deliverables into smaller units of work.

    C. The scope management plan describes how project scope will be developed and how changes will be managed.

    D. The scope management plan describes how cost and time estimates will be developed for project scope changes.

9. Which of the following statements regarding Ishikawa diagrams in the Identify Risks process is not true?

    A. Ishikawa diagrams are also called *cause-and-effect diagrams*.

    B. Ishikawa diagrams are also called *fishbone diagrams*.

    C. Ishikawa diagrams are part of the diagramming tool and technique of this process.

    D. Ishikawa diagrams show the steps needed to identify the risk.

10. All of the following are outputs of the Perform Integrated Change Control process except for which one?

    A. Change log

    B. Project management plan updates

    C. Organizational process assets updates

    D. Approved change requests

11. What is one of the most important skills a project manager can have?

    A. Negotiation skills

    B. Influencing skills

    C. Communication skills

    D. Problem-solving skills

12. All of the following are a type of project ending except for which one?

    A. Extinction

    B. Starvation

    C. Desertion

    D. Addition

13. You are the project manager for a construction company that is building a new city and county office building in your city. Your CCB recently approved a scope change. You know that scope change might come about as a result of all of the following except which one?

    A. Schedule revisions

    B. Product scope change

    C. Changes to the agreed-on WBS

    D. Changes to the project requirements

14. You are the project manager for Xylophone Phonics. It produces children's software programs that teach basic reading and math skills. You're performing cost estimates for your project and don't have a lot of details yet. Which of the following techniques should you use?

    A. Analogous estimating techniques, because this is a form of expert judgment that uses historical information from similar projects

    B. Bottom-up estimating techniques, because this is a form of expert judgment that uses historical information from similar projects

    C. Monte Carlo analysis, because this is a modeling technique that uses simulation to determine estimates

    D. Parametric modeling, because this is a form of simulation used to determine estimates

15. Project managers have the highest level of authority and the most power in which type of organizational structure?

    A. Projectized

    B. Strong matrix

    C. Functional

    D. Balanced matrix

16. This process is concerned with determining the engagement levels of the stakeholders.

    A. Plan Communications Management

    B. Control Communications

    C. Plan Stakeholder Management

    D. Manage Stakeholder Engagement

17. All of the following statements are true regarding risk events except which one?

   A. Project risks are uncertain events.

   B. If risks occur, they can have a positive or negative effect on project objectives.

   C. Unknown risks can be threats to the project objectives, and nothing can be done to plan for them.

   D. Risks that have more perceived rewards to the organization than consequences should be accepted.

18. The Conduct Procurement process applies evaluation criteria to bids and proposals and selects a vendor. It also uses independent estimates to compare vendor prices. This is also known as which of the following?

   A. Independent comparisons

   B. Analytical techniques

   C. Should cost estimates

   D. Expert judgment

19. You are the project manager for Xylophone Phonics. This company produces children's software programs that teach basic reading and math skills. You are ready to assign project roles, responsibilities, and reporting relationships. On which project Planning process are you working?

   A. Estimate Activity Resources

   B. Plan Human Resource Management

   C. Acquire Project Team

   D. Plan Organizational Resources

20. You know that PV – 470, AC = 430, EV = 460, EAC = 500, and BAC = 525. What is VAC?

   A. 65

   B. 20

   C. 25

   D. 30

21. You are a project manager who has recently held a project team kickoff meeting where all the team members were formally introduced to each other. Some of the team members know each other from other projects and have been working with you for the past three weeks. Which of the following statements is not true?

   A. Team building improves the knowledge and skills of team members.

   B. Team building builds feelings of trust and agreement among team members, which can improve morale.

   C. Team building can create a dynamic environment and cohesive culture to improve productivity of both the team and the project.

   D. Team building occurs throughout the life of the project and can establish clear expectations and behaviors for project team members, leading to increased productivity.

22. You are a project manager for the Swirling Seas Cruises food division. You're considering two different projects regarding food services on the cruise lines. The initial cost of Project Fish'n for Chips will be $800,000, with expected cash inflows of $300,000 per quarter. Project Picnic's payback period is six months. Which project should you recommend?

    A. Project Fish'n for Chips, because its payback period is two months shorter than Project Picnic's

    B. Project Fish'n for Chips, because the costs on Project Picnic are unknown

    C. Project Picnic, because Project Fish'n for Chips's payback period is four months longer than Project Picnic's

    D. Project Picnic, because Project Fish'n for Chips's payback period is two months longer than Project Picnic's

23. Which of the following compression techniques increases risk?

    A. Crashing

    B. Resource leveling

    C. Fast tracking

    D. Lead and lag

24. Name the ethical code you'll be required to adhere to as a PMP® credential holder.

    A. *Project Management Policy and Ethics Code*

    B. *PMI® Standards and Ethics Code of Conduct*

    C. *Project Management Code of Professional Ethics*

    D. *PMI® Code of Ethics and Professional Conduct*

25. You have been assigned to a project that will allow job seekers to fill out applications and submit them via the company website. You report to the VP of human resources. You are also responsible for screening applications for the information technology division and setting up interviews. The project coordinator has asked for the latest version of your changes to the online application page for his review. Which organizational structure do you work in?

    A. Functional organization

    B. Weak matrix organization

    C. Projectized organization

    D. Balanced matrix organization

26. You are the project manager for Lucky Stars Candies. You've identified the requirements for the project and documented them where?

    A. In the requirements document, which will be used as an input to the Create WBS process

    B. In the project scope statement, which is used as an input to the Create WBS process

    C. In the product requirements document, which is an output of the Define Scope process

    D. In the project specifications document, which is an output of the Define Scope process

27. What is the purpose of the project charter?

    A. To recognize and acknowledge the project sponsor

    B. To recognize and acknowledge the existence of the project and commit organizational resources to the project

    C. To acknowledge the existence of the project team, project manager, and project sponsor

    D. To describe the selection methods used to choose this project over its competitors

28. Which of the following are tools and techniques of the Identify Stakeholders process?

    A. Stakeholder analysis, expert judgment, and meetings

    B. Stakeholder analysis, expert judgment, and stakeholder register

    C. Stakeholder analysis and expert judgment

    D. Stakeholder analysis, stakeholder management strategy, and expert judgment

29. You are a project manager working on a software development project. You've developed the risk management plan, identified risks, and determined risk responses for the risks. A risk event occurs, and you implement the response. Then, another risk event occurs as a result of the response you implemented. What type of risk is this called?

    A. Trigger risk

    B. Residual risk

    C. Secondary risk

    D. Mitigated risk

30. You are working on a project that will upgrade the phone system in your customer service center. You have considered using analogous estimating, parametric estimating, bottom-up estimating, and three-point estimating to determine activity costs. Which process does this describe?

    A. Estimating Activity Resources

    B. Estimate Costs

    C. Determine Budget

    D. Estimating Activity Costs

31. Failure costs are also known as which of the following?

    A. Internal costs

    B. Cost of poor quality

    C. Cost of keeping defects out of the hands of customers

    D. Prevention costs

32. Feeding buffers and the project buffer are part of which of the following Develop Schedule tool and technique?

    A. Critical path method

    B. Schedule network analysis

    C. Applying leads and lags

    D. Critical chain method

33. You are working on a project that will upgrade the phone system in your customer service center. You have used bottom-up estimating techniques to assign costs to the project activities and have determined the cost baseline. Which of the following statements is true?

    A. You have completed the Estimate Cost process and now need to complete the Determine Budget process to develop the project's cost baseline.

    B. You have completed the Estimate Cost process and established a cost baseline to measure future project against.

    C. You have completed the Determine Budget process and now need to complete the Schedule Development process to establish a project baseline to measure future project performance against.

    D. You have completed the Determine Budget process, and the cost baseline will be used to measure future project performance.

34. Each of the following statements describes an element of the Develop Project Management Plan process except for which one?

    A. Project charter

    B. Outputs from other planning processes

    C. Configuration management system

    D. Organizational process assets

35. There are likely to be team loyalty issues in a matrixed environment. All of the following are true regarding this situation as it pertains to the Manage Project Team process except for which one?

    A. Two of the tools and techniques you might use to manage these relationships effectively are communications methods and conflict management.

    B. In this type of structure, team members report to both a functional manager and a project manager. Both managers should have input to the project performance appraisal for this team member, which is a tool and technique of this process.

    C. The project manager is generally responsible for managing this relationship.

    D. The effective management of these reporting relationships is often a critical success factor for the project.

36. Monte Carlo analysis can help predict the impact of risks on project deliverables. This is an element of one of the tools and techniques of which of the following processes?

    A. Plan Risk Responses

    B. Perform Quantitative Risk Analysis

    C. Identify Risks

    D. Perform Qualitative Risk Analysis

37. Which of the following statements regarding configuration management is not true?

    A. Configuration management involves managing changes to the project baselines.

    B. Change control systems are a subset of the configuration management system.

    C. Configuration management focuses on the specifications of the deliverables of the project.

    D. Configuration management validates and improves the project by evaluating the impact of each change.

38. Which performance measurement tells you what the projected total cost of the project will be at completion?

   A. ETC

   B. EV

   C. AC

   D. EAC

39. Which of the following contracts should you use for projects that have a degree of uncertainty and require a large investment early in the project life cycle?

   A. Fixed price

   B. Cost reimbursable

   C. Lump sum

   D. T&M

40. According to the *PMBOK® Guide*, the project manager is identified and assigned during which process?

   A. During the Develop Project Charter process

   B. At the conclusion of the Develop Project Charter process

   C. Prior to beginning the Planning processes

   D. Prior to beginning the Define Scope process

41. All of the following are tools and techniques of the Close Procurements process except for which one?

   A. Expert judgment

   B. Procurement audits

   C. Procurement negotiations

   D. Records management system

42. The inputs of the Control Communications process include all of the following except for which one?

   A. Work performance data

   B. Issue log

   C. Project communications

   D. Work performance information

43. All of the following statements are true regarding risks except for which one?

   A. Risks might be threats to the objectives of the project.

   B. Risks are certain events that may be threats or opportunities to the objectives of the project.

   C. Risks might be opportunities to the objectives of the project.

   D. Risks have causes and consequences.

44. Which performance measurement tells you the cost of the work that has been authorized and budgeted for a WBS component?

    A. PV

    B. EV

    C. AC

    D. BCWP

45. Which of the following statements is true regarding the Project Management Knowledge Areas?

    A. They include Initiation, Planning, Executing, Monitoring and Controlling, and Closing.

    B. They consist of 10 areas that bring together processes that have things in common.

    C. They consist of five processes that bring together phases of projects that have things in common.

    D. They include Planning, Executing, and Monitoring and Controlling processes because these three processes are commonly interlinked.

46. You have just prepared an RFP for release. Your project involves a substantial amount of contract work detailed in the RFP. Your favorite vendor drops by and offers to give you and your spouse the use of their company condo for your upcoming vacation. It's located in a beautiful resort community that happens to be one of your favorite places to go for a get-away. What is the most appropriate response?

    A. Thank the vendor, but decline the offer because you know this could be considered a conflict of interest.

    B. Thank the vendor, and accept. This vendor is always offering you incentives like this, so this offer does not likely have anything to do with the recent RFP release.

    C. Thank the vendor, accept the offer, and immediately tell your project sponsor so they're aware of what you're doing.

    D. Thank the vendor, but decline the offer because you've already made another arrangement for this vacation. Ask them whether you can take a rain check and arrange another time to use the condo.

47. What are the Define Scope process tools and techniques?

    A. Cost–benefit analysis, scope baseline, expert judgment, and facilitated workshops

    B. Product analysis, alternatives generation, and expert judgment

    C. Product analysis, alternatives generation, expert judgment, and facilitated workshops

    D. Alternatives generation, stakeholder analysis, and expert judgment

48. You are the project manager for Heartthrobs by the Numbers Dating Services. You're working on an updated Internet site that will display pictures as well as short bios of prospective heartbreakers. You have your activity list and resource requirements in hand and are planning to use parametric estimates and reserve analysis to determine activity durations. Which of the following statements is true?

    A. You are using inputs from the Estimate Activity Duration process.

    B. You are using tools and techniques of the Estimate Cost process.

    C. You are using tools and techniques of the Estimate Activity Durations process.

    D. You are using inputs of the Estimate Costs process.

49. Your team is developing the risk management plan. Which tool and technique of this process is used to develop risk cost elements and schedule activities that will be included in the project budget and schedule?

A. Meetings

B. Strategies for both threats and opportunities

C. Information gathering techniques

D. Risk data quality assessment

50. What type of organization experiences the least amount of stress during project closeout?

A. Projectized

B. Functional

C. Weak matrix

D. Strong matrix

51. You are the project manager for Xylophone Phonics. It produces children's software programs that teach basic reading and math skills. You are performing the Plan Quality Management process and are identifying nonproductive activities. Part of this involves capturing information such as process boundaries, process configurations, and process metrics. Which of the following does this describe?

A. The process improvement plan

B. The quality management plan

C. The quality metrics

D. The cost of quality

52. You need to convey some very complex, detailed information to the project stakeholders. What is the best method for communicating this kind of information?

A. Verbal

B. Vertical

C. Horizontal

D. Written

53. You are the project manager for Heartthrobs by the Numbers Dating Services. You're working on an updated Internet site that will display pictures as well as short bios of prospective heartbreakers. You've just completed your project staff assignments and published the project team directory. Which process are you in?

A. Plan Human Resource Management

B. Manage Project Team

C. Develop Project Team

D. Acquire Project Team

54. You are a project manager for Waterways Houseboats, Inc. You've been asked to perform a cost-benefit analysis for two proposed projects. Project A costs $2.4 million, with potential benefits of $12 million and future operating costs of $3 million. Project B costs $2.8 million, with potential benefits of $14 million and future operating costs of $2 million. Which project should you recommend?

    A. Project A, because the cost to implement is cheaper than Project B

    B. Project A, because the potential benefits plus the future operating costs are less in value than the same calculation for Project B

    C. Project B, because the potential benefits minus the implementation and future operating costs are greater in value than the same calculation for Project A

    D. Project B, because the potential benefits minus the costs to implement are greater in value than the same calculation for Project A

55. These diagrams rank-order factors for corrective action by frequency of occurrence. They are also a type of histogram.

    A. Control charts

    B. Process flowcharts

    C. Scatter diagrams

    D. Pareto diagrams

56. You are a project manager working in a foreign country. You observe that some of your project team members are having a difficult time adjusting to the new culture. You provided them with training on cultural differences and the customs of this country before arriving, but they still seem uncomfortable and disoriented. Which of the following statements is true?

    A. This is the result of working with teams of people from two different countries.

    B. This condition is known as *culture shock*.

    C. This is the result of jet lag and travel fatigue.

    D. This condition is known as *global culturalism*.

57. Your project involves the research and development of a new food additive. You're ready to release the product to your customer when you discover that a minor reaction might occur in people with certain conditions. The reactions to date have been very minor, and no known long-lasting side effects have been noted. As project manager, what should you do?

    A. Do nothing because the reactions are so minor that very few people will be affected.

    B. Inform the customer that you've discovered this condition and tell them you'll research it further to determine its impacts.

    C. Inform your customer that there is no problem with the additive except for an extremely small percentage of the population and release the product to them.

    D. Tell the customer you'll correct the reaction problems in the next batch, but you'll release the first batch of product to them now to begin using.

58. The project manager has the greatest influence over quality during which process?

    A. Plan Quality Management

    B. Perform Quality Assurance

    C. Control Quality

    D. Monitor Quality

59. You are the project manager for a construction company that is building a new city and county office building in your city. You recently looked over the construction site to determine whether the work to date conformed to the requirements and quality standards. Which tool and technique of the Control Quality process were you using?

    A. Defect repair review

    B. Inspection

    C. Sampling

    D. Quality audit

60. All of the following statements are true of the project Closing processes except for which one?

    A. Probability for success is greatest in the project Closing processes.

    B. The project manager's influence is greatest in the project Closing processes.

    C. The stakeholders' influence is least in the project Closing processes.

    D. Risk occurrence is greatest in the project Closing processes.

61. You are refining the product description for your company's new line of ski boots. Which of the following statements is true?

    A. You are in the Initiating processes of your project and know that the product description will contain more detail in this stage and that a decreasing amount of detail will be added to it as the project progresses.

    B. You are in the Planning processes of your project and know that the product description will contain less detail in this stage and greater detail as the project progresses.

    C. You are in the Planning processes of your project and know that the product description should contain the most detail possible at this stage because this is critical information for the Planning process.

    D. You are in the Initiating processes of your project and know that the product description will contain less detail in this stage and greater detail as the project progresses.

62. Every status meeting should have time allotted for reviewing risks. Which of the following sentences is not true?

    A. Risk identification and monitoring should occur throughout the life of the project.

    B. Risk audits should occur toward the later phases of the project.

    C. Risks should be monitored for their status and to determine whether the impacts to the objectives have changed.

    D. Technical performance measurement variances may indicate that a risk is looming and should be reviewed at status meetings.

63. The business need, product scope description, and strategic plan together describe elements of which of the following?

   A. Organizational process assets

   B. Tools and techniques of the Initiating processes

   C. The project statement of work

   D. The project charter

64. Which of the following statements is true regarding constraints and assumptions?

   A. Constraints restrict the actions of the project team, and assumptions are considered true for planning purposes.

   B. Constraints are considered true for planning purposes, and assumptions limit the options of the project team.

   C. Constraints consider vendor availability and resource availability to be true for planning purposes. Assumptions limit the project team to work within predefined budgets or timelines.

   D. Constraints and assumptions are inputs to the Initiation process. They should be documented because they will be used throughout the project Planning process.

65. People are motivated by the need for achievement, power, or affiliation according to which theory?

   A. Expectancy Theory

   B. Achievement Theory

   C. Contingency Theory

   D. Theory X

66. As a result of a face-to-face meeting you recently had to discuss the items in your issue log, you have resolved issues and come away with an approved corrective action and an update to the project management plan. Which process does this describe?

   A. Manage Stakeholder Engagement

   B. Control Communications

   C. Manage Project Communications

   D. Manage Project Team

67. You've just completed the WBS. Which of the following statements is true?

   A. The WBS breaks the project deliverables down to a level where alternatives identification can be used to determine how level-two assignments should be made.

   B. The WBS breaks the project deliverables down to a level where project constraints and assumptions can be identified easily.

   C. The WBS breaks the project deliverables down to the work package level, where product analysis can be documented.

   D. The WBS breaks the project deliverables down to the work package level, where cost and time estimates can be easily determined.

68. As a PMP® credential holder, one of your responsibilities is to ensure integrity on the project. When your personal interests are put above the interests of the project or when you use your influence to cause others to make decisions in your favor without regard for the project outcome, this is considered which of the following?

   A. Conflict of interest

   B. Using professional knowledge inappropriately

   C. Culturally unacceptable

   D. Personal conflict issue

69. Which of the following describes the Executing process group?

   A. Project plans are put into action.

   B. Project performance measurements are taken and analyzed.

   C. Project plans are developed.

   D. Project plans are published.

70. Which of the following statements regarding the ADM method is not true?

   A. The ADM method is a tool and technique of Sequence Activities.

   B. The ADM method uses one time estimate to determine durations.

   C. The ADM method is also called AOA.

   D. The ADM method is rarely used today.

71. You are a project manager working on gathering requirements and establishing estimates for the project. Which process group are you in?

   A. Planning

   B. Executing

   C. Initiating

   D. Monitoring and Controlling

72. According to the *PMBOK® Guide*, which of the following names all the components of a communication model?

   A. Encode, transmit, decode

   B. Encode, transmit, decode, acknowledge, feedback and/or response

   C. Encode, transmit, decode, feedback and/or response

   D. Encode, transmit, acknowledge, decode

Answers to Assessment Test

1. D. Fast-tracking is the best answer in this scenario. Budget was the original constraint on this project, so it's unlikely the project manager would get more resources to assist with the project. The next best thing is to compress phases to shorten the project duration. For more information, please see Chapter 1.

2. A. Discretionary dependencies can create arbitrary total float values, and they can also limit scheduling options. For more information, please see Chapter 4.

3. A. Project managers spend about 90 percent of their time communicating through status meetings, team meetings, email, verbal communications, and so on. For more information, please see Chapter 9.

4. B. Inspections are also called reviews, peer reviews, walk-throughs, and audits. For more information, please see Chapter 11.

5. C. The primary function of the Closing processes is to ensure that project records accurately reflect the final specifications of the product. It also analyzes project management processes for effectiveness, and roles and responsibilities documentation should be updated during these processes. For more information, please see Chapter 12.

6. C. The smoothing technique (also known as accommodate) does not usually result in a permanent solution. The problem is downplayed to make it seem less important than it is, which makes the problem tend to resurface later. For more information, please see Chapter 8.

7. B. Decision models are project selection methods that include benefit measurement methods and mathematical models. For more information, please see Chapter 2.

8. C. The scope management plan outlines how project scope will be managed and how changes will be incorporated into the project. For more information, please see Chapter 3.

9. D. Cause-and-effect diagrams—also called *Ishikawa* or *fishbone diagrams*—show the relationship between the effects of problems and their causes. Kaoru Ishikawa developed cause-and-effect diagrams. For more information, please see Chapter 6.

10. C. The outputs of this process are approved change requests, change log, project management plan updates, and project documents updates. For more information, please see Chapter 10.

11. C. Negotiation, influencing, and problem-solving skills are all important for a project manager to possess. However, good communication skills are the most important skills a project manager can have. For more information, please see Chapter 1.

12. C. The four types of project endings are addition, integration, starvation, and extinction. For more information, please see Chapter 12.

13. A. Scope changes will cause schedule revisions, but schedule revisions do not change the project scope. Project requirements are part of the project scope statement; therefore, option D is one of the correct responses. For more information, please see Chapter 11.

14. A. Analogous estimating—also called *top-down estimating*—is a form of expert judgment. Analogous estimating can be used to estimate cost or time and considers historical information from previous, similar projects. For more information, please see Chapter 4.

15. A. Project managers have the highest level of power and authority in a projectized organization. They also have high levels of power and authority in a strong matrix organization, but a matrix organization is a blend of functional and projectized organizations. Therefore, the project manager has the most authority and power in a projectized organization. For more information, please see Chapter 1.

16. C. Plan Stakeholder Management is concerned with determining the engagement levels of the stakeholders, understanding their needs and interests, and understanding how they might impact the project or how the project may impact them. For more information, please see Chapter 5.

17. C. Unknown risks might be threats or opportunities to the project, and the project manager should set aside contingency reserves to deal with them. For more information, please see Chapter 6.

18. C. Independent estimates are also known as should cost estimates. For more information, please see Chapter 9.

19. B. The Plan Human Resource Management process identifies project resources, documents roles and responsibilities of project team members, and documents reporting relationships. For more information, please see Chapter 7.

20. C. VAC is calculated this way: VAC = BAC − EAC. Therefore, 525 − 500 = 25. For more information, please see Chapter 11.

21. D. Team building does occur throughout the life of the project, but ground rules are what establish clear expectations and behaviors for project team members. For more information, please see Chapter 8.

22. D. The payback period for Project Fish'n for Chips is eight months. This project will receive $300,000 every three months, or $100,000 per month. The $800,000 will be paid back in eight months. For more information, please see Chapter 2.

23. C. Fast-tracking is a compression technique that increases risk and potentially causes rework. Fast-tracking is starting two activities previously scheduled to start one after the other at the same time. For more information, please see Chapter 4.

24. D. The *PMI® Code of Ethics and Professional Conduct* is published by PMI®, and all PMP® credential holders are expected to adhere to its standards. For more information, please see Chapter 12.

25. B. Functional managers who have a lot of authority and power working with project coordinators who have minimal authority and power characterizes a weak matrix organization. Project managers in weak matrix organizations are sometimes called *project coordinators*, *project leaders*, or *project expeditors*. For more information, please see Chapter 1.

26. A. The requirements document contains a list of requirements for the project along with other important information regarding the requirements. For more information, please see Chapter 3.

27. B. The purpose of a project charter is to recognize and acknowledge the existence of a project and commit resources to the project. The charter names the project manager and project sponsor, but that's not its primary purpose. For more information, please see Chapter 2.

28. A. Identify Stakeholders tools and techniques are stakeholder analysis, expert judgment, and meetings. For more information, please see Chapter 2.

29. C. Secondary risk events occur as a result of the implementation of a response to another risk. For more information, please see Chapter 6.

30. B. Estimate Costs is where activity costs are estimated using some of the tools and techniques listed in the question. The remaining tools and techniques of this process are expert judgment, reserve analysis, cost of quality, project management software, vendor bid analysis, and group decision-making techniques. For more information, please see Chapter 5.

31. B. Failure costs are associated with the cost of quality and are also known as cost of poor quality. For more information, please see Chapter 7.

32. D. The critical chain is a resource-constrained critical path that adds duration buffers to help protect schedule slippage. For more information, please see Chapter 4.

33. D. The Determine Budget process establishes the cost baseline, which is used to measure and track the project throughout the remaining process groups. For more information, please see Chapter 5.

34. C. The inputs to Develop Project Management Plan include project charter, outputs from other processes, enterprise environmental factors, and organizational process assets. The only tools and techniques of this process are expert judgment and facilitation techniques. For more information, please see Chapter 3.

35. A. The tools and techniques of the Manage Project Team process are observation and conversation, project performance appraisals, conflict management, and interpersonal skills. For more information, please see Chapter 8.

36. B. Monte Carlo analysis is a modeling and simulation technique that is part of the quantitative risk analysis and modeling techniques tool and technique of the Perform Quantitative Risk Analysis process. For more information, please see Chapter 6.

37. A. Change control systems are a subset of the configuration management system. Change control systems manage changes to the deliverables and/or project baselines. For more information, please see Chapter 10.

38. D. Estimate at completion (EAC) estimates the total cost of the project at completion based on the performance of the project to date. For more information, please see Chapter 11.

39. B. Cost-reimbursable contracts are used when the degree of uncertainty is high and when the project requires a large investment prior to completion. For more information, please see Chapter 7.

40. A. According to the *PMBOK® Guide*, the project manager should be assigned during the development of the project charter, which occurs in the Develop Project Charter process. For more information, please see Chapter 2.

41. A. The tools and techniques of Close Procurements are procurement audits, procurement negotiations, and records management systems. For more information, please see Chapter 12.

42. D. Work performance information is an output, not an input, of the Control Communications process. The remaining inputs of this process are project management plan and organizational process assets. For more information, please see Chapter 10.

43. B. Risks are uncertain events that may be threats or opportunities to the objectives of the project. For more information, please see Chapter 6.

44. A. Planned value is the cost of work that has been authorized and budgeted for a schedule activity or WBS component. For more information, please see Chapter 11.

45. B. The project management Knowledge Areas bring processes together that have commonalities. For example, the Project Quality Management Knowledge Area includes the Plan Quality Management, Perform Quality Assurance, and Control Quality processes. For more information, please see Chapter 2.

46. A. The best response is to decline the offer. This is a conflict of interest, and accepting the offer puts your own integrity and the contract award process in jeopardy. For more information, please see Chapter 12.

47. C. The tools and techniques of the Define Scope process include product analysis, alternatives generation, expert judgment, and facilitated workshops. For more information, please see Chapter 3.

48. C. Parametric estimating and reserve analysis are two of the tools and techniques of the Estimate Activity Durations process. The other tools are analogous estimating, group decision-making techniques, and three-point estimating. For more information, please see Chapter 4.

49. A. The Plan Risk Management process has three tools and techniques: analytical techniques, expert judgment, and meetings. For more information, please see Chapter 6.

50. C. Weak matrix organizational structures tend to experience the least amount of stress during the project closeout processes. For more information, please see Chapter 12.

51. A. This describes the process improvement plan, which is a subsidiary of the project management plan and an output of the Plan Quality Management process. For more information, please see Chapter 7.

52. D. Information that is complex and detailed is best conveyed in writing. A verbal follow-up would be good to answer questions and clarify information. Vertical and horizontal are ways of communicating within the organization. For more information, please see Chapter 9.

53. D. Project staff assignments are an output of the Acquire Project Team process, and it includes a team directory. For more information, please see Chapter 8.

54. C. Project B's cost–benefit analysis is a $9.2 million benefit to the company, compared to $6.6 million for Project A. Cost–benefit analysis takes into consideration the initial costs to implement and future operating costs. For more information, please see Chapter 2.

55. D. Pareto diagrams rank-order important factors for corrective action by frequency of occurrence. For more information, please see Chapter 11.

56. B. When people work in unfamiliar environments, culture shock can occur. Training and researching information about the country you'll be working in can help counteract this. For more information, please see Chapter 12.

57. B. Honesty and truthful reporting are required of PMP® credential holders. In this situation, you would inform the customer of everything you know regarding the problem and work to find alternative solutions. For more information, please see Chapter 12.

58. B. Perform Quality Assurance is the process where project managers have the greatest amount of influence over quality. For more information, please see Chapter 9.

59. B. Inspection involves physically looking at, measuring, or testing results to determine whether they conform to your quality standards. For more information, please see Chapter 11.

60. D. Risk occurrence is lowest during the Closing processes because you've completed the work of the project at this point. However, risk impacts are the greatest in the Closing process because you have much more at stake. For more information, please see Chapter 12.

61. D. Product descriptions are used during the Initiating process group and contain less detail now and more detail as the project progresses. For more information, please see Chapter 1.

62. B. Risk audits should be performed throughout the life of the project and are specifically interested in looking at the implementation and effectiveness of risk strategies. For more information, please see Chapter 11.

63. C. These elements are part of the project statement of work used as an input to the Develop Project Charter process. For more information, please see Chapter 2.

64. A. Constraints limit the options of the project team by restricting action or dictating action. Scope, time, and cost are the three most common constraints, and each of these has an effect on quality. Assumptions are presumed to be true for planning purposes. Always validate your assumptions. For more information, please see Chapter 3.

65. B. Achievement Theory conjectures that people are motivated by the need for achievement, power, or affiliation. For more information, please see Chapter 8.

66. A. The clues in this question are the face-to-face meetings (a communication method), the issue log, and the resolved issues, which is one of the primary purposes of the Manage Stakeholder Engagement process. For more information, please see Chapter 9.

67. D. The work package level is the lowest level in the work breakdown structure. Schedule and cost estimates are easily determined at this level. For more information, please see Chapter 3.

68. A. A conflict of interest is any situation that compromises the outcome of the project or ignores the impact to the project to benefit yourself or others. For more information, please see Chapter 12.

69. A. The Executing process group takes published project plans and turns them into actions to accomplish the goals of the project. For more information, please see Chapter 1.

70. B. The arrow diagramming method (ADM)—also called activity on arrow (AOA)—uses more than one time estimate to determine project duration. For more information, please see Chapter 4.

71. A. The Planning process group is where requirements are fleshed out and estimates on project costs and time are made.

72. B. The components of the communication model are encode, transmit, decode, acknowledge, and feedback and/or response.

Chapter

1

What Is a Project?

Congratulations on your decision to study for and take the Project Management Institute (PMI®) Project Management Professional (PMP®) certification exam (PMP® exam). This book was written with you in mind. The focus and content of this book revolve heavily around the information contained in *A Guide to the Project Management Body of Knowledge (PMBOK® Guide), Fifth Edition*, published by PMI®. I will refer to this guide throughout this book and elaborate on those areas that appear on the test. Keep in mind that the test covers all the project management processes, so don't skip anything in your study time.

When possible, I'll pass on hints and study tips that I collected while studying for the exam. My first tip is to familiarize yourself with the terminology used in the *PMBOK® Guide*. Volunteers from differing industries from around the globe worked together to come up with the standards and terms used in the guide. These folks worked hard to develop and define project management terms, and these terms are used interchangeably among industries. For example, *resource planning* means the same thing to someone working in construction, information technology, or healthcare. You'll find many of the *PMBOK® Guide* terms explained throughout this book. Even if you are an experienced project manager, you might find you use specific terms for processes or actions you regularly perform but the *PMBOK® Guide* calls them by another name. So, the first step is to get familiar with the terminology.

The next step is to become familiar with the processes as defined in the *PMBOK® Guide*. The process names are unique to PMI®, but the general principles and guidelines underlying the processes are used for most projects across industry areas.

This chapter lays the foundation for building and managing your project. I'll address project and project management definitions as well as organizational structures. Good luck!

Is It a Project?

Let's start with an example of how projects come about, and later in this section, we'll look at a definition of a project. Consider the following scenario: You work for a wireless phone provider, and the VP of marketing approaches you with a fabulous idea—"fabulous" because he's the big boss and because he thought it up. He wants to set up kiosks in local grocery and big-box stores as mini-offices. These offices will offer customers the ability to sign up for new wireless phone services, make their wireless phone bill payments, and purchase equipment and accessories. He believes that the exposure in grocery stores will increase awareness of the company's offerings. After all, everyone has to eat, right? He told you that the board of directors has already cleared the project, and he'll dedicate as many resources to this as he can. He wants the new kiosks in place in 12 stores by the end of this year. The best news is he has assigned you to head up this project.

Your first question should be "Is it a project?" This might seem elementary, but confusing projects with ongoing operations happens often. Projects are temporary in nature; have definite start and end dates; produce a unique product, service, or result; and are completed when their goals and objectives have been met and signed off by the stakeholders or when the project is terminated.

When considering whether you have a project on your hands, you need to keep some issues in mind. First, is it a project or an ongoing operation? Next, if it is a project, who are the stakeholders? And third, what characteristics distinguish this endeavor as a project? We'll look at each of these next.

Projects versus Operations

Projects are temporary in nature and have definitive start dates and definitive end dates. The project is completed when its goals and objectives are accomplished to the satisfaction of the stakeholders. Sometimes projects end when it's determined that the goals and objectives cannot be accomplished or when the product, service, or result of the project is no longer needed and the project is canceled. Projects exist to bring about a product, service, or result that didn't exist before. This might include tangible products, components of other products, services such as consulting or project management, and business functions that support the organization. Projects might also produce a result or an outcome, such as a document that details the findings of a research study. In this sense, a project is unique. However, don't get confused by the term *unique*. For example, Ford Motor Company is in the business of designing and assembling cars. Each model that Ford designs and produces can be considered a project. The models differ from each other in their features and are marketed to people with various needs. An SUV serves a different purpose and clientele than a luxury sedan or a hybrid. The initial design and marketing of these three models are unique projects. However, the actual assembly of the cars is considered an operation—a repetitive process that is followed for most makes and models.

Determining the characteristics and features of the different car models is carried out through what the *PMBOK® Guide* terms *progressive elaboration*. This means the characteristics of the product, service, or result of the project are determined incrementally and are continually refined and worked out in detail as the project progresses. More information and better estimates become available the further you progress in the project. Progressive elaboration improves the project team's ability to manage greater levels of detail and allows for the inevitable change that occurs throughout a project's life cycle. This concept goes along with the temporary and unique aspects of a project because when you first start the project, you don't know all the minute details of the end product. Product characteristics typically start out broad-based at the beginning of the project and are progressively elaborated into more and more detail over time until they are complete and finalized.

Exam Spotlight

Progressive elaboration is most often used when creating the project or product scope, developing requirements, determining human resources, scheduling, and defining risks and their mitigation plans.

 Real World Scenario

The New Website Project

You've just been charged with creating a new intranet site for your organization. At the beginning of the project, you don't know a lot of detail other than the high-level purpose of the project. One of the next steps is to discover the elements that should be included on the website. For example, you might need to make available human resources policies and procedures, travel request forms, expense reimbursement forms, and so on. At this point, you are progressively elaborating the scope of the project. Each of these elements will need its own progressive elaboration process to further define its requirements and develop estimates. For example, as you interview stakeholders, you discover that travel request forms require two electronic signatures, one from the employee's supervisor and one from the section manager. Progressive elaboration continues throughout the project life cycle, including defining the requirements and scope, delivering the end product or result, and obtaining acceptance from the stakeholders.

Operations are ongoing and repetitive. They involve work that is continuous without an ending date, and you often repeat the same processes and produce the same results. One way to think of operations is the transforming of resources (steel and fiberglass, for example) into outputs (cars). The purpose of operations is to keep the organization functioning, whereas the purpose of a project is to meet its goals and to conclude. At the completion of a project, or at various points throughout the project, the deliverables may get turned over to the organization's operational areas for ongoing care and maintenance. For example, let's say your company implements a new human resources software package that tracks employees' time, expense reports, benefits, and so on, like the example described in the sidebar, "The New Website Project." Defining the requirements and implementing the software is a project. The ongoing maintenance of the site, updating content, and so on are ongoing operations.

It's a good idea to include some members of the operational area on the project team when certain deliverables or the end product of the project will be incorporated into their future work processes. They can assist the project team in defining requirements, developing scope, creating estimates, and so on, helping to assure that the project will meet their needs. The process of knowledge transfer to the team is much simpler when they are involved throughout the project; they gain knowledge as they go and the formal handoff is more efficient. This isn't a bad strategy in helping to gain buy-ins from the end users of the product or service either. Often, business units are resistant to new systems or services, but getting them involved early in the project rather than simply throwing the end product over the fence when it's completed may help gain their acceptance.

Managing projects and managing operations require different skill sets. Operations management involves managing the business operations that support the goods and services the organization is producing. Operations managers may include line supervisors in manufacturing, retail sales managers, customer service call center managers, and more. The skills needed to manage a project include general management skills, interpersonal skills, planning and organization skills, and more. The remainder of this book will discuss project management skills in detail.

According to the *PMBOK® Guide*, several examples exist where projects can extend into operations up until and including the end of the product life cycle:

- At the end of each phase of the project

- Developing new products or services

- Upgrading and/or expanding products or services

- Improving the product development processes

- Improving operations

The preceding list isn't all inclusive. Whenever you find yourself working on a project that ultimately impacts your organization's business processes, I recommend you get people from the business units to participate on the project.

Stakeholders

A project is successful when it achieves its objectives and meets or exceeds the expectations of the stakeholders. *Stakeholders* are those folks (or organizations) with a vested interest in your project. They may be active or passive as far as participation on the project goes, but the one thing they all have in common is that each of them has something to either gain or lose as a result of the project. Stakeholder identification is not a onetime process. You should continue to ask fellow team members and stakeholders if there are other stakeholders who should be a part of the project.

Key stakeholders can make or break the success of a project. Even if all the deliverables are met and the objectives are satisfied, if your key stakeholders aren't happy, nobody is happy.

The *project sponsor*, generally an executive in the organization with the authority to assign resources and enforce decisions regarding the project, is a stakeholder. The project sponsor generally serves as the tie-breaker decision maker and is one of the people on your escalation path. The customer is a stakeholder, as are contractors and suppliers. The project manager, the project team members, and the managers from other departments, including the operations areas, are stakeholders as well. It's important to identify all the stakeholders in your project up front. Leaving out an important stakeholder or their department's function and not discovering the error until well into the project can be a project killer.

Figure 1.1 shows a sample listing of the kinds of stakeholders involved in a typical project.

FIGURE 1.1   Project stakeholders

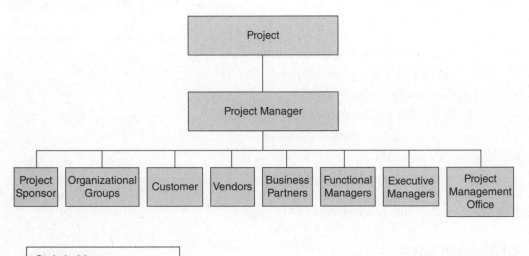

Many times, stakeholders have conflicting interests. It's the project manager's responsibility to understand these conflicts and try to resolve them. It's also the project manager's responsibility to manage stakeholder expectations. Be certain to identify and meet with all key stakeholders early in the project to understand their needs and constraints. When in doubt, you should always resolve stakeholder conflicts in favor of the customer.

Project Characteristics

You've just learned that a project has several characteristics:

- Projects are unique.
- Projects are temporary in nature and have a definite beginning and ending date.
- Projects are completed when the project goals are achieved or it's determined the project is no longer viable.
- A successful project is one that meets the expectations of your stakeholders.

Using these criteria, let's examine the assignment from the VP of marketing to determine whether it is a project:

Is it unique?　Yes, because the kiosks don't exist now in the local grocery stores. This is a new way of offering the company's services to its customer base. Although the service the company is offering isn't new, the way it is presenting its services is.

Does the project have a limited time frame?　Yes, the start date of this project is today, and the end date is the end of this year. It is a temporary endeavor.

Is there a way to determine when the project is completed?　Yes, the kiosks will be installed, and services will be offered from them. Once all the kiosks are intact and operating, the project will come to a close.

Is there a way to determine stakeholder satisfaction?　Yes, the expectations of the stakeholders will be documented in the form of deliverables and requirements during the Planning processes. Some of the requirements the VP noted are that customers can sign up for new services, pay their bills, and purchase equipment and accessories. These deliverables and requirements will be compared to the finished product to determine whether it meets the expectations of the stakeholders.

Houston, we have a project.

What Is Project Management?

You've determined that you indeed have a project. What now? The notes you scratched on the back of a napkin during your coffee break might get you started, but that's not exactly good project management practice.

We have all witnessed this scenario: An assignment is made, and the project team members jump directly into the project, busying themselves with building the product, service, or result requested. Often, careful thought is not given to the project-planning process. I'm sure you've heard coworkers toss around statements like, "That would be a waste of valuable time," or "Why plan when you can just start building?" Project progress in this circumstance is rarely measured against the customer requirements. In the end, the delivered product, service, or result doesn't meet the expectations of the customer. This is a frustrating experience for all those involved. Unfortunately, many projects follow this poorly constructed path.

Project management brings together a set of tools and techniques—performed by people—to describe, organize, and monitor the work of project activities. *Project managers* are the people responsible for managing the project processes and applying the tools and techniques used to carry out the project activities. All projects are composed of processes, even if they employ a haphazard approach. There are many advantages to organizing projects and teams around the project management processes endorsed by PMI®. We'll be examining those processes and their advantages in depth throughout the remainder of this book.

According to the *PMBOK® Guide*, project management involves applying knowledge, skills, tools, and techniques during the course of the project to accomplish the project's objective. It is the responsibility of the project manager to ensure that project management techniques are applied and followed.

Exam Spotlight

Remember that according to the *PMBOK® Guide*, the definition of project management is applying tools, techniques, skills, and knowledge to project activities to bring about successful results and meet the project requirements.

Project management is a collection of processes that includes initiating a new project, planning, putting the project management plan into action, and measuring progress and performance. It involves identifying the project requirements, establishing project objectives, balancing constraints, and taking the needs and expectations of the key stakeholders into consideration. Planning is one of the most important functions you'll perform during the course of a project. It sets the standard for the remainder of the project's life and is used to track future project performance. Before we begin the Planning process, let's look at some of the ways the work of project management is organized.

Programs

According to the *PMBOK® Guide*, *programs* are groups of related projects, subprograms, or other works that are managed using similar techniques in a coordinated fashion. When projects are managed collectively as programs, it's possible to capitalize on benefits that wouldn't be achievable if the projects were managed separately. This would be the case where a very large program exists with many subprojects under it—for example, building an urban live-work-shopping development. Many subprojects exist underneath this program, such as design and placement of living and shopping areas, architectural drawings, theme and design, construction, marketing, facilities management, and so on. Each of the subprojects is a project unto itself. Each subproject has its own project manager, who reports to a project manager with responsibility over several of the areas, who in turn reports to the head project manager who is responsible for the entire program. All the projects are related and are managed together so that collective benefits are realized and controls are implemented and managed in a coordinated fashion. Sometimes programs involve aspects of ongoing operations as well. After the shopping areas in our example are built, the management of the buildings and common areas becomes an ongoing operation. The management of this collection of projects—determining their interdependencies, managing among their constraints, and resolving issues among them—is called *program management*. Program management also involves centrally managing and coordinating groups of related projects to meet the objectives of the program.

Portfolios

Portfolios are collections of programs, subportfolios, operations, and projects that support strategic business goals or objectives. Let's say our company is in the construction business. Our organization has several business units: retail, single-family residential, and multi-family residential. Collectively, the projects within all of these business units make up the portfolio. The program I talked about in the preceding section (the collection of projects associated with building the new live-work urban area) is a program within our portfolio. Other programs and projects could be within this portfolio as well. Programs and projects within a portfolio are not necessarily related to one another in a direct way. However, the overall objective of any program or project in this portfolio is to meet the strategic objectives of the portfolio, which in turn should meet the strategic objectives of the department and ultimately the business unit or corporation.

Portfolio management encompasses managing the collections of programs, projects, other work, and sometimes other portfolios. It also entails facilitating effective management of all the work to meet the organization's strategic goals. Maximizing the portfolio is critical to increasing success. This includes weighing the value of each project, or potential project, against the business's strategic objectives, selecting the right programs and projects, eliminating projects that don't add value, and assuring resources are available to support the work. It also concerns monitoring active projects for adherence to objectives, balancing the portfolio among the other investments of the organization, and assuring the efficient use of resources. Portfolio managers also monitor the organizational planning activities of the organization to help prioritize projects according to fund availability, risk, the strategic mission, and more. Portfolio management is generally performed by a senior manager who has significant experience in both project and program management.

Table 1.1 compares the differences between projects, programs, and portfolios according to the *PMBOK® Guide*.

TABLE 1.1   Projects, programs, and portfolios

	Purpose	Area of focus
Project	Applies and uses project management processes, knowledge, and skills	Delivery of products, services, or results
Program	Collections of related projects, subprojects, or work managed in a coordinated fashion	Project interdependencies
Portfolio	Aligns projects/programs/portfolios/sub-portfolios/operations to the organization's strategic business objectives	Optimizing efficiencies, objectives, costs, resources, risks, and schedules

Exam Spotlight

Projects or programs within a portfolio are not necessarily related or dependent on each other.

Project Management Offices

The *project management office (PMO)* is usually a centralized organizational unit that oversees the management of projects and programs throughout the organization. The most common reason a company starts a project management office is to establish and maintain procedures and standards for project management methodologies and to manage resources assigned to the projects in the PMO. PMOs are often tasked with establishing an organizational project management (OPM) framework. OPM helps assure projects, programs, and portfolios are managed consistently and that they support the overall goals of the organization. OPM is used in conjunction with other organizational practices such as human resources, technology, and culture, to improve performance and maintain a competitive edge.

According to the *PMBOK® Guide*, the key purpose of a PMO is to provide support for project managers. This may include:

- Providing an established project management methodology including templates, forms, standards, and more
- Mentoring, coaching, and training project managers
- Facilitating communication within and across projects
- Managing resources

Not all PMOs are the same. Some PMOs may have a great deal of authority and control whereas another may only serve a supporting role. According to the *PMBOK® Guide*, there are three types of PMOs: supportive, controlling, and directive. Table 1.2 describes each type of PMO, their roles, and their levels of control.

TABLE 1.2   PMO organizational types

PMO type	Role	Level of control
Supportive	Consulting: Templates Project repository	Low
Controlling	Compliance: Project management framework Conformance to methodologies	Moderate
Directive	Controlling: PMO manages projects	High

A PMO can exist in all organizational structures—functional, projectized, or matrix. (These structures will be discussed later in this chapter.) It might have full authority to manage projects, including the authority to cancel projects, or it might serve only in an advisory role. PMOs might also be called *project offices* or *program management offices* or *Centers of Excellence*.

The PMO usually has responsibility for maintaining and archiving project documentation for future reference. This office compares project goals with project progress and gives feedback to the project teams and management. It assures projects are aligned with the strategic objectives of the organization, and it measures the performance of active projects and suggests corrective actions. The PMO evaluates completed projects for their adherence to the project management plan and asks questions like, "Did the project meet the time frames established?" and, "Did it stay within budget?" and, "Was the quality acceptable?"

Project managers are typically responsible for meeting the objectives of the project they are managing, controlling the resources within the project, and managing the individual project constraints. The PMO is responsible for managing the objectives of a collective set of projects, managing resources across the projects, and managing the interdependencies of all the projects within the PMO's authority.

Project management offices are common in organizations today, if for no other reason than to serve as a collection point for project documentation. Some PMOs are fairly sophisticated and prescribe the standards and methodologies to be used in all project phases across the enterprise. Still, others provide all these functions and also offer project management consulting services. However, the establishment of a PMO is not required in order for you to apply good project management practices to your next project.

There Ought to Be a Law

The importance of practicing sound project management techniques has grown significantly over the past several years. The state of Colorado passed legislation requiring project managers on large projects conducted by state employees or vendors working on behalf of the state to be certified in project management best practices. This was an attempt to increase the probability of project success and reduce negative risk. The state of Colorado has seen more projects delivered on time, on budget, and within scope because of the application of best practices in this area and because their project managers are highly trained and have a great deal of experience at managing projects.

Skills Every Good Project Manager Needs

Many times, organizations will knight their technical experts as project managers. The skill and expertise that made them stars in their technical fields are mistakenly thought to translate into project management skills. This is not necessarily so.

Project managers are generalists with many skills in their repertoires. They are also problem solvers who wear many hats. Project managers might indeed possess technical skills, but technical skills are not a prerequisite for sound project management skills. Your project team should include a few technical experts, and these are the people on whom the project manager will rely for technical details. Understanding and applying good project management techniques, along with a solid understanding of general management and interpersonal skills, are career builders for all aspiring project managers.

Project managers have been likened to small-business owners. They need to know a little bit about every aspect of management. General management skills include every area of management, from accounting to strategic planning, supervision, personnel administration, and more. Interpersonal skills are often called soft skills and include communications, leadership, decision making, and more. General management and interpersonal skills are called into play on every project. But some projects require specific skills in certain application areas. Application areas consist of categories of projects that have common elements. These elements, or application areas, can be defined several ways: by industry group (automotive, pharmaceutical), by department (accounting, marketing), and by technical (software development, engineering) or management (procurement, research and development) specialties. These application areas are usually concerned with disciplines, regulations, and the specific needs of the project, the customer, or the industry. For example, most governments have specific procurement rules that apply to their projects that wouldn't be applicable in the construction industry. The pharmaceutical industry is acutely interested in regulations set forth by the Food and Drug Administration. The automotive industry has little or no concern for either of these types of regulations. Having experience in the application area you're working in will give you a leg up when it comes to project management. Although you can call in the experts who have application area knowledge, it doesn't hurt for you to understand the specific aspects of the application areas of your project.

The interpersonal skills listed in the following sections are the foundation of good project management practices. Your mastery of them (or lack thereof) will likely affect project outcomes. The various skills of a project manager can be broken out in a more or less declining scale of importance. We'll look at an overview of these skills now, and I'll discuss each in more detail in subsequent chapters.

Communication Skills

One of the single most important characteristics of a first-rate project manager is excellent communication skills. Written and oral communications are the backbone of all successful projects. Many forms of communication will exist during the life of your project. As the creator or manager of most of the project communication (project documents, meeting updates, status reports, and so on), it's your job to ensure that the information is explicit, clear, and complete so that your audience will have no trouble understanding what has been communicated. Once the information has been distributed, it is the responsibility of the people receiving the information to make sure they understand it.

    Many forms of communication and communication styles exist. I'll discuss them more in depth in Chapter 8, "Developing the Project Team."

Organizational and Planning Skills

Organizational and planning skills are closely related and probably the most important skills, after communication skills, a project manager can possess. Organization takes on many forms. As project manager, you'll have project documentation, requirements information, memos, project reports, personnel records, vendor quotes, contracts, and much more to track and be able to locate at a moment's notice. You will also have to organize meetings, put together teams, and perhaps manage and organize media-release schedules, depending on your project.

Time management skills are closely related to organizational skills. It's difficult to stay organized without an understanding of how you're managing your time. I recommend you attend a time management class if you've never been to one. They have some great tips and techniques to help you prioritize problems and interruptions, prioritize your day, and manage your time.

I discuss planning extensively throughout the course of this book. There isn't any aspect of project management that doesn't first involve planning. Planning skills go hand in hand with organizational skills. Combining these two with excellent communication skills is almost a sure guarantee of your success in the project management field.

Conflict Management Skills

Show me a project, and I'll show you problems. All projects have some problems, as does, in fact, much of everyday life. Isn't that what they say builds character? But I digress.

Conflict management involves solving problems. Problem solving is really a twofold process. First, you must define the problem by separating the causes from the symptoms. Often when defining problems, you end up just describing the symptoms instead of getting to the heart of what's causing the problem. To avoid that, ask yourself questions like, "Is it an internal or external problem? Is it a technical problem? Are there interpersonal problems between team members? Is it managerial? What are the potential impacts or consequences?" These kinds of questions will help you get to the cause of the problem.

Next, after you have defined the problem, you have some decisions to make. It will take a little time to examine and analyze the problem, the situation causing it, and the alternatives available. After this analysis, the project manager will determine the best course of action to take and implement the decision. The timing of the decision is often as important as the decision itself. If you make a good decision but implement it too late, it might turn into a bad decision.

Negotiation and Influencing Skills

Effective problem solving requires negotiation and influencing skills. We all utilize negotiation skills in one form or another every day. For example, on a nightly basis I am asked, "Honey, what do you want for dinner?" Then the negotiations begin, and the fried chicken versus swordfish discussion commences. Simply put, negotiating is working with others to come to an agreement.

Negotiation on projects is necessary in almost every area of the project, from scope definition to budgets, contracts, resource assignments, and more. This might involve one-on-one negotiation or with teams of people, and it can occur many times throughout the project.

Influencing is convincing the other party that swordfish is a better choice than fried chicken, even if fried chicken is what they want. It's also the ability to get things done through others. Influencing requires an understanding of the formal and informal structure of all the organizations involved in the project.

Power and politics are techniques used to influence people to perform. *Power* is the ability to get people to do things they wouldn't do otherwise. It's also the ability to change minds and the course of events and to influence outcomes.

 I'll discuss power further in Chapter 8.

Politics involve getting groups of people with different interests to cooperate creatively even in the midst of conflict and disorder.

These skills will be utilized in all areas of project management. Start practicing now because, guaranteed, you'll need these skills on your next project.

Leadership Skills

Leaders and managers are not synonymous terms. *Leaders* impart vision, gain consensus for strategic goals, establish direction, and inspire and motivate others. *Managers* focus on results and are concerned with getting the job done according to the requirements. Even though leaders and managers are not the same, project managers must exhibit the characteristics of both during different times on the project. Understanding when to switch from leadership to management and then back again is a finely tuned and necessary talent.

Team-Building and Motivating Skills

Project managers will rely heavily on team-building and motivational skills. Teams are often formed with people from different parts of the organization. These people might or might not have worked together before, so some component of team-building groundwork might involve the project manager. The project manager will set the tone for the project team and will help the members work through the various stages of team development to become fully functional. Motivating the team, especially during long projects or when experiencing a lot of bumps along the way, is another important role the project manager fulfills during the course of the project.

An interesting caveat to the team-building role is that project managers many times are responsible for motivating team members who are not their direct reports. This has its own set of challenges and dilemmas. One way to help this situation is to ask the functional manager to allow you to participate in your project team members' performance reviews. Use the negotiation and influencing skills I talked about earlier to make sure you're part of this process.

> **Multiple Dimensions**
>
> Project managers are an interesting bunch. They know a little bit about a lot of topics and are excellent communicators. They have the ability to motivate people, even those who have no reason to be loyal to the project, and they can make the hard-line calls when necessary. Project managers can get caught in sticky situations that occasionally require making decisions that are good for the company (or the customer) but aren't good for certain stakeholders. These offended stakeholders will then drag their feet, and the project manager has to play the heavy in order to motivate and gain their cooperation again. Some organizations hire contract project managers to run their large, company-altering projects just because they don't want to burn out a key employee in this role. Fortunately, that doesn't happen often.

Role of a Project Manager

Project managers are responsible for assuring the objectives of the project are met. Projects create value, which in turn increases the business value of the organization. Business value is the total value of all the assets of the organization, including both tangible and intangible elements. The project manager must be familiar with the organization's strategic plan in order to marry those strategic objectives with the projects in the portfolio. This requires all of the skills we covered in this section. However, according to the *PMBOK® Guide*, applying the skills and techniques of project management to your next project is not enough—you must also have the following capabilities:

- Knowledge—of project management techniques
- Performance—the ability to perform as a project manager by applying your knowledge
- Personal—behavioral characteristics including leadership abilities, attitudes, ethics, and more

Now that you've been properly introduced to some of the skills you need in your tool kit, you'll know to be prepared to communicate, solve problems, lead, and negotiate your way through your next project.

Understanding Organizational Structures

Just as projects are unique, so are the organizations in which they're carried out. Organizations have their own styles, cultures, and ways of communicating that influence how project work is performed and influences their ability to achieve project success. One of the keys to determining the type of organization you work in is measuring how much authority senior management is willing to delegate to project managers. Although uniqueness abounds in business cultures, all organizations are structured in one of three ways: functional, projectized, or matrix. It's helpful to know and understand the organizational structure and the culture of the entity in which you're working. Companies with aggressive cultures that are comfortable in a leading-edge position within their industries are highly likely to take on risky projects. Project managers who are willing to suggest new ideas and projects that have never been undertaken before are likely to receive a warm reception in this kind of environment. Conversely, organizational cultures that are risk-averse and prefer the follow-the-leader position within their industries are highly unlikely to take on risky endeavors. Project managers with risk-seeking, aggressive styles are likely to receive a cool reception in a culture like this.

The level of authority the project manager enjoys is denoted by the organizational structure and by the interactions of the project manager with various levels of management. For example, a project manager within a functional organization has little to no formal authority. Their title might not be project manager; instead, they might be called a *project leader*, a *project coordinator*, or perhaps a *project expeditor*. And a project manager who primarily works with operations-level managers will likely have less authority than one who works with middle- or strategic-level managers.

Exam Spotlight

According to the *PMBOK® Guide*, the project managers' authority levels, availability of resources, control over the project budget, the role of the project manager, and the project team makeup are influenced by the structure of the organization; by the level of interaction the project manager has with strategic-level managers, middle managers, and operations-level managers; and by the project management maturity levels of the organization.

We'll now take a look at each of these types of organizations individually to better understand how the project management role works in each one.

Functional Organizations

One common type of organization is the *functional organization*. Chances are you have worked in this type of organization. This is probably the oldest style of organization and is, therefore, known as the traditional approach to organizing businesses.

Functional organizations are centered on specialties and grouped by function, which is why it's called *functional organization*. As an example, the organization might have a human resources department, finance department, marketing department, and so on. The work in these departments is specialized and requires people who have the skill sets and experiences in these specialized functions to perform specific duties for the department. Figure 1.2 shows a typical organizational chart for a functional organization.

FIGURE 1.2   Functional organizational chart

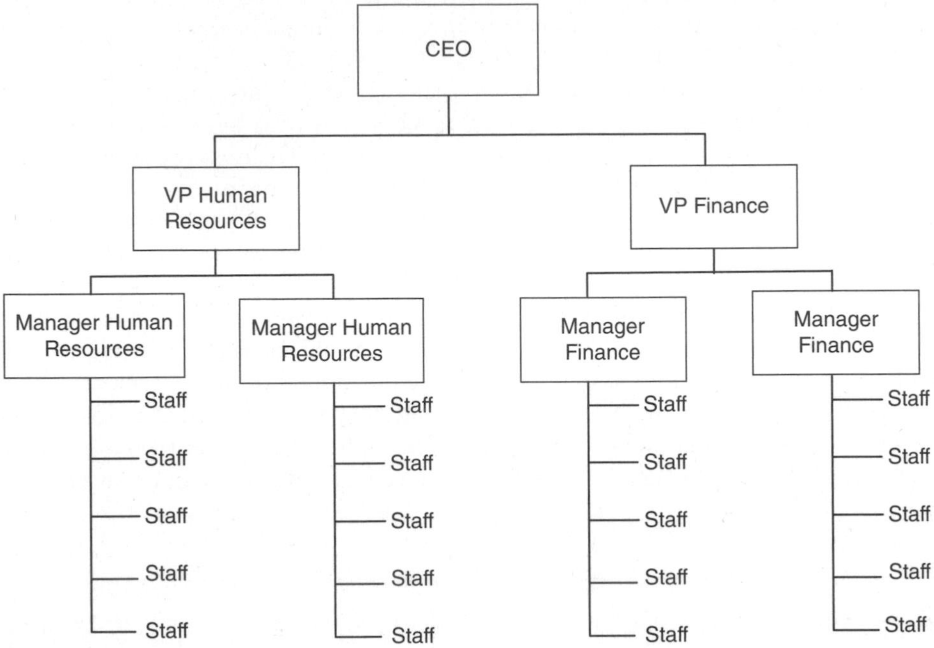

You can see that this type of organization is set up to be a hierarchy. Staff personnel report to managers who report to department heads who report to vice presidents who report to the CEO. In other words, each employee reports to only one manager; ultimately, one person at the top is in charge. Many companies today, as well as governmental agencies, are structured in a hierarchical fashion. In organizations like this, be aware of the chain of command. A strict chain of command might exist, and the corporate culture might dictate that you follow it. Roughly translated: *Don't talk to the big boss without first talking to your boss who talks to their boss who talks to the big boss.* Wise project managers should determine whether there is a chain of command, how strictly it's enforced, and how the chain is linked before venturing outside it.

Each department or group in a functional organization is managed independently and has a limited span of control. Marketing doesn't run the finance department or its projects, for example. The marketing department is concerned with its own functions and projects. If it were necessary for the marketing department to get input from the finance department on a project, the marketing team members would follow the chain of command. A marketing manager would speak to a manager in finance to get the needed information and then pass it back down to the project team.

Human Resources in a Functional Organization

Commonalities exist among the personnel assigned to the various departments in a functional organization. In theory, people with similar skills and experiences are easier to manage as a group. Instead of scattering them throughout the organization, it is more efficient to keep them functioning together. Work assignments are easily distributed to those who are best suited for the task when everyone with the same skill works together. Usually, the supervisors and managers of these workers are experienced in the area they supervise and are able to recommend training and career enrichment activities for their employees.

 Workers in functional organizations specialize in an area of expertise— finance or personnel administration, for instance—and then become very good at their specialty.

People in a functional organization can see a clear upward career path. An assistant budget analyst might be promoted to a budget analyst and then eventually to a department manager over many budget analysts.

The Downside of Functional Organizations

Functional organizations have their disadvantages. If this is the kind of organization you work in, you probably have experienced some of them.

One of the greatest disadvantages for the project manager is that they have little to no formal authority. This does not mean project managers in functional organizations are doomed to failure. Many projects are undertaken and successfully completed within this type of organization. Good communication and interpersonal and influencing skills on the part of the project manager are required to bring about a successful project under this structure.

In a functional organization, the vice president or senior department manager is usually the one responsible for projects. The title of project manager denotes authority, and in a functional structure, that authority rests with the VP.

Managing Projects in a Functional Organization

Projects are typically undertaken in a divided approach in a functional organization. For example, the marketing department will work on its portion of the project and then hand it off to the manufacturing department to complete its part, and so on. The work the marketing department does is considered a marketing project, whereas the work the manufacturing department does is considered a manufacturing project.

Some projects require project team members from different departments to work together at the same time on various aspects of the project. Project team members in this structure will more than likely remain loyal to their functional managers. The functional manager is responsible for their performance reviews, and their career opportunities lie within the functional department—not within the project team. Exhibiting leadership skills by forming a common vision regarding the project and the ability to motivate people to work toward that vision are great skills to exercise in this situation. As previously mentioned, it also doesn't hurt to have the project manager work with the functional manager in contributing to the employee's performance review.

Resource Pressures in a Functional Organization

Competition for resources and project priorities can become fierce when multiple projects are undertaken within a functional organization. For example, in my organization, it's common to have competing project requests from three or more departments all vying for the same resources. Thrown into the heap is the requirement to make, for example, mandated tax law changes, which automatically usurps all other priorities. This sometimes causes frustration and political infighting. One department thinks their project is more important than another and will do anything to get that project pushed ahead of the others. Again, it takes great skill and diplomatic abilities to keep projects on track and functioning smoothly. In Chapter 2, "Creating the Project Charter," I'll discuss the importance of gaining stakeholder buy-in, and in Chapter 5, "Developing the Project Budget and Communicating the Plan," I'll talk about the importance of communication to avert some of these problems.

Project managers have little authority in functional organizations, but with the right skills, they can successfully accomplish many projects. Table 1.3 highlights the advantages and disadvantages of this type of organization.

TABLE 1.3   Functional organizations

Advantages	Disadvantages
There is an enduring organizational structure.	Project managers have little to no formal authority.
There is a clear career path with separation of functions, allowing specialty skills to flourish.	Multiple projects compete for limited resources and priority.
Employees have one supervisor with a clear chain of command.	Project team members are loyal to the functional manager.

Projectized Organizations

Projectized organizations are nearly the opposite of functional organizations. The focus of this type of organization is the project itself. The idea behind a projectized organization is to develop loyalty to the project, not to a functional manager.

Figure 1.3 shows a typical organizational chart for a projectized organization.

FIGURE 1.3   Projectized organizational chart

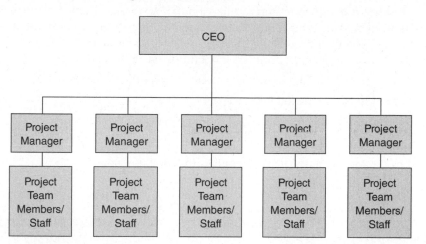

Organizational resources are dedicated to projects and project work in purely projectized organizations. Project managers almost always have ultimate authority over the project in this structure and report directly to the CEO. In a purely projectized organization, supporting functions such as human resources and accounting might report directly to the project manager as well. Project managers are responsible for making decisions regarding the project and acquiring and assigning resources. They have the authority to choose and assign resources from other areas in the organization or to hire them from outside if needed. For example, if there isn't enough money in the budget to hire additional resources, the project manager will have to come up with alternatives to solve this problem. This is known as a *constraint*. Project managers in all organizational structures are limited by constraints such as scope, schedule, and cost (or budget). Quality is also considered a constraint, and it's generally affected by scope, schedule, and/or cost. We'll talk more about constraints in Chapter 2.

You may come across the term *triple constraints* in your studies. The term refers to scope, schedule, and cost constraints. However, please note that the *PMBOK® Guide* also calls constraints, competing demands, and notes that the primary competing demands on projects are scope, schedule, cost, risk, resources, and quality.

Teams are formed and often *co-located*, which means team members physically work at the same location. Project team members report to the project manager, not to a functional or departmental manager. One obvious drawback to a projectized organization is that project team members might find themselves out of work at the end of the project. An example of this might be a consultant who works on a project until completion and then is put on the bench or let go at the end of the project. Some inefficiency exists in this kind of organization when it comes to resource utilization. If you have a situation where you need a highly specialized skill at certain times throughout the project, the resource you're using to perform this function might be idle during other times in the project.

In summary, you can identify projectized organizations in several ways:

- Project managers have high to ultimate authority over the project.
- The focus of the organization is the project.
- The organization's resources are focused on projects and project work.
- Team members are co-located.
- Loyalties are formed to the project, not to a functional manager.
- Project teams are dissolved at the conclusion of the project.

 Real World Scenario

The Projectized Graphic Artist

You've been appointed project manager for your company's website design and implementation. You're working in a projectized organization, so you have the authority to acquire and assign resources. You put together your team, including programmers, technical writers, testers, and business analysts. Julianne, a highly qualified graphic arts designer, is also part of your team. Julianne's specialized graphic arts skills are needed only at certain times throughout the project. When she has completed the graphic design portion of the screen she's working on, she doesn't have anything else to do until the next page is ready. Depending on how involved the project is and how the work is structured, days or weeks might pass before Julianne's skills are needed. This is where the inefficiency occurs in a purely projectized organization. The project manager will have to find other duties that Julianne can perform during these downtimes. It's not practical to let her go and then hire her back when she's needed again.

In this situation, you might assign Julianne to other project duties when she's not working on graphic design. Perhaps she can edit the text for the web pages or assist with the design of the upcoming marketing campaign. You might also share her time with another project manager in the organization.

During the Planning process, you will discover the skills and abilities of all your team members so that you can plan their schedules accordingly and eliminate idle time.

Matrix Organizations

Matrix organizations came about to minimize the differences between, and take advantage of, the strengths and weaknesses of functional and projectized organizations. The idea at play here is that the best of both organizational structures can be realized by combining them into one. The project objectives are fulfilled and good project management techniques are utilized while still maintaining a hierarchical structure in the organization.

Employees in a matrix organization oftentimes report to one functional manager and to at least one project manager. It's possible that employees could report to multiple project managers if they are working on multiple projects at one time. Functional managers pick up the administrative portion of the duties and assign employees to projects. They also monitor the work of their employees on the various projects. Project managers are responsible for executing the project and giving out work assignments based on project activities. Project managers and functional managers share the responsibility of performance reviews for the employee.

In a nutshell, in a matrix organization, functional managers assign employees to projects, whereas project managers assign tasks associated with the project.

Matrix organizations have unique characteristics. We'll look at how projects are conducted and managed and how project and functional managers share the work in this organizational structure next.

Project Focus in a Matrix Organization

Matrix organizations allow project managers to focus on the project and project work just as in a projectized organization. The project team is free to focus on the project objectives with minimal distractions from the functional department.

Project managers should take care when working up activity and project estimates for the project in a matrix organization. The estimates should be given to the functional managers for input before publishing. The functional manager is the one in charge of assigning or freeing up resources to work on projects. If the project manager is counting on a certain employee to work on the project at a certain time, the project manager should determine their availability up front with the functional manager. Project estimates might have to be modified if it's discovered that the employee they were counting on is not available when needed.

Balance of Power in a Matrix Organization

As we've discussed, a lot of communication and negotiation takes place between the project manager and the functional manager. This calls for a balance of power between the two, or one will dominate the other.

In a strong matrix organization, the balance of power rests with the project manager. They have the ability to strong-arm the functional managers into giving up their best resources for projects. Sometimes, more resources than necessary are assembled for the project, and then project managers negotiate these resources among themselves, cutting out the functional manager altogether, as you can see in Figure 1.4.

FIGURE 1.4   Strong matrix organizational chart

On the other end of the spectrum is the weak matrix (see Figure 1.5). As you would suspect, the functional managers have the majority of power in this structure. Project managers are really project coordinators or expeditors with part-time responsibilities on projects in a weak matrix organization. Project managers have limited authority, just as in the functional organization. On the other hand, the functional managers have a lot of authority and make all the work assignments. The project manager simply expedites the project.

FIGURE 1.5   Weak matrix organizational chart

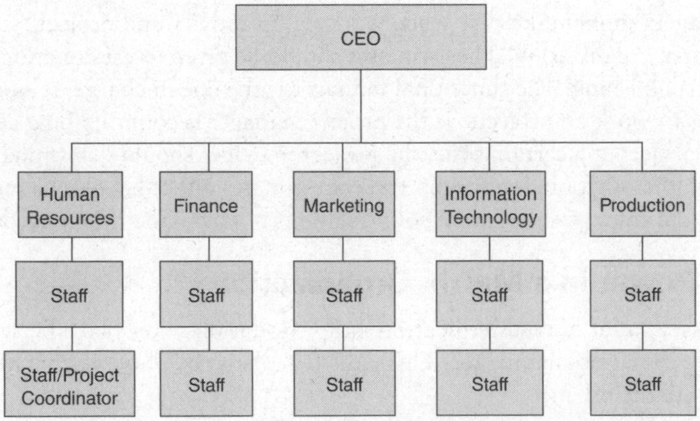

In between the weak matrix and the strong matrix is an organizational structure called the *balanced matrix* (see Figure 1.6). The features of the balanced matrix are what I've been discussing throughout this section. The power is balanced between project managers and functional managers. Each manager has responsibility for their parts of the project or organization, and employees get assigned to projects based on the needs of the project, not the strength or weakness of the manager's position.

FIGURE 1.6   Balanced matrix organizational chart

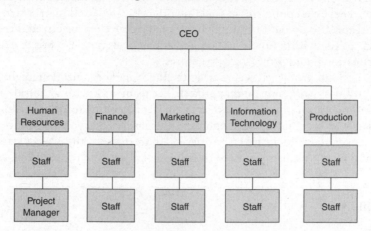

Matrix organizations have subtle differences, and it's important to understand their differences for the PMP® exam. The easiest way to remember them is that the weak matrix has many of the same characteristics as the functional organization, whereas the strong matrix has many of the same characteristics as the projectized organization. The balanced matrix is exactly that—a balance between weak and strong, where the project manager shares authority and responsibility with the functional manager. Table 1.4 compares all three structures.

TABLE 1.4   Comparing matrix structures

	Weak matrix	Balanced matrix	Strong matrix
Project manager's title	Project coordinator, project leader, or project expeditor	Project manager	Project manager
Project manager's focus	Split focus between project and functional responsibilities	Projects and project work	Projects and project work
Project manager's power	Minimal authority	Balance of authority and power	Significant authority and power
Project manager's time	Part-time on projects	Full-time on projects	Full-time on projects
Organization style	Most like functional organization	Blend of both weak and strong matrix	Most like a projectized organization
Project manager reports to	Functional manager	A functional manager, but shares authority and power	Manager of project managers

Most organizations today use some combination of the organizational structures described here. They're a *composite* of functional, projectized, and matrix structures. It's rare that an organization would be purely functional or purely projectized. Projectized structures can coexist within functional organizations, and most composite organizations are a mix of functional and projectized structures.

In the case of a high-profile, critical project, the functional organization might appoint a special project team to work only on that project. The team is structured outside the bounds of the functional organization, and the project manager has ultimate authority for the project. This is a workable project management approach and ensures open communication between the project manager and team members. At the end of the project, the project team is dissolved, and the project members return to their functional areas to resume their usual duties.

Exam Spotlight

Understand the characteristics of each organizational structure and their strengths and weaknesses for the exam.

Project-Based Organizations

There is one more structure we should talk about called a *project-based organization (PBO)*. A PBO is a temporary structure an organization puts into place to perform the work of the project. A PBO can exist in any of the organizational structure types we've just discussed. Most of the work of a PBO is project based and can involve an entire organization or a division within an organization. The important thing to note about PBOs for the exam is that a PBO measures the success of the final product, service, or result of the project by bypassing politics and position, and thereby weakening the red tape and hierarchy within the organization because the project team works within the PBO and takes its authority from there.

Organizations are unique, as are the projects they undertake. Understanding the organizational structure will help you, as a project manager, with the cultural influences and communication avenues that exist in the organization to gain cooperation and successfully bring your projects to a close.

Understanding Project Life Cycles and Project Management Processes

Project life cycles are similar to the life cycle that parents experience raising their children to adulthood. Children start out as infants and generate lots of excitement wherever they go. However, not much is known about them at first. So, you study them as they grow, and you assess their needs. Over time, they mature and grow (and cost a lot of money in the process) until one day the parents' job is done.

Projects start out just like this and progress along a similar path. Someone comes up with a great idea for a project and actively solicits support for it. The project, after being approved, progresses through the intermediate phases to the ending phase, where it is completed and closed out.

Project Phases and Project Life Cycles

Most projects are divided into phases, and all projects, large or small, have a similar project life cycle structure. Project phases generally consist of segments of work that allow for easier management, planning, and control of the work. The work and the deliverables produced during the phase are typically unique to that phase. Some projects may consist of one phase, and others may have many phases.

The number of phases depends on the project complexity and the industry. For example, information technology projects might progress through phases such as requirements, design, program, test, and implement. All the collective phases the project progresses through in concert are called the *project life cycle*. Project life cycles are similar for all projects regardless of their size or complexity.

The phases that occur within the project life cycle are sequential and sometimes overlap each other. Most projects consist of the following structure (not to be confused with the project management process groups that we'll discuss in the section titled, "Project Management Process Groups"):

- Beginning the project
- Planning and organizing the work of the project
- Performing the work of the project
- Closing out the project

Life Cycle Categories

According to the *PMBOK® Guide*, there are three categories of project life cycles. Each of these project life cycles contain the phases, or iterations, we just discussed (beginning, planning, performing, closing). The three types of project life cycles are as follows:

Predictive Cycles (Also Known As Fully Plan-Driven Approach or Waterfall)   The project scope is defined at the beginning of the project and changes are monitored closely. If changes are made, you must revisit and modify plans and formally accept the changes to the scope and subsequent project management plan. The work of each phase is usually distinct and not repeated in other phases. Schedules and budgets are defined early in the life cycle as well. Each phase has an emphasis on a different portion of the project activities and different project management process groups (described in the next section) are performed during each phase.

Iterative and Incremental Life Cycles   Project deliverables are defined early in the life cycle and progressively elaborated as the project progresses. Schedule and cost estimates are continually refined as the end product, service, or result of the project is more clearly defined.

Iterative life cycles are a perfect choice for large projects, complex projects (this life cycle process will reduce the complexity), for those where changing objectives and scope are known ahead of time, or for projects where deliverables need to be delivered incrementally. Each phase requires performing all of the project management process groups.

Adaptive Life Cycles (Also Known As Agile Methods or Change-Driven Methods)   Choose this method when active participation of your stakeholders is required throughout the project, when you are not certain of all the requirements at the beginning of the project, or when you work in a changing environment. This life cycle produces deliverables, or portions of deliverables, in short time periods of 2 to 4 weeks. Each iteration must produce something that is ready for release at the end of the time period, and as such, the time period and the resources are fixed. All iterations require the Planning process group and most will perform all of the project management process groups.

The end of each phase within the life cycle, regardless of the type of life cycle you are using, allows the project manager, stakeholders, and project sponsor the opportunity to determine whether the project should continue to the next phase. To progress to the next phase, the deliverable from the phase before it must be reviewed for accuracy and approved. As each phase is completed, it's handed off to the next phase. We'll look at handoffs and progressions through these phases next.

Handoffs

Project phases evolve through the life cycle in a series of phase sequences called *handoffs*, or technical transfers. For projects that consist of sequential phases, the end of one phase typically marks the beginning of the next. For example, in the construction industry, feasibility studies often take place in the beginning phase of a project and are completed prior to the beginning of the next phase.

The purpose of the *feasibility study* is to determine whether the project is worth undertaking and whether the project will be profitable to the organization. A feasibility study is a preliminary assessment of the viability of the project; the viability or perhaps marketability of the product, service, or result of the project; and the project's value to the organization. It might also determine whether the product, service, or result of the project is safe and meets industry or governmental standards and regulations. The completion and approval of the feasibility study triggers the beginning of the requirements phase, where requirements are documented and then handed off to the design phase, where blueprints are produced. The feasibility might also show that the project is not worth pursuing and the project is then terminated; therefore, the next phase never begins.

Phase Completion

You will recognize phase completion because each phase has a specific deliverable, or multiple deliverables, that marks the end of the phase. A *deliverable* is an output that must be produced, verified, and approved to bring the phase, life cycle process, or project to completion. Deliverables are unique and verifiable and may be tangible or intangible, such as the ability to carry out a service. Deliverables might also include things such as design documents, project budgets, blueprints, project schedules, prototypes, and so on.

A phase-end review allows those involved with the work to determine whether the project should continue to the next phase. For example, a deliverable produced in the beginning phase of a construction industry project might be the feasibility study. Producing, verifying, and accepting the feasibility study will signify the ending of this phase of the project. The successful conclusion of one phase does not guarantee authorization to begin the next phase. The feasibility study mentioned earlier might show that environmental impacts of an enormous nature would result if the construction project were undertaken at the proposed location. Based on this information, a go or no-go decision can be made at the end of the phase. Phase-end reviews give the project manager the ability to discover, address, and take corrective action against errors discovered during the phase.

 The *PMBOK® Guide* states that phase end reviews are also known by a few other names: *phase exits, phase gates, phase reviews, milestones, stage gates,* and *kill points.*

Multi-phased Projects

Projects may consist of one or more phases. The phases of a project are often performed sequentially, but there are situations where performing phases concurrently, or overlapping the start date of a sequential phase, can benefit the project. According to the *PMBOK® Guide* there are two types of phase-to-phase relationships:

Sequential Relationships   One phase must finish before the next phase can begin.

Overlapping Relationships   One phase starts before the prior phase completes.

Sometimes phases are overlapped to shorten or compress the project schedule. This is called *fast tracking*. Fast tracking means that a later phase is started prior to completing and approving the phase, or phases, that come before it. This technique is used to shorten the overall duration of the project.

Project phases are performed within a project life cycle, as I mentioned earlier in this section. Project life cycles typically consist of initiating the project, performing the work of the project, and so on. As a result, most projects have the following characteristics in common:

- In the beginning of the project life cycle, when the project is initiated, costs are low, and few team members are assigned to the project.

- As the project progresses, costs and staffing increase and then taper off at closing.

- The potential that the project will come to a successful ending is lowest at the beginning of the project; its chance for success increases as the project progresses through its phases and life cycle stages.

- Risk is highest at the beginning of the project and gradually decreases the closer the project comes to completion.

- Stakeholders have the greatest chance of influencing the project and the characteristics of the product, service, or result of the project in the beginning phases and have less and less influence as the project progresses.

This same phenomenon exists within the project management processes as well. We'll look at those next.

Project Management Process Groups

Project management processes organize and describe the work of the project. The *PMBOK® Guide* describes five process groups used to accomplish this end. These processes are performed by people and are interrelated and dependent on one another.

These are the five project management process groups that the *PMBOK® Guide* documents:

- Initiating
- Planning
- Executing
- Monitoring and Controlling
- Closing

All these process groups have individual processes that collectively make up the group. For example, the Initiating process group has two processes called Develop Project Charter and Identify Stakeholders. Collectively, these process groups—including all their individual processes—make up the project management process. Projects, or each phase of a project, start with the Initiating process and progress through all the processes in the Planning process group, the Executing process group, and so on, until the project is successfully completed or it's canceled. All projects must complete the Closing processes, even if a project is killed.

Let's start with a high-level overview of each process group. The remainder of this book will cover each of these processes in detail. If you want to peek ahead, Appendix B, "Process Inputs and Outputs," lists each of the process groups, the individual processes that make up each process group, and the Knowledge Areas in which they belong. (I'll introduce Knowledge Areas in the section, "Exploring the Project Management Knowledge Areas," in Chapter 2.)

Project Phases vs. Project Management Process Groups

Don't confuse project phases and life cycles with the project management process groups. Project phases and life cycles describe how the work associated with the product of the project will be completed. For example, a construction project might have phases such as feasibility study, design, build, inspection, and turnover. The five project management process groups (Initiating, Planning, Executing, Monitoring and Controlling, and Closing) organize and describe how the project activities will be conducted in order to meet the project requirements. These processes are generally performed for each phase of a large project. The five process groups are the heart of the *PMBOK® Guide* and the exam. As you progress through this book, be certain you understand each of these processes as they're described in the *PMBOK® Guide*.

Initiating   The *Initiating* process group, as its name implies, occurs at the beginning of the project and at the beginning of each project phase for large projects. Initiating acknowledges that a project, or the next project phase, should begin. This process group grants the approval to commit the organization's resources to working on the project or phase and authorizes the project manager to begin working on the project. The outputs of the Initiating process group, including the project charter and identification of the stakeholders, become inputs into the Planning process group.

Planning   The *Planning* process group is the process of formulating and revising project goals and objectives and creating the project management plan that will be used to achieve the goals the project was undertaken to address. The Planning process group also involves determining alternative courses of action and selecting from among the best of those to produce the project's goals. This process group is where the project requirements are fleshed out. Planning has more processes than any of the other project management process groups. To carry out their functions, the Executing, Monitoring and Controlling, and Closing process groups all rely on the Planning processes and the documentation produced during the Planning processes. Project managers will perform frequent iterations of the Planning processes prior to project completion. Projects are unique and, as such, have never been done before. Therefore, planning must encompass all areas of project management and consider budgets, activity definition, scope planning, schedule development, risk identification, staff acquisition, procurement planning, and more. The greatest conflicts a project manager will encounter in this process group are project prioritization issues.

Executing   The *Executing* process group involves putting the project management plan into action. It's here that the project manager will coordinate and direct project resources to meet the objectives of the project management plan. The Executing processes keep the project on track and ensure that future execution of project plans stays in line with project objectives. This process group is typically where approved changes are implemented. The Executing process group will utilize the most project time and resources, and as a result, costs are usually highest during the Executing processes. Project managers will experience the greatest conflicts over schedules in this cycle.

Monitoring and Controlling   The *Monitoring and Controlling* process group is where project performance measurements are taken and analyzed to determine whether the project is staying true to the project management plan. The idea is to identify problems as soon as possible and apply corrective action to control the work of the project and assure successful outcomes. For example, if you discover that variances exist, you'll apply corrective action to get the project activities realigned with the project management plan. This might require additional passes through the Planning processes to adjust project activities, resources, schedules, budgets, and so on.

Monitoring and Controlling is used to track the progress of work being performed and identify problems and variances within a process group as well as the project as a whole.

Closing   The *Closing* process group is probably the most often skipped process group in project management. Closing brings a formal, orderly end to the activities of a project phase or to the project itself. Once the project objectives have been met, most of us are ready to move on to the next project. However, Closing is important because all the project information is gathered and stored for future reference. The documentation collected during the Closing process group can be reviewed and used to avert potential problems on future projects. Contract closeout occurs here, and formal acceptance and approval are obtained from project stakeholders.

Exam Spotlight

The project manager and project team are responsible for determining which processes within each process group are appropriate for the project on which you're working. This is called *tailoring*. You should consider the size and complexity of the project and the various inputs and outputs of each of the processes when determining which processes to implement and perform. Small projects might not require all of the processes within a process group or the same level of rigor of a large project. Every process should be addressed and determined whether the process is appropriate for the project at hand and if so, what level of implementation is required. Use your judgment when deciding which processes to follow, particularly for small projects.

Characteristics of the Process Groups

The progression through the project management process groups exhibits the same characteristics as progression through the project phases. That is, costs are lowest during the Initiating processes, and few team members are involved. Costs and staffing increase in the Executing process group and then decrease as you approach the Closing process group. The chances for success are lowest during Initiating and highest during Closing. The chances for risks occurring are higher during Initiating, Planning, and Executing, but the impacts of risks are greater during the later processes. Stakeholders have the greatest influence during the Initiating and Planning processes and less and less influence as you progress through Executing, Monitoring and Controlling, and Closing. To give you a better idea of when certain characteristics influence a project, refer to Table 1.5.

TABLE 1.5   Characteristics of the project process groups

	Initiating	Planning	Executing	Monitoring and Controlling	Closing
Costs	Low	Low	Highest	Lower	Lowest
Staffing levels	Lowest	Low	High	High	Low

	Initiating	Planning	Executing	Monitoring and Controlling	Closing
Chance for successful completion	Lowest	Low	Medium	High	Highest
Stakeholder influence	Highest	High	Medium	Low	Lowest
Risk probability of occurrence	Highest	High	Medium	Low	Lowest

The Process Flow

You should not think of the five process groups as onetime processes that are performed as discrete elements. Rather, these processes interact and overlap with each other. They are *iterative* and might be revisited and revised several times as the project is refined throughout its life. The *PMBOK® Guide* calls this process of going back through the process groups an iterative process. The conclusion of each process group allows the project manager and stakeholders to reexamine the business needs of the project and determine whether the project is satisfying those needs—and it is another opportunity to make a go or no-go decision.

Figure 1.7 shows the five process groups in a typical project. Keep in mind that during phases of a project, the Closing process group outputs can provide inputs to the Initiating process group. For example, once the feasibility study discussed earlier is accepted or closed, it becomes an input to the Initiating process group of the design phase.

FIGURE 1.7   Project management process groups

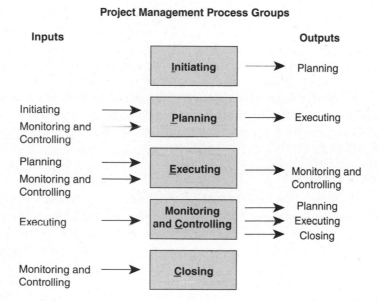

It's important to understand the flow of these processes for the exam. If you remember the processes and their inputs and outputs, it will help you when you're trying to decipher an exam question. The outputs of one process group may in some cases become the inputs into the next process group (or the outputs might be a deliverable of the project). Sometimes just understanding which process the question is asking about will help you determine the answer. One trick you can use to memorize these processes is to remember syrup of ipecac. This is an old-fashioned remedy for accidental poisoning that is no longer used today. If you think of the Monitoring and Controlling process group as simply "Controlling," when you sound out the first initial of each of the process, it sounds like IPECC (Initiating, Planning, Executing, Monitoring and Controlling, and Closing).

As I stated earlier, individual processes make up each of the process groups. For example, the Closing process group consists of two processes: Close Project or Phase and Close Procurements. Each process takes inputs and uses them in conjunction with various tools and techniques to produce outputs.

It's outside the scope of this book to explain all the inputs, tools and techniques, and outputs for each process in each process group (although each is listed in Appendix B). You'll find all the inputs, tools and techniques, and outputs detailed in the *PMBOK® Guide*, and I highly recommend you become familiar with them.

Exam Spotlight

Understand each project management process group and all the processes that make up these groups. Appendix B contains a table of all the processes, their inputs, their tools and techniques, their outputs, and the Knowledge Area in which they each belong.

You'll likely see test questions regarding inputs, tools and techniques, and outputs of many of the processes within each process group. One way to keep them all straight is to remember that tools and techniques usually require action of some sort, be it measuring, applying some skill or technique, planning, or using expert judgment. Outputs are usually in the form of a deliverable. Remember that a deliverable is characterized with results or outcomes that can be verified. Last but not least, outputs from one process oftentimes serve as inputs to another process.

Process Interactions

We've covered a lot of material, but I'll explain one more concept before concluding. As stated earlier, project managers must determine the processes that are appropriate for effectively managing a project based on the complexity and scope of the project, available resources, budget, and so on. As the project progresses, the project management processes might be revisited and revised to update the project management plan as more information becomes known. Underlying the concept that process groups are iterative is a cycle the

PMBOK® Guide describes as the Plan-Do-Check-Act cycle, which was originally defined by Walter Shewhart and later modified by Edward Deming. The idea behind this concept is that each element in the cycle is results oriented. The results from the Plan cycle become inputs into the Do cycle, and so on, much like the way the project management process groups interact. The cycle interactions can be mapped to work with the five project management process groups. For example, the Plan cycle maps to the Planning process group. Before going any further, here's a brief refresher:

- Project phases describe how the work required to produce the product of the project will be completed.

- Project management process groups organize and describe how the project activities will be completed in order to meet the goals of the project.

- The Plan-Do-Check-Act cycle is an underlying concept that shows the integrative nature of the process groups.

Figure 1.8 shows the relationships and interactions of the concepts you've learned so far. Please bear in mind that a simple figure can't convey all the interactions and iterative nature of these interactions; however, I think you'll see that the figure ties the basic elements of these concepts together.

FIGURE 1.8 Project management process groups

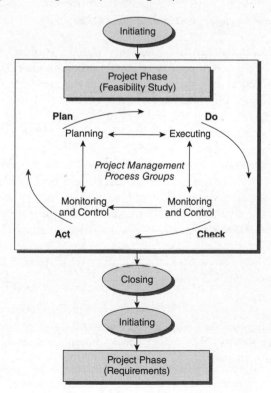

Understanding How This Applies to Your Next Project

As you can tell from this first chapter, managing projects is not for the faint of heart. You must master multiple skills and techniques in order to complete projects successfully. In your day-to-day work environment, it probably doesn't matter much if you're working in a functional or strong matrix organization. More important are your communication, conflict management, and negotiation and influencing skills. Good communications are the hallmark of successful projects. (We'll talk more about communication and give you some communication tips in the coming chapters.)

In any organizational structure, you'll find leaders, and you'll find people who have the title of leader. Again, the organizational structure itself probably isn't as important as knowing who the real leaders and influencers are in the organization. These are the people you'll lean on to help with difficult project decisions and hurdles.

I talked about the definition of a project in this chapter. You'd be surprised how many people think ongoing operations are projects. Here's a tip to help you explain the definition to your stakeholders: projects involve the five project management process groups (Initiating through Closing). Ongoing operations typically involve the Planning, Executing, and Monitoring and Controlling processes. But here's the differentiator—ongoing operations don't include Initiating or Closing process groups because ongoing operations don't have a beginning or an end.

Most projects I've worked on involved more than one stakeholder, and stakeholders often have conflicting interests. On your next project, find out what those stakeholder interests are. Resolving conflicts is easier at the beginning of the project than at the end. You'll likely need both negotiating and influencing skills.

I've made the mistake of thinking the project process groups are overkill for a small project. My team once embarked on a small project and thought that within a matter of weeks we'd have it wrapped up and delivered. We neglected to get signatures from the project requestor on the agreed-upon scope, and you guessed it, the scope grew and grew and changed several times before we were able to get the project back under control. If you're reading between the lines here, you can also tell we didn't have adequate change control in place. As you progress through the book, I'll highlight the important processes you'll want to include on all projects, large and small, so you don't get caught in this trap.

Summary

Phew! I covered a lot of ground in this chapter. You learned that projects exist to bring about a unique product, service, or result. Projects are temporary in nature and have definite beginning and ending dates.

Stakeholders are those people or organizations that have a vested interest in the outcome of the project. Stakeholders include people such as the project sponsor, the customer, key management personnel, operations managers, the project manager, contractors, suppliers, and more. Projects are considered complete when the project meets or exceeds the expectations of the stakeholders.

Project management is a discipline that brings together a set of tools and techniques to describe, organize, and monitor the work of project activities. Project managers are the ones responsible for carrying out these activities. Projects might be organized into programs or portfolios and might be managed centrally by a PMO.

Project managers have a wide variety of skills. They should be versed not only in the field they're working in but in general management skills as well. Communication is the most important skill a project manager will use in the course of a project.

Organizational structures come in variations of three forms: functional, projectized, and matrix. Functional organizations are traditional with hierarchical reporting structures. Project managers have little to no authority in this kind of organization. Projectized organizations are structured around project work, and staff personnel report to project managers. Project managers have full authority in this organizational structure. Matrix organizations are a combination of the functional and projectized. A project manager's authority varies depending on the structure of the matrix, be it a weak matrix, a balanced matrix, or a strong matrix.

A project manager's authority level, ability to manage the project budget, and availability of staff are also influenced by the project manager's interactions within the hierarchy of management (strategic, middle, and operations management) and the project management maturity level of the organization.

Projects progress through phases along a life cycle path to complete the product of the project. The project management process groups are performed throughout the project's life cycle. The process groups described in the *PMBOK® Guide* are Initiating, Planning, Executing, Monitoring and Controlling, and Closing.

Exam Essentials

Be able to describe the difference between projects and operations.   A project is temporary in nature with a definite beginning and ending date. Projects produce unique products, services, or results. Operations are ongoing and use repetitive processes that typically produce the same result over and over.

Be able to denote some of the interpersonal skills every good project manager should possess.   Communication, organizational, problem solving, negotiation and influencing, leading, and team building are skills a project manager should possess.

Be able to denote the three skills every project manager needs beyond their ability to apply project management skills, tools, and techniques.   The three skills are knowledge (of project management techniques), performance (the ability to perform as a project manager by applying your knowledge), and personal (the behavioral characteristics including leadership abilities, attitudes, ethics, and more).

Be able to differentiate the different organizational structures and the project manager's authority in each.   Organizations are usually structured in some combination of the following: functional, projectized, and matrix (including weak matrix, balanced matrix, and strong matrix). Project managers have the most authority in a projectized organization and the least amount of authority in a functional organization.

Be able to name the five project management process groups.   The five project management process groups are Initiating, Planning, Executing, Monitoring and Controlling, and Closing.

Key Terms

I've introduced the processes you'll use while managing projects. You need to understand each of these processes to be an effective project manager and know them by the names used in the *PMBOK® Guide* to be successful on the exam. I will discuss each in greater detail in the chapters to come:

Initiating

Planning

Executing

Monitoring and Controlling

Closing

You've learned many new key words in this chapter. PMI® has worked hard to develop and define standard project management terms that apply across industries. Here is a list of some of the terms you came across in this chapter:

balanced matrix	power
co-located	product scope
composite	program management
deliverable	programs
fast tracking	progressive elaboration
feasibility study	project based organization (PBO)
functional organization	project life cycle
handoffs	project management
iterative	project management office (PMO)
leaders	project managers
managers	project sponsor
matrix organizations	projectized organizations
operations	projects
politics	stakeholders
portfolio management	tailoring
portfolios	

Review Questions

You can find the answers to the questions in Appendix A.

1. Which organization has set the de facto standards for project management techniques?

    A. PMBOK®

    B. PMO

    C. PMI®

    D. PBO

2. The VP of marketing approaches you and requests that you change the visitor logon screen on the company's website to include a username with at least six characters. This is considered which of the following?

    A. Project initiation

    B. Ongoing operations

    C. A project

    D. Project execution

3. Your company manufactures small kitchen appliances. It is introducing a new product line of appliances in designer colors with distinctive features for kitchens in small spaces. These new products will be offered indefinitely starting with the spring catalog release. Which of the following is true?

    A. This is a project because this new product line has never been manufactured and sold by this company before.

    B. This is an ongoing operation because the company is in the business of manufacturing kitchen appliances. Introducing designer colors and features is simply a new twist on an existing process.

    C. This is an ongoing operation because the new product line will be sold indefinitely. It's not temporary.

    D. This is not a project or an ongoing operation. This is a new product introduction not affecting ongoing operations.

4. Your company manufactures small kitchen appliances. It is introducing a new product line of appliances in designer colors with distinctive features for kitchens in small spaces. These new products will be offered indefinitely starting with the spring catalog release. To determine the characteristics and features of the new product line, you will have to perform which of the following?

    A. Fast tracking

    B. Consulting with the stakeholders

    C. Planning the project life cycle

    D. Progressive elaboration

5. A project is considered successful when _____ .

    A. The product of the project has been manufactured.

    B. The project sponsor announces the completion of the project.

    C. The product of the project is turned over to the operations area to handle the ongoing aspects of the project.

    D. The project meets the expectations of the stakeholders.

6. The VP of customer service has expressed concern over a project in which you're involved. His specific concern is that if the project is implemented as planned, he'll have to purchase additional equipment to staff his customer service center. The cost was not taken into consideration in the project budget. The project sponsor insists that the project must go forward as originally planned or the customer will suffer. Which of the following is true?

    A. The VP of customer service is correct. Since the cost was not taken into account at the beginning of the project, the project should not go forward as planned. Project initiation should be revisited to examine the project plan and determine how changes can be made to accommodate customer service.

    B. The conflict should be resolved in favor of the customer.

    C. The conflict should be resolved in favor of the project sponsor.

    D. The conflict should be resolved in favor of the VP of customer service.

7. Which of the following applies a set of tools and techniques used to describe, organize, and monitor the work of project activities to meet the project requirements?

    A. Project managers

    B. The *PMBOK® Guide*

    C. Project management

    D. Stakeholders

8. All of the following are true regarding phase-to-phase relationships except for which one?

    A. Planning for an iterative phase begins when the work of the previous phase is progressing.

    B. Handoffs occur after a phase-end review in an overlapping phased project.

    C. During sequentially phased projects, the previous phase must finish before the next phase can begin.

    D. Fast tracking is a compression technique that can be applied as a phase-to-phase relationship.

9. All of the following statements are true except for which one?

    A. Programs are groups of related projects.

    B. Project life cycles are collections of sequential and occasionally overlapping project phases.

    C. A project may or may not be part of a program.

    D. Portfolios are collections of interdependent projects or programs.

10. You are the project manager for a large construction project. The project objective is to construct a set of outbuildings to house the Olympic support team that will be arriving in your city 18 months from the project start date. Resources are not readily available because they are currently assigned to other projects. Jack, an expert crane operator, is needed for this project two months from today. Which of the following skills will you use to get Jack assigned to your project?

   A. Negotiation and influencing skills

   B. Communication and organizational skills

   C. Communication skills

   D. Problem-solving skills

11. You've decided to try your hand at project management in the entertainment industry. You're working on a movie production and the phases are performed sequentially. The team has just completed the storyboard phase of the project. Which of the following is true?

   A. The storyboard is a deliverable that marks the end of the phase.

   B. The storyboard phase marks the end of the Initiating process group, and the next phase of the project should begin.

   C. The writing phase can begin once the majority of the storyboard phase is complete.

   D. The division of phases and determining which processes to use in each phase is called *tailoring*.

12. You are managing a project to install a new postage software system that will automatically print labels and administer postage for certified mailings, overnight packages, and other special mailing needs. You've attempted to gain the cooperation of the business analyst working on this project, and you need some answers. She is elusive and tells you that this project is not her top priority. What should you do to avoid situations like this in the future?

   A. Establish the business analyst's duties well ahead of due dates, and tell her you'll be reporting on her performance to her functional manager.

   B. Establish the business analyst's duties well ahead of due dates, and tell her you are expecting her to meet these expectations because the customer is counting on the project meeting due dates to save significant costs on their annual mailings.

   C. Negotiate with the business analyst's functional manager during the planning process to establish expectations and request to participate in the business analyst's annual performance review.

   D. Negotiate with the business analyst's functional manager during the planning process to establish expectations, and inform the functional manager of the requirements of the project. Agreement from the functional manager will assure the cooperation of the business analyst.

13. The amount of authority a project manager possesses can be related to all of following except which one?

   A. The organizational structure

   B. The key stakeholder's influence on the project

   C. The interaction with various levels of management

   D. The project management maturity level of the organization

14. What is one of the advantages of a functional organization?

   A. All employees report to one manager and have a clear chain of command.

   B. All employees report to two or more managers, but project team members show loyalty to functional managers.

   C. The organization is focused on projects and project work.

   D. Teams are co-located.

15. You have been assigned to a project in which the objectives are to direct customer calls to an interactive voice response system before being connected to a live agent. You are in charge of the media communications for this project. You report to the project manager in charge of this project and the VP of marketing, who share responsibility for this project. Which organizational structure do you work in?

   A. Functional organization

   B. Weak matrix organization

   C. Projectized organization

   D. Balanced matrix organization

16. You have been assigned to a project in which the objectives are to expand three miles of the north-to-south highway through your city by two lanes in each direction. You are in charge of the demolition phase of this project, and you report to the project manager in charge of this project. You have been hired on contract and will be released at the completion of the demolition phase. What type of organizational structure does this represent?

   A. Functional organization

   B. Weak matrix organization

   C. Projectized organization

   D. Balanced matrix organization

17. What are the five project management process groups, in order?

   A. Initiating, Executing, Planning, Monitoring and Controlling, and Closing

   B. Initiating, Monitoring and Controlling, Planning, Executing, and Closing

   C. Initiating, Planning, Monitoring and Controlling, Executing, and Closing

   D. Initiating, Planning, Executing, Monitoring and Controlling, and Closing

18. You have been assigned to a project in which the objectives are to expand three miles of the north-to-south highway through your city by two lanes in each direction. You are interested in implementing a new project process called Design-Build in order to speed up the project schedule. The idea is that the construction team will work on the first mile of the highway reconstruction at the same time the design team is coming up with plans for the third mile of the reconstruction rather than completing all design before any construction begins. This is an example of which of the following?

    A. Managing the projects as a program

    B. An overlapping phase-to-phase relationship

    C. Progressive elaboration

    D. Handoffs

19. During which project management process group are risk and stakeholder's ability to influence project outcomes the highest?

    A. Planning

    B. Executing

    C. Initiating

    D. Monitoring and Controlling

20. All of the following are true regarding a PMO except for which one?

    A. There are three types of PMOs, supportive, controlling, and directive.

    B. The PMO is often responsible for implementing the OPM.

    C. The key purpose of the PMO is to provide support to project managers.

    D. The PMO facilitates communication within and across projects.

Chapter 2

Creating the Project Charter

THE PMP® EXAM CONTENT FROM THE INITIATING THE PROJECT AND PLANNING THE PROJECT DOMAINS COVERED IN THIS CHAPTER INCLUDES THE FOLLOWING:

✓ Perform project assessment based on available information and meetings with the sponsor, customer, and other subject matter experts, in order to evaluate the feasibility of new products or services within the given assumptions and/or constraints.

✓ Define the high-level scope of the project based on business and compliance requirements in order to meet the customer's project expectations.

✓ Perform key stakeholder analysis using brainstorming, interviewing, and other data-gathering techniques in order to ensure expectation alignment and gain support for the project.

✓ Identify and document high-level risks, assumptions, and constraints based on current environment, historical data, and/or expert judgment in order to identify project limitations and propose an implementation approach.

✓ Develop Project Charter by further gathering and analyzing stakeholder requirements in order to document project scope, milestones, and deliverables.

✓ Obtain approval of the project charter from the sponsor and customer (if required) in order to formalize the authority assigned to the project manager and gain commitment and acceptance for the project.

✓ Conduct a kick-off meeting with all key stakeholders, in order to announce the start of the project, communicate the project milestones, and share other relevant information.

✓ **Knowledge and Skills:**

- Cost-benefit analysis

- Business case development

- Project selection criteria (for example, cost, feasibility, impact)

- Stakeholder identification techniques

- Risk identification techniques

- Elements of a project charter

Now that you're armed with a detailed overview of project management, you can easily determine whether your next assignment is a project or an ongoing operation. You've learned some of the basics of good project management techniques. Now you can start putting those techniques into practice during the Initiating process group, which is where all projects start. As you've probably already guessed, you'll be using some of the general management skills outlined in Chapter 1, "What Is a Project?"

One of the first skills you will put to use will be your communication skills. Are you surprised? Of course you're not. It all starts with communication. You can't start defining the project until you've first talked to the project sponsor, key stakeholders, and management personnel. All good project managers have honed their communication skills to a nice sharp edge.

You'll remember from Chapter 1 that *Initiating* is the first process group in the five project management process groups. You can think of it as the official project kickoff. Initiating acknowledges that the project, or the next phase in an active project, should begin. This process group culminates in the publication of a project charter and a stakeholder register. I'll cover each in this chapter. But before we dive into the Initiating processes, we have one more preliminary topic to cover regarding the 10 Knowledge Areas.

At the end of this chapter, I'll introduce a case study that will illustrate the main points of the chapter. I'll expand on this case study from chapter to chapter, and you'll begin building a project using each of the skills you learn.

Exploring the Project Management Knowledge Areas

We talked about the five process groups in Chapter 1. They are Initiating, Planning, Executing, Monitoring and Controlling, and Closing. Each process group is made up of a collection of processes used throughout the project life cycle. *A Guide to the Project Management Body of Knowledge (PMBOK® Guide), Fifth Edition* groups these processes into 10 categories that it calls the *Project Management Knowledge Areas*. These groupings, or Knowledge Areas, bring together processes that have characteristics in common. For example, the *Project Cost Management Knowledge Area* involves all aspects of the budgeting process, as you would suspect. Therefore, processes such as Estimate Costs, Determine Budget, and Control Costs belong to this Knowledge Area. Here's the tricky part: These processes don't belong to the same project management process groups (Estimate Costs and Determine Budget are part of the Planning process group, and Control Costs is part of the Monitoring and Controlling process group). Think of it this way: Knowledge Areas bring together processes by commonalities, whereas project management process groups are more or less the order in which you perform the project management processes (although remember that you can come back through these processes more than once). The *PMBOK® Guide* names the 10 Knowledge Areas as follows:

- Project Integration Management
- Project Scope Management
- Project Time Management
- Project Cost Management
- Project Quality Management
- Project Human Resource Management
- Project Communications Management
- Project Risk Management
- Project Procurement Management
- Project Stakeholder Management

Let's take a closer look at each Knowledge Area so you understand how they relate to the process groups. Included in each of the following sections are tables that illustrate the processes that make up the Knowledge Area and the project management process group to which each process belongs. This will help you see the big picture in terms of process groups compared to Knowledge Areas. I'll discuss each of the processes in the various Knowledge Areas throughout the book, but for now, you'll take a high-level look at each of them.

Exam Spotlight

The PMP® exam may have a question or two regarding the processes that make up a Knowledge Area. Remember that Knowledge Areas bring together processes by commonalities, so thinking about the Knowledge Area itself should tip you off to the processes that belong to it. Projects are executed in process group order, but the Knowledge Areas allow a project manager to think about groups of processes that require specific skills. This makes the job of assigning resources easier because team members with specific skills might be able to work on and complete several processes at once. To broaden your understanding of the Knowledge Areas, cross-reference the purposes and the processes that make up each Knowledge Area with the *PMBOK® Guide*.

The process names, inputs, tools and techniques, outputs, and descriptions of the project management process groups and related materials and figures in this chapter are based on content from *A Guide to the Project Management Body of Knowledge (PMBOK® Guide), Fifth Edition* (Sybex, 2010).

Project Integration Management

The *Project Integration Management Knowledge Area* comprises six processes, as shown in Table 2.1.

TABLE 2.1   Project Integration Management

Process name	Project management process group
Develop Project Charter	Initiating
Develop Project Management Plan	Planning
Direct and Manage Project Work	Executing
Monitor and Control Project Work	Monitoring and Controlling
Perform Integrated Change Control	Monitoring and Controlling
Close Project or Phase	Closing

The *Project Integration Management Knowledge Area* is concerned with coordinating all aspects of the project management plan and is highly interactive. This Knowledge Area involves identifying and defining the work of the project and combining, unifying, and integrating the appropriate processes. It is concerned with choosing among alternative projects and performing trade-offs among the competing objectives of several projects. This Knowledge Area also takes into account satisfactorily meeting the requirements of the customer and stakeholder and managing their expectations.

Project planning, executing, monitoring, and change-control occur throughout the project and are repeated continuously while you're working on the project. Project planning and executing involve weighing the objectives of the project against the alternatives to bring the project to a successful completion. This includes making choices about how to effectively use resources and coordinating the work of the project on a continuous basis. Monitoring the work of the project involves anticipating potential problems and issues and dealing with them before they reach the critical point. Change control can impact the project schedule, which in turn impacts the work of the project, which in turn can impact the project management plan, so you can see that these processes are tightly linked. The processes in this area, as with all the Knowledge Areas, also interact with other processes in the remaining Knowledge Areas. For example, the Identify Stakeholders process uses an output from the Develop Project Charter process as an input.

The *Project Integration Management Knowledge Area* has two tools for assisting with process integration: earned value management (EVM) and project management software. EVM is a project-integrating methodology used in this Knowledge Area to integrate the processes and measure project performance through a project's life cycle. I'll further define EVM and talk more about project management software tools in Chapter 4, "Creating the Project Schedule."

Project Scope Management

The *Project Scope Management Knowledge Area* has six processes, as shown in Table 2.2.

TABLE 2.2   Project Scope Management

Process name	Project management process group
Plan Scope Management	Planning
Collect Requirements	Planning
Define Scope	Planning
Create WBS	Planning
Validate Scope	Monitoring and Controlling
Control Scope	Monitoring and Controlling

Project Scope Management is concerned with defining all the work of the project and only the work needed to successfully produce the project goals. These processes are highly interactive. They define and control what is and what is not part of the project. Each process occurs at least once—and often many times—throughout the project's life.

Project Scope Management encompasses both product scope and project scope. *Product scope* concerns the characteristics of the product, service, or result of the project. It's measured against the product requirements to determine successful completion or fulfillment. The application area usually dictates the process tools and techniques you'll use to define and manage product scope. *Project scope* involves managing the work of the project and only the work of the project. Project scope is measured against the project management plan. The scope baseline is made up of the project scope statement, the work breakdown structure (WBS), and the WBS dictionary.

To ensure a successful project, both product and project scope must be well integrated. This implies that Project Scope Management is well integrated with the other Knowledge Area processes.

Collect Requirements, Define Scope, Create WBS, Validate Scope, and Control Scope involve the following:

- Defining and detailing the deliverables and requirements of the product of the project
- Creating a WBS
- Verifying deliverables using measurement techniques
- Controlling changes to the scope of the project

Project Time Management

The *Project Time Management Knowledge Area* has seven processes, as shown in Table 2.3.

TABLE 2.3 Project Time Management

Process name	Project management process group
Plan Schedule Management	Planning
Define Activities	Planning
Sequence Activities	Planning
Estimate Activity Resources	Planning
Estimate Activity Durations	Planning
Develop Schedule	Planning
Control Schedule	Monitoring and Controlling

This Knowledge Area is concerned with estimating the duration of the project activities, devising a project schedule, and monitoring and controlling deviations from the schedule. Collectively, this Knowledge Area deals with completing the project in a timely manner. Time management is an important aspect of project management because it concerns keeping the project activities on track and monitoring those activities against the project management plan to ensure that the project is completed on time.

Although most processes in this Knowledge Area occur at least once in every project (and sometimes more), in many cases—particularly on small projects—Sequence Activities, Estimate Activity Durations, and Develop Schedule are completed as one activity. Only one person is needed to complete these processes for small projects, and they're all worked on at the same time.

Project Cost Management

As its name implies, the *Project Cost Management Knowledge Area* centers around costs and budgets. Table 2.4 shows the processes that make up this Knowledge Area.

TABLE 2.4   Project Cost Management

Process name	Project management process group
Plan Cost Management	Planning
Estimate Costs	Planning
Determine Budget	Planning
Control Costs	Monitoring and Controlling

The activities in the Project Cost Management Knowledge Area establish cost estimates for resources, establish budgets, and keep watch over those costs to ensure that the project stays within the approved budget. The earlier you can develop and agree on the scope of the project, the earlier you can estimate costs. The benefit of this practice is that costs are more easily influenced early in the project.

This Knowledge Area is primarily concerned with the costs of resources, but you should think about other costs as well. For example, be certain to examine ongoing maintenance and support costs for software or equipment that may be handed off to the operations group at the end of the project.

Depending on the complexity of the project, these processes might need the involvement of more than one person. For example, the finance person might not have expertise about the resources documented in the staffing management plan, so the project manager will need to bring in a staff member with those skills to assist with the activities in this process.

Two techniques are used in this Knowledge Area to decide among alternatives and improve the project process: life cycle costing and value engineering. The *life cycle costing* technique considers a group of costs collectively (such as acquisition, operations, disposal, and so on) when deciding among or comparing alternatives. The *value engineering* technique helps improve project schedules, profits, quality, and resource usage and optimizes life cycle costs, among others. Value engineering, in a nutshell, involves optimizing project performance and cost and is primarily concerned with eliminating unnecessary costs. By examining the project processes, performance, or even specific activities, the project manager can identify those elements that are not adding value and could be eliminated, modified, or reduced to realize cost savings. These techniques can improve decision making, reduce costs, reduce activity durations, and improve the quality of the deliverables. Some application areas require additional financial analysis to help predict project performance. Techniques such as payback analysis, return on investment, and discounted cash flows are a few of the tools used to accomplish this.

Project Quality Management

The *Project Quality Management Knowledge Area* is composed of three processes, as shown in Table 2.5.

TABLE 2.5 Project Quality Management

Process name	Project management process group
Plan Quality Management	Planning
Perform Quality Assurance	Executing
Control Quality	Monitoring and Controlling

The Project Quality Management Knowledge Area assures that the project meets the requirements that it was undertaken to produce. This Knowledge Area focuses on product quality as well as on the quality of the project management processes used during the project. These processes measure overall performance and monitor project results and compare them to the quality standards set out in the project-planning process to ensure that the customers will receive the product, service, or result they commissioned.

Project Human Resource Management

The *Project Human Resource Management Knowledge Area* consists of four processes, as shown in Table 2.6.

TABLE 2.6 Project Human Resource Management

Process name	Project management process group
Plan Human Resource Management	Planning
Acquire Project Team	Executing
Develop Project Team	Executing
Manage Project Team	Executing

Project Human Resource Management involves all aspects of people management and personal interaction, including leading, coaching, dealing with conflict, conducting performance appraisals, and more. These processes ensure that the human resources assigned to the project are used in the most effective way possible. Some of the project participants on whom you'll practice these skills are stakeholders, team members, and customers. Each requires the use of different communication styles, leadership skills, and team-building skills. A good project manager knows when to enact certain skills and communication styles based on the situation.

Projects are unique and temporary, and project teams usually are too. Teams are built based on the skills and resources needed to complete the activities of the project, and many times project team members might not know one another. The earlier you can involve team members on the project, the better because you'll want the benefit of their knowledge and expertise during the planning processes. Their participation early on will also help assure their buy-in to the project. Because the makeup of each team is different and the stakeholders involved in the various stages of the project might change, you'll use different techniques at different times throughout the project to manage the processes in this Knowledge Area.

Project Communications Management

The processes in The *Project Communications Management Knowledge Area* are related to general communication skills, but they encompass much more than an exchange of information. Communication skills are considered interpersonal skills that the project manager utilizes on a daily basis. The processes in the Project Communications Management Knowledge Area seek to ensure that all project information—including plans, risk assessments, meeting notes, and more—is collected, organized, stored, and distributed to stakeholders, management, and project members at the proper time. When the project is closed, the information is archived and used as a reference for future projects. This is referred to as *historical information* in several project processes.

Everyone on the project has some involvement with this Knowledge Area because all project members will send and/or receive project communication throughout the life of the project. It is important that all team members and stakeholders understand how communication affects the project.

Three processes make up the Project Communications Management Knowledge Area, as shown in Table 2.7.

TABLE 2.7   Project Communications Management

Process name	Project management process group
Plan Communications Management	Planning
Manage Communications	Executing
Control Communications	Monitoring and Controlling

Time to Communicate

Project Communications Management is probably the most important Knowledge Area on any project, and most project managers understand the importance of good communication skills and making sure stakeholders are informed of project status. I know a project manager who had difficulties getting time with the project sponsor. The project sponsor agreed to meet with the project manager, even set up the meetings himself, and then canceled them or simply didn't show up. The poor project manager was at her wits' end about how to communicate with the sponsor and get some answers to the questions she had. Her desk was not far outside the project sponsor's office. One day as she peeked around the corner of her cube, she decided if the sponsor wouldn't come to her, she would go to him. From then on, every time the sponsor left his office, she would jump up from her chair and ride with him on the elevator. He was a captive audience. She was able to get some easy questions answered and finally convince him, after the fourth or fifth elevator ride, that they needed regular face-to-face meetings. She understood the importance of communication and went to great lengths to make certain the sponsor did too.

Project Risk Management

The *Project Risk Management Knowledge Area,* as shown in Table 2.8, contains six processes.

TABLE 2.8 Project Risk Management

Process name	Project management process group
Plan Risk Management	Planning
Identify Risks	Planning
Perform Qualitative Risk Analysis	Planning
Perform Quantitative Risk Analysis	Planning
Plan Risk Responses	Planning
Control Risk	Monitoring and Controlling

Risks include both threats to and opportunities to the project. The processes in this Knowledge Area are concerned with identifying, analyzing, and planning for potential risks, both positive and negative, that might impact the project. This means minimizing the probability and impact of negative risks while maximizing the probability and impact of positive risks. These processes are also used to identify the positive consequences of risks and exploit them to improve project objectives or discover efficiencies that might improve project performance.

Project managers will often combine several of these processes into one step. For example, Identify Risks and Perform Qualitative Risk Analysis might be performed at the same time. The important factor of the Project Risk Management Knowledge Area is that you should strive to identify all the risks and develop responses for those with the greatest consequences to the project objectives.

Project Procurement Management

Four processes are in the *Project Procurement Management Knowledge Area*, as shown in Table 2.9.

TABLE 2.9 Project Procurement Management

Process name	Project management process group
Plan Procurement Management	Planning
Conduct Procurements	Executing
Control Procurements	Monitoring and Controlling
Close Procurements	Closing

The Project Procurement Management Knowledge Area includes the processes involved with purchasing goods or services from vendors, contractors, suppliers, and others outside the project team. As such, these processes involve negotiating and managing contracts and other procurement vehicles, and managing changes to the contract or work order. When discussing the Project Procurement Management processes, it's assumed that the discussion is taking place from your perspective as a buyer, while sellers are external to the project team. Interestingly, the seller might manage their work as a project, particularly when the work is performed on contract, and you as the buyer become a key stakeholder in their project.

Project Stakeholder Management

There are four processes in the *Project Stakeholder Management Knowledge Area,* as shown in Table 2.10.

TABLE 2.10   Project Stakeholder Management

Process name	Project management process group
Identify Stakeholders	Initiating
Plan Stakeholder Management	Planning
Manage Stakeholder Engagement	Executing
Control Stakeholder Engagement	Monitoring and Controlling

The Project Stakeholder Management Knowledge Area is concerned with identifying all of the stakeholders associated with the project, both internal and external to the organization. These processes also assess stakeholder needs, expectations, and involvement on the project and seek to keep the lines of communication with stakeholders open and clear. Remember from Chapter 1 that the definition of a successful project is one where the stakeholders are satisfied. These processes assure that stakeholder expectations are met and that their satisfaction is a successful deliverable of the project.

The remainder of this book will deal with processes and process groups as they occur in order (that is, Initiating, Planning, Executing, Monitoring and Controlling, and Closing), because this is the way you will encounter and manage them during a project.

Understanding How Projects Come About

Your company's quarterly meeting is scheduled for today. You take your seat, and each of the department heads gets up and gives their usual "We can do it" rah-rah speech, one after the other. You sit up a little straighter when the CEO takes the stage. He starts his part of the program pretty much the same way the other department heads did, and before long, you find yourself drifting off. You are mentally reviewing the status of your current project when suddenly your daydreaming trance is shattered. You perk up as you hear the CEO say, "And the new phone system will be installed by Thanksgiving."

Wait a minute. You work in the telecom department and haven't heard a word about this project until today. You also have a funny feeling that you've been elected to manage this project. It's amazing how good communication skills are so important for project managers but not for... well, we won't go there.

Project *initiation* is the formal recognition that a project, or the next phase in an existing project, should begin and resources should be committed to the project. Unfortunately, many projects are initiated the way the CEO did in this example. Each of us, at one time or another, has experienced being handed a project with little to no information and told to "make it happen." The new phone system scenario is an excellent example of how *not* to initiate a project.

Taking one step back leads you to ask, "How do projects come about in the first place? Do CEOs just make them up like in this example?" Even though your CEO announced this new project at the company meeting with no forewarning, no doubt it came about as a result of a legitimate need. Believe it or not, CEOs don't dream up projects just to give you something to do. They're concerned about the future of the company and the needs of the business and its customers.

The business might drive the need for a project, customers might demand changes to products, or legal requirements might create the need for a new project. According to the *PMBOK® Guide*, projects come about as a result of one of seven needs or demands. Once those needs and demands are identified, the next logical step might include performing a feasibility study to determine the viability of the project. I'll cover these topics next.

Needs and Demands

Organizations exist to generate profits or serve the public. To stay competitive, organizations are always examining new ways of creating business, gaining efficiencies, or serving their customers. Sometimes laws are passed to force organizations to make their products safer or to make them less harmful to the environment. Projects might result from any of these needs as well as from business requirements, opportunities, or problems. According to the *PMBOK® Guide*, most projects will fit one of the seven needs and demands described next and are included in the business case, which is an input to the Develop Project Charter process. Let's take a closer look at each of these areas:

Market Demand　The demands of the marketplace can drive the need for a project. For example, a bank initiates a project to offer customers the ability to apply for mortgage loans over the Internet because of a drop in interest rates and an increase in demand for refinancing and new home loans.

Strategic Opportunity/Business Need　The new phone system talked about earlier that was announced at the quarterly meeting came about as a result of a business need. The CEO, on advice from his staff, was advised that call volumes were maxed on the existing system. Without a new system, customer service response times would suffer, and that would eventually affect the bottom line.

Customer Request   Customer requests run the gamut. Generally speaking, most companies have customers, and their requests can drive new projects. Customers can be internal or external to the organization. Government agencies don't have external customers per se (we're captive customers at any rate), but there are internal customers within departments and across agencies.

Perhaps you work for a company that sells remittance-processing equipment and you've just landed a contract with a local utility company. This project is driven by the need of the utility company to automate its process or upgrade its existing process. The utility company's request to purchase your equipment and consulting services is the project driver.

Technological Advance   Many of us own a smartphone that keeps names and addresses handy along with a calendar, a to-do list, and a plethora of other apps to help organize our day or add a little fun in between meetings. I couldn't live without mine. However, a newer, better version is always coming to market. Satellite communications, bigger screens, thinner bodies, touch screens, video streaming, and more are all examples of technological advances. Electronics manufacturers are continually revamping and reinventing their products to take advantage of new technology (thank you!).

Legal Requirement   Private industry and government agencies both generate new projects as a result of laws passed during every legislative season. For example, new sales tax or healthcare laws might require changes to the computer programs that support these systems. The requirement that food labels on packaging describe the ingredients in the product, the calories, and the recommended daily allowances is another example of legal requirements that drive a project.

Environmental Considerations   Many organizations today are undergoing a "greening" effort to reduce energy consumption, save fuel, reduce their carbon footprint, and so on. Another example might include manufacturing or processing plants that voluntarily remove their waste products from water prior to putting the water back into a local river or stream to prevent contamination. These are examples of environmental considerations that result in projects.

Social Need   The last need is a result of social demands. For example, perhaps a developing country is experiencing a fast-spreading disease that's infecting large portions of the population. Medical supplies and facilities are needed to vaccinate and treat those infected with the disease.

Exam Spotlight

Understand the needs and demands that bring about a project.

All of these needs and demands represent opportunities, business requirements, or problems that need to be solved. Each may also introduce risk to the project. Management must decide how to respond to these needs and demands, which will more often than not initiate new projects.

 Real World Scenario

Project Initiation

Corey is an information technology manager who works for the National Park Service. One warm spring Sunday morning he is perusing the local newspaper online and comes across an article about new services being offered at some of the national parks. He perks up when he sees his boss's name describing the changing nature of technology and how it impacts the types of services the public would like to see at the parks. Corey knows that the public has been asking when wireless Internet services will be available in some of the larger parks and has also been involved in the discussions about the resources needed to make this happen, but the project never has enough steam to get off the ground. It seems that a higher-priority project always takes precedence. However, all that changes when Corey sees the next sentence in the article: his boss promising wireless access in two of the largest parks in their region by July 4th. It looks like the customer requests have finally won out, and Corey has just learned he has a new project on his hands.

Feasibility Studies

After the opportunity for a project becomes evident, the next step might be to initiate it, which means you're ready to jump right into creating a project charter for the project. Before you take that plunge, you should know that some organizations will require a feasibility study prior to making a final decision about starting the project.

Feasibility studies are undertaken for several reasons. One is to determine whether the project is a viable project. A second reason is to determine the probability of the project succeeding. Feasibility studies can also examine the viability of the product, service, or result of the project. For example, the study might ask, "Will the new lemon-flavored soda be a hit? Is it marketable?" The study might also look at the technical issues related to the project and determine whether the technology proposed is feasible, reliable, and easily assimilated into the organization's existing technology structure.

Feasibility studies might be conducted as separate projects, as subprojects, or as the first phase of a project. Sometimes, you'll have a basic feel for the way the outcome of the study may turn out and you could consider making the feasibility study the first phase of the project. When you don't have any preconceived ideas about the outcome of the study, it's best to treat it as a separate project. The group of people conducting the feasibility study should not be the same people who will work on the project. Project team members might have built-in biases toward the project and will tend to influence the feasibility outcome toward those biases.

 It's always a good idea to meet with the sponsor, customer, and other subject matter experts when evaluating the feasibility of new products or services.

Performing Project Selection and Assessment

Most organizations don't have the luxury of performing every project that's proposed. Even consulting organizations that sell their project management services must pick and choose the projects on which they want to work. Selection and evaluation methods help organizations decide among alternative projects and determine the tangible benefits to the company of choosing or not choosing the project.

How projects are assessed will vary depending on the company, the people serving on the selection committee, the criteria used, and the project. Sometimes the criteria for selection methods will be purely financial, sometimes purely marketing, and sometimes they'll be based on public perception or political perception. In most cases, the decision is based on a combination of all these and more.

Most organizations have a formal, or at least semiformal, process for selecting and prioritizing projects. In my organization, a steering committee is responsible for project review, selection, and prioritization. A *steering committee* is a group of folks consisting of senior managers and sometimes mid-level managers who represent each of the functional areas in the organization.

 Real World Scenario

The Interactive Voice Response (IVR) Tax-Filing System

Jason, Sam, and Kate are web programmers working for the Department of Revenue in the State of Bliss. Ron, their manager, approaches them one day with an idea.

"Team, business unit managers think it would be a great idea to offer taxpayers the ability to file their income tax returns over the telephone. We already offer them the ability to file on the Internet, thanks to all your efforts on that project last year. It has been a fabulous success. No other state has had the success that Bliss has had with our Internet system."

"Kate, I know you've had previous experience with IVR technology, but I'm not sure about you guys, so this is new territory for us. I'd like to hear what each of you thinks about this project."

Jason speaks up first. "I think it's a great idea. You know me; I'm always up for learning new things, especially when it comes to programming. When can we start?"

Sam echoes Jason's comments.

"This technology is pretty sophisticated," Kate says. "Jason and Sam are excellent coders and could work on the programming side of things, but I would have to pick up the telephony piece on my own. After we're up and running, we could go over the telephony portions step by step, so Jason and Sam could help me support it going forward. I'd really like to take on this project. It would be good for the team and good for the department."

Ron thinks for a minute. "Let's not jump right into this. I know you're anxious to get started, but I think a feasibility study is in order. The senior director of the tax business unit doesn't know whether this project is cost justified and has some concerns about its life span. A feasibility study will tell us the answers to those questions. It should also help us determine whether we're using the right technology to accomplish our goals, and it will outline alternative ways of performing the project that we haven't considered. I don't want Kate going it alone without first examining all the issues and potential impacts to the organization."

Here's how our process works: The steering committee requests project ideas from the business staff and other subject matter experts prior to the beginning of the fiscal year. These project ideas are submitted in writing and contain a high-level overview of the project goals, a description of the deliverables, the business justification for the project, a desired implementation date, what the organization stands to gain from implementing the project, a list of the functional business areas affected by the project, and (if applicable) a cost-benefit analysis (I'll talk about that in a bit).

A meeting is called to review the projects, and a determination is made on each project about whether it will be included on the upcoming list of projects for the new year. Once the no-go projects have been weeded out, the remaining projects are prioritized according to their importance and benefit to the organization. The projects are documented on an official project list, and progress is reported on the active projects at the regular monthly steering committee meetings.

In theory, it's a great idea. In practice, it works only moderately well. Priorities can and do change throughout the year. New projects come up that weren't originally submitted during the call for projects, and they must be added to the list. Reprioritization begins anew, and resource alignment and assignments are shuffled. But again, I'm getting ahead of myself. Just be aware that organizations usually have a process to recognize and screen project requests, accept or reject those requests based on some selection criteria, and prioritize the projects based on some criteria.

Exam Spotlight

According to PMI®, project selection is outside the scope of the project manager's role. In reality, the project manager often participates in the decision and assists with analysis and selection methods. For the exam, remember that project selection is performed by the project sponsor, customer, or subject matter experts.

I'll discuss several project selection methods next. You may encounter a question or two on the exam regarding these methods, but keep in mind that selecting projects is outside the scope of the project manager's duties. Selection methods are one way the sponsor or customer may choose between projects. The individual opinion, and power, of selection committee members also plays a part in the projects the organization chooses to perform. Don't underestimate the importance of the authority, political standing, and individual aspirations of selection committee members. Those committee members who happen to carry a lot of weight in company circles, so to speak, are likely to get their projects approved just because they are who they are. This is sometimes how project selection works in my organization. How about yours?

Using Project Selection Methods

Project selection methods are concerned with the advantages or merits of the product of the project. In other words, selection methods measure the value of what the product, service, or result of the project will produce and how it will benefit the organization. Selection methods involve the types of concerns about which executive managers are typically thinking. This includes factors such as market share, financial benefits, return on investment, customer retention and loyalty, and public perceptions. Most of these are reflected in the organization's strategic goals. Projects, whether large or small, should always be weighed against the strategic plan. If the project doesn't help the organization reach its goals (increased market share, for example), then the project probably shouldn't be undertaken.

There are generally two categories of selection methods: *mathematical models* (also known as *calculation methods*) and *benefit measurement methods* (also known as *decision models*). Decision models examine different criteria used in making decisions regarding project selection, whereas calculation methods provide a way to calculate the value of the project, which is then used in project-selection decision making.

Mathematical Models

For the exam, all you need to understand about mathematical models is that they use linear, dynamic, integer, nonlinear, and/or multi-objective programming in the form of algorithms—or in other words, a specific set of steps to solve a particular problem.

These are complicated mathematical formulas and algorithms that are beyond the scope of this book and require an engineering, statistical, or mathematical background to fully understand. Organizations considering undertaking projects of enormous complexity might use mathematical modeling techniques to make decisions regarding these projects. Mathematical models are also known as *constrained optimization methods*. The vast majority of project selection techniques will use the benefit measurement methods to make project selection decisions.

Exam Spotlight

Project selection methods are also used to evaluate and choose between alternative ways of performing the project.

Benefit Measurement Methods

Benefit measurement methods employ various forms of analysis and comparative approaches to make project decisions. These methods include comparative approaches such as cost-benefit analysis, scoring models, and benefit contribution methods that include various cash flow techniques and economic models. You'll examine several of these methods, starting with cost-benefit analysis.

Cost-Benefit Analysis

One common benefit measurement method is the *cost-benefit analysis*. The name of this method implies what it does—it compares the cost to produce the product, service, or result of the project to the benefit (usually financial in the form of savings or revenue generation) that the organization will receive as a result of executing the project. Obviously, a sound project choice is one where the costs to implement or produce the product of the project are less than the financial benefits. How much less is the organization's decision. Some companies are comfortable with a small margin, whereas others are comfortable with a much larger margin between the two figures.

Cost-benefit analysis is also known as *benefit/cost analysis*. The techniques are the same. *Benefit/cost* has a more positive connotation because it shows the benefit, or the good stuff, before the cost, which is the not-so-good stuff.

When examining costs for a cost-benefit analysis, include the costs to produce the product or service, the costs to take the product to market, and the ongoing operational support costs. For example, let's say your company is considering writing and marketing a database software product that will allow banks to dissect their customer base, determine which types of customers buy which types of products, and then market more effectively to those customers. You will take into account some of the following costs:

- The costs to develop the software, such as programmer costs, hardware costs, and testing costs

- Marketing costs such as advertising, traveling costs to perform demos at potential customer sites, and so on

- Ongoing costs such as having a customer support staff available during business hours to assist customers with product questions and problems

Let's say the cost to produce this software, plus the ongoing support costs, total $5 million. Initial projections look like the demand for this product is high. Over a three-year period, which is the potential life of the software in its proposed form, projected revenues are $12 million. Taking only the financial information into account, the benefits outweigh the costs of this project. This project should receive a go recommendation.

Projects of significant cost or complexity usually involve more than one benefit measurement method when go or no-go decisions are being made or one project is being chosen over another. Keep in mind that selection methods can take subjective considerations into account as well—the project is a go because it's the new CEO's pet project; nothing else needs to be said.

Scoring Models

Another project selection technique in the benefit measurement category is a *scoring model*, or *weighted scoring model*. My organization uses weighted scoring models not only to choose between projects but also as a method to choose between competing bids on outsourced projects.

Weighted scoring models are quite simple. The project selection committee decides on the criteria that will be used on the scoring model—for example, profit potential, marketability of the product or service, ability of the company to quickly and easily produce the product or service, and so on. Each of these criteria is assigned a weight depending on its importance to the project committee. More important criteria should carry a higher weight than less important criteria.

Then each project is rated on a scale from 1 to 5 (or some such assignment), with the higher number being the more desirable outcome to the company and the lower number having the opposite effect. This rating is then multiplied by the weight of the criteria factor and added to other weighted criteria scores for a total weighted score. Table 2.11 shows an example that brings this together.

TABLE 2.11   Weighted scoring model

Criteria	Weight	Project A score*	Project A totals	Project B score*	Project B totals	Project C score*	Project C totals
Profit potential	5	5	25	5	25	3	15
Marketability	3	4	12	3	9	4	12
Ease to produce/ support	1	4	4	3	3	2	2
Weighted score	—	—	41	—	37	—	29

*5 = highest

In this example, Project A is the obvious choice.

Cash Flow Analysis Techniques

The remaining benefit measurement methods involve a variety of cash flow analysis techniques, including payback period, discounted cash flows, net present value, and internal rate of return. We'll look at each of these techniques individually, and I'll provide you with a crash course on their meanings and calculations.

PAYBACK PERIOD

The *payback period* is the length of time it takes the company to recoup the initial costs of producing the product, service, or result of the project. This method compares the initial investment to the cash inflows expected over the life of the product, service, or result. For example, say the initial investment on a project is $200,000, with expected cash inflows of $25,000 per quarter every quarter for the first two years and $50,000 per quarter from then on. The payback period is two years and can be calculated as follows:

Initial investment = $200,000

Cash inflows = $25,000 × 4 (quarters in a year) = $100,000 per year total inflow

Initial investment ($200,000) – year 1 inflows ($100,000) = $100,000 remaining balance

Year 1 inflows remaining balance – year 2 inflows = $0

Total cash flow year 1 and year 2 = $200,000

The payback is reached in two years.

The fact that inflows are $50,000 per quarter starting in year 3 makes no difference because payback is reached in two years.

The payback period is the least precise of all the cash flow calculations. That's because the payback period does not consider the value of the cash inflows made in later years, commonly called the *time value of money*. For example, if you have a project with a five-year payback period, the cash inflows in year 5 are worth less than they are if you received them today. The next section will explain this idea more fully.

DISCOUNTED CASH FLOWS

As I just stated, money received in the future is worth less than money received today. The reason for that is the time value of money. If I borrowed $2,000 from you today and promised to pay it back in three years, you would expect me to pay interest in addition to the original amount borrowed. If you were a family member or a close friend, maybe you wouldn't, but ordinarily this is the way it works. You would have had the use of the $2,000 had you not lent it to me. If you had invested the money (does this bring back memories of your mom telling you to save your money?), you'd receive a return on it. Therefore, the future value of the $2,000 you lent me today is $2,315.25 in three years from now at 5 percent interest per year. Here's the formula for future value calculations:

$$FV = PV(1 + i)^n$$

In English, this formula says the future value (FV) of the investment equals the present value (PV) times (1 plus the interest rate) raised to the value of the number of time periods (n) the interest is paid. Let's plug in the numbers:

$$FV = \$2,000(1 + .05)^3$$

$$FV = \$2,000(1.157625)$$

$$FV = \$2,315.25$$

The *discounted cash flow* technique compares the value of the future cash flows of the project to today's dollars. To calculate discounted cash flows, you need to know the value of the investment in today's terms, or the PV. PV is calculated as follows:

$$PV = FV / (1 + i)^n$$

This is the reverse of the FV formula talked about earlier. So, if you ask the question, "What is $2,315.25 in three years from now worth today given a 5 percent interest rate?" you'd use the preceding formula. Let's try it:

$$PV = \$2,315.25 / (1 + .05)^3$$

$$PV = \$2,315.25 / 1.157625$$

$$PV = \$2,000$$

$2,315.25 in three years from now is worth $2,000 today.

Discounted cash flow is calculated just like this for the projects you're comparing for selection purposes or when considering alternative ways of doing the project. Apply the PV formula to the projects you're considering, and then compare the discounted cash flows of all the projects against each other to make a selection. Here is an example comparison of two projects using this technique:

Project A is expected to make $100,000 in two years.

Project B is expected to make $120,000 in three years.

If the cost of capital is 12 percent, which project should you choose?

Using the PV formula used previously, calculate each project's worth:

The PV of Project A = $79,719

The PV of Project B = $85,414

Project B is the project that will return the highest investment to the company and should be chosen over Project A.

NET PRESENT VALUE

Projects might begin with a company investing some amount of money into the project to complete and accomplish its goals. In return, the company expects to receive revenues, or cash inflows, from the resulting project. *Net present value (NPV)* allows you to calculate an accurate value for the project in today's dollars. The mathematical formula for NPV is complicated, and you do not need to memorize it in that form for the test. However, you do need to know how to calculate NPV for the exam, so I've given you some examples of a less complicated way to perform this calculation in Table 2.12 and Table 2.13 using the formulas you've already seen.

TABLE 2.12   Project A

Year	Inflows	PV
1	10,000	8,929
2	15,000	11,958
3	5,000	3,559
Total	30,000	24,446
Less investment	—	24,000
NPV	—	**446**

TABLE 2.13   Project B

Year	Inflows	PV
1	7,000	6,250
2	13,000	10,364
3	10,000	7,118
Total	30,000	23,732
Less investment	—	24,000
NPV	—	**(268)**

Net present value works like discounted cash flows in that you bring the value of future monies received into today's dollars. With NPV, you evaluate the cash inflows using the discounted cash flow technique applied to each period the inflows are expected instead of in one sum. The initial investment is then deducted from the sum of the present value of the cash flows to determine NPV. NPV assumes that cash inflows are reinvested at the cost of capital.

Here's the rule: If the NPV calculation is greater than 0, accept the project. If the NPV calculation is less than 0, reject the project.

Look at the two project examples in Tables 2.12 and 2.13. Project A and Project B have total cash inflows that are the same at the end of the project, but the amount of inflows at each period differs for each project. We'll stick with a 12 percent cost of capital. Note that the PV calculations were rounded to two decimal places.

Project A has an NPV greater than 0 and should be accepted. Project B has an NPV less than 0 and should be rejected. When you get a positive value for NPV, it means that the project will earn a return at least equal to or greater than the cost of capital.

Another note on NPV calculations: Projects with high returns early in the project are better projects than projects with lower returns early in the project. In the preceding examples, Project A fits this criterion also.

INTERNAL RATE OF RETURN

The *internal rate of return (IRR)* is the most difficult equation to calculate of all the cash flow techniques we've discussed. It is a complicated formula and should be performed on a financial calculator or computer. IRR can be figured manually, but it's a trial-and-error approach to get to the answer.

Technically speaking, IRR is the discount rate when the present value of the cash inflows equals the original investment. When choosing between projects or when choosing alternative methods of doing the project, projects with higher IRR values are generally considered better than projects with low IRR values.

Exam Spotlight

Although the *PMBOK® Guide* doesn't specifically address project selection methods or cash flow techniques, you may see exam questions on these topics.

Exam Spotlight

For the exam, you need to know three facts concerning IRR:

- IRR is the discount rate when NPV equals 0.

- IRR assumes that cash inflows are reinvested at the IRR value.

- You should choose projects with the highest IRR value.

Applying Project Selection Methods

Now that we've discussed some of the project selection techniques, let's look at how to apply them when choosing projects or project alternatives. You can use one, two, or several of the benefit measurement methods alone or in combination to come up with a selection decision. Remember that payback period is the least precise of all the cash flow techniques, NPV is the most conservative cash flow technique, and NPV and IRR will generally bring you to the same accept/reject conclusion.

You can use project selection methods, and particularly the benefit measurement methods, to evaluate multiple projects or a single project. You might be weighing one project against another or simply considering whether the project you're proposing is worth performing.

 Real World Scenario

Fun Days Vacation Resorts

Nick is a project manager for Fun Days Vacation Resorts. He is working on three different project proposals to present to the executive steering committee for review. As part of the information-gathering process, Nick visits the various resorts pretending to be a guest. This gives him a feel for what Fun Days guests experience on their vacations, and it better prepares him to present project particulars and alternatives.

Nick has prepared the project overviews for three projects and called on the experts in marketing to help him out with the projected revenue figures. He works up the numbers and finds the following:

- Project A: payback period = 5 years; IRR = 8 percent

- Project B: payback period = 3.5 years; IRR = 3 percent

- Project C: payback period = 2 years; IRR = 3 percent

Funding exists for only one of the projects. Nick recommends Project A and predicts this is the project the steering committee will choose since the projects are mutually exclusive.

Nick's turn to present comes up at the steering committee. Let's listen in on the action:

"On top of all the benefits I've just described, Project A provides an IRR of 8 percent, a full 5 percent higher than the other two projects we discussed. I recommend the committee chooses Project A."

"Thank you Nick," Jane says. "Good presentation." Jane is the executive chairperson of the steering committee and has the authority to break ties or make final decisions when the committee can't seem to agree.

"However, here at Fun Days we like to have our fun sooner rather than later." Chuckles ensue from the steering committee. They've all heard this before. "I do agree that an 8 percent IRR is a terrific return, but the payback is just too far out into the future. There are too many risks and unknowns for us to take on a project with a payback period this long. As you know, our industry is directly impacted by the health of the economy. Anything can happen in five years' time. I think we're much better off going with Project C. I recommend we accept Project C. Committee members, do you have anything to add?"

Kicking Off the Project Charter

Your first stop in the Initiating group is a process called *Develop Project Charter*. As the name of the process suggests, your purpose is to create a project charter. As I talked about in Chapter 1, the purpose for the Initiating group is to authorize a project, or the next phase of a project, to begin. It also gives the project manager the authority to apply resources to the project. These are also the purposes of a project charter: formally authorizing the project to begin and committing resources.

 The charter contains several elements that I'll discuss in the section "Formalizing and Publishing the Project Charter" later in this chapter.

Exam Spotlight

The project charter (which is an output of the Develop Project Charter process) is the written acknowledgment that the project exists. The project charter documents the name of the project manager and gives that person the authority to assign organizational resources to the project. The project is officially authorized when the project charter is signed.

As you'll discover, every process has inputs, tools and techniques, and outputs, and this one is no exception. You'll start with the inputs. Let's get to it.

Inputs to the project processes are typically documents or other information that are key to the process. They come from one of two places: They are outputs from a previously completed process, or they are produced outside of the project. Inputs are used in combination with the tools and techniques to produce the outputs of each process. Process outputs are usually tangible, such as a report or an update or a list, for example. To get to the output, you have to start with the inputs. Let's take a look at the Develop Project Charter process inputs:

- Project statement of work
- Business case
- Agreements
- Enterprise environmental factors
- Organizational process assets

Project Statement of Work

The *project statement of work (SOW)* describes the product, service, or result the project was undertaken to complete. When the project is internal, this document is usually written by either the project sponsor or the initiator of the project. When the project is external to the organization, the buyer typically writes the SOW. For example, suppose you work for a consulting firm and have been assigned as the project manager for a project your company is performing on contract. The customer, the organization you'll be performing the project for, is the one who writes the SOW.

According to the *PMBOK® Guide*, a project SOW should contain or consider the following elements:

Business Need   The business need for the project relates to the needs of the organization itself. The need might be based on governmental regulation, technological advances, market demands, or a legal requirement.

Product Scope Description   The product scope description describes the characteristics of the product, service, or result of the project. The product scope description should be documented and should also include a description of the relationship between the business need or demand that's driving the project and the products being created.

Product descriptions contain less detail in the early phases of a project and more detail as the project progresses. Product scope descriptions, like the work of the project, are progressively elaborated. They will contain the greatest amount of detail in the project's Executing processes.

When a project is performed under contract, typically the buyer of the product or service will provide the product description to the vendor or contractor. The product description can serve as a statement of work when the project is contracted to a vendor. A statement of work describes the product, service, or result in enough detail so that the vendor can accurately price the contract and satisfactorily fulfill the requirements of the project.

Strategic Plan   Part of the responsibility of a project manager during the Initiating processes is to take into consideration the company's strategic plan. Perhaps the strategic plan states that one of the company goals is to build 15 new stores by the end of the next fiscal year. If your project entails implementing a new inventory software system, it makes sense to write the requirements for your project with the 15 new stores in mind. Your management team will refer to the strategic plan when choosing which new projects to initiate and which ones to drop, depending on their relationship to the strategic vision of the company.

Business Case

The purpose of a business case is to understand the business need for the project and determine whether the investment in the project is worthwhile. The business case often describes the cost-benefit analysis and the business need or demand that brought about the project.

Performing a feasibility study is a great first step in building the business case. The feasibility study will examine the needs and demands of the business, marketing opportunities, costs, risks, and more, while taking into account the given assumptions and constraints of the proposed products or services. Once the feasibility study is completed, it's easy to build a business case based on the findings of the study. Most sound business case documents contain the following elements:

- Description of the business need for the project including how the project aligns with the organization's strategic vision. This description should include the business need or demand that's driving the project and may note the feasibility study findings. This section should also include a description of the impact to the organization if the project is not undertaken.

- Description of any special requirements that must be met such as compliance requirements, legal requirements, government regulations, and so on.

- Description of alternative solutions. This should include a high-level description of costs, the feasibility of implementing each alternative, and a description of any impacts to the organization as a result of this solution. (Cost-benefit, payback, and other financial analyses are generally included in this section of the business case.)

- Description of the expected results of each alternative solution.

- Cost-benefit analysis.

- Recommended solution.

Remember that when your selection committee is analyzing the business case, discussing initial funding requirements, and approving the business case (and thus triggering the Develop Project Charter process), they are completing these activities outside of the boundaries of the project. Typically, the project team is not involved at this stage. In other words, the project isn't a project until the project charter is approved, and the project charter cannot be started until the business case is approved.

Agreements

Agreements refer to documents that define the intent of the project and are usually legal in nature. For example, a contract is an example of an agreement. Other agreements might include a memorandum of understanding, emails, an intergovernmental agency agreement, a verbal commitment, and so on. A contract is applicable when you are performing a project for a customer external to the organization. Agreements are an input to this process because they typically document the conditions under which the project will be executed, the time frame, and a description of the work.

Enterprise Environmental Factors

Enterprise environmental factors show up as input to many of the other processes we'll discuss throughout the book. This input refers to the factors outside the project that have (or might have) significant influence on the success of the project. According to the *PMBOK® Guide*, the environmental factors may include the following:

Organizational Culture, Structure, and Governance   I talked about organizational structures and their influence on the organization in Chapter 1.

Governmental or Industry Standards   These include elements such as regulatory standards and regulations (for instance, doctors must be licensed to practice medicine on people or pets), quality standards (International Standards Organization standards, for example), product standards, and workmanship standards.

Infrastructure   This refers to the organization's facilities and capital equipment. I'll also include information technology in this category.

Human Resources   This refers to the existing staff's skills and knowledge.

Personnel Administration   These are guidelines for hiring and firing, training, and employee performance reviews.

Organization's Work Authorization System   This defines how the work of the project is authorized.

Marketplace Conditions   The old supply-and-demand theory applies here along with economic and financial factors.

Stakeholder Risk Tolerances   This is the level of risk stakeholders are willing to take on. I'll talk more about this in Chapter 6, "Risk Planning."

Political Climate   This concerns both the internal and external political climate or influences on the project or organization.

Organization's Established Communications Channels   These are the mechanisms the organization uses to communicate both internally and externally.

Commercial Databases   These refer to industry-specific information, risk databases, and so on.

Project Management Information Systems   These refer to software tools that assist with managing projects, collecting and distributing project data, scheduling projects, managing and controlling changes, and more.

Some or all of these factors can influence the way you manage the project and, in some cases, the outcomes of the project. For example, perhaps the folks assigned to your project are junior level and don't have the skills, experience, or knowledge needed to complete the work of the project. It's up to the project manager to understand the organization's environmental factors and account for and consider how they can influence the management and outcomes of the project.

Organizational Process Assets

Organizational process assets are the organization's policies, guidelines, processes, procedures, plans, approaches, and standards for conducting work, including project work. Organizational process assets are divided into two categories: processes and procedures and corporate knowledge base. Processes and procedures refer to a wide range of elements that might affect several aspects of the project, such as project management policies, safety policies, performance measurement criteria, templates, financial controls, communication requirements, issue and defect management procedures, change control procedures, risk control procedures, and the procedures used for authorizing work.

Corporate knowledge base refers to items such as lessons learned, process measurement databases, project files, and the information the organization has learned on previous projects (including how to store and retrieve that information). For example, previous project risks, performance measurements, earned value data, and schedules for past projects are valuable resources of knowledge for the current project. This information is also known as *historical information* and it falls into the corporate knowledge base category. If you don't capture and store this information, however, it won't be available when you're starting a new project. You'll want to capture and store information such as project financial data (budgets, costs, overruns), historical information, lessons learned, project files, issues and defects, process measurements, and configuration management knowledge.

 There are too many organizational process assets to cover in this chapter. I'll discuss many of them throughout the Planning chapters when a certain organizational process asset pertains to a specific process.

Organizational process assets and historical information should be reviewed and examined when a new project is starting. Historical information can be useful to project managers and to stakeholders. When you're evaluating new projects, historical information about previous projects of a similar nature can be handy in determining whether the new project should be accepted and initiated. Historical information gathered and documented during an active project is used to assist in determining whether the project should proceed to the next phase. Historical information will help you with the project charter, project scope statement, development of the project management plan, the process of defining and estimating activities, and more during the project-planning processes.

Understanding previous projects of a similar nature—their problems, successes, issues, and outcomes—will help you avoid repeating mistakes while reusing successful techniques to accomplish the goals of this project to the satisfaction of the stakeholders. Many of the processes in the project management process groups have organizational process assets as an input, implying that you should review the pertinent organizational assets that apply for the process you're about to start. For example, when performing the Estimate Costs process, you might find it helpful to review the activity estimates and budgets on past projects of similar size and scope before estimating the costs for the activities on the new project.

Exam Spotlight

Remember that organizational process assets encompass many elements, including policies, guidelines, standards, historical information, and so on, and that they're divided into two categories: processes and procedures and corporate knowledge base. For the exam, make certain you understand what the organizational process assets entail and that you can differentiate them from the enterprise environmental factors input.

Tools and Techniques

Tools and techniques are multifaceted and include elements such as brainstorming, meetings, focus groups, alternatives analysis, and much more. Tools and techniques are used with the inputs of every process to produce the outputs of that process. For example, in Develop Project Charter, the SOW, business case, agreements, and other inputs are examined using the tools and techniques of this process (expert judgment and facilitation techniques) to produce the project charter, which is the only output of this process. Let's look at the two tools and techniques of this process in more detail.

The concept behind *expert judgment* is to rely on individuals, or groups of people, who have training, specialized knowledge, or skills in the areas you're assessing. These folks might be stakeholders, consultants, other experts in the organization, subject matter experts, the PMO, industry experts, or technical or professional organizations. Expert judgment is a tool and technique used in other processes as well.

In the case of developing a project charter, expert judgment would be helpful in assessing the inputs of this process, the environmental factors, organizational assets, and historical information. For example, as the project manager, you might rely on the expertise of your executive committee to help you understand how the proposed project gels with the strategic plan, or you might rely on team members who have participated on similar projects in the past to make recommendations regarding the proposed project.

Facilitation techniques is a tool used to help derive the final content of the project charter. According to the *PMBOK® Guide,* the key facilitation techniques you'll use in this process are brainstorming, managing meetings and keeping them on track, resolving conflict, and resolving problems. Project managers and others who serve as meeting facilitators should hone these skills as you will use them often throughout the course of the project.

Formalizing and Publishing the Project Charter

The approved *project charter* is the official, written acknowledgment and recognition that a project exists. It ties the work of the project with the ongoing operations of the organization. It's usually signed by a senior manager or project sponsor, and it gives the project manager the authority to assign organizational resources to the project.

The charter documents the business need or demand that the project was initiated to address, and it includes a description of the product, service, or result of the project. It is usually the first official document of the project once acceptance of the project has been granted. Project charters are often used as a means to introduce a project to the organization. Because this document outlines the high-level project description, the business opportunity or need, and the project's purpose, executive managers can get a first glance at the benefits of the project. Good project charters that are well documented will address many of the questions your stakeholders are likely to have up front.

Pulling the Project Charter Together

According to the *PMBOK® Guide*, to create a useful and well-documented project charter, you should include elements such as:

- Purpose or justification for the project
- Project objectives that are measurable
- High-level list of requirements
- High-level description of the project
- High-level list of risks
- Milestone schedule (summary level)
- Budget (summary level)
- Criteria for project approval
- Name of the project manager and their authority levels
- Name of the sponsor (or authorizer of the project) and their authority levels

For the exam, the important factors to remember about the project charter are that it authorizes the project to begin; it authorizes the project manager to assign resources to the project; it documents the business need, justification, and impact; it describes the customer's requirements; it sets stakeholder expectations; and it ties the project to the ongoing work of the organization.

Let's take a brief look at the key stakeholders who might be involved with the project charter and the role they'll play in its development and their role in the project in the future.

Key Stakeholders

The *PMBOK® Guide* states that the project charter forms a partnership between the organization requesting the project and the one performing the project. The project charter should always be written before you begin the Planning process group.

> The project charter will help assure that stakeholder's expectations are in alignment with the project scope and with the final results of the project. According to the *PMBOK® Guide*, a project charter assures a well-defined start date for the project and provides a way for senior management to formally accept the project.

According to the *PMBOK® Guide*, the project charter is a document issued by the person (or organization) who initiated the project or the project sponsor. My experience has been that the project charter requires input from the key stakeholders and is published and signed by the project sponsor. Once the charter is signed, the project is formally authorized and work can begin.

Let's take a look at the roles of some of the key stakeholders and how they can help contribute to creating a comprehensive project charter. I'll explain how to identify the right stakeholders for your project in the next main section, "Identifying Stakeholders."

Project Manager

The project manager is the person who assumes responsibility for the success of the project. The project manager should be identified as early as possible in the project and ideally should participate in writing the project charter.

The project charter identifies the project manager and describes the authority the project manager has in carrying out the project. The project manager's primary responsibilities are project planning and then executing and managing the work of the project. By overseeing the project charter and the project planning documents created later in the project, the project manager is assured that everyone knows and understands what's expected of them and what constitutes a successful project.

Project managers are responsible for setting the standards and policies for the projects on which they work. As a project manager, it is your job to establish and communicate the project procedures to the project team and stakeholders. In turn, the project team is responsible for supporting you by performing the work of the project.

Project managers will identify activities and tasks, resource requirements, project costs, project requirements, performance measures, and more. Communication and documentation must become the project manager's best friends. Keeping stakeholders, the project sponsor, the project team, and all other interested parties informed is "job one," as the famous car manufacturer's ads say.

Project Sponsor

Have you ever attended a conference or event that was put on by a sponsor? In the information technology field, software development companies often sponsor conferences and seminars. The sponsor pays for the event, the facilities, and the goodies and provides an opportunity for vendors to display their wares. In return, the sponsor comes out looking like a winner. Because it is footing the bill for all this fun, the sponsor gets to call the shots on conference content, and it gets the prime spots for discussing its particular solutions. Last but not least, it usually provides the keynote speaker and gets to present its information to a captive audience.

Project sponsors are similar to this. In their role as project champion, they rally support from stakeholders and the executive management team. They keep the project front and center at the higher levels of the organization and are the spokesperson for the project.

The project sponsor is usually an executive in the organization who has the power and authority to make decisions and settle disputes or conflicts regarding the project. The sponsor takes the project into the limelight, so to speak, and gets to call the shots regarding project outcomes. The project sponsor is also the one with the big bucks who provides funds for your project. The project sponsor should be named in the project charter and identified as the final authority and decision maker for project issues. Ultimately, the project sponsor is responsible for facilitating the project's success.

Sponsors are actively involved in the Initiating and Planning phases of the project and tend to have less involvement during the Execution and Monitoring and Controlling phases. It's up to the project manager to keep the project sponsor informed of all project activities, project progress, and any conflicts or issues that arise. The sponsor is the one with the authority to resolve conflicts and set priorities when these things can't be dealt with any other way.

Functional Managers

I covered functional managers briefly in Chapter 1. Project managers must work with and gain the support of functional managers in order to complete the project. Functional managers fulfill the administrative duties of the organization, provide and assign staff members to projects, and conduct performance reviews for their staff. It's a good idea to identify the functional managers who will be working on project tasks or assigned project responsibilities in the charter.

It's also a good idea to identify the key project stakeholders in the project charter. Although this isn't explicitly stated as part of this process, you'll see in the next section that stakeholder influences make up one of the components of the project charter. To identify stakeholder influences, it's also necessary to identify the stakeholders and describe their roles in high-level terms as I've done here.

Exam Spotlight

In some organizations, the project manager might write the project charter. However, if you (as the project manager) are asked to write the charter, remember that your name should not appear as the author. Because the project charter authorizes the project and authorizes you as the project manager, it doesn't make sense for you to write a document authorizing yourself to manage the project. The author of the charter should be an executive manager in your organization with the power and authority to assign resources to this project. This is usually the project sponsor or project initiator.

Project Charter Sign-Off

The project charter isn't complete until you've received sign-off from the project sponsor, senior management, and key stakeholders. Sign-off indicates that the document has been read by those signing it (let's hope so, anyway) and that they agree with its contents and are on board with the project. It also involves the major stakeholders right from the beginning and should win their continued participation in the project going forward. If someone has a problem with any of the elements in the charter, now is the time to speak up.

Prior to publishing the charter, I like to hold a kickoff meeting with the key stakeholders to discuss the charter and then obtain their sign-off. I think it's imperative for you to identify your key stakeholders as soon as possible and involve them in the creation of the project charter. Remember that stakeholder identification is an ongoing activity.

Signing the project charter document is the equivalent of agreeing to and endorsing the project. This doesn't mean the project charter is set in stone, however. Project charters will change throughout the course of the project. As more details are uncovered and outlined and as the Planning processes begin, more project issues will come to light. This is part of the iterative process of project management and is to be expected. The charter will occasionally be revised to reflect these new details, project plans will be revised, and project execution will change to incorporate the new information or direction.

The last step in this process is publishing the charter. Publishing, in this case, means distributing a copy of the project charter to the key stakeholders, the customer, the management team, and others who might be involved with the project. Publication can take several forms, including printed format or electronic format distributed via the company email system or on the company's intranet.

Next, we'll look at the Identify Stakeholders process.

Identifying Stakeholders

Think of stakeholders and project participants as a highly polished orchestra. Each participant has a part to play. Some play more parts than others, and, alas, some don't play their parts as well as others. An integral part of project management is getting to know your stakeholders and the parts they play. You'll remember from Chapter 1 that stakeholders are those people or organizations who have a vested interest in the outcome of the project. They have something to either gain or lose as a result of the project, and they have the ability to influence project results.

Identify Stakeholders Inputs

The *Identify Stakeholders* process involves identifying and documenting all the stakeholders on the project, including their interests, interdependencies, and potential positive or negative impacts on the project.

Identifying key stakeholders seems like it should be fairly easy, but once you get beyond the obvious stakeholders, the process can become difficult. Sometimes stakeholders, even key stakeholders, will change throughout the project's life. The key stakeholders on a project might include the project sponsor, the customer (who might also be the project sponsor), the project manager, project team members, management personnel, contractors, suppliers, and so on. The stakeholders involved in the project charter and the contract are obvious picks to be included in the stakeholder register, one output of this process.

The inputs of this process are as follows:

- Project charter
- Procurement documents
- Enterprise environmental factors
- Organizational process assets

According to the *PMBOK® Guide,* the environmental factors you'll want to pay particular attention to during this process are company culture, organizational structure, and governmental or industry standards. The organization structure will help you understand who has influence and power based on position and where they reside in the organization. The organizational process assets you should be concerned about include stakeholder register templates and lessons learned, including the stakeholder registers from previous projects. We'll talk more about stakeholder register templates later in this chapter.

The project charter and procurement documents can be helpful in identifying stakeholders. The signature pages of these documents, along with the descriptions and deliverables sections, may name stakeholders or business units you wouldn't ordinarily think about.

Don't forget important stakeholders. That could be a project killer. Leaving out an important stakeholder, or one whose business processes weren't considered particularly during the Initiating and Planning processes, could spell disaster for your project.

Exam Spotlight

Stakeholder identification should occur as early as possible in the project and continue throughout its life. Likewise, the stakeholder analysis and strategy should be reviewed periodically throughout the project and updated as needed. Remember to manage stakeholder satisfaction just as you would any key deliverable on the project. Identifying and analyzing their needs throughout the project will help make certain you are managing their expectations, and thus their satisfaction.

Stakeholder Analysis

The tools and techniques of Identify Stakeholders are stakeholder analysis, expert judgment, and meetings. We have already discussed expert judgment. Meetings in this case refer to profiling and analyzing stakeholders' involvement in the project, their roles, knowledge level, interests and more.

According to the *PMBOK® Guide,* stakeholder analysis involves using qualitative and quantitative data to analyze which stakeholders' interests should be considered throughout the project. Those with the most influence will also have the most impact.

During stakeholder analysis, you'll want to identify the influences stakeholders have in regard to the project and understand their expectations, needs, and desires. From there, you'll derive more specifics regarding the project goals and deliverables. Be warned that stakeholders are mostly concerned about their own interests and what they (or their organizations) have to gain or lose from the project. In all fairness, we all fall into the stakeholder category, so we're all guilty of focusing on those issues that impact us most.

According to the *PMBOK® Guide*, three steps are involved in stakeholder analysis: identifying stakeholders, analyzing potential impact, and assessing how stakeholders are likely to react to given situations. Let's look at each step independently.

The first step is identifying all potential stakeholders and capturing general information about them such as the department they work in, contact information, knowledge levels, and influence levels. Since the output of this process is the stakeholder register, you should devise a stakeholder register template now and capture all information about the stakeholders in one place. Here is an example of a stakeholder register template:

Name   Department   Knowledge Level   Expectations   Influence Levels   Phone Email

When we discuss the stakeholder register output later in this section, I'll tell you what additional elements you need to add to your chart.

Stakeholders can be internal or external to the organization. One way to uncover stakeholders whom you might not have thought about at the start is to ask known stakeholders if they know of anyone else who might be impacted by this project. Ask team members whether they're aware of stakeholders who haven't been identified. Stakeholders might also come to the forefront once you start uncovering some of the goals and deliverables of the project.

Understanding Stakeholder Roles

The second step in identifying stakeholders is identifying the potential impact on or support for the project each may have and then classifying them according to impact. That way, you can devise a strategy to deal with those impacts should they arise.

To determine potential impact, as project manager you must understand each stakeholder's role in the project and in the organization. Get to know them and their interests. Determine the relationship structure among the various stakeholders. Start cultivating partnerships with these stakeholders now, because it's going to get pretty cozy during the course of your project. If you establish good working relationships up front and learn a little about their business concerns and needs, it might be easier to negotiate or motivate them later when you have a pressing issue that needs action. Knowing which stakeholders work well together and which don't can also help you in the future. One stakeholder might have the authority or influence to twist the arm of another, figuratively speaking, of course. Conversely, you might know of two stakeholders who are like oil and water when put into the same room together. This can be valuable information to keep under your hat for future reference.

Some stakeholders may have a significant amount of influence over the project and its outcomes. Understanding the organizational structure, and where the stakeholders fit in that structure, should be your first step in determining the level of influence they have. For example, if Melanie in accounting wields a significant amount of power and influence over the organization, when you need input or decisions from her regarding costs or budgets for the project, you better believe that those decisions are not likely to be overridden. Conversely, if stakeholders with little influence provide direction that you don't verify, that input could be overridden at a later date by a more powerful stakeholder, causing changes to the project.

You can essentially classify the power and influence of each stakeholder on a simple four-square grid where power is on one axis and interest on the other. The *PMBOK®️ Guide* lists four classification models for this task:

▪ Power/Interest grid

▪ Power/Influence grid

▪ Influence/Impact grid

▪ Salience model

The first three grids are self-explanatory. The Salience model is more complicated than a four-square grid because it charts three factors: stakeholder power, urgency, and legitimacy. Urgency refers to a stakeholder's level of need for attention as immediate, occasional, or rarely. Legitimacy concerns the appropriateness of the stakeholder's participation at given times during the project.

Assessing Stakeholders

The third step in stakeholder analysis is assessing how your stakeholders may respond to different situations that arise throughout the project and how you might influence them to obtain the best possible outcome. As I said earlier, some stakeholders may have a significant amount of influence over the project and its outcomes and their level of influence may shed some light on how they may respond to various situations. Your first step in determining the level of influence they have should be to understand the organizational structure and where they fit in. Conducting informal interviews with project team members, other stakeholders, and the stakeholders themselves about their behaviors on past projects will also give you some insight on how they may react to your project.

Some of the elements you might want to consider when assessing stakeholders are:

▪ Identifying the key stakeholders who could have a significant impact on the project based on position, influence, and power

▪ Stakeholders' anticipated level of participation

▪ Stakeholders' groups or committees and their level of influence

Once the stakeholder assessment is complete, you should devise a plan to deal with any potential impacts and/or potential strategies for gaining their support.

Remember that the definition of a successful project is one that accomplishes the goals of the project and meets stakeholders' expectations. Understand and document those expectations, and you're off to a good start.

Stakeholder Register and Strategy

Stakeholder register is the only output of this process. The stakeholder register contains the information we discussed earlier in this section in the stakeholder register template. In addition to the elements we already discussed, the stakeholder register should contain at least the following details, according to the *PMBOK® Guide*:

Identifying Information   This includes items such as contact information, department, role in the project, and so on.

Assessment Information   This includes elements regarding influence, expectations, key requirements, and when the stakeholder involvement is most critical.

Stakeholder Classification   Stakeholders can be classified according to their relationship to the organization (internal or external for example) and, more important, whether they support the project, are resistant to the project, or have no opinion.

Remember that project documents are usually easily accessible by the project team and stakeholders. Use caution when documenting sensitive information regarding a stakeholder and your strategy for dealing with that stakeholder because it could become public knowledge.

Introducing the Kitchen Heaven Project Case Study

This chapter introduces a case study that we'll follow throughout the remainder of the book. The case study is updated at the end of every chapter. It's designed to show you how a project manager might apply the material covered in the chapter to a real-life project. As happens in real life, not every detail of every process is followed during all projects. Remember that the processes from the *PMBOK® Guide* that I'll cover in the remaining chapters are project management guidelines. You will often combine processes during your projects, which will allow you to perform several steps at once. The case studies will present situations or processes that you might find during your projects and describe how one project manager resolves them.

Real World Scenario

Project Case Study: New Kitchen Heaven Retail Store

You are a project manager for Kitchen Heaven, a chain of retail stores specializing in kitchen utensils, cookware, dishes, small appliances, and some gourmet foodstuffs, such as bottled sauces and spices. You're fairly new to the position, having been hired to replace a project manager who recently retired.

Kitchen Heaven currently owns 49 stores in 34 states and Canada. The world headquarters for Kitchen Heaven is in Denver, Colorado. Counting full-time and part-time employees, the company employs 1,500 people, 200 of whom work at headquarters.

The company's mission statement reads, "Great gadgets for people interested in great food."

Recently, the vice president of marketing paid you a visit. Dirk Perrier is a very nice, well-dressed man with the formal air you would expect a person in his capacity might have. He shakes your hand and gives you a broad, friendly smile.

"We've decided to go forward with our 50th store opening! Sales are up, and our new line of ceramic cookware is a hot seller, no pun intended. I don't know if you're familiar with our store philosophy, so let me take a moment to explain it. We like to place our stores in neighborhoods that are somewhat affluent. The plain fact is that most of our shoppers have incomes of more than $150,000 a year. So, we make an effort to place our stores in areas where those folks usually shop.

"We're targeting the type of customer who watches the Food Network channel and must have all the gadgets and tools they see the famous chefs using. So, the stores are upbeat and convey a fun, energetic feel, if you will.

"Our next store is going to be right here in our home area—Colorado Springs. Because this is going to be our 50th store, we plan on having a 50th grand-opening celebration, with the kind of surprises and activities you might expect for such a notable opening.

"Our stores generally occupy from 1,500 to 2,500 square feet of retail space, and we typically use local contractors for the build-out. A store build-out usually takes 120 days from the date the property has been procured until the doors open to the public. I can give you our last opening's project plan so you have a feel for what happens. Your job will be to procure the property, negotiate the lease, procure the shelving and associated store furnishings, get a contractor on the job, and prepare the 50th store festivities. My marketing folks will assist you with that last part.

"You have six months to complete the project. Any questions?

You take in a deep breath and collect your thoughts. Dirk has just given you a lot of information with hardly a pause between thoughts. A few initial ideas drift through your head while you're reaching for your notebook.

You work in a functional organization with a separate projectized department responsible for carrying out projects of this nature. You've been with the company long enough to know that Dirk is high up there in the executive ranks and carries the authority and power to make things happen. Therefore, Dirk is the perfect candidate for project sponsor.

You grab your notebook and start documenting some of the things Dirk talked about, clarifying with him as you write:

- The project objective is to open a new store in Colorado Springs six months from today.

- The store should be located in an affluent area.

- The store will carry the full line of products from utensils to gourmet food items.

- The grand opening will be accompanied by lots of fanfare because this is the 50th store opening.

You have a question or two for Dirk.

"Is there a special reason we have to open, let's see, six months from now, which is February 1?"

He responds, "Yes, we want the store open the first week in February. Early February is when the Garden and Home Show conference hits the Springs area. We'll have a trade show booth there. We know from experience in other areas that our stores generally see a surge in sales during this month as a result of the trade show. It's a great way to get a lot of advertising out there and let folks know where we're located."

"Another question, Dirk. Is there a budget set for this project yet?"

"We haven't set a hard figure," Dirk replies. "But again, from past experience we know it takes anywhere from $1.5 to $2 million to open a new store—and we don't want to forget the big bash for the grand opening."

"Thanks, Dirk. I'll get started writing the project charter right away. I'll put your name on the document because you're the project sponsor."

Dirk concludes with, "Feel free to come to me with questions or concerns at any time."

One week later.

You review your notes and reread the project charter you've prepared for the Kitchen Heaven retail store one last time before looking for Dirk. You finally run across Dirk in a hallway near the executive washroom.

"Dirk, I'm glad I caught you. I'd like to go over the project charter with you before the kick-off meeting tomorrow. Do you have a few minutes?"

"Sure," Dirk says to you. "Let's have it."

"The project charter states the purpose of the project, which of course is to open the 50th Kitchen Heaven store in Colorado Springs. I also documented some of the high-level requirements, many of which we talked about last time we met. I documented the assumptions and constraints you gave me with the understanding that we'll define these much more closely when I create the scope statement. I've included a section that out-lines a preliminary milestone schedule, and I've included some preliminary ROI [return on investment] calculations. Using your estimate of $2 million as our initial budget request and based on the projected inflows you gave me last week, I've calculated a payback period of 19 months, with an IRR [internal rate of return] of 6 percent."

"That's impressive," replies Dirk. "That's even better than our Phoenix store. If I recall, the payback period there was just over two years. Let's hope those numbers hold true."

"I think they're reliable figures," you say. "I researched our data based on recent store openings in similar-sized cities and factored in the economic conditions of the Colorado Springs area. Since they're on a growth pattern, we think the timing is perfect.

"As you know, the project kickoff is scheduled for tomorrow. What I'll need, then, is for you to talk about the project and the goals, talk about the commitment you'll need from the management team to support this project, and introduce me as the project manager. I've already forwarded a copy of the project charter to the meeting attendees so that they can review it before the meeting. I included a list of the assumptions we've made so far as an appendix to the charter. Lastly, I'll need you to ask everyone present to sign a copy of the project charter."

"Sounds like you've covered everything," Dirk says. "I don't anticipate any problems tomorrow, because everyone is looking forward to this store opening."

Project Case Study Checklist

- **Project objective:** To open a new store in Colorado Springs six months from today.

- **Business need or demand for project:** Company data concludes that the Kitchen Heaven consumers have incomes of more than $150,000 a year. The Colorado Springs area is home to a large number of people with that income. Currently, there is no Kitchen Heaven in the area, but there appears to be a demand for one.

- **Project sponsor:** Dirk Perrier, VP of marketing.

- **Organizational structure:** Functional organization with a separate projectized department.

- **Project selection methods:** Payback period calculated at 19 months and IRR calcu-lated at 6 percent.

- **Created project charter:** Project charter contains the following:

- High-level overview of project

- List of measurable project objectives

- High-level risks

- Summary milestone schedule with initial completion date of February 1

- Summary budget of $2 million

- Project manager authority levels

- Definition of roles of project sponsor and project manager

■ **Next steps:** Kickoff meeting set up to discuss charter and obtain sign-off.

Understanding How This Applies to Your Next Project

There are as many ways to select and prioritize projects as there are organizations. You might be profit driven, so money will be king. You might have a stakeholder committee that weighs the pros and cons, or you might have an executive director who determines which project is up next. Scoring models and cash flow analysis techniques are useful on the job. Whether your organization uses these methods or others, an organized, consistent way to select and prioritize projects is necessary. I know I could work the next 100 years straight and probably still not get all the projects completed my organization would like to see implemented. What I've found is that the selection method must be fair and reasonable. If your organization uses an arbitrary method—say you like Tara better than Joe, so Tara's projects always end up on the "yes" list—it won't be long before stakeholders demand that another method be devised to select projects that everyone can understand. Whatever method you're using, stick to it consistently.

If you're like me, when I'm faced with a new project I want to get right to the heart of the matter and understand the purpose of the project. Projects come about for many reasons. Most of the time, understanding the reason it came about will give you some insight into its purpose. For example, if a new law is passed that requires anyone applying for a driver's license to show two forms of identification but the existing system has the space to record verification of only one document, you immediately have a firm grasp on the purpose of the project—you'll have to update the system to include additional space for recording the second document.

It has been my experience in working with project teams that when the team understands the reason or the need that brought about the project and it understands the goal of the project, the project is more successful. I don't have any scientific evidence for this, but when the teams have a clear understanding of what they're working on and why, they tend to stay more focused and fewer unplanned changes make their way into the project. Don't assume everyone on the project team understands the goal of the project. It's good practice to review the project goal early in the project and again once the work of the project is under way. Reminding the team of the goal helps keep the work on track.

I usually write a project charter for all but the smallest of projects. I believe the most important sections of the charter are the objectives of the project, the summary milestone schedule, and the summary budget. If the project is so small that a charter seems like too much, I'll write a statement of work. It's important that the goal or objective of the project is written down, no matter how small the project, so that the team and the stakeholders know what they're working toward.

Identifying the stakeholders early in the project is imperative to project success. You won't want to write the charter without their involvement. The two processes described in this chapter are almost performed simultaneously when you're conducting a project. I won't begin writing the charter without stakeholder input first, and it's just as important to understand the role stakeholders will play in the project as well as their influence. If the CFO has ultimate influence over which projects proceed and what they'll include, you'll want the CFO's buy-in as soon as possible. Involvement in writing the charter and developing the future Planning process outputs helps to assure their buy-in. At a minimum, it helps reduce surprises midway through the project.

Always, and I mean *always*, get approval and signatures on the project charter. You will use this document as your basis for project planning, so you want to make certain the sponsor, key stakeholders, and the project manager understand the goals of the project the same way.

Summary

This chapter started with a discussion of the 10 Knowledge Areas. The Knowledge Areas bring together processes that have characteristics in common. They also help you understand what types of skills and resources are needed to complete the processes within them.

Next, I detailed how projects are initiated. Projects come about as a result of one of seven needs or demands: market demands, strategic opportunity/business needs, customer requests, technological advances, legal requirements, environmental considerations, or social needs.

Project selection methods include decision models in the form of benefit measurement methods and mathematical models (also called *constrained optimization methods*). The mathematical methods utilize mathematical models. Benefit measurement methods come in the form of cost-benefit analyses, scoring models, and economic analyses. These are primarily comparative approaches. Besides cost-benefit analysis, the most commonly used form of benefit measurement methods is cash flow analysis.

Analysis of cash flows includes payback period, discounted cash flows, net present value (NPV), and internal rate of return (IRR). These last three methods are concerned with the time value of money—or, in other words, converting future dollars into today's value. Generally, projects with a shorter payback period are desired over those with longer payback periods. Projects that have an NPV greater than 0 should be accepted. Projects with the highest IRR value are considered a better benefit to the organization than projects with lower IRR values.

The Develop Project Charter process is the first process in the Initiating process group. The project statement of work (SOW) is an input to this process that describes the product, service, or result the project was undertaken to complete. The SOW should include the business needs of the organization as well as a product scope description and should map to the organization's strategic plan.

Enterprise environmental factors are factors outside the project that might have significant influence on the success of the project. Organizational process assets refer to policies, guidelines, and procedures for conducting the project work.

Expert judgment and facilitation techniques are the two tools and techniques of this process. Experts usually have specialized knowledge or skills and can include staff from other departments in the company, external or internal consultants, and members of professional and technical associations or industry groups.

The output of this process is the project charter, which is the formal recognition that a project, or the next project phase, should begin. The charter authorizes the project to begin, it authorizes the project manager to assign resources to the project, it documents the business need and justification, it describes the customer's requirements, and it ties the project to the ongoing work of the organization.

The Identify Stakeholders process concerns identifying, assessing, and classifying stakeholders in a stakeholder register. Stakeholder involvement is critical to the success of the project. The more the project manager understands stakeholder influences, expectations, and impacts, the easier it is to prepare a strategy plan to deal with the impacts or issues, sometimes before they occur.

Exam Essentials

Be able to name the 10 Project Management Knowledge Areas.   The 10 Project Management Knowledge Areas are Project Integration Management, Project Scope Management, Project Time Management, Project Cost Management, Project Quality Management, Project Human Resource Management, Project Communications Management, Project Risk Management, Project Procurement Management, and Project Stakeholder Management.

Be able to distinguish between the seven needs or demands that bring about project creation.   The seven needs or demands that bring about project creation are market demand, strategic opportunity/business need, customer requests, technological advances, legal requirements, environmental considerations, and social needs.

Be able to define decision models.   Decision models are project selection methods that are used prior to the Develop Project Charter process to determine the viability of the project. Decision models include benefit measurement methods and mathematical models.

Be able to describe and calculate the payback period.   The payback period is the amount of time it will take the company to recoup its initial investment in the product of the project. It's calculated by adding up the expected cash inflows and comparing them to the initial investment to determine how many periods it takes for the cash inflows to equal the initial investment.

Be able to denote the decision criteria for NPV and IRR.   Projects with an NPV greater than 0 should be accepted, and those with an NPV less than 0 should be rejected. Projects with high IRR values should be accepted over projects with lower IRR values. IRR is the discount rate when NPV is equal to 0, and IRR assumes reinvestment at the IRR rate.

Be able to list the Develop Project Charter inputs.   The inputs for Develop Project Charter are project statement of work, business case, agreements, enterprise environmental factors, and organizational process assets.

Be able to describe the purpose of the business case.   The purpose of a business case is to understand the business need for the project and determine whether the investment in the project is worthwhile. It usually includes a cost-benefit analysis and the needs or demands that brought about the project.

Be able to describe the importance of the project charter.   The approved project charter is the document that officially recognizes and acknowledges that a project exists. The charter authorizes the project to begin, it authorizes the project manager to assign resources to the project, it documents the business need and justification, it describes the customer's requirements, and it ties the project to the ongoing work of the organization.

Understand the Identify Stakeholders process.   The purpose of this process is to identify the project stakeholders, assess their influence and level of involvement, and record stakeholder information in the stakeholder register.

Key Terms

You've learned just how important a charter is to every project. Be sure you understand the elements essential to the document and the processes used to ensure that your charter is complete. Skimping on the planning steps is almost certain to spell disaster down the road. Know these processes, and know them by the names used in the *PMBOK® Guide*:

Develop Project Charter

Identify Stakeholders

You'll also want to know these Knowledge Areas:

- Project Integration Management
- Project Scope Management
- Project Time Management
- Project Cost Management
- Project Quality Management
- Project Human Resource Management
- Project Communications Management
- Project Risk Management
- Project Procurement Management
- Project Stakeholder Management

You've also learned a lot of new keywords in this chapter. PMI® has worked hard to develop and define standard project management terms that apply across industries. Here is a list of some of the terms you came across in this chapter:

cost-benefit analysis	internal rate of return (IRR)
Develop Project Charter	net present value (NPV)
discounted cash flow	payback period
expert judgment	project charter
facilitation techniques	project statement of work (SOW)
feasibility studies	scoring model
historical information	steering committee
Identify Stakeholders	weighted scoring model

Review Questions

You can find the answers to the questions in Appendix A.

1. When a project is being performed under contract, the SOW is provided by which of the following?

    A. The buyer

    B. The project sponsor

    C. The project manager

    D. The contractor

2. You've been hired as a manager for the adjustments department of a nationwide bank based in your city. The adjustments department is responsible for making corrections to customer accounts. This is a large department, with several smaller sections that deal with specific accounts, such as personal checking or commercial checking. You've received your first set of management reports and can't make heads or tails of the information. Each section appears to use a different methodology to audit their work and record the data for the management report. You request that a project manager from the PMO come down and get started right away on a project to streamline this process and make the data and reports consistent. This project came about as a result of which of the following?

    A. Technological advance

    B. Strategic opportunity/business need

    C. Customer request

    D. Legal requirement

3. What are the inputs to the Develop Project Charter process?

    A. Agreements, project SOW, business case, enterprise environmental factors, and organizational process assets

    B. Project SOW, business case, and organizational process assets

    C. Agreements, enterprise environmental factors, and organizational process assets

    D. Project SOW, enterprise environmental factors, and organizational process assets

4. You work for a large manufacturing plant. Your firm is thinking of initiating a new project to release an overseas product line. This is the company's first experience in the overseas market, and it wants to make a big splash with the introduction of this product. The project entails producing your product in a concentrated formula and packaging it in smaller containers than the U.S. product uses. A new machine is needed in order to mix the first set of ingredients in the concentrated formula. Which of the following actions is the next best step the project manager should take?

    A. The project manager should document the project's high-level requirements in a project charter document and recommend that the project proceed.

    B. The project manager knows the project is a go and should document the description of the product in the statement of work.

   C. The project manager should document the business need for the project and recommend that a feasibility study be performed to determine the viability of the project.

   D. The project manager should document the needs and demands that are driving the project in a business case document.

5. You are the project manager for Fun Days Vacation Resorts. Your new project assignment is to head up the Fun Days resort opening in Austin, Texas. You are estimating the duration of the project management plan activities, devising the project schedule, and monitoring and controlling deviations from the schedule. Which of the Project Management Knowledge Areas are you working in?

   A. Project Scope Management

   B. Project Quality Management

   C. Project Integration Management

   D. Project Time Management

6. According to the *PMBOK® Guide*, the project statement of work should contain or reference which of the following elements?

   A. Strategic plan, product scope description, measurable project objectives, and business need

   B. Business need, strategic plan, product scope description

   C. Project purpose, measurable project objectives, business case, and product scope description

   D. Product scope description, project purpose, and business need

7. Your nonprofit organization is preparing to host its first annual 5 K run/walk in City Park. You worked on a similar project for the organization two years ago when it cohosted the 10 K run through Overland Pass. Which of the organizational process assets might be most helpful to you on your new project?

   A. The organization's marketing plans

   B. Historical information from a previous 10 K run or similar project

   C. The marketplace and political conditions

   D. The organization's project management information systems

8. Which of the following lists of processes belong to the Project Integration Management Knowledge Area?

   A. Define Scope, Close Procurements, and Perform Integrated Change Control

   B. Develop Project Management Plan, Direct and Manage Project Work, and Perform Integrated Change Control

   C. Define Scope, Direct and Manage Project Work, and Manage Stakeholders Expectations

   D. Define Scope, Collect Requirements, and Close Project or Phase

9. Comparative methods, scoring methods, and economic and cash flow analysis are all part of which of the following?

    A. Benefit measurement methods

    B. Constrained optimization methods

    C. Benefit measurement methods, which are a component of a tool and technique of the Develop Project Charter process

    D. Constrained optimization methods, which are a component of a tool and technique of the Develop Project Charter process

10. You are the project manager for the Late Night Smooth Jazz Club chain, with stores in 12 states. Smooth Jazz is considering opening a new club in Arizona or Nevada. You have derived the following information:

    Project Arizona: The payback period is 18 months, and the NPV is (250).

    Project Nevada: The payback period is 24 months, and the NPV is 300.

    Which project would you recommend to the selection committee?

    A. Project Arizona, because the payback period is shorter than the payback period for Project Nevada

    B. Project Nevada, because its NPV is a positive number

    C. Project Arizona, because its NPV is a negative number

    D. Project Nevada, because its NPV is a higher number than Project Arizona's NPV

11. You are the project manager for the Late Night Smooth Jazz Club chain, with stores in 12 states. Smooth Jazz is considering opening a new club in Kansas City or Spokane. You have derived the following information:

    Project Kansas City: The payback period is 27 months, and the IRR is 6 percent.

    Project Spokane: The payback period is 25 months, and the IRR is 5 percent.

    Which project should you recommend to the selection committee?

    A. Project Spokane, because the payback period is the shortest

    B. Project Kansas City, because the IRR is the highest

    C. Project Spokane, because the IRR is the lowest

    D. Project Kansas City, because the payback period is the longest

12. Which of the following is true regarding NPV?

    A. NPV assumes reinvestment at the cost of capital.

    B. NPV decisions should be made based on the lowest value for all the selections.

    C. NPV assumes reinvestment at the prevailing rate.

    D. NPV assumes reinvestment at the NPV rate.

13. You are the project manager for Insomniacs International. Since you don't sleep much, you get a lot of project work done. You're considering recommending a project that costs $575,000; expected inflows are $25,000 per quarter for the first two years and then $75,000 per quarter thereafter. What is the payback period?

   A. 40 months

   B. 38 months

   C. 39 months

   D. 41 months

14. Which of the following is true regarding IRR?

   A. IRR assumes reinvestment at the cost of capital.

   B. IRR is not difficult to calculate.

   C. IRR is a constrained optimization method.

   D. IRR is the discount rate when NPV is equal to zero.

15. Which of the following best describes the purpose of a business case?

   A. To determine project viability and probability of success

   B. To understand the need or demand that brought about the project

   C. To understand the business need for the project and determine whether the investment in the project is worthwhile

   D. To perform analysis using mathematical models and benefit measurement methods that will assist in project selection

16. You are in the process of identifying your stakeholders. You are using one of the tools and techniques of this process that according to the *PMBOK® Guide,* involves all of the following steps except for which one?

   A. Determining the level of stakeholder participation on the project

   B. Assessing how stakeholders are likely to react to certain situations

   C. Identifying stakeholders

   D. Analyzing potential impacts stakeholders may present

17. Your selection committee is debating between two projects. Project A has a payback period of 18 months. Project B has a cost of $125,000, with expected cash inflows of $50,000 the first year and $25,000 per quarter after that. Which project should you recommend?

   A. Either Project A or Project B, because the payback periods are equal

   B. Project A, because Project B's payback period is 21 months

   C. Project A, because Project B's payback period is 24 months

   D. Project A, because Project B's payback period is 20 months

18. Which of the following is true?

   A. Discounted cash flow analysis is the least precise of the cash flow techniques because it does not consider the time value of money.

   B. NPV is the least precise of the cash flow analysis techniques because it assumes reinvestment at the discount rate.

   C. Payback period is the least precise of the cash flow analysis techniques because it does not consider the time value of money.

   D. IRR is the least precise of the cash flow analysis techniques because it assumes reinvestment at the cost of capital.

19. You are a project manager for Zippy Tees. Your selection committee has just chosen a project you recommended for implementation. Your project is to manufacture a line of miniature stuffed bears that will be attached to your company's trendy T-shirts. The bears will be wearing the same T-shirt design as the shirt to which they're attached. Your project sponsor thinks you've impressed the big boss and wants you to skip to the manufacturing process right away. What is your response?

   A. Agree with the project sponsor because that person is your boss and has a lot of authority and power in the company.

   B. Require that a preliminary budget be established and a resource list be put together to alert other managers of the requirements of this project. This should be published and signed by the other managers who are impacted by this project.

   C. Require that a project charter be written and signed off on by all stakeholders before proceeding.

   D. Suggest that a preliminary statement of work be written to outline the objectives of the project.

20. Which of the following is true regarding the project charter?

   A. The project charter should be issued by a manager external to the project.

   B. The project charter should be issued by a key stakeholder's name.

   C. The project charter should be issued by the project manager.

   D. The project charter should be issued by the project sponsor.

Chapter

3

Developing the Project Scope Statement

THE PMP® EXAM CONTENT FROM THE PLANNING THE PROJECT PERFORMANCE DOMAIN COVERED IN THIS CHAPTER INCLUDES THE FOLLOWING:

✓ **Assess detailed project requirements, constraints, and assumptions with stakeholders based on the project charter, lessons learned from previous projects, and the use of requirement-gathering techniques (e.g., planning sessions, brainstorming, focus groups) in order to establish the project deliverables.**

✓ **Create the work breakdown structure with the team by deconstructing the scope in order to manage the scope of the project.**

✓ **Knowledge and Skills:**

- ※ Requirements gathering techniques
- ※ Work breakdown structure (WBS) tools and techniques
- ※ Scope management techniques
- ※ Elements, purpose, and techniques of project planning

Great job! You've successfully completed the project Initiating processes and published the project charter and the stakeholder register. The project is officially under way. Stakeholders have been identified and informed of the project, you have management buy-in on the project, the project manager has been assigned, and the project objectives and description have been identified. A solid foundation for the planning process is in place.

In this chapter, we will begin the Planning processes for the project. In fact, I will continue discussing the Planning processes through Chapter 7, "Planning Project Resources." Planning is a significant activity in any project and, if done correctly, will go a long way toward ensuring project success.

This chapter begins with the Develop Project Management Plan process. This process will describe the overall approach you'll use to manage the project. The result of this process is the project management plan document that describes how you'll execute, monitor, and control the project outcomes as the project progresses and how you'll close out the project once it concludes.

Then you'll move on to the Plan Scope Management process. Here we will examine documenting a plan that outlines how to define, validate, and control the project scope.

The Collect Requirements process is next. During this process quantified requirements are gathered and documented to assure stakeholder needs are met and expectations are managed.

During the Define Scope process, you'll use the project charter and the requirements documentation—plus some other inputs—and then apply the tools and techniques of this process to come up with the project scope statement. I'll talk in depth about project objectives, requirements, constraints, assumptions, and other elements of writing the project scope statement, which is an output of this process.

Once you have the deliverables and requirements well defined, you'll begin the process of breaking down the work of the project via a work breakdown structure (WBS). You'll accomplish this task in the Create WBS process. The WBS defines the scope of the project and breaks the work down into components that can be scheduled and estimated as well as easily monitored and controlled.

We have a lot to cover in this chapter so let's get started.

The process names, inputs, tools and techniques, outputs, and descriptions of the project management process groups and related materials and figures in this chapter are based on content from *A Guide to the Project Management Body of Knowledge (PMBOK® Guide), Fifth Edition* (Sybex, 2010).

Developing the Project Management Plan

The first process in the Planning process group is the *Develop Project Management Plan* process. It's first for good reasons. This process is part of the Project Integration Management Knowledge Area and is concerned with defining, preparing, coordinating, and then integrating all the various subsidiary project plans into an overall project management plan.

This process involves defining and documenting the processes you're going to use to manage this project. For example, let's say you and the project team have determined you will use project management processes involving costs, human resources, risks, and a project schedule. (Warning: This is a demonstration only—don't try this at home. In reality, professionals perform many more processes than this on a typical project.) Each particular process might have a management plan that describes it. For instance, a cost management plan (an example of a subsidiary plan) would describe how costs will be managed and controlled and how changes to costs will be approved and managed throughout the project. The Develop Project Management Plan process brings all these subsidiary plans together, along with the outputs of the Planning group processes, into one document called the *project management plan*.

> In Chapter 1, "What Is a Project?," I talked about *tailoring*—determining which processes within each process group are appropriate for the project on which you're working. Tailoring is used in the Develop Project Management Plan process because it's here you'll determine what processes to use to best manage the project.

To create and document the plan, you need to gather some inputs and build on the information you've already collected.

Developing Inputs

The Develop Project Management Plan process has four inputs:

- Project charter
- Outputs from other processes
- Enterprise environmental factors
- Organizational process assets

Let's take a look at each next.

Project Charter   You'll recall that the project charter describes the objectives of the project and the high-level requirements needed to satisfy stakeholder expectations. The reason it's an input into this process is because the content of the project charter—including project objectives, project description, high-level requirements, summary milestone schedule, summary budget, and so on—will help you and the team determine exactly which project management processes to use on the project.

Outputs from Other Processes   The project management processes include all the individual processes that make up the process groups we're talking about throughout this book. The Initiating group, for example, has two processes, Planning has a zillion (okay, not that many, but it seems like it), and so on. The outputs from other processes you use on the project become inputs to the Develop Project Management Plan process. For example, the cost management plan we talked about in the introduction is an input. Any processes you use that produce a baseline (such as schedule or cost) or a subsidiary management plan (such as a risk management plan, communication management plan, and so on) are included as inputs to this process.

 I'll talk more about baselines and the makeup of individual subsidiary management plans as we discuss the various Planning processes from now throughout Chapter 7 of this book.

Enterprise Environmental Factors   You've seen enterprise environmental factors before. Some of the key elements of the environmental factors you should consider when choosing the processes to perform for this project include standards and regulations (both industry and governmental), company culture and organizational structure, personnel administration, infrastructure, and the *project management information system (PMIS)*.

Organizational Process Assets   Some of the critical elements of the organizational process assets input you should consider when choosing the processes to perform for this project include project management plan template, change control procedures, performance measurement criteria, historical information, and the configuration management knowledge database that contains the official company policies, standards, procedures, and other project documents.

The PMIS is an automated (or manual) system used to document the project management plan and subsidiary plans, to facilitate the feedback process, and to revise the documents. It incorporates the configuration management system and the change control system, both of which I'll cover in Chapter 10, "Measuring and Controlling Project Performance." Later in the project, the PMIS can be used to control changes to any of the plans. When you're thinking about the PMIS as an input (that is, as part of the enterprise environmental factors), think of it as a collection and distribution point for information as well as an easy way to revise and update documents. When you're thinking about the PMIS as a tool and technique, think of it just that way—as a tool to facilitate the automation, collection, and distribution of data and to help monitor processes such as scheduling, resource leveling, budgeting, and web interfaces.

As I talked about in Chapter 1, the processes you choose to perform for the project will be based on the complexity of the project, the project scope, and the type of industry in which you work. Your organization's standards, guidelines, and policies or the project management office (PMO) might also dictate the types of processes you'll use for the project. You should also consider whether your organization has existing change control processes in place, templates that you're required to use, or financial controls and processes. Historical information and past project files are useful in helping you decide which processes to use for this project.

Exam Spotlight

The PMIS in the Develop Project Management Plan process includes a subsystem called the configuration management system and the change control system, which is a subsystem of the configuration management system.

The two tools and techniques of this process are expert judgment and facilitation techniques. We looked at facilitation techniques in Chapter 2, "Creating the Project Charter." According to the *PMBOK® Guide*, the types of expert judgment you'll need to complete this process include the following:

- Tailoring techniques
- Understanding technical and management details that need to be included in the project management plan
- Determining resources and assessing skill levels needed for project work
- Determining and defining the amount of configuration management to apply on the project
- Determining which project documents require formal change control processes

Documenting the Project Management Plan

The purpose of most processes is, of course, to produce an output. Outputs are usually a report or document of some type or a deliverable. In this case, you end up with a document—the project management plan—that describes, integrates, and coordinates baselines and subsidiary plans for the processes you've determined to use for the project. The project management plan can be detailed, or it can be a high-level summary based on the needs of the project.

According to the *PMBOK® Guide*, the project management plan defines how the project is executed, how it's monitored, and how it's controlled. It is progressively elaborated over the life of the project. It also documents the outputs of the Planning group processes, which

I'll cover over the next several chapters. The project management plan should include or discuss the following elements:

- Processes you'll use to perform each phase of the project and their level of implementation, the tools and techniques you'll use from these processes, and the interactions and dependencies among the processes. All this was determined as part of the tailoring exercise we talked about in Chapter 2.

- The life cycle you'll use for the project and for each phase of the project if applicable.

- Methods for executing the work of the project to fulfill the objectives.

- Change management plan describing methods for monitoring and controlling change.

- Configuration management plan.

- Methods for determining and maintaining the validity of performance baselines.

- Communication needs of the stakeholders and techniques to fulfill those needs.

- Management reviews of content, issues, and pending decisions.

In addition to these elements, the subsidiary plans that are associated with the processes you'll be using for this project should be documented in the project management plan. Each of these subsidiary management plans might contain the same elements that the overall project management plan does, but they're specifically related to the topic at hand. For example, the cost management plan should define how changes to cost estimates will be reflected in the project budget and how changes or variances with a significant impact should be communicated to the project sponsor and stakeholders. The schedule management plan describes how changes to the schedule will be managed, and so on.

The subsidiary plans might be detailed or simply a synopsis, depending on the needs of the project. I've listed the subsidiary plans along with a brief description next. I will cover each of these plans in more detail throughout the remainder of this book. According to the *PMBOK® Guide*, the subsidiary plans are as follows:

Scope Management plan   Describes the process for determining project scope, facilitates creating the work breakdown structure (WBS), describes how the product or service of the project is verified and accepted, and documents how changes to scope will be handled.

Requirements Management Plan   Describes how requirements will be analyzed, documented, traced, reported, and managed throughout the project.

Schedule Management Plan   Describes how the project schedule will be developed and controlled and how changes will be incorporated into the project schedule.

Cost Management Plan   Describes how costs will be managed and controlled and how changes to costs will be approved and managed.

Quality Management Plan   Describes how the organization's quality policy will be implemented. It should address and describe quality control procedures and measures, quality assurance procedures and measures, and continuous process improvement.

Communications Management Plan   Describes the communication needs of the stakeholders, including timing, frequency, and methods of communications.

Risk Management Plan   Describes how risks will be managed and controlled during the project. This should include risk management methodology; roles and responsibilities; definitions of probability and impact; when risk management will be performed; and the categories of risk, risk tolerances, and reporting and tracking formats.

Procurement Management Plan   Describes how the procurement processes will be managed throughout the project. This might include elements such as type of contract, procurement documents, and lead times for purchases.

Process Improvement Plan   Focuses on finding inefficiencies in a process or activity and eliminating them.

Human Resource Management Plan   Documents the roles and responsibilities for project team members, their reporting relationships, and how the team will be managed.

Stakeholder Management Plan   Documents what strategies to use to encourage stakeholder participation, documents the analysis of their needs and interests and impacts, and documents the process regarding project decision making.

The project management plan is not limited to the subsidiary plans listed here. You might include other plans and documentation that help describe how the project will be executed or monitored and controlled. Perhaps you're working on a project that requires precise calculations and exact adherence to requirements. You could include a plan that describes these calculations, how they'll be monitored and measured, and the processes you'll use to make changes or corrections.

The project management plan also includes project baselines, such as these:

- Schedule baseline
- Cost baseline
- Scope baseline

I'll talk about each of these documents in the remaining chapters as well.

Exam Spotlight

Understand that the purpose of the project management plan is to define how the project is executed, monitored and controlled, and closed, as well as to document the processes you'll use during the project.

As the project progresses and more and more processes are performed, the subsidiary plans and the project management plan itself might change. You will manage these changes using the Perform Integrated Change Control process. All changes should be reviewed following the processes outlined in the change control plan, and the project management plan should be updated to reflect the approved changes.

Exam Spotlight

In practice, you'll find that you'll prepare the project management plan after you've progressed through several of the other Planning processes. It's difficult to finalize some of these subsidiary plans without thinking through or sometimes performing the process they're associated with first. However, for the exam, remember that Develop Project Management Plan is the first process in the Planning group, and it should be performed first. Updates can and should occur to the project management plan as subsidiary plans are created or changed.

Plan Scope Management

Plan Scope Management is the first process in the Project Scope Management Knowledge Area. You might recall from Chapter 1 that the purpose of the Project Scope Management Knowledge Area is to describe and control what is and what is *not* work of the project. *Scope* is collectively the product, service, or result of the project and the deliverables the project intends to produce.

The primary purpose of this process is twofold: to write the scope management plan and to develop the requirements management plan. The scope management plan is a planning tool that documents how the project team will go about defining project scope, how changes to scope will be controlled, and how project scope will be verified. The requirements management plan addresses analyzing, documenting, and managing the project requirements.

I'll talk more about this in the section, "Documenting the Scope Management Plan," later in this chapter.

For now you'll concentrate on the inputs to this process, which will help you get started documenting the decisions about the Plan Scope Management process for your project.

Understanding the Plan Scope Management Inputs

You've seen the inputs to the Plan Scope Management process before. They are as follows:

- Project management plan
- Project charter
- Enterprise environmental factors
- Organizational process assets

Even though I've talked about these before, you'll want to look at specific elements of some of these inputs closely. Defining project scope, and managing that scope as you progress through the project, has a direct relationship to the success of the project. It's difficult to document how you'll define project scope if you don't first understand the purpose behind the project; the product, service, or result you're trying to produce; and the environmental factors and organizational process assets under which you're working. The process of how you'll go about defining and managing scope is what the scope management plan (which is what you're ultimately getting to with this process) is about.

The project charter describes the purpose and high-level requirements of the project. Analyzing the information in this document will help you determine the appropriate tools and methodologies to use (as well as which processes to perform) for the project. The idea here is that you want to understand the size and complexity of the project so that you don't spend more time documenting how you're going to go about defining and managing scope than what's needed.

One of the environmental factors that might influence the way scope is managed is personnel administration, or more specifically, the human resources involved on the project. Their skills, knowledge, and abilities to communicate and escalate issues appropriately might influence the way project scope is managed. Personnel policies governing those resources might also have an effect. For example, you might have a team member who has a close relationship with one of the stakeholders. Let's say the stakeholder wants a change to the project. The stakeholder and team member grab a cup of coffee together at the corner deli, and the next thing you know, the team member is incorporating the change into the project. Scope can't be managed efficiently when it's being changed without the knowledge of the project manager or project team.

Other environmental factors that might affect scope management are the organization's culture, economic conditions, market conditions, and physical and technological infrastructure.

Organizational process assets typically include policies and procedures, whether formal or informal. Your organization's policies or the policies and guidelines of your industry might have an effect on scope management, so make certain you're familiar with them. And don't forget historical information. You can review the scope management plan from previous projects of similar size and scope to help you craft the one for this project.

Real World Scenario

Scope Management Plan Requirements

Phil Reid is a gifted engineer. He works as an accident reconstructionist and has a 90 percent success rate at assisting his clients (who are attorneys) at winning court cases. Phil can intuitively and scientifically determine whether the scene of an accident is real or is insurance fraud. Most cases Phil works on are managed as projects because each accident is unique, the cause of each accident is unique, and each investigation has a definite beginning and ending. The attorneys that Phil's organization works with want the final results of the investigation delivered in different formats. Although Phil is exceptionally good at determining the forensic evidence needed to prove or disprove how the accident occurred, he is not at all gifted in oral communication skills. As a result, the scope management plan requires the client to define how the outcome of the investigation should be presented and whether the engineer might be required to testify regarding the results of the investigation. That way, Phil's organization can plan in advance how to use his talents on the project and assign a resource to work with him who has the communication skills and ability to testify if that's required.

Using Plan Scope Management Tools and Techniques

Plan Scope Management has two tools and techniques:

Expert Judgment   You'll rely on the expert judgment of people or groups with specific skills, knowledge, or training to help assess the process inputs. One expert you can count on in this process is the executive manager who wrote or contributed to the project charter. This person can clarify questions you might have about the project objectives as well as the product description. Stakeholders, industry experts, team members, people with specialized training, or other project managers with previous experience on projects similar to yours can help you determine how scope management should work for this project.

Meetings   You will use meetings with the experts just noted to determine and formalize the information contained in the scope management plan.

Documenting the Scope Management Plan

The first output of the Plan Scope Management process is the *scope management plan*. This plan describes how the project team will go about defining project scope, verifying the work of the project, and managing and controlling scope. According to the *PMBOK® Guide*, the scope management plan should contain the following:

- The process you'll use to prepare the project scope statement. The project scope statement (which I'll define later in this chapter) contains a detailed description of what the deliverables and requirements of the project are and is based on the information contained in the preliminary scope.

- A process for creating, maintaining, and approving the WBS. The WBS (I'll cover that in the next chapter) further defines the work of the project (as defined in the project scope statement) by breaking down the deliverables into smaller pieces of work.

- A definition of how the deliverables will be verified for accuracy and the process used for accepting deliverables.

- A description of the process for controlling scope change requests, including the procedure for requesting changes and how to obtain a change request form.

Exam Spotlight

The scope management plan is a planning tool that documents how the project team will go about defining project scope, how the work breakdown structure will be developed, how changes to scope will be controlled, and how the work of the project will be verified and accepted. And don't forget, the scope management plan is a component of (or a subsidiary of) the project management plan.

Documenting the Requirements Management Plan

The *requirements management plan* is much like the scope management plan but focuses on the project requirements. This plan details how to analyze, document, and manage the project requirements throughout all phases of the project. Managing the requirements is the key to this process and the phase-to-phase relationship you use to run the project will influence how you will manage the project requirements. For example, a sequential phase-to-phase relationship would dictate that all the requirements for each phase be completed before beginning the work of the phase and most certainly before moving on to the next phase of the project. An overlapping relationship might mean that the requirements are not fully defined before the work begins and are progressively elaborated as the project (or phase) progresses.

We talked about phase-to-phase relationships in Chapter 1. There are two types: sequential and overlapping.

Exam Spotlight

Make certain you document the phase-to-phase relationship you'll use during the project life cycle in the requirements management plan.

There are several components of a sound requirements management plan. According to the *PMBOK® Guide,* you should include the following factors in the plan (and you are always free to add more than those noted here):

- How planning, tracking, and reporting of requirements activities will occur
- How changes to the requirements will be requested, tracked, and analyzed along with other configuration management activities
- How requirements will be prioritized
- What metrics will be used to trace product requirements
- What requirements attributes will be documented in the traceability matrix (the last output of this process)
- What elements to include on the traceability matrix

Collecting Requirements

Now we are getting into the meat of the Planning processes. In the *Collect Requirements* process, we define what the final product or service of the project will look like. You will recall that scope management describes what is and what is not included in the project scope. In this case, we're starting off by defining what *is* included in the work of the project.

Exam Spotlight

The *PMBOK® Guide* notes that not all of the requirements gathered during this process will be included in the end result of the project. The Define Scope process is where you will determine which of the requirements gathered here will be included in the final project. We will look at Define Scope in the next section of this chapter.

Requirements describe the characteristics of the deliverables. They might also describe functionality that a deliverable must have or specific conditions a deliverable must meet to satisfy the objective of the project. Requirements are typically conditions that must be met or criteria that the product or service of the project must possess to satisfy the objectives of the project. Requirements quantify and prioritize the wants, needs, and expectations of the project sponsor and stakeholders. According to the *PMBOK® Guide* (and lots of personal experience), you must be able to measure, trace, and test requirements. It's important that they're complete and accepted by your project sponsor and key stakeholders.

Requirements can take many forms. According to the *PMBOK® Guide*, requirements can be classified into the categories listed below which may also assist you in elaborating them further:

- Business
- Stakeholder
- Solution
- Functional
- Nonfunctional
- Transition
- Project
- Quality

The primary purpose of the Collect Requirements process is to define and document the project sponsor, the customer, and the stakeholder's expectations and needs for meeting the project objectives. In my experience, understanding, documenting, and agreeing on requirements are critical factors to project success. Recording the requirements and attaining stakeholder approval of the requirements will help you define and manage their expectations throughout the project.

Exam Spotlight

Requirements must be documented, analyzed, and quantified in enough detail that they can be measured once the work of the project begins. Requirements become the basis for developing the WBS and are essential in estimating costs, developing the project schedule, and quality planning.

You've already learned about four of the five inputs to this process: the scope management plan, requirements management plan, project charter, and the stakeholder register. We will discuss the fifth, the stakeholder management plan in Chapter 5, "Developing the Project Budget and Communicating the Plan," so we'll move on to tools and techniques.

Using the Tools and Techniques of the Collect Requirements Process

Your communication skills are about to come in handy. Gathering and documenting requirements is not a task for the faint of heart. Because defining and producing requirements are so critical to the success of the project, I recommend using team members with excellent communication skills to perform this task. If they have the ability to read minds, all the better. Stakeholders almost always know what they want the end product to look like but often have difficulty articulating their needs. An expert communicator can read between the lines and ask probing questions that will draw the information out of the stakeholder.

Business process owners are those people who are experts in their particular area of the business. They are invaluable resources to the project manager and in gathering requirements for the project. They are usually the mid-level managers and line managers who still have their fingers in the day-to-day portion of the business. For example, it takes many experts in various areas to produce and market a great bottle of beer. Machinists regulate and keep the stainless steel and copper drums in top working order. Chemists check and adjust the secret formulas brewing in the vats daily. Graphic artists must develop colorful and interesting labels and ads to attract the attention of those thirsty patrons. Of course, those great TV commercials advertising the tasty brew are produced by yet another set of business experts. These are the kinds of people you'll interview and ask to assist you in identifying requirements.

There are several tools and techniques in this process you can use to help identify the requirements of the project. Some of these tools and techniques can also be used during the Identify Risk process and the Plan Quality Management process. We'll cover those processes in Chapter 6, "Risk Planning," and Chapter 7, "Planning Project Resources," respectively. The following tools and techniques are used for the Collect Requirements process:

Interviews   Interviews are typically one-on-one conversations with stakeholders. Interviews can be formal or informal and generally consist of questions prepared ahead of time. The advantages to this tool are that subject matter experts and experienced project participants can impart a lot of information in a short amount of time and typically have a good understanding of the features and functions needed from the project deliverables. You should record the responses during the interviews, and don't be afraid to ask spontaneous questions as they occur to you during the interview.

Focus Groups   Focus groups are usually conducted by a trained moderator. The key to this tool lies in picking the subject matter experts and stakeholders to participate in the focus group.

Facilitated Workshops   Cross-functional stakeholders come together in a facilitated workshop to discuss and define requirements that affect more than one department. For example, in the information technology industry you can use a technique called joint application design/development (JAD) to define requirements. Suppose you're implementing a software package that impacts several business units. You'll need representatives from each unit together in a workshop so that all of their needs are represented and prioritized. This way, all the participants understand the needs of other departments involved in the project and have a facilitated forum to discuss and resolve their issues. Other industries have similar techniques to bring together customers and/or business subject matter experts such as Quality Function Deployment (QFD) sessions used in the manufacturing industry.

Exam Spotlight

The primary difference between focus groups and facilitated workshops is that focus groups are gatherings of prequalified subject matter experts and stakeholders and facilitated workshops consist of cross-functional stakeholders who can define cross-functional requirements. Differences among stakeholders can be resolved more quickly and consensus is more easily attained in a facilitated workshop environment.

Group Creativity Techniques Group creativity involves several techniques, like brainstorming, the Nominal Group technique, affinity diagrams, and multicriteria decision analysis. We will cover each of these techniques in either the Identify Risk process (Chapter 6) or the Plan Quality Management process (Chapter 7).

Another group creativity technique, called idea/mind mapping, is a technique where participants first use brainstorming techniques to record their ideas. Whiteboards and flip charts are great tools to use with this process. The facilitator uses the whiteboard to map ideas and, using a mind-mapping layout, group similar topics together. There are a few mind-mapping software packages available on the market that can greatly assist with this process. Mind mapping allows the participants to gain an understanding of common ideas and themes, create new ideas, and understand differences.

Group Decision-Making Techniques According to the *PMBOK® Guide*, there are many methods groups can use to reach decisions. These methods can also be used with the group creativity techniques. The four methods mentioned include unanimity, where everyone agrees on the resolution or course of action; majority, where more than 50 percent of the members support the resolution; plurality, where the largest subgroup within the group makes the decision if majority is not reached; and dictatorship, where one person makes the decision on behalf of the group.

Questionnaires and Surveys This technique involves querying a large group of participants via questionnaires or surveys. These tools allow you to gather information quickly and apply statistical analysis, if needed, to the results.

Observations This technique is typically a one-on-one experience where an observer sits side by side with the participant to observe how the participant interacts with the product or service. This technique is also known as job shadowing. For example, you may use this technique to determine requirements for an upgrade to a software product. Sitting with users and watching their interactions with the product enables observers to uncover requirements they would not have ordinarily discovered. This technique can also involve participant observers who perform the job themselves in order to ascertain requirements.

Prototypes   Prototyping is a technique that involves constructing a working model or mock-up of the final product with which the participants can experiment. The prototype does not usually contain all the functionality the end product does, but it gives participants enough information that they can provide feedback regarding the mock-up. This is an iterative process where participants experiment and provide feedback and the prototype is revised and the cycle starts again.

Benchmarking   This technique is used in the Quality processes as well and involves comparing measurements against standards to determine performance. It can also compare processes, operations, management practices, and so on against other departments, organizations, or industries to help refine and promote best practices or come up with ideas to improve current practices.

Context Diagrams   Context diagrams use actors and business processes or equipment to visually show how interactions between them take place. Actors are people who use or interact with the business processes or equipment, which in turn produce outputs used by the actors.

Document Analysis   Document analysis comes into play when it's important to consider the organization's business plans, marketing plans, contracts, business rules, strategic plans, and so on when determining requirements.

Documenting Requirements

Now that you've employed the tools and techniques of this process to gather requirements, you'll want to record them in a requirements document. Stakeholders sometimes have short memories, particularly on long-term projects, so documenting requirements and obtaining their approval is essential for project success. You will use the requirements documentation throughout the project to manage stakeholder and customer expectations. This is a lot easier to accomplish when they've agreed to the requirements ahead of time and you have their approval documented.

I've already mentioned the first output of this process, which is requirements documentation. The other output of this process is the requirements traceability matrix. I'll describe each in detail next.

Requirements Documentation

As I mentioned in the opening to this section, requirements quantify and prioritize the wants, needs, and expectations of the project sponsor and stakeholders to achieve the project objectives. Requirements typically start out high level and are progressively elaborated as the project progresses. You must be able to track, measure, test, and trace the requirements of the project. You never want to find yourself at the end of the project (or phase) and discover you have no way to validate the requirements. If you can't measure or test whether the requirement satisfies the business need of the project, the definition of success is left to the subjective opinions of the stakeholders and team members.

You've worked hard to gather and define requirements and you don't want all that effort going to waste. This output involves recording the requirements in a requirements document. The *PMBOK® Guide* does not dictate the format of this document and acknowledges it can be formal with lots of detail or a simple list categorized by stakeholder and priority. However, it does state that the requirements document should include at least the following elements:

- Business need for the project and why it was undertaken
- Objectives of the project and the business objectives the project hopes to fulfill
- Functional requirements
- Nonfunctional requirements
- Quality requirements
- Acceptance criteria
- Transition requirements for the operations area or customer receiving the end result of the project
- Business rules
- Organizational areas and outside entities impacted
- Support and training requirements
- Assumptions and constraints

Functional requirements is a term used often in software development. It typically describes a behavior, such as calculations or processes that should occur once data is entered. In non-software terms, functional requirements might describe specifications, quantities, colors, and more. *Nonfunctional requirements* refer to elements that are related to the product but don't describe the product directly. In the case of a software product, this could be a security requirement or performance criteria.

One of the most important elements of the requirements document that isn't in the preceding list is the signatures of the key stakeholders indicating their acceptance of the requirements. They will also sign the scope statement, which we'll talk about in the section, "Defining Scope," later in this chapter.

Documenting the Requirements Traceability Matrix

The last output of the Collect Requirements process is the requirements traceability matrix. The idea behind the traceability matrix is to document where the requirement originated, document what the requirement will be traced to, and then follow it through to delivery or completion. Table 3.1 shows a sample traceability matrix with several attributes that identify the requirement.

TABLE 3.1   Requirements traceability matrix

Unique ID	Description of requirement	Source	Priority	Test scenario	Owner	Status
001	Requirement one	Project objective	B	User acceptance	HR specialist	Approved

Each requirement should have its own unique identifier. You could devise a numbering system that defines both the category of the requirement and a unique, ascending number—for example, HR (for human resources) 001—or a simple numbering system as shown in this example may suffice.

The description should be brief but have enough information to easily identify the requirement.

The source column refers to where the requirement originated. Requirements may come from many sources, including project objectives, business needs, product design, the work breakdown structure, deliverables, and so on.

Priority refers to the priority of the requirement. You can use any prioritization process like a simple numbering system or an alpha system as the example shows here. The definition of a "B" priority should be included in the requirements management plan. Perhaps an "A" is essential to project success and a "B" is highly desirable.

The test scenario in this example is where you record how the requirement will be tested or during which project phase, and the owner of the test item, who will also decide if the test scenario passes or fails.

Status may capture information about the requirement that refers to whether the requirement has been approved to be included in the project; if it was added, deferred, or canceled; and so on.

Exam Spotlight

According to the *PMBOK® Guide*, the requirements traceability matrix helps assure that business value is realized when the project is complete because each requirement is linked to a business and project objective.

The next process in the Planning process group is the Define Scope process. We'll look at that next.

Defining Scope

Now that you've documented the project requirements, you're ready to further define the needs of the project in the *Define Scope* process. Scope can refer to product scope (the features and characteristics that describe the product, service, or result of the project) or project scope (the project management work). We'll look at both product and project scope in this section. The project scope statement (an output of this process) is what you'll use to develop and document a detailed description of the deliverables of the project and the work needed to produce them. This process is progressively elaborated as more detail becomes known.

Exam Spotlight

You'll want to pay particular attention to the accuracy and completeness of this process. Defining project scope is critical to the success of the project because it spells out exactly what the product or service of the project looks like. Conversely, poor scope definition might lead to cost increases, rework, schedule delays, and poor morale.

First, you'll examine the inputs and tools and techniques of this process. The inputs to the Define Scope process are as follows:

- Scope management plan
- Project charter
- Requirements documentation
- Organizational process assets

Some of the important elements from the project charter that you'll want to consider when writing the project scope statement (we'll cover this output later) are the project description, project objectives, the characteristics of the product of the project, and the process for approving the project.

Objectives are quantifiable criteria used to measure project success. They describe "what" you're trying to do, accomplish, or produce. Quantifiable criteria should at least include schedule, cost, and quality measures. You might use business measures or quality targets as well. These objectives will be broken down shortly into deliverables that will describe the objectives outlined in the charter.

The requirements documentation is a starting point for developing the scope statement. During the Define Scope process, you will determine which requirements will be included in the final product, service, or result of the project. They will be progressively elaborated and then documented in detail in the scope statement. The idea here is that you know some information when the charter is being written and more information comes to light when you hold brainstorming sessions or other meetings with stakeholders to discover the requirements of the product of the project (during the Collect Requirements process).

Finally, those requirements are decided on, further elaborated, and documented (again) in much more detail in the scope statement. Keep in mind that not all of the requirements that you gathered and documented in the Collect Requirements process may be included in the scope statement. You will reexamine those requirements here and determine which ones are keepers and which ones are not.

Some of the other important information you'll want to key in on from these inputs are historical information, the product description, and the project assumptions and constraints. I'll cover each of these in the section, "Writing the Project Scope Statement," later in this chapter.

Exam Spotlight

If the project charter is missing or was not created, you'll need to develop the information normally found in the charter (or obtain it from other sources) to use as the foundation for creating the project scope statement.

You'll see some new tools and techniques in this process:

- Expert judgment
- Product analysis
- Alternatives generation
- Facilitated workshops

You learned about expert judgment and facilitated workshops in Chapter 2. I'll discuss product analysis and alternatives generation in the following sections.

Product Analysis

Product analysis goes hand in hand with the product scope description and, therefore, is most useful when the project's end result is a product. Product analysis is a method for converting the product description and project objectives into deliverables and requirements. According to the *PMBOK® Guide*, product analysis might include performing value analysis, product breakdown, systems-engineering techniques, systems analysis, or value-engineering techniques to further define the product or service.

Exam Spotlight

It's beyond the scope of this book to go into the various analysis techniques used in product analysis. For exam purposes, remember that product analysis is a tool and technique of the Define Scope process and memorize the list of analysis techniques that might be performed in this process.

Alternatives Generation

Alternatives generation is a technique used for discovering different methods or ways of accomplishing the work of the project. For example, brainstorming might be used to discover alternative ways of achieving one of the project objectives. Perhaps the project's budget doesn't allow for a portion of the project that the stakeholders think needs to be included. Brainstorming might uncover an alternative that would allow the needed portion to be accomplished.

Lateral thinking is a form of alternatives generation that can be used to help define scope. Edward de Bono created this term and has done extensive research and writing on the topic of lateral thinking. The simplest definition is that it's thinking outside the box. Lateral thinking is a process of separating the problem—or in our case the components of project scope (the deliverables and requirements)—looking at them from angles other than their obvious presentation and encouraging team members to come up with ways to solve problems or look at scope that are not apparently obvious.

Outside the Box

Lateral thinking is a way of reasoning and thinking about problems from perspectives other than the obvious. It challenges our perceptions and assumptions. Consider these two examples of lateral thinking that I crafted based on some puzzles I found at this website: www.folj.com/lateral/. Use your favorite search engine and run a query on "lateral thinking puzzles" to find many more examples.

Question: How could your pet Yorkie fall from the window of an 18-story building and live?

Answer: The question asks how your pet could fall from an 18-story building and live; however, the question doesn't state your pet fell from the 18th floor. So, your pet Yorkie fell from the basement-level window.

Question: Eight chocolates are arranged in an antique candy dish. Eight people each take one chocolate. There is one chocolate remaining in the dish. How can that be?

Answer: If there are eight chocolates in an antique dish, how can the last person take the last chocolate yet one remains in the dish? Well, the last person to take a chocolate took the dish as well—therefore, the last chocolate remained in the dish.

Remember these examples the next time you're defining scope or looking for alternative answers to a problem.

The use of pairwise comparisons is another alternatives generation technique. This is much like it sounds in that you compare any number of items against each other to determine which is preferred. This technique typically uses quantitative measures to determine the preferred option.

Writing the Project Scope Statement

The purpose of the *project scope statement* is to document the project objectives, deliverables, and the work required to produce the deliverables so that it can be used to direct the project team's work and as a basis for future project decisions. The scope statement is an agreement between the project management team and the project customer that states precisely what the work of the project will produce. Simply put, the scope statement tells everyone concerned with the project exactly what they're going to get when the work is finished.

Exam Spotlight

Understand that the purpose of the scope statement, according to the *PMBOK® Guide*, is to provide all the stakeholders with a foundational understanding of the project and product scope. It describes the project deliverables in detail. Also remember that the scope statement defines and progressively elaborates the work of the project. It guides the work of the project team during the Executing process, and all change requests will be evaluated against the scope statement. If the change request is outside the bounds of the project scope as documented in the project scope statement, it should be denied.

Since the scope statement serves as a baseline for the project, if questions arise or changes are proposed later in the project, they can be compared to what's documented in the scope statement. Making change decisions is easier when the original deliverables and requirements are well documented. You'll also know what is out of scope for the project simply because the work isn't documented in the scope statement (or conversely, deliverables or other elements are documented and noted as being specifically out of scope). The criteria outlined in the scope statement will also be used to determine whether the project was completed successfully. I hope you're already seeing the importance of documenting project scope.

Understanding the Scope Statement Components

According to the *PMBOK® Guide*, the project scope statement should include all of the following:

- Product scope description
- Acceptance criteria
- Project deliverables
- Project exclusions
- Project constraints
- Project assumptions

If the details surrounding these are spelled out in other documents, you don't have to reenter all the information in the scope statement. Simply reference the other document in the scope statement so that readers know where to find it.

Exam Spotlight

You may be thinking that the project scope statement has some of the same information as the project charter. Keep in mind the project charter is a high-level description of the project (and it names the project manager) whereas the project scope statement is a detailed description of the project and product scope and describes how the final product or result of the project will be accepted, along with the other items mentioned earlier.

Product Scope Description

The *product scope description* describes the characteristics of the product, service, or result of the project. I talked about this in Chapter 2. If the product scope description is contained in the project charter, you can reference the project charter in the project scope statement, or you can copy and paste the information from the project charter into the scope statement. It won't hurt anything to have it in both places and will make reading the scope statement easier.

Exam Spotlight

You'll use the project management plan as your measurement of project scope completion, and product scope completion will be measured against product requirements.

Acceptance Criteria

Acceptance criteria include the process and criteria that will be used to determine whether the deliverables and the final product, service, or results of the project are acceptable and satisfactory. Acceptance criteria help you describe project success because it defines the specifications the deliverables must meet in order to be acceptable to the stakeholder. Acceptance criteria might include any number of elements, such as quality criteria, fitness for use, and performance criteria. This component should also describe the process stakeholders will use to indicate their acceptance of the deliverables.

Project Deliverables

Deliverables are measurable outcomes, measurable results, or specific items that must be produced or performed to consider the project or project phase completed. Deliverables should be specific and verifiable. For example, one of your deliverables might include widgets with a 3" diameter that will in turn be assembled into the final product. This deliverable, a 3"-diameter widget, is specific and measurable. However, if the deliverable was not documented or not communicated to the manager or vendor responsible for manufacturing the widgets, there could be a disaster waiting to happen. If they deliver 2" widgets instead of the required 3" version, it would throw the entire project off schedule or perhaps cause the project to fail. This could be a career-limiting move for the project manager because it's the project manager's responsibility to document deliverables and monitor the progress of those deliverables throughout the project. Most projects have multiple deliverables. As in this example, if you are assembling a new product with many parts, each of the parts might be considered independent deliverables.

A project deliverable is typically a unique and verifiable product or result or a service that's performed. The product or service must be produced or performed in order to consider the project complete. The deliverables might also include supplementary outcomes such as documentation or project management reports.

The bottom line is this: No matter how well you apply your project skills, if the wrong deliverables are produced or the project is managed to the wrong objectives, you will have an unsuccessful project on your hands.

Project Exclusions

Project exclusions are, as you'd guess, anything that isn't included as a deliverable or work of the project. You'll want to note the project exclusions in the project scope statement so that you can continue to manage stakeholder expectations throughout the project.

Critical Success Factors

Deliverables and requirements are sometimes referred to as *critical success factors*. Critical success factors are those elements that must be completed in order for the project to be considered complete. For example, if you're building a bridge, one of the deliverables might be to produce a specific number of trusses that will be used to help support the bridge. Without the trusses, the bridge can't be completed; in fact, the bridge might not stand without them. The trusses, in this case, are a critical success factor. Not all deliverables are necessarily critical success factors, but many of them will fall into this category and should be documented as such.

Documenting *All* the Deliverables and Requirements

One of the project manager's primary functions is to accurately document the deliverables and requirements of the project and then manage the project so that they are produced according to the agreed-on criteria. Deliverables describe the components of the goals and objectives in a quantifiable way. Requirements are the specifications of the deliverables. (Remember for the exam that requirements are documented in the Collect Requirements process that occurs before the Define Scope process.)

The project manager should use the project charter as a starting point for identifying and progressively elaborating project deliverables, but it's possible that only some of the deliverables will be documented there. Remember that the charter was signed by a manager external to the project, and it was the first take at defining the project objectives and deliverables. As the project manager, it's your job to make certain *all* the deliverables are identified and documented in the project scope statement. That's because the scope statement (not the project charter) serves as the agreement among stakeholders—including the customer of the project—regarding what deliverables will be produced to meet and satisfy the business needs of the project.

Interview the stakeholders, other project managers, project team members, customers, management staff, industry experts, and any other experts who can help you identify all the deliverables of the project. Depending on the size of the project, you might be able to accomplish this in a group setting using simple brainstorming techniques, but large complex projects might have scope statements for each deliverable of the project. Remember that the project scope statement is progressively elaborated into finer detail and is used later to help decompose the work of the project into smaller tasks and activities.

Project Constraints

Constraints are anything that either restricts the actions of the project team or dictates the actions of the project team. Constraints put you in a box. (I hope you're not claustrophobic.) As a project manager, you have to manage *to* the project constraints, which sometimes requires creativity.

In my organization—and I'm sure the same is true in yours—we have far more project requests than we have resources to work on them. In this case, resources are a constraint. You'll find that a similar phenomenon occurs on individual projects as well. Almost every project you'll encounter must work within the triple constraint combination of scope, time, and cost. The quality of the project (or the outcomes of the project) is affected by how well these three constraints are managed. Usually, one or two triple constraints apply (and sometimes all three), which restricts the actions of the project team. You might work on projects where you have an almost unlimited budget (don't we wish!) but time is the limitation. For example, if the president mandated that NASA put an astronaut on Mars by the end of 2020, you'd have a time-constrained project on your hands.

Other projects might present the opposite scenario. You have all the time you need to complete the project, but the budget is fixed. Still other projects might incorporate two or more of the project constraints. Government agencies are notorious for starting projects that have at least two and sometimes all three constraints. For example, new tax laws are passed that impact the computer programs, requiring new programs to calculate and track the tax changes. Typically, a due date is given when the tax law takes effect, and the organization responsible is required to implement the changes with no additions to budget or staff. In other words, they are told to use existing resources to accomplish the objectives of the project, and the specific requirements, or scope, of the project are such that they cannot be changed to try to meet the time deadline.

As a project manager, one of your biggest jobs is to balance the project constraints while meeting the expectations of your stakeholders. In most projects, you usually will have to balance only one or two of the triple constraints. For example, if one of the project objectives is to complete the project by the end of the year and stay within a certain budget, you will need to balance the other two constraints: time and cost. As the saying goes, "I can give it to you fast or I can give it to you cheap, but I can't give it to you fast and cheap."

Constraints can take on many forms and aren't limited to time, cost, and scope. Anything that impedes your project team's ability to perform the work of the project or specifically dictates the way the project should be performed is considered a constraint. Constraints can come from inside or outside the project or organization. Let's say to fulfill some of the deliverables of your project you'll have to purchase a large amount of materials and equipment. Procurement processes may be so cumbersome that ordering supplies for a project adds months to the project schedule. The procurement process itself becomes a constraint because of the methods and procedures you're required to use to get the materials.

You're likely to encounter the following constraints on your future projects:

Time Constraint   As I said, time can be a project constraint. This usually comes in the form of an enforced deadline, commonly known as the "make it happen now" scenario. If you are in charge of the company's holiday bash scheduled for December 10, your project is time constrained. Once the invitations are out and the hall has been rented, you can't move the date. All activities on this project are driven by the due date.

Budget Constraints   Budgets, or cost, are another element of the classic triple constraint. Budgets limit the project team's ability to obtain resources and might potentially limit the scope of the project. For example, component X cannot be part of this project because the budget doesn't support it.

Scope Constraints   Scope is the third element of the original triple constraints. Scope defines the deliverables of the project, and you may have situations where scope is pre-defined by your project sponsor. Alternatively, sometimes budget constraints will impact the scope of the project and require you to cut back on the deliverables originally planned.

Quality Constraints   Quality constraints typically are restricted by the specifications of the product or service. The specifications for those 3" to widgets we talked about earlier could be considered a quality constraint. Most of the time, if quality is a constraint one of the other constraints—time or budget—has to have some give. You can't produce high quality on a restricted budget and within a tightly restricted time schedule. Of course, there are exceptions—but only in the movies.

Schedule Constraints   Schedule constraints can cause interesting dilemmas for the project manager. For example, say you're the project manager in charge of building a new football stadium in your city. The construction of the stadium will require the use of cranes—and crane operators—at certain times during the project. If crane operators are not available when your schedule calls for them, you'll have to make schedule adjustments so that the crane operators can come in at the right time.

Resource Constraints   Resources could be a constraint from a few different perspectives, including availability of key resources both internally and in the marketplace, skill levels, and personality. You may also have availability issues or quality problems with nonhuman resources, like materials and goods. Human resources constraints are something I deal with on every project.

Technology Constraints   Technology is marvelous. In fact, how did humans survive prior to the invention of computers and cell phones? However, it can also be a project constraint. For example, your project might require the use of new technology that is still so new it hasn't been released on a wide-scale basis or hasn't been adequately tested to determine stability in production. One impact might be that the project will take an additional six months until the new technology is ready and tested.

Directive Constraints   Directives from management can be constraints as well. Your department might have specific policies that management requires for the type of work you're about to undertake. This might add time to the project, so you must consider those policies when identifying project constraints. When you're performing work on contract, the provisions of the contract can be constraints

Constraints, particularly the classic triple constraints, can be used to help drive out the objectives and requirements of the project. If it's difficult to discern which constraint is the primary constraint, ask the project sponsor something like this: "Ms. Sponsor, if you could have only one of these two alternatives, which would you choose? The project is delivered on the date you've stated, or we don't spend one penny more than the approved budget." If Ms. Sponsor replies with the date response, you know your primary constraint is time. If push comes to shove during the project Planning processes for this project, the budget might have to give because time cannot.

You'll want to understand what the primary constraint is on the project. If you assume the primary constraint is budget when in actuality the primary constraint is time, in the immortal words of two-year-olds worldwide, "Uh-oh." Understanding the constraints and which one carries the most importance will help you later in the project Planning process group with details such as scope planning, scheduling, estimating, and project management plan development. That's assuming your project gets to the project Planning processes, which brings me to the next topic: project assumptions.

Project Assumptions

You've probably heard the old saying about the word *assume*, something about what it makes out of "u" and "me." In the case of project management, however, throw this old saying out the window, because it's not true.

Assumptions, for the purposes of project management, are things you believe to be true. For example, if you're working on a large construction project, you might make assumptions about the availability of materials. You might assume that concrete, lumber, drywall, and so on are widely available and reasonably priced. You might also assume that finding contract labor is either easy or difficult, depending on the economic times and the availability of labor in your locale. Each project will have its own set of assumptions, and the assumptions should be identified, documented, and updated throughout the project.

It's essential to understand and document the assumptions you're making, and the assumptions your stakeholders are making, about the project. It's also important to find out as many of the assumptions as you can up front. Projects can fail, sometimes after lots of progress has been made, because an important assumption was forgotten or the assumption was incorrect. Defining new assumptions and refining old ones are forms of progressive elaboration.

Let's say you make plans to meet your buddy for lunch at 11:30 on Friday at your favorite spot. When Friday rolls around, you assume he's going to show up, barring any catastrophes between the office and the restaurant. Project assumptions work the same way. For planning purposes, you presume the event or thing you've made the assumptions about is true, real, or certain. You might assume that key resources will be available when needed on the project. Document that assumption. If Sandy is the one and only resource who can perform a specific task at a certain point in the project, document your assumption that Sandy will be available and run it by her manager. If Sandy happens to be on a plane for Helsinki at the time you thought she was going to be working on the project, you could have a real problem on your hands.

Other assumptions could be factors such as vendor delivery times, product availability, contractor availability, the accuracy of the project plan, the assumption that key project members will perform adequately, contract signing dates, project start dates, and project phase start dates. This is not an exhaustive list, but it should get you thinking in the right direction. As you interview your stakeholders, ask them about their assumptions and add them to your list. Use brainstorming exercises with your team and other project participants to come up with additional assumptions.

Think about some of the factors you usually take for granted when you're trying to identify assumptions. Many times they're the elements everyone expects will be available or will behave in a specific way. Think about factors such as key team members' availability, access to information, access to equipment, management support, and vendor reliability.

Try to validate your assumptions whenever possible. When discussing assumptions with vendors, make them put those assumptions in writing. In fact, if the services or goods you're expecting to be delivered by your suppliers are critical to the project, include a clause in the contract to assure a contingency plan in case your suppliers fail to perform. For example, if you're expecting 200 computers to be delivered, configured, and installed by a certain date, require the vendor to pay the cost of rental equipment in the event the vendor can't deliver on the promised due date.

Remember, when assumptions are incorrect or not documented, it could cause problems partway through the project and might even be a project killer.

Approving and Publishing the Project Scope Statement

Just like the project charter, the project scope statement should be approved, agreed upon, published, and distributed to the stakeholders, key management personnel, and project team members. This isn't an official output of this process, nor is it noted in the *PMBOK®* *Guide.* You can accomplish this with a formal sign-off procedure that's documented as part of the *approval requirements* section of the scope statement. When stakeholders sign off and agree to the scope statement, they're agreeing to the deliverables and requirements of the project. As with the project charter, their agreement and endorsement of the project requirements and deliverables will likely sustain their participation and cooperation throughout the rest of the project. That doesn't mean they'll agree to everything as the project progresses, but it does mean the stakeholders are informed and will likely remain active project participants.

Remember that the definition of a successful project is one that accomplishes the goals of the project and meets stakeholders' expectations. Understand and document those expectations and you're off to a good start.

Updating the Project Documents

The last output of this process is project document updates. When you're in the midst of defining deliverables, you'll often find that changes to the original project objectives, requirements, or stakeholder register will occur. This may require updates to the stakeholder register, the requirements documentation, and requirements traceability matrix. Changes to scope may also occur later in the project. When the changes are approved, you'll need to update the scope statement and notify stakeholders that changes have been made.

Real World Scenario

Mountain Streams Services

Maria Sanchez is the CEO of Mountain Streams Services. She recently accepted a prestigious industry award on behalf of the company. Maria knows that without the dedication and support of her employees, Mountain Streams Services wouldn't have achieved this great milestone.

Maria wants to host a reception for the employees and their guests in recognition of all their hard work and contributions to the company. Maria has appointed you to arrange the reception.

The reception is scheduled for April 12, and Maria has given you a budget of $125 per person. The company employs 200 people. The reception should be semiformal.

You've documented the deliverables as follows:

- Location selection
- Food and beverage menu
- Invitations
- Entertainment
- Insurance coverage
- Decorations
- Photographer
- Agenda

In addition to the deliverables, you want to go over the following requirements with Maria to be certain you are both in agreement:

- The location should be in the downtown area.
- Employees are encouraged to bring one guest but no children.
- There will be an open bar paid for by Maria.
- The agenda will include a speech by Maria, followed by the distribution of bonus checks to every employee. This is to be kept secret until the reception.
- The decorations should include gold-trimmed fountain pens with the company logo at every place setting for the attendees to keep.

Once you've documented all the particulars, you ask to speak with Maria to go over this project scope statement and get her approval before proceeding with the project.

Creating the Work Breakdown Structure

Have you ever mapped out a family tree? In the *Create WBS* process, you'll construct something like it called a *work breakdown structure (WBS)*. It maps the deliverables of the project with subdeliverables and other components stemming from each major deliverable in a tree or chart format. Simply put, a WBS is a deliverable-oriented hierarchy that defines and organizes the entire scope of work of the project and only the work of the project. The items defined on the WBS come from the approved scope statement. Like the scope statement, the WBS serves as a foundational agreement among the stakeholders and project team members regarding project scope.

Exam Spotlight

Subdividing deliverables into smaller components is the purpose of the Create WBS process. The *PMBOK® Guide* calls this decomposition, which is also a tool and technique of this process.

The WBS will be used throughout many of the remaining Planning processes and is an important part of project planning. As you probably have concluded, everything you've done so far builds on the previous step. The project charter, requirements documentation, and project scope statement outline the project objectives, requirements, and deliverables. Now you'll use that comprehensive list of requirements and deliverables to build the framework of the WBS.

 I can't stress enough the importance of the work you've done up to this point. Your WBS will be only as accurate as your list of requirements and deliverables. The deliverables will become the groupings that will form the higher levels of the WBS from which activities will be derived later in the Planning processes.

The WBS should detail the full scope of work needed to complete the project. This breakdown will smooth the way for estimating project cost and time, scheduling resources, and determining quality controls later in the Planning processes. Project progress will be based on the estimates and measurements assigned to the WBS segments. So, again, accuracy and completeness are required when composing your WBS.

Before you begin constructing the WBS, you'll need to gather and review some important project documents. You'll look at those next.

Gathering the WBS Inputs

The inputs to the Create WBS process aren't new. They are as follows:

- Scope management plan
- Project scope statement
- Requirements documentation
- Enterprise environmental factors
- Organizational process assets

The scope management plan outlines how you will create the WBS from the elements listed in the scope statement, and it also describes how to obtain approval for and maintain the WBS. The important aspect to note about the inputs to this process is that the approved project scope statement is the document you will use to define and organize the work of the project in the WBS. Make certain you're using the most current version of the scope statement. Also note that the WBS, just like the project scope statement, contains the work of the project and only the work of the project.

Decomposing the Deliverables

The Create WBS process consists of two tools and techniques, decomposition and expert judgment. *Decomposition* involves breaking down the deliverables into smaller, more manageable components of work. The idea here is to break down the deliverables to a point where you can easily plan, execute, monitor and control, and close out the project deliverables. Decomposition typically pertains to breaking deliverables down into smaller deliverables, or component deliverables, where each level of the WBS (or each level of decomposition) is a more detailed definition of the level above it.

This breaking-down or decomposing process will accomplish several tasks for you, one of which is improving estimates. It's easier to estimate the costs, time, and resources needed for individual work components than it is to estimate them for a whole body of work or deliverable. Using smaller components also makes it easier to assign performance measures and controls. These give you a baseline to compare against throughout the project or phase. Finally, assigning resources and responsibility for the components of work makes better sense because several resources with different skills might be needed to complete one deliverable. Breaking them down assures that an assignment, and the responsibility for that assignment, goes to the proper parties.

According to the *PMBOK® Guide*, decomposition is a five-step process:

1. Identify the deliverables and work. This step involves identifying all the major project deliverables and related work. You can use the expert judgment technique to analyze the project scope statement and identify the major deliverables.

2. Organize the WBS. This step involves organizing the work of the project and determining the WBS structure. (I'll talk more about constructing the WBS in the next section.)

3. Decompose the WBS components into lower-level components. WBS components, like the deliverables and requirements, should be defined in tangible, verifiable terms so

that performance and successful completion (or delivery) are easily measured and verified. Each component must clearly describe the product, service, or result in verifiable terms, and it must be assigned to a unit in the organization that will take responsibility for completing the work and making certain of its accuracy.

4. Assign identification codes. This step is a process where you assign identification codes or numbers to each of the WBS components.

5. Verify the WBS. This step is a verification step. Examine the decomposition to determine whether all the components are clear and complete. Determine whether each component listed is absolutely necessary to fulfill the requirements of the deliverable, and verify that the decomposition is sufficient to describe the work.

I'll talk more about the process in step 4 in the section, "Understanding the Unique WBS Identifiers," later in this chapter.

Of course you won't perform this process alone. That's where the expert judgment tool and technique comes into play. You'll work with others such as team members, stakeholders, other experts with specific training or industry knowledge, those who have worked on similar projects in the past, and industry aides such as templates.

You can now plug the components you and the team have identified into the WBS. This all sounds like a lot of work. I won't kid you—it is, but it's essential to project success. If you don't perform the WBS process adequately and accurately, you might end up setting yourself up for a failed project at worst or for lots of project changes, delayed schedules, and increased costs at best—not to mention all those team members who'll throw up their hands when you return to them for the third or fourth time to ask that they redo work they've already completed. I know you won't let this happen, so let's move on to constructing the WBS.

The Create WBS process has several outputs, one of which is the WBS. You'll look at the specifics of how to create the WBS next.

Constructing the WBS

There is no "right" way to construct a WBS. In practice, the chart structure is used quite often. (This structure resembles an organization chart with different levels of detail.) But a WBS could be composed in outline form as well. The choice is yours. You'll look at a couple of ways shortly, along with some figures that depict the different levels of a WBS.

According to the *PMBOK® Guide*, you can organize the WBS in several ways:

Major Deliverables and Subprojects The major deliverables of the project are used as the first level of decomposition in this structure. If you're opening a new store, for example, the deliverables might include determining location, store build-out, furnishings, product, and so on. I'll talk about subprojects in the next section.

Subproject That May Be Executed Outside the Project Team   Another way to organize the work is by subprojects. Perhaps you're expanding an existing highway and several subprojects are involved. Some of your first level of decomposition might include these subprojects: demolition, design, bridgework, and paving. Each of the subproject managers will develop a WBS for their subproject that details the work required for that deliverable. When subproject work is involved, oftentimes the subproject work is contracted out. In this example, if you contracted out the bridgework deliverable, this subproject requires its own WBS, which the seller (the bridgework subcontractor) is responsible for creating as part of the contract and contract work.

Project Phases   Many projects are structured or organized by project phases. For example, let's say you work in the construction industry. The project phases used in your industry might include project initiation, planning, designing, building, inspection, and turnover. A feasibility study might be a deliverable under the project initiation phase, blueprints might be a deliverable under the planning phase, and so on. Each phase listed here would be the first level of decomposition (that is, the first level of the WBS); their deliverables would be the next level, and so on.

We'll take a look at some example WBS structures next.

Understanding the Various WBS Levels

Although the project manager is free to determine the number of levels in the WBS based on the complexity of the project, all WBS structures start with the project itself. Some WBS structures show the project as level one. Others show the level under the project, or the first level of decomposition, as level one. The *PMBOK® Guide* notes that level one is the project level, so I'll follow that example here.

The first level of decomposition might be the deliverables, phases, or subprojects, as I talked about earlier. (Remember that the first level of decomposition is actually the second level of the WBS because the project level is the first level.) The levels that follow show more and more detail and might include more deliverables followed by requirements. Each of these breakouts is called a *level* in the WBS. The lowest level of any WBS is called the *work package level*. The goal is to construct the WBS to the work package level where you can easily and reliably estimate cost and schedule dates. Keep in mind that not all of the deliverables may need the same amount of decomposition. Also realize that performing too much decomposition can be as unproductive as not decomposing enough. My rule of thumb is, when the work outlined in the work package level is easily understood by team members and can be completed within a reasonable length of time, you've decomposed enough. If you decompose to the point where work packages are describing individual activities associated with higher-level elements, you've gone too far.

Exam Spotlight

Remember that each descending level of the WBS is a more detailed description of
the project deliverables than the level above it. Each component of the WBS should be
defined clearly and completely and should describe how the work of the project will be
performed and controlled. Collectively, all the levels of the WBS roll up to the top so that
all the work of the project is captured (and no additional work is added). According to the
PMBOK® Guide, this is known as the 100-percent rule.

There is some controversy among project managers over whether activities should be listed on the WBS. In practice, I often include activities on
my work breakdown structure for *small* projects only because it facilitates
other Planning processes later. In this case, the activities are the work
package level. However, you should realize that large, complex projects
do not include activities on the WBS. For the exam, remember that you
will decompose activities during the Define Activities process that I'll talk
about in Chapter 4, "Creating the Project Schedule," and that activities are
not part of the WBS.

The easiest way to describe the steps for creating a WBS is with an example. Let's
suppose you work for a software company that publishes children's games. You're the
project manager for the new Billy Bob's Bassoon game, which teaches children about music,
musical rhythm, and beginning sight reading. The first box on the WBS is the project name;
it appears at the top of the WBS, as shown in Figure 3.1, and is defined as WBS Level One.

FIGURE 3.1   WBS levels one and two

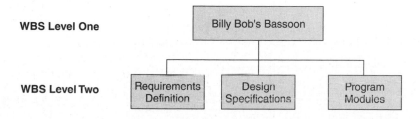

The next level is the first level of decomposition and should describe the major
deliverables for the project. In this example, some of the deliverables might be requirements
definition, design specifications, and programming. This isn't an exhaustive list
of deliverables; in practice, you would go on to place all of your major deliverables into the
WBS as level-one content. For illustration purposes, just look at a slice of the WBS for this
project. Refer to Figure 3.1 to see the WBS with level-one and level-two detail added.

Level-three content might be the component deliverables that are further broken out from the major deliverables of level two, or it might be the products or results that contribute to the deliverable. The Billy Bob's Bassoon example shows further deliverables as level-three content. See Figure 3.2 for an illustration of the WBS so far.

FIGURE 3.2   WBS levels one, two, and three

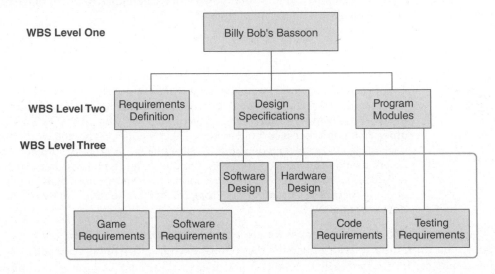

 Large, complex projects are often composed of several subprojects that collectively make up the main project. The WBS for a project such as the Billy Bob's Bassoon game would show the subprojects as level-one detail. These subprojects' major deliverables would then be listed as level-two content, perhaps more deliverables as level three, and so on.

The goal here is to eventually break the work out to the point where the responsibility and accountability for each work package can be assigned to an organizational unit or a team of people. In Figure 3.3, I've decomposed this WBS to the fourth level to show an even finer level of deliverable detail. Remember that activities are not usually included in the WBS. An easy way to differentiate between deliverables and activities is to use nouns as the deliverable descriptors and verbs as activity descriptors (we'll talk about activities in Chapter 4). Reaching way back to my grade-school English, I recall that a noun is a person, place, or thing. In this example, the deliverables are described using nouns. When we get to the activity list, you might use verbs like *define*, *design*, and *determine* to describe them.

FIGURE 3.3   WBS levels one, two, three, and four

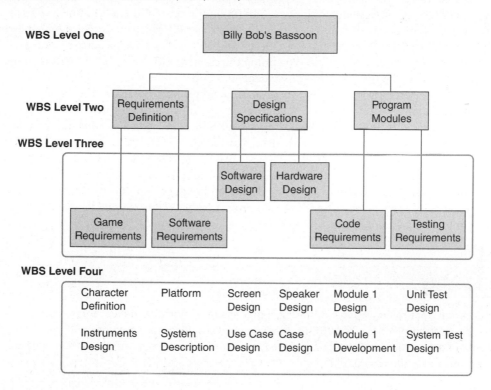

You can see from these illustrations how a poorly defined scope or inadequate list of deliverables will lead to a poorly constructed WBS. Not only will this make the WBS look sickly, but the project itself will suffer and might even succumb to the dreaded premature project demise. The final cost of the project will be higher than estimated, and lots of rework (translation: late nights and weekends) will be needed to account for the missing work not listed on the WBS. You can construct a good WBS and maintain a healthy project by taking the time to document all the deliverables during the Define Scope process.

WBS Templates

Work breakdown structures can be constructed using WBS templates or the WBS from a similar completed project. Although every project is unique, many companies and industries perform the same kind of projects repeatedly. The deliverables are similar from project to project, and they generally follow a consistent path. WBS templates can be used in a case like this as a tool to simplify the WBS process, saving the project manager time.

Don't get too carried away when creating a WBS. The object is to define the work of the project so you can easily plan, manage, monitor, and control the work. But you don't want to take this too far. If you decompose the work to the point that you're showing every minute detail, you've ventured into inefficiency and will find it more difficult to plan and manage. In addition, you're potentially stifling the creativity of the people working on the project because everything is so narrowly defined.

Sometimes, particularly when working on large projects that consist of several subprojects, some of the subprojects might not be scheduled until a future date. Obviously, it makes sense to develop the WBS in detail at that future date when the deliverables and subprojects are better known and more details are available. This technique is called *rolling wave planning*. The idea behind this technique is that you elaborate the work of the project to the level of detail you know about at the time. If a subproject or deliverable is scheduled sometime in the future, the only component that might appear on the WBS today is the subproject itself. As you get closer to the subproject, you'll elaborate the details of the subproject and record them on the WBS.

Exam Spotlight

Understand that rolling wave planning is a process of elaborating deliverables, project phases, or subprojects in the WBS to differing levels of decomposition depending on the expected date of the work. Work in the near term is described in more detail than work to be performed in the future.

Understanding the Unique WBS Identifiers

Each element at each level of the WBS is generally assigned a unique identifier according to the *PMBOK® Guide*. This unique identifier is typically a number, and it's used to sum and track the costs, schedule, and resources associated with the WBS elements. These numbers are usually associated with the corporation's chart of accounts, which is used to track costs by category. These codes are known as control accounts, and collectively, the control accounts are known as the *code of accounts*. The unique identifiers for the requirements definition branch of the WBS might look something like this:

10-1 Billy Bob's Bassoon

10-2 Requirements Definition

10-3 Game Requirements

    10-3-1 Character Definition

    10-3-2 Instruments Design

10-4 Software Requirements

    10-4-1 Platform

    10-4-2 System Description

Defining Work Packages

Work packages are the components that can be assigned to one person, or a team of people, with clear accountability and responsibility for completing the assignment, and they can be monitored and controlled throughout the project. Assignments are easily made at the work package level but can be made at any level in the WBS. The work package level is where time estimates, cost estimates, and resource estimates are determined.

As mentioned earlier, the project manager is free to determine the number of levels in the WBS based on the complexity of the project. You need to include enough levels to accurately estimate project time and costs but not so many levels that it's difficult to distinguish between the components. Regardless of the number of levels in a WBS, the lowest level in a WBS is called the *work package level*.

Work package levels on large projects can represent subprojects that are further decomposed into their own work breakdown structures. They might also consist of project work that will be completed by a vendor, another organization, or another department in your organization. If you're giving project work to another department in your organization, you'll assign the work packages to individual managers, who will in turn break them down into activities during the Define Activities process later in the Planning process group.

Work packages might be assigned to vendors or others external to the organization. For example, perhaps one of the deliverables in your project is special packaging and a vendor is responsible for completing this work. The vendor will likely treat this deliverable as a project within its own organization and construct its own WBS with several levels of decomposition. However, for your project, it's a deliverable listed at the work package level of the WBS.

 Real World Scenario

The Lincoln Street Office Building

Flagship International has just purchased a new building to house its growing staff. The folks at Flagship consider themselves very lucky to have won the bid on the property located in a prime section of the downtown area. The building is a historic building and is in need of some repairs and upgrades to make it suitable for office space. Constructing the renovations will require special handling and care, as outlined in the *Historical Society Building Revisions Guide.*

Alfredo Martini is the project manager assigned to the renovation project. Alfredo has already determined the deliverables for this project. In so doing, he has discovered that he will not be able to manage all the work himself. He will need several subproject managers working on individual deliverables, all reporting to him. Alfredo calls a meeting with the other project managers to develop the WBS. Let's eavesdrop on the meeting.

"As you all know, we're planning to move into the Lincoln Street building by November 1. There is quite a bit of work to do between now and then, and I'm enlisting each of you to manage a segment of this project. Take a look at this WBS."

Here's how a portion of the WBS that Alfredo constructed looks.

Lincoln Street Building Renovation

2.0 Facility Safety

    2.1 Sprinkler System

    2.2 Elevators

    2.3 Emergency Evacuation Plans

3.0 Asbestos Abatement

    3.1 Inspection and Identification

    3.2 Plans for Removal

4.0 Office Space

    4.1 Building Floor Plans

    4.2 Plans for Office Space Allocation

    4.3 Plans for Break Room Facilities

    4.4 Plans for Employee Workout Room

Alfredo continues, "I'm going to manage the Facility Safety project. Adrian, I'd like you to take the Asbestos Abatement project, and Orlando, you're responsible for the Office Space project."

"Alfredo," Adrian says, "asbestos abatement is going to take contractors and specialized equipment. We don't have staff to do these tasks."

"I understand. You'll need to take charge of securing the contractor to handle this. Your responsibility will be to manage the contractor and keep them on schedule," Alfredo answers.

Orlando reminds Alfredo that he has missed a deliverable on the WBS. "Part of the Office Space project needs to include the network communications and telecommunications equipment rooms. I don't see that on here."

"Good point, Orlando," Alfredo says. "The level-two and level-three elements of this WBS are not complete. Each of you has been assigned to the subproject level, level one. Your first assignment is to meet back here in two weeks with a WBS for your subproject. I'd like to see some ideas about the staff assignments you'd make at the work package level and how long you think these components will take. We'll refine those after we meet next."

This might seem self-evident, but work packages not shown on the WBS are not included in the project. The same holds true for the project scope statement—if the deliverable isn't noted there, it isn't part of the project.

Creating WBS Process Outputs

The Create WBS process has two outputs: the scope baseline and project documents updates. We'll look at both of these next.

Scope Baseline

Remember how I said that everything you've done so far has built upon itself? This is an important concept you should know for this output. The *scope baseline* for the project is the approved project scope statement, the WBS, and the WBS dictionary. (You'll recall from Chapter 2 that the project scope statement serves as a baseline for future project decisions because it helps the team determine whether requested changes are inside or outside of scope.) In other words, these documents together describe in detail all the work of the project. From these documents, you'll develop schedules, assign resources, and monitor and control the work of the project according to what's described here. We've already talked about the project scope statement and the WBS, but let's look at the WBS dictionary.

Exam Spotlight

The scope baseline is defined as the approved version of the detailed project scope statement, the WBS, and the WBS dictionary. Understand this concept for the exam. This process does not name the WBS as an output; the WBS is included as part of the scope baseline output.

WBS Dictionary

The *WBS dictionary*, an element of the scope baseline, is where work component descriptions listed on the WBS are documented. According to the *PMBOK® Guide*, the WBS dictionary should include the following elements for each component of the WBS:

- Code of accounts identifier
- Description of the work of the component
- Organization responsible for completing the component
- List of schedule milestones
- Schedule activities associated with the schedule milestones

- Required resources
- Cost estimates
- Quality requirements
- Criteria for acceptance
- Technical references
- Contract or agreements information
- Constraints and assumptions

Let's look at an example of what some of the elements of a WBS dictionary entry might look like. You'll use the work package level called Inspection and Identification defined in the sidebar, "The Lincoln Street Office Building," earlier. The WBS dictionary entry for this might look like the following:

3.1 Inspection and Identification

Description of work—Inspect the building for asbestos, and identify all areas where it's found. Update the plan for removal (WBS 2.2) with each location identified.

Responsible organization—Adrian in facilities will hire and oversee a contractor to perform this work.

Schedule milestones—Inspection and identification to start after contractor is identified and hired (no later than July 1). Work should be completed no later than September 15.

Contract information—Two contractors have been identified as qualified and experienced in this type of work. Contract process should close no later than June 12.

If the WBS and the WBS dictionary are constructed well, you've given yourself a huge helping hand with the remaining Planning processes. The completion of many of the remaining processes depends on the project scope statement and WBS being accurate and complete. In Chapter 4, for example, you'll use the work packages created here to further elaborate the work into activities. From there, you can estimate costs, develop schedules, and so on. The WBS is an essential tool for project planning, so keep it handy.

Project Document Updates

Project documents updates might include updates to the requirements document, which can come about as a result of changes that occur when you're creating the WBS. You can see from the examples you've walked through in this chapter how new deliverables or requirements might surface as a result of working on the WBS. These requested changes should be reviewed and either approved or denied using your change control processes. The approved changes will likely change the project scope statement, the project management plan, and other project documents. These documents should be updated to reflect the approved changes.

Project Case Study: New Kitchen Heaven Retail Store

The project charter kickoff meeting was held and well attended. You're ready to start gathering requirements and writing the project scope statement, and you have a question or two for Dirk. You knock on his door, and he invites you in.

"Shoot," he says.

"I'm ready to define the deliverables and requirements for this project. I want to make sure I get the right folks involved in the meeting. Who are key stakeholders you recommend I speak with?"

"I can think of a few people right off that you don't want to miss. There's Jake Peterson over in facilities. He's in charge of store furnishings, shelving, things like that—any supplies for the stores that aren't retail products. He can help out with store build-outs too. He supervised our last eight stores and did a terrific job."

"Anyone else?" you ask.

"You should also talk to Jill Overstreet, the director in charge of retail products. She can help with the initial store stocking, and once the store is open, her group will take over the ongoing operations. All the district managers report to Jill."

You thank Dirk and tell him you're going to contact Jake and Jill and set up a brainstorming session to determine requirements.

A few days later.

You review your notes and reread the first draft of the project scope statement you've prepared for the Kitchen Heaven retail store before looking for Dirk. After your meetings with the stakeholders, you were better able to refine the project objectives and deliverables.

"Dirk, I'm glad I caught you. I'd like to go over the project scope statement with you before I give it to the stakeholders. Do you have a few minutes?"

"Sure," Dirk says. "Let's have it."

"The project objective is to open the 50th Kitchen Heaven store in Colorado Springs by February 1. When I met with Jake, he confirmed it takes 120 days to do the store build-out. That includes having the shelves set up and in place, ready to stock with inventory."

Dirk asks whether Jake told you about his store location idea.

"Yes, Jake gave me a contact name of the leasing agent, and I've left her a voicemail. The sooner we can get that lease signed, the better. It takes Jake 120 days to do the build-out, and Jill said she needs two weeks lead time to order the initial inventory and stock the shelves. That puts us pretty close to our February 1 deadline, counting the time to get the lease papers signed."

"Sounds good so far," Dirk replies. "What else?"

You continue, "I've included an updated description of the products and services the new store will offer, based on the documentation that was written from the last store opening. Jill reviewed the updates to the description, so we should be in the clear there. The store will include some new lines that we've decided to take on—cookware from famous chefs, that kind of thing.

"Jake has already made contact with a general contractor in Colorado Springs, and he is ready to roll once we've signed the lease.

"One more thing, Dirk. Since we're including the big bash at the grand opening as part of the deliverables, I talked to some of your folks in marketing to get some ideas. They are thinking we should have some great giveaways as door prizes and that we will want the food catered. They also thought having some live cooking demonstrations with some local chefs would be a good attraction."

"Sounds like you're on the right track. So, what's next?" Dirk asks.

"Once you approve the scope statement, I'd like to send a copy to the stakeholders. My next step is to break down the deliverables and requirements I've documented here into the WBS so we can get rolling on the work of the project."

Project Case Study Checklist

The main topics discussed in the case study are as follows:

Stakeholder analysis for requirements gathering: Jake Peterson and Jill Overstreet interviewed. Needs, wants, and expectations recorded and requirements prioritized.

Organizational structure: Functional organization with a separate projectized department.

Constraints: February 1 date to coincide with home and garden show.

Assumptions: These are the assumptions:

- A store build-out usually takes 120 days.

- Jill Overstreet will help with the initial store stocking.

- Jake Peterson will provide supplies for the stores that aren't retail products, such as store furnishings, shelving, and so on, and can help with the store build-out as well.

- The budget for the project will be between $1.5 and $2 million.

The project scope statement includes the following:

Project objectives: Open 50th store by February 1 in Colorado Springs.

Project deliverables:

- Build out storefront, including shelving.

- Retail product line will be delivered two weeks prior to grand opening.

- Have grand-opening party with cooking demos.

Project requirements:

- Sign lease within 14 days.

- Offer new line of gourmet food products.

- Have classroom space in back of store for cooking demos and classes.

Constraints: February 1 date will coincide with home and garden show.

Fund limitations: Spend no more than $2 million on the project.

Assumptions: (These are the same as listed earlier.) Decomposed deliverables into a WBS.

The WBS includes the following:

- Level one is the project.

- Level two is subprojects or deliverables.

- Level three is deliverables.

- Last level of WBS is the work package level, where time and cost estimates can be defined in the next process.

Understanding How This Applies to Your Next Project

In this chapter, you dealt with the realities of life on the job. The reality is, many project managers I know are managing several projects at once as opposed to one large project. Although every concept presented in this chapter is a sound one, it's important to note that you have to balance the amount of effort you'll put into project management processes against the size and complexity of the project.

As a manager who prides herself and my team on excellent customer service, I have once or twice gotten my team into precarious situations because I was so focused on helping the customer that I hurt them and our department in the process. If you're wondering how that happened, it was because we didn't take the time to document the scope of the project and the final acceptance criteria. In one case, in the interest of getting the project completed quickly because of our customer's own internal deadlines, we decided the project was straightforward enough that we didn't need to document deliverables. The customer promised to work side by side with us as we produced the work of the project. Unfortunately, that wasn't the case, and we didn't meet the expectations of our customer. Further, after we did implement the project (two months behind schedule), we went through another six weeks of "fixes" because of the miscommunication between the customer and the project team on what constituted some of the features of the final product. There's always a great reason for cutting corners—but they almost always come back to haunt you. My advice is to always create a scope statement and a requirements document and get stakeholder signatures on both. (In practice, small projects can include both the deliverables and requirements within the scope statement.)

Decomposing the deliverables is the first step toward determining resource requirements and estimates. A WBS is always a good idea, no matter the size of the project. I have to admit I have cheated a time or two on small projects and used the project schedule as the WBS. In all fairness, that worked out fine when the team was small and there weren't more than three or four people working on the project. If you get many more than four people on the project team, it can be a little cumbersome to track deliverables with a schedule only. The WBS is the perfect tool to use to assign names to work packages, and it's the foundation for determining estimates for the work of the project.

The five-step process outlined by the *PMBOK® Guide* works very well. Starting with the 50,000-foot view, the team determines the major deliverables of the project. From there, the deliverables are decomposed into ever smaller units of work. The trick here is to break the work down into measurable units so that you can verify the status of the work and the completion and acceptance of the work when you're finished. If you have "fuzzy" WBS levels or work packages, you won't be able to determine status accurately. In the information technology field, we have a saying about the status of projects: "It's 90 percent complete." The problem is it always seems that the last 10 percent takes twice as long to complete as the first 90 did. If you've taken the time to document a WBS, you'll have a much better idea of what that 90 percent constitutes. The last step is the verification step where you determine whether everything you've identified in the WBS is absolutely necessary to fulfill the work of the project and whether it's decomposed enough to adequately describe the work. It has been my experience that documenting the WBS will save you time later in the Planning processes, particularly developing the project schedule and determining the project budget.

I believe the most important idea to take from this chapter is a simple one: Always use a scope statement and requirements document, and always get them signed.

Summary

This chapter started you on the road to project planning via the Develop Project Management Plan process, the Plan Scope Management process, the Collect Requirements process, the Define Scope process, and the Create WBS process. We covered a lot of material in this chapter. Everything you've learned so far becomes the foundation for further project planning.

The output of the Develop Project Management Plan process is the project management plan, which is concerned with defining, coordinating, and integrating all the ancillary project plans and baselines. The purpose of this plan is to define how the project is executed, how it's monitored and controlled, and how it's closed.

The primary output of the Plan Scope Management process is the scope management plan. This plan is an element of the project management plan that describes how the project team will go about defining project scope, verifying the work of the project, and managing and controlling scope.

The Collect Requirements process involves gathering and documenting the requirements of the project. It's important that requirements be measurable, traceable, testable, and so on. Measurement criteria for project requirements are agreed upon by the stakeholders and project manager. Additionally, requirements should be tracked in a traceability matrix that documents where they originated, the results of the tests, the priority of the requirement, and more.

The project scope statement is produced during the Define Scope process. It describes the project deliverables. The scope statement, along with the WBS and WBS dictionary, forms the scope baseline that you'll use to weigh future project decisions, most particularly change requests. The scope statement contains a list of project deliverables that will be used in future Planning processes.

The project scope statement contains many elements, including product scope description, product acceptance criteria, deliverables, exclusions from scope, constraints, and assumptions.

Constraints restrict or dictate the actions of the project team. Constraints usually involve time, cost, and scope but can also include schedules, technology, quality, resources, risk, and more.

Assumptions are things believed to be true. You'll want to document project assumptions and validate them as the project progresses.

A WBS is a deliverable-oriented hierarchy of project essentials. The highest levels of the WBS are described using nouns, and the lowest levels are described with verbs. Each element in the WBS has its own set of objectives and deliverables that must be met in order to fulfill the deliverables of the next highest level and ultimately the project itself. In this way, the WBS validates the completeness of the work.

The lowest level of the WBS is known as the work package level. This breakdown allows the project manager to determine cost estimates, time estimates, resource assignments, and quality controls.

Exam Essentials

Be able to state the purpose of the Develop Project Management Plan process.   It defines, coordinates, and integrates all subsidiary project plans.

Understand the purpose of the project scope statement.   The scope statement serves as a common understanding of project scope among the stakeholders. The project objectives and deliverables and their quantifiable criteria are documented in the scope statement and are used by the project manager and the stakeholders to determine whether the project was completed successfully. It also serves as a basis for future project decisions.

Be able to define project constraints and assumptions.   Project constraints limit the options of the project team and restrict their actions. Sometimes constraints dictate actions. Time, budget, and scope are the most common constraints. Assumptions are conditions that are presumed to be true or real.

Be able to describe the purpose of the scope management plan.   The scope management plan has a direct influence on the project's success and describes the process for determining project scope, facilitates creating the WBS, describes how the product or service of the project is verified and accepted, and documents how changes to scope will be handled. The scope management plan is a subsidiary plan of the project management plan.

Be able to define a WBS and its components.   The WBS is a deliverable-oriented hierarchy. It uses the deliverables from the project scope statement or similar documents and decomposes them into logical, manageable units of work. The first level of decomposition is the major deliverable level or subproject level, the second level of decomposition is a further elaboration of the deliverables, and so on. The lowest level of any WBS is called a work package.

Key Terms

Planning, planning, planning... I can't stress enough how important the planning processes are to a successful project. In this chapter, you learned about the processes involved in developing your project scope statement. Understand these processes well, and know them by the names used in the *PMBOK® Guide*:

Develop Project Management Plan

Plan Scope Management

Collect Requirements

Define Scope

Create WBS

Before you take the exam, also be certain you are familiar with the following terms:

acceptance criteria	project management information system (PMIS)
alternatives generation	project management plan
approval requirements	project scope statement
assumptions	requirements
code of accounts	requirements management plan
constraints	rolling wave planning
critical success factors	scope
decomposition	scope baseline
deliverables	scope management plan
objectives	WBS dictionary
product analysis	work breakdown structure (WBS)
product scope description	work packages
project exclusions	

Review Questions

You can find the answers to the questions in Appendix A.

1. You are a project manager for Laredo Pioneer's Traveling Rodeo Show. You're heading up a project to promote a new line of souvenirs to be sold at the shows. You are getting ready to write the project management plan and know that all the following are true regarding the PMIS except for one. Which of the following is not true?

   A. The PMIS is a tool and technique of this process.

   B. The configuration management system is a subsystem of the PMIS.

   C. The PMIS includes a change control system.

   D. The PMIS is an automated system.

2. Which of the following is true?

   A. You are a project manager for Laredo Pioneer's Traveling Rodeo Show. You're heading up a project to promote a new line of souvenirs to be sold at the shows. You're ready to document the processes you'll use to perform the project as well as define how the project will be executed, controlled, and closed. You are working on the project scope management plan.

   B. You are a project manager for Laredo Pioneer's Traveling Rodeo Show. You're heading up a project to promote a new line of souvenirs to be sold at the shows. You're ready to document the processes you'll use to perform the project as well as define how the project will be executed, controlled, and closed. You are working on the product scope statement.

   C. You are a project manager for Laredo Pioneer's Traveling Rodeo Show. You're heading up a project to promote a new line of souvenirs to be sold at the shows. You're ready to document the processes you'll use to perform the project as well as define how the project will be executed and controlled and how changes will be monitored and controlled. You are working on the project management plan.

   D. You are a project manager for Laredo Pioneer's Traveling Rodeo Show. You're heading up a project to promote a new line of souvenirs to be sold at the shows. You're ready to document the processes you'll use to perform the project as well as define how the project will be executed, controlled, and closed. You are working on the project scope statement.

3. You are a project manager responsible for the construction of a new office complex. You are taking over for a project manager who recently left the company. The prior project manager completed the scope statement and scope management plan for this project. In your interviews with some key team members, you conclude which of the following?

   A. They understand that the scope statement assesses the stability of the project scope and outlines how scope will be verified and used to control changes. They also know that project scope is measured against the product requirements.

   B. They understand that the scope management plan describes how project scope will be managed and controlled and how the WBS will be created and defined. They also know that product scope is measured against the product requirements.

    C. They understand that the scope management plan is deliverables oriented and includes cost estimates and stakeholder needs and expectations. They understand that project scope is measured against the project management plan.

    D. They understand that the scope statement describes how the high-level deliverables and requirements will be defined and verified. They understand that product scope is measured against the project management plan.

4. Unanimity, majority, plurality, and dictatorship are four examples of which of the following techniques?

    A. Group creativity techniques, which is a tool and technique of the Collect Requirements process

    B. Interviews, which is a tool and technique of the Define Scope process

    C. Facilitated workshops technique, which is a tool and technique of the Define Scope process

    D. Group decision-making techniques, which is a tool and technique of the Collect Requirements process

5. Which of the following is true regarding the project scope statement?

    A. The project scope statement includes a change control system that describes how to make changes to the project scope.

    B. The project scope statement further elaborates the details from the Initiating and Planning processes and serves as a basis for future project decisions.

    C. The project scope statement describes how the team will define and develop the work breakdown structure.

    D. The project scope statement assesses the reliability of the project scope and describes the process for verifying and accepting completed deliverables.

6. You are a project manager for an agricultural supply company. You have interviewed stakeholders and gathered requirements. Which of the following is true regarding the process to which this question refers?

    A. The requirements document lists the requirements and describes how they will be analyzed, documented, and managed throughout the project.

    B. Requirements documentation consist of formal, complex documents that include elements such as the business need of the project, functional requirements, nonfunctional requirements, impacts to others inside and outside the organization, and requirements assumptions and constraints.

    C. The requirements documentation details the work required to create the deliverables of the project, including deliverables description, product acceptance criteria, exclusions from requirements, and requirements assumptions and constraints.

    D. The requirements traceability matrix ties requirements to project objectives, business needs, WBS deliverables, product design, test strategies, and high-level requirements and traces them through to project completion.

7. Which of the following makes up the scope baseline?

   A. The approved project scope statement

   B. The approved scope management plan and WBS

   C. The WBS, approved project scope statement, and WBS dictionary

   D. The approved scope management plan, the WBS, and the WBS dictionary

8. Which of the following statements is true regarding brainstorming and lateral thinking?

   A. They are forms of expert judgment used to help define and develop requirements and develop the project scope statement.

   B. They are tools and techniques used to elaborate the product scope description.

   C. They are group decision-making techniques, which are a tool and technique of the Collect Requirements process.

   D. They are alternatives generation techniques, which are a tool and technique of the Define Scope process.

9. Your company, Kick That Ball Sports, has appointed you as project manager for its new Cricket product line introduction. This is a national effort, and all the retail stores across the country need to have the new products on the shelves before the media advertising blitz begins. The product line involves three new products, two of which will be introduced together and a third one that will follow within two years. You are ready to create the WBS. All of the following are true except for which one?

   A. The WBS may be structured using each product as a level-one entry.

   B. The WBS should be elaborated to a level where costs and schedule are easily estimated. This is known as the work package level.

   C. Rolling wave refers to how all levels of the WBS collectively roll up to reflect the work of the project and only the work of the project.

   D. Each level of the WBS represents verifiable products or results.

10. You are a project manager for Giraffe Enterprises. You've recently taken over for a project manager who lied about his PMI® certification and was subsequently fired. Unfortunately, he did a poor job of defining the scope. Which of the following could happen if you don't correct this?

   A. The stakeholders will require overtime from the project team to keep the project on schedule.

   B. The poor scope definition will adversely affect the creation of the work breakdown structure, and costs will increase.

   C. The project management plan's process for verification and acceptance of the deliverables needs to be updated as a result of the poor scope definition.

   D. The project costs could increase, there might be rework, and schedule delays might result.

11. You are the project manager for Lucky Stars nightclubs. They specialize in live country and western band performances. Your newest project is in the Planning processes group. You are working on the WBS. The finance manager has given you a numbering system to assign to the WBS. Which of the following is true?

    A. The numbering system is a unique identifier known as the WBS dictionary, which is used to assign quality control codes to the individual work elements.

    B. The numbering system is a unique identifier known as the WBS dictionary, which is used to track the descriptions of individual work elements.

    C. The numbering system is a unique identifier known as the code of accounts, which is used to track time and resource assignments for individual work elements.

    D. The numbering system is a unique identifier known as the code of accounts, which is used to track the costs of the WBS elements.

12. You are a project manager working on a large, complex project. You've constructed the WBS for this project and all of the work package levels are subprojects of this project. You've requested that the subproject managers report to you in three weeks with their individual WBSs constructed. Which statement is not true regarding your WBS?

    A. The work package level is decomposed to create the activity list.

    B. The work package level is the lowest level in the WBS.

    C. The work package level facilitates resource assignments.

    D. The work package level facilitates cost and time estimates.

13. You are a project manager working on a new software product your company plans to market to businesses. The project sponsor told you that the project must be completed by September 1. The company plans to demo the new software product at a trade show in late September and, therefore, needs the project completed in time for the trade show. However, the sponsor has also told you that the budget is fixed at $85,000, and it would take an act of Congress to get it increased. You must complete the project within the given time frame and budget. Which of the following is the primary constraint for this project?

    A. Budget

    B. Scope

    C. Time

    D. Quality

14. Which of the following statements about decomposition is the least true?

    A. Decomposition involves structuring and organizing the WBS so that deliverables are always listed at level one.

    B. Decomposition requires a degree of expert judgment and also requires close analysis of the project scope statement.

    C. Decomposition is a tool and technique used to create a WBS.

    D. Decomposition subdivides the major deliverables into smaller components until the work package level is reached.

15. You are in the process of translating project objectives into tangible deliverables and requirements. All of the following are techniques used in the product analysis tool and technique of the Define Scope process except which one?

A. Value engineering and value analysis

B. Product configuration and specification analysis

C. Systems analysis and systems engineering

D. Product breakdown and functional analysis

16. You are a project manager for a documentary film company. In light of a recent regional tragedy, the company president wants to produce a new documentary on the efforts of the heroic rescue teams to air as soon as possible. She's looking to you to make this documentary the best that has ever been produced in the history of this company. She guarantees you free rein to use whatever resources you need to get this project done quickly. However, the best photographer in the company is currently working on another assignment. Which of the following is true?

A. The primary constraint is time because the president wants the film done quickly. She told you to get it to air as soon as possible.

B. Resources are the primary constraint. Even though the president has given you free rein on resource use, you assume she didn't mean those actively assigned to projects.

C. The schedule is the primary constraint. Even though the president has given you free rein on resource use, you assume she didn't mean those actively assigned to projects. The photographer won't be finished for another three weeks on his current assignment, so schedule adjustments will have to be made.

D. The primary constraint is quality because the president wants this to be the best film ever produced by this company. She's given you free rein to use whatever resources needed to get the job done.

17. Your project depends on a key deliverable from a vendor you've used several times before with great success. You're counting on the delivery to arrive on June 1. This is an example of a/an _____ .

A. Constraint

B. Objective

C. Assumption

D. Requirement

18. What limits the options of the project team?

A. Technology

B. Constraints

C. Deliverables

D. Assumptions

19. Your company provides answering services for several major catalog retailers. The number of calls coming into the service center per month has continued to increase over the past 18 months. The phone system is approaching the maximum load limits and needs to be upgraded. You've been assigned to head up the upgrade project. Based on the company's experience with the vendor who worked on the last phone upgrade project, you're confident they'll be able to assist you with this project as well. Which of the following is true?

  A. You've made an assumption about vendor availability and expertise. The project came about because of a business need.

  B. Vendor availability and expertise are constraints. The project came about because of a business need.

  C. You've made an assumption about vendor availability and expertise. The project came about because of a market demand.

  D. Vendor availability and expertise are constraints. The project came about because of a market demand.

20. Which of the following is not a major step of decomposition?

  A. Identify major deliverables.

  B. Identify resources.

  C. Identify components.

  D. Verify correctness of decomposition.

Chapter

4

Creating the Project Schedule

THE PMP® EXAM CONTENT FROM THE PLANNING THE PROJECT PERFORMANCE DOMAIN COVERED IN THIS CHAPTER INCLUDES THE FOLLOWING:

✓ Create the schedule management plan.

✓ Develop project activity duration estimates.

✓ Develop project resource estimates.

✓ Develop a project schedule based on the project timeline, scope, and resource plan in order to manage timely completion of the project.

✓ Knowledge and Skills:

  ▪ Work breakdown structure (WBS) tools and techniques

  ▪ Time, budget, and cost estimation techniques

  ▪ Workflow diagramming techniques

  ▪ Elements, purpose, and techniques of project planning

The Planning process group has more processes than any other process group. As a result, a lot of time and effort goes into the Planning processes of any project. On some projects, you might spend almost as much time planning the project as you do executing and controlling it. This isn't a bad thing. The better planning you do up front, the more likely you'll have a successful project. Speaking of planning, together the Planning, Executing, and Monitoring and Controlling process groups account for almost 70 percent of the PMP® exam questions, so *plan* on spending about the same percentage of your study time on these areas.

This is another fun-filled, action-packed chapter. We'll start off by defining the schedule management plan and then move on to the activities that become the work of the project. The WBS will come in handy here, so keep it close. Then we'll sequence the activities in their proper order, estimate the resources we'll need to complete the work, and estimate how long each activity will take. Last but not least, we'll develop the project schedule.

Everything you've done up to this point and the processes we'll discuss in this chapter will help you create an accurate project schedule. You'll use these documents (along with several other documents you've created along the way) throughout the Executing and Monitoring and Controlling processes to help measure the progress of the project. Let's get going.

The process names, inputs, tools and techniques, outputs, and descriptions of the project management process groups and related materials and figures in this chapter are based on content from *A Guide to the Project Management Body of Knowledge (PMBOK® Guide), Fifth Edition* (Sybex, 2010).

Creating the Schedule Management Plan

The *Plan Schedule Management* process describes how the project schedule will be developed, executed, and controlled, as well as how changes will be incorporated into the project schedule. According to *A Guide to the Project Management Body of Knowledge (PMBOK® Guide), Fifth Edition,* the primary benefit of this process is that the tools and techniques for time management and the processes used to develop, manage, and control the schedule are documented. The only output of this process is the *schedule management plan.* Let's first look at the inputs and the tools and techniques of this process and spend most of our time examining the schedule management plan itself.

The inputs of this process include the project management plan, project charter, enterprise environmental factors, and organizational process assets. The project management plan includes the scope baseline, which in turn is made up of the project scope statement, WBS, and WBS dictionary. The project schedule will be derived from the WBS (which includes deliverables and work package levels) so the scope baseline is key to defining the processes you'll use to develop the schedule management plan.

Enterprise environmental factors include the culture of the organization and availability of resources, as well as the project management software, and work authorization system the organization uses to assign and track work components. The organizational process assets that are important to this process are templates, change control processes, historical information, policies and guidelines for schedule control, control tools for managing schedules, and risk control processes and procedures.

We have seen all of the tools and techniques before. They are expert judgment, analytical techniques, and meetings.

The key to this process, as I stated earlier, is the schedule management plan, which is an element of the project management plan. It is the only output of this process and it serves to describe how the project schedule will be developed, monitored, controlled, and changed. According to the *PMBOK® Guide,* several elements make up the schedule management plan. Be certain to review all of them. I have highlighted the most important elements here:

Schedule Model Development   This refers to the methodologies and tools you'll use to develop the schedule (for example, Oracle Primavera or Microsoft Project), along with the data they contain.

Accuracy Levels   This element describes the rounding you'll use when deriving activity duration estimates. For example, you might round to the nearest week, day, or hour depending on the complexity of the project.

Units of Measure   This element also concerns activity duration estimates as well as schedule activities. This describes what measure you'll use when developing the schedule, such as hours, days, weeks, or some other measure.

Control Thresholds   Control thresholds refer to the level of variance the schedule can experience before you take action. Again, depending on the complexity of the project, this might be a generous amount of time or a very limited amount of time. You can express thresholds in terms of hours or days (as an example, a slippage of greater than three days requires action) or, most typically, as a percentage of time.

Performance Measurement Rules   This refers to where and what types of measures you'll use to verify schedule performance. This could include designating levels on the WBS and/or determining what type of earned value measurement technique you'll use.

Defining Activities

Now you're off and running toward the development of your project schedule. To develop the schedule, you first need to define the activities, sequence them in the right order, estimate resources, and estimate the time it will take to complete the tasks. I'll cover the

Define Activities process here and the Sequence Activities process next, and I'll pick up with the estimating processes in the next chapter.

> Define Activities and Sequence Activities are separate processes, each with their own inputs, tools and techniques, and outputs. In practice, especially for small to medium-sized projects, you can combine the Create WBS process we talked about in Chapter 3, "Developing the Project Scope Statement," with these processes and complete them all at once.

The *Define Activities* process is a further breakdown of the work package elements of the WBS. It documents the specific activities needed to fulfill the deliverables detailed on the WBS and the project scope statement. Much like the work package level of the WBS, activities can be easily assigned, estimated, scheduled, and controlled. The Define Activities process might be performed by the project manager, or when the WBS is broken down to the subproject level, this process (and all the activity-related processes that follow) might be assigned to a subproject manager.

Define Activities Process Inputs

The following are inputs (including the key elements of each input) to the Define Activities process:

- Schedule management plan
- Scope baseline (including deliverables, constraints, and assumptions)
- Enterprise environmental factors (project management information systems, organizational culture, published commercial databases)
- Organizational process assets (existing guidelines and policies, templates, lessons learned knowledge base, and historical information)

Tools and Techniques for Defining Activities

The tools and techniques of the Define Activities process are as follows:

- Decomposition
- Rolling wave planning
- Expert judgment

We covered most of these topics in the previous chapter. Decomposition in this process involves breaking the work packages into smaller, more manageable units of work called *activities*. These are not deliverables but the individual units of work that must be completed to fulfill the work packages and the deliverables listed in the WBS. Activities will help in later Planning processes to define estimates and create the project schedule. Activity lists (which are one of the outputs of this process) from prior projects can be used as templates in this process. Rolling wave planning involves planning near-term work in more detail than future-term work. As we discussed in Chapter 3, this is a form of progressive elaboration. Expert judgment, in the form of project team members with prior experience developing project scope statements and WBSs, can help you define activities.

Exam Spotlight

The purpose of the Define Activities process is to decompose the work packages into schedule activities where the basis for estimating, scheduling, executing, and monitoring and controlling the work of the project is easily supported and accomplished.

Define Activities Outputs

Define Activities has three outputs:

- Activity list
- Activity attributes
- Milestone list

We'll look at each of these outputs next.

Activity List

One primary output of the Define Activities process is an *activity list*. The activity list should contain all the schedule activities that will be performed for the project, with a scope of work description of each activity and an identifier (such as a code or number) so that team members understand what the work is and how it is to be completed. The schedule activities are individual elements of the project schedule, and the activity list document is part of the project documents. To keep your sanity, and those of your team members, make certain to enter the activity names onto the schedule the same way they appear on the activity list.

Activity Attributes

Activity attributes describe the characteristics of the activities and are an extension of the activity list. Activity attributes will change over the life of the project as more information is known. In the early stages of the project, activity attributes might include the activity ID, the WBS identification code it's associated with, and the activity name. As you progress through the project and complete other Planning processes, you might add predecessor and successor activities, logical relationships, leads and lags, resource requirements, and constraints and assumptions associated with the activity. We'll cover these topics throughout the remainder of this chapter.

The activity attributes are used as input to several processes, including the Develop Schedule process that we'll talk about in the section "Developing the Project Schedule," later in this chapter.

> In practice, I like to tie the activity list to the WBS. Remember from Chapter 3 that each WBS element has a unique identifier, just like the activities in the activity list. When recording the identifier code for the activity list, I'll use a system whereby the first three or four digits represent the WBS element the activity is tied to and the remaining digits refer to the activity itself.

Milestone Lists

Milestones are typically major accomplishments of the project and mark the completion of major deliverables or some other key event in the project. For example, approval and sign-off on project deliverables might be considered milestones. Other examples might be the completion of a prototype, system testing, contract approval, and so on. The milestone list records these accomplishments and documents whether the milestone is mandatory or optional. The milestone list is part of the project documentation and is also used to help develop the project schedule.

Understanding the Sequence Activities Process

Now that you've identified the schedule activities, you need to sequence them in a logical order and find out whether dependencies exist among the activities. The interactivity of logical relationships must be sequenced correctly in order to facilitate the development of a realistic, achievable project schedule.

Consider a classic example. Let's say you're going to paint your house, but unfortunately, it's fallen into a little disrepair. The old paint is peeling and chipping and will need to be scraped before a coat of primer can be sprayed on the house. After the primer dries, the painting can commence. In this example, the primer activity depends on the scraping. You can't—okay, you *shouldn't*—prime the house before scraping off the peeling paint. The painting activity depends on the primer activity in the same way. You really shouldn't start painting until the primer has dried.

During *Sequence Activities*, you will use a host of inputs and tools and techniques to produce the primary output, and project schedule network diagrams. You've already seen all the inputs to this process. They are the schedule management plan, activity list, activity attributes, milestone list, project scope statement, enterprise environmental factors, and organizational process assets. We'll look at several new tools and techniques next.

Sequence Activities Tools and Techniques

Sequence Activities has three tools and techniques, all of which are new to you:

- Precedence diagramming method (PDM)
- Dependency determination
- Leads and lags

I'll switch the order of these and cover dependency determination first. In practice, you'll define dependencies either before or while you're using the PDM to draw your schedule network. To make sure you're on the same page with the *PMBOK® Guide* terminology regarding dependencies, I'll cover them first and then move on to the other tools and techniques.

Dependency Determination

Dependencies are relationships between the activities in which one activity is dependent on another to complete an action, or perhaps an activity is dependent on another to start an action before it can proceed. Dependency determination is a matter of determining where those dependencies exist. Thinking back to the house-painting example, you couldn't paint until the scraping and priming activities were completed. You'll want to know about four types of dependencies for the exam:

- Mandatory dependencies
- Discretionary dependencies
- External dependencies
- Internal dependencies

As you've probably guessed, the *PMBOK® Guide* defines dependencies differently depending on their characteristics:

Mandatory Dependencies   *Mandatory dependencies*, also known as *hard logic* or *hard dependencies*, are defined by the type of work being performed. The scraping, primer, and painting sequence is an example of mandatory dependencies. The nature of the work itself dictates the order in which the activities should be performed. Activities with physical limitations are a telltale sign that you have a mandatory dependency on your hands.

Discretionary Dependencies   *Discretionary dependencies* are defined by the project team. Discretionary dependencies are also known as *preferred logic*, *soft logic*, or *preferential logic*. These are usually process- or procedure-driven or "best-practice" techniques based on past experience. For example, both past experience and best practices on house-painting projects have shown that all trim work should be hand-painted whereas the bulk of the main painting work should be done with a sprayer.

Exam Spotlight

Discretionary dependencies have a tendency to create arbitrary total float values that will limit your options when scheduling activities that have this type of dependency. If you are fast tracking to compress your schedule, you should consider changing or removing these dependencies.

External Dependencies   *External dependencies* are, well, external to the project. This might seem obvious, but the *PMBOK® Guide* points out that even though the dependency is external to the project (and, therefore, a non-project activity), it impacts project activities. For example, perhaps your project is researching and marketing a new drug. The FDA must approve the drug before your company can market it. This is not a project activity, but the project cannot move forward until approval occurs. That means FDA approval is an external dependency.

Internal Dependencies   *Internal dependencies*, another somewhat obvious dependency, are internal to the project or the organization. They may, however, still be outside of your control. For example, perhaps before implementing a new time tracking system in your maintenance shop, the operations department has decided to study the business rules regarding time tracking. Examining and updating the business rules and processes needs to be completed before the time tracking system can be installed and your project can proceed.

Once you've identified the dependencies and assembled all the other inputs for the Sequence Activities process, you'll take this information and produce a diagram—or schematic display—of the project activities. The project schedule network diagram shows the dependencies—or logical relationships—that exist among the activities. You can use one of the other tools and techniques of this process to produce this output. You'll now examine each in detail.

Precedence Diagramming Method (PDM)

The *precedence diagramming method (PDM)* is what most project management software programs use to sequence activities. Precedence diagrams use boxes or rectangles to represent the activities (called *nodes*). The nodes are connected with arrows showing the dependencies between the activities. This method is also called *activity on node (AON)*.

The minimum information that should be displayed on the node is the activity name, but you might put as much information about the activity on the node as you'd like. Sometimes the nodes are displayed with activity name, activity number, start and stop dates, due dates, slack time, and so on. (I'll cover slack time in the section "Develop Schedule Tools and Techniques," later in this chapter.)

Exam Spotlight

For the exam, remember that the PDM uses only one time estimate to determine duration.

The following graphic shows a PDM—or AON—of the house-painting example.

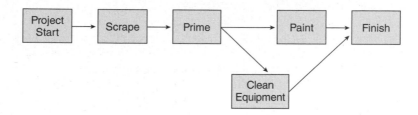

The PDM is further defined by four types of *logical relationships*. The terms *dependencies* and *precedence relationships* also are used to describe these relationships. You might already be familiar with these if you've used Microsoft Project or similar project management software. The four dependencies, or logical relationships, are as follows:

Finish-to-Start (FS)   The finish-to-start relationship is the most frequently used relationship. This relationship says that the predecessor—or *from* activity—must finish before the successor—or *to* activity—can start. In PDM diagrams, this is the most often used logical relationship.

Start-to-Finish (SF)   The start-to-finish relationship says that the predecessor activity must start before the successor activity can finish. This logical relationship is seldom used.

Finish-to-Finish (FF)   The finish-to-finish relationship says that the predecessor activity must finish before the successor activity finishes.

Start-to-Start (SS)   I think you're getting the hang of this. The start-to-start relationship says that the predecessor activity depends on starting before the successive activity can start.

Exam Spotlight

For the exam, know that finish-to-start is the most commonly used dependency in the PDM method and that start-to-finish is rarely used. Also remember that according to the *PMBOK® Guide*, each activity and/or milestone on the network diagram are connected by either at least one predecessor and/or a successor activity *except* the first and last activity and/or milestone.

Keep these logical relationships (or dependencies) in mind when constructing your project schedule network diagram.

Arrow Diagramming Method (ADM)

This is not a listed tool and technique of the Sequence Activities process, but there is a possibility you could see a question on the exam regarding the *arrow diagramming method (ADM)*. It's an old technique that's rarely used anymore, but nonetheless you should have some familiarity with it.

The ADM is visually the opposite of the PDM. The arrow diagramming method places activities on the arrows, which are connected to dependent activities with nodes. This method is also called *activity on arrow (AOA)* and activity on line (AOL). This technique isn't used nearly as often as the PDM, but some industries prefer the ADM to the PDM. For the record, note that the ADM allows for more than one time estimate to determine duration and uses only the finish-to-start dependency. There's one more unique note about the ADM to tuck away: Sometimes dummy activities must be plugged into the diagram to accurately display the dependencies. Dummy activities are commonly depicted using a dotted arrow.

The following example shows the ADM method applied to the house-painting example.

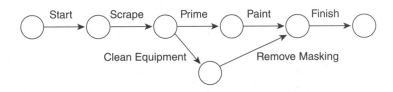

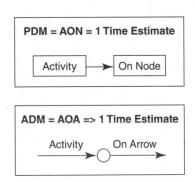

Exam Spotlight

I recommend that you memorize the following graphic to help you remember the tools and techniques of the Sequence Activities process and their characteristics for the exam.

PDM = AON = 1 Time Estimate

| Activity | → | On Node |

ADM = AOA => 1 Time Estimate

Activity → On Arrow

This might look a little strange, but I think it will work for you now that you understand what each of these diagramming methods is. This is information you need to know for the exam. If this graphic isn't useful for you, come up with your own mnemonic or sample that will help you remember which of these is which. Don't say I didn't warn you.

There is one other diagramming method you could potentially see a question about on the exam. It's called GERT, which stands for Graphical Evaluation and Review Technique. What you should know for the exam is that this diagramming method allows for conditions, branches, and loops.

Applying Leads and Lags

Leads and lags should be considered when determining dependencies. *Lags* occur when time elapses between two activities, which delays *successor activities* (those that follow a predecessor activity) from starting, and as a result, time is added either to the start date or to the finish date of the activity you're scheduling. *Leads*, conversely, speed up the successor activities, and as a result, time needs to be subtracted from the start date or the finish date of the activity you're scheduling.

Exam Spotlight

Leads and lags speed up or delay successor activities but should not replace schedule logic.

Let's revisit the house-painting example to put all this in perspective. In order to paint, you first need to scrape the peeling paint and then prime. However, you can't begin painting until the primer has dried, so you shouldn't schedule priming for Monday and painting for Tuesday if you need the primer to dry on Tuesday. Therefore, the priming activity generates the need for lag time at the end of the activity to account for the drying time needed before you can start painting.

Lead time works just the opposite. Suppose, for this example, you could start priming before the scraping is finished. Maybe certain areas on the house don't require scraping, so you don't need to wait until the scraping activity finishes to begin the priming activity. In this example, lead time is subtracted from the beginning of the priming activity so that this activity begins prior to the previous activity finishing.

Another tool you might use in this process are schedule network templates. These are not a named tool and technique of this process but may come in handy on your next project. Schedule network templates are like the templates I've talked about in previous processes. Perhaps the project you're working on is similar to a project that has been completed in the past. You can use a previous project schedule network diagram as a template for the current project. Or you might be working on a project with several deliverables that are fairly identical to projects you've performed in the past, or the deliverables on the existing project are fairly similar, and you can use the old schedule network diagrams, or the same schedule network diagrams, as templates for the project. Templates can be used for certain portions of the project schedule or for the entire project. If you are using templates for portions of the project schedule, they are known as subnetwork templates or fragment network templates.

Sequence Activities Outputs

There are only two outputs of the Sequence Activities process: project schedule network diagrams and project documents updates. I've just spent a good deal of time describing the different types of project schedule network diagrams you can construct using the PDM or ADM techniques. You can generate project schedule network diagrams on a computer, or you can draw them by hand. Like the WBS, these diagrams are visual representations of the work of the project and might contain all the project details or they might contain only summary-level details, depending on the complexity of the project. Summary-level activities are a collection of related activities, also known as *hammocks*. Think of hammocks as a group of related activities rolled up into a summary heading that describes the activities likely to be contained in that grouping.

Keep in mind that the construction of these project schedule network diagrams might bring activities to light that you missed when defining your activity list, or it might make you break an activity down into two activities in places where you thought one activity might work. If this is the case, you will need to update the activity list and the activity attributes. The other project document update that may be required as a result of this process is an update to the risk register. (We'll talk about the risk register in Chapter 6, "Risk Planning.")

After the activities are sequenced, the next steps involve estimating the resources and estimating the durations of the activities so that they can be plugged into the project schedule. We'll look at these topics in the next sections of this chapter.

Estimating Activity Resources

All projects, from the smallest to the largest, require resources. The term *resources*, in this case, does not mean just people; it means all the physical resources required to complete the project. The *PMBOK® Guide* defines resources as people, equipment, materials, and supplies. In reality, this includes people, equipment, supplies, materials, software, hardware—the list goes on depending on the project on which you're working. The *Estimate Activity Resources* process is concerned with determining the types of resources needed (both human and materials) and in what quantities for each schedule activity within a work package.

Remember, the activity resource requirements output from the Estimate Activity Resources process is an input to the Plan Human Resource Management process.

The *PMBOK® Guide* notes that Estimate Activity Resources should be closely coordinated with the Estimate Costs process (I'll talk about Estimate Costs in Chapter 5, "Developing the Project Budget and Communicating the Plan"). That's because resources—whether people or material or both—are typically the largest expense you'll have on any project. Identifying the resources becomes a critical component of the project planning process so estimates—and ultimately the project budget—can be accurately derived. You'll look at the inputs and tools and techniques that will help you document these requirements next.

Estimate Activity Resources Inputs

The Estimate Activity Resources process has several inputs, most of which you already know:

- Schedule management plan
- Activity list
- Activity attributes
- Resource calendars
- Risk register
- Activity cost estimates
- Enterprise environmental factors
- Organizational process assets

The only inputs you haven't seen before are resource calendars, risk register, and activity cost estimates.

Resource calendars are an output of the Acquire Project Team and Conduct Procurements processes. Both of these processes are performed during the Executing process group, so you may find this input perplexing here. However, you may have some resource availability information (resource calendars) on a preliminary basis during the Estimate Activity Resources process, and you'll further define it when resources are assigned to the project later in the Executing processes. In practice, you may find that you perform the Acquire Project Team process during the later stages of the Planning portion of the project rather than in the Executing process.

The *resource calendars* input describes the time frames in which resources (both human and material) are available. They look at a particular resource or groups of resources and their skills, abilities, quantity, and availability. Perhaps your project calls for a marketing resource and the person assigned to the marketing activities is on an extended vacation in October. The resource calendar would show this person's vacation schedule. (The overall project calendar shows the holidays the company recognizes.)

Resource calendars also examine the quantity, capability, and availability of equipment and material resources that have a potential to impact the project schedule. For example, suppose your project calls for a hydraulic drill and your organization owns only one. The resource calendar will tell you whether it's scheduled for another job at the same time it's needed for your project.

The risk register is an output of the Identify Risks process. It is a list of identified risks and their potential responses. We will discuss the risk register in more depth in Chapter 6, "Risk Planning."

Activity cost estimates are an output of the Estimate Costs process. These are the costs that are determined for each activity. We will look at activity cost estimates in more depth in Chapter 5.

Estimate Activity Resources Tools and Techniques

Your goal with the Estimate Activity Resources process is to determine the activity resource requirements, including quantity and availability. This process has five tools and techniques to help accomplish this output: expert judgment, alternative analysis, published estimating data, bottom-up estimating, and project management software. You already know what expert judgment entails, so take a look at the remaining tools:

Alternative Analysis   Alternative analysis is used when thinking about the methods you might use to accomplish the activities your resources have been assigned. Many times, you can accomplish an activity in more than one way, and alternative analysis helps decide among the possibilities. For example, a subcompact car drives on the same roads a six-figure sports car travels. The sports car has a lot more features than the subcompact, it's faster, it's probably more comfortable, and it has a visual appeal that the subcompact doesn't. The sports car might be the valid resource choice for the project, but you should consider all the alternatives. The same idea applies to human resources in that you might apply senior-level resources versus junior-level resources, or you could add resources to speed up the schedule. You may also use make-rent-or-buy analysis when determining alternative resources.

Published Estimating Data   Estimating data might include organizational guidelines, industry rates or estimates, production rates, resource rates, and so on. For example, your organization might have established price agreements with vendors that outline rates by resource types, or there might be industry estimates for production rates for your particular activity or your particular geographical region.

Bottom-Up Estimating   Bottom-up estimating is a process of estimating individual schedule activity costs and then adding them together to come up with a total estimate for the work package. Here you estimate every schedule activity individually and then roll up that estimate, or add them all together, to come up with a total. This is an accurate means of estimating, provided the estimates at the schedule activity level are accurate. However, it takes a considerable amount of time to perform bottom-up estimating because every activity must be assessed and estimated accurately to be included in the bottom-up calculation. The smaller and more detailed the activity, the greater the accuracy and cost of this technique. If it isn't possible to estimate the activity cost, you'll need to decompose the activity to a lower level of detail so that an estimate can be performed. Bottom-up estimating may also be used to determine activity durations and is a good technique to use when you aren't confident about the type or quantity of resources you'll need for the project.

Project Management Software   Project management software can help plan, organize, and estimate resource needs and document their availability. It might also help you to produce resource breakdown structures, resource rates, resource calendars, and availability.

Estimate Activity Resources Outputs

The purpose of the Estimate Activity Resources process is to develop the activity resource requirements output. This output describes the types of resources and the quantity needed for each activity associated with a work package. You should prepare a narrative description for this output that describes how you determined the estimate, including the information you used to form your estimate and the assumptions you made about the resources and their availability.

Work package estimates are derived by taking a cumulative total of all the schedule activities within the work package.

You'll use the activity resource requirements in the next process (Estimate Activity Durations) to determine the length of time each activity will take to complete. That, of course, depends on the quantity and skill level of the resources assigned, which is the reason you estimate resources before you try to determine duration.

The two other outputs of this process are resource breakdown structure and project documents updates.

The *resource breakdown structure (RBS)* is much like an organizational breakdown structure, but the RBS lists the resources by category and type. You may have several categories of resources, including labor, hardware, equipment, supplies, and so on. *Type* describes the types of resources needed, such as skill levels or quality grades of the material and so on.

The project documents updates portion of this output refers to updating the activity list, activity attributes, and the resource calendars with changes to any of the elements you've recorded here.

You can see how these "Activity" processes have built on each other. First you defined the activities; then you determined dependencies and sequenced them in the correct order; and next you determined what types and quantities of resources are required to complete the activities. Now you're ready to begin estimating the duration of these activities so you can plug them into the project schedule.

Estimating Activity Durations

The *Estimate Activity Durations* process attempts to estimate the work effort, resources, and number of work periods needed to complete each activity. The *activity duration estimates* are the primary output of this process. These are quantifiable estimates expressed as the number of work periods needed to complete a schedule activity. Work periods are usually expressed in hours or days. However, larger projects might express duration in weeks or months. Work periods are the activity duration estimates, and they become inputs to the Develop Schedule process.

When estimating activity duration, be certain to include all the time that will elapse from the beginning of the activity until the work is completed. For example, consider the earlier example of the house-painting project. You estimate that it will take three days, including drying time, to prime the house. Now, let's say priming is scheduled to begin on Saturday, but your crew doesn't work on Sunday. The activity duration in this case is four days, which includes the three days to prime and dry plus the Sunday the crew doesn't work. Most project management software programs will handle this kind of situation automatically once you've keyed in the project calendar and work periods.

Progressive elaboration comes into play during this process also. Estimates typically start at a fairly high level, and as more details are known about the deliverables and their associated activities, the estimates become more accurate. You should rely on those folks who have the most knowledge of the activities you're trying to estimate to help you with this process.

Estimate Activity Durations Inputs

The inputs to this process include the schedule management plan, activity list, activity attributes, activity resource requirements, resource calendars, project scope statement, risk register, resource breakdown structure, enterprise environmental factors, and organizational process assets.

A few of the important elements regarding these inputs apply here as you've seen in past processes: databases, productivity metrics, historical information regarding durations on similar projects, project calendars, scheduling methodology, and lessons learned. The *project calendars* (which list company holidays, shift schedules, and so on) are considered a part of the organizational process assets, and activity resource requirements are especially useful during this process.

Estimate Activity Durations Tools and Techniques

The Estimate Activity Durations process has several new tools and techniques:

- Expert judgment
- Analogous estimating
- Parametric estimating
- Three-point estimating
- Group decision-making techniques
- Reserve analysis

You'll take a look at each of these tools and techniques next.

Expert Judgment

The staff members who will perform activities will most accurately estimate them. In this case, team members use expert judgment because of their experience with similar activities in the past. You should be careful with these estimates, though, because they are subject to bias and aren't based on any scientific means. Your experts should consider that resource levels, resource productivity, resource capability, risks, and other factors can impact estimates. It's good practice to combine expert judgment with historical information and use as many experts as you can.

Analogous Estimating

Analogous estimating, also called *top-down estimating*, is a form of expert judgment. With this technique, you will use the actual duration of a similar activity completed on a previous project to determine the duration of the current activity—provided the information was documented and stored with the project information on the previous project. This technique is most useful when the previous activities you're comparing are similar to the activity you're estimating and don't just appear to be similar. You want the folks who are working on the estimate to have experience with these activities so they can provide reasonable estimates. This technique is especially helpful when detailed information about the project is not available, such as in the early phases of the project.

Top-down estimating techniques are also used to estimate total project duration, particularly when you have a limited amount of information about the project. The best way to think about top-down techniques is to look at the estimate as a whole. Think about being on a mountaintop where you can see the whole picture as one rather than all the individual items that make up the picture.

For instance, let's return to the house-painting example. You would compare a previous house-painting project to the current house-painting project, where the houses are of similar size and the paint you're using is the same quality. You can use the first house-painting project to estimate the project duration for the second house-painting project because of the similarities in the project.

Top-down techniques are useful when you're early in the project Planning processes and are just beginning to flesh out all the details of the project. Sometimes during the project selection process, the selection committee might want an idea of the project's duration. You can derive a project estimate at this stage by using top-down techniques.

Exam Spotlight

The *PMBOK® Guide* states that analogous estimating is a gross value estimating technique. It also notes that you can use analogous estimating to determine overall project duration and cost estimates for the entire project (or phases of the project). For the exam, remember that the analogous technique is typically less time-consuming and less costly than other estimating techniques, but it's also less accurate.

Parametric Estimating

Parametric estimating is a quantitatively based estimating method that multiplies the quantity of work by the rate or uses an algorithm in conjunction with historical data to determine cost, budget, or duration estimates. The best way to describe it is with an example. Suppose you are working on a companywide network upgrade project. This requires you to run new cable to the switches on every floor in the building. To come up with an estimate, you can use parametric estimates to determine activity duration estimates by taking a known element—in this case, the amount of cable needed—and multiplying it by the amount of time it takes to install a unit of cable. In other words, suppose you have 10,000 meters of new cable to run. You know from past experience it takes 1 hour to install 100 meters. Using this measurement, you can determine an estimate for this activity of 100 hours to run the new cable. Therefore, the cable activity duration estimate is 100 hours.

Exam Spotlight

The *PMBOK® Guide* states that you can also use parametric estimating to determine time estimates for the entire project or portions of the project. For the exam, remember that a statistical relationship exists between historical data and other variables (as explained in the cable example earlier) when using parametric estimates and that this technique can be highly accurate if the data you are using is reliable.

Three-Point Estimating

Three-point estimating, as you can probably guess, uses three estimates that, when averaged, come up with a final estimate. The three estimates you'll use in this technique are the most likely estimate, an optimistic estimate, and a pessimistic estimate. The most likely estimate assumes there are no disasters and the activity can be completed as planned. The optimistic estimate is the fastest time frame in which your resource can complete the activity. The pessimistic estimate assumes the worst happens, and it takes much longer than planned to get the activity completed. You'll want to rely on experienced folks to give you these estimates. Then you can choose to use one of two formulas to calculate the expected duration estimate (E). The first formula, called the triangular distribution, consists of summing the most likely, the optimistic, and the pessimistic estimates and then dividing that sum by 3. The formula looks like this:

$$E = (O + P + M) / 3$$

The second formula is called a beta distribution, which is taken from the program evaluation and review technique (PERT) that we will review in depth in the Develop Schedule process later in this process. The formula for beta distribution or PERT looks like this:

$$E = (O + P + 4M) / 6.$$

Group Decision-Making Techniques

Group decision-making techniques include brainstorming and the Delphi or nominal group techniques. These techniques get your team members involved and will help improve the accuracy of your estimates. Brainstorming is an age-old technique where all participants have an opportunity to speak up. No idea is a bad idea with this technique, and it's essential that the facilitator not allow participants to get into judging contests or debates on the merits of the ideas proposed during the brainstorming session.

The Delphi technique is similar to brainstorming in that you involve subject matter experts in determining estimates. Their experiences with the organization and on similar past projects will help improve the accuracy of the estimates. Because you have them involved in the process and they know that the estimates derived from this exercise will be attached to the project schedule, they are likely to provide more accurate estimates and work hard to meet or beat them.

Reserve Analysis

Contingency reserves—also called *buffers* or *time reserves* in the *PMBOK® Guide*—means a portion of time (or money when you're estimating budgets) that is added to the schedule to account for risk or uncertainty. You might choose to add a percentage of time or a set number of work periods to the activity or the overall schedule or both. Contingency reserves are calculated for known risks that have documented contingency or mitigation response plans to deal with the risk event should it occur, but you don't necessarily know how much time it will take to implement the mitigation plan and potentially perform rework. For example, you know it will take 100 hours to run new cable based on the quantitative estimate you came up with earlier. You also know that sometimes you hit problem areas when running the cable. To make sure you don't impact the project schedule, you build in a reserve time of 10 percent of your original estimate to account for the problems you might encounter. This brings your activity duration estimate to 110 hours for this activity. Contingency reserves can be and should be modified as the project progresses. As you use the time, or find you don't need the time, you will modify the reserve amounts.

Management reserves are a type of reserve used for unknown events. Since they are unknown, you have not identified them as risks. Management reserves are for that funny feeling you have that something could come up that you haven't thought about during the Planning process. Management reserves set aside periods of time for this unknown work but are not included in the schedule baseline. Keep in mind this is not time that is available to throw in extra deliverables that didn't make it into the scope statement. Management reserves must be used for project work that is within scope. If you do use management reserves during the project, you must change the schedule baseline to reflect the time used.

Exam Spotlight

Contingency reserves are included in the schedule baseline; management reserves are not. Contingency reserves are for potential work identified during the Risk Planning processes. Management reserves are for unknown circumstances that have not been previously identified but require work that is within scope of the project. Management reserves that are used on the project require a change to the schedule baseline.

Estimate Activity Durations Outputs

Everything I've discussed to this point has brought you to the primary output of this process: the activity duration estimates. You use the inputs and tools and techniques to establish these estimates. As mentioned earlier, activity duration estimates are estimates of the required work periods needed to complete the activity. This is a quantitative measure usually expressed in hours, weeks, days, or months.

One factor to note about your final estimates as an output to this process is that they should contain a range of possible results. In the cable-running example, you would state the activity duration estimates as "100 hours ± 10 hours" to show that the actual duration will take at least 90 hours and might go as long as 110 hours—or you could use percentages to express this range.

The other output of Estimate Activity Durations is project documents updates. The information that may need to be revisited and updated as a result of this process includes the activity attributes and the assumptions you made regarding resource availability and skill levels.

Now that you have all the activity information in hand, along with a host of other inputs, you're ready to develop the project schedule.

Exam Spotlight

Remember that you perform the Activity processes in this order: Define Activities, Sequence Activities, Estimate Activity Resources, and Estimate Activity Durations. Develop Schedule comes after you've completed all of these processes.

DSU has hired a contract agency to create its new registration website. The website will allow students in good academic standing to register for classes over the Internet. You have been appointed as the project manager for the DSU side of this project. You'll be working with Henry Lu from Websites International to complete this project.

Henry has given you an activity list and asked for time estimates that he can plug into the project plan.

Your first stop is Mike Walter's desk. He's the expert on the mainframe registration system and he'll be writing the interface programs to accept registration data from the new website. Mike will also create the download that the Internet program will use to verify a student's academic standing. Mike has created other programs just like this in the past. His expertise and judgment are very reliable.

The next stop is Kate Langdon. She's the new team leader of the testing group. Kate has been with DSU for only one month. Since she has no experience working with DSU data and staff members, she tells you she'll get back to you within a week with estimates for the testing activities. She plans to read through the project binders of some similar projects and base her estimates against the historical information on similar projects. She'll run the estimates by her lead tester before giving them to you.

You've asked both of your resources to provide you with three-point estimates. Mike Walter's estimates are an example of using the tool and technique of expert judgment to derive activity duration estimates. The estimates expected from Kate Langdon will be derived using historical information (implied by the research she's going to do into past similar projects) and expert judgment because she's involving her lead tester to verify the estimates.

Developing the Project Schedule

The *Develop Schedule* process is the heart of the Planning process group. This is where you lay out the schedule for your project activities, determine their start and finish dates, and finalize activity sequences and durations. Develop Schedule, along with Estimate Activity Resources and Estimate Activity Durations, is repeated several times before you come up with the project schedule. Most project management software programs today can automatically build a schedule for you once you've entered the needed information for the activities. The project schedule, once it's approved, serves as the *schedule baseline* for the project that you can track against in later processes.

Remember that you cannot perform Develop Schedule until you have completed at least the following processes in the Planning group (some of these can be performed at the same time for smaller, less complex projects): Collect Requirements, Define Scope, Create WBS, Define Activities, Sequence Activities, Estimate Activity Resources, Estimate Activity Durations, and Develop Human Resource Plan. In practice, it's also beneficial to perform Identify Risks, Perform Qualitative Risk Analysis, Perform Quantitative Risk Analysis, Plan Risk Responses, and Plan Procurements prior to developing the schedule.

There is a lot of material to cover in this process, so grab a cup of coffee or a soda now. I'll start with the inputs to the Develop Schedule process and then follow up with an in-depth discussion of the tools and techniques of the process. These techniques will help you get to the primary output of this process: the project schedule.

Develop Schedule Inputs

Develop Schedule has 13 inputs, 9 of which are outputs from other Planning processes. The inputs are as follows:

- Schedule management plan
- Activity list
- Activity attributes
- Project schedule network diagrams
- Activity resource requirements
- Resource calendars
- Activity duration estimates
- Project scope statement
- Risk register
- Project staff assignments
- Resource breakdown structure
- Enterprise environmental factors
- Organizational process assets

You can see how important it is to perform all the Planning processes accurately because the information you derive from almost every process in the Planning group is used somewhere else in Planning, many of them here. Your project schedule will reflect the information you know at this point in time. If you have incorrectly estimated activity durations or didn't identify the right dependencies, for example, the inputs to this process will be distorted and your project schedule will not be correct. It's definitely worth the investment of time to correctly plan your project and come up with accurate outputs for each of the Planning processes.

As with several other processes, you should pay particular attention to constraints and assumptions when performing Develop Schedule. Constraints are with you throughout the life of the project. The most important constraints to consider in the Develop Schedule process are time constraints, and they fall into two categories: imposed dates and key events/major milestones.

Imposed dates restrict the start or finish date of activities. The two most common constraints, *start no earlier than* and *finish no later than*, are used by most computerized project management software programs. Let's look once again at the house-painting example. The painting activity cannot start until the primer has dried. If the primer takes 24 hours to dry and is scheduled to be completed on Wednesday, this implies the painting activity can *start no earlier than* Thursday. This is an example of an imposed date.

Key events or milestones refer to the completion of specific deliverables by a specific date. Stakeholders, customers, or management staff might request that certain deliverables be completed or delivered by specific dates. Once you've agreed to those dates (even if the agreement is only verbal), it's often cast in stone and difficult to change. These dates, therefore, become constraints.

 Be careful of the delivery dates you commit to your stakeholders or customers. You might think you're simply discussing the matter or throwing out ideas, whereas the stakeholder might take what you've said as fact. Once the stakeholder believes the deliverable or activity will be completed by a specific date, there's almost no convincing them that the date needs changing.

Develop Schedule Tools and Techniques

The primary outputs of Develop Schedule are the schedule baseline and the project schedule. The schedule baseline is the approved version of the project schedule. You can employ several tools and techniques to produce these outputs. The tools and techniques you choose depend on the complexity of the project. For the exam, however, you'll need to know them all.

Develop Schedule has eight tools and techniques:

- Schedule network analysis
- Critical path method
- Critical chain method
- Resource optimization techniques
- Modeling techniques
- Leads and lags
- Schedule compression
- Scheduling tool

A lot of information is packed into some of these tools and techniques, and you should dedicate study time to each of them for the exam. We'll look at each one next.

Schedule Network Analysis

Schedule network analysis produces the project schedule. It involves calculating early and late start dates and early and late finish dates for project activities (as does the critical path method). It uses a schedule model and other analytical techniques such as critical path and critical chain method, what-if analysis, and resource leveling (all of which are other tools and techniques in this process) to help calculate these dates and create the schedule. These calculations are performed without taking resource limitations into consideration, so the dates you end up with are theoretical. At this point, you're attempting to establish the time periods within which the activities can be scheduled. Resource limitations and other constraints will be taken into consideration when you get to the outputs of this process.

Critical Path Method

The *critical path method (CPM)* is a schedule network analysis technique that estimates the minimum project duration. It determines the amount of float, or schedule flexibility, for each of the network paths by calculating the earliest start date, earliest finish date, latest start date, and latest finish date for each activity (without taking resource availability into account). This is a schedule network analysis technique that relies on sequential networks (one activity occurs before the next, a series of activities occurring concurrently is completed before the next series of activities begins, and so on) and on a single duration estimate for each activity. The precedence diagramming method (PDM) can be used to perform CPM. Keep in mind that CPM is a method to determine schedule durations without regard to resource availability.

The *critical path (CP)* is generally the longest full path on the project. Any project activity with a float time that equals 0 or has negative float is considered a critical path task. The critical path can change under a few conditions. When activities with float time use up all their float, they can become critical path tasks. Or you might have a milestone midway through the project with a *finish no later than* constraint that can change the critical path if it isn't met.

Float time is also called *slack time*, and you'll see these terms used interchangeably. There are two types of float: total float and free float. *Total float (TF)* is the amount of time you can delay the earliest start of a task without delaying the ending of the project. *Free float (FF)* is the amount of time you can delay the start of a task without delaying the earliest start of a successor task.

In the following section, you'll calculate the CP for a sample project, and I'll illustrate how you derive all the dates, the CP, and the float times.

Gathering Activity and Dependency Information

Let's say you are the project manager for a new software project. Your team will be developing a custom application that manages, tracks, and analyzes charitable contributions to a variety of organizations managed by your parent company. You need to devise a software system that tracks all the information related to the contributions, the donors, and the receivers and also supplies the management team with reports that will help them make good business decisions. For purposes of illustration, I'm showing only a limited portion of the tasks that you would have on a project like this.

You'll start this example by plugging information from the processes you've already completed into a table (a complete example is shown later in Table 4.1 in the section "Calculating the Critical Path"). The list of activities comes from the Define Activities process. The durations for each activity are listed in the Duration column and were derived during the Estimate Activity Durations process. The duration times are listed in days.

The Dependency column lists the activities that require a previous activity to finish before the current activity can start. You're using only finish-to-start relationships. For example, you'll see that activity 2 and activity 4 each depend on activity 1 to finish before they can begin. The dependency information came from the Sequence Activities process. Now, you'll proceed to calculating the dates.

Calculating the Forward and Backward Pass

Project Deliverables is the first activity and, obviously, where the project starts. This activity begins on April 1. Project Deliverables has a 12-day duration. So, take April 1 and add 12 days to this to come up with an early finish date of April 12. Watch out, because you need to count day 1, or April 1, as a full workday. The simplest way to do this calculation is to take the early start date, add the duration, and subtract 1. Therefore, the early finish date for the first activity is April 12. By the way, we are ignoring weekends and holidays for this example. Activity 2 depends on activity 1, so it cannot start until activity 1 has finished. Its earliest start date is April 13 because activity 1 finished at the end of the previous day. Add the duration to this date minus 1 to come up with the finish date.

You'll notice that, since activity 4 depends on activity 1 finishing, its earliest start date is also April 13. Continue to calculate the remaining early start and early finish dates in the same manner. This calculation is called a *forward pass*.

To calculate the latest start and latest finish dates, you begin with the last activity. The latest finish for activity 9 is July 10. Since the duration is only one day, July 10 is also the latest start date. You know that activity 8 must finish before activity 9 can begin, so activity 8's latest finish date, July 9, is one day prior to activity 9's latest start date, July 10. Subtract the duration of activity 8 (three days) from July 9 and add one day to get the latest start date of July 7. You're performing the opposite calculation that you did for the forward pass. This calculation is called a *backward pass*, as you might have guessed. Continue calculating the latest start and latest finish through activity 4.

Activity 3 adds a new twist. Here's how it works. Activity 7 cannot begin until activity 3 and activity 6 are completed. No other activity depends on the completion of activity 3. If activity 7's latest start date is June 29, activity 3's latest finish date must be June 28. June 28 minus eight days plus one gives you a latest start date of June 21. Activity 3 depends on activity 2, so activity 2 must be completed prior to beginning activity 3. Calculate these dates just as you did for activities 9 through 4.

Activity 1 still remains. Activity 4 cannot start until activity 1 is completed. If activity 4's latest start date is April 13, the latest finish date for activity 1 must be April 12.

Subtract the duration of activity 1, and add 1 to come up with a latest start date of April 1. Alternatively, you can calculate the forward pass and backward pass by saying the first task starts on day 0 and then adding the duration to this. For example, activity number 1's earliest start date is April 1, which is day 0. Add 12 days to day 0, and you come up with an earliest finish date of April 12.

You determine the calculation for float/slack time by subtracting the earliest start date from the latest start date. If the float time equals 0, the activity is on the critical path.

Calculating the Critical Path

To determine the CP duration of the project, add the duration of every activity with zero float. You should come up with 101 days because you're adding the duration for all activities except for activity 2 and activity 3. A critical path task is any task that cannot be changed without impacting the project end date. By definition, these are all tasks with zero float.

Another way to determine the critical path is by looking at the network diagram. If the duration is included with the information on the node or if start and end dates are given, you simply calculate the duration and then add the duration of the longest path in the diagram to determine the CP. However, this method is not as accurate as what's shown in Table 4.1. Figure 4.1 shows the same project in diagram form. The duration is printed in the top-right corner of each node. Add the duration of each path to determine which one is the critical path.

FIGURE 4.1 Critical path diagram

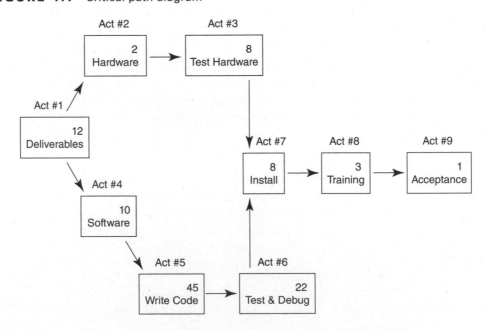

TABLE 4.1 CPM calculation

Activity number	Activity description	Dependency	Duration	Early start	Early finish	Late start	Late finish	Float/ slack
1	Project Deliverables	—	12	4/1	4/12	4/1	4/12	0
2	Procure Hardware	1	2	4/13	4/14	6/19	6/20	67
3	Test Hardware	2	8	4/15	4/22	6/21	6/28	67
4	Procure Software Tools	1	10	4/13	4/22	4/13	4/22	0
5	Write Programs	4	45	4/23	6/6	4/23	6/6	0
6	Test and Debug	5	22	6/7	6/28	6/7	6/28	0
7	Install	3, 6	8	6/29	7/6	6/29	7/6	0
8	Training	7	3	7/7	7/9	7/7	7/9	0
9	Acceptance	8	1	7/10	7/10	7/10	7/10	0

Remember that CP is usually the path with the longest duration. In Figure 4.1, path 1-2-3-7-8-9 equals 34 days. Path 1-4-5-6-7-8-9 equals 101 days; therefore, this path is the critical path.

Calculating Expected Value Using PERT

Program Evaluation and Review Technique (PERT) is a method that the United States Navy developed in the 1950s. The Navy was working on one of the most complex engineering projects in history at the time—the Polaris Missile Program—and needed a way to manage the project and forecast the project schedule with a high degree of reliability. PERT was developed to do just that.

PERT and CPM are similar techniques. The difference is that CPM uses the most likely duration to determine project duration, whereas PERT uses what's called *expected value* (or the weighted average). Expected value is calculated using the three-point estimates for activity duration (I talked about three-point estimates earlier in this chapter) and then finding the weighted average of those estimates (I'll talk about weighted average in the next section, "Calculating Expected Value"). If you take this one step further and determine the standard deviation of each activity, you can assign a confidence factor to your project estimates. Without getting too heavily involved in the mathematics of probability, understand that for data that fits a bell curve—which is what you're about to calculate with the PERT technique—the following is true:

- Work will finish within plus or minus three standard deviations 99.73 percent of the time.

- Work will finish within plus or minus two standard deviations 95.44 percent of the time.

- Work will finish within plus or minus one standard deviation 68.26 percent of the time.

Calculating Expected Value

The three-point estimates used to calculate expected value are the optimistic estimate, the pessimistic estimate, and the most likely estimate. Going back to the software example, let's find out what these three time estimates might look like for the activity called Write Programs. You get these estimates by asking the lead programmer, or key team member, to estimate the optimistic, pessimistic, and most likely duration for the activity based on past experience. Other historical information could be used to determine these estimates as well. Say in this case that you're given 38 days for the optimistic time, 57 days for the pessimistic, and 45 days for the most likely. (Forty-five days was derived from the Estimate Activity Durations process and is the estimate you used to calculate CPM.)

The formula to calculate expected value is as follows:

$$(\text{optimistic} + \text{pessimistic} + (4 \times \text{most likely})) / 6$$

The expected value for the Write Programs activity is as follows:

$$(38 + 57 + (4 \times 45)) / 6 = 45.83$$

The formula for standard deviation, which helps you determine confidence level, is as follows:

$$(\text{pessimistic} - \text{optimistic}) / 6$$

The standard deviation for your activity is as follows:

$$(57 - 38) / 6 = 3.17$$

You could say the following, given the information you now have:

- There is a 68.26 percent chance that the Write Programs activity will be completed in 42.66 days to 49 days.

- There is a 95.44 percent chance that the Write Programs activity will be completed in 39.49 days to 52.17 days.

You calculated the range of dates for the 68.26 percent chance by adding and subtracting one standard deviation, 3.17, from the expected value, 45.83. You calculated the 95.44 percent chance by multiplying the standard deviation times 2, which equals 6.34, and adding and subtracting that result from the expected value to come up with the least number of days and the most number of days it will take to finish the activity. Generally speaking, two standard deviations, or 95.44 percent, is a close enough estimate for most purposes.

Determining Date Ranges for Project Duration

Let's bring your table of activities back and plug in the expected values and the standard deviation for each (see Table 4.2).

TABLE 4.2   PERT calculation

Activity number	Activity description	Optimistic	Pessimistic	Most likely	Expected value	Standard deviation (SD)	SD squared
1	Project Deliverables	10	14	12	12.00	0.67	0.45
2	Procure Hardware	—	—	—	—	—	—
3	Test Hardware	—	—	—	—	—	—
4	Procure Software Tools	8	14	10	10.33	1.00	1.0
5	Write Programs	38	57	45	45.83	3.17	10.05
6	Test and Debug	20	30	22	23.00	1.67	2.79
7	Install	5	10	8	7.83	0.83	0.69
8	Training	3	3	3	3.00	0	0
9	Acceptance	1	1	1	1.00	0	0
Totals for CP Tasks					102.99		14.98

The higher the standard deviation is for an activity, the higher the risk. Because standard deviation measures the difference between the pessimistic and the optimistic times, a greater spread between the two, which results in a higher number, indicates a greater risk. Conversely, a low standard deviation means less risk.

Now let's look at the total project duration using PERT and the standard deviation to determine a range of dates for project duration. You should add only the tasks that are on the critical path. Remember from the CPM example that activities 2 and 3 are not on the critical path, so their expected value and standard deviation calculations have been left blank in this table. When you add all the remaining tasks, the total expected value duration is 102.99 days, or 103 days rounded to the nearest day.

Your next logical conclusion might be to add the Standard Deviation column to get the standard deviation for the project. Unfortunately, you cannot add the standard deviations because you will come out with a number that is much too high. Totaling the standard deviations assumes that all the tasks will run over schedule, and that's not likely. It is likely that a few tasks will run over but not every one of them. So now you're probably wondering how to calculate the magic number.

You might have noticed an extra column at the right called SD Squared (or variance). This is the standard deviation squared—or for those of you with math phobias out there, the standard deviation multiplied by itself.

Once you have calculated the standard deviation squared for each activity, add the squares, for a total of 14.98. There's one more step, and you're done. Take the square root of 14.98 (you'll need a calculator) to come up with 3.87. This is the standard deviation you will use to determine your range of projected completion dates. Here's a recap of these last few calculations:

$$\text{Total expected value} = 103.00$$

$$\text{Sum of SD Squared} = 14.98$$

$$\text{Square root of SD Squared} = 3.87$$

You can now make the following predictions regarding your project:

- There is a 68.26 percent chance that the project will be completed in 99.13 days to 106.87 days.
- There is a 95.44 percent chance that the project will be completed in 95.26 days to 110.74 days.

Exam Spotlight

For the exam, I recommend that you know that one standard deviation gives you a 68 percent (rounded) probability and two standard deviations gives you a 95 percent (rounded) probability. Also, know how to calculate the range of project duration dates based on the expected value and standard deviation calculation. You probably don't need to memorize how to calculate the standard deviation because most of the questions give you this information. You should, however, memorize the PERT formula and know how it works. It wouldn't hurt to memorize the standard deviation formula as well—you never know what might show up on the exam.

PERT is not used often today. When it is, it's used for very large, highly complex projects. However, PERT is a useful technique to determine project duration when your activity durations are uncertain. It's also useful for calculating the duration for individual tasks in your schedule that might be complex or risky. You might decide to use PERT for a handful of the activities (those with the highest amount of risk, for example) and use other techniques to determine duration for the remaining activities.

Critical Chain Method

Critical chain method is a schedule network analysis technique that will modify the project schedule by accounting for limited or restricted resources, or for unforeseen project issues, by adding buffers to any schedule path. First construct the project schedule network diagram using the critical path method. You will apply the duration estimates, dependencies, and constraints, and then enter resource availability. Buffers, called feeding buffers, are added at this time as well. The idea behind feeding buffers is similar to that of contingencies. Adding buffer activities (which are essentially non-work activities) to the schedule gives you a cushion of time that protects the critical path and thus the overall project schedule from slipping. Feeding buffers are added to noncritical chain-dependent tasks that feed into the critical chain. Project buffers are a type of buffer that is added at the end of the critical chain. According to the *PMBOK® Guide,* after adding these buffer activities you should schedule your critical path tasks at their latest start and finish dates.

Once this modified schedule is calculated, you'll often find that it changes the critical path. The new critical path showing the resource restrictions and feeding buffers is called the *critical chain.*

Critical chain uses both deterministic (step-by-step) and probabilistic approaches. A few steps are involved in the critical chain process:

- Construct the schedule network diagram using activity duration estimates (you'll use nonconservative estimates in this method).
- Define dependencies.
- Define constraints.
- Calculate critical path.
- Enter resource availability into the schedule.
- Recalculate for the critical chain.

The critical chain method typically schedules high-risk tasks early in the project so that problems can be identified and addressed right away. It allows for combining several tasks into one task when one resource is assigned to all the tasks.

Exam Spotlight

CPM manages the total float of schedule network paths, whereas critical chain manages buffer activity durations. Critical chain is built on CPM and protects the schedule from slipping.

Resource Optimization Techniques

Earlier, I said that CPM and PERT do not consider resource availability. Now that you have a schedule of activities and have determined the critical path, it's time to plug in resources for those activities and adjust the schedule or resources according to any resource constraints you discover. Remember that you identified resource estimates during the Estimate Activity Resources process. Now during Develop Schedule, resources are assigned to specific activities. Usually, you'll find that your initial schedule has periods of time with more activities than you have resources to work on them. You will also find that it isn't always possible to assign 100 percent of your team members' time to tasks. Sometimes your schedule will show a team member who is overallocated, meaning they're assigned to more work than they can physically perform in the given time period. Other times, they might not be assigned enough work to keep them busy during the time period. This problem is easy to fix. You can assign underallocated resources to multiple tasks to keep them busy. Adjusting the schedule for overallocated resources is a harder problem to fix. We will look at three techniques that optimize resources to prevent overallocation where possible, including resource leveling, resource smoothing, and reverse resource allocation scheduling. You should use these techniques with CPM-based schedules.

Resource Leveling

Resource leveling—also called the *resource-based method*—is used when resources are overallocated, are only available at certain times, or when they are assigned to more than one activity at a time. In a nutshell, resource leveling attempts to balance out the resource assignments to get tasks completed without overloading the individual. You accomplish this by adjusting the start and finish dates of schedule activities based on the availability of resources. This typically means allocating resources to critical path tasks first, which often changes the critical path and, in turn, the overall project end date.

The project manager can accomplish resource leveling in a couple of other ways as well. You might delay the start of a task to match the availability of a key team member, or you might adjust the resource assignments so that more tasks are given to team members who are underallocated. Generally speaking, resource leveling of overallocated team members extends the project end date. If you're under a date constraint, you'll have to rework the schedule after assigning resources to keep the project on track with the committed completion date. You can accomplish this with resource smoothing, which we'll look at next.

Resource Smoothing

Resource smoothing accommodates resource availability by modifying activities within their float times without changing the critical path or project end date. That means you'll also use this technique when you need to meet specific schedule dates and are concerned about resource availability.

There are several ways you can accomplish this. You can adjust the resource assignments so that more tasks are given to team members who are underallocated. You could also require the resources to work mandatory overtime—that one always goes over well! Perhaps you can split some tasks so that the team member with the pertinent knowledge or skill performs the critical part of the task and the noncritical part of the task is given to a less-skilled team member. Other methods might include moving key resources from noncritical tasks and assigning them to critical path tasks or adjusting assignments. Reallocating those team members with slack time to critical path tasks to keep them on schedule is another option. Don't forget, fast tracking is another way to keep the project on schedule.

Reverse Resource Allocation Scheduling

Reverse resource allocation scheduling is a technique used when key resources—like a thermodynamic expert, for example—are required at a specific point in the project and they are the only resource, or resources, available to perform these activities. This technique requires the resources to be scheduled in reverse order (that is, from the end date of the project rather than the beginning) in order to assign this key resource at the correct time.

Exam Spotlight

Resource leveling can cause the original critical path to change and can delay the project's completion date. Resource smoothing modifies activities within their floats without changing the critical path or project end date. It's used when changes to the critical path cannot or should not be made. Reverse resource allocation scheduling is used when specific resources are needed at certain times.

Modeling Techniques

Modeling techniques typically include the use of what-if scenario analysis and simulation.

What-if scenario analysis uses different sets of activity assumptions to produce multiple project durations. For example, what would happen if a major deliverable is delayed or the weather prevents you from completing a deliverable on time? What-if analysis literally asks the question, "What-if (fill in the blank) happens on the project?" and attempts to determine the potential positive and/or negative impacts to the project. What-if questions help determine the feasibility of the project schedule under adverse conditions. They are also useful to the project team in preparing risk responses or contingency plans to address the what-if situations. Worst-case what-if scenarios may result in a no-go decision.

Simulation techniques use a range of probable activity durations for each activity (often derived from the three-point estimates), and those ranges are then used to calculate a range of probable duration results for the project itself. Monte Carlo is a simulation technique that runs the possible activity durations and schedule projections many, many times to come up with the schedule projections and their probability, critical path duration estimates, and float time.

Exam Spotlight

For the exam, remember that Monte Carlo is a simulation technique that shows the probability of all the possible project completion dates.

Leads and Lags

I talked about leads and lags earlier in this chapter. You'll recall that lags delay successor activities and require time added either to the start date or to the finish date of the activity you're scheduling. Leads require time to be subtracted from the start date or the finish date of the activity. Keep in mind that as you go about creating your project schedule, you might need to adjust lead and lag time to come up with a workable schedule.

Schedule Compression

Schedule compression is a form of mathematical analysis that's used to shorten the project schedule duration without changing the project scope. Compression is simply shortening the project schedule to accomplish all the activities sooner than estimated.

Schedule compression might happen when the project end date has been predetermined or if, after performing the CPM or PERT techniques, you discover that the project is going to take longer than the original promised date. In the CPM example, you calculated the end date to be July 10. What if the project was undertaken and a July 2 date was promised? That's when you'll need to employ one or both of the duration compression techniques: crashing and fast tracking.

Crashing

Crashing is a compression technique that looks at cost and schedule trade-offs. Crashing the schedule is accomplished by adding resources—from either inside or outside the organization—to the critical path tasks. It wouldn't help you to add resources to noncritical path tasks; these tasks don't impact the schedule end date anyway because they have float time. Crashing could be accomplished by requiring mandatory overtime for critical path tasks or requiring overnight deliveries of materials rather than relying on standard shipping times. You may find that crashing the schedule can lead to increased risk and or increased costs.

Be certain to check the critical path when you've used the crashing technique because crashing might have changed the critical path. Also consider that crashing doesn't always come up with a reasonable result. It often increases the costs of the project as well. The idea with crashing is to try to gain the greatest amount of schedule compression with the least amount of cost.

Fast Tracking

I talked about fast tracking in Chapter 1, "What Is a Project?" *Fast tracking* is performing two tasks or project phases in parallel that were previously scheduled to start sequentially. Fast tracking can occur for the entire duration of the task or phase, or for a portion of the task or phase duration. It can increase project risk and might cause the project team to have to rework tasks. Fast tracking will work only for activities that can be overlapped. For example, it is often performed in object-oriented programming. The programmers might begin writing code on several modules at once, out of sequential order and prior to the completion of the design phase. However, if you remember our house-painting example, you couldn't start priming and painting at the same time, so fast tracking isn't a possibility for those activities.

Scheduling Tool

Given the examples you've worked through on Develop Schedule and resource leveling, you have probably already concluded how much a scheduling tool might help you with these processes. The scheduling tools I've used are in the form of project management software programs. They will automate the mathematical calculations (such as forward and backward pass) and perform resource-leveling functions for you. Obviously, you can then print the schedule that has been produced for final approval and ongoing updates. It's common practice to email updated schedules with project notes so that stakeholders know what activities are completed and which ones remain to be done.

It's beyond the scope of this book to go into all the various software programs available to project managers. Suffice it to say that scheduling tools and project management software range from the simple to the complex. The level of sophistication and the types of project management techniques that you're involved with will determine which software product you should choose. Many project managers that I know have had great success with Microsoft Project software and use it exclusively. It contains a robust set of features and reporting tools that will serve most projects well.

Don't forget that you are the project manager, and your good judgment should never be usurped by the recommendation of a software product. Your finely tuned skills and experience will tell you whether relationship issues between team members might cause bigger problems than what the resource-leveling function indicates. Constraints and stakeholder expectations are difficult for a software package to factor in. Rely on your expertise when in doubt. If you don't have the experience yet to make knowledge-based decisions, seek out another project manager or a senior stakeholder, manager, or team member and ask them to confirm whether you're on the right track. Here's a word of caution: Don't become so involved with the software that you're managing the software instead of managing the project. Project management software is a wonderful tool, but it is not a substitute for sound project management practices or experience.

Scheduling Process Outputs

The Develop Schedule process has six outputs:

- Schedule baseline
- Project schedule
- Schedule data
- Project calendars
- Project management plan updates
- Project documents updates

We'll take a look at a few of the outputs of this process next, starting with the project schedule first. Take note that the two primary outputs from this process that will carry forward throughout the rest of the project are the project schedule and the schedule baseline.

 Real World Scenario

Sunny Surgeons, Inc.

Kate Newman is a project manager for Sunny Surgeons, Inc. Sunny Surgeons, Inc. is a software company that produces software for handheld devices for the medical profession. The software allows surgeons to keep notes regarding patients, upcoming surgeries, and ideas about new medicines and techniques to research. Kate's latest project is to write an enhanced version of the patient-tracking program with system integration capabilities to a well-known desktop software product used by the medical industry.

The programming department has had some recent turnover. Fortunately, Stephen, the senior programmer who led the development effort on the original version of the patient tracker, still works for Sunny. His expertise with handheld technologies, as well as his knowledge of the desktop software product, makes him an invaluable resource for this project.

Kate discovered a problem during the development of the project schedule. Stephen is overallocated for three key activities. Kate decides to see what his take is on the situation before deciding what to do.

Stephen, the eternal optimist programmer who loves his job and does all but sleep in his office at night, says he can easily complete all the activities and that Kate shouldn't give it a second thought. He also suggests to Kate that Karen Wong, a junior programmer on his team who worked on the last project with him, might be able to handle the noncritical path task on her own, with a little direction from Stephen.

Kate thinks better of the idea of overallocating her key project resource, even if he does think he can do the entire thing single-handedly. She decides to try some resource leveling to see what turns up.

Kate discovers that rearranging the order of activities, along with assigning Karen to handle the noncritical path activity, might be a possible solution. However, this scenario lengthens the project by a total of eight days. Since Kate knows the primary constraint on this project is quality, she's fairly sure she can get a buy-off from the project sponsor and stakeholders on the later schedule date. She can also sell the resource-leveled schedule as a low-risk option as opposed to assigning Stephen to all the activities and keeping the project end date the same. Overallocating resources can cause burnout and stress-related illnesses, which will ultimately have a negative impact on the project schedule.

Project Schedule

The purpose of the Develop Schedule process is to analyze most of the steps we've talked about so far, including sequencing activities, determining their durations, considering schedule constraints, and analyzing resource requirements. One of the primary outputs of this process is the *project schedule*, which presents the start and finish dates for each of the project activities, the duration of activities, dependencies among activities, milestones, and resources in a project schedule model. Determining resource assignments occurs in the Acquire Project Team process, and depending on the size and complexity of your project or your organization's culture, this process might not be completed yet. If that's the case, the project schedule is considered preliminary until the resources are assigned to the activities.

WARNING

In *PMBOK® Guide* terms, the project schedule is considered preliminary until resources are assigned. In reality, keep in mind that once you've published the project schedule (even though it's in a preliminary state), some stakeholders might regard it as the actual schedule and expect you to keep to the dates shown. Use caution when publishing a schedule in its preliminary form.

The project schedule should be approved by stakeholders and functional managers, who should sign off on it. This assures you that they have read the schedule, understand the dates and resource commitments, and will likely cooperate. You'll also need to obtain confirmation that resources will be available as outlined in the schedule when you're working in a functional organization. The schedule cannot be finalized until you receive approval and commitment for the resource assignments outlined in it.

Once the schedule is approved, it will become your baseline for the remainder of the project. Project progress and task completion will be monitored and tracked against the project schedule to determine whether the project is on course as planned.

Exam Spotlight

For the exam, remember that the project schedule is based on the timeline (derived from the activity estimates we calculated earlier in this chapter), the scope document (to help keep track of major milestones and deliverables), and resource plans. These plans are all used as references when creating the schedule.

According to the *PMBOK® Guide*, the schedule models are called presentations. You can present the schedule in a variety of ways, some of which are variations on what you've already seen. Project schedule network diagrams, like the ones discussed earlier, will work as schedule diagrams when you add the start and finish dates to each activity. These diagrams usually show the activity dependencies and critical path. Figure 4.2 shows a sample portion of a project schedule network diagram highlighting the programming activities.

FIGURE 4.2   Project schedule network diagram with activity dates

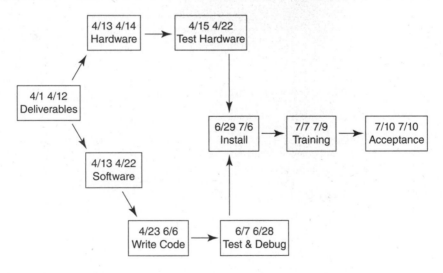

Gantt charts are easy to read and commonly used to display schedule activities. Depending on the software you're using to produce the Gantt chart, it might also show activity sequences, activity start and end dates, resource assignments, activity dependencies, and the critical path. Figure 4.3 is a simple example that plots various activities against time. These activities do not relate to the activities in the tables or other figures shown so far. Gantt charts are also known as *bar charts*.

FIGURE 4.3   Gantt chart

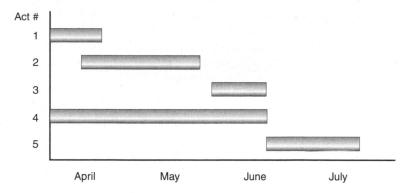

Milestone charts are another way to depict schedule information. Milestones mark the completion of major deliverables or some other key events in the project. For example, approval and sign-off on project deliverables might be considered a milestone. Other examples might be completion of a prototype, system testing, and contract approval.

Milestone charts might show the key events and their start or completion dates in a bar chart form similar to a Gantt chart. Or they can be written in a simple table format with milestones listed in the rows and expected schedule dates in one column and actual completion dates in another, as shown in Table 4.3. As the milestones are met, the Actual Date column is filled in. This information can be included with the project status reports.

TABLE 4.3   Milestone chart

Milestone	Scheduled date	Actual date
Sign-off on deliverables	4/12	4/12
Sign-off on hardware test	4/22	4/25
Programming completed	6/06	
Testing completed	6/28	
Acceptance and sign-off	7/10	
Project closeout	7/10	

Milestone charts are an ideal way to present information to the executive team. They are high level, easy to read, and to the point. Bar charts (or Gantt charts) are great for presenting the schedule to the management level. They have a bit more detail and are a quick way to see at a glance what resources are required when.

Schedule Baseline

The schedule baseline is the final, approved version of the project schedule with baseline start and baseline finish dates and resource assignments. The approved project schedule becomes a part of the project management plan we talked about in Chapter 3 and, once approved, must follow change control procedures if changes are needed.

As I've noted during discussions of some of the other Planning processes, project planning and project management are iterative processes. Rarely is anything cast in cement. You will continue to revisit processes throughout the project to refine and adjust. Eventually, processes do get put to bed. You wouldn't want to return to the Planning process at the conclusion of the project, for example, but keep in mind that the Planning, Executing, and Monitoring and Controlling process groups are iterative, and it's not unusual to have to revise processes within these process groups as you progress on the project.

In practice, for small- to medium-sized projects, you can complete Define Activities, Sequence Activities, Estimate Activity Resources, Estimate Activity Durations, and Develop Schedule at the same time with the aid of a project management software tool. You can produce Gantt charts; you can produce the critical path, resource allocation, activity dependencies; you can perform what-if analysis; and you can produce various reports after plugging your scheduling information into most project management software tools. Regardless of your methods, be certain to obtain sign-off on the project schedule and provide your stakeholders and project sponsor with regular updates. Keep your schedule handy—there will likely be changes and modifications as you go. While you're at it, be certain to save a schedule baseline for comparative purposes. Once you get into the Executing and Monitoring and Controlling processes, you'll be able to compare what you planned to do against what actually happened.

Schedule Data

The schedule data refers to documenting the supporting data for the schedule. The minimum amount of information in this output includes the milestones, schedule activities and activity attributes, and the assumptions and constraints regarding the schedule. You should document any other information that doesn't necessarily fit into the other categories. Always err on the side of too much documentation rather than not enough.

You will have to be the judge of what other information to include here because it will depend on the nature of the project. The *PMBOK® Guide* suggests that you might include schedule contingencies, alternative schedules, and resource histograms. Chapter 7, "Planning Project Resources," contains an example of a resource histogram if you want to peek ahead. Resource histograms typically display hours needed on one axis and period of time (days, weeks, months, years) on the other axis. You might also include alternative schedules or contingency schedule reserves in the schedule data section.

Project Documents Updates

As with many of the other processes you've seen in this chapter, creating the project schedule may require updates to the activity resource requirements document, activity attributes, calendars, and the risk register.

Real World Scenario

Project Case Study: New Kitchen Heaven Retail Store

You worked with the stakeholders to document the activity list last week. After creating the first draft of the project schedule network diagram, you went back to each of them to ask for time estimates for each of the activities. Ricardo's estimates are shown here:

1. Procure the T1 connection. This takes 30 to 45 days. This activity can be done concurrently with the other activities listed here. Ricardo will perform this activity.

2. Run Ethernet cable throughout the building. This activity depends on the lease being signed and must finish before the build-out can start. The estimated time to complete is 16 hours, which was figured using parametric estimating techniques. Ricardo has one person on staff who can complete this specialized activity. His first available date is October 5.

3. Purchase the router, switch, server, and rack for the equipment room and the four point-of-service terminals. Delivery time is two weeks. Ricardo will perform this activity.

4. Install the router and test the connection. Testing depends on the T1 installation at demarcation. The time estimate to install is eight hours. Ricardo's staff will perform this activity.

5. Install the switch. Based on past experience, the time estimate to install is two hours. Ricardo's staff will do this activity.

6. Install the server and test. The testing depends on the T1 connection installation. Based on past experience, the time estimate to install is six hours. Ricardo's staff will do this activity.

7. The web team will add the new store location and phone number to the lookup function on the Internet site. The time estimate is two hours. Ricardo will assign his applications programming manager to this activity. This activity depends on the lease being signed.

Jake and Jill have each written similar lists with estimates and potential resource assignments. You begin to align all the activities in sequential order and discover a problem. Jill needs 14 days to hire personnel and stock shelves, meaning that the build-out must be finished by January 16. Build-out takes approximately 120 days and can't start before September 20 because of the contractor's availability. This is a problem because Ricardo's Ethernet cable expert isn't available until October 5, and he needs 2 days to complete the cabling. This pushes out the build-out start date by almost 2 weeks, which means the project completion date, or store-opening date, is delayed by 2 weeks.

After gathering more information from Ricardo, you head to Dirk's office.

"So, Dirk," you conclude after filling him in on all the details, "we have two options. Hire a contractor to perform the cable run since Ricardo's person isn't available or push the store opening out by two weeks."

Dirk asks, "How much will the contractor charge to run the cable, and are they available within the time frame you need?"

"Yes, they are available, and I've already requested that Ricardo book the week of September 18 to hold this option open for us. They've quoted a price of $10,000."

"Okay, let's bring in the contractor. At this point, $10,000 isn't going to break the budget. How is that planning coming anyway? Signed a lease yet?"

"Yes, we've signed the lease. Jake has been meeting with Gomez construction on the build-out. We've used Gomez on three out of the last five new stores and have had good luck with them."

You spend the next couple of days working on the project schedule in Microsoft Project, clarifying tasks and activities with Jake, Ricardo, and Jill. You decide that a Gantt chart will work excellently for reporting status for this project. You stare intensely at the problem you see on the screen. The Grand Opening task is scheduled to occur 13 days later than when you need it! The grand opening must happen February 1 and 2, not February 14 and 15 as the schedule shows. You trace the problem back and see that the Grand Opening task depends on Train Store Personnel, which itself depends on several other tasks, including Hire Store Personnel and Install and Test Hardware. Digging deeper, build-out can't begin until the Ethernet cable is run throughout the building. Ricardo already set up the time with the contractor to run the cable on September 18. This date cannot move, which means build-out cannot start any sooner than September 20, which works with Gomez's availability.

You pick up the phone and dial Jake's number. "Jake," you say into the receiver, "I'm working on the project schedule, and I have some issues with the Gomez activity."

"Shoot," Jake says.

"Gomez Construction can't start work until the Ethernet cable is run. I've already confirmed with Ricardo that there is no negotiation on this. Ricardo is hiring a contractor for this activity, and the earliest they can start is September 18. It takes them two days to run the cable, which puts the start date for build-out at September 20."

"What's the problem with the September 20 date?" Jake asks

"Jill wants to have the build-out finished prior to hiring the store personnel. During the last store opening, those activities overlapped, and she said it was unmanageable. She wants to hire folks and have them stock the shelves in preparation for store opening but doesn't want contractors in there while they're doing it. A September 20 start date for Gomez puts us at a finish date of January 26, which is too late to give Jill time to hire and stock shelves. My question is this: Is 120 days to finish a build-out a firm estimate?"

"Always—I've got this down to a science. Gomez has worked with me on enough of these build-outs that we can come within just a couple of days of this estimate either way," Jake says.

You pick up your schedule detail and continue, "I've scheduled Gomez's resource calendar as you told me originally. Gomez doesn't work Sundays, and neither do we. Their holidays are Labor Day, a couple of days at Thanksgiving, Christmas, and New Year's, but this puts us too far out on the schedule. Our February 1 opening must coincide with the Home and Garden Show dates."

"I can't change the 120 days. Sounds like you have a problem."

"I need to crash the schedule," you say. "What would the chances be of Gomez agreeing to split the build-out tasks? We could hire a second contractor to come in and work alongside Gomez's crew to speed up this task. That would shorten the duration to 100 days, which means we could meet the February 1 date."

"Won't happen. I know Gomez. They're a big outfit and have all their own crews. We typically work with them exclusively. If I brought another contractor into the picture, I might have a hard time negotiating any kind of favors with them later if we get into a bind."

"All right," you say. "How about this? I'm making some changes to the resource calendar while we're talking. What if we authorize Gomez's crew to work six 10-hour days, which still leaves them with Sundays off, and we ask them to work on Labor Day and take only one day at Thanksgiving instead of two?"

"I think Gomez would go for that. You realize it's going to cost you?"

"Project management is all about trade-offs. We can't move the start date, so chances are the budget might take a hit to accommodate schedule changes or risk. Fortunately, I'm just now wrapping up the final funding requirements, so if you can get me the increased cost from Gomez soon, I'd appreciate it. This change will keep us on track and resolve Jill's issues too."

"I don't think Gomez's crew will mind the overtime during the holiday season. Everyone can use a little extra cash at that time of year, it seems. I'll have the figures for you in a day or two."

Project Case Study Checklist

The main topics discussed in the case study are as follows:

Estimate Activity Durations
Estimate Activity Resources
Developing project schedule
    Calendars
    Lead and lag time
    Critical path
Duration compression
    Crashing
    Fast tracking
Utilizing project management software
Producing project schedule
    Milestones
    Gantt chart
    Resource leveling

Understanding How This Applies to Your Next Project

The schedule management plan documents how you will define, monitor, control, and change the project schedule. It is the only output of the Plan Schedule Management process. Define Activities and Sequence Activities are the first two processes in the "Activity" sequence you'll complete on the road to Develop Schedule. You perform Estimate Activity Resources to determine the resource requirements and quantity of resources needed for each schedule activity. For small- to medium-sized projects, I've found that you can perform this process at the same time as the Estimate Activity Durations process. If you work in an organization where the same resource pool is used for project after project, you already know the people's skills sets and availability, so you can perform this process at the same time you're creating the project schedule. The same logic holds for projects where the material resources are similar for every project you conduct. If you don't have the need to perform this process, I do recommend that you create a resource calendar at a minimum so that you can note whether team members have extended vacations or family issues that could impact the project schedule. Needless to say, if you're working on a large project or your project teams are new for every project, you should perform the Estimate Activity Resources process rather than combining it with Develop Schedule. It will come in handy later when you're ready to plug names into the activities listed on the project schedule.

Estimate Activity Durations is a process you'll perform for most projects on which you'll work. For larger projects, I'm a big fan of PERT estimates. PERT gives you estimates with a high degree of reliability, which are needed for projects that are critical to the organization, projects that haven't been undertaken before, or projects that involve complex processes or scope. It's easy to create a spreadsheet template to automatically calculate these estimates for you. List your schedule activities in each row, and in the individual columns to the right, record the most likely, pessimistic, and optimistic estimates. The final column can hold the calculation to perform the weighted average of these three estimates, and you can transfer the estimates to your schedule. You can easily add columns to calculate standard deviation as well.

In theory, if you've performed all the "Activity" processes, the schedule should almost be a no-brainer. You can plug the activity list, resources, estimates, and successor and predecessor tasks into the schedule. From there, you will want to take the next step and determine the critical path. The critical path is, well, critical to your project's success. If you don't know which activities are on the critical path, you won't know what the impacts that delays or risk events will have on the project. No matter how big or small the project, be sure you know and understand the critical path activities.

Summary

Great job! You've made it through the Planning activities associated with the Project Time Management Knowledge Area. I covered several processes in this chapter, including Plan Schedule Management, Define Activities, Sequence Activities, Estimate Activity Resources, Estimate Activity Durations, and Develop Schedule.

Define Activities uses the scope baseline (which includes the project scope statement, WBS, and WBS dictionary) to help derive activities. Activities are used to help derive a basis for estimating and scheduling project work during the Planning processes and for executing and monitoring and controlling the work of the project in later processes.

The Sequence Activities process takes the activities and puts them in a logical, sequential order based on dependencies. Dependencies exist when the current activity relies on some action from a predecessor activity or it impacts a successor activity. Four types of dependencies exist: mandatory, discretionary, external, and internal. PDM (also known as AON) and ADM (also known as AOA) are two methods for displaying project schedule network diagrams. PDM has four logical relationships, or dependencies: finish-to-start, start-to-finish, finish-to-finish, and start-to-start.

The Estimate Activity Resources process considers all the resources needed and the quantity of resources needed to perform project activities. This information is determined for each activity and is documented in the activity resource requirements output.

Duration estimates are produced as a result of the Estimate Activity Durations process. Activity duration estimates document the number of work periods needed for each activity, including their elapsed time. Analogous estimating—also called *top-down estimating* or gross value estimating—is one way to determine activity duration estimates. You can also use top-down techniques to estimate project durations and total project costs. Parametric estimating techniques multiply a known element—such as the quantity of materials needed—by the time it takes to install or complete one unit of materials. The result is a total estimate for the activity. Three-point estimates use two formulas to calculate estimates including triangular distributions (an average estimate based on the most likely estimate, a pessimistic estimate, and an optimistic estimate) and beta distributions (the PERT formula). Reserve analysis takes schedule risk into consideration by adding a percentage of time or another work period to the estimate just in case you run into trouble.

PERT calculates a weighted average estimate for each activity by using the optimistic, pessimistic, and most likely times. It then determines variances, or standard deviations, to come up with a total project duration within a given confidence range. Work will finish within plus or minus one standard deviation 68.26 percent of the time. Work will finish within plus or minus two standard deviations 95.44 percent of the time.

Develop Schedule is the process in which you assign beginning and ending dates to activities and determine their duration. You might use CPM to accomplish this. CPM calculates early start, early finish, late start, and late finish dates. It also determines float time. All tasks with zero float are critical path tasks. The critical path is the longest path of tasks in the project.

Schedules sometimes need to be compressed to meet promised dates or to shorten the schedule times. Crashing looks at cost and schedule trade-offs. Adding resources to critical path tasks or approving over time are two ways to crash the schedule. Fast tracking involves performing tasks (or phases) in parallel that were originally scheduled to start one after the other. Crashing may change the critical path; fast tracking does not. Fast tracking usually increases project risk. You can use Monte Carlo analysis in the Develop Schedule process to determine multiple, probable project durations.

Resource leveling is used when resources are overallocated and may create changes to the critical path and project end date. Resource smoothing modifies activities within their floats without changing the critical path or project end date.

The project schedule presents the activities in graphical form through the use of project schedule network diagrams with dates, Gantt charts, milestone charts, and project schedule network diagrams.

Exam Essentials

Be able to name the purpose of the Estimate Activity Resources process.   The purpose of Estimate Activity Resources is to determine the types of resources needed (human, equipment, and materials) and in what quantities for each schedule activity within a work package.

Be familiar with the tools and techniques of Estimate Activity Durations.   The tools and techniques of Estimate Activity Durations are expert judgment, analogous estimating, parametric estimating, three-point estimating, group decision-making techniques, and reserve analysis.

Know the difference between analogous estimating and bottom-up estimating.   Analogous estimating is a top-down technique that uses expert judgment and historical information. Bottom-up estimating performs estimates for each work item and rolls them up to a total.

Be able to calculate the critical path.   The critical path includes the activities with durations that add up to the longest path of the project schedule network diagram. Critical path is calculated using the forward pass, backward pass, and float calculations.

Be able to define a critical path task.   A critical path task is a project activity with zero or negative float.

Be able to describe and calculate PERT duration estimates.   This is a weighted average technique that uses three estimates: optimistic, pessimistic, and most likely. The formula is as follows: (optimistic + pessimistic + (4 × most likely)) / 6.

Be able to describe the difference between resource leveling and resource smoothing.   Resource leveling can change the critical path and project end date. Resource smoothing does not change the critical path or project end date.

Be familiar with the duration compression techniques.   The duration compression techniques are crashing and fast tracking.

Be able to describe a critical chain.   The critical chain is the new critical path in a modified schedule that accounts for limited resources and feeding buffers.

Know the key outputs of the Develop Schedule process.   The key outputs are the project schedule and schedule baseline.

Key Terms

Accurately planning a project budget and schedule is one of the most difficult tasks you'll face as a project manager. Know the processes I've discussed and the terms used to identify them in the *PMBOK® Guide*. Here's a list of the schedule planning processes you'll need to be successful:

Plan Schedule Management

Define Activities

Sequence Activities

Estimate Activity Resources

Estimate Activity Durations

Develop Schedule

You've also learned a lot of new key words in this chapter. PMI® has worked hard to develop and define standard project management terms that apply across industries. Here is a list of some of the terms you came across in this chapter:

activity attributes	mandatory dependencies
activity duration estimates	milestone charts
activity list	milestones
activity on arrow (AOA)	parametric estimating
activity on node (AON)	precedence diagramming method (PDM)
analogous estimating	precedence relationships
arrow diagramming method (ADM)	preferential logic
backward pass	preferred logic
bar charts	Program Evaluation and Review Technique (PERT)
buffers	project calendars
contingency reserves	project schedule
crashing	resource breakdown structure (RBS)
critical chain	resource calendars
critical chain method	resource leveling

critical path (CP)

critical path method (CPM)

dependencies

discretionary dependencies

expected value

external dependencies

fast tracking

float time

forward pass

free float (FF)

Gantt charts

hammocks

hard dependencies

hard logic

internal dependencies

lags

leads

logical relationships

resource smoothing

resource-based method

resources

reverse resource allocation scheduling

schedule baseline

schedule compression

schedule management plan

schedule network analysis

simulation

slack time

soft logic

successor activities

three-point estimating

time reserves

top-down estimating

total float (TF)

what-if scenario analysis

Review Questions

You can find the answers to the questions in Appendix A.

1. You are the project manager for Changing Tides video games. You have gathered the inputs for the Estimate Activity Durations process. Which of the following tools and techniques will you employ to produce the outputs for this process?

    A. Activity list, expert judgment, alternatives analysis, analogous estimating, parametric estimating, three-point estimating, and reserve analysis

    B. Activity list, expert judgment, analogous estimating, parametric estimating, group decision-making techniques, and three-point estimating

    C. Expert judgment, analogous estimating, parametric estimating, three-point estimating, group decision-making techniques, and reserve analysis

    D. Expert judgment, alternatives analysis, analogous estimating, parametric estimating, three-point estimating, and group decision-making techniques

2. You are the project manager for Changing Tides video games. You have produced a project schedule network diagram and have updated the activity list. Which process have you just finished?

    A. The Define Activities process, which identifies all the specific activities of the project

    B. The Sequence Activities process, which identifies all the activity dependencies

    C. The Develop Schedule process, which diagrams project network time estimates

    D. The Estimate Activity Durations process, which estimates activity durations

3. Your project's primary constraint is quality. To make certain the project team members don't feel too pressed for time and to avoid schedule risk, you decide to use which of the following activity estimating tools?

    A. Three-point estimates

    B. Analogous estimating

    C. Reserve analysis

    D. Parametric estimating

4. You have been hired as a contract project manager for Grapevine Vineyards. Grapevine wants you to design an Internet wine club for its customers. One of the activities for this project is the installation and testing of several new servers. You know from past experience it takes about 16 hours per server to accomplish this task. Since you're installing 10 new servers, you estimate this activity to take 160 hours. Which of the estimating techniques have you used?

    A. Parametric estimating

    B. Analogous estimating

    C. Bottom-up estimating

    D. Reserve analysis

5. All of the following statements describe the activity list except which one?

   A. The activity list is an output of the Define Activities process.

   B. The activity list includes all activities of the project.

   C. The activity list is an extension of and a component of the WBS.

   D. The activity list includes an identifier and description of the activity.

6. You have been hired as a contract project manager for Grapevine Vineyards. Grapevine wants you to design an Internet wine club for its customers. Customers must register before being allowed to order wine over the Internet so that legal age can be established. You know that the module to verify registration must be written and tested using data from Grapevine's existing database. This new module cannot be tested until the data from the existing system is loaded. This is an example of which of the following?

   A. Preferential logic

   B. Soft logic

   C. Discretionary dependency

   D. Hard logic

7. You are the project manager for Design Your Web Site, Inc. Your company is designing the website for a national grocery store chain. You have your activity list in hand and are ready to diagram the activity dependencies using the PDM technique. Which of the following statements is true?

   A. PDM is also the AON diagramming method and it uses one time estimate.

   B. PDM is also the AOA diagramming method and uses logical relationships.

   C. PDM is also the ADM diagramming method and its most common logical relationship is finish-to-start.

   D. PDM is also the GERT method, which allows for conditions, branches, and loops.

8. You are working on a project that requires resources with expertise in the areas of hospitality management and entertainment. You are preparing your project schedule network diagram and know that you will use only finish-to-start dependencies. Which of the following diagramming methods does this describe?

   A. PDM

   B. ADM

   C. AON

   D. Network template

9. Which logical relationship does the PDM use most often?

   A. Start-to-finish

   B. Start-to-start

   C. Finish-to-finish

   D. Finish-to-start

10. You are a project manager for Picture Shades, Inc. Your company manufactures window shades that have replicas of Renaissance-era paintings for hotel chains. Picture Shades is taking its product to the home market, and you're managing the new project. It will offer its products at retail stores as well as on its website. You're developing the project schedule for this undertaking and have determined the critical path. Which of the following statements is true?

   A. You calculated the most likely start date and most likely finish dates, float time, and weighted average estimates.

   B. You calculated the activity dependency and the optimistic and pessimistic activity duration estimates.

   C. You calculated the early and late start dates, the early and late finish dates, and float times for all activities.

   D. You calculated the optimistic, pessimistic, and most likely duration times, and the float times for all activities.

11. You are a project manager for Picture Shades, Inc. Your company manufactures window shades that have replicas of Renaissance-era paintings for hotel chains. Picture Shades is taking its product to the home market, and you're managing the new project. It will offer its products at retail stores as well as on its website. You're developing the project schedule for this undertaking. Looking at the following graph, which path is the critical path?

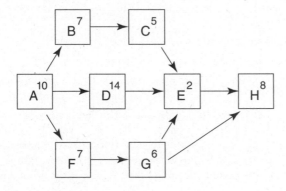

   A. A-B-C-E-H

   B. A-D-E-H

   C. A-F-G-H

   D. A-F-G-E-H

12. Use the following graphic to answer this question. If the duration of activity B was changed to 10 days and the duration of activity G was changed to 9 days, which path is the critical path?

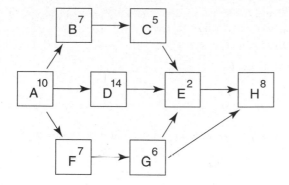

A. A-B-C-E-H
B. A-D-E-H
C. A-F-G-H
D. A-F-G-E-H

13. Which of the following statements is true regarding the critical path?
   A. It should not be compressed.
   B. It allows for looping and branching.
   C. The critical path technique is the same as PERT.
   D. It's the duration of all tasks with zero or negative float.

14. You are a project manager for Move It Now trucking company. Your company specializes in moving household goods across the city or across the country. Your project involves upgrading the nationwide computer network for the company. Your lead engineer has given you the following estimates for a critical path activity: 60 days most likely, 72 days pessimistic, 48 days optimistic. What is the weighted average or expected value?
   A. 54
   B. 66
   C. 60
   D. 30

15. You are a project manager for Move It Now trucking company. Your company specializes in moving household goods across the city or across the country. Your project involves upgrading the nationwide computer network for the company. Your lead engineer has given you the following estimates for a critical path activity: 60 days most likely, 72 days pessimistic, 48 days optimistic. What is the standard deviation?
   A. 22
   B. 20
   C. 2
   D. 4

16. If you know the expected value is 500 and the standard deviation is 12, you can say with approximately a 95 percent confidence rating which of the following?

    A. The activity will take from 488 to 512 days.

    B. The activity will take from 464 to 536 days.

    C. The activity will take from 494 to 506 days.

    D. The activity will take from 476 to 524 days.

17. If your expected value is 110 and the standard deviation is 12, which of the following is true?

    A. There is approximately a 99 percent chance of completing this activity in 86 to 134 days.

    B. There is approximately a 68 percent chance of completing this activity in 98 to 122 days.

    C. There is approximately a 95 percent chance of completing this activity in 98 to 122 days.

    D. There is approximately a 75 percent chance of completing this activity in 86 to 134 days.

18. You are the project manager working on a research project for a new drug treatment. Your preliminary project schedule runs past the due date for a federal grant application. The manager of the R&D department has agreed to release two resources to work on your project to meet the federal grant application date. This is an example of _____.

    A. crashing

    B. fast tracking

    C. resource leveling

    D. adjusting the resource calendar

19. You are the project manager for Rivera Gourmet Adventure Vacations. Rivera combines the wonderful tastes of great gourmet food with outdoor adventure activities. Your project involves installing a new human resources software system. Your stakeholders understand this is a large undertaking and that you might experience some schedule slippage. Jason, the database analyst working on this project, is overallocated. He is critical to the success of the project and you don't want to burn him out by overscheduling him. Which of the following actions should you take?

    A. You should use fast tracking to smooth out resource overallocation.

    B. You should use crashing to resource level the critical path tasks.

    C. You should use resource leveling to balance out resource assignments.

    D. You should use resource smoothing to smooth out resource assignments.

20. What is one of the problems with project management software?

    A. The project manager manages the software instead of the project.

    B. Project duration calculations are sometimes approximate.

    C. You cannot override the project management software decisions regarding schedules.

    D. It's expensive and difficult to use.

Chapter

5

Developing the Project Budget and Communicating the Plan

THE PMP® EXAM CONTENT FROM PLANNING THE PROJECT PERFORMANCE DOMAIN COVERED IN THIS CHAPTER INCLUDES THE FOLLOWING:

✓ Develop a project budget based on the project scope using estimating techniques in order to manage project cost.

✓ Develop a communication plan based on the project organization structure and external stakeholder requirements in order to manage the flow of project information.

✓ Communicate project status to stakeholders for their feedback, in order to ensure the project aligns with business needs.

✓ Create a stakeholder management plan to document needs, interests, and impacts of stakeholders.

✓ Knowledge and Skills:

  ▪ Requirements gathering techniques

  ▪ Work breakdown structure (WBS) tools and techniques

  ▪ Time, budget, and cost estimation techniques

  ▪ Elements, purpose, and techniques of project planning

  ▪ Elements, purpose, and techniques of communications planning

Two of the most important documents you'll prepare for any project are the project schedule and the project budget. You'll use the schedule and budget documents throughout the Executing and Monitoring and Controlling processes to measure progress and determine if the project is on track. I believe the budget is easier to prepare after the activities have been defined and the resource estimates calculated. So now that we have the schedule in hand, we're going to spend our time in this chapter developing the budget.

There are three processes we'll perform that will lead us to the cost baseline output. The cost baseline is the authorized budget. The processes are Plan Cost Management, Estimate Costs, and Determine Budget. There are several tools and techniques to cover in these processes that you'll want to understand for the exam. Before we get into the details of the Estimate Costs and Determine Budget processes, we'll talk about the cost management plan and its importance in guiding the development of the budget.

Next, we'll talk about the stakeholder management plan, which documents stakeholder interests, needs, and their potential impacts to the project. We'll wrap up the chapter discussing how project information is documented and communicated. I've talked a lot about documentation so far, and I will discuss it more in this chapter. Documentation is something you will do throughout the remainder of the project, and the Plan Communications Management process details how to collect information, how to store it, and when and how to distribute it to stakeholders.

The process names, inputs, tools and techniques, outputs, and descriptions of the project management process groups and related materials and figures in this chapter are based on content from *A Guide to the Project Management Body of Knowledge (PMBOK® Guide), Fifth Edition* (Sybex, 2010).

Creating the Project Cost Management Plan

You now have an exhaustive breakdown of project activities, and you have some pretty good duration estimates. Now here's the question that's forever on the mind of the executive management staff: How much is it going to cost? The purpose of the Estimate Costs process is to answer that question.

Every project has a budget, and part of completing a project successfully is completing it within the approved budget. Sometimes project managers are not responsible for the budget portion of the project. Instead, this function is assigned to a functional manager who is responsible for tracking and reporting all the project costs. I believe project managers will have more and more responsibility in this area as the project management discipline evolves. Keep in mind that if you, as the project manager, don't have responsibility for the project budget, your performance evaluation for the project should not include budget or cost measurements.

Before diving into the Estimate Costs and Determine Budget process particulars, you should know that these processes are governed by a cost management plan that is created when you perform the *Plan Cost Management* process. You should know a couple of facts about this process and the plan for the exam.

Performing Plan Cost Management

The purpose of the Plan Cost Management process is to produce the cost management plan, and we will look at that in detail in the next section. Stakeholders are almost always concerned about costs. And remember that each of them, or the departments they represent, may have a different perspective on the costs of the project, including accounting for costs at different times in the project and in differing ways.

Let's take a quick look at the inputs and tools and techniques of this process.

This process has four inputs: project management plan, project charter, enterprise environmental factors, and organizational process assets. The two components of the project management plan that can impact project costs are the scope baseline and the schedule baseline, so be certain they are accurate and kept up-to-date.

The tools and techniques of the Plan Cost Management process are expert judgment, analytical techniques, and meetings. Analytical techniques include methods of funding (funding with debt, equity, or a project that is self-funded), whether items should be leased or purchased, and the same techniques we discussed in Chapter 2, "Creating the Project Charter," such as payback period, ROI, IRR, discounted cash flows, and net present value.

Creating the Cost Management Plan

The only output of this process is the cost management plan. The *cost management plan* establishes the policies and procedures you'll use to plan and execute project costs. It also documents how you will estimate, manage, and control project costs. Like all the other management plans, the cost management plan is a subsidiary of the project management plan.

According to the *PMBOK® Guide*, this plan includes, but is not limited to, the following elements:

Level of Accuracy   This refers to the precision level you'll use to round activity estimates— for example, hundreds, thousands, and so on. Level of accuracy is based on the scope and complexity of the activities and the project itself. It also describes the acceptable ranges for establishing cost estimates (for example, plus or minus 5 percent).

Units of Measure This refers to the unit of measure you'll use to estimate resources—for example, hours, days, weeks, or a lump sum amount.

Organizational Procedures Links In Chapter 3, "Developing the Project Scope Statement," we talked about the WBS and the identifiers associated with each component of the WBS. These identifiers are called the code of accounts. A *control account (CA)* is a point where several factors such as actual cost, schedule, and scope can be used to determine earned value performance measures. (We'll talk more about earned value in Chapter 10, "Measuring and Controlling Project Performance.") The control account is used in the Project Cost Management Knowledge Area to monitor and control project costs. The control account is typically associated with the work package level of the WBS, but control accounts could be established at any level of the WBS. The control account also has a unique identifier that's linked to the organization's accounting system, sometimes known as a *chart of accounts.*

> **Exam Spotlight**
>
> The cost management plan is established using the WBS and its associated control accounts.

Control Thresholds Most actual project costs do not match the estimate exactly. The control threshold refers to the amount of variance the sponsor or stakeholders are willing to allow before action is required. Document the threshold amount as a percentage of deviation allowed from the cost baseline.

Rules of Performance Measurement This component of the cost management plan refers to how you will set the earned value management measurements. It's here you'll document where the control accounts exist within the WBS, the earned value management (EVM) techniques you'll use to measure performance, and the equations you'll use for calculating estimate at completion forecasts and other measurements. We'll talk about EVM and estimate at completion forecasts in detail in Chapter 10.

Reporting Formats This refers to the types of cost reports you'll produce for this project and how often they'll be created.

Process Descriptions This describes the Estimate Cost, Determine Budget, and Control Costs processes and how you'll use these processes to manage project cost.

Additional Details This refers to any other information you might want to capture regarding cost activities, including items such as who will perform the cost activities, how a cost is recorded, and a description of the funding alternatives and choices used for the project.

The key to determining accurate cost estimates (and accurate time estimates as we discovered in Chapter 4, "Creating the Project Schedule") is the work breakdown structure (WBS). Next, we'll look at how to determine cost estimates for the WBS components.

Estimating Costs

The *Estimate Costs* process develops a cost estimate for the resources (human and material) required for each schedule activity. This includes weighing alternative options and examining risks and trade-offs. Some alternatives you may consider are make-versus-buy, buy-versus-lease, and sharing of resources across either projects or departments.

Let's look at an example of trade-offs. Many times software development projects take on a life of their own. The requested project completion dates are unrealistic; however, the project team commits to completing the project on time and on budget anyway. How do they do this? They do this by cutting things such as design, analysis, and documentation. In the end, the project might get completed on time and on budget, but was it really? The costs associated with the extended support period because of a lack of design and documentation and the hours needed by the software programmers to fix the reported bugs weren't included in the original cost of the project (but they should have been). Therefore, the costs actually exceed what was budgeted. You should examine trade-offs such as these when determining cost estimates.

When you are determining cost estimates, be certain to include all the costs required to complete the work of the project over its entire life cycle. Additionally, the project team should take into consideration the costs of ongoing support or recurring costs such as maintenance, support, and service costs after the project is complete. As in the preceding example, software projects often have warranty periods that guarantee bug fixes or problem resolution within a certain time frame. After the warranty period expires, you move into the yearly maintenance and support period. These costs are typically calculated as a percentage of the total software cost. The management team should be made aware that these costs will continue to recur for the length of time you own the software. It's also good practice to understand these costs prior to making go/no-go project decisions.

Don't confuse pricing with Estimate Costs. If you are working for a company that performs consulting services on contract, for example, the price you will charge for your services is not the same as the costs to perform the project. The costs are centered on the resources needed to produce the product, service, or result of the project. The price your company might charge for the service includes not only these costs but a profit margin as well.

Estimate Costs Inputs

Many of the inputs of the Estimate Costs process are already familiar to you. We talked about the cost management plan earlier in this chapter. We'll look briefly at the other inputs next so you can see the key elements that should be considered when creating the project budget. The inputs to this process are as follows:

- Cost management plan
- Human resource management plan

- Scope baseline
- Project schedule
- Risk register
- Enterprise environmental factors
- Organizational process assets

Human Resource Management Plan

We will look more closely at the human resource management plan (an output of the Plan Human Resource Management process) in Chapter 7, "Planning Project Resources." For the purposes of the Estimate Costs process, understand that the human resource management plan includes elements such as personnel rates, project staffing attributes, and employee recognition or rewards programs. All of these elements should be considered when determining cost estimates.

Scope Baseline

It's pop quiz time. Do you remember the elements of the scope baseline? They are the project scope statement, the WBS, and the WBS dictionary. You'll want to consider a few key elements from the project scope statement in this process, including key deliverables, constraints, assumptions, and acceptance criteria. I can safely say that every project I've ever worked on had a limited budget, which is a classic example of a project constraint. You should also understand other constraints that have the potential to impact costs, such as required delivery dates or availability of resources. Project assumptions regarding costs might include whether to include indirect costs in the project estimate. We'll talk more about this in the "Determine Budget Inputs" section later in this chapter.

The WBS, as we've discussed, serves as the basis for estimating costs. It contains all the project deliverables and the control accounts that are typically established at the work package level (but can be assigned to any level of the WBS). The WBS dictionary describes the deliverables, work components, and other elements of the WBS.

When you're considering deliverables, think about those that may have contractual obligations that should be considered when determining cost estimates. Perhaps you have deliverables that have legal or governmental regulations that will require additional expenses to fulfill. Health, safety, security, licenses, performance, intellectual property rights, and environmental factors are some of the other elements of the scope baseline you should consider when estimating costs, according to the *PMBOK® Guide*.

Exam Spotlight

Scope definition is a key component of determining the estimated costs and should be completed as early in the project as possible because it's easier to influence costs in the beginning phases of the project. But you can't influence costs if you don't understand the project scope.

Project Schedule

We determined the types and quantities of resources we needed in Chapter 4 using the Estimate Activity Resources (this process is closely associated with the Estimate Costs process, according to the *PMBOK® Guide*) and Estimate Activity Durations processes. Activity resource requirements and activity duration estimates are the key outputs you should consider when estimating costs.

Be aware that activity duration estimates can affect costs. For example, you must account for costs such as interest charges when you're financing the work of the project. Also consider fluctuations in costs that can occur due to seasonal or holiday demands or collective bargaining agreements. Watch for duration estimates that are calculated for resources who are scheduled to work for a per-unit period of time. These duration estimates can be incorrect (not too far off, you hope) and can end up costing you more. For example, I recently bought a new home requiring a move of about eight miles. The moving company told me that the work was performed on a per-hour basis. The person providing the estimate assured me he had been doing this for over 25 years and his estimates were typically right on the money. Unfortunately, I swallowed that line and the estimate I was given was wildly incorrect. It took them almost twice the amount of time I was quoted, and you guessed it, the total ended up being almost twice the original estimate.

Risk Register

The risk register is an output of the Identify Risks process that we'll discuss in Chapter 6, "Risk Planning." When developing project cost estimates you should consider the cost of implementing risk response plans (identified in the risk register), particularly those with negative impacts to the project. Generally, negative risk events that occur early in the project are more costly than those that occur later in the project.

Enterprise Environmental Factors

According to the *PMBOK® Guide*, the enterprise environmental factors you should consider in this process are market conditions and published commercial information. Market conditions help you understand the materials, goods, and services available in the market and what terms and conditions exist to procure those resources. Published commercial information refers to resource cost rates. You can obtain these rates from commercial databases or published seller price lists.

Organizational Process Assets

The organizational process assets considered in the process are similar to those we've seen before. Historical information and lessons learned on previous projects of similar scope and complexity can be useful in determining estimates for the current project—particularly if the past projects occurred recently. Your organization's business office or PMO may also have cost estimating templates you can use to help with this process. You could use cost-estimating worksheets from past projects as templates for the current project as well.

Tools and Techniques to Estimate Costs

The Estimate Costs process has 10 tools and techniques used to derive estimates:

- Expert judgment
- Analogous estimating
- Parametric estimating
- Bottom-up estimating
- Three-point estimating
- Reserve analysis
- Cost of quality
- Project management software
- Vendor bid analysis
- Group decision-making techniques

I covered analogous estimating, parametric estimating, three-point estimating, reserve analysis, and group decision-making techniques in Chapter 4. The majority of these are also tools and techniques of the Estimate Activity Durations process used to help determine schedule estimates. All of the information we discussed in Chapter 4 applies here as well, except you're using the tools and techniques to derive cost estimates. Three-point estimates (either triangular distribution, a simple averaging or weighted averaging, and beta distribution [PERT] formulas) are used in this process when you want to improve your estimates and account for risk and estimation uncertainty. In the case of reserve analysis, you're adding cost reserves (or contingencies), not schedule reserves, during this process. Contingency reserves, like schedule reserves, might be calculated for the whole project, one or more activities, or both and may be calculated as a percentage of the cost or as a fixed amount. Contingency reserves are used for known-unknown risk or issues that may impact the project. The risk is known but the consequences are unknown. And as with the schedule reserve, you should add contingency reserves to the cost baseline but should not add management reserves to the cost baseline. Management reserves are considered a part of the project budget. You could aggregate these cost contingencies and assign them to a schedule activity or a WBS work package level. As more information becomes known further into the project, you may be able to reduce the contingency reserves, turn them back to the organization, or eliminate them altogether.

The project management software tool can help you quickly determine estimates given different variables and alternatives. Some systems are quite sophisticated and use simulation and statistical techniques to determine estimates, whereas others are less complex. A simple spreadsheet program can do the trick much of the time. We'll look at the remaining tools and techniques next.

Bottom-Up Estimating

You learned about this technique in Chapter 4, but there are a few pointers to consider for this process. This technique estimates costs associated with every activity individually and then rolls them up to derive a total project cost estimate. You wouldn't choose this technique to provide a cost estimate for the project during Initiating if one were requested because you don't have enough information at that stage to use it. Instead, use the top-down estimating technique (analogous estimating) when a project cost estimate is needed early in the project selection stage. Bottom-up estimating will generally provide you with the most accurate cost estimates, but it is the most time-consuming estimating technique of all those mentioned here. However, the size and complexity of the project impacts the accuracy you can achieve using this technique.

Cost of Quality

The *cost of quality (COQ)* is the total cost to produce the product or service of the project according to the quality standards. Cost of quality is a topic that we will cover when we look at the quality topics in more depth. For this process, understand that quality is not free and you will need to include cost of quality estimates in your final project budget.

Vendor Bid Analysis

As the name implies, this is a process of gathering information from vendors to help you establish cost estimates. You can accomplish this by requesting bids or quotes or working with some of your trusted vendor sources for estimates. You should compare vendor bids when using this tool and technique and not rely solely on one vendor to provide you with estimates.

Estimate Costs Process Outputs

The primary output of the Estimate Costs process is activity cost estimates. These are quantitative amounts—usually stated in monetary units—that reflect the cost of the resources needed to complete the project activities. The tools and techniques I just described help you derive these estimates. Resources in this case include human resources, material, equipment, services, information technology needs, facilities, leases, rentals, exchange rates (if it applies), financing and/or interest costs (if it applies), and so on, as well as any contingency reserve amounts and inflation factors (if you're using them).

Estimates should be updated throughout the course of the project as more information comes to light. Estimates are performed at a given period of time with a limited amount of information. As more information becomes available, your cost estimates, and therefore your overall project estimate, will become more accurate over time and should be updated to reflect this new information. According to the *PMBOK® Guide,* the accuracy of estimates during the Initiating phase of a project have a rough order of magnitude (ROM) of –25% to +75%, and as more information becomes available over the course of the project, the definitive estimate moves to a range of –5% to +10%.

The remaining outputs of the Estimate Costs process are the basis of estimates and project documents updates. The *basis of estimates* is the supporting detail for the activity cost estimates and includes any information that describes how the estimates were developed, what assumptions were made during the Estimate Costs process, and any other details you think are needed. According to the *PMBOK® Guide*, the basis of estimates should include at least the following:

- A description of how the estimate was developed or the basis for the estimate.
- A description of the assumptions made about the estimates or the method used to determine them.
- A description of the constraints.
- A range of possible results. You should state the cost estimates within ranges such as: $5,000 ± 10%.
- The confidence level regarding the final estimates.

 Real World Scenario

This Older House

Janie is an accomplished project manager. She and her husband recently purchased an 80-year-old home in need of several repairs and modern updates. She decided to put her project management skills to work on the house project. First, they hired a general contractor to oversee all the individual projects needed to bring the house up-to-date. Janie worked with the general contractor to construct a WBS, and she ended up with 23 work packages. With each work package (or multiple work packages in some cases) assigned to a subcontractor, it was easy to track who was responsible for completing the work and for determining duration estimates. Janie and the general contractor worked together to determine schedule dependencies and make certain the work was performed in the correct order and that each subcontractor knew when their activity was to begin and end.

Some of the cost estimates for certain work packages were easy to determine using the parametric estimating method. Others required expert judgment and the experience of the general contractor (analogous techniques) to determine a cost estimate. Resource rates for laborers for some of the work packages were agreed to when the subcontractors bid on the work. Once Janie had all the cost estimates, she used the bottom-up estimating technique to come up with an overall cost estimate for the project. She added a contingency reserve in addition to the overall estimate for unforeseen risk events.

The last output of this process is project documents updates. Cost variances will occur and estimates will be refined as you get further into your project. As a result, you'll update cost estimates and ultimately the project budget to reflect these changes. The risk register may also require an update after cost estimates are complete.

Estimate Costs uses several techniques to make an accurate assessment of the project costs. In practice, using a combination of techniques is your best bet to come up with the most reliable cost estimates. The activity cost estimates will become an input to the Determine Budget process, which allows you to establish a baseline for project costs to track against.

Establishing the Cost Baseline

The next process involves determining the authorized cost baseline, which is the primary output of the Determine Budget process. The *Determine Budget* process aggregates the cost estimates of activities and establishes a cost baseline for the project that is used to measure performance of the project throughout the remaining process groups. Only the costs associated with the project become part of the authorized project budget. For example, future period operating costs are not project costs and therefore aren't included in the project budget.

The *cost baseline* is the total expected cost for the project. According to the *PMBOK® Guide,* the cost baseline is a time-phased budget, and it must be approved by the project sponsor (and key stakeholders if appropriate for your project). As we discussed earlier, the cost baseline does not include management reserves. And if the cost baseline is not approved, it is not valid. When you're using earned value management techniques to measure project performance, the cost baseline is also known as the performance measurement baseline (PMB). We'll talk about budget at completion and earned value management techniques in detail in Chapter 11, "Controlling Work Results." Remember that costs are tied to the financial system through the chart of accounts—or code of accounts—and are assigned to project activities at the work package level or to control accounts at various points in the WBS. The budget will be used as a plan for allocating costs to project activities.

 As we've discussed with several other processes, in practice you can sometimes perform the Estimate Costs and Determine Budget processes at the same time.

Determine Budget Inputs

Outputs from other Planning processes, including the Create WBS, Develop Schedule, and Estimate Costs processes, must be completed prior to working on Determine Budget because some of their outputs become the inputs to this process. The inputs for Determine Budget are as follows:

Cost Management Plan The cost management plan documents how the project costs will be developed, managed, and controlled throughout the project.

Scope Baseline Scope baseline includes the project scope statement, WBS, and WBS dictionary. The scope statement describes the constraints of the project you should consider when developing the budget. The WBS shows how the project deliverables are related to their components, and the work package level typically contains control account information (although control accounts can be assigned at any level of the WBS).

Activity Cost Estimates These are an output of the Estimate Costs process. Activity cost estimates are determined for each activity within a work package and then summed to determine the total estimate for a work package.

Basis of Estimates This is also an output of the Estimate Costs process and contains all the supporting detail regarding the estimates. You should consider assumptions regarding indirect costs and whether they will be included in the project budget. Indirect costs cannot be directly linked to any one project. They are allocated among several projects, usually within the department or division in which the project is being performed. Indirect costs can include items like building leases, management and administrative salaries (those not directly assigned full time to a specific project), and so on.

Project Schedule The schedule contains information that is helpful in developing the budget, such as start and end dates for activities, milestones, and so on. Based on the information in the schedule, you can determine budget expenditures for calendar periods.

Resource Calendars Resource calendars help you determine costs in calendar periods and over the length of the project because they describe what resources are needed when on the project.

Risk Register The risk register contains a list of risks that could occur on the project. Risks with a high impact and/or high probability of occurring will likely have response plans that could add costs to the project, so you should review them before preparing the budget.

Agreements   Agreements include cost information for purchased goods or services that you should include in the overall project budget.

Organizational Process Assets   The organizational process assets that will assist you with the work of this process include cost budgeting tools, the policies and procedures your organization (or PMO) may have regarding budgeting exercises, and reporting methods.

Determine Budget Tools and Techniques

The Determine Budget process has five tools and techniques, including two you haven't seen before:

- Cost aggregation
- Reserve analysis
- Expert judgment
- Historical relationships
- Funding limit reconciliation

I've covered expert judgment previously. Let's look at the remaining tools and techniques.

Cost Aggregation   Cost aggregation is the process of tallying the schedule activity cost estimates at the work package level and then totaling the work package levels to higher-level WBS component levels (such as the control accounts). Then all of the costs can be aggregated to obtain a total project cost.

Reserve Analysis   We talked about reserve analysis in the Estimate Cost section of this chapter. Reserve analysis works the same for the Determine Budget process. Contingency costs are considered and included in the aggregation of control accounts for both activity cost estimates and work package estimates. Management reserves are not included as part of the cost baseline (an output of this process) but should be included in the project budget. Management reserves are also not considered when calculating earned value measurements.

Reserve analysis should also contain appropriations for risk responses. I'll talk about several categories and tools of Plan Risk Responses in Chapter 6. Additionally, you'll want to set aside money for management reserves for unknown risks. This is for the unforeseen, unplanned risks that might occur. Even with all the time and effort you spend on planning, unexpected issues do crop up. It's better to have the money set aside and not need it than to need it and not have it.

Historical Relationships   Analogous estimates and parametric estimates can be used to help determine total project costs. Remember from Chapter 4 that analogous estimates are a form of expert judgment. Actual costs from previous projects of similar size, scope, and complexity are used to estimate the costs for the current project. This is helpful when detailed information about the project is not available or it's early in the project phases and not much information is known.

Parametric estimates are quantitatively based and, for example, multiply the amount of time needed to perform an activity by the resource rate to determine total cost. Quantifiable measures used with the parametric method are easily defined and are easily scalable from large to small projects. Analogous and parametric estimating techniques are more accurate when the historical data you're using is accurate.

Funding Limit Reconciliation   Funding limit reconciliation involves reconciling the amount of funds to be spent with the amount of funds budgeted for the project. The organization or the customer sets these limits. Reconciling the project expenses will require adjusting the schedule so that the expenses can be smoothed. You do this by placing imposed date constraints (I talked about these in the Develop Schedule process in Chapter 4) on work packages or other WBS components in the project schedule.

Determine Budget Process Outputs

The goal of Determine Budget is to develop a cost baseline (an output of this process) for the project that you can use in the Executing and Monitoring and Controlling processes to measure performance. You now have all the information you need to create the cost baseline. In addition, you'll establish the project funding requirements.

The following are the outputs of the Determine Budget process:

- Cost baseline
- Project funding requirements
- Project documents updates

We've covered the project documents updates in other processes. For Determine Budget, you may need to update the risk register, cost estimates, and/or the project schedule. Let's look at the other two outputs next.

Documenting the Cost Baseline

You develop the cost baseline, the first output of Determine Budget, by aggregating the costs of the WBS work packages, including contingency reserves, into control accounts. All the control accounts are then aggregated and together, they make up the cost baseline. Most projects span some length of time, and most organizations time the release of funding with the project. In other words, you won't get all the funds for the project at the beginning of the project; they'll likely be disbursed over time. The cost baseline provides the basis for measurement, over time, of the expected cash flows (or funding disbursements) against the requirements, including contingency reserves. This is also known as the project's *time-phased budget.*

The project budget consists of several components: the activity costs plus contingency reserves (these are aggregated to the work package level), the work package costs plus contingency reserves (these are aggregated to the control accounts), and the management reserves for the cost baseline. Figure 5.1 depicts all of the elements contained in the project budget.

FIGURE 5.1   Project budget

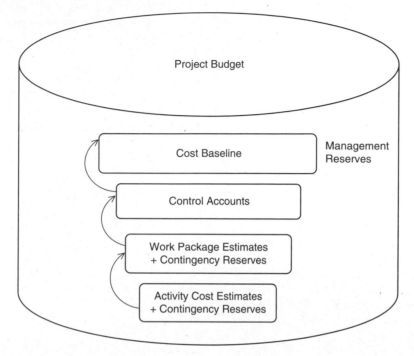

Cost baselines can be displayed graphically, with time increments on one axis and dollars expended on the other axis, as shown in Figure 5.2. The costs shown on this graph are cumulative costs, meaning that what you spent this period is added to what was spent last period and then charted. Many variations of this graph exist showing dollars budgeted against dollars expended to date and so on. Cost budgets can be displayed using this type of graph as well, by plotting the sum of the estimated costs excepted per period.

FIGURE 5.2   Cost baseline

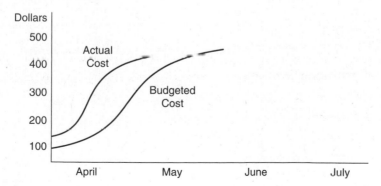

The cost baseline should contain the costs for all of the expected work on the project. You would have identified these costs in the Estimate Costs process. You'll find most projects' largest expense is resource costs (as in labor costs). In the case of projects where you're purchasing the final product, the purchase price is the largest cost.

Exam Spotlight

For the exam, remember that cost baselines are displayed as an S curve. The reason for this is that project spending starts out slowly, gradually increases over the project's life until it reaches a peak, and then tapers off again as the project wraps up. Large projects are difficult to graph in this manner because the timescale isn't wide enough to accurately show fluctuations in spending. Also remember the cost baseline does *not* include management reserves but the project budget does include them.

 Large projects might have more than one cost baseline. For example, you might be required to track human resources costs, material costs, and contractor costs separately.

You'll revisit the cost baseline when you learn about the Cost Control process and examine different ways to measure costs in Chapter 10.

Gathering the Project Funding Requirements

Project funding requirements describe the need for funding over the course of the project, and they are derived from the cost baseline. Funding for a project is not usually released all at once. Some organizations may release funds monthly, quarterly, or in annual increments or other increments that are appropriate for your project.

As I said earlier, spending usually starts out slowly on the project and picks up speed as you progress. Sometimes, the expected cash flows don't match the pace of spending. Project funding requirements account for this by releasing funds in increments based on the cost baseline plus management reserves that may be needed for unanticipated events. Figure 5.3 shows the cost baseline, the funding requirements, and the actual expenses plotted on the S curve. You can see in this figure that actual costs have exceeded the authorized cost baseline. The difference between the funding requirements and the cost baseline at the end of the project is the management reserve.

FIGURE 5.3   Cost baseline, funding requirements, and cash flow

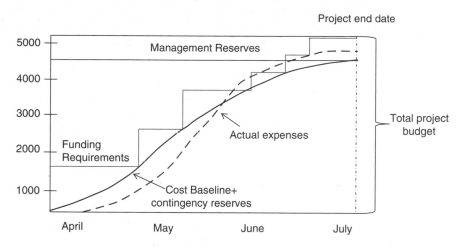

We've now completed two critical components of the project management plan: the project schedule and the project budget. Several times throughout the book I've mentioned the need for documenting, publishing, and communicating project information. As you can imagine, the *PMBOK® Guide* has a process for communications. We'll discuss it next.

Understanding Stakeholders

The *Plan Stakeholder Management* process (a part of the Project Stakeholder Management Knowledge Area) focuses on effectively engaging stakeholders, understanding their needs and interests, understanding the good and bad things they might bring to the project, and how the project will impact them. The primary output of this process is the stakeholder management plan, which documents all of the items I just mentioned.

Stakeholder management is almost a full-time job. Stakeholders are a diverse group with their own personalities, interests, expectations, and more. It is critical to the success of the project that you, as the project manager, understand all of the key stakeholders' needs and devise a plan to engage them in the project, and manage their expectations. In my experience, the most successful projects are those where the key stakeholders and I have established a strong, professional relationship. That means we trust each other, are able to ask questions, and can discuss constructive alternative ideas without feeling threatened. It also means that I often need to put myself in their shoes and understand how the project impacts them and their departments and devise ways to work together to meet their day-to-day needs while also completing the work of the project.

Stakeholder involvement will vary as the project progresses. I make it a point to meet with the key stakeholders as early in the project as possible. Their involvement early on is important because you'll need them to make decisions about scope, budgets, and timelines and, more importantly, to help smooth the way and remove obstacles that are impeding progress. As the work gets under way and the project progresses, their involvement may lessen, but it's important to note that their continued engagement, even on a limited level, is critical to the success of the project.

Exam Spotlight

For the exam, remember that stakeholder involvement must occur throughout the life of the project and is a critical success factor for overall project success.

We have seen all of the inputs to this process before. They are project management plan, stakeholder register, enterprise environmental factors, and organizational process assets.

Next we'll take a look at the tools and techniques of this process.

Analyzing Stakeholders

There are three tools and techniques of this process: expert judgment, meetings, and analytical techniques. Expert judgment, as you recall, means meeting with others who know something about the project. In this case, that likely includes senior managers, key stakeholders, other project managers who have worked with your key stakeholders in the past, consultants, industry experts, and more.

Analytical techniques allow you to classify the engagement levels of your stakeholders and monitor and modify them throughout the project. According to the *PMBOK® Guide,* there are five levels of classifications of stakeholder engagement:

Unaware   Stakeholders are not engaged in the project.

Resistant   Stakeholders are not supportive of the project and may actively resist engaging.

Neutral   Stakeholders are neither supporting nor resisting the project and may be minimally engaged.

Supportive   Stakeholders have positive expectations of the project and are supportive and engaged.

Leading   Stakeholders are actively engaged in the project and helping to assure its success.

The purpose behind the classification is to document what levels of engagement your stakeholders are at during each phase of the project. It helps you to plan what levels are needed for coming phases and to create action plans for those stakeholders who are not at the desired level of engagement for the given phase of the project. You might construct a simple spreadsheet like the one shown in Table 5.1 to indicate the level of engagement of each stakeholder.

TABLE 5.1   Stakeholder engagement

	Unaware	Resistant	Neutral	Supportive	Leading
Stakeholder A		Existing level		Preferred level	
Stakeholder B			Existing level		Preferred level
Stakeholder C					Existing level

Stakeholder Management Plan

The primary output of this process is the stakeholder management plan. This plan documents the engagement levels of stakeholders (the stakeholder engagement table we talked about in the last section gets documented here). According to the *PMBOK® Guide,* other elements that might be a part of this plan include but are not limited to the following:

- Relationships between and among stakeholders

- Communication requirements for stakeholders engaged in the current phase of the project

- Details regarding the distribution of information, such as the language of the various stakeholders, the format of the information, and the level of detail needed

- Reasons for distributing the information, including how the stakeholders may react and/or the potential for changing their level of engagement

- Timing of the information distributions and their frequency

- The process for updating and modifying the stakeholder management plan due to the changing needs of the stakeholders and changes as the project progresses

The stakeholder management plan is a subsidiary of the project management plan.

Communicating the Plan

I've talked a good deal about documentation so far, and this topic will continue to come up throughout the remainder of the book. "Is that documented?" should be an ever-present question on the mind of the project manager. Documentation can save your bacon, so to speak, later in the project. Documentation is only one side of the equation, though—communication is the other. You and your stakeholders need to know who gets what information and when.

The *Plan Communications Management* process involves determining the communication needs of the stakeholders by defining the types of information needed, the format for communicating the information, how often it's distributed, and who prepares it. All of this is documented in the communications management plan, which is an output of this process.

Pop quiz: Do you remember where else the communications management plan belongs? I'll give you the answer later in the next section, "Plan Communications Management Outputs."

Plan Communications Management Inputs

The inputs to the Plan Communications Management process will look familiar to you. They are as follows:

- Project management plan
- Stakeholder register
- Enterprise environmental factors
- Organizational process assets

You'll recall that the project management plan defines how the subsidiary plans will be defined and integrated into the overall project management plan. As such, it's rich with constraints and assumptions that you should review as they pertain to stakeholder communication needs. We talked about the stakeholder register in the last section.

The *PMBOK® Guide* notes that all the elements described in the enterprise environmental factors and in the organizational process assets are inputs to this process. However, special note is made of the lessons learned and historical information elements of the organizational process assets input. Information you learn as you're progressing through the project is documented as lessons learned. This information is helpful for future projects of similar scope and complexity. Historical information is also useful to review when starting the Plan Communications Management process. Either of these documents might contain information about communication decisions on past projects and their results. Why reinvent the wheel? If something didn't work well on a past project, you'd want to know that before implementing that procedure on this project, so review past project documentation.

Exam Spotlight

The *PMBOK® Guide* notes that there is a difference between effective and efficient communication. Effective communication refers to providing the information in the right format for the intended audience at the right time. Efficient communication refers to providing the appropriate information at the right time—that is, only the information that's needed at the time.

Tools and Techniques for Plan Communications Management

The Plan Communications Management process concerns defining and documenting the types of information you're going to deliver, the format it will take, to whom it will be delivered, and when. The process consists of five tools and techniques to help determine these elements: communications requirements analysis, communication technology, communication models, communication methods, and meetings. Meetings, the last tool and technique of this process, are used to help gather information to determine the communication needs of the stakeholders and other information for the communications management plan. You'll look at the remainder of the tools and techniques for this process next.

Communications Requirements Analysis

Communications requirements analysis involves analyzing and determining the communication needs of the project stakeholders. According to the *PMBOK® Guide*, you can examine several sources of information to help determine these needs, including the following:

- Company and departmental organizational charts.
- Stakeholder responsibility relationships.
- Other departments and business units involved on the project.
- The number of resources involved on the project and where they're located in relation to project activities.
- Internal needs that the organization may need to know about the project.
- External needs that organizations such as the media, government, or industry groups might have that require communication updates.
- Stakeholder information. (This was documented in the stakeholder register, and output of Identify Stakeholders.)

This tool and technique requires an analysis of the items in the preceding list to make certain you're communicating information that's valuable to the stakeholders. Communicating valuable information doesn't mean you always paint a rosy picture. Communications to stakeholders might consist of either good or bad news—the point is that you don't want to bury stakeholders in too much information but you want to give them enough so that they're informed and can make appropriate decisions.

Project communication will always involve more than one person, even on the tiniest of projects. As such, communication network models have been devised to explain the relationships between people and the number or type of interactions needed between project participants. What you need to remember for the exam is that network models consist of nodes with lines connecting the nodes that indicate the number of communication channels, also known as *lines of communication*. Figure 5.4 shows an example of a network communication model with six channels of communication.

FIGURE 5.4 Network communication model

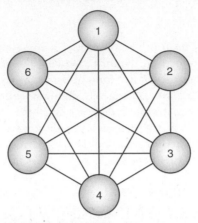

Nodes = participants
Lines = lines of communication between participants

The nodes are the participants, and the lines show the connections between them all. You'll need to know how to calculate the number of communication channels when you take the exam. You could draw them out as in this example and count up the lines, but there's an easier way. The formula for calculating the lines of communication is as follows:

(number of participants × (number of participants less 1)) divided by 2

Here's the calculation in mathematical terms:

$$n\,(n-1)\,/\,2$$

Figure 5.4 shows six participants, so let's plug that into the formula to determine the lines of communication:

$$6\,(6-1)\,/\,2 = 15$$

Exam Spotlight

I recommend you memorize the communications channel formula before taking the exam.

🌐 **Real World Scenario**

Stakeholder Relationships

Bill is an information technology manager working on an enterprise resource planning project. He's one of the key stakeholders on this project. Bill reports to the CIO, who in turn reports to the executive vice president, who also happens to be the project sponsor. Bill is close friends with the human resources director but doesn't get along so well with the accounting department director. This project requires heavy involvement from the accounting department and medium-level involvement from the human resources department.

You are the project manager for this project and are new to the organization. You know Bill's relationship with both the accounting and human resources directors. What you don't know is the relationship the two directors have with each other. Because all three stakeholders are key to the success of this project, it's important that all three communicate with you as well as with each other. You set up an interview with each of these stakeholders to determine several pieces of information: other departments that might need to be involved on the project, stakeholder communication needs and timing, external needs, timing of status updates for the company newsletter, and other department members aside from the stakeholders who need to be involved in the project. You also plant a few surreptitious questions that will give you insight into the relationships the stakeholders have with each other and with the project sponsor.

You discover that the human resources and accounting directors have known each other for several years and worked together at another organization prior to coming to work here. This tells you that if you can get one of them to buy in on project decisions, the other will likely follow suit. They both have the utmost respect for Bill and his technical capabilities, even though the accounting director doesn't care for his abrupt, direct communication style. You also learn that although they both have respect for the position of the executive vice president, they don't believe the person filling that role is competent to do the job. They question his decision-making ability—or lack thereof—and warn you that you need to write down his answers and direction so that he doesn't change his story halfway through the project. Although you won't formally document this valuable piece of information, you'll definitely put it into action right away.

Communication Technology

The second tool and technique of this process is communication technology. This examines the methods (or technology) used to communicate the information to, from, and among the stakeholders. Methods of communicating can take many forms, such as written, spoken, email, formal status reports, meetings, online databases, online schedules, and so on. This tool and technique examines the technology elements that might affect project communications. You should consider several factors before deciding what methods you'll choose to transfer information. The timing of the information exchange or need for updates is the first factor. The availability of the technology you're planning on using to communicate project information is important as well. Do you need to procure new technology or systems, or are there systems already in place that will work? Staff experience with the technology is another factor. Are the project team members and stakeholders experienced at using this technology, or will you need to train them? Consider the duration of the project and the project environment. Will the technology you're choosing work throughout the life of the project, or will it have to be upgraded or updated at some point? How does the project team function? Are the members located together or spread out across several campuses or locations? Is the information you're distributing confidential or sensitive in nature? If so, consider what security measures should be put in place to protect the information and assure it is delivered only to the intended recipients.

The answers to these questions should be documented in the communications management plan output. I'll cover that in the next section.

Communication Models

Communication models depict how information is transmitted from the sender and how it's received by the receiver. According to the *PMBOK® Guide*, a communication model includes the following key components:

- Encode
- Transmit
- Decode
- Acknowledge
- Feedback and/or response

Encoding the message simply means putting the information or your thoughts or ideas into a language that the receiver will understand. The message is the result or output of the encoding.

The sender transmits the message using any number of methods, including written, oral, email, and so on. Barriers can exist that compromise this information, such as cultural differences, distance the message must travel, technology used to transmit and receive, and more. Any barrier, including those just mentioned, that keeps the message from either being transmitted or understood is called noise.

Decode is performed by the receiver and it refers to translating the information that was sent.

Acknowledge is when the receiver lets the sender know they have received the message. This is not an indication of agreement.

Last but not least, feedback and/or response is provided after the receiver has decoded the original message. Then, the receiver encodes their response and sends it back to the sender, starting the cycle all over again.

The sender is responsible for encoding the message, for transmitting the message, and decoding the feedback message. The receiver is responsible for decoding the original message from the sender and encoding and sending the feedback message.

Communication Methods

Communication methods refer to how the project information is shared among the stakeholders. According to the *PMBOK® Guide*, there are three classifications of communication methods. We'll briefly look at each of them:

Interactive Communication   Interactive communication involves multi-directional communication where two or more parties must exchange thoughts or ideas. This method includes videoconferencing, phone or conference calls, meetings, and so on.

Push Communications   Push communications is one way and refers to sending information to intended receivers. It includes methods such as letters, memos, reports, emails, voicemails, and so on. This method assures the communication was sent but is not concerned with whether it was actually received or understood by the intended receivers.

Pull Communications   This is the opposite of push communications. The likely recipients of the information access the information themselves using methods such as websites, e-learning sites, knowledge repositories, shared network drives, and so on.

 We'll discuss communication models and communication methods in more detail in Chapter 9, "Conducting Procurements and Sharing Information."

Plan Communications Management Outputs

There are two outputs to the Plan Communications Management process. They are the communications management plan and project documents updates. The updates that may be required as a result of performing this process are the project schedule, the stakeholder register, and the stakeholder management strategy. Let's take a closer look at the details of the communications management plan.

All projects require sound communication plans, but not all projects will have the same types of communication or the same methods for distributing the information. The *communications management plan* documents the types of information needs the stakeholders have, when the information should be distributed, how the information will be delivered, and how communications will be monitored and controlled throughout the project. The answer to the pop quiz posed earlier in this chapter is the communications management plan is a subsidiary plan of the project management plan I talked about in Chapter 3.

The type of information you will typically communicate includes project status, project scope statements and scope statement updates, project baseline information, risks, action items, performance measures, deliverable acceptance, and so on. What's important to know for this process is that the information needs of the stakeholders should be determined as early in the Planning process group as possible so that as you and your team develop project planning documents, you already know who should receive copies of them and how they should be delivered.

According to the *PMBOK® Guide*, the communications management plan typically describes the following elements:

- The communication requirements of each stakeholder or stakeholder group
- Purpose for communication
- Frequency of communications, including time frames for distribution
- Name of the person responsible for communicating information
- Format of the communication and method of transmission
- Method for updating the communications management plan
- Flowcharts
- Glossary of common terms

 I've included only some of the most important elements of the communications management plan in the list of elements for the communications management plan. I recommend you review the entire list in the *PMBOK® Guide*.

The information that will be shared with stakeholders and the distribution methods are based on the needs of the stakeholders, the project complexity, and the organizational policies. Some communications might be informal—a chat by the coffeemaker, for instance—while other communications are more formal and are kept with the project files for later reference. The communications management plan may also include guidelines for conducting status meetings, team meetings, and so on.

You might consider setting up an intranet site for your project and posting the appropriate project documentation there for the stakeholders to access any time they want. If you use this method, be sure to document it in the communications management plan and notify your stakeholders when updates or new communication is posted.

Exam Spotlight

For the exam, know that the communications management plan documents how the communication needs of the stakeholders will be met, including the types of information that will be communicated, who will communicate it, who receives the communication, the methods used to communicate, the timing and frequency, the method for updating this plan as the project progresses, the escalation process, and a glossary of common terms.

🌐 Real World Scenario

Project Case Study: New Kitchen Heaven Retail Store

After creating the first draft of the project schedule network diagram, you went back to each stakeholder to ask for cost estimates for each of the activities. Ricardo's estimates are shown here with the activities he gave you last time:

1. Procure the T1 connection. This takes 30 to 45 days and will have ongoing costs of $3,000 per month. Procurement costs are covered in the monthly expense.

2. Run Ethernet cable throughout the building. The estimated time to complete is 16 hours at $100 per hour, which was figured using parametric estimating techniques.

3. Purchase the router, switch, server, and rack for the equipment room and four point-of-service terminals. The estimated costs are $17,000.

4. Install the router and test the connection. Testing depends on the T1 installation at demarcation. The time estimate to install is eight hours. Ricardo's staff will perform this activity at an average estimated cost of $78 per hour.

5. Install the switch. Based on past experience, the time estimate to install is two hours. Ricardo's staff will perform this activity at an average estimated cost of $78 per hour.

6. Install the server and test. Based on past experience, the estimate to install is six hours at $84 per hour.

7. The web team will add the new store location and phone number to the lookup function on the Internet site. The time estimate is two hours at $96 per hour.

Jake and Jill have each written similar lists with time and cost estimates. Using this information, you create the activity cost estimates and are careful to document the basis of estimates. The following list includes some of the information you document in the basis of estimates:

- Ricardo's use of parametric estimates for his cost estimates.

- Jake's use of both analogous and parametric estimating techniques.

- Jill's use of reserve analysis to include contingencies for unplanned changes involving vendor deliveries.

- Assumptions made about vendor deliveries and availability of the T1 and assumptions made regarding when lease payments begin.

- The range of possible estimates is stated as plus or minus 10 percent.

You also document the cost management plan and the cost baseline along with the project funding requirements. Since this project will occur fairly quickly, only two funding requirement periods are needed.

The stakeholder management plan is written and describes the relationships between the stakeholders, their communication requirements, and the format, reasons, and timing of the distribution of information.

The communications management plan is also complete, and you've asked the key stakeholder to review it before posting it to the intranet site for the project. You want to make certain you've identified stakeholder communication needs, the method of communication, and the frequency with which they will occur.

Project Case Study Checklist

The main topics discussed in the case study are as follows:

Estimate Costs

Determine Budget

    Cost aggregation

    Reserve analysis

    Expert judgment

    Parametric estimates

    Cost baseline

    Project funding requirements

Plan Communications Management

    Determine effective and efficient communications

    Review stakeholder register and stakeholder management strategy

    Communications requirements analysis

    Communication technology

    Communication models

    Communication methods

Communications management plan

    Stakeholder needs

    Format and language for information

    Time frame and frequency of communication

    Person responsible for communication

    Methods for communicating

    Glossary of terms

Understanding How This Applies to Your Next Project

The Plan Cost Management and Estimate Costs processes are something I have to do rather early in the project because of our long procurement cycle. Our cost management plan (the policies and procedures used to plan and execute project costs) is set in legislation and government rulings so there isn't a lot of flexibility around this process in my situation. The way our funding request process works is that I must have an estimated cost for the project before I can request funding. If funding is approved, the project is approved. If I'm not awarded funding, the project dies and we move on to the next one.

I rely on expert judgment and parametric estimating techniques to determine activity and total project costs. I often engage vendors and my own project team to help determine the costs. When I have a large project that must go out for bid, I have a well-defined scope and some idea of schedule dates and overall costs, but I won't complete the schedule until after the contract is awarded. In an ideal world, I would prefer to create the schedule prior to determining cost estimates and budgets…but we don't live in an ideal world and sometimes Planning processes have to be performed out of order.

The authorized project budget becomes one of the key measurements of project success. In a later chapter, we'll talk about monitoring the budget to determine whether we're tracking with our estimates.

I generally create a stakeholder management plan and a communications plan together as one document (I call it a communications plan). The reason for this is because the stakeholder management plan contains a lot of information about communication needs, timing, distribution methods, distribution formats, and so on. I find it easier to keep this information together in one plan. This plan is a must-have for every project. I can't stress enough how often I've seen the root cause of project issues end up being communication problems. Never assume keeping the stakeholders informed or engaged is an easy job. Even if you know the stakeholders well, always create a communication plan. Document how you'll communicate status, baseline information, risks, and deliverables acceptance. That way, there's no question as to how information will be relayed, who's going to receive it, or when it will be delivered.

Summary

The cost management plan is the only output of the Plan Cost Management process. This documents the policies and procedures you'll use to plan and execute project costs as well as how you will estimate, manage, and control project costs. The Estimate Costs process determines how much the project resources will cost, and these costs are usually stated in monetary amounts. Some of the techniques used specifically for estimating costs are analogous estimating, parametric estimating, bottom-up estimating, three-point estimates, and reserve analysis. You can also use bottom-up estimating for total project cost estimates. This involves estimating the cost of each activity and then rolling these up to come up with a total work package cost. The output of this process is the activity cost estimates and the basis of estimates that details all the support information related to the estimates.

The tools and techniques of the Determine Budget process include cost aggregation, reserve analysis, expert judgment, historical relationships, and funding limit reconciliation. These tools together help you produce the final, authorized project budget known as the cost baseline, which is an output of this process. You will use the cost baseline throughout the remainder of the project to measure project expenditures, variances, and project performance. The cost baseline is graphically displayed as an S curve.

The cost baseline is also known as a performance measurement baseline (PMB) when you're calculating earned value management formulas. PMBs are management controls that should change only infrequently. Examples of the performance measurement baselines you've looked at so far are the scope, schedule, and cost baselines. The completed project plan itself also becomes a baseline. If changes in scope or schedule do occur after Planning is complete, you should go through a formalized process (which I'll cover in Chapter 10) to implement the changes.

The Plan Stakeholder Management process focuses on effectively engaging stakeholders, understanding their needs and interests, understanding the good and bad things they might bring to the project, and how the project will impact them. The primary output of this process is the stakeholder management plan.

The purpose of the communications management plan is to determine and document the communication needs of the stakeholders by defining the types of information needed, the format for communicating the information, how often it's distributed, and who prepares it. This plan is a subsidiary plan of the project management plan and is created in the Plan Communications Management process.

Exam Essentials

Be able to state the purpose of the cost management plan.   The cost management plan is the only output of the Plan Cost Management process. It establishes policies and procedures for planning and executing project costs and documents the processes for estimating, managing, and controlling project costs.

Be able to identify and describe the primary output of the Estimate Costs process.   Activity cost estimates are the primary output of Estimate Costs. These estimates are quantitative amounts—usually stated in monetary units—that reflect the cost of the resources needed to complete the project activities.

Be familiar with the tools and techniques of the Estimate Costs process.   The tools and techniques of Estimate Costs are expert judgment, analogous estimating, parametric estimating, bottom-up estimating, three-point estimating, reserve analysis, cost of quality, project management software, vendor bid analysis, and group decision-making techniques.

Be able to identify additional general management techniques that can be used in the Project Cost Management Knowledge Area.   Some of the general management techniques that can be used in this Knowledge Area are return on investment, discounted cash flow, and payback analysis.

Know the tools and techniques of the Determine Budget process.   The tools and techniques of Determine Budget are cost aggregation, reserve analysis, expert judgment, historical relationships, and funding limit reconciliation.

Be able to describe the cost baseline.   The cost baseline is the authorized, time-phased cost of the project when using budget-at-completion calculations. The cost baseline is displayed as an S curve.

Be able to describe project funding requirements.   Project funding requirements are the output of the Determine Budget process. They detail the funding requirements needed on the project by time period (monthly, quarterly, annually).

Be able to describe the purpose of the Plan Stakeholder Management process.   The Plan Stakeholder Management process concerns effectively engaging stakeholders, understanding their needs and interests, understanding how they may help or hurt the project, and understanding how the project will impact them. The primary output of this process is the stakeholder management plan.

Be able to describe the primary purpose of the stakeholder management plan.   The stakeholder management plan documents engagement levels of the stakeholders.

Be able to describe the purpose of the communications management plan.   The communications management plan determines the communication needs of the stakeholders. It documents what information will be distributed, how it will be distributed, to whom, and the timing of the distribution.

Key Terms

Here's a list of the processes from the Planning process group we talked about in this chapter that you'll need to help bring about a successful project:

  Plan Cost Management

  Estimate Costs

  Determine Budget

  Plan Communications Management

  Plan Stakeholder Management

Here is a list of some of the terms you came across in this chapter:

basis of estimates	cost baseline
chart of accounts	cost management plan
communications management plan	cost of quality (COQ)
control account (CA)	time-phased budget

Review Questions

You can find the answers to the questions in Appendix A.

1. All of the following are true regarding the Project Cost Management Knowledge Area processes except for which one?

   A. The primary concern of the Project Cost Management Knowledge Area is determining the amount of resources needed to complete project activities.

   B. The Estimate Costs and Determine Budget processes can be combined into one process for small projects.

   C. The Estimate Cost process is closely linked with the Estimate Activity Resources process.

   D. General management techniques such as ROI, discounted cash flow, and payback analysis can be used to help derive cost estimates.

2. This document is used to establish the criteria for planning, estimating, budgeting, and controlling costs.

   A. Cost baseline, an output of the Determine Budget process.

   B. Performance management baseline, an output of the Plan Cost Management process.

   C. Project funding requirements, an output of the Determine Budget process.

   D. Cost management plan, an output of the Plan Cost Management process.

3. You are a project manager working for iTrim Central and you're preparing your cost management plan. You know that all of the following are true regarding this plan except for which one?

   A. The WBS provides the framework for this plan.

   B. Units of measure should be described in the plan usually as hours, days, weeks, or lump sum.

   C. This plan is a subsidiary of the project management plan.

   D. Control thresholds should be described in the plan as to how estimates will adhere to rounding ($100 or $1,000, and so on).

4. You are a project manager working for iTrim Central. Your organization has developed a new dieting technique that is sure to be the next craze. One of the deliverables of your feasibility study was an analysis of the potential financial performance of this new product, and your executives are very pleased with the numbers. You will be working with several vendors to produce products, marketing campaigns, and software that will track customers' progress with the new techniques. For purposes of performing earned value measurements for project costs, you are going to place which of the following in the WBS?

   A. Chart of accounts

   B. Code of accounts

   C. Control account

   D. Reserve account

5. All of the following are inputs of the Estimate Costs process except for which one?

   A. Resource calendars

   B. Scope baseline

   C. Project schedule

   D. Human resource management plan

6. You want to improve your activity cost estimates by taking into account estimation uncertainty and risk. Which of the following tools and techniques will you use?

   A. Analogous estimates

   B. Three-point estimating

   C. Parametric estimates

   D. Bottom-up estimates

7. You have received estimates for activity costs associated with one work package of the WBS. Additional contingencies have been added to the estimates to account for cost uncertainty. Which of the following tools and techniques of Estimate Costs does this describe?

   A. Reserve analysis

   B. Three-point estimates

   C. Vendor bid analysis

   D. Analogous estimates

8. You have received the following estimates for a complex activity that is critical to the success of your project. The three-point estimates are: most likely estimate is $42, the optimistic estimate is $35, and the pessimistic estimate is $54. What is the expected activity cost of this activity using the beta distribution formula (rounded to the nearest dollar)?

   A. 49

   B. 39

   C. 43

   D. 44

9. You are the project manager for a custom home-building construction company. You are working on the model home project for the upcoming Show Homes Tour. The model home includes Internet connections in every room, talking appliances, and wiring for home theaters. You are working on the cost baseline for this project. All of the following statements are true except which one?

   A. This process aggregates the estimated costs of project activities.

   B. The cost baseline will be used to measure variances and future project performance.

   C. This process assigns cost estimates for expected future period operating costs.

   D. The cost baseline is the time-phased budget at completion for the project.

10. Your project sponsor has requested a cost estimate for the project. She would like the cost estimate to be as accurate as possible because this might be her one and only chance to secure the budget for this project because of recent cuts in special projects. You decide to use _____.

    A. analogous estimating techniques

    B. bottom-up estimating techniques

    C. top-down estimating techniques

    D. expert judgment techniques

11. You are the project manager for a custom-home-building construction company. You are working on the model home project for the upcoming Show Homes Tour. The model home includes Internet connections in every room, talking appliances, and wiring for home theaters. You are working on the Determine Budget process. All of the following statements are true except which one?

    A. You document the funding limit reconciliation to include a contingency for unplanned risks.

    B. You discover that updates to the risk register are needed as a result of performing this process.

    C. You document that funding requirements are based on a quarterly basis and are derived from the cost baseline.

    D. The performance measurement baseline will be used to perform earned value management calculations.

12. Which of the following is displayed as an S curve?

    A. Funding requirements

    B. Cost baseline

    C. Cost estimates

    D. Expenditures to date

13. All of the following are tools and techniques of the Determine Budget process except for which one?

    A. Reserve analysis

    B. Expert judgment

    C. Historical relationships

    D. Cost of quality

14. Your project sponsor has requested a cost estimate for the project on which you're working. This project is similar in scope to a project you worked on last year. She would like to get the cost estimates as soon as possible. Accuracy is not her primary concern right now. She needs a ballpark figure by tomorrow. You decide to use _____.

    A. analogous estimating techniques

    B. bottom-up estimating techniques

   C.   parametric estimating techniques

   D.   three-point estimating techniques

15. You have eight key stakeholders (plus yourself) to communicate with on your project. Which of the following is true?

   A.   There are 36 channels of communication, and this should be a consideration when using the communications technology tool and technique.

   B.   There are 28 channels of communication, and this should be a consideration when using the communications requirements analysis tool and technique.

   C.   There are 28 channels of communication, and this should be a consideration when using the communications technology tool and technique.

   D.   There are 36 channels of communication, and this should be a consideration when using the communications requirements analysis tool and technique.

16. All of the following are true regarding Plan Communications Management except for which one?

   A.   The communications management plan is a subsidiary plan of the project management plan.

   B.   This process should be completed as early in the project as possible.

   C.   It's tightly linked with enterprise environmental factors and all organizational process assets are used as inputs for this process.

   D.   Communications requirements analysis, communication technology, communication methods, and expert judgment are tools and techniques of this process.

17. You are preparing your communications management plan and know that all of the following are true except for which one?

   A.   Decode means to translate thoughts or ideas so they can be understood by others.

   B.   Transmit concerns the method used to convey the message.

   C.   Acknowledgment means the receiver has received and agrees with the message.

   D.   Encoding and decoding are the responsibility of both the sender and receiver.

18. Which of the following ensures that information is distributed but does not acknowledge or certify that it was understood by intended receiver(s)?

   A.   Push communication

   B.   Interactive communication

   C.   Transmit

   D.   Message and feedback message

19. You need to communicate information in a multi-directional fashion with several stakeholders. Which of the following is true?

   A.   This describes push communication, which is a communication model.

    B. This describes interactive communication, which is a communication method.

    C. This describes communication requirements analysis, which is a communication model.

    D. This describes pull communication, which is a communication method.

20. Communication technology takes into account all of the following factors that can affect the project except for which one?

    A. Urgency of the need for information

    B. Project environment

    C. Reasons for the distribution of information

    D. Duration of the project

Chapter

6

Risk Planning

THE PMP® EXAM CONTENT FROM THE PLANNING THE PROJECT PERFORMANCE DOMAIN COVERED IN THIS CHAPTER INCLUDES THE FOLLOWING:

✓ **Develop a risk management plan by identifying, analyzing, and prioritizing project risks and defining risk response strategies in order to manage uncertainty throughout the project life cycle.**

✓ **Identify risks and create risk register to monitor existing risks and add new risks throughout the project.**

✓ **Perform analysis to determine probability and impact of risks occurring.**

✓ **Prepare responses to risks.**

✓ **Knowledge and Skills:**

- Elements, purpose, and techniques of risk management planning

- Elements, purpose, and techniques of project planning

Risk is evident in everything we do. When it comes to project management, understanding risk and knowing how to minimize its impacts (or take full advantage of its opportunities) on your project are essential for success. This entire chapter is dedicated to project risk. Five of the six risk processes, all contained in the Risk Management Knowledge Area, fall in the Planning process group. I'll cover Plan Risk Management, Identify Risks, Perform Qualitative Risk Analysis, Perform Quantitative Risk Analysis, and Plan Risk Responses in this chapter. I'll follow up with the last risk process, Control Risks, in Chapter 10, "Measuring and Controlling Project Performance."

Hold on to your hats! I'm going to cover a lot of material in this chapter, but it will go fast. I promise.

The process names, inputs, tools and techniques, outputs, and descriptions of the project management process groups and related materials and figures in this chapter are based on content from *A Guide to the Project Management Body of Knowledge (PMBOK® Guide), Fifth Edition* (Sybex, 2010).

Planning for Risks

Every one of us takes risks on a daily basis. Just getting out of bed in the morning is a risk. You might stub your toe in the dark on the way to the light switch or trip over the dog and break a leg. These events don't usually happen, but the possibility exists. The same is true for your project. Risk exists on all projects, and the potential that a particular risk event will occur depends on the nature of the risk.

Risk, like most of the elements of the other Planning processes, changes as the project progresses and should be monitored throughout the project. As you get close to a risk event, that's the time to reassess your original assumptions about the risk and your plans to deal with the risk and to make any adjustments as required.

Not all risks are bad. Risks can present future opportunities as well as future threats to a project. Risk events may occur due to one reason or several reasons, and they may have multiple impacts. All risks have causes, and if the risk event occurs during a project, there are consequences. Those consequences will likely impact one or more of the project objectives, and you'll need to know whether the consequences have positive or negative impacts.

Risk is, after all, uncertainty. The more you know about risks and their impacts beforehand, the better equipped you will be to handle a risk event when it occurs. The processes that involve risk, probably more than any other project Planning process, concern balance. You want to find that point where you and the stakeholders are comfortable with the risk based on the benefits you can potentially gain. In a nutshell, you're balancing the action of taking a risk against avoiding the consequences or impacts of a risk event, or enjoying the benefits it may bring. The rest of this chapter will deal with finding out what risk events might occur (and how to deal with those risks that are unknown), determining an organization's tolerance for risk taking, and developing action plans for those risks you've determined have hefty impacts. The first step is performing the Plan Risk Management process. Here, you determine the approach you'll use for risk management activities and document your plans for them in a risk management plan. You'll look at that process now.

Exam Spotlight

According to the *PMBOK® Guide*, once a risk event occurs, it's considered an issue and is no longer a risk.

Planning Your Risk Management

Risks come about for many reasons. Some are internal to the project, and some are external. The project environment, the planning process, the project management process, inadequate resources, and so on can all contribute to risk. Some risks you'll know about in advance and plan for during this process; others risk events will occur unannounced during the project. The *Plan Risk Management* process determines how you'll prepare for and perform risk management activities on your project.

Exam Spotlight

The *PMBOK® Guide* contends that the Plan Risk Management process should begin as soon as the project begins and it should be concluded early in the Planning process. The risk management plan, the only output of this process, assures that the appropriate amount of resources and the appropriate time are dedicated to risk management. "Appropriate" is determined based on the levels, the importance, and the types of risks. The most important function the risk management plan serves is that it's an agreed-upon baseline for evaluating project risk.

To document the risk management plan, you need to gather some inputs that will help you determine your organization's risk policies and tolerance for risk. You'll look at those inputs next.

Plan Risk Management Inputs

Risks associated with a project generally concern four project objectives—time, cost, scope, and quality—or any combination of the four. As you might have guessed, the project management plan is an input to this process and it includes the scope statement, which describes your project deliverables. The inputs of this process are as follows:

- Project management plan
- Project charter
- Stakeholder register
- Enterprise environmental factors
- Organizational process assets

The *risk attitude* of the organization and the stakeholders is a key element of the enterprise environmental factors input. Risk attitude consists of three elements:

Risk Appetite   *Risk appetite* is the level of uncertainty the stakeholders are willing to accept in exchange for the potential positive impacts of the risk. For example, let's say your organization is a multinational manufacturing firm that is implementing a new inventory system. The end users are grumbling and have expressed their concerns for the new system. The old system does everything they want it to do, and they are not interested in this new technology. There is a potential for the represented employees to protest this new system, and such a reaction could impact production. Your stakeholders are willing to accept this risk even though they don't know if, or to what extent, production may be impacted because the benefits of the new system far outweigh the potential unknown impacts of employees protesting.

Risk Tolerance   *Risk tolerance* is that balance I talked about earlier where stakeholders are comfortable taking a risk because the known benefits to be gained outweigh what could be lost—or just the opposite. They will avoid taking a risk because the cost or impact is too great given the amount of benefit that can be derived. Here's an example to describe risk tolerance: Suppose you're a 275-pound brute who's surrounded by three bodyguards of equal proportion everywhere you go. Chances are, walking down a dark alley in the middle of the night doesn't faze you in the least. That means your risk tolerance for this activity is high. However, if you're a petite 90-pounder without the benefit of bodyguards or karate lessons, performing this same activity might give you cause for concern. Your risk tolerance is low, meaning you wouldn't likely do this activity. The higher your tolerance for risk, the more you're willing to take on risk and its consequences.

Risk tolerance is different than risk appetite because risk appetite concerns the amount of uncertainty you are willing to take on to gain a benefit whereas risk tolerance concerns the amount of risk, and hence the potential consequences or benefits you might gain or lose if the risk event occurs.

Risk Threshold   *Risk thresholds* are measures or levels of uncertainty or impact the organization is willing to operate within. For example, a monetary risk threshold might state if the risk poses a threat that could cost more than 5 percent of the total project budget, the risk should not be accepted. If it's below 5 percent, it may be accepted.

Organizations and stakeholders, as well as individuals, all have different tolerances for risk. One organization might believe that the risk of a potential 7 percent cost overrun is high, whereas another might think it's low. However, either one of these organizations might decide to accept the risk if it believes the risk is in balance with the potential rewards. It's important for the project manager to understand the tolerance level that the organization and the stakeholders have for risk before evaluating and ranking risk.

Remember that organizational process assets include policies and guidelines that might already exist in the organization. Your organization's risk categories, risk statement formats, and risk templates should be considered when planning for risks. Also when developing the risk management plan, consider the defined roles and responsibilities and the authority levels the stakeholders and project manager have for making decisions regarding risk planning.

The project management plan includes all of the subsidiary plans and baselines for the project. This is the first place you'll start looking when identifying risks, and it should be considered when determining the process you'll use to evaluate risks. The risk management plan (the only output of this process) will also become part of the project management plan.

Tools and Techniques for Plan Risk Management

The Plan Risk Management process has three tools and techniques: analytical techniques, expert judgment, and meetings.

Analytical techniques in this case refer to understanding stakeholder risk appetites and tolerances, developing a method for scoring risks, and determining the risk exposure of the project. We will cover these topics in more depth throughout the remainder of this chapter.

The purpose of meetings—which are held with project team members, stakeholders, functional managers, and others who might have involvement in the risk management process—is to contribute to the risk management plan. During these meetings, the fundamental plans for performing risk management activities will be discussed and determined and then documented in the risk management plan.

The key outcomes of performing these planning meetings are as follows:

- Risk cost elements are developed for inclusion in the project budget.
- Schedule activities associated with risk are developed for inclusion in the project schedule.
- Risk responsibilities are assigned.
- The risk contingency reserve process is established or reviewed.
- Templates for risk categories are defined or modified for this project.
- Definitions of terms (*probability, impact, risk types, risk levels,* and so on) are developed and documented.
- The probability and impact matrix is defined or modified for this project.

I'll discuss risk responsibilities, define the terms associated with risk management, and help you construct your own probability and impact matrix in the remaining sections of this chapter.

Real World Scenario

Do We Need a Risk Management Plan?

Julia is the project manager for a small project her department is undertaking. The project objective is to give customers the ability to download videos of the properties her organization has listed for lease. Two programmers from the information technology department will be working on the updates to the website, programming the links, and so on. The project sponsor wants to fast-track this project. She'd like to skip most of the Planning processes, and she sees no need for a risk management plan. Julia explains to the sponsor that the risk management plan for a project this size might be only a paragraph or two long. She emphasizes the importance of documenting how they'll identify risks, how they'll quantify them, and how they'll monitor the risks as the project progresses. Julia has project management experience on projects of all sizes and knows firsthand that ignoring this step could bring some unexpected surprises to the sponsor later in the project. She explains a bad past experience where this step was ignored and then assures the sponsor they can probably agree to the plan, identify and quantify the risks, and determine response plans in an hour and a half or less. The sponsor now understands the issues and agrees to the meeting.

Ultimately, your goal for this process is documenting the risk management plan. This document is the basis for understanding the remaining risk processes. Because the risk management plan encompasses a wealth of information, I've given this topic its own section. Let's get to it.

Creating the Risk Management Plan

The purpose of the Plan Risk Management process is to create a *risk management plan*, which describes how you will define, monitor, and control risks throughout the project. The risk management plan is a subsidiary of the project management plan, and it's the only output of this process.

The risk management plan details how risk management processes (including Identify Risks, Perform Qualitative Risk Analysis, Perform Quantitative Risk Analysis, Plan Risk Responses, and Control Risks) will be implemented, monitored, and controlled throughout the life of the project. It details how you will manage risks but does not attempt to define responses to individual risks.

NOTE   I'll talk about how to develop the risk response plans in the section, "Developing a Risk Response Plan" later in this chapter.

According to the *PMBOK® Guide*, the risk management plan should include the following elements:

- Methodology
- Roles and responsibilities
- Budgeting
- Timing
- Risk categories
- Definitions of risk probability and impact
- Probability and impact matrix
- Revised stakeholder tolerances
- Reporting formats
- Tracking

Exam Spotlight

It's important to spend time developing the risk management plan, because it's an input to every other risk-planning process and it enhances the probability of risk management success.

You'll take a look at most of these elements next. However, risk categories, probability and impact, and probability and impact matrix are pretty meaty topics, so I'll cover those in their own sections following this one:

Methodology   Methodology is a description of how you'll perform risk management, including elements such as methods, tools, and where you might find risk data that you can use in the later processes.

Roles and Responsibilities   Roles and responsibilities describe the people who are responsible for managing the identified risks and their responses for each type of activity identified in the risk management plan. These risk teams might not be the same as the project team. Risk analysis should be unbiased, which might not be possible when project team members are involved.

Budgeting   The budget for risk management is included in the plan as well. In this section, you'll assign resources and estimate the costs of risk management and its methods, including contingency reserves. These costs are then included in the project's cost baseline.

Timing   Timing documents the timing of the risk management processes (including when and how often they'll be performed on the project) and includes the activities associated with risk management in the project schedule.

Revised Stakeholder Tolerances   This is just as it implies. As you proceed through the risk management processes, you might find that risk tolerances will change. Document those new tolerance levels in the risk management plan.

Reporting Formats   Reporting formats describe the content of the risk register and the format of this document. (I'll talk more about the risk register later in this chapter.) Reporting formats also detail how risk management information will be maintained, updated, analyzed, and reported to project participants.

Tracking   This includes a description of how you'll document the history of the risk activities for the current project and how the risk processes will be audited. You can reference this information when you're performing risk-planning processes later in the current project or on future projects. This information is also helpful for lessons learned, which I'll cover in Chapter 11, "Controlling Work Results."

Risk Categories

Risk categories are a way to systematically identify risks and provide a foundation for understanding. When determining and identifying risks, the use of risk categories helps improve the process by giving everyone involved a common language or basis for describing risk.

Risk categories should be identified during this process and documented in the risk management plan. These categories will assist you in making sure the next process, Identify Risks, is performed effectively and produces a quality output. The following list includes some examples of the categories you might consider during this process (or modify based on previous project information):

- Technical, quality, or performance risks
- Project management risks
- Organizational risks
- External risks

You can go about describing categories of risk in a couple of ways. One way is simply listing them. You could, and should, review prior projects for risk categories and then tailor them for this project.

You could also construct a *risk breakdown structure (RBS)*, which lists the categories and subcategories. Figure 6.1 shows a sample of an RBS.

FIGURE 6.1 Risk breakdown structure

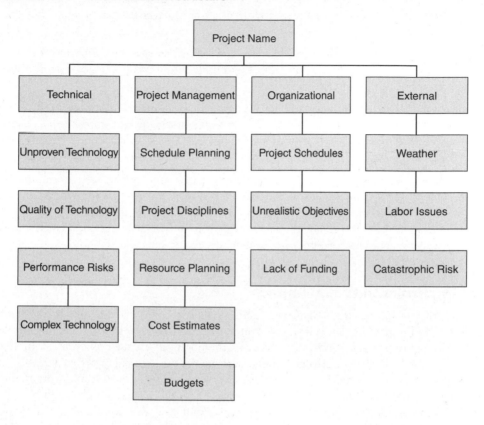

 The organizational process assets input might include an RBS that you can reference for this project. Don't forget your PMO. The project management office might have templates or an RBS already developed.

Risk categories might reflect the type of industry or application area in which the project exists. For example, information technology projects will likely have many risks that fall into the technical category, whereas construction projects might be more subject to risks that fall into the external risks category. The categories do not have to be industry specific, however. Keep in mind that project management, for example, is a risk for every project in every industry. You can find a description of each of the categories next:

Technical/Quality/Performance Risks   Technical, quality, or performance risks include risks associated with unproven technology, complex technology, or changes to technology anticipated during the course of the project. Performance risks might include unrealistic performance goals. Perhaps one of the project deliverables concerns a component manufactured to specific performance standards that have never been achieved. That's a performance risk.

Project Management Risks   The project management risk category includes improper schedule and resource planning, poor project planning, and improper or poor project management disciplines or methodologies.

Organizational Risks   The organizational risk category can include resource conflicts because of multiple projects occurring at the same time in the organization; scope, time, and cost objectives that are unrealistic given the organization's resources or structure; and lack of funding for the project or diverting funds from this project to other projects.

External Risks   The external risk category includes those aspects that are external to the project, such as new laws or regulations, labor issues, weather, changes in ownership, and foreign policy for projects performed in other countries. Catastrophic risks—known as *force majeure*—are usually outside the scope of Plan Risk Management and instead require disaster recovery techniques. Force majeure includes events such as earthquakes, meteorites, volcanoes, floods, civil unrest, terrorism, and so on.

Defining Probability and Impact

When you're writing the risk management plan, you'll want to document the definitions for probability and impact as they relate to potential negative risk events and their impacts on the four project objectives. Probability describes the potential for the risk event occurring, whereas impact describes the effects or consequences the project will experience if the risk event occurs. This definition can be sophisticated or simple. For example, you might use numeric values to define probability and impact or simply assign a high-medium-low rating to each risk. What's important to note now is that you don't use these probability and impact definitions here. You use these definitions later in the Perform Qualitative Risk Analysis process. (I'll talk in depth about probability and impact in the section, "Analyzing Risks Using Qualitative Techniques" later in this chapter.) But you should define and document them here in the risk management plan.

Probability and Impact Matrix

A *probability and impact matrix* prioritizes the combination of probability and impact scores and helps you determine which risks need detailed risk response plans. For example, a risk event with a high probability of occurring and a high impact will likely need a response plan. This matrix is typically defined by the organization, but if you don't have one, you'll need to develop this now—during your planning meetings (a tool and technique of this process). You'll use this matrix in the Perform Qualitative Risk Analysis process, and I'll talk more in depth about it in the section, "Analyzing Risks Using Qualitative Techniques" later in this chapter. Again, you want to define (or modify) and document the probability and impact matrix in the risk management plan.

The key point about this process is that you'll define what the probability and impact tools look like now during Plan Risk Management so that the team has an agreed-upon basis for evaluating the identified risks later during the Perform Qualitative Risk Analysis process.

To recap, the steps associated with these last few elements of the risk management plan are as follows:

1. Define the risk categories (these will assist the risk team in the Identify Risks process).

2. Determine how probability and impact will be defined (to be used in the Perform Qualitative Risk Analysis process).

3. Develop or modify the probability and impact matrix (to be used in the Perform Qualitative Risk Analysis process).

Doing all these steps, together with the other elements of the risk management plan, gives you and the risk management team a common understanding for evaluating risks throughout the remainder of the project.

Identifying Potential Risk

The *Identify Risks* process involves identifying all the risks that might impact the project, documenting them, and documenting their characteristics. Identify Risks is an iterative process that continually builds on itself. As you progress through the project, more risks might present themselves. Once you've identified or discovered a potential new risk, you should analyze it to determine whether a response plan is needed. You can see that the risk management cycle starts again with Identify Risks and progresses through the remaining risk processes to determine what to do about them.

You can include several groups of folks to help identify risks, including project team members, risk team members, stakeholders, subject matter experts, users of the final product or service, and anyone else who you think might help in the process. Perhaps in the first round of Identify Risks you could include just the project team and subject matter experts and then bring in the stakeholders or risk management team to further flesh out risks during the second round of identification. Risk events can occur at any time during the project, and all project participants should be encouraged to continually watch for and report potential risk events.

I'll talk more about the techniques you can use to identify risks in the section, "Tools and Techniques for Identify Risk."

Risks might or might not adversely affect the project. Some risks have positive consequences, whereas others have negative consequences. However, you should identify all risk events and their consequences. Here's a partial list to get you thinking about where risk might be found:

- Budgets/funding
- Schedules
- Scope or requirements changes
- Project plan
- Project management processes
- Technical issues
- Personnel issues
- Hardware
- Contracts
- Political concerns
- Business risk
- Legal risk
- Environmental risk
- Management risk

This is by no means an exhaustive list. Remember that risk is uncertainty, and realize that risk (uncertainty) is lurking almost anywhere on your project. It's your job to discover as many of the potential risks as possible using the tools and techniques of this process and to document these risks.

Identify Risks Inputs

The inputs to the Identify Risks process are as follows:

- Risk management plan
- Cost management plan
- Schedule management plan
- Quality management plan
- Human resource management plan
- Scope baseline
- Activity cost estimates
- Activity duration estimates
- Stakeholder register

- Project documents
- Procurement documents
- Enterprise environmental factors
- Organizational process assets

We have covered each of these inputs previously, with the exception of the quality management plan and the human resource management plan. We'll talk about both of these inputs in Chapter 7, "Planning Project Resources," where we will discuss quality planning and human resource planning in depth. For purposes of the Identify Risk process, understand that the quality management process, identified in the quality management plan, has the potential to produce or prevent risks itself. We'll touch on a few of the key elements of some of these other inputs also.

You should pay particular attention to the roles and responsibilities section of the risk management plan and the budget and schedule for risk activities. Don't forget to examine the categories of risks as well. This is a great place to start when you get the team together and begin brainstorming your list of risks.

The project scope statement, part of the scope baseline, contains a list of project assumptions. You'll recall that assumptions are things believed to be true. During the risk-planning stages of your project and throughout the work of the project, it's imperative to revisit and revalidate your project assumptions. At the time you recorded an assumption about vendor deliveries, for example, the vendor had a great track record and never missed a date. Months later on the project, that vendor merges with one of its competitors. Now you'll need to reexamine your assumptions about delivery times and determine whether the assumption is still valid or whether you have a risk on your hands.

The cost, schedule, and human resource management plans can be helpful sources when identifying risks. You should also consider network diagrams, baselines, work performance reports, and other project information during this process.

The enterprise environmental-factors input concerns aspects from outside the project that might help you determine or influence project outcomes. Be certain to check for industry information (commercial databases, checklists, benchmarking studies, and so on) or academic research that might exist for your application areas regarding risk information.

As always, don't forget about historical information such as previous project experiences via the project files. You might find risk templates and lessons learned in these files that will help with the current project. Project team knowledge is another form of historical information.

Although the *PMBOK® Guide* doesn't mention it, I've found that other elements of your project are helpful when identifying risk, such as the work breakdown structure (WBS), the staffing management plan, project staff assignments, and resource availability. In practice, you should examine the outputs of most of the Planning processes when attempting to identify risks.

Tools and Techniques for Identify Risks

The Identify Risks process is undertaken using seven tools and techniques:

- Documentation reviews
- Information gathering
- Checklist analysis
- Assumptions analysis
- Diagramming techniques
- SWOT analysis
- Expert judgment

You'll learn more about each of these in the following sections.

Documentation Reviews

Documentation reviews involve reviewing project plans, assumptions, procurement documents, and historical information from previous projects from both a total project perspective and an individual deliverables and activities level. This review helps the project team identify risks associated with the project objectives. Pay attention to the quality of the plans (is the content complete, or does it seem to lack detail?) and the consistency between plans. An exceptionally documented schedule is great, but if the budget isn't as well documented, you might have some potential risks.

Information Gathering

Information gathering encompasses several techniques, including brainstorming, the Delphi technique, interviewing, and root cause analysis. The goal of these techniques is to end up with a comprehensive list of risks at the end of the meeting. Let's take a quick look at each of these techniques.

Brainstorming

Brainstorming is probably the most often used technique of the Identify Risks process. You've probably used this technique many times for many purposes. Brainstorming involves getting subject matter experts, team members, risk management team members, and anyone else who might benefit the process in a room and asking them to start identifying possible risk events. The trick here is that one person's idea might spawn another idea, and so on, so that by the end of the session you've identified all the possible risks. The facilitator could start the group off by going through the categories of risks to get everyone thinking in the right direction. Edward de Bono devised a method of brainstorming called Six Thinking Hats (based on his book by the same name) that you might want to investigate. You may recall that Edward de Bono is also noted for lateral thinking techniques, which we discussed in Chapter 3, "Developing the Project Scope Statement."

Nominal Group Technique

The Nominal Group Technique is not included as part of the information gathering techniques in the *PMBOK® Guide*. However, it's possible you may see a question about it on the exam. The *Nominal Group technique* is a brainstorming technique or it can be conducted as a mass interview technique.

This technique requires the participants to be together in the same room. Each participant has paper and pencil in front of them, and they are asked to write down what risks they think the project faces. Using sticky-backed notes is a good way to do this. Each piece of paper should contain only one risk. The papers are given to the facilitator, who sticks them up to the wall or a whiteboard. The panel is then asked to review all the risks posted on the board; rank them and prioritize them, in writing; and submit the ranking to the facilitator. Once this is done, you should have a complete list of risks.

Delphi Technique

The *Delphi technique* is a lot like brainstorming, except that the people participating in the meeting don't know one another. In fact, the people participating in this technique don't all have to be located in the same place and usually participate anonymously. You can use email to facilitate the Delphi technique easily.

What you do is assemble your experts, from both inside and outside the company, and provide them with a questionnaire to identify potential risks. The questionnaire is often designed with forced choices that require the experts to select between various options. The questionnaire asks participants about risks associated with the project, the business process, and the product of the project, and it asks the readers to rank their answers in regard to the potential impacts of the risks. They in turn send their responses back to you (or to the facilitator of this process). All the responses are organized by content and sent back to the Delphi members for further input, additions, or comments. The participants then send their comments back one more time, and the facilitator compiles a final list of risks.

The Delphi technique is a great tool that allows consensus to be reached quickly. It also helps prevent one person from unduly influencing the others in the group and, therefore, prevents bias in the outcome because the participants are usually anonymous and don't necessarily know how others in the group responded.

Interviewing

Interviews are question-and-answer sessions held with others, including other project managers, subject matter experts, stakeholders, customers, the management team, project team members, and users. These folks provide you with possible risks based on their past experiences with similar projects.

This technique involves interviewing those folks with previous experience on projects similar to yours or those with specialized knowledge or industry expertise. Ask them to tell you about any risks that they've experienced or that they think might happen on your project. Show them the WBS and your list of assumptions to help get them started thinking in the right direction.

Root Cause Analysis

Did you ever hear someone say you're looking at the symptoms and not at the problem? That's the idea here. *Root cause analysis* involves digging deeper than the risk itself and looking at the cause of the risk. This helps define the risk more clearly, and it also helps you later when it's time to develop the response plan for the risk.

> **Exam Spotlight**
>
> Be aware that there might be questions about any of the techniques I've shown here. Understand the difference between the various information-gathering techniques for the exam.

Checklist Analysis

Checklists used during the Identify Risks process are usually developed based on historical information and previous project team experience. If you typically work on projects that are similar in nature, begin to compile a list of risks. You can then convert this to a checklist that will allow you to identify risks on future projects quickly and easily. You can also use the lowest level of the RBS as a checklist. However, don't rely solely on checklists for Identify Risks because you might miss important risks. It isn't possible for a single checklist to be an exhaustive source for all projects. You can improve your checklists at the end of the project by adding the new risks that were identified.

Assumptions Analysis

Assumptions analysis is a matter of validating the assumptions you identified and documented during the course of the project-planning processes. Assumptions should be accurate, complete, and consistent. Examine all your assumptions for these qualities. Assumptions are also used as jumping-off points to further identify risks.

The important point to note about the project assumptions is that all assumptions are tested against two factors:

- The strength of the assumption or the validity of the assumption
- The consequences that might impact the project if the assumption turns out to be false

All assumptions that turn out to be false should be evaluated and scored just as risks.

Diagramming Techniques

Three types of diagramming techniques are used in Identify Risks: cause-and-effect, system or process flowcharts, and influence diagrams. *Cause-and-effect diagrams* show the relationship between the effects of problems and their causes. This diagram depicts every potential cause and subcause of a problem and the effect that each proposed solution will have on the problem. This diagram is also called a *fishbone diagram* or *Ishikawa diagram* after its developer, Kaoru Ishikawa. Figure 6.2 shows an example cause-and-effect diagram.

FIGURE 6.2   Cause-and-effect diagram

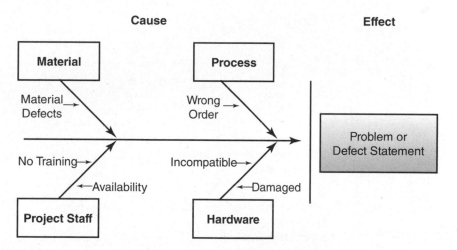

The *system or process flowchart* shows the logical steps needed to accomplish an objective, how the elements of a system relate to each other, and what actions cause what responses. This flowchart is probably the one with which you're most familiar. It's usually constructed with rectangles and parallelograms that step through a logical sequence and allow for "Yes" and "No" branches (or some similar type of decision). Figure 6.3 shows a flowchart to help determine whether risk response plans should be developed for the risk (I'll talk about response plans in the section, "Developing a Risk Response Plan" later in this chapter).

FIGURE 6.3 Flowchart diagram

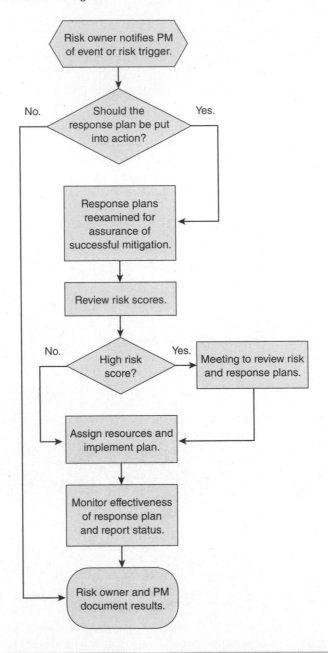

 Cause-and-effect diagrams and system or process flowcharts are used in the Identify Risks process, as well as in the Perform Quality Control process.

A third diagramming technique used during Identify Risks is called *influence diagramming*. According to the *PMBOK® Guide*, influence diagrams typically show the causal influences among project variables, the timing or time ordering of events, and the relationships among other project variables and their outcomes. Simply put, they visually depict risks (or decisions), uncertainties or impacts, and how they influence each other. Figure 6.4 shows an influence diagram for a product introduction decision. The weather is a variable that could impact delivery time, and delivery time is a variable that can impact when revenues will occur.

FIGURE 6.4   Influence diagram

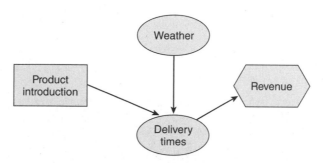

Each of these techniques provides a way for you to help identify project risks. It's important that you identify all the risks early in the process. The better job you do of identifying the project's risks at the Planning stage, the more comprehensive the risk response plan will be. Identify Risks is not an area of project planning that you should skip.

Strengths, Weaknesses, Opportunities, and Threats (SWOT)

Strengths, weaknesses, opportunities, and threats (also known as *SWOT analysis*) is a technique that examines the project from each of these viewpoints. It also requires examining the project from the viewpoint of the project itself and from project management processes, resources, the organization, and so on to identify risks, including those that are generated internally to the project. Strengths and weaknesses are generally related to issues that are internal to the organization. Strengths examine what your organization does well and what your customers, or the marketplace, view as your strengths. Weaknesses are areas the organization could improve upon. Typically, negative risks are associated with the organization's weaknesses and positive risks are associated with its strengths. Opportunities and threats are usually external to the organization. SWOT analysis is sometimes known as internal-external analysis and can be used in combination with brainstorming techniques to help discover and document potential risks.

Expert Judgment

Experts for risk identification purposes can include anyone who has experience working on similar projects, experience working in the business area for which the project was undertaken, or specific industry experience. When using this technique, you should consider any bias your experts may have regarding the project or potential risk events.

Identify Risks Outputs

The output of the Identify Risks process is the *risk register*. Everything you've done in this process up to this point will get documented here. The risk register contains the following elements:

- List of identified risks
- List of potential responses

The risk register also often contains warning signs or triggers, although they aren't listed as an official part of the register. You'll take a look at each of these next. Understand that all risks should be documented, tracked, reviewed, and managed throughout the project.

List of Identified Risks

Risks are all the potential events and their subsequent consequences that could occur as identified by you and others during this process. You might want to consider logging your risks in a risk database or tracking system to organize them and keep a close eye on their status. This can easily be done in spreadsheet format or whatever method you choose. List the risks, assign each risk a tracking number, and note the potential cause or event and the potential impact. This list gives you a means to track the risks, their occurrence, and the responses implemented.

List of Potential Responses

You might identify potential responses to risk at the same time you're identifying the risks. Sometimes just identifying the risk will tell you the appropriate response. Document those responses here. You'll refer to them again in the Plan Risk Responses process a little later in this chapter.

A sample risk register is shown in Table 6.1. As you progress through the risk, planning processes, and through the project itself, more risks may be identified and more information will become known about the risks. You should update the risk register with new information as it becomes known.

TABLE 6.1   Risk register

ID	Risk	Trigger	Event	Cause	Impact	Owner	Response plan
1	Infra-structure team is not avail-able when needed	Prede-cessor tasks not com-pleted on time	Oper-ating system upgrade delayed	Equip-ment was not deliv-ered on time	Sched-ule delay	Brown	Compress the schedule by beginning tasks in the next mile-stone while working on operat-ing system upgrade

Triggers

Triggers are warning signs or symptoms that a risk event is about to occur. For example, if you've ever suffered from a hay fever attack, you can't mistake the itchy, runny nose and scratchy throat that can come on suddenly and send you into a sneezing frenzy. Signals like this are known as *triggers* and work the same way when determining whether a risk event is about to occur. For example, if you're planning an outdoor gathering and rain clouds start rolling in from the north on the morning of the activity, you probably have a risk event waiting to happen. A key team member hinting about job hunting is a warning sign that the person might be thinking of leaving, which in turn can cause schedule delays, increased costs, and so on. This is another example of a trigger.

Triggers are *not* listed as one of the risk register elements until the Plan Risk Responses process is carried out, but in practice this is an appropriate time to list them. You will likely encounter questions on the exam about triggers, so don't say I didn't warn you. Also, throughout the remainder of the project, be on the alert for triggers that might signal that a risk event is about to occur.

Analyzing Risks Using Qualitative Techniques

The *Perform Qualitative Risk Analysis* process involves determining what impact the identified risks will have on the project objectives and the probability they'll occur. It also ranks the risks in priority order according to their effect on the project objectives so that you can spend your time efficiently by focusing on the high-priority risks. This helps the team determine whether Perform Quantitative Risk Analysis should be performed or whether you can skip right to developing response plans. The Perform Qualitative Risk Analysis process also considers risk tolerance levels, especially as they relate to the project constraints (scope, time, cost, and quality) and the time frames of the potential risk events.

The Perform Qualitative Risk Analysis process should be performed throughout the project. This process is the one you'll find you'll use most often when prioritizing project risks because it's fast, relatively easy to perform, and cost effective. The *PMBOK® Guide* notes that you should identify and manage the risk attitudes of those assisting with this process, and if bias is introduced, you should evaluate it and correct it if necessary. It also notes that simply conducting the Perform Qualitative Risk Analysis process and evaluating the impact and probability of risks can help to keep bias at a minimal level.

Perform Qualitative Risk Analysis Inputs

The Perform Qualitative Risk Analysis process has five inputs:

- Risk management plan
- Scope baseline
- Risk register
- Enterprise environmental factors
- Organizational process assets

The critical element in this process, as with most of the processes where the risk register is an input, is the list of risks contained in the risk register. The risk management plan documented the roles and responsibilities of risk team members, budget and schedule factors for risk activities, the stakeholder risk tolerances, the definitions for probability and impact, and the probability and impact matrix, all of which should be utilized when prioritizing risks. You'll examine probability and impact more closely in the next section, "Tools and Techniques for Perform Qualitative Risk Analysis."

The scope baseline describes the deliverables of the project, and from there you should be able to determine whether you're dealing with a high level of uncertainty or a project that's similar in size and scope to one you've performed before. Projects with high levels of uncertainty or that are more complex than what the team has undertaken before require more diligence during the Perform Qualitative Risk Analysis process.

As with the Identify Risks process, you should examine historical information and lessons learned from past projects as a guide for prioritizing the risks for this project. Risk databases from your industry or application area can be used here as well. These are part of the organizational process assets input.

The real key to this process lies in the tools and techniques you'll use to prioritize risks. Hold on tight because you're going in the deep end.

Tools and Techniques for Perform Qualitative Risk Analysis

The Perform Qualitative Risk Analysis process's tools and techniques are primarily concerned with discovering the probability of a risk event and determining the impact (or consequences) the risk will have if it does occur. The output of this process is project documents updates (that will include risk register updates) where you'll document the prioritized risks you've scored using these tools and techniques. All the information you gather regarding risks and probability needs to be as accurate as possible. It's also important that you gather unbiased information so that you don't unintentionally overlook risks with great potential or consequences.

The purpose of this process is to determine risk event probability and risk impact and to prioritize the risks and their responses. You'll use the tools and techniques of this process to establish risk scores, which is a way of categorizing the probability and risk impact. The Perform Qualitative Risk Analysis process includes the following tools and techniques:

- Risk probability and impact assessment
- Probability and impact matrix
- Risk data quality assessment
- Risk categorization
- Risk urgency assessment
- Expert judgment

We'll look at each of these tools and techniques next.

Risk Probability and Impact Assessment

This tool and technique assesses the probability that the risk events you've identified will occur, and it determines the effect their impacts have on the project objectives, including time, scope, quality, and cost. Analyzing risks in this way allows you to determine which risks require the most aggressive management. When determining probabilities and impacts, you'll refer to the risk management plan element called "definitions of risk probability and impact."

Probability

Probability is the likelihood that an event will occur. The classic example is flipping a coin. There is a 0.50 probability of getting heads and a 0.50 probability of getting tails on the flip. Note that the probability that an event will occur plus the probability that the event will not occur always equals 1.0. In this coin-flipping example, you have a 0.50 chance that you'll get heads on the flip. Therefore, you have a 0.50 chance you will not get heads on the flip. The two responses added together equal 1.0. Probability is expressed as a number from 0.0— which means there is no probability of the event occurring—to 1.0—which means there is 100 percent certainty the event will occur.

Determining risk probability can be difficult because it's most commonly accomplished using expert judgment. In non-project management terms, this means you're guessing (or asking other experts to guess) at the probability a risk event will occur. Granted, you're basing your guess on past experiences with similar projects or risk events, but no two risk events (or projects) are ever the same. It's best to fully develop the criteria for determining probability and get as many experts involved as you can. Carefully weigh their responses to come up with the best probability values possible.

Impact

Impact is the amount of pain (or the amount of gain) the risk event poses to the project. The risk *impact scale* can be a relative scale (also known as an ordinal scale) that assigns values such as high-medium-low (or some combination of these) or a numeric scale known as a *cardinal scale*. Cardinal scale values are actual numeric values assigned to the risk impact. Cardinal scales are expressed as values from 0.0 to 1.0 and can be stated in equal (linear) or unequal (nonlinear) increments.

Table 6.2 shows a typical risk impact scale for cost, time, and quality objectives based on a high-high to low-low scale. You'll notice that each of the high-medium-low value combinations on this impact scale has been assigned a cardinal value. I'll use these in the next section when I talk about the probability and impact matrix.

When you're using a high-medium-low scale, it's important that your risk team understands what criteria were used to determine a high score versus a medium or low score and how they should be applied to the project objectives.

TABLE 6.2   Risk impact scale

Objectives	Low-low	Low	Medium	High	High-high
	0.05	0.20	0.40	0.60	0.80
Cost	No significant impact	Less than 6% increase	7–12% increase	13–18% increase	More than 18% increase
Time	No significant impact	Less than 6% increase	7–12% increase	13–18% increase	More than 18% increase
Quality	No significant impact	Few components impacted	Significant impact requiring customer approval to proceed	Unacceptable quality	Product not usable

Assessing Probability and Impact

The idea behind both probability and impact values is to develop predefined measurements that describe what value to place on a risk event.

Exam Spotlight

For the exam, don't forget that you define probability and impact values during the Plan Risk Management process and document them in the risk management plan.

If the risk impact scale has not been previously defined, develop one for the project as early in the Planning processes as possible. You can use any of the techniques I talked about earlier in the section, "Tools and Techniques for Identify Risk," such as brainstorming or the Delphi technique, to come up with the values for probability and impact.

During the Perform Qualitative Risk Analysis process, you'll determine and assess probability and impact for every risk identified during the Identify Risks process. You could interview or hold meetings with project team members, subject matter experts, stakeholders, or others to help assess these factors. During this process, you should document not only the probability and impact but also the assumptions your team members used to arrive at these determinations. The next technique—probability and impact matrix—takes the probability and impact values one step further by assigning an overall risk score.

Probability and Impact Matrix

The outcome of a probability and impact matrix is an overall risk rating for each of the project's identified risks. The combination of probability and impact results in a classification usually expressed as high, medium, or low. Typically, high risks are considered a red condition, medium risks are considered a yellow condition, and low risks are considered a green condition. This type of ranking is known as *an ordinal scale* because the values are ordered by rank from high to low. (In practice, ordinal values might also include ranking by position. In other words, the risks are listed in order by rank as the first, the second, the third, and so on.)

Exam Spotlight

The *PMBOK® Guide* notes that risk rating rules and the probability and impact matrix values and steps are usually set by the organization and are part of the organizational process assets.

Now let's look at an example. You have identified a risk event that could impact project costs, and your experts believe costs could increase by as much as 9 percent. According to the risk impact rating matrix in Table 6.2, this risk carries a medium impact, with a value of 0.40. Hold on to that number because you're going to plug it into the probability impact matrix—along with the probability value—to determine an overall risk value next.

You'll remember from the discussion previously that probability values should be assigned numbers from 0.0 to 1.0. In this example, the team has determined that there is a 0.2 probability of this risk event occurring. The risk impact scale shows a medium or 0.4 impact should the event occur.

Now, to determine whether the combination of the probability and impact of this risk is high, medium, or low, you'll need to check the probability impact matrix. Table 6.3 shows a sample probability and impact matrix.

TABLE 6.3   Sample probability and impact matrix

Probability	Impact values* low-low.05	Low .20	Medium .40	High .60	High-high .80
.8	.04	.16	*.32*	*.48*	*.64*
.6	.03	.12	.24	*.36*	*.48*
.4	.02	.08	.16	.24	*.32*
.2	.01	.04	.08	.12	.16

*No formatting = low assignment or green condition; **bold** = medium assignment or yellow condition; ***bold italic*** = high assignment or red condition.

First, look at the probability column. Your risk event has a probability of .2. Now, follow that row across until you find the column that shows the impact score of .40 (it's the Medium column). According to your probability and impact matrix values, this risk carries an overall score of .08 and falls in the low threshold, so this risk is assigned a low (or green condition) value.

The values assigned to the risks determine how Plan Risk Responses is carried out for the risks later during the risk-planning processes. Obviously, risks with high probability and high impact are going to need further analysis and formal responses. Remember that the values for this matrix (and the probability and impact scales discussed earlier) are determined prior to the start of this process and documented in the risk management plan. Also keep in mind that probability and impact do not have to be assigned the same values as I've done here. You might use 0.8, 0.6, 0.4, and 0.2 for probability, for example, and assign .05, 0.1, .3, 0.5, and 0.7 for impact scales.

 Real World Scenario

Screen Scrapers, Inc.

Screen Scrapers is a software-manufacturing company that produces a software product that looks at your mainframe screens, commonly called *green screens*, and converts them to browser-based screens. The browser-based screens look like any other Windows-compatible screens with buttons, scroll bars, and drop-down lists.

Screen Scrapers devised this product for companies that use mainframe programs to update and store data because many of the entry-level workers beginning their careers today are not familiar with green screens. They're cumbersome and difficult to learn, and no consistency exists from screen to screen or from program to program. Pressing the F5 key in one program might mean go back one page, whereas pressing F5 in another program might mean clear the screen. New users are easily confused, make a lot of mistakes, and have to write tablets full of notes on how to navigate all the screens.

Your company has purchased the Screen Scraper product and has appointed you the project manager over the installation. This project consists of a lot of issues to address, and you've made great headway. You're now at the Identify Risks and Perform Qualitative Risk Analysis stage. You decide to use the Delphi technique to assist you in identifying risk and assigning probability and impact rankings. Some experts are available in your company to serve on the Delphi panel, as well as some folks in industry organizations you belong to outside the company.

You assemble the group, set up a summary of the project, and send it out via email, requesting responses to your questions about risk. After the first pass, you compile the list of risks as follows (this list is an example and isn't exhaustive because your list will be project specific):

- Vendor viability (will the software company stay in business?)

- Vendor responsiveness with problems after implementation

- Software compatibility risks with existing systems

- Hardware compatibility risk

- Connection to the mainframe risk

- Training IT staff members to maintain the product

You send this list back to the Delphi members and ask them to assign a probability of 0.0 to 1.0 and an impact of high-high, high, medium, low, or low-low to each risk. The Delphi members assign probability and impact based on a probability scale and an impact scale designed by the risk management team. The values of the impact scale are as follows:

- High-high = 0.8

- High = 0.6

- Medium = 0.4

- Low = 0.2

- Low-low = 0.05

The results are compiled to determine the following probability and impact values:

- Vendor viability = 0.6 probability, high impact

- Vendor responsiveness = 0.4 probability, medium impact

- Software compatibility = 0.4 probability, medium impact

- Hardware compatibility = 0.6 probability, high-high impact

- Mainframe connection = 0.2 probability, high-high impact

- Training = 0.2 probability, low-low impact

The probability and impact matrix you used to assign the overall risk scores were derived from the probability and impact matrix shown in the following table.

Based on the probability and impact matrix thresholds, the project risks are assigned the following overall probabilities:

- Vendor viability = high
- Vendor responsiveness = medium
- Software compatibility = medium
- Hardware compatibility = high
- Mainframe connection = medium
- Training = low

PI Matrix for Screen Scrapers, Inc.

Probability	Impact scores*.05	.20	.40	.60	.80
.8	.04	.16	*.32*	*.48*	*.64*
.6	.03	.12	.24	*.36*	*.48*
.4	.02	.08	.16	.24	*.32*
.2	.01	.04	.08	**.12**	**.16**

*No formatting = low assignment or green condition; **bold** = medium assignment or yellow condition; ***bold italic*** = high assignment or red condition.

Risk Data Quality Assessment

The risk data quality assessment involves determining the usefulness of the data gathered to evaluate risk. Most important, the data must be unbiased and accurate. You will want to examine elements such as the following when using this tool and technique:

- The quality of the data used
- The availability of data regarding the risks
- How well the risk is understood
- The reliability and integrity of the data
- The accuracy of the data

Low-quality data will render the results from the Perform Qualitative Risk Analysis process almost useless. Spend the time to validate and verify the information you've collected about risks so that your prioritization and analysis is as accurate as it can be. If you find that the quality of the data is questionable, you guessed it—go back and get better data.

Risk Categorizations

This tool and technique is used to determine the effects risk has on the project. You can examine not only the categories of risk determined during the Plan Risk Management process (and described in the RBS) but also the project phase and the WBS to determine the elements of the project that are affected by risk.

Risk Urgency Assessment

Using this tool you'll determine how soon the potential risk events might occur and quickly determine responses for those risk events that could occur soon. You should consider the risk triggers, the time to develop and implement a response, and the overall risk rating when deciding how quickly responses are needed.

Expert Judgment

Because this process determines qualitative values, by its very nature you must rely on expert judgment to determine the probability, impact, and other information we've derived so far. The more knowledge and similar experience your experts have, the better your assessments will be. Interviews and facilitated workshops are two techniques you can use in conjunction with expert judgment to perform this process. As with the Identify Risks process, make certain to take into account any bias your experts have and to correct it when necessary.

Ranking Risks in the Risk Register

The goal of the Perform Qualitative Risk Analysis process is to rank the risks and determine which ones need further analysis and, eventually, risk response plans. The output of this process is project documents updates. This almost always involves updating the risk register. According to the *PMBOK® Guide*, you'll update the risk register with the following information:

- Risk ranking (or priority) for the identified risks
- Risk scores
- Updated probability and impact analysis
- Risk urgency information
- Causes of risk
- List of risks requiring near-term responses

- List of risks that need additional analysis and response
- Watch list of low-priority risks
- Trends in qualitative risk analysis results

Each element becomes a new entry in the risk register. For example, risk ranking assigns the risk score or priority you determined using the probability and impact matrix to the list of identified risks previously recorded in the risk register. I discussed the categories and the list of risks requiring near-term responses earlier. Note these in the risk register.

You should also note those risks that require further analysis (including using the Perform Quantitative Risk Analysis process), you'll create a list of risks that have low risk scores to review periodically, and you should note any trends in Perform Qualitative Risk Analysis that become evident as you perform this process.

The assumptions log is another project document that should be updated as new information is discovered throughout this process. Assumptions are generally documented in the project scope statement or can be kept in a separate document so that they are easier to update. Assumptions can and do change throughout the course of the project, and the process of identifying and prioritizing risks may require updates to the assumptions.

Quantifying Risk

The *Perform Quantitative Risk Analysis* process evaluates the impacts of risk prioritized during the Perform Qualitative Risk Analysis process. It is typically performed for those risks that were identified in Perform Qualitative Risk Analysis that could have a significant impact on the project. Perform Quantitative Risk Analysis quantifies the aggregate risk exposure for the project by assigning numeric probabilities to risks and their impacts on project objectives. This quantitative approach is accomplished using techniques such as Monte Carlo simulation and decision tree analysis. To paraphrase the *PMBOK® Guide*, the purpose of this process is to perform the following:

- Quantify the project's possible outcomes and probabilities.
- Determine the probability of achieving the project objectives.
- Identify risks that need the most attention by quantifying their contribution to overall project risk.
- Identify realistic and achievable schedule, cost, or scope targets.
- Determine the best project management decisions possible when outcomes are uncertain.

Perform Quantitative Risk Analysis—like Perform Qualitative Risk Analysis—examines risk and its potential impact on the project objectives. You might choose to use both of these processes to assess all risks or only one of them, depending on the complexity of the project and the organizational policy regarding risk planning. The Perform Quantitative Risk Analysis process follows the Perform Qualitative Risk Analysis process. If you use this process, be sure to repeat it every time the Plan Risk Responses process is performed and as part of the Control Risks process so that you can determine whether overall project risk has decreased.

I've already covered many of the inputs to the Perform Quantitative Risk Analysis process in previous sections of this chapter. They are as follows:

- Risk management plan
- Cost management plan
- Schedule management plan
- Risk register
- Environmental enterprise factors
- Organizational process assets

The elements of the enterprise environmental factors you'll want to pay close attention to as an input to this process are risk databases and risk specialists' studies performed on similar projects. The elements of the organizational process assets input include historical information from previous projects of a similar nature.

Tools and Techniques for Perform Quantitative Risk Analysis

The Perform Quantitative Risk Analysis process includes three tools and techniques: data-gathering and representation techniques, quantitative risk analysis and modeling techniques, and expert judgment.

Data-Gathering and Representation Techniques

The data-gathering and representation techniques include interviewing techniques and probability distributions.

Interviewing

This technique is like the interviewing technique discussed earlier in the section, "Identifying Potential Risk." Project team members, stakeholders, and subject-matter experts are prime candidates for risk interviews. Ask them about their experiences on past projects and about working with the types of technology or processes you'll use during this project.

 For the exam, remember that interviewing is a tool and technique of the Perform Quantitative Risk Analysis process. Although you can use this technique in the Identify Risks process, keep in mind that it's part of the data-gathering and representation techniques and not a named tool and technique itself.

When using this technique, you should first determine what methods of probability distribution (described next) you'll use to analyze your information. The technique you choose will dictate the type of information you need to gather. For example, you might use a three-point scale that assesses the low, high, and most likely risk scenarios or take it a step further and use standard deviations calculations.

Make certain you document how the interviewees decided on the risk ranges, the criteria they used to place risks in certain categories, and the results of the interview. This information will help you later in developing risk responses.

Exam Spotlight

For the exam, you should know that several types of probability distributions exist that are useful in determining and displaying risk information. The type of distribution you use determines the type of information you should gather during the interviewing process.

Probability Distributions

It's beyond the scope of this book to delve into probability distributions and calculations, so I'll point out a few aspects of them that you should remember for the exam.

Continuous probability distributions (particularly beta and triangular distributions) are commonly used in Perform Quantitative Risk Analysis. According to the *PMBOK® Guide*, continuous probability distributions include normal, lognormal, triangular, beta, and uniform distributions. Distributions are graphically displayed and represent both the probability and time or cost elements.

Triangular distributions use estimates based on the three-point estimate (the pessimistic, most likely, and optimistic values). This means that during your interviews, you'll gather these pieces of information from your experts. Then you'll use them to quantify risk for each WBS element.

Normal and lognormal distributions use mean and standard deviations to quantify risk, which also require gathering the optimistic, most likely, and pessimistic estimates.

Discrete distributions represent possible scenarios in a decision tree (we'll discuss this in the next section), outcomes of a test, results of a prototype, and other uncertain events.

Quantitative Risk Analysis and Modeling Techniques

For the exam, you should know the four analysis and modeling techniques within the Quantitative Risk Analysis tool and technique: sensitivity analysis, expected monetary value analysis, decision tree analysis, and modeling and simulation. Let's take a brief look at each of them.

Sensitivity Analysis

Sensitivity analysis is a quantitative method of analyzing the potential impact of risk events on the project and determining which risk event (or events) has the greatest potential for impact by examining all the uncertain elements at their baseline values. One of the ways sensitivity analysis data is displayed is a tornado diagram. Figure 6.5 shows a sample *tornado diagram*.

FIGURE 6.5   Tornado diagram

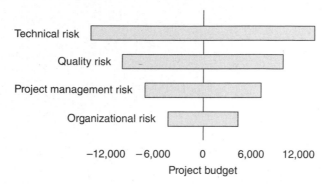

You can see by the arrangement of horizontal bars (each representing a sensitivity variable) how the diagram gets its name. The idea is that each sensitivity bar displays the low and high value possible for the element the bar represents. It's beyond the scope of this book to explain how these values are determined. The questions you might encounter on the exam are focused on the context of this type of analysis. The variables with the greatest effect on the project appear at the top of the graph and decrease in impact as you progress down through the graph. This gives you a quick overview of how much the project can be affected by uncertainty in the various elements. It also allows you to see at a glance which risks might have the biggest impacts on the project and will require carefully crafted, detailed response plans. You can use tornado diagrams to determine sensitivity in cost, time, and quality objectives or for risks you've identified during this process. Sensitivity analysis can also be used to determine stakeholder risk tolerance levels.

Expected Monetary Value (EMV) Analysis

Expected monetary value (EMV) analysis is a statistical technique that calculates the average, anticipated future impact of the decision. EMV is calculated by multiplying the probability of the risk by its impact for two or more potential outcomes (for example, a good outcome and a poor outcome) and then adding the results of the potential outcomes together. EMV is used in conjunction with the decision tree analysis technique, which is covered next. I'll give you an example of the EMV formula in the next section. Positive results generally mean the risks you're assessing pose opportunities to the project, whereas negative results generally indicate a threat to the project.

Decision Tree Analysis

Unfortunately, this isn't a tree outside your office door that produces "yes" and "no" leaves that you can pick to help you make a decision. *Decision trees* are diagrams that show the sequence of interrelated decisions and the expected results of choosing one alternative over the other. Typically, more than one choice or option is available when you're faced with a decision or, in this case, potential outcomes from a risk event. The available choices are depicted in tree form starting at the left with the risk decision branching out to the right with possible outcomes. Decision trees are usually used for risk events associated with time or cost.

Figure 6.6 shows a sample decision tree using expected monetary value (EMV) as one of its inputs.

FIGURE 6.6 Decision tree

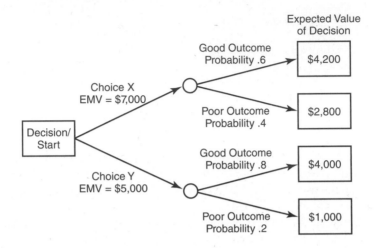

The expected monetary value of the decision is a result of the probability of the risk event multiplied by the impact for two or more potential outcomes and then summing their results. The squares in this figure represent decisions to be made, and the circles represent the points where risk events might occur.

The decision with an expected value of $7,000 is the correct decision to make because the resulting outcome has the greatest value.

Modeling and Simulation

Modeling and simulation techniques are often used for schedule risk analysis and cost analysis. For example, modeling allows you to translate the potential risks at specific points in the project into their impacts so you can determine how the project objectives are affected. Simulation techniques compute the project model using various inputs, such as cost estimates or activity durations, to determine a probability distribution for the variable chosen. (Cost risks typically use either a work breakdown structure or a cost breakdown structure as the input variable. Schedule risks always use the schedule network diagram and duration estimates as the input variable. I'll cover schedule diagramming methods in Chapter 7.) If you used simulation techniques to determine project cost and use the cost of the project elements as the input variable, a probability distribution for the total cost of the project would be produced after running the simulation numerous times. Modeling and simulation techniques examine the identified risks and their potential impacts on the project objectives from the perspective of the whole project.

Monte Carlo analysis is an example of a simulation technique. Monte Carlo analysis is replicated many times, typically using cost or schedule variables. Every time the analysis is performed, the values for the variable are changed using a probability distribution for each variable. Monte Carlo analysis can also be used during the Develop Schedule process.

Exam Spotlight

Simulation techniques are recommended for predicting schedule or cost risks because they're more powerful than EMV and less likely to be misused. For the exam, remember that simulation techniques are used to predict schedule or cost risks.

Expert Judgment

I've talked about this tool and technique before. Experts can come from inside or outside the organization and should have experience that's applicable to your project. For example, if your project involves manufacturing a new product or part, you might want to consider experts such as engineers or statisticians. If you're dealing with sensitive data in an information technology project, consider bringing in a security expert. When evaluating risk, use experts who understand the tools associated with analyzing risk including the benefits and drawbacks of the tools or methods you'll use.

Perform Quantitative Risk Analysis Outputs

The output of the Perform Quantitative Risk Analysis process is—I'll bet you can guess—project documents updates. As with the Perform Qualitative Risk Analysis process, you'll record the following new elements in the risk register:

Probabilistic Analysis of the Project   Probabilistic analysis of the project is the forecasted results of the project schedule and costs as determined by the outcomes of risk analysis. These results include projected completion dates and costs, along with a confidence level associated with each. According to the *PMBOK® Guide*, this output is often expressed as a cumulative frequency distribution, and you'll use these results along with stakeholder risk tolerances to quantify the time and cost contingency reserves. (I'll talk about contingency reserves in the next section, "Developing a Risk Response Plan.")

Confidence levels can also be used to describe the level of confidence placed on the outcome of the forecasted results. For example, suppose the projected schedule completion date is July 12 and the confidence level is .85. This says you believe the project will finish on or before July 12 and that you have an 85-percent level of confidence that this date is accurate.

Probability of Achieving the Cost and Time Objectives   Using the tools and techniques of Perform Quantitative Risk Analysis allows you to assign a probability of achieving the cost and time objectives of the project. This output documents those probabilities and as such requires a thorough understanding of the current project objectives and knowledge of the risks.

Prioritized List of Quantified Risks   The prioritized list in this process is similar to the list produced during the Perform Qualitative Risk Analysis process. The list of risks includes those that present the greatest risk or threat to the project and their impacts. It also lists those risks that present the greatest opportunities to the project. This list should also indicate which risks are most likely to impact the critical path and those that have the largest cost contingency.

Trends in Perform Quantitative Risk Analysis Results   Trends in Perform Quantitative Risk Analysis will likely appear as you repeat the risk analysis processes. This information is useful as you progress, making those risks with the greatest threat to the project more evident, which gives you the opportunity to perform further analysis or go on to develop risk response plans.

Exam Spotlight

Understand the differences between the Perform Qualitative Risk Analysis and Perform Quantitative Risk Analysis processes for the exam.

Developing a Risk Response Plan

The *Plan Risk Responses* process is the last process covered in this chapter. (I hear you cheering out there!) Plan Risk Responses is a process of deciding what actions to take to reduce threats and take advantage of the opportunities discovered during the risk analysis processes. This process also includes assigning departments or individual staff members the responsibility of carrying out the risk response plans you'll outline in this process. These folks are known as *risk owners*.

 The more effective your risk response plans are, the better your chances for a successful project. Well-developed and well-written risk response plans will likely decrease overall project risk.

Generally, you'll want to develop risk response plans for those risks with a combination of high probability of occurrence and significant impact to the project, those ranked high (or red) on the probability/impact matrix, or those ranked high as a result of Perform Quantitative Risk Analysis. Developing risk response plans for risks of low severity or insignificant impact is not an efficient or good use of the project team's time. Spend your time planning responses that are appropriate given the impact the risk itself poses (or the opportunity the risk presents), and don't spend more time, money, or energy to produce a response than the risk event itself would produce if it occurred.

The inputs you'll use to assist you in this process are the risk register and the risk management plan. Several strategies are used in this process to reduce or control risk. It's important that you choose the right strategy for each risk so that the risk and its impacts are dealt with effectively. After deciding on which strategy to use, you'll develop an action plan to put this strategy into play should the risk event occur. You might also choose to designate a secondary or backup strategy.

Exam Spotlight

The rank of the risk will dictate the level at which the Plan Risk Responses should be performed. For example, a risk with low severity wouldn't warrant the time it takes to develop a detailed risk response plan. Risk responses should be cost effective—if the cost of the response is more than the consequences of the risk, you might want to examine a different risk response. Risk responses should also be timely, agreed to by all the project stakeholders, and assigned to an individual (risk owner) who is responsible for monitoring and carrying out the risk response plan if needed.

Tools and Techniques for Plan Risk Responses

The Plan Risk Responses process consists of four tools and techniques, and each one of them involves a strategy. The tools and techniques are as follows:

- Strategies for negative risks or threats
- Strategies for positive risks or opportunities
- Contingent response strategies
- Expert judgment

You'll take a look at the first three next.

Strategies for Negative Risks or Threats

Four strategies exist to deal with negative risks or threats to the project objectives: avoid, transfer, mitigate, and accept. Accept is a strategy you can use for positive risks or opportunities also.

Avoid

To *avoid* a risk means you'll evade it altogether by eliminating the cause of the risk event or by changing the project management plan to protect the project objectives from the risk event. Let's say you're going to take a car trip from your home to a point 800 miles away. You know—because your friends who just took the same trip told you—that there is a long stretch of construction on one of the highways you're planning on using. To avoid the risk of delay, you plan the trip around the construction work and use another highway for that stretch of driving. In this way, you change your plans, avoid the risk of getting held up in construction traffic, and arrive at your destination on time.

With risk avoidance, you essentially eradicate the risk by eliminating its cause. Here's another example: Suppose your project was kicked off without adequate scope definition and requirements gathering. You run a high probability of experiencing scope creep—ever-changing requirements—as the project progresses, thereby impacting the project schedule. You can avoid this risk by adequately documenting the project scope and requirements during the Planning processes and taking steps to monitor and control changes to scope so it doesn't get out of hand.

Risks that occur early in the project might easily be avoided by improving communications, refining requirements, assigning additional resources to project activities, refining the project scope to avoid risk events, and so on.

Transfer

The idea behind a risk *transfer* is to transfer the risk and the consequences of that risk to a third party. The risk hasn't gone away, but the responsibility for the management of that risk now rests with another party. Most companies aren't willing to take on someone else's risk without a little cash thrown in for good measure. This strategy will impact the project budget and should be included in the cost estimate exercises if you know you're going to use it.

Transfer of risk can occur in many forms but is most effective when dealing with financial risks. Insurance is one form of risk transfer. You are probably familiar with how insurance works. Car insurance is a good example. You purchase car insurance so that if you come upon an obstacle in the road and there is no way to avoid hitting it, the cost to repair the damage to the car is paid by the insurance company...okay, minus the deductible and all the calculations for the age of the car, the mileage, the color and make of the car, the weather conditions the day you were driving—but I digress.

Another method of risk transfer is contracting. Contracting transfers specific risks to the vendor, depending on the work required by the contract. The vendor accepts the responsibility for the cost of failure. Again, this doesn't come without a price. Contractors charge for their services, and depending on the type of contract you negotiate, the cost might be quite high. For example, in a fixed-price contract, which I'll talk more about in Chapter 7, the vendor (or seller) increases the cost of the contract to compensate for the level of risk they're accepting. A cost reimbursable contract, however, leaves the majority of the risk with you, the buyer. This type of contract might reduce costs if project changes occur midway through the project.

Keep in mind that contracting isn't a cure-all. You might just be swapping one risk for another. For example, say you hire a driver to go with you on your road trip, and that person's job is to do all the driving. If the driver becomes ill or in some way can't fulfill their obligation, you aren't going to get to your destination on time. You've placed the risks associated with the trip on the contract driver; however, you've taken on a risk of delay because of nonperformance, which means you've just swapped one risk for another. You'll have to weigh your options in cases like this and determine which side of the risk coin your organization can more readily accept.

Other forms of transference include warranties, guarantees, and performance bonds.

Mitigate

When you *mitigate* a risk, you attempt to reduce the probability of a risk event occurring or reduce its impacts to an acceptable level. This strategy is a lot like defensive driving. You see an obstacle in the road ahead, survey your options, and take the necessary steps to avoid the obstacle and proceed safely on your journey. Seeing the obstacle ahead (identifying risk) allows you to reduce the threat by planning ways around it or planning ways to reduce its impact if the risk does occur (mitigation strategies).

According to the *PMBOK® Guide*, the purpose of mitigation is to reduce the probability that a risk will occur and/or reduce the impact of the risk to a level where you can accept the risk and its outcomes. It's easier to take actions early on that will reduce the probability of a risk event or its consequences than it is to fix the damage once it has occurred. Some examples of risk mitigation include performing more tests, using less complicated processes, creating prototypes, and choosing more reliable vendors.

Accept

The acceptance strategy is used when you aren't able to eliminate all the threats on the project. *Acceptance* of a risk event is a strategy that can be used for risks that pose either threats or opportunities to the project. There are two alternatives to the acceptance strategy. *Passive acceptance* means you won't make any plans to try to avoid or mitigate the risk. You're willing to accept the consequences of the risk should it occur. This strategy is often used when it's more cost-effective to accept the impacts of the risk than to spend time or resources developing plans to deal with the consequences. Passive acceptance might also be used because the project team was unable to come up with an adequate response strategy and must accept the risk and its consequences. *Active acceptance* is the second strategy and might include developing contingency plans and reserves to deal with risks should they occur. (You'll look at contingency reserves in the next section.)

Let's revisit the road trip example. You could plan the trip using the original route and just accept the risk of running into construction. If you get to that point and you're delayed, you'll just accept it. This is passive acceptance. You could also go ahead and make plans to take an alternative route but not enact those plans until you actually reach the construction and know for certain that it is going to impede your progress. This is active acceptance and might involve developing a contingency plan.

Exam Spotlight

Understand all the strategies and their characteristics in each Plan Risk Response tool and technique for the exam.

Real World Scenario

New Convention Center Wing

You work for a small hotel and resort in western Colorado. Your company has taken on a project to expand the convention center by adding another wing. This wing will add six more meeting rooms (four of which can be combined into a large room by folding back the movable walls to accommodate large groups). This is a popular resort, and one of the risks identified with this project was an increase in demand for conference reservations after the construction finishes. The marketing team members decide they'll mitigate this risk by contacting the organizations who've consistently reserved space with them over the past three years and offer them incentives on their next reservation if they book their convention before the construction is completed. That way, their most important customers won't be turned away when the new reservations start pouring in.

Strategies for Positive Risk or Opportunities

Four strategies exist to deal with opportunities or positive risks that might present themselves on the project: exploit, share, enhance, and accept. We already covered accept, so we'll look at the remaining strategies next.

Exploit

When you *exploit* a risk event, you're looking for opportunities for positive impacts. This is the strategy of choice when you've identified positive risks that you want to make certain will occur on the project. Examples of exploiting a risk include reducing the amount of time to complete the project by bringing on more qualified resources or by providing even better quality than originally planned.

Share

The *share* strategy is similar to transferring because you'll assign the risk to a third-party owner who is best able to bring about the opportunity the risk event presents. For example, perhaps what your organization does best is investing. However, it isn't so good at marketing. Forming a joint venture with a marketing firm to capitalize on a positive risk will make the most of the opportunities.

Enhance

The *enhance* strategy closely watches the probability or impact of the risk event to assure that the organization realizes the benefits. The primary point of this strategy is to attempt to increase the probability and/or impact of positive risks. This entails watching for and emphasizing risk triggers and identifying the root causes of the risk to help enhance impacts or probability.

Contingency Planning

The last tool and technique of the Plan Risk Responses process we'll address is called the *contingent response strategy*, better known as *contingency planning*. Contingency planning involves planning alternatives to deal with certain risks (such as those with accept strategies) should they occur. This is different from mitigation planning in that mitigation looks to reduce the probability of the risk and its impact, whereas contingency planning doesn't necessarily attempt to reduce the probability of a risk event or its impacts.

Contingency comes into play when the risk event occurs. This implies you need to plan for your contingencies well in advance of the threat or opportunity occurring. After the risks have been identified and quantified, contingency plans should be developed and kept at the ready.

Contingency reserves are a common contingency response. We talked about this topic in the last chapter as well. Contingency reserve strategies for risk events are similar to those for cost and activity durations. This may include setting aside funding, resources, or adding contingency time to the project schedule.

Fallback plans should be developed for risks with high impact or for risks with identified strategies that might not be the most effective at dealing with the risk. Fallback plans are not contingency plans. For example, in the information technology field, we often have high impact risks associated with upgrading operating systems or implementing new applications. A contingency plan may include calling the vendor to assist in the middle of the night (that's always when things fall apart) when we can't figure out a solution. A fallback plan in this case may describe how we are going to bring the old system back online so users can still do their work while we figure out what went wrong with the implementation.

In practice, you'll find that identifying, prioritizing, quantifying, and developing responses for potential threats might happen simultaneously. In any case, you don't want to be taken by surprise, and that's the point of the risk processes. If you know about potential risks early, you can often mitigate them or prepare appropriate response plans or contingency plans to deal with them.

Plan Risk Responses Outputs

As you've no doubt concluded, the purpose of the Plan Risk Responses process is to develop risk responses for those risks with the highest threat to or best opportunity for the project objectives. The Plan Risk Responses process has two outputs: project management plan updates and project documents updates.

Remember that you might need to revisit other Planning processes after performing Plan Risk Responses to modify project plans as a result of risk responses.

Project Management Plan Updates

As we've discussed throughout the book, the management plans created to document how the schedule, budget, quality, procurement, and human resources will be defined, managed, and controlled on the project become subsidiary plans to the project management plan. Any and all of these management plans may require updates after you perform the risk processes. In addition, the WBS, the scope baseline, the schedule baseline, and cost baseline may require updates as well.

Other project documents, such as technical documentation and the assumptions documented in the project scope statement, could need an update after performing these processes as well.

Project Documents Updates

For this output, you may need to update project documents, including the risk register, technical documents, the assumptions log, and change requests. The risk register is updated at the end of this process with the information you've discovered during this process. The response plans are recorded in the risk register. You'll recall that the risk register lists the risks in order of priority (those with the highest potential for threat or opportunity first), so it makes sense that the response plans you have for these risks will be more detailed than the remaining lists. Some risks might not require response plans at all, but you should put them on a watch list and monitor them throughout the project.

Let's take a look at what the risk register should contain at this point. According to the *PMBOK® Guide*, after Identify Risks, Perform Qualitative Risk Analysis, and Perform Quantitative Risk Analysis are performed, the following elements should appear in the risk register:

- Prioritized list of identified risks, including their descriptions, what WBS element they impact (or area of the project), categories (RBS), root causes, and how the risk impacts the project objectives
- Risk ranking
- Risk owners and their responsibility
- Outputs from the Perform Qualitative Analysis
- Agreed-upon response strategies
- Actions needed to implement response plans
- Cost and schedule activities needed to implement risk responses
- Contingency plans
- Fallback plans
- List of residual and secondary risks
- Contingency reserves

The only elements in the preceding list I haven't talked about so far are residual and secondary risks. A *residual risk* is a leftover risk, so to speak. After you've implemented a risk response strategy—say mitigation, for example—some minor risk might still remain. The contingency reserve is set up to handle situations like this.

Secondary risks are risks that come about as a result of implementing a risk response. The example given previously where you transferred risk by hiring a driver to take you to your destination but the person became ill along the way is an example of a secondary risk. The driver's illness delayed your arrival time, which is a risk directly caused by hiring the driver or implementing a risk response. When planning for risk, identify and plan responses for secondary risks.

Risks exist on all projects, and risk planning is an important part of the project Planning processes. Just the act of identifying risks and planning responses can decrease their impact if they occur. Don't take the "What I don't know won't hurt me" approach to risk planning. This is definitely a case where not knowing something can be devastating. Risks that are easily identified and have planned responses aren't likely to kill projects or your career. Risks that you should have known about but ignored could end up costing the organization thousands or millions of dollars, causing schedule delays, causing loss of competitive advantage, or ultimately killing the project. There could be a personal cost as well, because cost and schedule overruns due to poor planning on your part are not easily explained.

 Real World Scenario

Project Case Study: New Kitchen Heaven Retail Store

Ricardo knocks on your office door and asks whether you have a few minutes to talk. "Of course," you reply, and he takes a seat on one of the comfy chairs at the conference table. You have a feeling this might take a while.

"I think you should know that I'm concerned about the availability of the T1 line. I've already put in the call to get us on the list because, as I said last week, there's a 30- to 45-day lead time on these orders."

"We're only part way through the Planning processes. Do you need to order the T1 so soon? We don't even know the store location yet," you say.

"Even though they say lead time is 30 to 45 days, I've waited as long as five or six months to get a T1 installed in the past. I know we're really pushing for the early February store opening, so I thought I'd get the ball rolling now. What I need from you is the location address, and I'll need that pretty quick."

"We're narrowing down the choices between a couple of properties, so I should have that for you within the next couple of weeks. Is that soon enough?"

"The sooner, the better," Ricardo replies.

"Great. I'm glad you stopped by, Ricardo. I wanted to talk with you about risk anyway, and you led us right into the discussion. Let me ask you, what probability would you assign to the T1 line installation happening six months from now?"

"I'd say the probability for six months is low. It's more likely that if there is a delay, it would be within a three- to four-month time frame."

"If they didn't get to it for six months, would it be a showstopper? In other words, is there some other way we could transfer Jill's data until the T1 did get installed?"

"Sure, we could use other methods. Jill won't want to do that for very long, but work-arounds are available."

"Good. Now, what about the risk for contractor availability and hardware availability and delivery schedules?" you ask.

You and Ricardo go on to discuss the risks associated with the IT tasks. Later, you ask Jill and Jake the same kinds of questions and compile a list of risks. In addition, you review the project information for the Atlanta store opening because it's similar in size and scope to this store. You add the risks from that store opening to your list as well. You divide some of the risks into the following categories: IT, Facilities, and Retail. A sample portion of your list appears as follows, with overall assignments made based on Perform Qualitative Risk Analysis and the probability and impact matrix:

- Category: IT
    - T1 line availability and installation. Risk score: Low
    - Contractor availability for Ethernet installation. Risk score: Medium
    - POS and server hardware availability. Risk score: Medium
- Category: Facilities
    - Desirable location in the right price range. Risk score: High
    - Contractor availability for build-out. Risk score: Low
    - Availability of fixtures and shelving. Risk score: Low
- Category: Retail
    - Product availability. Risk score: Medium
    - Shipment dates for product. Risk score: Medium

After examining the risks, you decide that response plans should be developed for the last two items listed under the IT source, the first item under Facilities, and both of the risks listed under Retail.

Ricardo has already mitigated the T1 connection and installation risk by signing up several months ahead of the date when the installation is needed. The contractor availability can be handled with a contingency plan that specifies a backup contractor should the first choice not be available. For the POS terminals and hardware, you decide to use the transfer strategy. As part of the contract, you'll require these vendors to deliver on time, and if they cannot, they'll be required to provide and pay for rental equipment until they can get your gear delivered.

The Facilities risk and Retail risks will be handled with a combination of acceptance, contingency plans, and mitigation.

You've calculated the expected monetary value for several potential risk events. Two of them are detailed here.

Desirable location has an expected monetary value of $780,000. The probability of choosing an incorrect or less than desirable location is 60 percent. The potential loss in sales is the difference between $2.5 million in sales per year that a high-producing store generates versus $1.2 million in sales per year that an average store generates.

The expected monetary value of the product availability event is $50,000. The probability of the event occurring is 40 percent. The potential loss in sales is $125,000 for not opening the store in conjunction with the Home and Garden Show.

Project Case Study Checklist

- Plan Risk Management
- Identify Risks
  - Documentation reviews
  - Information-gathering techniques
- Perform Qualitative Risk Analysis
  - Risk probability and impact
  - Probability and impact rating
  - List of prioritized risks
- Perform Quantitative Risk Analysis
  - Interviewing
  - Expected monetary value
- Plan Risk Responses
  - Avoidance, transference, mitigation, and acceptance strategies
  - Risk response plans documented

Understanding How This Applies to Your Next Project

Risk management, and all the processes it involves, is not a process I recommend you skip on a project of any size. This is where the Boy Scouts of America motto, "Be Prepared," is wise advice. If you haven't examined what could be lurking around the corner on your project and come up with a plan to deal with it, then you can be assured you're in for some surprises. Then again, if you like living on the edge, never knowing what might occur next, you'll probably find yourself back on the job-hunting scene sooner than you planned (oh, wait, you didn't plan because you're living on the edge).

In all seriousness, as with most of the Planning processes I've discussed so far, risk management should be scaled to match the complexity and size of your project. If you're working on a small project with a handful of team members and a short timeline, it doesn't make sense to spend a lot of time on risk planning. However, it does warrant spending *some* time identifying project risk, determining impact and probability, and documenting a plan to deal with the risk.

My favorite Identify Risks technique is brainstorming. I like its cousin the Nominal Group technique, too. Both techniques help you quickly get to the risks with the greatest probability and impact because, more than likely, these are the first risks that come to mind. Identify Risks can also help the project team find alternative ways of completing the work of the project. Further digging and the ideas generated from initial identification might reveal opportunities or alternatives you wouldn't have thought about during the regular Planning processes.

After you've identified the risks with the greatest impact to the project, document response plans that are appropriate for the risk. Small projects might have only one or two risks that need a response plan. The plans might consist of only a sentence or two, depending on the size of the project. I would question a project where no risks require a response plan. If it seems too good to be true, it probably is.

The avoid, transfer, and mitigate strategies are the most often used strategies to deal with risk, along with contingency planning. Of these, mitigation and contingency planning are probably the most common. Mitigation generally recognizes that the risk will likely occur and attempts to reduce the impact.

I have used brainstorming and the Nominal Group technique to strategize response plans for risks on small projects. When you're working on a small project, you can typically identify, quantify, and create response plans for risks at one meeting.

Identifying positive risk, in my experience, is fairly rare. Typically, when my teams perform Identify Risks, it's to determine what can go wrong and how bad the impact will be if it does. The most important concept from this chapter that you should apply to your next project is that you and your team should identify risks and create response plans to deal with the most significant ones.

Summary

Congratulations! You've completed another fun-filled, action-packed chapter, and all of it on a single topic—risk. Risk is inherent in all projects, and risks pose both threats to and opportunities for the project. Understanding the risks facing the project better equips you to determine the appropriate strategies to deal with those risks and helps you develop the response plans for the risks (and the level of effort you should put into preparing those plans).

The Plan Risk Management process determines how you will plan for risks on your project. Its only output is the risk management plan, which details how you'll define, monitor, and control risks throughout the project. The risk management plan is a subsidiary of the project management plan.

The Identify Risks process seeks to identify and document the project risks using information-gathering techniques such as brainstorming, the Delphi technique, interviewing, and root cause analysis. This list of risks gets recorded in the risk register, the only output of this process.

Perform Qualitative Risk Analysis and Perform Quantitative Risk Analysis involve evaluating risks and assigning probability and impact values to the risks. Many tools and techniques are used during these processes, including risk probability and impact assessment, probability and impact matrix, interviewing, probability distributions, expert judgment, sensitivity analysis, decision tree analysis, and simulation.

A probability and impact matrix uses the probability multiplied by the impact value to determine the risk score. The threshold of risk based on high, medium, and low tolerances is determined by comparing the risk score based on the probability level to the probability and impact matrix.

Monte Carlo simulation is a technique used to quantify schedule or cost risks. Decision trees graphically display decisions and their various choices and outcomes, and they are typically used in combination with expected monetary value.

The Plan Risk Responses process is the last Planning process and culminates with an update to the risk register documenting the risk response plans. The risk response plans detail the strategies you'll use to respond to risk and assign individuals to manage each risk response. Risk response strategies for negative risks include avoidance, mitigation, and transference. Risk strategies for positive risks include exploit, share, and enhance. Acceptance is a strategy for both negative and positive risks.

Contingency planning involves planning alternatives to deal with risk events should they occur. Contingency reserves are set aside to deal with risks associated with cost and time according to the stakeholder tolerance levels.

Exam Essentials

Be able to define the purpose of the risk management plan.   The risk management plan describes how you will define, monitor, and control risks throughout the project. It details how risk management processes (including Identify Risks, Perform Qualitative Risk Analysis, Perform Quantitative Risk Analysis, Plan Risk Responses, and Control Risks) will be implemented, monitored, and controlled throughout the life of the project. It describes how you will manage risks but does not attempt to define responses to individual risks. The risk management plan is a subsidiary of the project management plan, and it's the only output of the Plan Risk Management process.

Be able to name the purpose of Identify Risks.   The purpose of the Identify Risks process is to identify all risks that might impact the project, document them, and identify their characteristics.

Be able to define the purpose of Perform Qualitative Risk Analysis.   Perform Qualitative Risk Analysis determines the impact the identified risks will have on the project and the probability they'll occur, and it puts the risks in priority order according to their effects on the project objectives.

Be able to define the purpose of Perform Quantitative Risk Analysis.   Perform Quantitative Risk Analysis evaluates the impacts of risk prioritized during the Perform Qualitative Risk Analysis process and quantifies risk exposure for the project by assigning numeric probabilities to each risk and their impacts on project objectives.

Be able to define the purpose of the Plan Risk Responses process.   Plan Risk Responses is the process where risk response plans are developed using strategies such as avoid, transfer, mitigate, accept, exploit, share, enhance, develop contingent response strategies, and apply expert judgment. The risk response plan describes the actions to take should the identified risks occur. It should include all the identified risks, a description of the risks, how they'll impact the project objectives, and the people assigned to manage the risk responses.

Be able to define the risk register and some of its primary elements.   The risk register is an output of the Identify Risks process, and updates to the risk register occur as an output of every risk process that follows this one. By the end of the Plan Risk Responses process, the risk register contains these primary elements: identified list of risks, risk owners, risk triggers, risk strategies, contingency plans, and contingency reserves.

Key Terms

Life is a risky business, but with proper planning, your project doesn't have to be. Using processes I've discussed in this chapter, you'll be prepared for the foreseeable and the not so foreseeable. Understand them well, and know each process by the name used in the *PMBOK® Guide*:

Perform Qualitative Risk Analysis	Plan Risk Management
Perform Quantitative Risk Analysis	Plan Risk Responses
Identify Risks	

Before you take the exam, also be certain you are familiar with the following terms:

acceptance	passive acceptance
active acceptance	Nominal Group technique
assumptions analysis	ordinal scale
avoid	probability
brainstorming	probability and impact matrix
cardinal scale	residual risk
cause-and-effect diagrams	risk appetite
contingency planning	risk attitude
contingent response strategy	risk breakdown structure (RBS)
decision trees	risk categories
Delphi technique	risk management plan
enhance	risk owners
expected monetary value (EMV)	risk register
exploit	risk thresholds
fishbone diagram	risk tolerance
force majeure	root cause analysis
impact	secondary risks
impact scale	sensitivity analysis
influence diagramming	share
interviews	SWOT analysis
Ishikawa diagram	system or process flowchart
mitigate	transfer
Monte Carlo analysis	triggers

Review Questions

You can find the answers to the questions in Appendix A.

1. You are a project manager for Fountain of Youth Spring Water bottlers. Your project involves installing a new accounting system, and you're performing the risk-planning processes. You have identified several problems along with the causes of those problems. Which of the following diagrams will you use to show the problem and its causes and effects?

   A. Decision tree diagram

   B. Fishbone diagram

   C. Benchmark diagram

   D. Simulation tree diagram

2. Assessing the probability and consequences of identified risks to the project objectives, assigning a risk score to each risk, and creating a list of prioritized risks describe which of the following processes?

   A. Perform Quantitative Risk Analysis

   B. Identify Risks

   C. Perform Qualitative Risk Analysis

   D. Plan Risk Management

3. Each of the following statements is true regarding the risk management plan except for which one?

   A. The risk management plan is an output of the Plan Risk Management process.

   B. The risk management plan includes a description of the responses to risks and triggers.

   C. The risk management plan includes thresholds, scoring and interpretation methods, responsible parties, and budgets.

   D. The risk management plan is an input to all the remaining risk-planning processes.

4. You are using the interviewing technique of the Perform Quantitative Risk Analysis process. You intend to use normal and lognormal distributions. All of the following statements are true regarding this question except which one?

   A. Interviewing techniques are used to quantify the probability and impact of the risks on project objectives.

   B. Normal and lognormal distributions use mean and standard deviation to quantify risks.

   C. Distributions graphically display the impacts of risk to the project objectives.

   D. Triangular distributions rely on optimistic, pessimistic, and most likely estimates to quantify risks.

5. The information-gathering techniques used in the Identify Risks process include all of the following except _____.

   A. root cause analysis

   B. the Delphi technique

   C. brainstorming

   D. checklist analysis

6. Which of the following processes assesses the likelihood of risk occurrences and their consequences using a numerical rating?

   A. Perform Qualitative Risk Analysis

   B. Identify Risks

   C. Perform Quantitative Risk Analysis

   D. Plan Risk Responses

7. You are the project manager for a new website for the local zoo. You need to perform the Perform Qualitative Risk Analysis process. When you've completed this process, you'll produce all of the following as part of the risk register update output except which one?

   A. Priority list of risks

   B. Watch list of low-priority risks

   C. Probability of achieving time and cost estimates

   D. Risks grouped by categories

8. You've identified a risk event on your current project that could save $100,000 in project costs if it occurs. Which of the following is true based on this statement?

   A. This is a risk event that should be accepted because the rewards outweigh the threat to the project.

   B. This risk event is an opportunity to the project and should be exploited.

   C. This risk event should be mitigated to take advantage of the savings.

   D. This is a risk event that should be avoided to take full advantage of the potential savings.

9. You've identified a risk event on your current project that could save $500,000 in project costs if it occurs. Your organization is considering hiring a consulting firm to help establish proper project management techniques in order to assure it realizes these savings. Which of the following is true based on this statement?

   A. This is a risk event that should be accepted because the rewards outweigh the threat to the project.

   B. This risk event is an opportunity to the project and should be exploited.

   C. This risk event should be mitigated to take advantage of the savings.

   D. This is a risk event that should be shared to take full advantage of the potential savings.

10. Your hardware vendor left you a voicemail saying that a snowstorm in the Midwest might prevent your equipment from arriving on time. She wanted to give you a heads-up and asked that you return the call. Which of the following statements is true?

    A. This is a trigger.

    B. This is a contingency plan.

    C. This is a residual risk.

    D. This is a secondary risk.

11. You are constructing a probability and impact matrix for your project. Which of the following statements is true?

    A. The probability and impact matrix multiplies the risk's probability by the cost of the impact to determine an expected value of the risk event.

    B. The probability and impact matrix multiplies the risk's probability—which fall from 0.0 to 1.0—and the risk's impact for each potential outcome and then adds the result of the potential outcomes together to determine a risk score.

    C. The probability and impact matrix are predetermined thresholds that use the risk's probability multiplied by the impact of the risk event to determine an overall risk score.

    D. The probability and impact matrix multiplies the risk's probability by the risk impact—which both fall from 0.0 to 1.0—to determine a risk score.

12. Your stakeholders have asked for an analysis of the cost risk. All of the following are true except for which one?

    A. Monte Carlo analysis is the preferred method to use to determine the cost risk.

    B. Monte Carlo analysis is a modeling technique that computes project costs one time.

    C. A traditional work breakdown structure can be used as an input variable for the cost analysis.

    D. Monte Carlo usually expresses its results as probability distributions of possible costs.

13. Your hardware vendor left you a voicemail saying that a snowstorm in the Midwest will prevent your equipment from arriving on time. You identified a risk response strategy for this risk and have arranged for a local company to lease you the needed equipment until yours arrives. This is an example of which risk response strategy?

    A. Transfer

    B. Acceptance

    C. Mitigate

    D. Avoid

14. Risk attitude is an enterprise environmental factor that you should evaluate when performing the Plan Risk Management process. Risk attitude consists of all of the following elements except for which one?

    A. Risk appetite

    B. Risk threshold

    C. Risk urgency

    D. Risk tolerance

15. You work for a large manufacturing plant. You are working on a new project to release an overseas product line. This is the company's first experience in the overseas market, and it wants to make a big splash with the introduction of this product. The stakeholders are a bit nervous about the project and historically proceed cautiously and take a considerable amount of time to examine information before making a final decision. The project entails producing your product in a concentrated formula and packaging it in smaller containers than the U.S. product uses. A new machine is needed in order to mix the ingredients into a concentrated formula. After speaking with one of your stakeholders, you discover this will be the first machine your organization has purchased from your new supplier. Which of the following statements is true given the information in this question?

    A. The question describes risk tolerance levels of the stakeholders, which should be considered when performing the Plan Risk Management process.

    B. This question describes the interviewing tool and technique used during the Identify Risks process.

    C. This question describes risk triggers that are derived using interviewing techniques and recorded in the risk register during the Perform Qualitative Risk Analysis process.

    D. This question describes a risk that requires a response strategy from the positive risk category.

16. Your project team has identified several potential risks on your current project that could have a significant impact if they occurred. The team examined the impact of the risks by keeping all the uncertain elements at their baseline values. What type of diagram will the team use to display this information?

    A. Fishbone diagram

    B. Tornado diagram

    C. Influence diagram

    D. Process flowchart

17. Your project team is in the process of identifying project risks on your current project. The team has the option to use all of the following tools and techniques to diagram some of these potential risks except for which one?

    A. Ishikawa diagram

    B. Decision tree diagram

    C. Process flowchart

    D. Influence diagram

18. All of the following statements are true regarding the RBS except for which one?

    A. The RBS is contained in the risk management plan.

    B. It describes risk categories, which are a systematic way to identify risks and provide a foundation for understanding for everyone involved on the project.

    C. The lowest level of the RBS can be used as a checklist, which is a tool and technique of the Identify Risks process.

    D. The RBS is similar to the WBS in that the lowest levels of both are easily assigned to a responsible party or owner.

19. Your team has identified the risks on the project and determined their risk score. The team is in the midst of determining what strategies to put in place should the risks occur. After some discussion, the team members have determined that the risk of losing their network administrator is a risk they'll just deal with if and when it occurs. Although they think it's a possibility and the impact would be significant, they've decided to simply deal with it after the fact. Which of the following is true regarding this question?

    A. This is a negative response strategy.

    B. This is a positive response strategy.

    C. This is a response strategy for either positive or negative risk known as *contingency planning*.

    D. This is a response strategy for either positive or negative risks known as *passive acceptance*.

20. All of the following are true regarding the Perform Qualitative Risk Analysis process except which one?

    A. Probability and impact and expert interviews are used to help correct biases that occur in the data you've gathered during this process.

    B. The probability and impact matrix is used during this process to assign red, yellow, and green conditions to risks.

    C. Perform Qualitative Risk Analysis is an easy method of determining risk probability and impact that usually takes a good deal of time to perform.

    D. Risk urgency assessment is a tool and technique of this process used to determine which risks need near-term response plans.

Chapter

7

Planning Project Resources

THE PMP® EXAM CONTENT FROM THE PLANNING THE PROJECT PERFORMANCE DOMAIN COVERED IN THIS CHAPTER INCLUDES THE FOLLOWING:

✓ Develop a human resource management plan that defines the roles and responsibilities of the project team members and provides guidance regarding how resources will be utilized and managed.

✓ Develop a procurement management plan in order to ensure that the required project resources will be available.

✓ Develop a quality management plan in order to prevent the occurrence of defects and reduce the cost of quality.

✓ Present the project plan to the key stakeholders (if required) in order to obtain approval to execute the project.

✓ Knowledge and Skills:
- Resource planning process
- Elements, purpose, and techniques of project planning
- Elements, purpose, and techniques of procurement planning
- Elements, purpose, and techniques of quality management planning

We're closing in on finishing up the Planning group processes. We're at a place where we need to talk about some processes that aren't necessarily related to each other but need to be completed before you can construct the project schedule and budget. So, we'll start out this chapter by discussing resources.

All projects require resources. Some may require materials or goods, but all projects require human resources to perform the activities to bring them to completion. We'll discuss the Plan Procurement Management process, which deals with the goods and services procurements and then move on to Plan Human Resource Management, where you will develop the staffing management plan. This plan will help guide you later when acquiring your project team members in the Executing processes.

We'll wrap up the chapter with the Plan Quality Management process. This process focuses on determining the quality standards that are necessary for the project and for documenting how you'll go about meeting them. Let's get going.

The process names, inputs, tools and techniques, outputs, and descriptions of the project management process groups and related materials and figures in this chapter are based on content from *A Guide to the Project Management Body of Knowledge (PMBOK® Guide), Fifth Edition* (Sybex, 2010).

Procurement Planning

Plan Procurement Management is a process of identifying what goods or services you're going to purchase from outside the organization and which needs the project team can meet. Part of what you'll accomplish in this process is determining whether you should purchase the goods or services and, if so, how much, when, and from which sellers. Keep in mind that I'm discussing the procurement from the buyer's perspective, because this is the approach used in the *PMBOK® Guide.*

The Plan Procurement Management process can influence the project schedule, and the project schedule can influence this process. For example, the availability of a contractor or special-order materials might have a significant impact on the schedule. Conversely, your organization's business cycle might have an impact on the Plan Procurement Management process if the organization is dependent on seasonal activity. The Estimate Activity Resources process can also be influenced by this process, as will make-or-buy decisions (I'll get to those shortly).

You need to perform each process in the Project Procurement Management Knowledge Area (beginning with Plan Procurement Management and ending with Close Procurements) for each product or service that you're buying outside the organization. If you're procuring all your resources from within the organization, the only process you'll perform in this Knowledge Area is the Plan Procurement Management process.

Sometimes, you'll procure all the materials and resources for your project from a vendor. In cases like these, the vendor will have a project manager assigned to the project. Your organization might have an internal project manager assigned as well to act as the conduit between your company and the vendor and to provide information and monitor your organization's deliverables. When this happens, the vendor or contracting company is responsible for fulfilling all the project management processes as part of the contract. In the case of an outsourced project, the seller—also known as the *vendor, supplier*, or *contractor*—manages the project and the buyer becomes the stakeholder. If you're hiring a vendor, don't forget to consider permits or professional licenses that might be required for the type of work you need them to perform.

Several inputs are needed when planning for purchases. You'll look at them next.

Plan Procurement Management Inputs

The Plan Procurement Management process has nine inputs:

- Project management plan
- Requirements documentation
- Risk register
- Activity resource requirements
- Project schedule
- Activity cost estimates
- Stakeholder register
- Enterprise environmental factors
- Organizational process assets

The important component of the project management plan for this process is the scope baseline. You will recall the scope baseline includes the project scope statement that describes the need for the project and lists the deliverables and the acceptance criteria for the product or service of the project. Obviously, you'll want to consider these when thinking about procuring goods and services. You'll also want to consider the constraints (issues such as availability and timing of funds, availability of resources, delivery dates, and vendor availability) and assumptions (issues such as reliability of the vendor, assuming availability of key resources, and adequate stakeholder involvement). The product scope description is included in the project scope statement as well and might alert you to special considerations (services, technical requirements, and skills) needed to create the project's product.

As part of the scope baseline, the WBS and WBS dictionary identify the deliverables and describe the work required for each element of the WBS.

The risk register, which includes risk-related contract decisions, will guide you in determining the types of services or goods needed for risk management. For example, the transference strategy might require the purchase of insurance. You should review each of these elements when determining which goods and services will be performed within the project and which will be purchased. Marketplace conditions are the key element of enterprise environmental factors you should consider for this process. The organization's guidelines and organizational policies (including any formal procurement policies), along with the organization's supplier system that contains prequalified sellers, are the elements of the organizational process assets you should pay attention to here.

Many organizations have procurement departments that are responsible for procuring goods and services and writing and managing contracts. Some organizations also require that all contracts be reviewed by their legal department prior to signing. These are organizational process assets that you should consider when you need to procure goods and services.

It's important for the project manager to understand organizational policies because they might impact many of the Planning processes, including the Procurement Planning processes. For example, the organization might have purchasing approval processes that must be followed. Perhaps orders for goods or services that exceed certain dollar amounts need different levels of approval. As the project manager, you need to be aware of policies like this so you're certain you can execute the project smoothly. It's frustrating to find out later that you should have followed a certain process or policy and now, because you didn't, you've got schedule delays or worse. You could consider using the "Sin now, ask forgiveness later" technique in extreme emergencies, but you didn't hear that from me. (By the way, that's not a technique that's authorized by the *PMBOK® Guide*.)

The project manager and the project team will be responsible for coordinating all the organizational interfaces for the project, including technical, human resources, purchasing, and finance. It will serve you well to understand the policies and politics involved in each of these areas in your organization.

My organization is steeped in policy. (A government organization steeped in policy? Go figure!) It's so steeped in policy that we have to request the funds for large projects at least two years in advance. There are mounds and mounds of request forms, justification forms, approval forms, routing forms—you get the idea. My point is, if you miss one of the forms or don't fill out the information correctly, you can set your project back by a minimum of a year, if not two. Then once the money is awarded, there are more forms to fill out and policies to follow. Again, if you don't follow the policies correctly, you can jeopardize future project funds. Many organizations have a practice of not giving you all the project money up front in one lump sum. In other words, you must meet major milestones or complete a project phase before they'll fund your next phase. Know what your organizational policies are well ahead of time. Talk to the people who can walk you through the process and ask them to check your work to avoid surprises.

Keep in mind that if you are a seller, you may be managing the sale of your goods or services as a project. If that's the case, you will be following all of the processes in all of the Knowledge Areas and will want to assure you thoroughly understand the terms and conditions of the procurement documents (contracts, purchase orders, statement of work and so on) associated with the project.

Teaming agreements are not an official input of any of the processes. However, teaming agreements by themselves are an input to the Planning Process group. Teaming agreements are contractual agreements between multiple parties that are forming a partnership or joint venture to work on the project. Teaming agreements are often used when two or more vendors form a partnership to work together on a particular project. If teaming agreements are used on the project, typically the scope of work, requirements for competition, buyer and seller roles, and other important project concerns should be predefined.

Be aware that when teaming agreements are in force on a project, the planning processes are significantly impacted. For example, the teaming agreement predefines the scope of work, and that means that elements such as the requirements and the deliverables may change the completion dates, thereby impacting the project schedule, or they may affect the project budget, quality, human resources availability, procurement decisions, and so on.

Tools and Techniques for Plan Procurement Management

The Plan Procurement Management process consists of four tools and techniques. They are make-or-buy analysis, expert judgment, market research, and meetings. I've already covered expert judgment and meetings, so you'll look at make-or-buy analysis followed by market research. We'll close out this section with a discussion of contract types. Contracts are not a tool and technique of this process, but they are a mechanism you might use to conduct business with vendors.

Make-or-Buy Analysis

The main decision you're trying to get to in *make-or-buy analysis* is whether it's more cost effective to buy the products and services or more cost effective for the organization to produce the goods and services needed for the project. Costs should include both direct costs (in other words, the actual cost to purchase the product or service) and indirect costs, such as the salary of the manager overseeing the purchase process or ongoing maintenance costs. Costs don't necessarily mean the cost to purchase. In make-or-buy analysis, you might weigh the cost of leasing items against the cost of buying them. For example, perhaps your project requires using a specialized piece of hardware that you know will be outdated by the end of the project. In a case like this, leasing might be a better option so that when the project is ready to be implemented, a newer version of the hardware can be tested and put into production during rollout.

Other considerations in make-or-buy analysis might include elements such as capacity issues, skills, availability, and trade secrets. Strict control might be needed for a certain process, and therefore, the process cannot be outsourced. Perhaps your organization has the skills in-house to complete the project but your current project list is so backlogged that you can't get to the new project for months, so you need to bring in a vendor.

Make-or-buy analysis is considered a general management technique and concludes with the decision to do one or the other.

Market Research

Market research can consist of a variety of methods to assist you or the team in determining vendors, their capabilities, and experience. My first go-to is using my favorite search engine. This can reveal information about experience, market presence, customer reviews, and more. Conferences are my second favorite method of discovering new vendors or new services from vendors I know. I am generally concerned with a few key items when engaging vendor services. First, I need to know their experience levels with my particular project or industry. I also want to know the team members they are proposing for the project and the depth and breadth of knowledge they have in the subject matter. I want to interview them before they start work on the project and learn the financial stability of the company.

Contract Types

A *contract* is a compulsory agreement between two or more parties and is used to acquire products or services from outside the organization. Typically, money is exchanged for the goods or services. Contracts are enforceable by law and require an offer and an acceptance. Generally speaking, most organizations require a more extensive approval process for contracts than for other types of procurements. For example, contracts may require a signature from someone in the legal department, an executive in the organization, the CFO, the procurement director, and the senior manager from the department that is having the work performed.

There are different types of contracts for different purposes. The *PMBOK® Guide* divides contracts into three categories:

- Fixed price
- Cost reimbursable
- Time and materials (T&M)

Within the fixed-price and cost-reimbursable categories are different types of contracts. You'll look at each in the following sections. Keep in mind that several factors will determine the type of contract you should use. The product requirements (or service criteria) might drive the contract type. The market conditions might drive availability and price—remember back in the dot-com era when trying to hire anyone with programming skills was next to impossible? Also, the amount of risk—for the seller, the buyer, and the project itself—will help determine contract type.

Exam Spotlight

Contract types help determine the risk the buyer and seller will bear during the life of the contract. The project manager should take this into consideration when purchasing goods and services outside the organization and make certain it is in keeping with the risk attitudes of the organization and stakeholders. (We talked about this in Chapter 6, "Risk Planning.") There could always be an exam question or two regarding contract types, so spend some time getting familiar with them.

Fixed-Price Contracts

Fixed-price contracts can either set a specific, firm price for the goods or services rendered (known as a *firm fixed-price contract,* or *FFP*) or include incentives for meeting or exceeding certain contract deliverables.

Fixed-price contracts can be disastrous for both the buyer and the seller if the scope of the project is not well defined or the scope changes dramatically. It's important to have accurate, well-defined deliverables when you're using this type of contract. Conversely, fixed-price contracts are relatively safe for both buyer and seller when the original scope is well defined and remains unchanged. They typically reap only small profits for the seller and force the contractor to work productively and efficiently. This type of contract also minimizes cost and quality uncertainty. For the exam, you should know three types of fixed-price contracts:

Firm Fixed-Price (FFP)   In the FFP contract, the buyer and seller agree on a well-defined deliverable for a set price. The good news for the buyer is the price never goes up. However, if the deliverables are not well defined, the buyer can incur additional costs in the form of change orders. It's important that you clearly describe the work to avoid additional cost.

In this kind of contract, the biggest risk is borne by the seller. The seller—or contractor—must take great strides to assure they've covered their costs and will make a comfortable profit on the transaction. The seller assumes the risks of increasing costs, nonperformance, or other problems. However, to counter these unforeseen risks, the seller builds in the cost of the risk to the contract price. This is the most common type of contract and the most often used.

Fixed-Price Incentive Fee (FPIF)   *Fixed-price incentive fee (FPIF) contracts* are another type of fixed-price contract. The difference here is that the contract includes an incentive—or bonus—for early completion or for some other agreed-upon performance criterion that meets or exceeds contract specifications. The criteria for early completion, or other performance enhancements, are typically related to cost, schedule, or technical performance and must be spelled out in the contract so both parties understand the terms and conditions. The fixed-price, much like the FFP, is set and never goes up. The seller assumes the risk for completing the work no matter the cost.

Another aspect of fixed-price incentive fee contracts to consider is that some of the risk is borne by the buyer, unlike the firm fixed-price contract where most of the risk is borne by the seller. The buyer takes some risk, albeit minimal, by offering the incentive to, for example, get the work done earlier. Suppose the buyer would like the product delivered 30 days prior to when the seller thinks they can deliver. In this case, the buyer assumes the risk for the early delivery via the incentive.

Fixed-Price with Economic Price Adjustment (FP-EPA) There's one more type of fixed-price contract, known as a *fixed-price with economic price adjustment contract (FP-EPA)*. This contract allows for adjustments due to changes in economic conditions such as cost increases or decreases, inflation, and so on. These contracts are typically used when the project spans many years. This type of contract protects both the buyer and seller from economic conditions that are outside of their control.

Exam Spotlight

The economic adjustment section of an FP-EPA contract should be tied to a known financial index.

Cost-Reimbursable Contracts

Cost-reimbursable contracts are as the name implies. The allowable costs—allowable is defined by the contract—associated with producing the goods or services are charged to the buyer. All the costs the seller takes on during the project are charged back to the buyer; therefore, the seller is reimbursed.

Cost-reimbursable contracts carry the highest risk to the buyer because the total costs are uncertain. As problems arise, the buyer has to shell out even more money to correct the problems. However, the advantage to the buyer with this type of contract is that scope changes are easy to make and can be made as often as you want—but it will cost you.

Cost-reimbursable contracts have a lot of uncertainty associated with them. The contractor has little incentive to work efficiently or be productive. This type of contract protects the contractor's profit because increasing costs are passed to the buyer rather than taken out of profits, as would be the case with a fixed-price contract. Be certain to audit your statements when using a contract like this so that charges from some other project the vendor is working on don't accidentally end up on your bill.

Cost-reimbursable contracts are used most often when the project scope contains a lot of uncertainty, such as for cutting-edge projects and research and development. They are also used for projects that have large investments early in the project life. Incentives for completing early, or not so early, or meeting or exceeding other performance criteria may be included in cost-reimbursable contracts much like the FPIF. We'll look at four types of cost-reimbursable contracts:

Cost Plus Fixed Fee (CPFF) *Cost plus fixed fee (CPFF) contracts* charge back all allowable project costs to the buyer and include a fixed fee upon completion of the contract. This is how the seller makes money on the deal; the fixed fee portion is the seller's profit. The fee is always firm in this kind of contract, but the costs are variable. The seller doesn't necessarily have a lot of motivation to control costs with this type of contract, as you can imagine, and one of the strongest motivators for completing the project is driven by the fixed fee portion of the contract.

Cost Plus Incentive Fee (CPIF)   The next category of cost-reimbursable contract is *cost plus incentive fee (CPIF)*. This is the type of contract in which the buyer reimburses the seller for the seller's allowable costs and includes an incentive for meeting or exceeding the performance criteria laid out in the contract. An incentive fee actually encourages better cost performance by the seller, and a possibility of shared savings exists between the seller and buyer if performance criteria are exceeded. The qualification for exceeded performance must be written into the contract and agreed to by both parties, as should the definition of allowable costs; the seller can possibly lose the incentive fee if agreed-upon targets are not reached.

There is moderate risk for the buyer under the cost plus incentive fee contract, and if well written, it can be more beneficial for both the seller and the buyer than a cost-reimbursable contract.

Cost Plus Percentage of Cost (CPPC)   In the *cost plus percentage of cost (CPPC)* contract, the seller is reimbursed for allowable costs plus a fee that's calculated as a percentage of the costs. The percentage is agreed upon beforehand and documented in the contract. Because the fee is based on costs, the fee is variable. The lower the costs, the lower the fee, so the seller doesn't have a lot of motivation to keep costs low. This is not a commonly used contract type.

Cost Plus Award Fee (CPAF)   The *cost plus award fee (CPAF) contract* is the riskiest of the cost plus contracts for the seller. In this contract, the seller will recoup all the costs expended during the project but the award fee portion is subject to the sole discretion of the buyer. The performance criteria for earning the award is spelled out in the contract, but these criteria can be subjective and the awards are not usually contestable.

Time and Materials (T&M) Contracts

Time and materials (T&M) contracts are a cross between fixed-price and cost-reimbursable contracts. The full amount of the material costs is not known at the time the contract is awarded. This resembles a cost-reimbursable contract because the costs will continue to grow during the contract's life and are reimbursable to the contractor. The buyer bears the biggest risk in this type of contract.

T&M contracts can resemble fixed-price contracts when unit rates are used, for example. Unit rates might be used to preset the rates of certain elements or portions of the project. For example, a contracting agency might charge you $150 per hour for a .NET programmer, or a leasing company might charge you $2,000 per month for the hardware you're leasing during the testing phase of your project. These rates are preset and agreed upon by the buyer and seller ahead of time. T&M contracts are most often used when you need human resources with specific skills and when you can quickly and precisely define the scope of work needed for the project.

Plan Procurement Management Outputs

The Plan Procurement Management process consists of seven outputs. The first is the *procurement management plan*. You've seen a few of the other management plan outputs, so you're probably already ahead of me on this one. But hold the phone—I'll be sure to touch on the important points. The other outputs are the procurement statement of work, make-or-buy decisions, procurement documents, source selection criteria, change requests, and project documents updates.

Procurement Management Plan

The procurement management plan details how the procurement process will be managed. The procurement management plan is based primarily on the project scope and schedule. According to the *PMBOK® Guide*, it includes the following information:

- The types of contract to use
- The authority of the project team in the procurement process
- How the procurement process will be integrated with other project processes
- Where to find standard procurement documents (provided your organization uses standard documents)
- How many vendors or contractors are involved and how they'll be managed
- How the procurement process will be coordinated with other project processes, such as performance reporting and scheduling
- How the constraints and assumptions might be impacted by purchasing
- How independent estimates and make-or-buy decisions will be used during these processes and in developing activity resource estimates and the project schedule
- Coordinating scheduled dates in the contract with the project schedule
- How multiple vendors or contractors will be managed
- The coordination of purchasing lead times with the development of the project schedule
- The schedule dates that are determined in each contract
- Identification of prequalified sellers (if known)
- Risk management issues
- Procurement metrics for managing contracts and for evaluating sellers

The procurement management plan, like all the other management plans, is a component of the project management plan.

 Real World Scenario

Streamlining Purchases

Russ is a project manager for a real estate development company in Hometown, USA. Recently he transferred to the office headquarters to develop a process for streamlining purchases and purchase requests for the construction teams in the field. His first step was to develop a procurement management plan for the construction managers to use when ordering materials and equipment. Russ decided the procurement management plan could be used as a template for all new projects. That meant the project managers in the field didn't have to write their own procurement management plans when starting new construction projects. They could use the template, which had many of the fields prepopulated with corporate headquarters processes, and then they could fill in the information specific to their project. For example, the Types of Contracts section states that all equipment and materials purchases require fixed-price contracts. When human resources are needed for the project on a contract basis, a T&M contract should be used with the unit rates stated in the contract. A "not to exceed" amount should also be written into the contract so that there are no surprises as to the total amount of dollars the company will be charged for the resources.

Procurement Statement of Work

A *procurement statement of work (SOW)* contains the details of the procurement item in clear, concise terms. It includes the following elements:

- The project objectives
- A description of the work of the project and any post-project operational support needed
- Concise specifications of the products or services required
- The project schedule, time period of services, and work location

The procurement SOW might be prepared by either the buyer or the seller. Buyers might prepare the SOW and give it to the sellers, who in turn rewrite it so that they can price the work properly. If the buyer does not know how to prepare an SOW or the seller would be better at creating the SOW because of their expertise about the product or service, the seller might prepare it and then give it to the buyer to review. In either case, the procurement statement of work is developed from the project scope statement and the WBS and WBS dictionary.

The seller uses the SOW to determine whether they are able to produce the goods or services as specified. In addition, it wouldn't hurt to include a copy of the WBS with the SOW.

Any information the seller can use to properly price the goods or services helps both sides understand what's needed and how it will be provided.

Projects might require some or all of the work of the project to be provided by a vendor. The Plan Procurement Management process determines whether goods or services should be produced within the organization or procured from outside, and if goods or services are procured from outside, it describes what will be outsourced and what kind of contract to use and then documents the information in the SOW and procurement management plan. The SOW will undergo progressive elaboration as you proceed through the procurement processes. There will likely be several iterations of the SOW before you get to the actual contract award.

> You used an SOW during the Develop Project Charter process. You can use that SOW as the procurement SOW during this process if you're contracting out the entire project. Otherwise, you can use just those portions of the SOW that describe the work you've contracted.

Make-or-Buy Decisions

The *make-or-buy decision* is a document that outlines the decisions made during the process regarding which goods and/or services will be produced by the organization and which will be purchased. This can include any number of items, including services, products, insurance policies, performance, and performance bonds.

Procurement Documents

Procurement documents are used to solicit vendors and suppliers to bid on your procurement needs. You're probably familiar with some of the titles of procurement documents. They might be called request for proposal (RFP), request for information (RFI), invitation for bid (IFB), request for quotation (RFQ), and so on.

Procurement documents should clearly state the description of the work requested, they should include the contract SOW, and they should explain how sellers should format and submit their responses. These documents are prepared by the buyer to ensure as accurate and complete a response as possible from all potential bidders. Any special provisions or contractual needs should be spelled out as well. For example, many organizations have data concerning their marketing policies, new product introductions planned for the next few years, trade secrets, and so on. The vendor will have access to this private information, and to guarantee that they maintain confidentiality, you should require that they sign a nondisclosure agreement.

A few terms that you should understand are used during this process; they are usually used interchangeably even though they have distinct definitions. When your decision is going to be made primarily on price, the terms *bid* and *quotation* are used, as in IFB or RFQ. When considerations other than price (such as technology or specific approaches to the project) are the deciding factors, the term *proposal* is used, as in RFP. These terms are used interchangeably in practice, even though they have specific meanings in the *PMBOK®
Guide.*

In my organization, all solicitation requests are submitted as RFPs, even though our primary decision factor is price.

Exam Spotlight

Understand the difference between *bid* and/or *quotation* and *proposal* for the exam. Bids or quotations are used when price is the only deciding factor among bidders. Proposals are used when there are considerations other than price.

Procurement documents are posted or advertised according to your organizational policies. This might include ads in newspapers and magazines or ads/posts on the Internet.

Source Selection Criteria

The term *source selection criteria* refers to the method your organization will use to choose a vendor from among the proposals you receive. The criteria might be subjective or objective. In some cases, price might be the only criteria, and that means the vendor that submits the lowest bid will win the contract. You should use purchase price (which should include costs associated with purchase price, such as delivery and setup charges) as the sole criterion only when you have multiple qualified sellers from which to choose.

Other projects might require more extensive criteria than price alone. In this case, you might use scoring models as well as rating models, or you might use purely subjective methods of selection. I described an example weighted-scoring method in Chapter 2, "Creating the Project Charter." You can use this method to score vendor proposals.

Sometimes, the source selection criteria are made public in the procurement process so that vendors know exactly what you want in a vendor. This approach has pros and cons. If the organization typically makes known the source selection criteria, you'll find that almost all the vendors that bid on the project meet every criteria you've outlined (in writing, that is). When it comes time to perform the contract, however, you might encounter some surprises. The vendor might have done a great job of writing the bid based on your criteria, but in reality they don't know how to put the criteria into practice. On the other hand, having all the criteria publicly known beforehand gives ground to great discussion points and discovery later in the procurement processes.

The following list includes some of the criteria you can consider using for evaluating proposals and bids:

- Comprehension and understanding of the needs of the project as documented in the contract SOW

- Cost, up front as well as total cost of ownership over the life of the product or service

- Technical ability of vendor and its proposed team

- Technical approach

- Risk

- Experience on projects of similar size and scope, including references

- Project management approach

- Management approach

- Business type and size

- Financial stability and capacity

- Production capacity

- Warranty or guarantee

- Reputation, references, and past performance

- Intellectual and proprietary rights

You could include many of these in a weighted scoring model and rate each vendor on how well they responded to these issues.

 When considering business type and size, also consider whether the business is a small business, a disadvantaged or minority-owned business, or a women-owned business. Government organizations in particular may require awarding a certain percentage of procurements to businesses that fall within these categories.

 Real World Scenario

The Customer Relationship Management System Response

Ryan Hunter is preparing the source selection criteria for an RFP for a customer relationship management (CRM) software system. After meeting with key stakeholders and other project managers in the company who've had experience working on projects of this size and scope, he devised the first draft of the source selection criteria. A partial list is as follows:

- Successful bidder's response must detail how business processes (as documented in the RFP page 24) will be addressed with their solution.

- Successful bidder must document their project management approach, which must follow the *PMBOK® Guide* project practices. They must provide an example project management plan based on a previous project experience of similar size and scope to the one documented in the RFP.

- Successful bidder must document previous successful implementations, including integration with existing organization's PBX and network operating system, and must provide references.

- Successful bidder must provide financial statements for the previous three years.

Change Requests

As you perform the Plan Procurement Management process, the project management plan, including its subsidiary plans, may require changes due to vendor availability, vendor capability, or the vendor's proposed solution, as well as cost and quality considerations. Change requests must be processed through the Perform Integrated Change Control process that we'll discuss in Chapter 10, "Measuring and Controlling Project Performance."

Project Documents Updates

We've seen this output several times before. Some of the documents that may require updating as a result of the procurement processes are the requirements document, the requirements traceability matrix, the risk register, and others as needed.

Now we'll switch our focus to the human resource needs for the project and discuss the Plan Human Resource Management process next.

Developing the Human Resource Management Plan

All projects require human resources, from the smallest project to the largest. The *Plan Human Resource Management* process documents the roles and responsibilities of individuals or groups for various project elements and then documents the reporting relationships for each. Reporting relationships can be assigned to groups as well as to individuals, and the groups or individuals might be internal or external to the organization or a combination of both. Plan Communications Management goes hand in hand with Plan Human Resource Management because the organizational structure affects the way communications are carried out among project participants and the project interfaces.

When developing the human resource management plan, the only output of this process, you'll have to consider factors such as the availability of resources, skill levels, training needs, and more. Each of these factors can have an impact on the project cost, schedule, and quality and may introduce risks not previously considered.

Plan Human Resource Management Inputs

Plan Human Resource Management has four inputs: project management plan, activity resource requirements, enterprise environmental factors, and organizational process assets. We'll look at the key elements of each of these next.

Project Management Plan

The project management plan consists of many of the subsidiary plans we have already discussed. During this process, you might want to consider several of them, including the stakeholder management plan and the stakeholder register. These documents describe the communication needs of the stakeholders. Another document to consider is the risk register. It lists the risk owners and their responsibility, so be certain to check this document when outlining roles and responsibilities. The change control and configuration management plans are important to understand as well as the project life cycle processes you'll use in each phase of the project.

Activity Resource Requirements

Human resources are needed to perform and complete the activities outlined in the activity resource requirements output of the Estimate Activity Resources process. During the Plan Human Resource Management process, you'll define those resource needs in further detail.

Key Environmental Factors

Enterprise environmental factors play a key role in determining human resource roles and responsibilities. The type of organization you work in, the reporting relationships, and the technical skills needed to complete the project work are a few of the factors you should consider when developing the staffing management plan, which is a subset of the human resource management plan. Here is a list of some of the factors you should consider during this process:

Organizational Factors   Consider what departments or organization units will have a role in the project, the interactions between and among departments, organizational culture, and the level of formality among these working relationships.

Existing Human Resources and Marketplace Conditions   The existing base of human resources that are employed, or available to, the organization should be considered when developing the human resource management plan. Marketplace conditions will dictate the availability of resources you're acquiring outside the organization and their going rate.

Personnel Policies   Be certain you have an understanding of the personnel policies in the organization regarding hiring, firing, and tasking employees. Other considerations include holiday schedules, leave time policies, and so on.

Technical Factors   Consider the types of specialized skills needed to complete the work of the project (for example, programming languages, engineering skills, knowledge of pharmaceuticals) and any technical considerations during handoff from phase to phase or from project completion to production.

Interpersonal Factors   Interpersonal factors have to do with potential project team members. You should consider their experience, skills, current reporting relationships, cultural considerations, and perceptions regarding their levels of trust and respect for coworkers and superiors.

Location and Logistics   Consider where the project team is physically located and whether they are all located together or at separate facilities (or cities or countries).

Political Factors   Political factors involve your stakeholders. Consider the amount of influence the stakeholders have, their interactions and influence with each other, and the power they can exert over the project.

In addition to these factors, you should consider constraints that pertain to project teams, including the following:

Organizational Structures   Organizational structures can be constraints. For example, a strong matrix organization provides the project manager with much more authority and power than the weak matrix organization does. Functional organizations typically do not empower their project managers with the proper authority to carry out a project. If you work in a functional organization as I do, it's important to be aware that you'll likely face power struggles with other managers and, in some cases, a flat-out lack of cooperation. Don't tell them I said this, but functional managers tend to be territorial and aren't likely to give up control easily. Here's the best advice I have for you in this case:

- Establish open communications early in the project.

- Include all the functional managers with key roles in important decisions.

- Get the support of your project sponsor to empower you (as the project manager) with as much authority as possible. It's important that the sponsor makes it clear to the other managers that their cooperation on project activities is expected.

Collective Bargaining Agreements   Collective bargaining agreements are actually contractual obligations of the organization to the employees. Collective bargaining is typically associated with unions and organized employee associations. Other organized employee associations or groups might require specialized reporting relationships as well—especially if they involve contractual obligations. You will not likely be involved in the negotiations of collective bargaining agreements, but if you have an opportunity to voice opinions regarding employee duties or agreements that would be helpful to your project or future projects, by all means take it.

Economic Conditions   These conditions refer to the availability of funds for the project team to perform training, hire staff, and travel. If funds are severely limited and your project requires frequent trips to other locations, you have an economic constraint on your hands.

Exam Spotlight

For the exam, understand the key environmental factors (organizational factors, existing human resources and market conditions, personnel policies, technical factors, interpersonal, location and logistics, and political factors) and the three constraints (organizational structures, collective bargaining agreements, and economic conditions) that can impact the Plan Human Resource Management process.

Organizational Process Assets

You should consider four primary elements of the organizational process assets input during this process. They are organizational processes and standardized role descriptions, templates and checklists, historical information, and escalation procedures for the team and the organization as a whole.

The term *templates*, in this case, refers to documentation such as project descriptions, organizational charts, performance appraisals, and the organization's conflict management process. Checklists might include elements such as training requirements, project roles and responsibilities, skills and competency levels, and safety issues.

Exam Spotlight

Using templates and checklists is one way to ensure that you don't miss any key responsibilities when planning the project and will help reduce the amount of time spent on project planning.

Plan Human Resource Management Tools and Techniques

The Plan Human Resource Management process consists of five tools and techniques. Remember that your goal is to produce the human resource management plan output of this process that includes a description of the team's roles and responsibilities, organizational charts, and a staffing management plan. You'll see that the tools and techniques of this process directly contribute to the components of the human resource management plan. They are organization charts and position descriptions, networking, organizational theory, expert judgment, and meetings. We'll look at the first three of these tools and techniques in the following sections.

Organization Charts and Position Descriptions

We've all seen an organization chart. It usually documents your name, your position, your boss, your boss's boss, your boss's boss's boss, and so on. The important point to note about this tool and technique is that this information might be presented in one of three ways:

Hierarchical Charts   Hierarchical charts, like a WBS, are designed in a top-down format. For example, the organization or department head is at the top, the management employees who report to the organization head are next, and so on, descending down the structure. An *organization breakdown structure (OBS)* is a form of organization chart that shows the departments, work units, or teams within an organization (rather than individuals) and their respective work packages.

A *resource breakdown structure (RBS)* is another type of hierarchical chart that breaks down the work of the project according to the types of resources needed. (RBS also stands for *risk breakdown structure*, as you learned in the previous chapter.) For example, you might have programmers, database analysts, and network analysts as resource types on the RBS. However, they won't all necessarily work on the project team. You might have programmers reporting to the project team, the finance department, and the customer service department, for example. An RBS can help track project costs because it ties to the organization's accounting system. Let's suppose you have programming resources in the RBS at the junior, advanced, and senior levels. Each of these levels of programmer has an average hourly salary recorded in the accounting system that makes it easy for you to track project costs. Ten senior programmers, 14 advanced, and 25 junior-level programmers are easy to calculate and track.

Matrix-Based Charts   Matrix-based charts are used to show the type of resources and the responsibility they have on the project. Many times a project manager will use a *responsibility assignment matrix (RAM)* to graphically display this information. A RAM is usually depicted as a chart with resource names listed in each row (for example, programmers, testers, and trainers) and project phases or WBS elements listed as the columns. (It can also be constructed using team member names.) Indicators in the intersections show where the resources are needed. However, the level of detail is up to you. One RAM might be developed showing only project phases; another RAM might show level-two WBS elements for a complex project, with more RAMs subsequently produced for the additional WBS levels; or a RAM might be constructed with level-three elements only.

Exam Spotlight

The RAM relates the OBS to the WBS to ensure that every component of the work of the project is assigned to an individual.

Table 7.1 shows a type of RAM called an *RACI chart* for a software development team. In this example, the RACI chart shows the level of accountability each of the participants has on the project. The letters in the acronym RACI are the designations shown in the chart:

R = Responsible for performing the work
A = Accountable, the one who is responsible for producing the deliverable or work package and approves or signs off on the work
C = Consult, someone who has input to the work or decisions
I = Inform, someone who must be informed of the decisions or results

TABLE 7.1   Sample RAM[x]

	Olga	Rae	Jantira	Nirmit
Design	R	A	C	C
Test	I	R	C	A
Implement	C	I	R	A

*R = Responsible, A = Accountable, C = Consult, I = Inform

In this example, Olga is responsible for design, meaning she creates the software programming design document, but Rae is accountable and is the one who must make sure the work of the project is completed and approved. This is a great tool because it shows at a glance not only where a resource is working but what that resource's responsibility level is on the project.

Keep in mind this is only one type of RAM chart. You may choose to use other designations in place of R-A-C-I.

Text-Oriented Formats   Text-oriented formats are used when you have a significant amount of detail to record. These are also called *position descriptions* or *role-responsibility-authority forms*. These forms detail (as the name implies) the role, responsibility, and authority of the resource, and they make great templates to use for future projects.

Networking

Networking in this process doesn't refer to the technical kind of networking with servers, switches, and fiber. It means human resource networking; that is, you know someone who knows someone and you can share information, learn new techniques, and interact with each other. According to the *PMBOK® Guide*, several types of networking activities exist, including proactive communication, lunch meetings (my personal favorite), informal conversations (ah, the information you learn by hanging out at the espresso machine), and trade conferences (another favorite because they get you out of the office). Networking might help when you have a specific resource need on the project but can't seem to locate someone with that set of skills.

Organizational Theory

Organizational theory refers to all the theories that attempt to explain what makes people, teams, and work units perform the way they do. I'll talk more about motivation techniques (which are a type of organizational theory) in Chapter 8, "Developing the Project Team." Organizational theory improves the probability that planning will be effective and helps shorten the amount of time it takes to produce the Plan Human Resource Management outputs.

Plan Human Resource Management Outputs

The Plan Human Resource Management process has one output, the human resource management plan. According to the *PMBOK® Guide,* the human resource management plan, a subsidiary or component of the project management plan, documents how human resources should be defined, staffed, managed and controlled, and released from the project when their activities are complete. It also helps in establishing an effective project team by defining the types of resources needed during the project, documenting when they're needed, and providing direction regarding how the resources should be managed.

This output has three components:

- Roles and responsibilities
- Project organizational charts
- Staffing management plan

I've already covered organizational charts in detail, so we'll look at the other two components of the human resource management plan now.

Roles and Responsibilities

This output is the list of roles and responsibilities for the project team. It can take the form of the RAM or RACI chart I talked about earlier, or the roles and responsibilities can be recorded in text format. According to the *PMBOK® Guide*, the following are the key elements you should include in the roles and responsibilities documentation:

Role   Describes the parts of the project for which the individuals or teams are accountable. This should also include a description of authority levels, responsibilities, and what work is not included as part of the role.

Authority   Describes the amount of authority the resource has to make decisions, dictate direction, and approve the work.

Responsibility   Describes the work required to complete the project activities.

Competency   Describes the skills and ability needed to perform the project activities.

Staffing Management Plan

The *staffing management plan* is a part of the human resource management plan that documents how and when human resources are introduced to the project and the criteria for releasing them. As with the other management plans I've discussed, the level and amount of detail contained in this plan are up to you. It can be formal or informal, and it can contain lots of detail or only high-level detail.

The staffing management plan should be updated throughout the project. According to the *PMBOK® Guide,* you should consider several elements for inclusion in the staffing management plan, including the following:

Staff Acquisition   This describes how team members are acquired (from inside or outside the organization), where they're located, and the costs for specific skills and expertise. I'll talk more about staff acquisition in Chapter 8.

Resource Calendars   This describes the time frames in which the resources will be needed on the project and when the recruitment process should begin. The resources can be described individually, by teams, or by function (programmers, testers, and so on). Many staffing management plans use a resource histogram. This is usually drawn in chart form, with project time along the horizontal axis and hours needed along the vertical axis. The following example histogram shows the hours needed for an asphalt crew on a construction project.

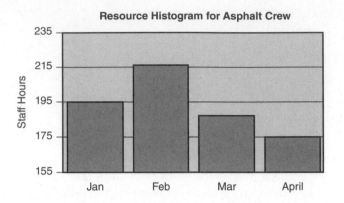

Resource Histogram for Asphalt Crew

Staff Release Plan   Attention should be given to how you'll release project team members at the end of their assignments. You should have reassignment procedures in place to move folks on to other projects or back to assignments they had before the project. This reduces overall project costs because you pay them only for the time they work and then release them. You won't have a tendency to simply keep them busy between assignments or until the end of their scheduled end date if they complete their activities early. Having these procedures in place will also improve morale because everyone will be clear about how reassignment will occur. This should reduce anxiety about their opportunities for employment at the conclusion of the project or their assignments.

Training Needs   This describes any training plans needed for team members who don't have the required skills or abilities to perform project tasks.

Recognition and Rewards   This describes the systems you'll use to reward and reinforce desired behavior. I'll talk more about recognition and rewards in Chapter 8.

Compliance   If your project involves regulations that must be met or contractual obligations (such as union contracts), the staffing management plan should detail these and any human resource policies the organization has in place that deal with compliance issues.

Safety   Any safety policies and procedures that are applicable to the project or industry you work in should be included in the staffing management plan.

Exam Spotlight

Be sure you understand the roles and responsibilities and the staffing management elements of the human resource management plan for the exam.

In the next section, we'll shift our focus once again but to a completely new topic. We'll look at quality and its effect on the project planning processes.

Quality Planning

Quality is affected by the triple constraints (project scope, schedule, and cost), and quality concerns are found in all projects. Quality typically defines whether stakeholder expectations were met. Being on time and on budget is one thing; if you deliver the wrong product or an inferior product, on time and on budget suddenly don't mean much.

The *Plan Quality Management* process is concerned with targeting quality standards that are relevant to the project at hand and devising a plan to meet and satisfy those standards. The quality management plan is an output of this process that describes how the quality policy will be implemented by the project management team during the course of the project. Another key output of this process is the process improvement plan, which documents the actions for analyzing processes to ultimately increase customer value. Everything discussed in this section, including the inputs and tools and techniques of this process, will be used to help develop these two primary outputs.

Exam Spotlight

Plan Quality Management is a key process performed during the Planning processes and when developing the project management plan. It should be performed in conjunction with other Planning processes. According to the *PMBOK® Guide*, quality should be planned, designed, and built in—not inspected.

Plan Quality Management Inputs

The Plan Quality Management process has several inputs:

- Project management plan
- Stakeholder register
- Risk register

- Requirements documentation
- Enterprise environmental factors
- Organizational process assets

One of the key components of the project management plan is the scope baseline. We talked about the scope baseline in Chapter 3, "Developing the Project Scope Statement"; recall that the scope baseline consists of the approved project scope statement, the WBS, and the WBS dictionary. For the exam, remember that the scope baseline is based on the project scope and requirements. The other baselines you should consider are the schedule baseline, which includes the project and activity start and finish dates, and the cost baseline.

The two key elements I'll cover regarding inputs are standards and regulations, which are part of the enterprise environmental factors input, and the quality policy, which is part of the organizational process assets input.

Standards and Regulations

The project manager should consider any standards, regulations, guidelines, or rules that exist concerning the work of the project when writing the quality plan. A *standard* is something that's approved by a recognized body and that employs rules, guidelines, or characteristics that should be followed. For example, the Americans with Disabilities Act (ADA) has established standards for web page designers that outline alternative viewing options of web pages for people with disabilities. PMI® guidelines regarding project management are another example of standards.

Standards aren't legally mandatory, but it's a good idea to follow them. Many organizations (or industries) have standards in place that are proven best practice techniques. Disregarding accepted standards can have significant consequences. For example, if you're creating a new software product that ignores standard protocols, your customers won't be able to use it. Standards can be set by the organization, independent bodies, organizations such as the International Organization for Standardization (ISO), and so on. ISO develops and publishes international standards on various subjects, including mathematics, information technology, railway engineering, construction materials and building, and much more. There are 160 countries that have participating members (one member per country) in ISO's national standards institutes. ISO is not a government organization, but they work closely with government and the private sector to establish standards in many disciplines to meet the needs of business and society. You can find out more about ISO at: www.iso.org. According to the *PMBOK® Guide*, the Project Quality Management Knowledge Area is designed to be in alignment with the ISO.

A *regulation* is mandatory. Regulations are almost always imposed by governments or institutions such as the American Medical Association. Organizations might have their own self-imposed regulations that you should be aware of as well. Regulations require strict adherence, particularly in the case of government-imposed regulations, or stiff penalties and fines could result—maybe even jail time if the offense is serious enough. Hmm, it might be tough to practice project management from behind bars—not a recommended career move.

If possible, it's a good idea to include information from the quality policy (I'll cover this in the next section) and any standards, regulations, or guidelines that affect the project in the quality management plan. If it's not possible to include this information in the quality management plan, then at least refer to the information and where it can be found. It's the project management team's responsibility to be certain all stakeholders are aware of and understand the policy issues and standards or regulations that might impact the project.

 Contracts might have certain provisions for quality requirements that you should account for in the quality management plan. If the quality management plan was written prior to the Plan Procurement Management process, you should update the quality plan to reflect it.

Quality Policy

The quality policy is part of the organizational process assets input. It's a guideline published by executive management that describes what quality policies should be adopted for projects the company undertakes. It's up to the project manager to understand this policy and incorporate any predetermined company guidelines into the quality plan. If a quality policy does not exist, it's up to the project management team to create one for the project.

Exam Spotlight

It is the responsibility of the project management team to ensure that all key project stakeholders are aware of and have received copies of the quality policy.

Tools and Techniques for Plan Quality Management

The Plan Quality Management process has eight tools and techniques used to help construct the quality management plan:

- Cost-benefit analysis
- Cost of quality
- Seven Basic Quality Tools
- Benchmarking
- Design of experiments
- Statistical sampling
- Additional quality planning tools
- Meetings

Make sure you understand each of these tools and techniques and its purpose for the exam. We'll take a look at them now with the exception of meetings.

Cost-Benefit Analysis

You've seen the cost-benefit analysis technique before in the Initiating process group. In the case of quality management, you'll want to consider the trade-offs of the cost of quality. It's cheaper and more efficient to prevent defects in the first place than to spend time and money fixing them later. The benefits of meeting quality requirements are as follows:

- Stakeholder satisfaction is increased.

- Costs are lower.

- Productivity is higher.

- There is less rework.

The primary cost of meeting quality requirements for a project is the expense incurred while performing project quality management activities.

Cost of Quality

The *cost of quality (COQ)* is the total cost to produce the product or service of the project according to the quality standards and/or the cost to make a product or service that does not meet the quality requirements. These costs include all the work necessary to meet the product requirements whether the work was planned or unplanned. It also includes the costs of work performed due to nonconforming quality requirements, assessing whether the product or service meets requirements, and rework.

Three costs are associated with the cost of quality:

Prevention Costs   Prevention means keeping defects out of the hands of customers. *Prevention costs* are the costs associated with satisfying customer requirements by creating a product without defects. These costs are manifested early in the process and include aspects such as Plan Quality Management, training, equipment, documenting, and taking the time to do things right.

Appraisal Costs   *Appraisal costs* are the costs expended to examine the product or process and make certain the requirements are being met. Appraisal costs might include costs associated with aspects such as inspections and testing. Prevention and appraisal costs are often passed on to the acquiring organization because of the limited duration of the project.

Failure Costs   *Failure costs* are what it costs when things don't go according to plan. Failure costs are also known as cost of poor quality. Two types of failure costs exist:

Internal Failure Costs   These result when customer requirements are not satisfied while the product is still in the control of the organization. Internal failure costs might include corrective action, rework, scrapping, and downtime.

External Failure Costs   External failure costs, unfortunately, are when the customer determines that the requirements have not been met. Costs associated with external failure costs might include inspections at the customer site, warranty work, returns, liabilities, lost business, and additional customer service costs.

There are two categories of costs within COQ, the cost of conformance and the cost of nonconformance. Conformance costs are associated with activities undertaken to avoid failures, whereas nonconformance costs are those undertaken because a failure has occurred. All of the types of costs of quality we just covered fall into one of these categories. Table 7.2 is a quick reference.

TABLE 7.2   Cost of conformance and nonconformance

Conformance costs	Nonconformance costs
Prevention costs	Internal failure costs
Appraisal costs	External failure costs

The cost of quality can be affected by project decisions. Let's say you're producing a new product. Unfortunately, the product scope description or project scope statement was inadequate in describing the functionality of the product. The project team created the product exactly as specified in the project scope statement, the WBS, and other planning documents. Once the product hit the store shelves, the organization was bombarded with returns and warranty claims because of the poor quality. Therefore, your project decisions impacted the cost of quality. Recalls of products can also impact the cost of quality.

Cost of quality is a topic you'll likely encounter on the exam. The following sections will discuss some of the pioneers in this field. To make sure the product or service meets stakeholders' expectations, quality must be planned into the project and not inspected in after the fact.

Four people in particular are responsible for the rise of the modern quality management movement and the theories behind the cost of quality: Philip B. Crosby, Joseph M. Juran, W. Edwards Deming, and Walter Shewhart. Each of these men developed steps or points that led to commonly accepted quality processes that we use today and either developed or were the foundation for the development of quality theories such as Total Quality Management, Six Sigma, cost of quality, and continuous improvement. I'll also cover a quality technique called the Kaizen approach that originated in Japan.

Philip B. Crosby

Philip B. Crosby devised the *zero defects* practice, which means, basically, do it right the first time. (Didn't your dad use to tell you that?) Crosby says that costs will increase when quality planning isn't performed up front, which means you'll have to engage in rework, thereby affecting productivity. Prevention is the key to Crosby's theory. If you prevent the defect from occurring in the first place, costs are lower, conformance to requirements is easily met, and the cost measurement for quality becomes the cost of nonconformance rather than the cost of rework.

Joseph M. Juran

Joseph M. Juran is noted for his *fitness for use* premise. Simply put, this means the stakeholders' and customers' expectations are met or exceeded. This says that conformance to specifications—meaning the product of the project that was produced is what the project set out to produce—is met or exceeded. Fitness for use specifically reflects the customers' or stakeholders' view of quality and answers the following questions:

Did the product or service produced meet the quality expectation?

Did it satisfy a real need?

Is it reliable and safe?

Juran also proposed that there could be grades of quality. However, you should not confuse grade with quality. *Grade* is a category for products or services that are of the same type but have differing technical characteristics. *Quality* describes how well the product or service (or characteristics of the product or service) fulfills the requirements. Low quality is usually not an acceptable condition; however, low grade might be. For example, your new Dad's Dollars Credit Card software tracking system might be of high quality, meaning it has no bugs and the product performs as advertised, but of low grade, meaning it has few features. You'll almost always want to strive for high quality, regardless of the acceptable grade level.

Exam Spotlight

Understand the difference between quality and grade for the exam.

W. Edwards Deming

W. Edwards Deming suggested that as much as 85 percent of the cost of quality is management's problem and responsibility. Once the quality issue has hit the floor, or the worker level, the workers have little control. For example, if you're constructing a new highway and the management team that bid on the project proposed using inferior-grade asphalt, the workers laying the asphalt have little control over its quality. They're at the mercy of the management team responsible for purchasing the supplies.

Deming also proposed that workers cannot figure out quality on their own and, therefore, cannot perform at their best. He believed that workers need to be shown what acceptable quality is and that they need to be made to understand that quality and continuous improvement are necessary elements of any organization—or project, in your case.

Many consider Deming to be a major contributor to the *Total Quality Management (TQM)* theory. TQM, like Deming, says that the process is the problem, not people. Every person and all activities the company undertakes are involved with quality. TQM stipulates that quality must be managed in and that quality improvement should be a continuous way of doing business, not a onetime performance of a specific task or process.

Exam Spotlight

There is some controversy surrounding who is the actual founder of TQM. Some say Deming, but others say Armand V. Feigenbaum. For the exam, I recommend knowing that Feigenbaum is the founder of TQM and Deming believes quality is a management issue. *Six Sigma* is a quality management approach that is similar to TQM and is typically used in manufacturing and service-related industries. Six Sigma is a measurement-based strategy that focuses on process improvement and variation reduction, which you can achieve by applying Six Sigma methodologies to the project. There are two Six Sigma methodologies. The first is known as DMADV (define, measure, analyze, design, and verify) and is used to develop new processes or products at the Six Sigma level. The second is called DMAIC (define, measure, analyze, improve, and control) and is used to improve existing processes or products. Another tidbit you should know about Six Sigma is that it aims to eliminate defects and stipulates that no more than 3.4 defects per million are produced.

Walter Shewhart

Some sources say that Walter Shewhart is the grandfather of TQM, which was further popularized by Feigenbaum and Deming. Shewhart developed statistical tools to examine when a corrective action must be applied to a process. He invented control chart techniques (control charts are a tool and technique of the Perform Quality Control process) and was also the inventor of the Plan-Do-Check-Act cycle that I talked about in Chapter 1, "What Is a Project?"

Kaizen Approach

The *Kaizen approach* is a quality technique from Japan. In fact, *Kaizen* means *continuous improvement* in Japanese. With this technique, all project team members and managers should be constantly watching for quality improvement opportunities. The Kaizen approach states that you should improve the quality of the people first and then the quality of the products or service.

Continuous improvement involves everyone in the organization watching for ways to improve quality, whether incrementally or by incorporating new ideas into the process. This involves taking measurements, improving processes by making them repeatable and systemized, reducing variations in production or performance, reducing defects, and improving cycle times. TQM and Six Sigma are examples of continuous improvement.

Capability Maturity Model Integration

The *Capability Maturity Model Integration (CMMI)* is used to help organizations assess and improve performance. CMMI is used in many areas such as engineering, project management, organizational development, and more. CMMI models are based on five stages of development ranging from almost no formal processes to the fifth stage, where a state of continuous, sustained improvements is reached. You may have heard about CMMI as it relates to project management. There are differing measures and stages of development depending on the industry, but most CMMI models have the following stages:

1. No formal processes are in place.

2. Basic processes exist but aren't standardized across the organization.

3. Best practices are in place and are standardized across the organization.

4. Best practices are in place and standardized across the organization, and they are measurable using quantifiable methods.

5. Continuous, sustained improvements are realized.

You can measure your organization's maturity regarding project management practices as a whole, and or you can take it one step further and measure maturity in each of the nine Knowledge Areas. Since we're discussing quality in this chapter, remember that CMMI can also be used to measure quality processes.

Exam Spotlight

For the exam, understand each of these theories on the cost of quality. Here's a key to help you remember:

- Crosby = Zero defects and prevention or rework results.

- Juran = Fitness for use, conformance. Quality by design.

- Deming = Quality is a management problem.

- Feigenbaum = Founder of TQM.

- Shewhart = Plan-Do-Check-Act cycle.

- TQM = Quality must be managed and must be a continuous process.

- Six Sigma = Six Sigma is a measurement-based strategy; no more than 3.4 defects per million opportunities.

- Kaizen = Continuous improvement; improve quality of people first.

- Continuous improvement = Watch continuously for ways to improve quality.

- CMMI = Assesses and improves performance by measuring the maturity levels of the organization.

Seven Basic Quality Tools

The term "Seven Basic Quality Tools" refers to seven techniques used to graphically display and diagnose quality issues. According to the *PMBOK® Guide*, the Seven Basic Quality Tools are used in conjunction with the plan-do-check-act cycle we talked about in Chapter 1. The charts and diagrams within this tool you should understand for the exam are as follows:

- Cause-and-effect diagrams
- Flowcharts (also known as stratification charts)
- Checksheets
- Pareto diagrams
- Histograms
- Control charts
- Scatter diagrams

We talked about histograms earlier in this chapter. I will cover control charts, Pareto diagrams, and scatter diagrams in more depth in Chapter 11, "Controlling Work Results."

Cause-and-effect diagrams, also known as Ishikawa diagrams or fishbone diagrams, associate the source of the problem back to a root cause. We discussed cause-and-effect diagrams in Chapter 6.

Flowcharts are another tool associated with the Seven Basic Quality Tools that we discussed in Chapter 6. You will recall that a flowchart graphically depicts the relationships between and among steps. They typically show activities, decision points, and the flow or order of steps in a process. Flowcharts may point out possible quality issues and are a great tool for the project team to use when reviewing quality results. They can also be helpful in determining the cost of quality by estimating the expected costs of conformance and nonconformance. According to the *PMBOK® Guide*, flowcharts are useful to understand the processes that exist within the Supplier, Input, Process, Output, Customer (SIPOC) model.

Checksheets are similar to checklists and are used during the quality processes to gather or verify data regarding quality problems. They are particularly useful when inspecting quality results.

Benchmarking

Benchmarking is a process of comparing previous similar activities to the current project activities to provide a standard to measure performance against. This comparison will also help you derive ideas for quality improvements on the current project. For example, if your current printer can produce 8 pages per minute and you're considering a new printer that produces 14 pages per minute, the benchmark is 8 pages per minute.

Design of Experiments

Design of experiments (DOE) is a statistical technique that identifies the elements—or variables—that will have the greatest effect on overall project outcomes. It is used most often concerning the product of the project but can also be applied to project management processes to examine trade-offs. DOE designs and sets up experiments to determine the ideal solution for a problem using a limited number of sample cases. It analyzes several variables at once, allowing you to change all (or some of) the variables at the same time and determine which combination will produce the best result at a reasonable cost.

Exam Spotlight

For the exam, remember that the key to DOE is that it equips you with a statistical framework that allows you to change the variables that have the greatest effect on overall project outcomes at once instead of changing one variable at a time.

Statistical Sampling

Statistical sampling involves taking a sample number of parts from the whole population and inspecting them to determine whether they fall within acceptable variances. We will discuss statistical sampling in more detail in Chapter 9, "Conducting Procurements and Sharing Information."

Additional Quality Planning Tools

The *PMBOK® Guide* lists the following tools as part of the additional quality planning tools tool and technique:

- Brainstorming
- Force field analysis
- Nominal Group technique
- Quality management and control tools

We've already covered brainstorming and the Nominal Group technique. Let's briefly look at the remaining tools next.

Force field analysis is a method of examining the drivers and resistors of a decision. You could use the old T-square approach and list all the drivers down the left column and all the resistors in the right. Determine which of the elements in the list are barriers and which are enablers to the project. Assign a priority or rank to each, and develop strategies for leveraging the strengths of the high-priority enablers while minimizing the highest-ranked barriers.

Quality management and control tools consists of several tools, including affinity diagrams, process decision program charts, interrelationship digraphs, tree diagrams, prioritization matrices, activity network diagrams, and matrix diagrams. We will cover each of these in Chapter 11.

You should memorize the names of these additional Plan Quality Management tools for the exam, but more important, you should know both the names and concepts of the other tools and techniques I talked about earlier in this chapter, as well as when to use them.

Plan Quality Management Outputs

Plan Quality Management uses many techniques to determine the areas of quality improvement that can be implemented, controlled, and measured throughout the rest of the project, as you've seen. These are recorded in the primary output of this process, which is called the *quality management plan*. The following list includes all the outputs of this process:

- Quality management plan
- Process improvement plan
- Quality metrics
- Quality checklists
- Project documents updates

Project documents updates include updates to the stakeholder register and the RAM and may also involve updates to the WBS and WBS dictionary. We'll talk about the Perform Quality Assurance process in Chapter 9. We'll look at the remaining outputs of Plan Quality Management next.

Quality Management Plan

The quality management plan describes how the project management team will carry out the quality policy. It should document the resources needed to carry out the quality plan, the responsibilities of the project team in implementing quality, and all the processes and procedures the project team and organization should use to satisfy quality requirements, including quality control, quality assurance techniques, and continuous improvement processes.

The project manager, in cooperation with the project staff, writes the quality management plan. You can assign quality actions to the activities listed on the WBS based on the quality plan requirements. Isn't that WBS a handy thing? Later in the Control Quality process, measurements will be taken to determine whether the quality to date is on track with the quality standards outlined in the quality management plan.

Exam Spotlight

The Project Quality Management Knowledge Area, which includes the Plan Quality Management, Perform Quality Assurance, and Control Quality processes, involves the quality management of the project as well as the quality aspects of the product or service the project was undertaken to produce. We'll discuss Quality Assurance and Quality Control in later chapters.

Process Improvement Plan

The *process improvement plan* focuses on finding inefficiencies in a process or activity and eliminating them. The idea here is that if you're doing activities or performing processes that don't add any value, you'll want to either stop doing what you're doing or modify the process so that you are adding value. You should note that the process improvement plan is a subsidiary plan of the project management plan. Some of the elements you should consider when thinking about process improvement are the process boundaries, which describe the purpose for the process and its expected start and end dates; the process configuration so that you know what processes are performed when and how they interact; the process metrics; and any specific elements you want to target for improvement.

Quality Metrics

A *quality metric*, also known as an *operational definition*, describes what is being measured and how it will be measured during the Control Quality process. For example, let's say you're managing the opening of a new restaurant in July of next year. Perhaps one of the deliverables is the procurement of flatware for 500 place settings. The operational definition in this case might include the date the flatware must be delivered and a counting or inventory process to ensure you received the number of place settings you ordered. Measurements of this variable consist of actual values, not "yes" or "no" results. In our example, receiving the flatware is a "yes" or "no" attribute result (you have it or you don't), but the date it was delivered and the number of pieces delivered are actual values. Failure rates are another type of quality metric that is measurable, as are reliability, availability, test coverage, and defect density measurements.

Quality Checklists

If you're like me, you start your day at the office with a big to-do list that has so many items on it you won't be able to finish them all. Nevertheless, you faithfully write the list every day and check off the items that you accomplish throughout the day. *Checklists* are like this in that they provide a means to determine whether the required steps in a process have been followed. As each step is completed, it's checked off the list. Checklists can be activity specific or industry specific and might be complex or easy to follow. Sometimes, organizations might have standard checklists they use for projects. You might also be able to obtain checklists from professional associations.

 Real World Scenario

Candy Works

Juliette Walters is a contract project manager for Candy Works. She is leading a project that will introduce a new line of hard candy drops in various exotic flavors: café latte, hot buttered popcorn, and jalapeño spice, just to name a few.

Juliette is writing the quality management plan for this project. After interviewing stakeholders and key team members, she has found several quality factors of importance to the organization. Quality will be measured by the following criteria:

Candy Size   Each piece should measure 3 mm.

Appearance   No visible cracks or breaks should appear in the candy.

Flavor   Flavor must be distinguishable when taste tested.

Number Produced   The production target is 9,000 pieces per week. The current machine has been benchmarked at 9,200 candies per week.

Intensity of Color   There should be no opaqueness in the darker colors.

Wrappers   Properly fitting wrappers cover the candies, folding over twice in back and twisted on each side. There is a different wrapper for each flavor of candy, and they must match exactly.

The candy is cooked and then pulled into a long cylinder shape roughly 6' long and 2" in diameter. This cylinder is fed into the machine that molds and cuts the candy into drops. The cylinders vary a little in size because they're hand-stretched by expert candy makers, who then feed the candies into the drop maker machine. As a result, the end of one flavor batch—the café latte flavor—and the beginning of the next batch—the hot buttered popcorn flavor—merge. This means the drops that fall into the collection bins are intermingled during the last run of the first flavor batch. In other words, the last bin of the café latte flavor run has some hot buttered popcorn drops mixed in. There is no way to separate the drops once they've hit the bin. From there, the drops go on to the candy-wrapping machine, where brightly colored wrappers are matched to the candy flavor. According to the quality plan, hot buttered popcorn drops cannot be wrapped as café latte drops. Juliette ponders what to do.

As she tosses and turns that night thinking about the problem, it occurs to her to present this problem to the company as an opportunity rather than as a problem. To keep production in the 9,000 candies per week category, the machines can't be stopped every time a new batch is introduced. So, Juliette comes up with the idea to wrap candies from the intermixed bins with wrappers that say, "Mystery Flavor." This way, production keeps pace with the plan, and the wrapper/flavor quality problem is mitigated.

Exam Spotlight

Be aware that a checklist shows up as an input, an output, and a tool and technique. Quality checklists are an output of the Plan Quality Management process and an input to the Control Quality process, and checklist analysis is a tool and technique of the Identify Risks process.

NOTE   One of the results of the Plan Quality Management process is that your product or process might require adjustments to conform to the quality policy and standards. These changes might result in cost changes and schedule changes. You might also discover that you'll need to perform risk analysis techniques for problems you uncover or when making adjustments as a result of this process.

Bringing It All Together

Believe it or not, you have officially completed the Planning process group. Along the way, I've mentioned gaining approvals for portions of the project plan such as the schedule and budget.

The *project management plan* is the approved, formal, documented plan that's used to guide you throughout the project Executing process group. The plan consists of all the outputs of the Planning process groups, including the subsidiary plans and baselines. It's the map that tells you where you're going and how to perform the activities of the project plan during the Direct and Manage Project Work process. It serves several purposes, the most important of which is tracking and measuring project performance through the Executing and Monitoring and Controlling processes and making future project decisions. The project management plan is critical in all communications you'll have from here forward with the stakeholders, management, and customers. The project management plan also documents all project planning assumptions, all project planning decisions, and important management reviews needed.

The project management plan encompasses everything I've talked about up to now and is represented in a formal document, or collection of documents. This document contains the project scope statement, deliverables, assumptions, risks, WBS, milestones, project schedule, resources, and more. It becomes the baseline you'll use to measure and track progress against. It's also used to help you control the components that tend to stray from the original plan so you can get them back in line.

The project management plan is used as a communication and information tool for stakeholders, team members, and the management team. They will use the plan to review and gauge progress as well.

Exam Spotlight

Performance measurement baselines are management controls that should change only infrequently. Examples of the performance measurement baselines you've looked at so far are budget, scope, and schedule baselines. However, the project management plan itself also becomes a baseline. If changes in scope or schedule do occur after Planning is complete, you should go through a formalized process (which I'll cover in Chapter 10) to implement the changes.

Don't forget that sign-off on the project management plan is important to the project's success. It isn't necessary for the sponsor and key stakeholders to sign off on every individual project document, but you should obtain signatures on the project management plan. PMI® notes that the project management plan should be signed off, "if required." In reality, I would never embark on a project of any size without sign-off from at least the project sponsor and maybe a few key stakeholders depending on the size, risk, and complexity of the project as well. If they've been an integral part of the Planning processes all along (and I know you know how important this is), obtaining sign-off on the project management plan should simply be a formality.

The project management plan consists of several components and I've recapped them here for your reference. You can find the differences between project management plan components and project documents on a handy table (Table 4-1) in the *PMBOK® Guide* on page 77:

- Change Management Plan
- Communications Management Plan
- Configuration Management Plan
- Cost Management Plan
- Cost Baseline
- Human Resource Management Plan
- Process Improvement Plan
- Procurement Management Plan
- Quality Management Plan
- Requirements Management Plan
- Risk Management Plan
- Schedule Baseline
- Schedule Management Plan
- Scope Baseline
- Scope Management Plan
- Stakeholder Management Plan

"But wait," I hear you saying, "we didn't discuss the change management plan or the configuration management plan." In a nutshell, the change management plan describes how you will document and manage change requests, the process for approving changes, and how to document and manage the final recommendation for the change requests. Configuration management is similar, but configuration changes deal with the components of the product of the project, such as functional ability or physical attributes, rather than the project process itself. I will cover these topics in much more depth in Chapter 10.

Note that you will use all the management plans I discussed during the Planning processes—all those just listed—throughout the Executing process group to manage the project and keep the performance of the project on track with the project objectives. If you don't have a project management plan, you'll have no way of managing the process. You'll find that even with a project management plan, project scope has a way of changing. Stakeholders and others tend to sneak in a few of the "Oh, I didn't understand that before" statements and hope that they slide right by you. With that signed, approved project management plan in your files, you are allowed to gently remind them that they read and agreed to the project plan and you're sticking to it.

 Real World Scenario

Project Case Study: New Kitchen Heaven Retail Store

You're just finishing a phone conversation with Jill, and you see Dirk headed toward your office.

Dirk walks in, crosses his arms over his chest, and stands next to your desk with an "I'm here for answers" look.

"I thought I'd drop by and see whether you have signed a lease and gotten Jake started on that build-out yet," says Dirk.

"I just got off the phone with Jill," you reply. "The realtor found a great location, and we've set up a tour for tomorrow."

"What has been the holdup?" Dirk asks. "I thought we'd be ready to start the build-out about now."

"I've been working on the project plans."

"Project plans," Dirk interrupts. "We already have a plan. That schedule thing and risk stuff and the budget you drew up over the last couple of weeks spelled things out pretty clearly."

"I'm almost finished with the project plans. I'd like you to take a look at the human resource management plan after I review with you what we've done to date."

"I don't understand why you're wasting all this time planning. We all know what the objectives are."

"Dirk," you reply, "if we put the right amount of effort and time into planning, the actual work of the project should go pretty smoothly. Planning is probably one of the most important things we can do on this project. If we don't plan correctly, we might miss something very important that could delay the store opening. That date is pretty firm, I thought."

"Yes, the date is firm. But I don't see how we could miss anything. You and I have met several times, and I know you've met with Jill and Jake. They're the other key players on this."

"Let me finish," you reply. "I have met with all the key stakeholders and after you review these last few documents I have for you, we're finished with the planning phase of this project. Ricardo drafted a procurement statement of work. He needs to hire some external resources—and I noted that in the human resource management plan by the way—to help run Ethernet cable, procure a T1 line, and purchase some routers and switches. The purchase of the routers and switches will be accomplished using a fixed-price contract, and the human resources he needs will be procured using a time and materials contract. Jill also drew up a procurement statement of work for the gourmet and cookware lines purchase. I documented a lot of the human resource management plan when we worked through the activity estimating and duration exercise and put some finishing touches on it yesterday. It includes an RACI chart for all our project key deliverables." You sneak in a quick breath because you don't want Dirk to interrupt. "And the quality management plan is complete. After your review, I'll distribute it to the key stakeholders. The quality management plan describes how we'll implement our quality policy. You know the old saying, 'Do it right the first time.' I took the time to write down the specific quality metrics we're looking for, including the lease signing date (this one must start and finish on time) and the IT equipment specifications, and Jill has documented the gourmet products and the cookware line specifications."

Dirk looks impressed but you can't tell for sure.

"After I look at the last of these planning documents, are we ready to actually start working?"

"Yes, as soon as the lease is signed. I anticipate that happening by the end of this week. Tomorrow's tour is the fifth location Jill will look at. She's very happy with the third property she saw but wants to look at this last property before she makes her final decision."

"Great. Let's take a look at that human plan or whatever it is."

After reviewing the last of the planning documents, Dirk signs off on the project plan.

- Procurement
  - Fixed-price contract
  - Time and materials contract
  - Procurement documents prepared
  - Procurement statement of work prepared
- Plan Human Resource Management

- Roles and responsibilities documented
- RACI chart developed
- Organizational chart developed
- Quality Management Plan and Quality Metrics
  - Lease signing start and end dates
  - IT equipment specifications
  - Gourmet products—availability rates and defects
  - Cookware products—availability rates
  - Organizational chart developed
- Obtain approval and sign-off on project plan

Understanding How This Applies to Your Next Project

In my organization, the Plan Procurement Management process comes right after finalizing project scope because it takes a great deal of time and effort to procure goods and services. That means we have to start procuring resources as early in the project as possible in order to meet the project deadlines.

In all the organizations I've worked in, someone has always been responsible for procurement—whether it was a single person or an entire department. Typically, the procurement department defines many elements of the procurement management plan. Sure, the project team determines how many vendors need to be involved and how they'll be managed along with the schedule dates, but many other elements are predetermined, such as the type of contract to use, the authority of the project team regarding the contract, how multiple vendors will be managed, and the identification of prequalified sellers.

The procurement department also determines what type of procurement document you should use depending on the types of resources you're acquiring and the amount of money you're spending. Typically, they'll have a template for you to use with all the legalese sections prepopulated, and you'll work on the sections that describe the work or resources you need for the project, milestones or schedule dates, and evaluation criteria.

Don't make the mistake of thinking your procurement department will take care of all the paperwork for you. At a minimum, you will likely be responsible for writing the statement of work, writing the RFP, writing the contract requirements (as they pertain to the work of the project), creating the vendor selection criteria, and determining the schedule dates for contract work.

Plan Human Resource Management is a process you might not need to complete, depending on the size and complexity of the project. I typically work with the same team members over and over again, so I know their skills, capabilities, and availability. However, if you're hiring contract resources for the project or you typically work with new team members on each project, I recommend creating a staffing management plan.

The quality management plan is another important element of your project management plan. You should take into consideration the final result or product of the project and the complexity of the project to determine if you need a multi-page document with detailed specifications or if the plan can be more informal and broad in nature. Again, depending on the project complexity, the measurements or criteria you'll use to determine the quality objective could be a few simple sentences or bullet items or a more formal, detailed document. The quality baseline should be documented during this process as well.

Summary

This chapter's focus was on planning for project resources. Several aspects are involved in these planning activities, including procuring goods and services, planning human resources, and defining the activities in which human resources will be involved.

This chapter started with the Plan Procurement Management process. This process identifies the goods or services you're going to purchase from outside the organization and determines which goods or services the project team can meet. This involves tools and techniques such as make-or-buy decisions, expert judgment, and contract types. The procurement management plan is one of the outputs of this process and describes how procurement services will be managed throughout the project. The procurement SOW (another output of this process) describes the work that will be contracted.

In our discussion of contract types, we covered fixed-price, cost plus, and time and materials contracts and the benefits and risks of using them.

The Plan Human Resource Management process identifies and assigns roles and responsibilities and reporting relationships. Many times the roles and responsibilities assignments are depicted in a responsibility assignment matrix (RAM) or an RACI chart. The staffing management plan describes how and when project team members will be acquired and is part of the human resource management plan output of this process.

Plan Quality Management targets the quality standards that are relevant to your project. The quality management plan outlines how the project team will enact the quality policy.

You need to take into account the cost of quality when considering stakeholder needs. Four men led to the rise of the cost of quality theories. Crosby is known for his zero-defects theory, Juran for the fitness for use theory, Deming for attributing 85 percent of cost of quality to the management team, and Shewhart for the Plan-Do-Check-Act cycle. The Kaizen approach says that the project team should continuously be on the lookout for ways to improve the process and that people should be improved first and then the quality of the products or services. TQM and Six Sigma are examples of continuous improvement techniques.

Cost-benefit analysis considers trade-offs in the Plan Quality Management process. Benchmarking compares previous similar activities to the current project activities to provide a standard to measure performance against. Design of experiments is an analytical technique that determines what variables have the greatest effect on the project outcomes. This technique equips you with a statistical framework, allowing you to change all the important variables at once instead of changing one variable at a time.

Cost of quality involves three types of costs: prevention, appraisal, and failure costs; the latter is also known as the cost of poor quality. Failure costs include the costs of both internal and external failures.

The process improvement plan is a subsidiary plan of the project management plan and targets inefficiencies in a process or activity. The quality baseline is used to document the quality objectives of the project and is used as a basis for future Quality processes.

Exam Essentials

Be able to name the purpose of the Plan Procurement Management process. The purpose of the Plan Procurement Management process is to identify which project needs should be obtained from outside the organization. Make-or-buy analysis is used as a tool and technique to help determine this.

Be familiar with the contract types and their usage. Contract types are a tool and technique of the Plan Procurement Management process and include fixed-price and cost-reimbursable contracts. Use fixed-price contracts for well-defined projects with a high value to the company, and use cost-reimbursable contracts for projects with uncertainty and large investments early in the project life. The three types of fixed-price contracts are FFP, FPIF, and FP-EPA. The four types of cost-reimbursable contracts are CPFF, CPIF, CPF (or CPPC), and CPAF. Time and materials contracts are a cross between fixed-price and cost-reimbursable contracts.

Know the outputs of the Plan Procurement Management process. The outputs of Plan Procurement Management are procurement management plan, procurement statement of work, make-or-buy decisions, procurement documents, source selection criteria, change requests, and project documents updates.

Be able to name the purpose of the Plan Human Resource Management process. Plan Human Resource Management involves determining roles and responsibilities, reporting relationships for the project, and creating the staffing management plan, which describes how team members are acquired and the criteria for their release.

Be able to list the benefits of meeting quality requirements. The benefits of meeting quality requirements include increased stakeholder satisfaction, lower costs, higher productivity, and less rework and are discovered during the Plan Quality Management process.

Be able to define the cost of quality.   The COQ is the total cost to produce the product or service of the project according to the quality standards. These costs include all the work necessary to meet the product requirements for quality. The three costs associated with cost of quality are prevention, appraisal, and failure costs (also known as cost of poor quality).

Be able to name four people associated with COQ and some of the techniques they helped establish.   The four are Crosby, Juran, Deming, and Shewhart. Some of the techniques they helped to establish are TQM, Six Sigma, cost of quality, and continuous improvement. The Kaizen approach concerns continuous improvement and says people should be improved first.

Be able to name the tools and techniques of the Plan Quality Management process.   The Plan Quality Management process consists of cost-benefit analysis, cost of quality, Seven Basic Quality Tools, benchmarking, design of experiments, statistical sampling, flowcharting, proprietary quality management methodologies, additional quality planning tools, and meetings.

Key Terms

In this chapter, you began to see just how important communication is to every successful project. You learned about planning what work needs to be done, how you will communicate during the project, and how you will judge whether or not the project is successful. The processes that follow allow you to accomplish those portions of project planning.

Understand them well, and know each process by the name used in the *PMBOK®️ Guide:*

Plan Quality Management

Plan Procurement Management

Plan Human Resource Management

Before you take the exam, also be certain you are familiar with the following terms:

appraisal costs	make-or-buy decision
benchmarking	operational definition
Capability Maturity Model Integration (CMMI)	organization breakdown structure (OBS)
checklists	prevention costs
contract	process improvement plan
cost of quality (COQ)	procurement documents
cost plus award fee (CPAF) contract	procurement statement of work (SOW)
cost plus fixed fee (CPFF) contracts	quality management plan
cost plus incentive fee (CPIF)	quality metric
cost plus percentage of cost (CPPC)	RACI chart
cost-reimbursable contracts	regulation
design of experiments (DOE)	resource breakdown structure (RBS)
failure costs	responsibility assignment matrix (RAM)
firm fixed-price contract (FFP)	Six Sigma
fitness for use	source selection criteria
fixed-price contracts	staffing management plan
fixed-price incentive fee (FPIF) contracts	standard

fixed-price with economic price adjustment
contract (FP-EPA)

Kaizen approach

make-or-buy analysis

time and materials (T&M) contracts

Total Quality Management (TQM)

zero defects

Review Questions

You can find the answers to the questions in Appendix A.

1. You are the project manager for an upcoming outdoor concert event. You're working on the procurement plan for the computer software program that will control the lighting and screen projections during the concert. You're comparing the cost of purchasing a software product to the cost of your company programmers writing a custom software program. You are engaged in which of the following?

    A. Procurement planning

    B. Using expert judgment

    C. Creating the procurement management plan

    D. Make-or-buy analysis

2. You are the project manager for an outdoor concert event scheduled for one year from today. You're working on the procurement documents for the computer software program that will control the lighting and screen projections during the concert. You've decided to contract with a professional services company that specializes in writing custom software programs. You want to minimize the risk to the organization, so you'll opt for which contract type?

    A. FPIF

    B. CPFF

    C. FFP

    D. CPIF

3. You are the project manager for the Heart of Texas casual clothing company. Your company is introducing a new line of clothing called Black Sheep Ranch Wear. You will outsource the production of this clothing line to a vendor. The vendor has requested a procurement SOW. All of the following statements are true except for which one?

    A. The procurement SOW contains a description of the new clothing line.

    B. As the purchaser, you are required to write the procurement SOW.

    C. The procurement SOW contains the objectives of the project.

    D. The vendor requires a procurement SOW to determine whether it can produce the clothing line given the detailed specifications of this product.

4. You are the project manager for the Heart of Texas casual clothing company. Your company is introducing a new line of clothing called Black Sheep Ranch Wear. You will outsource the production of this clothing line to a vendor. Your legal department has recommended you use a contract that reimburses the seller's allowable costs and builds in a bonus based on the vendor achieving the performance criteria they've outlined in their memo. Which of the following contract types will you use?

    A. CPIF

    B. CPFF

    C. CPF

    D. FPIF

5. All of the following statements are true regarding the Plan Human Resource Management process except for which one?

   A. The Plan Human Resource Management process involves determining roles and responsibilities.

   B. Included in the Plan Human Resource Management output are project organization charts that show the project's reporting relationships.

   C. The staffing management plan created in this process describes how and when resources will be acquired and released.

   D. A RAM (or RACI chart) is an output of this process that allows you to see all the people assigned to an activity.

6. Sally is a project manager working on a project that will require a specially engineered machine. Only three manufacturers can make the machine to the specifications Sally needs. The price of this machine is particularly critical to this project. The budget is limited, and there's no chance of securing additional funds if the bids for the machine come in higher than budgeted. She's developing the source selection criteria for the bidders' responses and knows all of the following are true except for which one?

   A. Sally will use understanding of need and warranties as two of the criteria for evaluation.

   B. Sally will review the project management plan, requirements documents, and risk register as some of the inputs to this process.

   C. Sally will base the source selection criteria on price alone because the budget is a constraint.

   D. Sally will document an SOW, the desired form of response, and any required contractual provisions in the RFP.

7. Which of the following are constraints that you might find during the Plan Human Resource Management process?

   A. Organizational structures, collective bargaining agreements, and economic conditions

   B. Organizational structures, technical interfaces, and interpersonal interfaces

   C. Organizational interfaces, collective bargaining agreements, and economic conditions

   D. Organizational interfaces, technical interfaces, and interpersonal interfaces

8. You have been hired as a contract project manager for Grapevine Vineyards. Grapevine wants you to design an Internet wine club for its customers. Customers must register before being allowed to order wine over the Internet so that legal age can be established. You know this project will require new hardware and an update to some existing infrastructure. You will have to hire an expert to help with the infrastructure assessment and upgrades. You also know that the module to verify registration must be written and tested using data from Grapevine's existing database. This new module cannot be tested until the data from the existing system is loaded. You are going to hire a vendor to perform the programming and testing tasks for this module to help speed up the project schedule. The vendor will be reimbursed for all their costs, and you want to use a contract type that will allow you to give the vendor a little something extra if you are satisfied with the work they do. You know all of the following apply in this situation except for which one?

    A. Contract type is determined by the risk shared between the buyer and seller.

    B. You'll use a CPAF contract for the programming vendor.

    C. Fixed-price contracts can include incentives for meeting or exceeding performance criteria.

    D. Each procurement item needs an SOW.

9. You are the project manager for BB Tops, a nationwide toy store chain. Your new project involves creating a prototype display at several stores across the country. You are using a RACI chart to display individuals and activities. What does RACI stand for?

    A. Responsible, accountable, consult, inform

    B. Responsible, assignment, control, inform

    C. Resource, activity, control, identify

    D. Resource, accountable, consult, identify

10. Which process has the greatest ability to directly influence the project schedule?

    A. Plan Human Resource Management

    B. Plan Procurement Management

    C. Plan Communications

    D. Plan Quality Management

11. You are the project manager for BB Tops, a nationwide toy store chain. Your new project involves creating a prototype display at several stores across the country. You are hiring a contractor for portions of the project. The contract stipulates that you'll pay all allowable costs and a 6 percent fee over and above the allowable costs at the end of the contract. Which of the following describes this contract type?

    A. CPPF

    B. CPPC

    C. CPF

    D. CPIF

12. All of the following are true regarding the Plan Quality Management process except for which one?

    A. DOE is a tool and technique of this process that provides statistical analysis for changing product or process elements one at a time to optimize the process.

    B. This is one of the key processes performed during the Planning process group and during the development of the project management plan.

    C. Changes to the product as a result of meeting quality standards might require cost or schedule adjustments.

    D. Some of the tools and techniques of this process are cost-benefit analysis, COQ, Seven Basic Quality Tools, benchmarking, DOE, and statistical sampling.

13. Four people are responsible for establishing cost of quality theories. Crosby and Juran are two them, and their theories are _____, respectively.

    A. grades of quality, fitness for use

    B. fitness for use, zero defects

    C. zero defects, fitness for use

    D. cost of quality, zero defects

14. The theory that 85 percent of the cost of quality is a management problem is attributed to _____?

    A. Deming

    B. Shewhart

    C. Juran

    D. Crosby

15. All of the following are benefits of meeting quality requirements except which one?

    A. An increase in stakeholder satisfaction

    B. Less rework

    C. Lower risk

    D. Higher productivity

16. Which of the following describes the cost of quality associated with scrapping, rework, and downtime?

    A. Internal failure costs

    B. External failure costs

    C. Prevention costs

    D. Appraisal costs

17. The quality management plan documents how the project team will implement the quality policy. It should address at least all of the following except which one?

    A. The resources needed to carry out the quality plan

    B. The quality metrics and tolerances and what will be measured

    C. The responsibilities the project team has in implementing quality

    D. The processes to use to satisfy quality requirements

18. You work for a furniture manufacturer. Your project is going to design and produce a new office chair. The chair will have the ability to function as a regular chair and also the ability to move its occupant into an upright, kneeling position. The design team is trying to determine the combination of comfort and ease of transformation to the new position that will give the chair the best characteristics while keeping the costs reasonable. Several different combinations have been tested. This is an example of which of the following tools and techniques of Plan Quality Management?

    A. Benchmarking

    B. Quality metrics

    C. COQ

    D. DOE

19. Which of the following best characterizes Six Sigma?

    A. Stipulates that quality must be managed in

    B. Focuses on process improvement and variation reduction by using a measurement-based strategy

    C. Asserts that quality must be a continuous way of doing business

    D. Focuses on improving the quality of the people first, then improving the quality of the process or project

20. Your organization is embarking on a long-term project that will require additional human resources on a contract basis to complete the work of the project. Since the project will span several years, you know one vendor probably can't supply all the resources you'll need over the course of the contract. However, you want to work with only one vendor throughout the project to minimize the amount of procurement documents you'll have to produce. So, you'll specify in your procurement documents that contractors will have to form partnerships to work on this project. You know all of the following are true regarding this question except for which one?

    A. You will use an RFP, which is part of the procurement documents output of the Plan Procurement Management process, as your procurement document for this project.

    B. You'll use an FP-EPA contract because this project spans several years.

    C. You should consider teaming agreements, which are an input to the Plan Procurement Management process.

    D. Some of the quality metrics you'll use for this project include on-time performance, failure rates, budget control, and test coverage. Quality metrics are an output of the Plan Quality Management process.

Chapter

8

Developing the Project Team

✓ Execute the tasks as defined in the project plan in order to achieve the project deliverables within budget and schedule.

✓ Maximize team performance through leading, mentoring, training, and motivating team members.

✓ Communicate project status to stakeholders for their feedback, in order to ensure the project aligns with business needs.

✓ Knowledge and Skills:

  ▪ Project monitoring tools and techniques

  ▪ Interaction of work breakdown structure elements within the project schedule

This chapter begins the project Executing process group. I'll cover four of the processes in this chapter: Direct and Manage Project Work, Acquire Project Team, Develop Project Team, and Manage Project Team. I'll cover the remaining four Executing processes in the next chapter.

Direct and Manage Project Work is the action process. This is where you'll put the plans into action and begin working on the project activities. Execution also involves keeping the project in line with the original project management plan and bringing wayward activities back into alignment.

The Acquire, Develop, and Manage Project Team processes are all interrelated, as you can imagine, and work together to help obtain the best project team available.

Several things happen during the Executing processes. The majority of the project budget will be spent during this process group, and often the majority of the project time is expended here as well. The greatest conflicts you'll see during the project Executing processes are schedule conflicts. In addition, the product description will be finalized here and contain more detail than it did in the Planning processes.

There might be several exam questions from every process within the Executing process group. Don't skip studying these processes and the ones in Chapter 9, "Conducting Procurements and Sharing Information," because 30 percent of the exam questions concern the Executing process group. Are you ready to dive into Executing? Let's go.

 The process names, inputs, tools and techniques, outputs, and descriptions of the project management process groups and related materials and figures in this chapter are based on content from *A Guide to the Project Management Body of Knowledge (PMBOK® Guide), Fifth Edition* (Sybex, 2010).

Directing and Managing Project Work

The purpose of the *Direct and Manage Project Work* process is to carry out the project management plan and perform the work of the project. This is where your project comes to life and the work of the project happens. The work is authorized to begin and activities are performed. Resources are committed and people carry out their assigned activities to create the product, result, or service of the project. Funds are spent to accomplish project objectives. Performing project activities, training, selecting sellers, collecting project data, utilizing resources, and so on are all integrated with or are part of this process.

Direct and Manage Project Work is where the rubber meets the road. If you've done a good job planning the project, things should go relatively smoothly for you during this process. The deliverables and requirements are agreed on, the resources have been identified and are ready to go, and the stakeholders know exactly where you're headed because you had them review, agree to, and approve the project plan.

Some project managers think this is the time for them to kick back and put their feet up. After all, the project management plan is done, everyone knows what to do and what's expected of them, and the work of the project should almost carry itself out because your plan is a work of genius, right? Wrong! You must stay involved. Your job now is a matter of overseeing the actual work, producing deliverables, communicating, issuing change requests, implementing approved changes, managing the schedule, managing risks, managing stakeholders, staying on top of issues and problems, and keeping the work lined up with the project management plan.

Exam Spotlight

The project management plan serves as the project baseline. During the Executing processes, you should continually compare and monitor project performance against the baseline so that corrective actions can be taken and implemented at the right time to prevent disaster. This information will also be fed into the Monitoring and Controlling processes for further analysis.

One of the most difficult aspects of this process is coordinating and integrating all the elements of the project. Although you do have the project management plan as your guide, you still have a lot of balls in the air. You'll find yourself coordinating and monitoring many project elements—occasionally all at the same time—during the course of the Direct and Manage Project Work process. You might be negotiating for team members at the same time you're negotiating with vendors at the same time you're working with another manager to get a project component completed so your deliverables stay on schedule. You should monitor risks and risk triggers closely. The Plan Procurement Management process might need intervention or cause you delays. The organizational, technical, and interpersonal interfaces might require intense coordination and oversight. Of course, you should always be concerned about the pulse of your stakeholders. Are they actively involved in the project? Are they throwing up roadblocks now that the work has started?

According to the *PMBOK® Guide*, this process also requires implementing corrective actions to bring the work of the project back into alignment with the project management plan, preventive actions to reduce the probability of negative consequences, and defect repairs to correct product defects discovered during the quality processes.

As you can see, your work as project manager is not done yet. Many elements of the project require your attention, so let's get to work.

Later in this chapter I'll also talk about Develop Project Team because this is an integral part of the Direct and Manage Project Work process as well. You'll want to monitor the team's performance, the status of their work, and their interactions with you and other team members as you execute the project management plan.

Executing Inputs

Direct and Manage Project Work has four inputs:

- Project management plan
- Approved change requests
- Enterprise environmental factors
- Organizational process assets

The project management plan documents the collection of outputs of the Planning processes and describes and defines how the project should be executed, monitored, controlled, and closed. The project management plan documents the goals of the project and the actual work you and the team will execute in order to meet those goals. Once the project management plan is complete, you will know all of the work and actions needed to meet the deliverables of the project and will have a plan for executing those actions. You'll take a brief look at each of the other inputs next.

Approved Change Requests

Approved change requests come about as a result of the approved change requests output of the Perform Integrated Change Control process. (We'll cover this process in Chapter 10, "Measuring and Controlling Project Performance.") Change requests are approved or denied during this process, and once the decision has been made, approved changes come back through the Direct and Manage Project Work process for the project team to implement.

Approved changes might either expand or reduce project scope and may also cause revisions to project budgets, schedules, procedures, the project management plan, and so on. Change requests can be internal or external to the project or organization. For example, you may need to make changes because of a new law that affects your project.

Enterprise Environmental Factors

When performing this process, you will need to consider several enterprise environmental factors, including the company culture and organizational structure, the facilities available to the project team, personnel guidelines and hiring practices, risk tolerance levels, and project management information systems.

Organizational Process Assets

Like many of the other processes we've covered, historical information from past projects, organizational guidelines, and work processes are some of the organizational process assets you should consider when performing this process. In addition, measurement databases and issue and defect databases can be used in this process to compare past projects to the current project and to capture information about the current project for future reference.

Tools and Techniques of Direct and Manage Project Work

The tools and techniques of the Direct and Manage Project Work process are expert judgment, project management information system, and meetings. You've looked at all of these before. Remember that in the Executing processes, you'll be actively using all of these tools; consulting and meeting with stakeholders, professionals, and others; employing the project management methodology you developed in the Planning processes; and using the project management information system to update and track progress.

Some of the outputs of this process are going to look familiar and some are new. We'll examine them next.

Outputs of Direct and Manage Project Work

The outputs of the Direct and Manage Project Work process are as follows:

- Deliverables
- Work performance data
- Change requests
- Project management plan updates
- Project documents updates

The three most important outputs of this process are deliverables (meaning actually accomplishing the activities leading to the completion of the product, result, or service you set out to produce), work performance data, and change requests. Almost every process you've performed up to this point has defined and outlined what the work of the project entails and what the final results should look like. Now you're ready to begin performing the work. Let's look at these three outputs that will help us document our progress.

Deliverables

During Direct and Manage Project Work, you'll gather and record information regarding the outcomes of the work, including activity completion dates, milestone completions, the status of the deliverables, the quality of the deliverables, costs, schedule progress and updates, and so on. Deliverables aren't always tangible, but they are always unique and verifiable. For example, perhaps your team members require training on a piece of specialized equipment. Completion of the training is recorded as a work result. Capabilities required to perform a service that's described in the project management plan are also considered a deliverable. All of this information gets used during the Control Communications process, which I'll discuss during the Monitoring and Controlling processes.

Executing and Monitoring and Controlling are two process groups that work hand in hand. As you gather the information from work results, you'll measure the outputs and take corrective actions where necessary. This means you'll loop back through the Executing processes to put the corrections into place. The *PMBOK® Guide* breaks these processes up for ease of explanation, but in practice, you'll work through several of the Executing and Monitoring and Controlling processes together.

Work Performance Data

Work performance data concerns observing, gathering, documenting, and recording the status of project activities. The types of information you might gather during this process include some of the following:

- Schedule status and progress
- Status of deliverable completion
- Progress and status of schedule activities including start and end dates
- Percent of overall work complete
- Adherence to quality standards
- Number of change requests
- Status of costs (those authorized and costs incurred to date)
- Schedule activity completion estimates for those activities started
- Schedule activities percent complete
- Lessons learned
- Resource consumption and utilization

Work performance data becomes an input to a few of the Monitoring and Controlling processes where you'll perform further analysis on the data. It's important that you document this information so that when you get to the Monitoring and Controlling processes, you don't have to backtrack.

Change Requests

As a result of working through activities and producing your product, service, or result, you will inevitably come upon things that need to be changed. Changes can also come about from stakeholder requests, external sources, technological advances, and so on. These change requests might encompass schedule, scope, requirement, or resource changes. The list could go on. Your job as project manager, if you choose to accept it, is to collect the *change requests* and make determinations about their impact on the project.

Exam Spotlight

According the *PMBOK® Guide*, a change request is a formal request to bring about a change that will require revising a document, a project baseline, a deliverable, or some combination of all three.

Implementation of change requests may incorporate two types of actions: corrective actions or preventive actions. They may also require defect repairs or updates. Each of these topics is described next.

Corrective Actions   In my organization, a corrective action means an employee is in big trouble. Fortunately, this isn't what's meant here. *Corrective actions* are taken to get the anticipated future project outcomes to align with the project management plan. Maybe you've discovered that one of your programmers is adding an unplanned feature to the software project because he's friends with the user. You'll have to redirect him to the activities assigned to him originally to avoid schedule delays. Perhaps your vendor isn't able to deliver the laboratory equipment needed for the next project phase. You'll want to exercise your contract options (let's hope there's a clause in the contract that says the vendor must provide rental equipment until they can deliver your order), put your contingency plan into place, and get the lab the equipment that's needed to keep the project on schedule.

Preventive Actions   A *preventive action* involves anything that will reduce the potential negative impacts of risk events should they occur. Contingency plans and risk responses are examples of preventive actions. I described these and other risk responses while talking about the Plan Risk Response process in Chapter 6, "Risk Planning." You should be aware of contingency plans and risk responses so that you're ready to implement them at the first sign of trouble.

Defect Repairs   A defect occurs when a project component does not meet the requirements or specifications. Defects might be discovered when conducting quality audits in the Perform Quality Assurance process or when performing inspections during the Control Quality process.

For the exam, you should understand the difference between a validated defect repair and a defect repair. A validated defect repair is the result of a reinspection of the original defect repair. In other words, you found a problem with the product during the Quality processes, you corrected the problem (defect repair), and now you're reinspecting that repair (validated defect repair) to make certain the fix is accurate, correct, and fixed the problem.

Updates   Changes may require updates to the project documents so that the new information is captured and recorded. For example, some of the documents that might require an update could include the scope statement, budget documents, the schedule, risk management plan or risk response plans, and so on may need updating.

I'll discuss change requests more in the coming chapters as well. Change requests are an output of several processes, including the Direct and Manage Project Work process and the Control Communications process in the Monitoring and Controlling process group. Remember that the Executing process group outputs and the Monitoring and Controlling process group outputs feed each other as inputs. In this particular case, approved change requests are an input, and change requests are an output of the same process.

Exam Spotlight

Direct and Manage Project Work is where the work of the project is performed and the project management plan is put into action and carried out. In this process, the project manager is like an orchestra conductor signaling the instruments to begin their activities, monitoring what should be winding down, and keeping that smile going to remind everyone that they should be enjoying themselves. I recommend that you know the outputs of the Direct and Manage Project Work process for the exam.

I told you the Executing process group is about performing the work of the project, and in order to do that, you need resources. You'll look at two processes, Acquire Project Team and Develop Project Team, in the next few sections.

 ### Real World Scenario

We All Scream for Ice Cream

Heather is a pharmaceutical salesperson who is fed up with the rat race. She ran the numbers, decided to quit her day job, and bought an ice cream shop in a quaint tourist town. Having been involved in a few research and development projects, she understands the value of project management planning and using that plan as her guide to perform the work of the project.

Heather documented the deliverables needed to prepare for opening day in her scope statement. Some of those deliverables are as follows: remodel, develop staffing plan, procure equipment, and procure materials. Confident in her planning, Heather hired a contractor and began remodeling the shop. Then real life happened. The contractors discovered a water problem in the storage room. They installed a sump pump, which took care of the water, but discovered an even bigger problem when they moved the storage shelves. Mold was growing up the drywall. The drywall had to be removed, as did the insulation behind it, and the mold remaining on permanent fixtures had to be eliminated. Then new insulation and drywall had to be installed. The drywall had to be primed and painted. Because that portion of the storage room was getting a fresh coat of paint, Heather decided the contractors might as well paint the entire room.

All of these actions required another pass through the Planning processes. The schedule didn't require much modification because other work could be started while the water problem was being addressed, but the budget needed to be modified as a result of the additional work. To avoid more surprises, Heather requested that the contractor perform a thorough inspection of the property and determine whether there were any other hidden issues. Armed with the inspection report, Heather could knowledgeably plan corrective action for other items that needed to be addressed.

Acquiring the Project Team

The *Acquire Project Team* process involves attaining and assigning human resources to the project. Project staff might come from inside the company or from outside the company in the form of employees hired specifically for the project or as contract help. In any case, it's your job as the project manager to ensure that resources are available and skilled in the project activities to which they're assigned. However, in practice, you might find that you don't always have control over the selection of team members. Someone else, the big boss for example, might handpick the folks they want working on the project, and it's up to you to assess their skills and decide where they best fit on the project.

The Acquire Project Team process inputs are as follows:

- Human resource management plan
- Enterprise environmental factors
- Organizational process assets

The human resource management plan describes the roles and responsibilities, project organization charts, and staffing management plan, including the time periods needed by team members on the project. Keep in mind that you may not have direct authority over the project resources due to matrix managed organizations, collective bargaining agreements, the use of contractors and subcontractors, and so on. You should document this in the human resource management plan.

Enterprise environmental factors in this process account for project activities that might require special skills or knowledge in order to be completed. They may also consider personal interests, cost rates, prior experience, and availability of potential team members before making assignments. For example, consider the previous experience of the staff member you're thinking of assigning to a specific activity. Have they performed this function before? Do they have the experience necessary for the level of complexity this project activity requires? Are they competent and proficient at these skills?

Personal interests and personal characteristics play a big role as well. If the person you're thinking of just isn't interested in the project, they aren't likely to perform at their best. If you can, think about assigning someone else in a case like this. Unfortunately, some people just don't play well with others. When you're assigning staff, if at all possible, don't put the only two people in the whole company who can't get along together on the same project. If a staff member you need has a skill no one else has or they can perform a function like no one else can, you might not have a choice. In this case, you'll have to employ other techniques to keep the team cohesive and working well together despite the not-so-friendly relationship between the two staff members.

Here's one final consideration: Check on the availability of key team members. If the team member you must have for the activity scheduled in February is on their honeymoon, you probably aren't going to win the toss.

The organizational process assets input refers to standard processes, policies, and procedures the organization has in place. Recruitment practices are one example to watch for in this process. You'll want to make certain you're following the organization's recruitment procedures and processes when hiring and assigning staff. You should also note that organizational policies that dictate recruitment practices are constraints.

We've looked at the other inputs in previous processes, so we'll move on to the tools and techniques of this process.

Tools and Techniques of Acquire Project Team

The tools and techniques of the Acquire Project Team process are as follows:

- Preassignment
- Negotiation
- Acquisition
- Virtual teams
- Multi-criteria decision analysis

Preassignment   *Preassignment* can happen when the project is put out for bid and specific team members are promised as part of the proposal or when internal project team members are promised and assigned as a condition of the project. When staff members are promised as part of the project proposal—particularly on internal projects—they should be identified in the project charter.

Negotiation   As the project manager, you will use the negotiation technique a lot, so brush up on those skills every chance you get. You'll have to negotiate with functional managers and other organizational department managers—and sometimes with the vendor to get some of their best people—for resources for your project and for the timing of those resources.

Availability is one part of the negotiating equation. You'll have to work with the functional manager or other project managers to ensure that the staff member you're requesting is available when the schedule says they're needed.

The second part of the equation is the competency level of the staff member they're assigning to your project. I remember hearing someone once say that availability is not a skill set. Be wary of functional managers who are willing to offer up certain individuals "any time" while others are "never available." Be certain your negotiations include discussions about the skills and personal characteristics of the team members you want on your project.

Acquisition   Acquisition involves hiring individuals or teams of people for certain project activities, either as employees or as contract help during the course of the project or project phase or for specific project activities. Procurement is usually required when the organization does not have employees with the required skills and competencies available to work on the project.

We talked about Plan Procurement Management in Chapter 7, "Planning Project Resources."

Virtual Teams   *Virtual teams* don't usually work in the same location, but their members all share the goals of the project and have a role to fulfill. This type of team allows you to include folks from different geographic locations, those who work different hours or shifts than the other team members, those with mobility limitations, and so on. The idea is that virtual teams can meet the objectives of the project and perform their roles without meeting face to face. In today's wonderful world of technology, team members can use the Internet, email, videoconferencing, teleconferencing, and more to meet and communicate on a regular basis. This of course brings to light the importance of communication. Make certain all team members are aware of the protocols for communicating in a virtual team environment, understand the expectations, and are clear regarding decision-making processes.

It's vital in this type of team structure that you, as the project manager, give credit to the appropriate team members for their performance and actions on the project. You might be the only one who fully understands the contributions individual team members have made. When teams are co-located, members have the opportunity to see for themselves the extraordinary efforts others are making on the project. Virtual team members don't necessarily know what their teammates have contributed to the project (or the level of effort they've exerted), so it's up to you to let everyone know about outstanding performance.

Multicriteria Decision Analysis   Selecting team members, just like selecting vendors, requires some type of criteria and analysis to determine whether the potential candidate is a fit. You could use any number of factors, including experience, education, skills, availability, and more, to rank and score candidates and choose among them.

Outputs of Acquire Project Team

The resulting outputs of the Acquire Project Team process are as follows:

- Project staff assignments
- Resource calendars
- Project management plan updates

Project Staff Assignments   Your ability to influence the selection of resources (using the negotiating technique) will impact the project staff assignments output. After determining elements such as the roles and responsibilities, reviewing recruitment practices, and negotiating for staff, you assign project team members to project activities. Along with this output, a project team directory is published listing the names of all project team members and stakeholders. Don't forget to also include team member names in project organization charts, RAM charts, and other planning documents if their assignments or names weren't known when you created those documents.

Resource Calendars   Resource calendars show the team members' availability and the times they are scheduled to work on the project. A composite resource calendar includes availability information for potential resources as well as their capabilities and skills. (Resource calendars are an input to the Estimate Activity Resources process.) This comes in handy when you're creating the final schedule and assigning resources to activities.

Project Management Plan Updates   The time periods your project staff are available are documented in the resource calendars output. The human resource management plan and staffing management plan might require updates to document the project roles and responsibilities of the staff assigned to the project. These documents might require updates throughout the project if staff members leave because of a promotion or, heaven forbid, if they leave for employment in another company (unless you want them to leave—that's another story).

Now that you have the team, what do you do with them? You'll look at topics such as motivation, rewards, and recognition in the next process, Develop Project Team.

Real World Scenario

The Only Candidate

"Hey, did you hear?" your friend Story asks, "Roger has been assigned to the project team."

"Over my dead body," you reply, pushing away from your computer screen. You head straight for the project manager's office and don't wait for a response from Story.

Ann sets the phone into the cradle just as you walk through the door. Fortunately for you, Ann's door is always open, and she welcomes drop-ins.

"Seems like something is on your mind," Ann says. "What can I help with?"

"Story just told me that Roger has been assigned to the project team. I can't work with Roger. He's arrogant and doesn't respect anyone's work but his own. He belittles me in front of others, and I don't deserve that. I write good code, and I don't need Roger looking over my shoulder. I want to be on this team, but not if Roger is part of it."

Ann thinks for a minute and replies, "I want you to work on this project; it's a great opportunity for you. But there isn't anyone else who can work on the analysis phase of this project except Roger. He's the only one left who has a solid understanding of the mainframe legacy code. Unfortunately, those old programs were never documented well, and they've evolved over the years into programs on top of programs. Without Roger's knowledge of the existing system, we'd blow the budget and time estimates already established for this project. Since I need both of you on this project, here's what I propose. I will clearly outline the roles and responsibilities for all the key team members at the kickoff meeting. I'll also make it clear that negative team interactions won't be allowed. If you have a problem with Roger that you can't resolve on your own, you should get me involved right away."

Developing the Project Team

Projects exist to create a unique product, result, or service within a limited time frame. Projects are performed by people, and most projects require more than one person to perform all of the activities. If you've got more than one person working on your project, you've got a team. If you've got a team, you've got a wide assortment of personalities, skills, needs, and issues in the mix. Couple this with part-time team members, teams based in functional organizations whose loyalty lies with the functional manager, teams based in matrix organizations that report to you for project-related activities and another manager for their functional duties, or teams with members who are scattered around the globe, and you could have some real challenges on your hands. Good luck! Okay, I won't leave you hanging like that.

The *Develop Project Team* process is about creating an open, encouraging environment for your team and developing it into an effective, functioning, coordinated group. Projects are performed by individuals, and the better they work together, the smoother and the more efficient the execution of the project will be. I'm sure you have had the experience of working with a team who pitched in and shared workloads when the work became unbalanced. I'm also sure you have worked with teams who didn't do this—teams whose members took on a "me first" attitude and couldn't care less about the plight of their fellow team members. I'd much rather work with a team like the first example.

The proper development of the team is critical to a successful project, and as the project manager, you should know that developing the team is one of your most important duties. Because teams are made up of individuals, individual development becomes a critical factor to project success. Individual team members need the proper development and training to perform the activities of the project or to enhance their existing knowledge and skills. The development needed will depend on the project. Perhaps you have a team member who's ready to make the jump into a lead role but they don't have any experience at lead work. Give them some exposure by assigning them a limited amount of activities in a lead capacity, provide them with some training if needed, and be available to coach and mentor where needed. The best option is to work with the management team to provide this person with the development they need prior to the start of the project (if you're lucky enough to know early on who your resources might be and what their existing skills are).

Develop Project Team inputs include human resource management plan, project staff assignments, and resource calendars. Funny thing is, two of these inputs are outputs that I discussed in the Acquire Project Team process, and the human resource management plan was covered previously, so we'll move on.

Tools and Techniques of Develop Project Team

The tools and techniques of Develop Project Team are as follows:

- Interpersonal skills
- Training
- Team-building activities
- Ground rules
- Co-location
- Recognition and rewards
- Personnel assessment tools

I'll cover all these tools and techniques next.

Interpersonal Skills

Interpersonal skills are often referred to as soft skills or emotional intelligence. *Soft skills* include such things as leadership, influence, negotiation, communications, empathy, and creativity. For example, it's important for you as the project manager to understand your project team members' attitudes and opinions about their work. Bad attitudes, like the saying goes, are contagious. It doesn't mean the person who has the attitude is bad, but if you're paying attention to your team members and taking the appropriate amount of time to listen to their legitimate concerns and issues, and taking action on them, you can go a long way toward stemming bad attitudes.

Soft skills can be learned, but in my experience they are more often inherent in project managers' personalities. However, just because certain soft skills may not be in your nature, it doesn't mean you can't observe this behavior in others and incorporate those skills into your management techniques.

One other issue to consider regarding this tool and technique is that you'll have resources from other departments who have assignments on the project that you're responsible for overseeing. For example, the finance department and the marketing department might have assigned project activities, and as the project manager, you'll manage their progress. This implies that you'll need general knowledge management skills to understand what the assignments entail and strong leadership and negotiation skills to influence the departments to stay on schedule.

Training

Training is a matter of assessing your team members' skills and abilities, assessing the project needs, and providing the training necessary for the team members to carry out their assigned activities. Training can be formal or informal. Formal training may include classroom training, online training, or training performed on the job. Informal training might occur by observing others or asking others how to perform a task. Training can sometimes be a reward as well. In the software industry, programmers seek out positions that offer training on the latest and greatest technologies, and they consider it a benefit or bonus to attend training on the company dollar and time. If you know early in the Planning processes that training is necessary, include the details of this in the staffing management plan. During the course of the project, you might observe team members who need training, or they might ask for training. Update the staffing management plan with this information.

Team-Building Activities

Many times, project teams consist of folks who don't know each other. They aren't necessarily aware of the project objectives and might not even want to be a part of the team. The project manager might not have worked with the people assigned to the project team before either. Does this sound like a recipe for disaster? It's not. Thousands of projects are started with team members and project managers who don't know each other, and those projects come to a successful completion. How is that done? It's a result of the project manager's team-building and communication skills.

The project manager's job is to bring the team together, get its members all headed in the right direction, and provide motivation, reward, and recognition to keep the team in tip-top shape. This is done using a variety of team-building techniques and exercises. *Team building* is simply getting a diverse group of people to work together in the most efficient and effective manner possible. This might involve events organized by the management team or individual actions designed to improve team performance. There are entire volumes on this subject, and it's beyond the scope of this book to go into all the team-building possibilities. The exam tends to focus more on the theories behind team building and the characteristics of effective teams, so that's what you'll spend your time exploring.

Dr. Bruce Tuckman and Mary Ann Jensen developed a model that describes how teams develop and mature. According to Tuckman-Jensen, all newly formed teams go through five stages of development:

1. Forming

2. Storming

3. Norming

4. Performing

5. Adjourning

Tuckman-Jensen originally devised this theory using the first four stages of development. Based on later research by the Tuckman-Jensen team, a fifth stage of development was added called adjourning. You've probably seen this model elsewhere, but because these stages might show up on the exam, you'll want to memorize them. Take a brief look at each of them:

Forming   This one is easy. Forming is the beginning stage of team formation, when all the members are brought together, introduced, and told the objectives of the project. This is where team members learn why they're working together. During this stage, team members tend to be formal and reserved and take on an "all-business" approach.

Your role as the project manager in this stage of development is communication. If the team is small, I recommend meeting with each of the members one-on-one and as a group to discuss the questions (and answers) previously outlined. In my experience, team members who clearly understand why they are assigned to the project, what's expected of them regarding individual and team deliverables, and how to inform the project manager of their needs and issues will generally outperform their peers who do not have or understand this information.

Storming   Storming is where the action begins. Team members become confrontational with each other as they're vying for position and control during this stage. They're working through who is going to be the top dog and jockeying for status.

Your role as the project manager during this stage is to remind the team of the project goals and keep everyone centered on those goals. Conflicts aren't bad in this case; they're necessary to get the team into the next stage. During this stage, it is best if you can limit your intervention and let team members resolve their own issues as often as possible. Team members need to get a feel for where they stand, where the extent of their responsibility lies, and how they'll accomplish their tasks working with the other personalities of the team, and that usually involves some tussles. Questioning and conflict help clarify the goals of the project for everyone on the team, not just the person in conflict, so encourage your team members to ask questions and discuss conflicts openly. However, you won't progress to the next stage until the team has resolved the conflicts.

Norming   Now things begin to calm down. Team members know each other fairly well by now. They're comfortable with their positions in the team, and they begin to deal with project problems instead of people problems. In the norming stage, they confront the project concerns and problems instead of each other. Decisions are made jointly at this stage, and team members exhibit mutual respect and familiarity with one another.

As the project manager, you should continue to hold team meetings, especially during this stage, because team members can fall back into the storming stage if left to their own devices. During this stage, you should intervene more often when conflicts arise to keep the team moving forward. Monitor each team member's participation, and encourage the team to continue to remain focused on the project's goals and alert you of any problems as soon as they arise.

Teams in the norming stage are efficient, functioning teams. If your team has progressed to this stage, they'll likely be productive and work effectively toward meeting the project goals. They still aren't performing at their absolute best, though—that happens in the next stage.

Performing Ahh, perfection. Well, almost, anyway. This is where great teams end up. This stage is where the team is productive and effective. The level of trust among team members is high, and great things are achieved. This is the mature development stage.

Your role as project manager during this stage should be more focused on the project management processes than on the team itself. Teams in this stage are usually self-directed and will hum along smoothly, provided you continue to update them on project progress and keep the lines of communication open.

Adjourning As the name implies, this phase refers to the breakup of the team after the work is completed.

As the project manager, you need to realize that many team members may experience a sense of loss at the end of the project, particularly long-term projects. Guide the team through a closure process. Team celebrations at the conclusion of the project are one way to accomplish this. Acknowledge their contributions and let them know you are grateful for their efforts and for any sacrifices they've made during the course of the project.

Exam Spotlight

Different teams progress through the stages of development at different rates. When new team members are brought onto the team, the development stages start all over again. It doesn't matter where the team is in the first four phases of the development process—a new member will start the cycle all over again.

According to Tuckman-Jensen, leaders adapt their leadership styles as the teams develop maturity and progress through the development stages. For example, early in the forming stage, leaders take on a direct style of leadership. As the team progresses, their leaders will employ a coaching, participating, and then delegating style of leadership to match the level of development the team has achieved.

You'll now take a closer look at focusing your team members throughout these stages of development, along with some of the characteristics of effective teams.

Team Focus

Have you ever watched any of those old pirate movies on late-night TV? Remember the scenes where the captain goes down into the bowels of the ship to check on the teams of rowers? He scrutinizes the crew and literally whips the rowers who aren't pulling their weight into shape. I don't recommend this as a team-building technique, but imagine for a minute that your project team members are like those rowing teams. If the members on the left are rowing one way and the members on the right are rowing another, you're creating a lot of energy and looking busy, but in the end you aren't making any progress.

It's paramount that the team members know and understand the goals and objectives of the project. They should all understand the direction you're headed and work toward that end. After all, that's the reason they were brought together in the first place. Keep in mind that people see and hear things from their own perspective. A room full of people attending a speech will each come away with something a little different because what was said speaks to their particular situation in life at the time. In other words, their own perceptions filter what they hear. It's your job as project manager to make sure the team members understand the project goals and their own assignments correctly. I suggest you use solid communication skills to get your point across. Ask your team members to tell you in their own words what they believe the project goals are. This is a great way to know whether you've got everyone on board and a great opportunity for you to clarify any misunderstandings regarding the project goals.

Effective Team Characteristics

Effective teams are typically very energetic teams. They often are characterized as high-performance teams and are motivated by results and the successful completion of tasks. Their enthusiasm is contagious, and it feeds on itself. They generate a lot of creativity and become good problem solvers. Teams like this are every project manager's dream. Investing yourself in team building as well as relationship building—especially when you don't think you have the time to do so—will bring many benefits. Here's a sample of the benefits:

- Better conflict resolution
- Commitment to the project
- Commitment to the project team members and project manager
- High job satisfaction
- Enhanced communication
- A sense of belonging and purpose
- Enhanced feelings of trust
- Lower project costs
- Improved productivity
- Improved quality
- A successful project

Dysfunctional teams will typically produce the opposite results of the benefits just listed. Dysfunctional teams don't just happen by themselves any more than great teams do. Sure, sometimes you're lucky enough to get the right combination of folks together right off the bat. But usually, team building takes work and dedication on the part of the project manager. Even in the situations where you do get that dynamite combination of people, they will benefit from team-building exercises and feedback.

Unfortunately, sour attitudes are just as contagious as enthusiasm. Watch for these symptoms among your team members, and take action to correct the situation before the entire team is affected:

- Lack of motivation or "don't care" attitudes
- Project work that isn't satisfactory
- Status meetings that turn into whining sessions
- Poor communication
- Lack of respect and lack of trust for the project manager

 No amount of team building will make up for poor project planning or ineffective project management techniques. Neglecting these things and fooling yourself into thinking that your project team is good enough to make up for the poor planning or poor techniques could spell doom for your project. Besides that, it's not fair to your project team to put them in that position.

Ground Rules

Ground rules are expectations set by the project manager and project team that describe acceptable team behavior. For example, one of my pet peeves is team members who interrupt each other. In this case, one of the ground rules is one person speaks at a time during a meeting. Another ground rule might be reporting potential issues as soon as the team member becomes aware of them. Outlining ground rules like this helps the team understand expectations regarding acceptable behavior and increases productivity.

Co-location

Co-location, also known as *tight matrix*, brings team members together in one physical location for the entire project, or for important periods during the project life cycle. Many times on large projects the project manager will make provisions in the project budget to bring the team together at the same location. One way to achieve co-location might be to set aside a common meeting room, sometimes called a *war room*, for team members who are located in different buildings or across town to meet and exchange information.

Multiple locations can also be a big time-waster for you as the project manager and for your team members. If some team members are located in one part of town and another set of team members are located across town, you'll find yourself in the car (or the bus) driving back and forth to make face-to-face contact and get status updates. Conducting team meetings also becomes a hassle as one set of team members or the other must drive to another location (or both to a central location) to have a meeting.

Our busy, conflicting schedules and differences in location don't always allow for face-to-face communication, so email is the next best thing. Email can keep the information flowing when you aren't able to meet in person, and it can even help take the heat out of conflicts that might escalate if you were meeting one on one. However, email cannot reveal tone of voice, facial expressions, or body language and sometimes words alone are misinterpreted. Sometimes those nonverbal cues are more important than what's being said. If you don't know your team members or stakeholders well, I recommend meeting with them personally whenever you can. Once you've established good relationships with them, you should be able to balance the use of email and personal interactions and know when it's time to call a face-to-face meeting. In reality, it's often difficult to get your team together physically. A good solution in lieu of having people relocate is videoconferencing or Internet meetings. Team members scattered across the country have access to the Internet, and it's relatively easy to find a time everyone can meet via the Web. Videoconferencing or video web conferencing are the best options if available because they allow intonation and nonverbal behaviors to be part of the communication process.

Recognition and Rewards

I have quite a bit of ground to cover with recognition and rewards. As I said earlier, you could see several exam questions regarding team building, so dig out all your favorite memorization techniques and put them to use.

Team building starts with project planning and doesn't stop until the project is completed. It involves employing techniques to improve your team's performance and keeping team members motivated. Motivation helps people work more efficiently and produce better results. If clear expectations, clear procedures, and the right motivational tools are used, project teams will excel.

Motivation can be extrinsic or intrinsic. Intrinsic motivators are specific to the individual. Some people are just naturally driven to achieve—it's part of their nature. (I suspect this is a motivator for you since you're reading this book.) Cultural and religious influences are forms of intrinsic motivators as well.

Extrinsic motivators are material rewards and might include bonuses, the use of a company car, stock options, gift certificates, training opportunities, extra time off, and so on. Reward and recognition—a tool and technique of the Develop Project Team process—are examples of extrinsic motivators. We'll look at them next.

Recognition and rewards are important parts of team motivation. They are formal ways of recognizing and promoting desirable behavior and are most effective when carried out by the management team and the project manager. You should develop and document the criteria for rewards, especially monetary awards. Although rewards and recognition help build a team, they can also kill morale if you don't have an established method or criteria for handing them out. Track who is receiving awards throughout the project. For example, if you have consistent overachievers on the team, you could kill morale by consistently rewarding the same one or two people repeatedly. It could also be perceived that you're playing favorites. If team members believe the rewards are win-lose (also known as *zero-sum*) and that only certain team members will be rewarded, you might end up hurting morale more than helping. If you find yourself in this position, consider team awards. This is a win-win because all team members are recognized for their contributions. Recognition and rewards should be proportional to the achievement. In other words, appropriately link the reward to the performance. For example, a project manager who has responsibility for the project budget and the procurement process and keeps the costs substantially under budget without sacrificing the results of the project should be rewarded for this achievement. However, if these responsibilities are assigned to a functional manager in the organization, it wouldn't be appropriate to reward a project manager who was not the one responsible for keeping the costs in line.

 Real World Scenario

Baker's Gift Baskets

You're a contract project manager for Baker's Gift Baskets. This company assembles gift baskets of all styles and shapes with every edible treat imaginable. The company has recently experienced explosive growth, and you've been brought on board to manage its new project. The owners of the company want to offer "pick-your-own" baskets that allow customers to pick the individual items they want included in the baskets. In addition, they're introducing a new line of containers to choose from, including items such as miniature golf bags, flowerpots, serving bowls, and the like. This means changes to the catalog and the website to accommodate the new offerings.

The deadline for this project is the driving constraint. The website changes won't cause any problems with the deadline. However, the catalog must go to press quickly to meet holiday mailing deadlines, which in turn are driving the project deadline.

Your team members put their heads together and came up with an ingenious plan to meet the catalog deadline. It required lots of overtime and some weekend work on their part to pull it off, but they met the date.

You decide this is a perfect opportunity to recognize and reward the team for their outstanding efforts. You've arranged a slot on the agenda at the next all-company meeting to bring your team up front and praise them for their cooperation and efforts to get the catalog to the printers on time. You'll also present each of them with two days of paid time off and a gift certificate for a dinner with their family at an exclusive restaurant in the city.

Team members should be rewarded for going above and beyond the call of duty. Perhaps they put in a significant amount of overtime to meet a project goal or spent nights round-the-clock babysitting ill-performing equipment. These types of behaviors should be rewarded and formally recognized by the project manager and the management team. On the other hand, if the ill-performing equipment was a direct result of mistakes made or if it happened because of poor planning, rewards would not be appropriate, obviously.

Consider individual preferences and cultural differences when using rewards and recognitions. Some people don't like to be recognized in front of a group; others thrive on it. Some people appreciate an honest thank-you with minimal fanfare, and others just won't accept individual rewards because their culture doesn't allow it. Keep this in mind when devising your reward system.

There are many theories on motivation. As a project manager, it's important to understand them so that you can tailor your recognition and rewards programs to take into account the reasons people do what they do. You might encounter questions on these theories on the exam, so we'll discuss their primary points in the following sections.

Motivational Theories

Motivational theories came about during the modern age. Prior to today's information- and service-type jobs and yesterday's factory work, the majority of people worked the land and barely kept enough food on the table to feed their family. No one was concerned about motivation at work. You worked because you wouldn't have anything to eat if you didn't. Fortunately, that isn't the only reason most people work today.

Today we have a new set of problems in the workplace. Workers in the service- and knowledge-based industries aren't concerned with starvation—that need has been replaced with other needs such as job satisfaction, a sense of belonging and commitment to the project, good working conditions, and so on. Motivational theories present ideas on why people act the way they do and how you can influence them to act in certain ways to get the results you want. Again, there are libraries full of books on this topic. I'll cover four of those theories here.

MASLOW'S HIERARCHY OF NEEDS

You have probably seen this classic example of motivational theory. Abraham Maslow theorized that humans have five basic needs arranged in hierarchical order. The first needs are physical needs, such as the need for food, clothing, and shelter. The idea is that these needs must be met before the person can move to the next level of needs in the hierarchy, which includes safety and security needs. Here, the concern is for the person's physical welfare and the security of their belongings. Once that need is met, they progress to the next level, and so on.

Maslow's hierarchy of needs theory suggests that once a lower-level need has been met, it no longer serves as a motivator and the next higher level becomes the driving motivator in a person's life. Maslow conjectures that humans are always in one state of need or another. Here is a recap of each of the needs, starting with the highest level and ending with the lowest:

Self-Actualization   Performing at your peak potential

Self-Esteem Needs   Accomplishment, respect for self, capability

Social Needs   A sense of belonging, love, acceptance, friendship

Safety and Security Needs   Your physical welfare and the security of your belongings

Basic Physical Needs   Food, clothing, shelter

The highest level of motivation in this theory is the state of self-actualization. A few years ago, the United States Army had a slogan that I think encapsulates self-actualization very well: "Be all that you can be." When all the physical, safety, social, and self-esteem needs have been met, a person reaches a state of independence where they're able to express themselves and perform at their peak. They'll do good work just for the sake of doing good work. Recognition and self-esteem are the motivators at lower levels; now the need for being the best they can be is reached.

In Maslow's later work, he discussed three additional aspects of motivation: cognitive, aesthetic, and transcendence. The five key needs are the ones you'll most likely need to know for the exam, but it wouldn't hurt to be familiar with the names of the three additional motivational levels. Also note that people are not "stuck" at a certain level forever. You will traverse the pyramid, up and down, throughout your life and career.

HYGIENE THEORY

Frederick Herzberg came up with the *Hygiene Theory*, also known as the *Motivation-Hygiene Theory*. He postulates that two factors contribute to motivation: hygiene factors and motivators. Hygiene factors deal with work environment issues. The thing to remember about hygiene factors is that they prevent dissatisfaction. Examples of hygiene factors are pay, benefits, the conditions of the work environment, and relationships with peers and managers. Pay is considered a hygiene factor because Herzberg believed that over the long term, pay is not a motivator. Being paid for the work prevents dissatisfaction but doesn't necessarily bring satisfaction in and of itself. He believed this to be true as long as the pay system is equitable. If two workers performing the same functions have large disparities in pay, then pay can become a motivator.

Motivators deal with the substance of the work itself and the satisfaction one derives from performing the functions of the job. Motivators lead to satisfaction. The ability to advance, the opportunity to learn new skills, and the challenges involved in the work are all motivators, according to Herzberg.

Exam Spotlight

For the exam, remember that Herzberg was the inventor of the Hygiene Theory and that this theory claims that hygiene factors (pay, benefits, and working conditions) prevent dissatisfaction while motivators (challenging work, opportunities to learn, and advancement) lead to satisfaction.

EXPECTANCY THEORY

The *Expectancy Theory,* first proposed by Victor Vroom, says that the expectation of a positive outcome drives motivation. People will behave in certain ways if they think there will be good rewards for doing so. Also note that this theory says the strength of the expectancy drives the behavior. This means the expectation or likelihood of the reward is linked to the behavior. For example, if you tell your two-year-old to put the toys back in the toy box and you'll give her a cookie to do so, chances are she'll put the toys away. This is a reasonable reward for a reasonable action. However, if you promise your project team members vacations in Hawaii if they get the project done early and they know there is no way you can deliver that reward, there is little motivation to work toward it. Also make certain you are using rewards that motivate your team members. If you make a trip to Hawaii the reward, and you can make good on that promise in this example, but your team members are deathly afraid of flying, the reward won't have a motivating effect.

This theory also says that people become what you expect of them. If you openly praise your project team members and treat them like valuable contributors, you'll likely have a high-performing team on your hands. Conversely, when you publicly criticize people or let them know that you have low expectations regarding their performance, they'll likely live up (or down as the case might be) to that expectation as well.

ACHIEVEMENT THEORY

The *Achievement Theory,* attributed to David McClelland, says that people are motivated by the need for three things: achievement, power, and affiliation. The achievement motivation is obviously the need to achieve or succeed. The power motivation involves a desire for influencing the behavior of others, and the need for affiliation is relationship oriented. Workers want to have friendships with their coworkers and a sense of camaraderie with their fellow team members. The strength of your team members' desire for each of these will drive their performance on various activities.

Exam Spotlight

Make certain you understand the theories of motivation and their premises for the exam. Here's a summary to help you memorize them:

Maslow's Hierarchy of Needs   Abraham Maslow. Needs must be satisfied in a hierarchical order.

Hygiene Theory   Frederick Herzberg. Work environment (pay, benefits, and working conditions) prevents dissatisfaction.

Expectancy Theory   Victor Vroom. Expectation of positive outcomes drives motivation.

Achievement Theory   David McClelland. People are motivated by achievement, power, and affiliation.

I'll cover two more theories in the leadership section, which is next. They deal specifically with how leaders interact with their project team members.

Leadership versus Management

Chapter 1, "What Is a Project?" introduced the differences between leaders and managers. I'll add a bit more information here regarding leadership theories and the types of power leaders possess, but first I'll recap leadership and management.

Recall that leadership is about imparting vision and rallying people around that vision. Leaders motivate and inspire and are concerned with strategic vision. Leaders have a knack for getting others to do what needs to be done.

Two of the techniques they use to do this are power and politics. *Power* is the ability to get people to do what they wouldn't do ordinarily. It's also the ability to influence behavior. *Politics* imparts pressure to conform regardless of whether people agree with the decision. Leaders understand the difference between power and politics and when to employ each technique. I'll talk more about power shortly.

Good leaders have committed team members who believe in the vision of the leader. Leaders set direction and time frames and have the ability to attract good talent to work for them. Leaders inspire a vision and get things done through others by earning loyalty, respect, and cooperation from team members. They set the course and lead the way. Good leaders are directive in their approach but allow for plenty of feedback and input. Good leaders commonly have strong interpersonal skills and are well respected.

Managers are generally task-oriented and concerned with issues such as plans, controls, budgets, policies, and procedures. They're generalists with a broad base of planning and organizational skills, and their primary goal is satisfying stakeholder needs. They also possess motivational skills and the ability to recognize and reward behavior.

Project managers need to use the traits of both leaders and managers at different times during a project. On large projects, a project manager will act more like a leader inspiring the subproject managers to get on board with the objectives. On small projects, project managers will act more like managers because they're responsible for all the planning and coordinating functions.

I'll discuss six theories regarding leadership and management. They are Douglas McGregor's Theory X and Theory Y, Dr. William Ouchi's Theory Z, the Contingency Theory, the Tannenbaum and Schmidt Continuum Management Theory, and the Situational Leadership Theory. Then I'll discuss the types of power leaders use and leadership styles.

THEORY X, THEORY Y, AND THEORY Z

Douglas McGregor defined two models of worker behavior, Theory X and Theory Y, that attempt to explain how different managers deal with their team members. *Theory X* managers believe most people do not like work and will try to steer clear of it; they believe people have little to no ambition, need constant supervision, and won't actually perform the duties of their job unless threatened. As a result, Theory X managers are like dictators and impose very rigid controls over their people. They believe people are motivated only by punishment, money, or position. Unfortunately for the team members, Theory X managers unknowingly also subscribe to the Expectancy Theory. If they expect people to be lazy and unproductive and treat them as such, their team members probably will be lazy and unproductive.

Theory Y managers believe people are interested in performing their best given the right motivation and proper expectations. These managers provide support to their teams, are concerned about their team members, and are good listeners. Theory Y managers believe people are creative and committed to the project goals, that they like responsibility and seek it out, and that they are able to perform the functions of their positions with limited supervision.

Theory Z was developed by Dr. William Ouchi. This theory is concerned with increasing employee loyalty to their organizations. It came about in Japan in the 1980s when jobs were often offered for life. This theory results in increased productivity, it puts an emphasis on the well-being of the employees both at work and outside of work, it encourages steady employment, and it leads to high employee satisfaction and morale.

CONTINGENCY THEORY

The *Contingency Theory* builds on a combination of Theory Y behaviors and the Hygiene Theory. The Contingency Theory, in a nutshell, says that people are motivated to achieve levels of competency and will continue to be motivated by this need even after competency is reached.

TANNENBAUM AND SCHMIDT CONTINUUM MANAGEMENT THEORY

Robert Tannenbaum and Warren Schmidt developed a leadership theory, called the *Tannenbaum and Schmidt Continuum Management Theory,* that describes the level of authority a manager exerts on the team versus the freedom a team has to make decisions (under the guidance of the manager.) They outline seven levels of delegated freedom ranging from the manager making all decisions and announcing them to the team, to the manager allowing the team to identify the problem, determine alternatives, and make the final recommendation regarding the action needed to solve the problem. The level of freedom you use depends on the maturity and experience of the team and the manager. As the team progresses, their decision making matures, and more and more freedom can be delegated. The manager is always engaged at all levels of this model, but their authority level will decrease as they delegate decision-making responsibility to the team.

SITUATIONAL LEADERSHIP THEORY

Paul Hersey and Ken Blanchard developed the *Situational Leadership Theory* during the mid-1970s. This theory's main premise is that the leadership style you use depends on the situation. For example, perhaps you have a new employee fresh out of school, and they are learning a new task. Obviously, this employee will need a lot more guidance and direction than an employee who has been with the organization for some time and knows how to perform the task at hand. Both Hersey and Blanchard went on to develop their own situational leadership models. Blanchard's model, Situational Leadership II, describes four styles of leadership that depend on the situation: directing, coaching, supporting, and delegating.

The Power of Leaders

As stated earlier, power is the ability to influence others to do what you want them to do. Power can be used in a positive manner or a negative one. But that old saying of your grandmother's about attracting more flies with honey than vinegar still holds true today.

Leaders, managers, and project managers use power to convince others to do tasks in a specific way. The kind of power they use to accomplish this depends on their personality, their personal values, and the company culture.

A project manager might use several forms of power. I've already talked about reward power, which is the ability to grant bonuses or incentive awards for a job well done. Here are a few more:

Punishment Power   Punishment, also known as *coercive* or *penalty power*, is just the opposite of reward power. The employee is threatened with consequences if expectations are not met.

Expert Power   Expert power occurs when the person being influenced believes the manager, or the person doing the influencing, is knowledgeable about the subject or has special abilities that make them an expert. The person goes along just because they think the influencer knows what they're doing and it's the best thing for the situation.

Legitimate Power   Legitimate, or formal, power comes about as a result of the influencer's position. Because that person is the project manager, executive vice president, or CEO, they have the power to call the shots and make decisions.

Referent Power   Referent power is inferred to the influencer by their subordinates. Project team members who have a great deal of respect and high regard for their project managers willingly go along with decisions made by the project manager because of referent power.

Punishment power should be used as a last resort and only after all other forms have been exhausted. Sometimes, you'll have to use this method, but I hope much less often than the other three forms of power. Sometimes, you'll have team members who won't live up to expectations and their performance suffers as a result. This is a case where punishment power is enacted to get the employee to correct their behavior.

Leadership Styles

Extensive research has been done in the area of leadership styles. I will highlight a few of the well-known styles for exam purposes, but I encourage you to read more about leadership on your own. You can train almost anyone to follow the principles and practices of sound project management, but you won't have much of a team to lead if you haven't mastered the art of great leadership.

Autocratic   Autocratic leaders are essentially dictators. All decisions are made by the leader with little to no input from the team.

Laissez-faire   This leadership style is the opposite of the autocratic style. The leader allows the team to drive decisions and recommend actions and has little involvement in the process.

Democratic   Democratic, or participative, driven leaders gather all the facts and ask for input from the team before making a decision. In this style, all team members participate in the decision-making process.

Situational   As we discussed in the last section, the Blanchard theory of situational leadership has four styles. Directive is used when a team member needs to know the step-by-step procedures for the problem. Coaching is used with team members who have limited experience with the task at hand. They can perform some minor functions of the task but need direction with the majority of the task. Supporting is used with team members who have completed the same types of tasks in the past and are able to complete the majority of the task at hand on their own. They may need to ask a question or two to obtain guidance along the way. Delegating is used when team members have performed the same tasks in the past and are capable of making decisions regarding unexpected issues that may occur. Delegating involves little to no input from the leader.

Transactional and Transformational   Transactional and transformational leadership styles were first developed by Bernard Bass, who was a professor emeritus in the School of Management at Binghamton. He describes transactional leaders as autocratic, activity focused, and autonomous, and they use contingent reward systems and manage by exception.

Transformational leaders tend to focus on relationships rather than activities; they are collaborative, influential, and inspire and motivate their teams to perform. Bass describes transformational leaders as empowering and concerned with social justice, equity, and fairness.

Exam Spotlight

Know the difference between leaders and managers, the motivational and leadership theories, and the types of power for the PMP® exam. Here's a summary to help you memorize them:

Leaders   Leaders motivate, inspire, and create buy-ins for the organization's strategic vision. Leaders use power and politics to accomplish the vision.

Managers   Managers are task-oriented and concerned with satisfying stakeholder needs.

Theory X – McGregor   Most people don't like work.

Theory Y – McGregor   People are motivated to perform their best given proper expectations and motivation.

Theory Z – Ouchi   The implementation of this theory increases employee loyalty and leads to high satisfaction and morale.

Contingency Theory   People are motivated to achieve levels of competency and will continue to be motivated after competency is reached.

Tannenbaum and Schmidt Continuum Management Theory   You use seven levels of delegated freedom when working with the team.

Situational Leadership Theory   Hersey and Blanchard developed this theory, which states that different situations call for different leadership styles. Blanchard describes the styles in the Situational Leadership II Model as directive, coaching, supportive, and delegating.

Reward Power   You reward desirable behavior with incentives or bonuses.

Punishment Power   You threaten team members with consequences if expectations are not met (also known as *penalty or coercive power*).

Expert Power   The person doing the influencing has significant knowledge or skills regarding the subject.

Legitimate Power   This is the power of the position held by the influencer (the president or vice president, for example), also known as *formal* power.

Referent Power   This is power that's inferred to the influencer.

Personnel Assessment Tools

The final tool and technique of this process is personnel assessment tools. These tools help highlight the strengths and weaknesses of the team by assessing various aspects of the team such as communication techniques, interpersonal skills and preferences, organizational skills, decision-making skills, and more.

Outputs of Develop Project Team

You're now ready to close out the Develop Project Team process. This process has only two outputs: team performance assessments and enterprise environmental factors updates. Team performance assessment involves determining a team's effectiveness. As a result of positive team-building experiences, you'll see individuals improving their skills, team behaviors and relationships improving, conflict resolutions going smoothly, reduced turnover, and team members recommending ways to improve the work of the project. I talked about effective team characteristics earlier in this chapter. Assessing these characteristics will help you determine where (or whether) the project team needs improvements.

Project managers wear a lot of hats. This is one of the things that make this job so interesting. You need organization and planning skills to plan the project. You need motivation and sometimes disciplinary skills to execute the project plans. You need to exercise leadership and power where appropriate—and all the while, you have a host of relationships to manage, involving team members, stakeholders, managers, and customers. It's a great job and brings terrific satisfaction.

Managing Project Teams

The *Manage Project Team* process is concerned with tracking and reporting on the performance of individual team members. During this process, performance appraisals are prepared and conducted, issues are identified and resolved, and feedback is given to the team members. Some team behavior is also observed during this process, but the main focus here is on individuals and their performance.

Exam Spotlight

Take note that the *PMBOK® Guide* states that one of the outcomes or results of the Manage Project Team process is an update to the human resource management plan, which is part of the project management plan updates output of this process. Other outcomes to note are that issues are resolved, and information is provided for performance appraisals and lessons learned.

With the exception of issue log and work performance reports, you've seen all the inputs to this process before:

- Human resource management plan
- Project staff assignments
- Team performance assessments
- Issue log
- Work performance reports
- Organizational process assets

The issue log is a place to document the issues that keep the project team from meeting project goals. These issues can range from differences of opinion to newly surfaced responsibilities that need to be assigned to a project team member. Each issue should be recorded in the log along with the person responsible for resolving it. You should also note the date the resolution is needed.

Work performance reports document the status of the project compared to the forecasts, including but not limited to cost control, scope validation, schedule control, and quality control. Keep in mind that work performance reports are an output of the Monitor and Control Project Work process and an input to this one (an Executing process).

Tools and Techniques for Managing Teams

Most of the tools and techniques for this process are new. Don't skip studying any of them because you'll likely see exam questions regarding them. The tools and techniques of the Manage Project Team process are as follows:

- Observation and conversation
- Project performance appraisals
- Conflict management
- Interpersonal skills

We'll take a closer look at each of these tools in the following sections.

Observation and Conversation

Observation and conversation is another one of those tools and techniques that is self-evident. To assess team member performance, you have to observe it. I hope you've also learned how important communication is to the success of the project. This includes communicating with your team members. I know project managers who are reticent to engaging their teams in conversation unless it's official project business. I've even known project managers who've instructed their administrative assistants to give specific directions to other team members. It's difficult to understand a team member's attitude or viewpoint toward the project if you're communicating through someone else. Establish an open door policy with your team members and live up to it. The benefits are so great that it's worth a few minutes a day of chitchat to establish that feeling of trust and camaraderie. If your team perceives you as open, honest, and willing to listen, you'll be the first person they come to when issues arise.

 Real World Scenario

What Not to Do

Tina is a newly minted project manager. She has worked on many projects as the assistant project manager, but this is the first time she has led the charge. Tina is so shy she finds it difficult to give team members any kind of direction or to assign tasks, so she has her administrative assistant do it for her. Tina tells her administrative assistant what needs to be done and who needs to do it and leaves it to the assistant to inform the appropriate team members.

As the project progresses, schedule milestone dates are missed, and Tina discovers tasks that haven't started that were scheduled to begin two weeks ago. Coming in from lunch one day she sees several project team members huddled around her administrative assistant's desk. From what she overhears, they are discussing a risk event that occurred on the project.

Fortunately for Tina, one of the project managers she has worked for in the past understands what is happening. Because the administrative assistant is the one who has established relationships with the team and is in effect giving the orders, the team is treating her as the project manager instead of Tina. Tina's friend has a one-on-one coaching session with Tina about her management style and the importance of conversation and observation. Together they are able to get the project back on track.

Project Performance Appraisals

Project performance appraisals are typically annual or semiannual affairs where managers let their employees know what they think of their performance over the past year and rate them accordingly. They are also the perfect time to review the employee's job description and clarify roles and responsibilities. Appraisals are usually manager-to-employee exchanges but can incorporate a *360-degree review*, which takes in feedback from just about everyone the team member interacts with, including stakeholders, customers, project manager, peers, subordinates, and the delivery person if they have a significant amount of project interaction. I'm not a fan of 360-degree reviews because they make most nonmanager types uncomfortable. "I don't want to rate my peer," is a typical response. I also find 360-degree reviews are biased. At best you'll get a response like this: "Oh, Ken is great, just great. No problems—a good guy." Or you'll get exactly the opposite if the person you're speaking with doesn't like the team member you're reviewing. Performance appraisal should be a bit more constructive than this. Nonetheless, understand the 360-degree concept for the exam.

No matter what type of appraisal is conducted, project managers should contribute to the performance appraisals of all project team members. You should be aware of potential loyalty issues when you're working in a matrix organizational structure. The team member in this structure reports to both you (as the project manager) and a functional manager. If the project manager does not have an equal say, or at least some say about the employee's performance, it will cause the team member to be loyal to the functional manager and show little loyalty to the project or project manager. Managing these dual reporting relationships is often a critical success factor for the project, and it is the project manager's responsibility to ensure that these relationships are managed effectively.

Performance appraisal time is also a good time to explore training needs, clarify roles and responsibilities, set goals for the future, and so on.

Conflict Management

I said earlier in this chapter that if you have more than one person working on your project, you have a team. Here's another fact: If you have more than one person working on your project, you'll have conflict.

Everyone has desires, needs, and goals. Conflict comes into the picture when the desires, needs, or goals of one party are incompatible with the desires, needs, or goals of another party (or parties). *Conflict*, simply put, is the incompatibility of goals, which often leads to one party resisting or blocking the other party from attaining their goals. Wait—this doesn't sound like a party!

Exam Spotlight

The *PMBOK® Guide* notes that conflict can be reduced by implementing team ground rules, group norms, and utilizing well-grounded project management processes. Regular and effective communication, and clear definitions of roles and responsibilities of team members, will also go a long way in keeping conflict to a minimum.

There are five styles of resolving conflict that might show up on the exam:

Force/Direct   *Force* or *direct* is just as it sounds. One person forces a solution on the other parties. This is where the boss puts on the "Because I'm the boss and I said so" hat. Although this is a permanent solution, it isn't necessarily the best solution. People will go along with it because, well, they're forced to go along with it. It doesn't mean they agree with the solution. This isn't the best technique to use when you're trying to build a team. This is an example of a win-lose conflict resolution technique. The forcing party wins, and the losers are those who are forced to go along with the decision.

Smooth/Accommodate   The *smooth* or *accommodate* technique does not lead to a permanent solution. It's a temporary way to resolve conflict where the areas of agreement are emphasized over the areas of difference so the real issue stays buried. Smoothing can also occur when someone attempts to make the conflict appear less important than it is. Everyone looks at each other and scratches their head and wonders why they thought the conflict was such a big deal anyway. As a result, a compromise is reached, and everyone feels good about the solution until they get back to their desk and start thinking about the issue again. When they realize that the conflict was smoothed over and is more important than they were led to believe, or that they never dealt with the issue at hand, they'll be back at it, and the conflict will resurface. This is an example of a lose-lose conflict resolution technique because neither side wins. Smoothing is also known as accommodating.

Compromise/Reconcile   Parties that *compromise* or *reconcile* each give up something to reach a solution. Everyone involved decides what they will give on and what they won't give on, and eventually through all the give and take, a solution is reached. Neither side wins or loses in this situation. As a result, neither side is gung ho about the decision that was reached. They will drag their feet and reluctantly trudge along. If, however, both parties make firm commitments to the resolution, then the solution becomes a permanent one.

Collaborate/Problem Solve   The *collaborate* technique is also called *problem solve* and is the best way to resolve conflict. One of the key actions you'll perform with this technique is a fact-finding mission. The thinking here is that one right solution to a problem exists and the facts will bear out the solution. Once the facts are uncovered, they're presented to the parties and the decision will be clear. Thus, the solution becomes a permanent one and the conflict expires. This is a win-win solution. Multiple viewpoints are discussed and shared using this technique, and team members have the opportunity to examine all the perspectives of the issue. Collaborating will lead to true consensus where team members commit to the decision. This is the conflict resolution approach project managers use most often and is an example of a win-win conflict resolution technique.

Withdraw/Avoid   When parties *withdraw* or *avoid*, they never reach resolution. The withdraw or avoid technique occurs when one of the parties gets up and leaves and refuses to discuss the conflict. It is probably the worst of all the techniques because nothing gets resolved. This is an example of a lose-lose conflict resolution technique.

Exam Spotlight

Know each of the conflict resolution techniques for the exam. Also remember that these techniques will not necessarily yield long-term results. The smoothing and withdrawal techniques have temporary results and aren't always good techniques to use to resolve problems. Resolutions reached through forcing and compromise might not always be satisfying for all parties, but they tend to produce longer-lasting results. Collaborating techniques are often successful and produce commitment to the decision provided all parties believe they had the opportunity to provide their opinions and ideas.

During the Manage Project Team process, it's important to note that, as in any situation, you'll want to deal with conflict as soon as it arises. According to the *PMBOK® Guide*, when you have successfully resolved conflict, it will result in increased productivity and better, more positive working relationships.

Most conflicts come about in the Manage Project Team process as a result of schedule issues, availability of resources (usually the lack of availability), or personal work styles. When project team members are having a conflict, address them first in private with the person who has the issue. Work in a direct and collaborative manner, but be prepared to escalate the issue into a more formalized procedure (potentially even disciplinary action) if needed.

If conflicts exist between the team members, encourage resolution between them without intervention on your part. The best conflict resolution will come about when they can work out the issues between them. When that isn't possible, you'll have to step in and help resolve the matter.

Remember that solid ground rules and established policies and procedures will help mitigate conflict before it arises.

Interpersonal Skills

We talked about interpersonal skills in the Develop Project Team process, but you should know for the exam that the *PMBOK® Guide* points out three types of interpersonal skills used most often in this process: leadership, influencing, and effective decision making. We've already covered leadership and influencing. Effective decision making involves making decisions in a timely manner and making decisions that reflect and support the goals of the project. Effective decisions should bring about a good result for the project, the stakeholders, and the team members. They also help you take advantage of opportunities and minimize negative risks. As project managers, and good leaders, we have a responsibility to put the good of the project and the organization over our own needs, so use sound judgment when making decisions.

In the course of my career, I have seen many project managers drag their feet when it comes to making a decision or downright refuse to make a decision. No decision is a decision—in effect, you're choosing to do nothing. This can have disastrous consequences for your project. Sometimes, it's better to make a misguided decision than no decision at all. Be sure to examine all the information known at the time, consult your experts, and finally, make the decision.

Managing Project Team Outputs

The outputs of the Manage Project Team process are the result of the conversations, performance appraisals, and conflict resolution I've talked about previously. This process has five outputs:

- Change requests
- Project management plan updates
- Project documents updates
- Enterprise environmental factors updates
- Organizational process assets updates

Remember that the elements of these outputs pertain to human resources. For example, change requests might come about as a result of a change in staffing, corrective actions might come about because of disciplinary actions or training needs, and preventive actions might be needed to reduce the impact of potential human resource issues. Any of these actions might cause changes to the staffing management plan or the human resource management plan, which means you should update the project management plan. The issue log, roles and responsibilities descriptions, and/or project staff assignments are examples of project document updates that might need to be changed.

The enterprise environmental process updates has two components that may need updating as a result of this process: input to organizational performance appraisals and personnel skill updates. The input to organizational performance appraisals comes from team members with significant interactions with the project and each other.

The organizational process asset updates output has three components: historical information/lessons learned documentation, templates, and organizational standard processes.

Lessons learned encompasses everything you've learned about the human resources aspect during this project, including documentation that can be used as templates on future projects (such as org charts, position descriptions, and the staffing management plan), techniques used to resolve conflict, the types of conflict that came up during the project, ground rules, when and how virtual teams were used on the project and the procedures associated with them, the staffing management plan, special skills needed during the project that weren't known about during the Planning processes, and the issue log.

In the next chapter, we'll wrap up the Executing process group and examine the processes associated with conducting procurements: providing quality assurance, distributing information, and managing the expectations of stakeholders.

Real World Scenario

Project Case Study: New Kitchen Heaven Retail Store

You are in Dirk's office giving him some good news.

"The lease is signed and the work of the project has started. Ricardo has several of his staff members assigned to perform tasks related to the information technology deliverables, as do Jill and Jake for their areas.

"I held a kickoff meeting with all the key project team members. We started out with some team-building exercises, and I explained the five stages of team development. It's normal to have some conflict as we're starting out, and I let them all know my door is always open and if they have issues they can't resolve, they can come to me directly. I explained the goals of the project, laid some ground rules for team interaction, and talked with them about the conflict resolution techniques we'll use as we get further into the project."

"I'm just glad to hear we're finally doing something," Dirk replies.

"Even though Gomez construction doesn't start until next week, they sent their crew leader to the kickoff meeting. I was impressed with that."

Dirk asks, "Why isn't Gomez starting work now?"

"They aren't scheduled to start until September 20 and we need to get our procurement documents signed. We have a week to finish up the signatures before they get here, so we're in fine shape. But Ricardo's group has already prepared their procurement documents to purchase the switches and other equipment they need to start work. Bryan, Ricardo's team lead, finished his other project sooner than anticipated, and since they have Ethernet cable on hand, he started running cable today."

The key stakeholder from the marketing department peeks her head in Dirk's door. "I saw you both in here and thought I'd ask you when someone from the project team is going to work with me on the website announcement. I haven't heard anything, and I don't want to cut this so close that we put something subpar on the website. The 50th anniversary deserves a little splash."

"Okay," you reply. "I'll set up a meeting with you to get more information, and then I'll work with Ricardo to determine who the best fit is. I've noted we need to assign someone to this activity in the issue log. The person he thought he was going to assign to this task is out on family leave, and we don't know when he's expected back."

"Thanks," the stakeholder replies. "I also heard you lost a valuable team member last week. I was really sorry to see Madelyn go. What happened? And will her loss impact the project?"

"I don't want to go into all the details, but she violated our Internet acceptable use policy. She was placed on disciplinary action on this very issue once before. This may impact the project schedule because her activities were on the critical path. I've already interviewed two internal candidates who've expressed interest in working on the project. I believe either one would work out nicely. They have the skills we need and are very interested. However, some ramp-up time is needed. I've added this to the risk list because we could have an impact to the schedule if we don't get Madelyn replaced by the end of this week. I've got a change request ready also, in case there is a schedule impact. I won't know more until next week."

DIrk glances at his desk clock.

You stand and on your way to the door tell him, "Next week I'll hold a formal status meeting with all the stakeholders and will begin distributing written weekly status reports."

Project Case Study Checklist

The processes and concepts discussed in the case study include:

- Direct and Manage Project Work
    - Deliverables
    - Work results
    - Work performance data
- Develop Project Team
    - Interpersonal skills
    - Team-building
    - Ground rules
    - Team performance assessments
- Acquire Project Team
    - Negotiation
    - Acquisition
    - Resource calendars
- Manage Project Team
    - Observation and conversation
    - Conflict management
    - Change requests

Understanding How This Applies to Your Next Project

The topics in this chapter are some of my favorites because this is where project management shines—dynamic teams working under the direction of a capable, responsible leader who can effectively balance the needs of the team with the needs of the project (and ultimately the organization) and pull it all off successfully. There aren't many things better in an organization than a high-performing team working together to accomplish a well-understood goal. It doesn't matter whether the team members are all in the same company, department, or country. When they're working toward a common goal and functioning at the performing level, there's almost nothing they can't accomplish. The movies *Ocean's Eleven, Ocean's Twelve,* and *Ocean's Thirteen* are good examples of strong leadership and dynamic teamwork at play. Although I'm certainly not advocating you turn to a life of crime, you can pick up a few pointers on how effective teams work from George Clooney and the gang.

So, how does this apply? As the project manager, it's your responsibility, and dare I say duty, to acquire the best team members possible for your project. In my experience, this doesn't always mean all my team members are highly qualified. To me, team fit and team dynamics are as important as the team members' skills. I know some will disagree with me on this next point, but I believe it's easier to train someone on a new skill (given they have the aptitude) than it is to take on a team member with an abrasive personality who is imminently qualified but can't get along with anyone else on the team. Sometimes you don't have much choice when it comes to picking team members, as referenced in the sidebar, "The Only Candidate" earlier in this chapter. When you find yourself in this situation, I recommend you lay down clear ground rules for communication, problem escalation, work assignments, and so on.

Make it a habit to read at least a couple of leadership books a quarter. You may already be familiar with the topic and think there is nothing new to learn. However, staying current on the topic will reinforce concepts that you already know and will remind you of other points that you forgot about and haven't yet developed but know you should. Occasionally, you will pick up a gold nugget of information that is new and immediately applicable to your situation.

Leadership skills are invaluable, but communication skills are just as important. In my opinion, it's difficult to be an effective leader without also being an effective communicator. My guess is that if you take a close look at the leaders you respect and admire, you'll discover they are also good communicators—and communication is mostly listening, not talking. I make it a habit to practice active listening. It's amazing what people will tell you when you smile politely and ask an open-ended question or two.

Let me stress again that you cannot successfully manage a project team without communicating with them on a regular basis. The last thing you want is for a stakeholder to follow you into the elevator to inform you about a major problem with the project that you weren't aware of. That will happen if you haven't established a relationship with your team. If they don't believe you're trustworthy or they don't know you well enough to know whether you'll stand by them, you'll be one of the last people to find out what's happening. I know managers and project managers who subscribe to the "don't get too close to your team" theory. I subscribe to the "all things in moderation" theory. You do want to establish relationships and prove your loyalty to the team, but you also have to know where to draw the line. When it comes time to hold a team member accountable, it can be difficult to do if you have become very close on a personal basis. However, I advocate erring on the side of developing a relationship with the team. My teams have to trust me to the point that they know they can come to me—at any time, with all types of news, good or bad—and I'll help them resolve the problem.

Summary

This chapter described four processes from the Executing process group: Direct and Manage Project Work, Acquire Project Team, Develop Project Team, and Manage Project Team.

In Direct and Manage Project Work, the project management plan comes to life; activities are authorized to begin; and the product, result, or service of the project is produced. Status review meetings are held to inform stakeholders of project progress and updates.

Acquire Project Team involves negotiation with other functional managers, project managers, and organizational personnel to obtain human resources to complete the work of the project. The project manager might not have control over who will be a part of the team. Availability, ability, experience, interests, and costs are all enterprise environmental factors that should be considered when you are able to choose team members.

Develop Project Team involves creating an open, inviting atmosphere where project team members will become efficient and cooperative, increasing productivity during the course of the project. It's the project manager's job to bring the team together into a functioning, productive group.

According to the Tuckman-Jensen model, team development has five stages: forming, storming, norming, performing, and adjourning. All groups proceed through these stages, and the introduction of a new team member will always start the process over again.

Co-location, also known as tight matrix, is physically placing team members together in the same location. This might also include a common meeting room or gathering area, known as a war room, where team members can meet and collaborate on the project.

Several motivational theories exist, including reward and recognition, Maslow's hierarchy of needs, the Hygiene Theory, the Expectancy Theory, and the Achievement Theory. These theories conjecture that motivation is driven by several desires; including physical, social, and psychological needs; anticipation of expected outcomes; and needs for achievement, power, or affiliation. The Hygiene Theory proposes that hygiene factors prevent dissatisfaction.

Leaders inspire vision and rally people around common goals. Theory X leaders think most people are motivated only through punishment, money, or position. Theory Y leaders think most people want to perform the best job they can. The Contingency Theory says that people naturally want to achieve levels of competency and will continue to be motivated by the desire for competency even after competency is reached. The Tannenbaum-Schmidt Continuum Management Theory involves seven levels of delegated freedom regarding decision making and problem solving. The Blanchard version of the Situational Leadership Theory describes four leadership styles to use depending on the situation.

Leaders exhibit five types of power: reward, punishment, expert, legitimate, and referent power.

Manage Project Teams involves tracking and reporting on project team member performance. Performance appraisals are performed during this process, and feedback is provided to the team members.

Exam Essentials

Be able to identify the distinguishing characteristics of Direct and Manage Project Work.   Direct and Manage Project Work is where the work of the project is performed, and the majority of the project budget is spent during this process.

Be able to name the five stages of group formation.   The five stages of group formation are forming, storming, norming, performing, and adjourning.

Be able to define Maslow's highest level of motivation.   Self-actualization occurs when a person performs at their peak and all lower-level needs have been met.

Know the five types of power.   The five levels of power are reward, punishment, expert, legitimate, and referent.

Be able to identify the five styles of conflict resolution.   The five styles of conflict resolution are force/direct, smooth/accommodate, compromise/reconcile, collaborate/problem solve, and withdraw/avoid.

Be familiar with the tools and techniques of the Manage Project Team process.   The tools and techniques of Manage Project Team are observation and conversation, project performance appraisals, conflict management, and interpersonal skills.

Key Terms

I've discussed in detail the processes you'll use while developing your project team. You need to understand each of these processes to effectively build your team and know them by the names used in the *PMBOK® Guide* to be successful on the exam:

Acquire Project Team

Develop Project Team

Direct and Manage Project Work

Manage Project Team

You learned a lot of new key words in this chapter. PMI® has worked hard to develop and define standard project management terms that apply across industries. Here is a list of some of the terms you came across in this chapter:

360-degree review	power
accommodate	preassignment
Achievement Theory	preventive action
avoid	problem solve
change requests	recognition and rewards
co-location	reconcile
collaborate	Situational Leadership Theory
compromise	smooth
conflict	Tannenbaum and Schmidt Continuum Management Theory
Contingency Theory	team building
corrective actions	Theory X
direct	Theory Y
Expectancy Theory	Theory Z
force	tight matrix
Hygiene Theory	training
Maslow's hierarchy of needs	virtual teams
Motivation-Hygiene Theory	war room
motivational theories	withdraw
politics	

Review Questions

You can find the answers to the questions in Appendix A.

1. You are a project manager for a growing dairy farm. It offers organic dairy products regionally and is expanding its operations to the West Coast. It is in the process of purchasing and leasing dairy farms to get operations underway. You are in charge of the network operations part of this project. An important deadline that depends on the successful completion of the testing phase is approaching. You've detected some problems with your hardware in the testing phase and discover that the hardware is not compatible with other network equipment. You take corrective action and exchange the hardware for more compatible equipment. Which of the following statements is true?

    A. This is not a corrective action because corrective action involves human resources, not project resources.

    B. Corrective action is taken here to make sure the future project outcomes are aligned with the project management plan.

    C. Corrective action is not necessary in this case because the future project outcomes aren't affected.

    D. Corrective action serves as the change request to authorize exchanging the equipment.

2. You are a project manager for a growing dairy farm. It offers organic dairy products regionally and is expanding its operations to the West Coast. It's in the process of purchasing and leasing dairy farms to get operations under way. The subproject manager in charge of network operations has reported some hardware problems to you. You're also having other problems coordinating and integrating other elements of the project. Which of the following statements is true?

    A. You are in the Direct and Manage Project Work process.

    B. Your project team doesn't appear to have the right skills and knowledge needed to perform this project.

    C. You are in the norming stage of team development.

    D. Your project team could benefit from some team-building exercises.

3. Which of the following process groups serve as inputs to each other?

    A. Executing, Monitoring and Controlling

    B. Executing, Closing

    C. Planning, Monitoring and Controlling

    D. Executing, Initiation

4. Your team members have just completed training on specialized equipment. This is one of the work results you've gathered and recorded. Which of the following outputs of the Direct and Manage Project Work process does this describe?

    A. Work performance data

    B. Deliverable

    C. Preventive action

    D. Project documents updates

5. You are reporting on project elements such as schedule status, deliverables completion, lessons learned, and resource utilization. Which of the following outputs of the Direct and Manage Project Work does this describe?

   A. Project management plan updates

   B. Project documents updates

   C. Preventive action

   D. Work performance data

6. You are in the process of making project staff assignments. You have several candidates for a position on the project team that requires specific qualifications. All the candidates seem to meet the qualifications. You also consider prior experience, their interest in the project, cost rates, and availability of these potential candidates. Which of the following is true?

   A. You are considering the resource calendars input of the Develop Project Team process.

   B. You are considering the project staff assignments input of the Develop Project Team process.

   C. You are considering the enterprise environmental factors input of the Acquire Project Team process.

   D. You are considering the project management plan input of the Acquire Project Team process.

7. During a recent team meeting, you reached a resolution to a problem that's been troubling the team for several weeks. It turned out that there was a problem with one of the manufactured parts required for the project. Once this was corrected, the remaining production run went off without a hitch. You took responsibility for searching out the facts of this problem and implemented a change request to resolve the issue. Which of the following is true regarding this question?

   A. This is a defect repair, which is performed during the Direct and Manage Project Work process.

   B. This is a corrective action, which is performed during the Direct and Manage Project Work process.

   C. This is a preventive action, which is performed during the Direct and Manage Project Work process.

   D. This is an unapproved change request and must first go through the Perform Integrated Change Control process.

8. You are the project manager for a cable service provider. Your team members are amiable with each other and are careful to make project decisions jointly. Which of the following statements is true?

   A. They are in the forming stage of team development.

   B. They are in the norming stage of team development.

   C. They are in the storming stage of team development.

   D. They are in the adjourning stage of team development.

9. You are the project manager for a cable service provider. Your project team is researching a new service offering. They have been working together for quite some time and are in the performing stage of team development. A new member has been introduced to the team. Which of the following statements is true?

    A. The team will start all over again with the storming stage.

    B. The team will continue in the performing stage.

    C. The team will start all over again with the forming stage.

    D. The team will start all over again at the storming stage but quickly progress to the performing stage.

10. You are the project manager for a cable service provider. Your project team is researching a new service offering. They have been working together for quite some time and have a good understanding of the task at hand. They will not likely need any direction from you to complete this task. According to Blanchard, what type of leadership style does this describe?

    A. Supporting

    B. Autocratic

    C. Laissez-faire

    D. Delegating

11. You've promised your team two days of paid time off plus a week's training in the latest technology of their choice if they complete their project ahead of schedule. This is an example of which of the following?

    A. Achievement Theory

    B. Expectancy Theory

    C. Maslow's Theory

    D. Contingency Theory

12. Your team is split between two buildings on either side of town. As a result, the team isn't very cohesive because the members don't know each other very well. The team is still in the storming stage because of the separation issues. Which of the following should you consider?

    A. Corrective action

    B. Co-location

    C. Training

    D. Conflict resolution

13. Which conflict resolution technique offers project managers the best option for resolution?

    A. Smooth/accommodate

    B. Collaborate/problem solve

    C. Compromise/reconcile

    D. Force/direct

14. You are a fabulous project manager, and your team thinks highly of you. You are well respected by the stakeholders, management team, and project team. When you make decisions, others follow your lead as a result of which of the following?

   A. Referent power

   B. Expert power

   C. Legitimate power

   D. Punishment power

15. Theory Y managers believe which of the following?

   A. People are motivated only by money, power, or position.

   B. People will perform their best if they're given proper motivation and expectations.

   C. People are motivated to achieve a high level of competency.

   D. People are motivated by expectation of good outcomes.

16. When working in a matrix environment, all of the following are true regarding the Manage Project Team process except for which one?

   A. Improving competencies, team interactions, and the team environment can help enhance project performance.

   B. Managing project teams in a matrix environment is often a critical success factor for the project.

   C. It's the project manager's responsibility to make certain this dual reporting relationship is managed effectively.

   D. Loyalty issues might arise when managing projects in a matrix environment.

17. You are preparing project performance appraisals and have decided you'd like each team member to receive feedback regarding their performance from several sources, including peers, superiors, and subordinates. Which of the following is true?

   A. This is called *360-degree feedback* and is part of the input to the organizational project performance appraisals, which is part of the organizational process assets updates input of the Manage Project Team process.

   B. This is called *360-degree feedback* and is considered part of the team performance assessment input of the Manage Project Team process.

   C. This is called *360-degree feedback* and is considered part of the Work performance data input of the Manage Project Team process.

   D. This is called *360-degree feedback* and is part of the project performance appraisals tool and technique of the Manage Project Team process.

18. Specific team members were promised for your project as part of the project proposal. You speak with the functional managers to assure their availability. All of the following are true regarding this question except for which one?

    A. This is a preassignment, which is a tool and technique of the process to which this question refers.

    B. Team members promised as part of the project proposal should be noted in the project charter.

    C. The other tools and techniques of the process this question refers to are negotiation, virtual teams, and resource availability.

    D. Team members might be promised as part of a project that's put out for bid or of internal projects.

19. These two conflict resolution techniques are known as lose-lose techniques.

    A. Accommodating and forcing

    B. Smoothing and withdrawal

    C. Compromise and reconcile

    D. Avoidance and forcing

20. You are a project manager who believes people will have high productivity, morale, and satisfaction if offered a job for life. Which theory do you subscribe to?

    A. Theory X

    B. Hygiene Theory

    C. Theory Y

    D. Theory Z

Chapter

9

Conducting Procurements and Sharing Information

THE PMP® EXAM CONTENT FROM THE EXECUTING THE PROJECT PERFORMANCE DOMAIN COVERED IN THIS CHAPTER INCLUDES THE FOLLOWING:

✓ **Obtain and manage project resources, both internal and external to the organization, by following the procurement plan in order to ensure successful project execution.**

✓ **Execute the tasks as defined in the project plan in order to achieve the project deliverables within budget and schedule.**

✓ **Implement the quality management plan, using the appropriate tools and techniques, in order to ensure that work is being performed according to required quality standards.**

✓ **Implement approved actions (e.g., workarounds) by following the risk management plan in order to minimize the impact of the risks on the project.**

✓ **Use effective communication tools and techniques to convey project information and properly gather, document, and store project information.**

✓ **Continue to engage stakeholders on the project, manage their expectations, manage and engage them in issues, and communicate project information.**

✓ **Knowledge and Skills:**

- Project monitoring tools and techniques

- Elements of a statement of work

- Interaction of work breakdown structure elements within the project schedule

- Project budgeting tools and techniques

- Quality standard tools

- Continuous improvement processes

This chapter wraps up the Executing process group. We'll look at four processes in this chapter: Conduct Procurements, Perform Quality Assurance, Manage Communications, and Manage Stakeholder Engagement.

Most of these processes aren't related to each other, but all are necessary to conduct the work of the project. They work in coordination with all the other Executing processes and are extensions of the Planning processes that preceded them (such as Plan Procurement Management, Plan Quality Management, and so on). Conduct Procurements and Perform Quality Assurance, in particular, work hand in hand with their Monitoring and Controlling processes (Control Procurements and Control Quality) to implement, measure, and report services and results.

The Conduct Procurements process is where sellers respond to the bids prepared in the Plan Procurement Management process. Contract awards are made here also. In Perform Quality Assurance, we'll look at several techniques to audit the project's quality requirements against the quality results. Manage Communications will cover more communication topics, including status reports, and last but not least we'll talk about Managing Stakeholder Engagement, which is critical during the Executing processes. Grab your favorite beverage and let's get started.

 The process names, inputs, tools and techniques, outputs, and descriptions of the project management process groups and related materials and figures in this chapter are based on content from *A Guide to the Project Management Body of Knowledge (PMBOK® Guide), Fifth Edition* (Sybex, 2010).

Conducting Procurements

Many times project managers must purchase goods or services to complete some or all of the work of the project. Sometimes the entire project is completed on contract. The *Conduct Procurements* process is concerned with obtaining responses to bids and proposals from potential vendors, selecting a vendor, and awarding the contract.

This process has several inputs:

- Procurement management plan
- Procurement documents

- Source selection criteria
- Seller proposals
- Project documents
- Make-or-buy decisions
- Procurement statement of work
- Organizational process assets

We've talked about most of these inputs in previous chapters. Procurement documents include requests for proposals (RFPs), requests for information (RFIs), requests for quotations (RFQs), and so on. The responses to those proposals become inputs to this process. Source selection criteria were defined in the Plan Procurement Management process that we talked about in Chapter 7, "Planning Project Resources." In the tools and techniques section for this process, we'll talk more about how seller proposals are evaluated. Seller proposals are responses to your procurement requests. Most organizations have a preferred format for seller responses so that the selection committee has a little of an easier time comparing proposals.

One element of the organizational process assets input you might consider during this process is a *qualified sellers list*. Qualified sellers lists are lists of prospective sellers who have been preapproved or prequalified to provide contract services (or provide supplies and materials) for the organization. For example, your organization might require vendors to register and maintain information regarding their experience, offerings, and current prices on a qualified seller list. Usually, vendors must go through the procurement department to be placed on the list. Project managers are then required to choose their vendors from the qualified seller list published by the procurement department. However, not all organizations have qualified seller lists. If a list isn't available, you'll have to work with the project team to come up with your own requirements for selecting vendors.

The Conduct Procurements process is used only if you're obtaining goods or services from outside your own organization. If you have all the resources you need to perform the work of the project within the organization, you won't use this process.

In the following sections, you'll examine some new tools and techniques that will help vendors give you a better idea of their responses, and then you'll move on to the outputs of this process, two of which are the selected seller and agreements.

Conduct Procurements Tools and Techniques

Remember that the purpose of the Conduct Procurements process is to obtain responses to your RFP (or similar procurement document), select the right vendor for the job, and award the contract. The tools and techniques of this process are designed to assist the vendors in getting their proposals to you and include techniques for evaluating those proposals. The tools and techniques are as follows:

- Bidder conferences
- Proposal evaluation techniques
- Independent estimates
- Expert judgment
- Advertising
- Analytical techniques
- Procurement negotiations

We'll look at each of these tools and techniques next with the exception of expert judgment, which we've covered in previous chapters.

Bidder Conferences

Bidder conferences (also known as vendor conferences, prebid conferences, and contractor conferences according to the *PMBOK® Guide*) are meetings with prospective vendors or sellers that occur prior to the completion of their response proposal. You or someone from your procurement department arranges the bidder conference. The purpose is to allow all prospective vendors to meet with the buyers to ask questions and clarify issues they have regarding the project and the RFP. The facilitator of the meeting should ensure that the meeting is orderly and that all questions and answers are restated in front of the entire group so all potential vendors have an equal chance at the bid. The meeting is held once, and all vendors attend at the same time. The bidder conference is held before the vendors prepare their responses so that they are sure their RFP responses will address the project requirements.

Proposal Evaluation Techniques

There are several techniques you might use to evaluate proposals. Simple procurements may not need much more than a quick check against the statement of work or a price comparison. Complex procurements may need several rounds of evaluation to begin narrowing the list of sellers. This is where you might use one or more of the following evaluation techniques to get to the final winner.

You can use source selection criteria as one method of rating and scoring proposals. We discussed source selection criteria in Chapter 7. You may recall that these criteria include several elements such as an understanding of the work, costs, technical capability, risk, warranty, and so on. We'll get into more detail on some of these criteria here. Keep in mind this is an input to the Conduct Procurements process, not a tool and technique, even though you'll be using it as you would a tool and technique.

The types of goods and services you're trying to procure will dictate how detailed your evaluation criteria are. (Of course, if your organization has policies in place for evaluating proposals, then you'll use the format or criteria already established.) The selection of some goods and services might be price driven only. In other words, the bidder with the lowest price will win the bid. This is typical when the items you're buying are widely available.

When you're purchasing goods, you might request a sample from each vendor in order to compare quality (or some other criteria) against your need. For example, perhaps you need a special kind of paper stock for a project you're working on at a bank. This stock must have a watermark; it must have security threads embedded through the paper; and when the paper is used for printing, the ink must not be erasable. You can request samples of stock with these qualities from the vendors and then test them to see whether they'll work for your project.

It's always appropriate to ask the vendor for references, especially when you're hiring contract services. It's difficult to assess the quality of services because it's not a tangible product. References can tell you whether the vendor delivered on time, whether the vendor had the technical capability to perform the work, and whether the vendor's management approach was appropriate when problems surfaced. Create a list of questions to ask the references before you call.

You can request financial records to assure you—the buyer—that the vendor has the fiscal ability to perform the services they're proposing and that the vendor can purchase whatever equipment is needed to perform the services. If you examine the records of the company and find that it's two steps away from bankruptcy, that company might not be a likely candidate for your project. (Remember those general management skills? Here's another example where they come into play.)

One of the most important criteria is the evaluation of the response itself to determine whether the vendor has a clear understanding of what you're asking them to do or provide. If they missed the mark (remember, they had an opportunity at the bidder conferences to ask clarifying questions) and didn't understand what you were asking them to provide, you'll probably want to rank them very low.

Now you can compare each proposal against the criteria and rate or score each proposal for its ability to meet or fulfill these criteria. This can serve as your first step in eliminating vendors that don't match your criteria. Let's say you received 18 responses to an RFP. After evaluating each one, you discover that six of them don't match all the evaluation criteria. You eliminate those six vendors in this round. The next step is to apply the tools and techniques of this process to further evaluate the remaining 12 potential vendors.

Weighting Systems

Weighting systems assign numerical weights to evaluation criteria and then multiply them by the weights of each criteria factor to come up with total scores for each vendor. This technique provides a way to quantify the data and assist in keeping personal biases to a minimum. Weighting systems are useful when you have multiple vendors to choose from because they allow you to rank the proposals to determine the sequence of negotiations.

You'll find an example of a weighted scoring system in Chapter 2, "Creating the Project Charter." These systems are commonly used to evaluate vendor proposals.

Screening Systems

Screening systems use predefined performance criteria or a set of defined minimum requirements to screen out unsuitable vendors. Perhaps your project requires board-certified engineers. One of the screening criteria would be that vendors propose project team members who have this qualification. If they don't, they're eliminated from the selection process.

Screening systems can be used together with some of the other tools and techniques of this process, weighting systems, and independent estimates, to rank vendor proposals.

Seller Rating Systems

Seller rating systems use information about the sellers—such as past performance, delivery, contract compliance, and quality ratings—to determine seller performance. Your organization might have seller rating systems in place, and you should check with your procurement department to see whether they exist for the bidders on your project. Part of the Control Procurements process (I'll talk about this in Chapter 10, "Measuring and Controlling Project Performance") concerns gathering and recording this type of information. Don't use seller rating systems as your sole criterion for evaluating vendors.

> Proposal evaluation techniques are a combination of all the techniques I've discussed in this section. All techniques use some form of expert judgment and evaluation criteria—whether it's objective or subjective criteria. The evaluation criteria are usually weighted, much like a weighted scoring system, and those participating as reviewers provide their ratings (usually to the project manager) to compile into a weighted proposal to determine an overall score. Scoring differences are also resolved using this technique. Some or all of the evaluation techniques described here can be used in combination with the remaining tools and techniques of this section to evaluate seller responses.

Independent Estimates

Your procurement department might conduct *independent estimates* (also known as *should cost estimates*) of the costs of the proposal and compare these to the vendor prices. If there are large differences between the independent estimate and the proposed vendor cost, one of two things is happening: Either the statement of work (SOW) or the terms of the contract or both are not detailed enough to allow the vendor to come up with an accurate cost, or the vendor simply failed to respond to all the requirements laid out in the contract or SOW. Independent estimates can also be used to verify schedule estimates and other project estimates as well.

Advertising

Advertising is letting potential vendors know that an RFP is available. Advertising can be used as a way of expanding the pool of potential vendors or it may be a requirement, such as in the case of government projects. The company's Internet site, professional journals, or newspapers are examples of where advertising might appear. In reality, most organizations, including government organizations, have replaced advertising in the newspaper with advertising on their own websites.

Analytical Techniques

Analytical techniques are used to help research potential vendors' capabilities, get an idea of cost, analyze past performance, forecast future performance, and learn from others who have undergone similar projects. Internet searches are an analytical technique that has several useful features. You can use Internet searches to find vendors, perform research on their past performance, and compare prices. You can also use the Internet to purchase items that are readily available and are generally offered for a fixed price. Internet searches are probably not useful when you're conducting high-risk or complex procurements, but you could do some research on company performance and reputation to help in choosing a vendor.

Procurement Negotiation

In *procurement negotiation*, both parties come to an agreement regarding the contract terms. Negotiation skills are put into practice here as the details of the contract are ironed out between the parties. At a minimum, contract language should include price, responsibilities, regulations or laws that apply, and the overall approach to the project.

The complexity of the contract will determine how extensive the contract negotiations will be. Simple contracts may have predetermined nonnegotiable elements that only require seller acceptance. Complex contracts may include any number of elements, including financing options, overall schedule, proprietary rights, service-level agreements, technical aspects, and more. In either case, once agreement is reached and the negotiations are finished, the contract is signed by both buyer and seller and then it is executed.

You might see the term *fait accompli* show up on the exam. Fait accompli tactics are used during contract negotiation when one party tries to convince the other party discussing a particular contract item that it is no longer an issue. It can be a distraction technique, when the party practicing fait accompli tactics is purposely trying to keep from negotiating an issue and claims the issue cannot be changed. For example, during negotiations the vendor tells you that the key resource they're assigning to your project must start immediately or you'll lose that resource and they'll get assigned work elsewhere. However, you don't know—because the vendor didn't tell you—that the vendor can reserve this resource for your project and hold them until the start date. In this instance, they used fait accompli tactics to push you into starting the project, or hiring this resource, sooner than you would have otherwise.

Exam Spotlight

Procurement negotiations, according to the *PMBOK® Guide*, can be performed as a process itself with inputs and outputs.

🌐 Real World Scenario

Vendor Selection for Fitness Counts HR System

Amanda Jacobson is the project manager for Fitness Counts, a nationwide chain of gyms containing all the latest and greatest fitness equipment, aerobics classes, swimming pools, and such. Fitness Counts is converting its human resources data management system. The RFP addressed several requirements, including the following:

- The new system must run on a platform that's compatible with the company's current operating system.

- Hardware must be compatible with company standards.

- Data conversion of existing HR data must be included in the price of the bid.

- Fitness Counts wants to have the ability to add custom modules using internal programmers.

- Training for the Fitness Counts programmers must be included in the bid.

The project team is in the Conduct Procurements process and has received bids based on the RFP published earlier this month. Fitness Counts is using a combination of selection criteria and a weighted scoring model to choose a vendor.

One of the evaluation criteria states that the vendor must have prior experience with a project like this. Four vendors met that criteria and proceeded to the weighted scoring selection process.

Amanda is one of the members of the selection committee. She and four other members on the committee rated the four vendors who met the initial selection criteria. They read all of the proposals and rated the criteria using factors they had predetermined for each. For example, vendors who proposed an SQL database as part of the "Platform" criteria (along with the other predetermined factors) should receive a total weighted score of 5. Table 9.1 shows their results.

TABLE 9.1   A Weighted Scoring Model

	Platform	Hardware	Data conversion	Custom modules/ training	Totals
Weighting factor *	5	4	5	4	
Vendor A					
Raw score	*3*	*3*	*3*	*4*	
Weighted score	15	12	15	16	**58**

	Platform	Hardware	Data conversion	Custom modules/ training	Totals
Vendor B					
Raw score	*2*	*3*	*4*	*3*	
Weighted score	10	12	20	12	**54**
Vendor C					
Raw score	*4*	*4*	*4*	*3*	
Weighted score	20	16	20	12	**68**
Vendor D					
Raw score	*3*	*3*	*2*	*4*	
Weighted score	15	12	10	16	**53**

*1–5, with 5 being highest

Vendor C is the clear winner of this bid. Based on the weighted scoring model, their responses to the RFP came out ahead of the other bidders. Amanda calls them with the good news and also calls the other vendors to thank them for participating in the bid. Vendor C is awarded the contract, and Amanda moves on to the Contract Administration process.

Conduct Procurements Outputs

The Conduct Procurements process has six outputs:

- Selected sellers
- Agreements
- Resource calendars
- Change requests
- Project management plan updates
- Project documents updates

The selected sellers output is obvious: You choose the seller (or sellers) to whom you'll award the project and execute the contract. I'll talk more about the agreements output next. I've discussed all the other outputs previously.

> According to the *PMBOK® Guide*, a negotiated draft contract is one of the requirements of the selected sellers output. Also note that senior management signatures may be required on complex, high-risk, or high-dollar contracts. Be sure to check your organization's procurement policies regarding the authority level and amounts for which you are authorized to sign. In my organization, not only do our contracts require senior management signatures, they also require signatures from two other external departments. We have to account for the multiple reviews, signatures, and question-and-answer sessions required to get contract signature. This has a definite impact on the project schedule and must be accounted for in time estimates for these tasks.

Elements of a Procurement Agreement

Procurement agreements take different forms depending on what you are procuring, who you are procuring it from, and the nature of the goods or services themselves. You might use a purchase order, a contract, a work order against an existing contract, or other forms. You might recall that a contract is a legally binding agreement between two or more parties, typically used to acquire goods or services. Contracts have several names, including agreements, memorandums of understanding (MOUs), subcontracts, and purchase orders.

The type of contract you'll award will depend on the product or services you're procuring and your organizational policies. I talked about the types of contracts—fixed price, cost reimbursable, and so on—in Chapter 7. If you need a refresher, you can refer back to it. If your project has multiple sellers, you'll award contracts for each of them.

The contract or procurement agreement should clearly address the elements of the SOW, time period of performance, pricing and payment plan, acceptance criteria, warranty periods, dispute resolution procedures, status or performance reporting procedures, limitations of liabilities, change request process, penalties and incentives, and so on.

Because contracts are legally binding and obligate your organization to fulfill the terms, they'll likely be subject to some intensive review, often by several different people. Be certain you understand your organization's policies on contract review and approval before proceeding.

Contracts, like projects, have a life cycle of their own. You might encounter questions on the exam regarding the stages of the contract life cycles, so we'll look at this topic next.

Contract Life Cycles

The contract life cycle consists of four stages:

- Requirement
- Requisition

- Solicitation
- Award

These stages are closely related to the following Project Procurement Management Knowledge Area processes from the *PMBOK® Guide*:

- Plan Procurement Management
- Conduct Procurements

A description of each of the contract life cycles follows:

Requirement   The requirement stage is the equivalent of the Plan Procurement Management process I discussed in Chapter 7. You establish the project and contract needs in this cycle, and you define the requirements of the project. The SOW defines the work of the project, the objectives, and a high-level overview of the deliverables. You develop a work breakdown structure (WBS), a make-or-buy analysis takes place, and you determine cost estimates.

The buyer provides the SOW to describe the requirements of the project when it's performed under contract. The product description can serve as the SOW.

Requisition   In the requisition stage, the project objectives are refined and confirmed. Solicitation materials such as the request for proposals (RFP), request for information (RFI), and request for quotations (RFQ) are prepared during this phase. Generally, the project manager is responsible for preparing the RFP, RFI, and RFQ. A review of the potential qualified vendors takes place, including checking references and reviewing other projects the vendors have worked on that are similar to your proposed project. Requisition occurs during the Plan Procurement Management process.

Solicitation   The solicitation stage is where vendors are asked to compete for the contract and respond to the RFP. You can use the tools and techniques of the Conduct Procurements process during this contract stage. The resulting output is the proposals. Solicitation occurs during the Conduct Procurements process.

Award   Vendors are chosen and contracts are awarded and signed during the award stage. The Conduct Procurements process is the equivalent of the award phase.

The project manager—or the selection committee, depending on the organizational policy—receives the bids and proposals during the award phase and applies evaluation criteria to each in order to score or rank the responses. After ranking each of the proposals, an award is made to the winning vendor, and the contract is written.

Once you have a contract, someone has to administer it. In large organizations, this responsibility will fall to the procurement department. The project manager should still have a solid understanding of administering contracts because that person will work with the procurement department to determine the satisfactory fulfillment of the contract.

Now we're going to switch courses and discuss the quality assurance aspects of the project. We discussed the Plan Quality Management process back in Chapter 7, which prepared you for the Perform Quality Assurance process that's conducted during the Executing process group. We'll look at it next.

Laying Out Quality Assurance Procedures

The Plan Quality Management process laid out the quality standards for the project and determined how those standards are to be satisfied. The *Perform Quality Assurance* process involves performing systematic quality activities and uses quality audits to determine which processes should be used to achieve the project requirements and to ensure they are performed efficiently and effectively.

The project team members, the project manager, and the stakeholders are all responsible for the quality assurance of the project. Continuous process improvement can be achieved through this process, bringing about improved process performance and eliminating unnecessary actions.

A quality assurance department or organization may be assigned to the project to oversee these processes. In that case, quality assurance might be provided to (rather than by) the project team. The project manager will have the greatest impact on the quality of the project during this process.

You'll review the inputs to this process next and then spend some time exploring a few new tools and techniques for ensuring a quality product and project.

Inputs to Perform Quality Assurance

The inputs to Perform Quality Assurance are what you use to measure the organizational project quality management processes against. The quality management processes were defined during Quality Planning. The inputs to the Perform Quality Assurance process are as follows:

- Quality management plan
- Process improvement plan
- Quality metrics
- Quality control measurements
- Project documents

You've heard about the inputs to Perform Quality Assurance before, so we'll move right into the tools and techniques of this section.

Exam Spotlight

The most important point to remember about Perform Quality Assurance is that quality management processes are what you use to verify that the project satisfies the quality standards laid out in the project management plan.

Perform Quality Assurance Tools and Techniques

The Perform Quality Assurance process has three tools and techniques: quality management and control tools, quality audits, and process analysis.

Quality management and control tools consist of the tools and techniques from both the Plan Quality Management and Control Quality processes. We will look at the Control Quality tools and techniques in Chapter 11, "Controlling Work Results." In addition to all of the tools mentioned in those processes, the *PMBOK® Guide* notes the following tools are included within this tool and technique:

Affinity Diagrams   Affinity diagrams, also known as KJ Methods, are used to group and organize thoughts and facts and can be used in conjunction with brainstorming. After you've gathered all ideas possible with brainstorming, you group similar ideas together on an affinity diagram. You may be familiar with mind-mapping techniques where the primary concept is captured in the middle of the diagram and related ideas are branched off the middle into their own segments. This is an example of an affinity diagram. This technique is useful when decomposing the scope of the project. Put a brief scope statement in the middle circle or bubble, and then identify all of the deliverables that make up the scope on independent branches (and bubbles). You could use this technique to decompose each deliverable as well.

Process Decision Program Charts (PDPC)   PDPC charts are constructed like organizational charts. The project or primary idea is in the top box, and related ideas are branched off from the main box, with more boxes branching off from them. This technique may be used for contingency planning to help identify all the possible results that could impact the project.

Interrelationship Digraphs   Interrelationship digraphs are problem-solving tools used for complex situations. They involve relating up to 50 factors, processes, or areas of focus. Each factor is interconnected to many other factors, making it easier to identify those elements that have the biggest impact on the project. The idea behind this tool is to start by writing down the main issue and draw a circle or square around the issue. From there, identify all of the elements involved with the issue and connect them to the main issue and to each other where a relationship exists. It can look a bit like a misshaped spider web when you are finished. The factors with the most connecting lines are the ones you'll want to pay particular attention to because they likely have the biggest impact on the project.

Tree Diagrams   Examples of tree diagrams include work breakdown structures, risk breakdown structures, and objectives breakdown structures. The common theme with these diagrams is they depict hierarchies and parent-child relationships. If you flip back to Chapter 3, "Developing the Project Scope Statement," and look at the WBS for Billy Bob's Bassoon, you'll see there are nested branches that all lead to a single point (ultimately the project itself). For example, "Requirements definition" requires both "Game Requirements" and "Software Requirements" to be completed before this deliverable is complete. And both of these deliverables have work packages that must be completed. Uncomplicated structures such as this allow you to easily determine expected values for any level on the structure. (We talked about expected values in Chapter 4, "Creating the Project Schedule.") Tree diagrams are also known as systematic diagrams.

Prioritization Matrices   We've talked quite a bit about prioritization matrices, including probability and impact matrix and weighted scoring systems. Prioritization matrices are also applicable to the Perform Quality Assurance process.

Activity Network Diagrams   We talked about activity network diagrams in Chapter 4. They include both activity on nodes and activity on arrow diagrams and are used to help construct the project schedule.

Matrix Diagrams   In Chapter 7, we talked about RAMs and RACI charts. These are examples of matrix diagrams. The *PMBOK® Guide* points out two types of matrix diagrams you should be aware of for the exam: two-dimensional diagrams that consist of L-Type, T-Type, and X-Type, and three-dimensional diagrams such as C-Type.

We'll look at the remaining tools and techniques in the following sections.

Quality Audits

Quality audits are independent reviews performed by trained auditors or third-party reviewers. The purpose of a quality audit is the same as the purpose of the Perform Quality Assurance process—to identify ineffective and inefficient activities or processes used on the project. These audits might examine and uncover inefficient processes and procedures as well as processes that are not in compliance with organizational practices.

You can perform quality audits on a regular schedule or at random, depending on the organizational policies. Quality audits performed correctly will provide the following benefits:

- The product of the project is fit for use and meets safety standards.
- Applicable laws and standards are followed.
- Corrective action is recommended and implemented where necessary.
- The quality plan for the project is followed.
- Quality improvements are identified.
- Confirms the implementation of approved change requests, corrective actions, preventive actions, and defect repairs are confirmed.
- Gaps or shortcomings in the process are identified.
- Good and best practices are implemented and shared within the organization or industry.

Quality improvements come about as a result of the quality audits. During the course of the audit, you might discover ways of improving the efficiency or effectiveness of the project, thereby increasing the value of the project and more than likely exceeding stakeholder expectations.

Quality improvements are implemented by submitting change requests and/or taking corrective action. Quality improvements interface with the Monitoring and Controlling processes because of the need to submit change requests.

You'll look at change requests and change request procedures in Chapter 10.

Experienced specialists generally perform quality audits. The specialist's job is to produce an independent evaluation of the quality process. Some organizations are large enough to have their own quality assurance departments or quality assurance teams; others might have to hire contract personnel to perform this function. Internal quality assurance teams report results to the project team and management team of the organization. External quality assurance teams report results to the customer.

Process Analysis

Process analysis looks at process improvement from an organizational and technical perspective. According to the *PMBOK® Guide*, process analysis follows the steps in the process improvement plan and examines the following:

- Problems experienced while conducting the project
- Constraints experienced while conducting the work of the project
- Inefficient and ineffective activities identified during process operation

One of the techniques of process analysis includes performing root cause analysis. (I talked about root cause analysis in the Identify Risks process in Chapter 6, "Risk Planning.") While you're examining problems and constraints, for example, you should look for what's causing the underlying issue. The result of this exercise will allow you to understand what caused the problem and develop preventive actions for problems that are similar to the one you're examining or that have the similar root causes.

Perform Quality Assurance Outputs

The Perform Quality Assurance process has four outputs:

- Change requests
- Project management plan updates
- Project documents updates
- Organizational process assets updates

These aren't new, but there is one new idea embedded in the change requests output. During this process, any recommended corrective actions, whether they are a result of a quality audit or process analysis, should be acted on immediately and processed through the change control process. Let's say you're manufacturing parts for one of the deliverables of your project. Obviously, the moment you discover that the parts are not correct, you'd correct the process by calibrating the machine perhaps, or by using different raw materials, to make certain the parts are produced accurately.

Quality Improvements

Although it isn't stated as an output, one of the overarching goals of the Perform Quality Assurance process is to provide a foundation for continuous process improvements. As the name implies, continuous improvements are iterative. This process of continuous improvements sets the stage, so to speak, for improving the quality of all the project processes. This can mean project management processes, but it also means the processes and activities involved in accomplishing the work of the project.

The advantage of continuous process improvement is that it reduces the time the project team spends on ineffective or inefficient processes. If the activities don't help you meet the goals of the project or, worse yet, hinder your progress, it's time to look at ways to improve them.

Once again we're going to shift gears and talk about a new process. We'll look at best practices regarding sharing and distributing information next.

Managing Project Information

The *Manage Communications* process is concerned with gathering, creating, storing, distributing, retrieving, and disposing of project communications. One of the primary functions of this process is distributing information about the project to the stakeholders in a timely manner. This can come about in several ways: status reports, project meetings, review meetings, and so on. Status reports inform stakeholders about where the project is today in regard to project schedule and budget, for example. They also describe what the project team has accomplished to date. This might include milestones completed to date, the percentage of schedule completion, and what remains to be completed. The Manage Communications process describes how this report and other information are distributed and to whom.

In the Manage Communications process, the communications management plan that was defined during the Plan Communication Management process is put into action. Remember that this plan is a subsidiary of the project management plan, which is an input to this process. The other inputs include work performance reports, enterprise environmental factors, and organizational process assets. Plan Communications Management and Manage Communications work together to report the progress of the project team.

Manage Communications has some new tools and techniques, which we'll look at next.

Tools and Techniques of Manage Communications

The tools and techniques of this process are as follows:

- Communication technology
- Communication models
- Communication methods
- Information management systems
- Performance reporting

We talked about communication technology, models, and methods in Chapter 5, "Developing the Project Budget and Communicating the Plan." We'll explore communication models in a little more depth in the next section.

Communication skills are probably the single most important skill in your project management toolbox. You can't employ communication methods or use communication models effectively without some sound communication skills, so let's take a look at this topic next.

Developing Great Communication Skills

Every aspect of your job as a project manager will involve communications. It has been estimated that project managers spend as much as 90 percent of their time communicating in one form or another. Therefore, communication skills are arguably one of the most important skills a project manager can have. They are even more important than technical skills. Good communication skills foster an open, trusting environment, and excellent communication skills are a project manager's best asset.

Throughout this book I've emphasized how important good communication skills are. Now I'll discuss the act of communication, listening behaviors, and conflict resolution. You'll employ each of these techniques with your project team, stakeholders, customers, and management team.

Information Exchange

Communication is the process of exchanging information. All communication includes three elements:

Sender   The sender is the person responsible for putting the information together in a clear and concise manner. The information should be complete and presented in a way that the receiver will be able to correctly understand it. Make your messages relevant to the receiver. Junk mail is annoying, and information that doesn't pertain in any way whatsoever to the receiver is nothing more than that.

Message   The message is the information being sent and received. It might be written, verbal, nonverbal, formal, informal, internal, external, horizontal, or vertical. *Horizontal communications* are messages sent and received to peers. *Vertical communications* are messages sent and received down to subordinates and up to executive management.

Make your messages as simple as you can to get your point across. Don't complicate messages with unnecessary detail and technical jargon that others might not understand. A simple trick that helps clarify your messages, especially verbal messages, is to repeat the key information periodically. Public speakers are taught that the best way to organize a speech is to first tell the audience what you're going to tell them; second, tell them; and third, tell them what you just told them.

Receiver   The receiver is the person for whom the message is intended. They are responsible for understanding the information correctly and making sure they've received all the information.

Keep in mind that receivers filter the information they receive through their knowledge of the subject, cultural influences, language, emotions, attitudes, and geographic locations. The sender should take these filters into consideration when sending messages so that the receiver will clearly understand the message that was sent.

This book is an example of the sender-message-receiver model. I'm the sender of the information. The message concerns topics you need to know to pass the PMP® exam (and if I've done my job correctly, is written in a clear and easily understood format). You, the reader, are the receiver.

ELEMENTS OF A COMMUNICATION MODEL

Senders, receivers, and messages are the elements of communication. The way the sender packages or encodes the information and transmits it and the way the receiver unpacks or decodes the message are the models of communication exchange.

Senders encode messages. Encoding is a method of putting the information into a format the receiver will understand. Language, pictures, and symbols are used to encode messages. Encoding formats the message for transmitting.

Transmitting is the way the information gets from the sender to the receiver. Spoken words, written documentation, memos, email, and voicemail are all transmitting methods.

Decoding is what the receiver does with the information when they get it. They convert it into an understandable format. Usually, this means they read the memo, listen to the speaker, read the book, and so on.

Acknowledging involves the receiver informing the sender they have received the message. This is not, however, an indication of agreement or that the receiver understands the message. It serves only to let the sender know the message has been received.

Feedback/Response implies the message was not only received and decoded, but the message from the sender was understood. In response, the receiver crafts a message and sends it back to the sender, starting the cycle all over again.

FORMS OF COMMUNICATION

Communication occurs primarily in written or verbal form. Granted, you can point to something or indicate what you need with motions, but usually you use the spoken or written word to get your message across.

Verbal communication is easier and less complicated than written communication, and it's usually a fast method of communication. Written communication, on the other hand, is an excellent way to get across complex, detailed messages. Detailed instructions are better provided in written form because it gives the reader the ability to go back over information about which they're not quite sure.

Both verbal and written communication might take a formal or an informal approach. Speeches and lectures are examples of formal verbal communication. Most project status meetings take more of a formal approach, as do most written project status reports. Generally speaking, the project manager should take an informal approach when communicating with stakeholders and project team members outside of the status meetings. This makes you appear more open and friendly and easier to approach with questions and issues.

Formal and informal approaches may also include techniques such as fact finding, asking questions, motivating team members, providing performance feedback to team members, and setting and managing stakeholder (and team) expectations.

Effective Listening Skills

What did you say? Often we think we're listening when we really aren't. In all fairness, we can take in only so much information at one time. However, it is important to perform active listening when someone else is speaking. As a project manager, you will spend the majority of your time communicating with team members, stakeholders, customers, vendors, and others. This means you should be as good a listener as you are a communicator.

You can use several techniques to improve your listening skills. Many books are devoted to this topic, so I'll try to highlight some of the most common techniques here:

- Appear interested in what the speaker is saying. This will make the speaker feel at ease and will benefit you as well. By acting interested, you become interested and thereby retain more of the information being presented.

- Making eye contact with the speaker is another effective listening tool. This lets the speaker know you are paying attention to what they're saying and are interested.

- Put your speaker at ease by letting them know beforehand that you're interested in what they're going to talk about and that you're looking forward to hearing what they have to say. While they're speaking, nod your head, smile, or make comments when and if appropriate to let the speaker know you understand the message. If you don't understand something and are in the proper setting, ask clarifying questions.

- Another great trick that works well in lots of situations is to recap what the speaker said in your own words and tell it back to them. Start with something like this, "Let me make sure I understand you correctly, you're saying…," and ask the speaker to confirm that you did understand them correctly.

- Just as your mother always said, it's impolite to interrupt. Interrupting is a way of telling the speaker that you aren't really listening and you're more interested in telling them what you have to say than listening to them. Interrupting gets the other person off track, they might forget their point, and it might even make them angry.

Not to disagree with Mom, but there probably are some occasions where interrupting is appropriate. For example, if you're in a project status meeting and someone wants to take the meeting off course, sometimes the only way to get the meeting back on track is to interrupt them. You can do this politely. Start first by saying the person's name to get their attention. Then let them know that you'd be happy to talk with them about their topic outside of the meeting or add it to the agenda for the next status meeting if it's something everyone needs to hear. Sorry, Mom.

Resolving Conflicts

We discussed conflict resolution techniques in Chapter 8, "Developing the Project Team." They are also a form of communication skills. You may recall the conflict resolution techniques:

- Force/direct
- Smooth/accommodate
- Compromise/reconcile
- Collaborate/problem solve
- Withdraw/avoid

Keep in mind that group size makes a difference when you're trying to resolve conflicts or make decisions. Remember the channels of communication you learned about in Chapter 5? The larger the group, the more lines of communication and the more difficult it will be to reach a decision. Groups of 5 to 11 people have a manageable number of participants and have been shown to make the most accurate decisions.

Use communication, listening, and conflict resolution skills wisely. As a project manager, you'll find that your day-to-day activities encompass these three areas the majority of the time. Project managers with excellent communication skills can work wonders. Communication won't take the place of proper planning and management techniques, but a project manager who communicates well with their team and the stakeholders can make up for a lack of technical skills any day, hands down. If your team and your stakeholders trust you and you can communicate the vision and the project goals and report on project status accurately and honestly, the world is your oyster.

Information Management Systems

Information management systems are ways of getting the project information to the project team or stakeholders. As the name implies, these are ways to distribute the information, including email, hard copy, voice mail, videoconferencing, websites, project management software, collaborative work management tools, and so on. You can also use electronic project management tools such as schedules and meeting software to maintain project records.

Performance Reporting

This tool and technique involves collecting and distributing the project information, which can include status reports, measurements regarding the progress of the project, and forecasts concerning future performance. I'm certain you're all familiar with status reports. These can take many forms, but most project status reports include the progress of the project to date, the expected activities for the next period, schedule and budget updates, risk and issues updates, and change requests. Most project management software systems can produce dashboards with information about the project schedule, budget, quality, and other criteria the management team might like to see. The dashboards typically grade the health of these areas of the project with numeric scores or colors such as red, yellow, and green to indicate that area is in trouble, is headed into trouble and should be watched, or is in good shape.

Output of Manage Communications

The Manage Communications process has four outputs, including project communications, project management plan updates, project documents updates, and organizational process asset updates.

The project communications output involves all of the work required for gathering, creating, storing, distributing, retrieving, and disposing of project communications. A few key elements you should consider regarding this output are the urgency of the message, the impact the message may have on the receiver (and perhaps the project as well), the delivery method you'll use for the message, and whether the message is sensitive or confidential and how to ensure the message goes only to the intended receivers. According to the *PMBOK® Guide*, project communications typically consists of performance reports, deliverables status, schedule progress, and cost incurred.

The project management plan updates may include updating the project baselines (scope, schedule, and/or cost), the communications management plan, and the stakeholder management plan. Remember that together, the approved scope, schedule, and cost baselines are known as the performance measurement baseline. It's essential that you as the project manager update the project sponsor and key stakeholders of any changes to the performance management baseline.

There are six elements of the organizational process assets updates you should know:

Stakeholder Notifications   Remember that the focus of this process is distributing information. Stakeholder notifications involve notifying stakeholders when you have implemented solutions and approved changes, have updated project status, have resolved issues, and so on.

Project Reports   *Project reports* include the project status reports and minutes from project meetings, lessons learned, closure reports, and other documents from all the process outputs throughout the project. If you're keeping an issue log, the issues should be included with the project reports as well.

Project Presentations *Project presentations* involve presenting project information to the stakeholders and other appropriate parties when necessary. The presentations might be formal or informal and depend on the audience and the information being communicated.

Project Records As you might guess, *project records* include memos, correspondence, and other documents concerning the project. The best place to keep information like this is in a project notebook or in a set of project notebooks, depending on the size of the project. The project notebooks are ordinary three-ring binders where project information gets filed. They are maintained by the project manager or project office and contain all information regarding the project. You could also keep the information on a project website, the company intranet, or CDs. If you're keeping the information electronically, make certain it's backed up regularly. Individual team members might keep their own project records in notebooks or electronically as well. These records serve as historical information once the project is closed.

Feedback from Stakeholders Feedback you receive from the stakeholders that can improve future performance on this project or future projects should be captured and documented. If the information has an impact on the current project, distribute it to the appropriate team members so that future project performance can be modified to improve results.

Lessons Learned Documentation *Lessons learned* are information that you gather and document throughout the course of the project that can be used to benefit the current project, future projects, or other projects currently being performed by the organization. Lessons learned might include positive as well as negative lessons.

During the Manage Communications process, you'll begin conducting lessons-learned meetings focusing on many different areas, depending on the nature of your project. These areas might include project management processes, product development, technical processes, project team performance, stakeholder involvement, and so on.

Lessons learned meetings should always be conducted at the end of project phases and at the end of the project at minimum. Team members, stakeholders, vendors, and others involved with the project should participate in these meetings. It's important to understand, and to make your team members understand, that this is not a finger-pointing meeting. The purpose of lessons learned is to understand what went well and why—so you can repeat it on future projects—and what didn't go so well and why—so you can perform differently on future projects. These meetings can make good team-building sessions because you're creating an atmosphere of trust and sharing and you're building on each other's strengths to improve performance.

You should document the reasons or causes for the issues, the corrective action taken and why, and any other information from which future projects might benefit.

Exam Spotlight

According to the *PMBOK® Guide*, it's a project manager's professional obligation to hold lessons learned meetings.

We're making one last switch of focus in this chapter and will examine how to Manage Stakeholder Engagement next.

Managing Stakeholder Engagement

The *Manage Stakeholder Engagement* process is about satisfying the needs of the stakeholders by managing communications with them, resolving issues, engaging them on the project, managing their expectations, improving project performance by implementing requested changes, and managing concerns in anticipation of potential problems.

 If you need a refresher on the definition and role of stakeholders, please see Chapter 1, "What Is a Project?"

In my experience, managing stakeholder expectations is much more difficult than managing project team members. Stakeholders are often managers or directors in the organization who might be higher in the food chain than the project manager and aren't afraid to let you know it. Having said that, you *can* manage stakeholder expectations, and you do so using communication.

Stakeholders need lots of communication in every form you can provide. If you are actively engaged with your stakeholders and interacting with them, providing project status, and resolving issues, your chances of a successful project are much greater than if you don't do these things.

Exam Spotlight

According to the *PMBOK® Guide*, it's the project manager's responsibility to manage stakeholder expectations. Doing so will decrease the potential for project failure. Managing the expectations of your stakeholders will also increase the chance of meeting the project goals because issues are resolved in a timely manner and disruptions during the project are limited.

Manage Stakeholder Engagement Inputs

The inputs of Manage Stakeholder Engagement include the following:

- Stakeholder management plan
- Communications management plan
- Change log
- Organizational process assets

We have discussed each of these inputs previously with the exception of the change log. We'll look more closely at change logs in the next chapter, but for purposes of this process understand that this is a log that documents all the changes made during the course of the project. In terms of stakeholder expectations, you'll want to keep stakeholders updated on changes and their impacts on the project.

Tools and Techniques for Manage Stakeholder Engagement

The tools and techniques of this process include communication methods, interpersonal skills, and management skills. It's been a while since we talked about management skills, but for purposes of this process, they refer primarily to maintaining consensus regarding the project objectives, influencing others to support the project, negotiating, and helping to shape organizational behavior to accept the project outcomes. Other management skills you may need to polish are presenting, writing, and public speaking skills. Keep in mind that face-to-face communications are the most effective with stakeholders.

Manage Stakeholder Engagement Outputs

The outputs of the Manage Stakeholder Engagement process are the issue log, change requests, project management plan updates, project documents updates, and organizational process assets updates.

One thing to note about the issue log in this process is that it acts more like an action item log where you record the actions needed to resolve stakeholder concerns and project issues they raise. Issues should be ranked according to their urgency and potential impact on the project. As with the issue log in the Manage Project Team process, you'll assign a responsible party and a due date for resolution.

Exam Spotlight

According to the *PMBOK® Guide*, the issue log (or action item log) can be used to promote communication with stakeholders and to ensure that stakeholders and the project team have the same understanding of the issues.

Organizational process assets updates in this process include some of the same updates we talked about in the Manage Communications process: stakeholder notifications, project reports, project presentations, project records, feedback from stakeholders, and lessons learned documentation.

You've successfully completed the Executing process group. Remember that the Executing processes and Monitoring and Controlling processes serve as inputs to each other and that Executing and Monitoring and Controlling are both iterative process groups. As your project progresses and it becomes evident that you need to exercise controls to get the project back on track, you'll come back through the Executing process group and then proceed through the Monitoring and Controlling processes again. You'll move on to the Monitoring and Controlling process group now and find out what it's all about.

🌐 Real World Scenario

Project Case Study: New Kitchen Heaven Retail Store

Dirk Perrier logs on and finds the following status report addressed to all the stakeholders and project team members from you:

Project Progress Report

Project Name Kitchen Heaven Retail Store

Project Number 081501-1910

Prepared By Project manager

Date October 8

Section 1: Action Items

- *Action Item 1*: Call cable vendor. Responsible party: Ricardo. Resolution date: 9/14

- *Action Item 2*: Check T1 connection status. Responsible party: Ricardo. Resolution date: Pending

- *Action Item 3*: Build-out begins. Responsible party: Jake. Resolution date: Pending

Section 2: Scheduled and Actual Completion Dates

- *Sign lease*: Scheduled: 8/21. Completed: 8/21

- *Gomez contract signed*: Scheduled: 9/12. Completed: 9/12

- *Ethernet cable run*: Scheduled: 9/18. Completed: 9/19

- *Build-out started*: Scheduled: 9/20. Completed: In progress

Section 3: Activity That Occurred in the Project This Week

The Ethernet cable run was completed without a problem.

Section 4: Progress Expected This Reporting Period Not Completed

None. Project is on track to date.

Section 5: Progress Expected Next Reporting Period

Build-out will continue. Jake reports that Gomez expects to have electrical lines run and drywall started prior to the end of the next reporting period.

Ricardo should have a T1 update. There's a slim possibility that the T1 connection will have occurred by next reporting period.

Section 6: Issues

We had to start the build-out on the last day of the cable run (this is called *fast tracking*) to keep the project on schedule. Jake and Ricardo reported only minor problems with this arrangement in that the contractors got into each other's way a time or two. This did not impact the completion of the cable run because most of day two this team was in the back room and Gomez's crew was in the storefront area.

A key member of the Gomez construction crew was out last week because of a family emergency. Gomez assures us that it will not impact the build-out schedule. They replaced the team member with someone from another project, so it appears so far that the build-out is on schedule.

Ricardo is somewhat concerned about the T1 connection because the phone company won't return his calls inquiring about status. We're still ahead of the curve on this one because hardware isn't scheduled to begin testing until January 21. Hardware testing depends on the T1 connection. This is a heads-up at this point, and we'll carry this as an issue in the status report going forward until it's resolved.

One of the gourmet food item suppliers Jill uses regularly went out of business. She is in the process of tracking down a new supplier to pick up the slack for the existing stores and supply the gourmet food products for the new store.

Status Meeting in Early December

"Thank you all for coming," you begin. You note those stakeholders who are present and pass out the agendas. "First, we have a contract update. Jake, would you give us the update, please?"

"Gomez Construction has submitted a seller payment request for the work completed through November 30. Shelly in our contract management office manages the payment system and handles all payment requests. She'll get a check cut and out to Gomez by the end of this month. They are doing an outstanding job as always. As you know, I've also hired an independent inspector, aside from the city and county types, so that we make sure we're up to code before the city types get there. I don't want to get caught in that trap and end up delaying the project because we can't get the city inspector back out to reinspect quickly enough."

"Thank you, Jake. Any problems with those inspections so far?"

Jake clears his throat. "It turned out to be a good move because the contractor did find some things that we were able to correct before bringing out the official inspectors."

"Ricardo, do you have a contract update for us today?"

"Yes. The contract management office used a fixed-price contract on the hardware and IT supplies order. That contract is just now making its way through the sign-off processes. My group will manage the quality control and testing once all this equipment arrives."

"Jill, can you give us the update on the store?" you ask.

"I've ordered all the retail products, have ordered the cookware line, and have lined up the chef demos. The costs for the new gourmet supplier we're using are higher than our original vendor. This impacts ongoing operations, but the hit to the project budget is minimal. I should also mention that a change request was submitted."

You point everyone's attention to the issues list. "In the last meeting I reported that Gomez had an important crew member out on a family emergency. Gomez was able to replace the team member with no impact to the schedule. The next issue was the T1 connection—I reported that Ricardo was not receiving return phone calls. Good news— that issue has been cleared, the date has been set, and we can close this issue. Are there any new issues to be added this week?"

No additional issues were reported.

"What's the forecast?" Dirk asks. "Are we on track for meeting the grand opening date given all these issues?"

"I'll have performance figures for you at the next status meeting, and I have some ideas on how we can make up this time in other ways so that we still meet the date."

You thank everyone for coming and remind them of the next meeting time.

Project Case Study Checklist

- Conduct Procurements
    - Procurement negotiations
    - Agreements
- Perform Quality Assurance
    - Quality audits
    - Making certain the project will meet and satisfy the quality standards of the project
- Manage Communications
    - Project information is delivered to stakeholders in a timely manner.
    - The Manage Communications method is status reports via email and project meetings.
    - The status report is part of the project reports filed in the project notebook or filed for future reference as historical information.
- Manage Stakeholder Engagement
    - Communications methods
    - Issue log
    - Resolved issues

Understanding How This Applies to Your Next Project

This chapter is jammed with information you need to know for the exam as well as on the job. Depending on the size of your organization, many of the processes I discussed in the Executing process group might actually be handled by another department in your organization. I've worked in small companies (fewer than 100 people) as well as very large companies and have always had either a person or a department that was responsible for the vendor selection, contract negotiation, and contract administration. In all these situations and in my current role as project manager, I have significant input to these processes, but the person or department responsible for procurement has the ultimate control. For example, we use only RFPs (and occasionally RFIs) to solicit vendors. We typically use a weighted scoring model in combination with a screening and rating system to choose a vendor. For small projects, we have a list of prequalified vendors from which to choose.

Someone who is skilled at writing contracts can best handle the contracts, which ideally should be reviewed by the legal team. The legal team should also review changes proposed by the vendor before someone signs on the dotted line. Clear, concise, and specific contracts, in my experience, are critical success factors for any project. I've too often seen contract issues bring a project to a sudden halt. Another classic contract faux pas allows the vendor to think the work is complete while the buyer believes the vendor is weeks or months away from meeting the requirements. These types of disputes can almost always be traced back to an unclear, imprecise contract. It's important to be specific in your statement of work. Make sure that the project requirements are clear and broken down far enough to be measurable and that deliverables are defined with criteria that allow you to inspect for contract compliance prior to final acceptance.

I'll emphasize one last time the importance of communication, good communication skills, and getting that information into the appropriate hands at the right time. Enough said.

Engaging your stakeholders on the project and managing their expectations is as important as managing the project team. Stakeholders need plenty of communication, and issues need to be discussed and resolutions agreed on. Remember the old adage that most people need to hear the same information six times before it registers with them. Stakeholders, understandably, are notorious for hearing what they want to hear. Here's an example: If I asked you to picture an elephant, you would likely picture an elephant in your mind. It might be live or the stuffed variety and it could be gray, brown, or pink, but you'd clearly understand the concept. *Elephant* is a word that's pretty hard to misinterpret. But what if I asked you to picture a three-bedroom house? There's lots of room for interpretation there. When I said *three-bedroom house*, I meant ranch style with the master on one end of the house and the other two bedrooms at the other end of the house. What did you picture? Make certain you're using language your stakeholders understand, and repeat it often until you're certain they get it.

Summary

This chapter finished up the Executing process group. We looked at Conduct Procurements, Perform Quality Assurance, Manage Communications, and Manage Stakeholder Engagement.

Conduct Procurements involves obtaining responses to bids and proposals from potential vendors, selecting a vendor, and awarding the contract. In this process, the selection committee will use proposal evaluation techniques to prioritize the bids and proposals, and the outcome is that a seller (or sellers) is selected and contracts awarded.

Contracts have cycles of their own, much like projects. Phases of the contracting life cycle include requirement, requisition, solicitation, and award. Changes to the contract are managed with change requests.

Changes that cannot be agreed on are contested changes. These take the form of disputes, claims, or appeals. They might be settled among the parties directly, through a court of law, or through arbitration.

During the Perform Quality Assurance process, quality audits are performed to ensure that the project will meet and satisfy the project's quality standards set out in the quality management plan.

The Manage Communications process is concerned with making sure project information is available to stakeholders at the right time and in the appropriate format. This process is performed throughout the life of the project.

The Manage Stakeholder Engagement process involves making certain communication needs and expectations of the stakeholders are met, managing any issues stakeholders might raise that could become future issues, and resolving previously identified issues.

Exam Essentials

Be able to describe the purpose of the Conduct Procurements process.   Conduct Procurements involves obtaining bids and proposals from vendors, selecting a vendor, and awarding a contract.

Be able to name the tools and techniques of the Conduct Procurements process.   The tools and techniques of the Conduct Procurements process are bidder conferences, proposal evaluation techniques, independent estimates, expert judgment, advertising, analytical techniques, and procurement negotiations.

Be able to name the contracting life cycle stages.   Contracting life cycles include requirement, requisition, solicitation, and award stages.

Be able to describe the purpose of the Perform Quality Assurance process.   The Perform Quality Assurance process is concerned with making certain the project will meet and satisfy the quality standards of the project.

Be able to differentiate between senders and receivers of information.   Senders are responsible for clear, concise, complete messages, whereas receivers are responsible for understanding the message correctly.

Be able to describe the purpose of the Manage Stakeholder Engagement process.   Manage Stakeholder Engagement involves satisfying the needs of the stakeholders and successfully meeting the goals of the project by managing communications with stakeholders, resolving issues, engaging them on the project, managing their expectations, improving project performance by implementing requested changes, and managing concerns in anticipation of potential problems.

Key Terms

I've discussed the processes you'll use while measuring and evaluating project performance. You need to understand each of these processes to effectively evaluate progress, recognize variances from the plan, and make adjustments to keep the project on track. Know them by the names used in the *PMBOK® Guide* so you'll recognize them on the exam.

Conduct Procurements

Manage Stakeholder Engagement

Manage Communications

Perform Quality Assurance

You learned a lot of new key words in this chapter as well. PMI® has worked hard to develop and define terms that apply across industries. Here is a list of some of the terms you came across in this chapter:

advertising	project presentations
bidder conferences	project records
communication	project reports
fait accompli	qualified sellers list
independent estimates	quality audits
information management systems	screening systems
lessons learned	seller rating systems
process analysis	should cost estimates
procurement negotiation	

Review Questions

You can find the answers to the questions in Appendix A.

1. You have been hired as a contract project manager for Grapevine Vineyards. Grapevine wants you to design an Internet wine club for its customers. Customers must register before being allowed to order wine over the Internet so that legal age can be established. You know that the module to verify registration must be written and tested using data from Grapevine's existing database. This new module cannot be tested until the data from the existing system is loaded. You are going to hire a vendor to perform the programming and testing tasks for this module to help speed up the project schedule. You decide to use an IFB and include a detailed SOW. This is an example of which of the following?

   A. Source selection criteria

   B. Seller proposals

   C. Advertising

   D. Procurement documents

2. Receivers in the communication model filter their information through all of the following, except:

   A. Culture

   B. Knowledge of subject

   C. Habits

   D. Language

3. You have accumulated project information throughout the project and need to distribute some important information you just received. Which of the following is not an information distribution tool?

   A. Project reports

   B. Electronic databases

   C. Electronic mail

   D. Manual filing system

4. You know that the next status meeting will require some discussion and a decision for a problem that has surfaced on the project. To make the most accurate decision, you know that the number of participants in the meeting should be limited to:

   A. 1 to 5

   B. 5 to 11

   C. 7 to 16

   D. 10 to 18

5. You are holding end-of-phase meetings with your team members and key stakeholders to learn what has hindered and helped the project team's performance of the work. All of the following are true regarding this situation except for which one?

   A. These meetings are called lessons learned meetings. Lessons learned documentation is part of the organizational process assets output of the Manage Communications process. These meetings are also a good team-building activity.

   B. The information learned from these meetings concerns processes and activities that have already occurred, so it will be most useful to document the lessons learned and use it for future projects.

   C. The project-reports component of the organizational process assets updates output includes status meetings and lessons learned.

   D. These meetings should be documented and should always include the cause of the issue, the reasons for corrective actions, and other appropriate information about the issues.

6. You are a project manager for Dakota Software Consulting Services. You're working with a major retailer that offers its products through mail-order catalogs. The company is interested in knowing customer characteristics, the amounts of first-time orders, and similar information. As a potential bidder for this project, you worked on the RFP response and submitted the proposal. When the selection committee received the RFP responses from all the vendors bidding on this project, they used a weighted system to make a selection. Which tool and technique is this a part of?

   A. A proposal evaluation technique in the Conduct Procurements process

   B. A seller proposal technique in the Conduct Procurements process

   C. A make-or-buy decision technique in the Conduct Procurements process

   D. A procurement negotiations technique in the Conduct Procurements process

7. You have been asked to submit a proposal for a project that has been put out for bid. First you attend the bidder conference to ask questions of the buyers and to hear the questions some of the other bidders will ask. Which of the following statements is not true?

   A. Bidder conferences are also known as contractor conferences.

   B. Bidder conferences also known as vendor conferences.

   C. Bidder conferences are also known as prebid conferences.

   D. Bidder conferences are also known as procurement conferences.

8. You have been asked to submit a proposal for a project that has been put out for bid. Prior to submitting the proposal, your company must register so that its firm is on the qualified seller list. Which of the following statements is true?

   A. The qualified seller list provides information about the sellers and is a tool and technique of the Conduct Procurements process.

   B. The qualified seller list provides information about the project and the company that wrote the RFP and is an output of the Conduct Procurements process.

    C. The qualified seller list provides information about the project and the company that wrote the RFP and is a component of the procurement documents input of the Conduct Procurements process.

    D. The qualified seller list provides information about the sellers and is a component of the organizational assets input to Conduct Procurements.

9. Which of the following tools and techniques of the Conduct Procurements process is used to check and compare proposed pricing to the benchmark?

    A. Expert judgment

    B. Seller rating systems

    C. Independent estimates

    D. Proposal evaluation technique

10. During the opening rounds of contract negotiation, the other party uses a fait accompli tactic. Which of the following statements is true about fait accompli tactics?

    A. One party agrees to accept the offer of the other party but secretly knows they will bring the issue back up at a later time.

    B. One party claims the issue was documented and accepted in the issue log but they're willing to reopen it for discussion.

    C. One party claims the issue under discussion has already been decided and can't be changed.

    D. One party claims to accept the offer of the other party, provided a contract change request is submitted describing the offer in detail.

11. The tools and techniques of the Conduct Procurements process include all of the following except which one?

    A. Bidder conferences

    B. Market research

    C. Advertising

    D. Analytical techniques

12. The purpose of a quality audit includes all of the following except which one?

    A. To determine which project processes or activities are inefficient or ineffective

    B. To examine the work of the project, or the results of a process, and accept the work results

    C. To improve processes and reduce the cost of quality

    D. To improve processes and increase the percentage of product or service acceptance

13. You are a contract project manager for a wholesale flower distribution company. Your project involves developing a website for the company that allows retailers to place their flower orders online. You will also provide a separate link for individual purchases that are ordered, packaged, and mailed to the consumer directly from the grower's site. This project involves coordinating the parent company, growers, and distributors. You've discovered a problem with one of the technical processes needed to perform this project. You decide to perform root cause analysis to determine the cause of this problem and recommended preventive actions. Which of the following is true?

   A. You are using the process analysis technique.

   B. You are using the quality audit technique.

   C. You are using the root cause identification technique.

   D. You are using a design of experiments tool and technique.

14. You are using the Quality Management and Control Tools tool and technique of the Perform Quality Assurance process that will help you establish expected values for the dependent relationships in the hierarchy. Which tool within this tool and technique are you using?

   A. Affinity diagrams

   B. PDPC

   C. Tree diagrams

   D. Interrelationship digraphs

15. You are working on a project and discover that one of the business users responsible for testing the product never completed this activity. She has written an email requesting that one of your team members drop everything to assist her with a problem that could have been avoided if she had performed the test. This employee reports to a stakeholder, not to the project team. All project team members and stakeholders are co-located. Because your team also needs her to participate in an upcoming test, you decide to do which of the following?

   A. You decide to record the issue in the issue log and bring it up at the next status meeting. Everyone can benefit from understanding the importance of stakeholders fulfilling their roles and responsibilities on the project.

   B. You decide to record the issue in the issue log and then phone the stakeholder to explain what happened. You know speaking with the stakeholder directly is the most effective means for resolving issues.

   C. You decide to have a face-to-face meeting with the stakeholder because this is the most effective means for resolving issues with them.

   D. You decide to email the stakeholder and explain what happened in a professional manner so you can incorporate their response in the next status report.

16. Your project is progressing as planned. The project team has come up with a demo that the sales team will use when making presentations to prospective clients. You will do which of the following at your next stakeholder project status meeting?

  A. Preview the demo for stakeholders, and obtain their approval and sign-off.

  B. Report on the progress of the demo, and note that it's a completed task.

  C. Review the technical documentation of the demo, and obtain approval and sign-off.

  D. Report that the demo has been noted as a completed task in the project information system.

17. Negotiated draft contracts that will be used as the final contract are a requirement of which of the following outputs of the Conduct Procurements process?

  A. Agreements

  B. Project document updates

  C. Procurement statement of work

  D. Selected sellers

18. According to the *PMBOK® Guide*, this party is responsible for managing stakeholder expectations.

  A. Project manager, because actively managing stakeholder expectations will reduce project risk and help unresolved issues get resolved quickly.

  B. Project sponsor, because the overall success or failure of the project rests on this individual.

  C. All stakeholders have the responsibility to make sure their expectations are managed and they receive the proper information at the right time.

  D. Project manager and the project team members together have the responsibility because the project manager alone cannot manage all the stakeholders on a large, complex project.

19. This activity can become its own process with inputs and outputs on large or complex projects.

  A. Independent estimates

  B. Procurement negotiations

  C. Procurement agreements

  D. Proposal evaluations

20. Which of the following statements is false regarding contract life cycles?

    A. The requirement phase is the first contract life cycle phase and is performed during the Plan Procurement Management process. The buyer prepares the SOW during this phase.

    B. The award phase is the fourth contract life cycle phase and is performed during the Conduct Procurements process. The buyer awards the contract in this phase.

    C. The solicitation phase is the third contract life cycle phase and is performed during the Conduct Procurements process. This phase receives the bids and proposals and applies evaluation criteria to each in order to score or rank the responses.

    D. The requisition phase is the second contract life cycle phase and is performed during the Plan Procurement Management process. The buyer prepares the RFP during this phase.

Chapter 10

Measuring and Controlling Project Performance

THE PMP® EXAM CONTENT
FROM THE EXECUTING THE PROJECT,
AND THE MONITORING AND
CONTROLLING THE PROJECT
PERFORMANCE DOMAIN COVERED
IN THIS CHAPTER INCLUDES
THE FOLLOWING:

✓ Measure project performance using appropriate tools and techniques in order to identify and quantify any variances, perform approved corrective actions, and communicate with relevant stakeholders.

✓ Manage changes to the project scope, schedule, and costs by updating the project plan and communicating approved changes to the team in order to ensure that revised project goals are met.

✓ Implement approved changes according to the change management plan, in order to meet project requirements.

✓ Assess corrective actions on the issue register and determine next steps for unresolved issues by using appropriate tools and techniques in order to minimize the impact on project schedule, cost, and resources.

✓ Control stakeholder engagement by managing expectations, informing stakeholders of project issues, and obtaining feedback.

✓ **Knowledge and Skills:**

- Performance measurement and tracking techniques (for example, EV, CPM, and PERT)

- Project control limits (for example, thresholds and tolerance)

- Project performance metrics (for example, efforts, costs, and milestones)

- Variance and trend analysis techniques

- Project plan management techniques

- Change management techniques

- Integrated change control processes

This chapter introduces the Monitoring and Controlling process group. The Monitoring and Controlling process group involves taking measurements and performing inspections to find out whether there are variances in the plan. If you discover variances, you need to take corrective action to get the project back on track and repeat the affected project Planning processes to make adjustments to the plan as a result of resolving the variances.

We'll start with the Monitor and Control Project Work process. This process involves tracking, reviewing, adjusting, and controlling progress to meet the project performance objectives. We'll also look at Control Procurements, Control Communications, Perform Integrated Change Control, and Control Stakeholder Engagement.

Control Procurements is where contract performance is monitored, procurement relationships are managed, and corrections or changes are implemented where needed.

Work performance information is an output of the Control Communications process and this output is used and maintained during the Monitoring and Controlling processes, along with tools and techniques, to monitor and control project communication throughout the life of the project. This information allows the project manager to take corrective action during the Monitoring and Controlling processes and to remedy wayward project results and realign future project results with the project management plan.

Perform Integrated Change Control lays the foundation for all the control processes—such as Control Risks, Control Costs, and Control Schedule—that we'll talk about in Chapter 11, "Controlling Work Results." During this discussion, I'll take time to explain how change control and configuration management works. When you read these sections, remember that the information from the Perform Integrated Change Control process applies to all the control processes we'll talk about in Chapter 11.

Control Stakeholder Engagement is about continuing your relationship with the stakeholders and maintaining their engagement on the project. Stakeholders sometimes lose interest once you get into the later stages of the project, and you don't want that to happen. You've learned a lot about project management by this point and have just a few more topics to add to your study list. Keep up the good work. You're getting closer to exam day.

The process names, inputs, tools and techniques, outputs, and descriptions of the project management process groups and related materials and figures in this chapter are based on content from *A Guide to the Project Management Body of Knowledge (PMBOK® Guide), Fifth Edition* (Sybex, 2010).

Monitoring and Controlling Project Work

The processes in the Monitoring and Controlling process group concentrate on monitoring and measuring project performance at regular intervals to identify variances from the project management plan and get it back on track.

The *Monitor and Control Project Work* process is concerned with monitoring all the processes in the Initiating, Planning, Executing, and Closing process groups. Collecting data, measuring results, comparing results to what was planned, and reporting on performance information are some of the activities you'll perform during this process. Many key outputs from other Monitoring and Controlling processes are inputs to this process.

According to the *PMBOK® Guide*, the Monitor and Control Project Work process involves the following:

- Reporting and comparing actual project results against the project management plan

- Analyzing performance data and determining whether corrective or preventive action should be recommended

- Monitoring the project for risks to make certain they're identified and reported, their status is documented, and the appropriate risk response plans have been put into action

- Documenting all appropriate product information throughout the life of the project

- Gathering, recording, and documenting project information that provides project status, measurements of progress, and forecasting to update cost and schedule information that is reported to stakeholders, project team members, management, and others

- Monitoring approved change requests

Keep in mind that the *PMBOK® Guide* presents information according to Knowledge Areas. In this chapter, for example, the Monitor and Control Project Work process is presented first because it is the first process in the Project Integration Management Knowledge Area that discusses a Monitoring and Controlling process. Monitor and Control Project Work is a process that encompasses all aspects of monitoring and controlling the work of the project. Unfortunately, we can't cover every process that this process refers to in the same chapter. (For example, outputs from the Control Costs process are inputs to this process.) I have attempted to arrange these processes in the most logical format possible so an all-encompassing process will be presented first, followed by other processes within this group. Rest assured we will cover everything this process touches either in this chapter or Chapter 11.

Monitor and Control Project Work Inputs

The inputs of this process include the project management plan, schedule forecasts, cost forecasts, validated changes, work performance information, enterprise environmental factors, and organizational process assets. We will look at each of these next.

Project Management Plan

The Monitor and Control Project Work process is broad reaching and is concerned with all of the work of the project rather than a specific area like schedule or cost or human resources. To monitor and control the work, you'll need the project management plan, which includes all of the subsidiary plans we've talked about so far, so that you know what was planned and can take action where needed to get the project back in line with the plan. As a reminder, some of those subsidiary plans include the scope management plan, the cost management plan, the human resource plan, the communications plan, and more. And don't forget the important baselines: scope, schedule, and cost.

Schedule Forecasts

Schedule forecasts are an output of the Control Schedule process. Schedule forecasts help determine the progress of the project schedule as it compares to the schedule baseline. This can involve a series of formulas to determine elements such as when a milestone was scheduled to be completed versus when it was actually completed. We will look at all of the formulas in the next chapter when we talk about controlling the project schedule.

Cost Forecasts

Cost forecasts are an output of the Control Costs process. Much like the schedule forecasts, cost forecasts help us determine project progress as far as costs are concerned. This includes formulas to determine factors such as what we anticipated spending at this point in time versus what was actually spent. These formulas are known as earned value management formulas, and we will look at them as well as the cost forecasts formulas in the next chapter when we talk about controlling project costs.

Forecasting involves examining the project performance data to date and making predictions about future project performance based on this data. According to the *PMBOK® Guide*, cost forecasts are determined using earned value management formulas such as estimate to complete and estimate at completion. Forecasting can also include methods such as time series, scenario building, and simulation. These forecasting methods fall into four different categories, and each category has several types of forecasting methods. We'll look at a brief description of each of the categories next, but it is beyond the scope of this book to go into detail on each one. Keep in mind these are not discussed in the *PMBOK® Guide,* but they are methods you should know as you may see them in practice.

Time Series Methods   These forecasting methods use historical data to predict future performance. Earned value, moving average, extrapolation, trend estimation, linear prediction, and growth curve are some of the methods that fall into this category. We'll cover earned value in Chapter 11.

Causal/Econometric Methods   Causal methods are based on the ability to identify variables that may cause or influence the forecast. A drop in interest rates, for example, may spur an increase in home sales. The methods included in this category are regression analysis, autoregressive moving average (ARMA), and econometrics.

Judgmental Methods   If your mom is anything like mine, you were taught not to be judgmental. This category of forecasting does just that, only it doesn't judge people. It uses opinions, intuitive judgments, and probability estimates to determine possible future results. Methods within this category include composite forecasts, the Delphi method, surveys, technology forecasting, scenario building, and forecast by analogy.

Other Methods   Other types of forecasting methods include simulation (like Monte Carlo analysis), probabilistic forecasting, and ensemble forecasting.

Validated Changes

Validated changes are an output of the Control Quality process. Validated changes are those changes that have been inspected and determined to be correct.

Work Performance Information

Work performance information concerns gathering and analyzing the performance data, or work results, from the Monitoring and Controlling processes. This might include performance information such as the status of deliverables, schedule forecast data, cost forecast data, the status of change requests, costs incurred to date, and more. Work performance information is reported to the stakeholders according to the requirements laid out in the communications management plan and the stakeholder management plan.

Enterprise Environmental Factors

Some of the enterprise environmental factors to consider in this process include the project management information system, government or industry standards, the risk tolerance levels of your stakeholders, and work authorization systems.

A *work authorization system* is a subsystem of the project management system. This is a formal, documented procedure that describes how to authorize work and how to begin that work in the correct sequence and at the right time. This system describes the steps needed to issue a work authorization, the documents needed, the method or system you'll use to record and track the authorization information, and the approval levels required to authorize the work. You should understand the complexity of the project and balance the cost of instituting a work authorization system against the benefit you'll receive from it. This might be overkill on small projects, and verbal instructions might work just as well. For purposes of the exam, understand that project work is assigned and committed via a work authorization system.

Work is usually authorized using a form that describes the task, the responsible party, anticipated start and end dates, special instructions, and whatever else is particular to the activity or project. Depending on the organizational structure, the work is generally assigned and authorized by either the project manager or the functional manager. Remember that the system includes documentation on who has the authority to issue work authorization orders.

The *PMBOK® Guide* glossary lists work authorization systems as a subsystem of the overall project management system, but it's noted as part of the enterprise environmental factors input in the Monitor and Control Project Work process. For the exam, I recommend that you understand what a work authorization system is and how you use it. For the record, you'll use these systems during the Executing processes.

Organizational Process Assets

The organizational process assets that the *PMBOK® Guide* notes should be considered during this process include financial controls, the communication needs for the organization, change control processes, issue management, process measurements, risk control processes, and lessons learned.

There are four tools and techniques of this process: expert judgment, analytical techniques, project management information system, and meetings, all of which we've covered previously, so we'll move right to the outputs next.

Monitor and Control Project Work Outputs

The outputs of the Monitor and Control Project Work process will also look familiar. They are as follows:

- Change requests
- Work performance reports
- Project management plan updates
- Project documents updates

Change Requests

Remember from Chapter 9, "Conducting Procurements and Sharing Information," that change requests may take the form of corrective actions, preventive actions, or defect repairs. Corrective actions bring the work of the project into alignment with expected future performance. Preventive actions are implemented to help reduce the probability of negative project risks. Defect repairs either correct or replace components that are substandard or malfunctioning.

Work Performance Reports

Work performance reports are the primary output of this process. It's here that the work performance data and work performance information gathered and analyzed throughout the Monitoring and Controlling processes are documented and reported to the stakeholders as outlined in the communications management plan. Work performance reports might take many forms, including status reports, issues or action item logs, project documents, and so on. They may be represented in hardcopy form or electronic form or both.

Work performance reports may range from simply stated status reports to highly detailed reports. Dashboards are an example of a simple report that may use indicators like red-yellow-green to show the status of each area of the project at a glance. Red means the item being reported is in trouble or behind schedule, yellow means it's in danger and corrective action should be taken, and green means all is well.

Exam Spotlight

According to the *PMBOK® Guide*, the work performance reports produced as a result of this process are used by the project management team and stakeholders to create awareness of issues, make decisions about those issues, and determine actions to take to resolve the issues. They are a subset of project documents.

More detailed reports may include the following elements according to the *PMBOK® Guide*:

- Analysis of project performance for previous periods
- Risk and issue status
- Work completed in the current reporting period
- Work expected to be completed during the next reporting period
- Changes approved in the current reporting period (or a summary if there are numerous changes)
- Results of variance analysis
- Time completion forecasts and cost forecasts
- Other information stakeholders want or need to know

The information contained in these reports is used at status meetings or in meetings with the project sponsor to generate action, make decisions, or to inform. This information should be in written format (such as a status report or memo) and stored electronically with other project documents. Work performance reports are considered a subset of project documents and should be shared and distributed according to your communications plan.

Project Management Plan and Document Updates

Project management plan updates may include updates to one or more of the management plans, including schedule, cost, or quality, and may require updates to the baselines, including scope, schedule, and cost.

Project documents updates may include updates to forecasts, performance reports, and the issue log.

Controlling Procurements

We'll now take another look at the procurement arena. You learned about Conduct Procurements in Chapter 9. Now that the contract has been awarded, you need to administer it.

The *Control Procurements* process involves monitoring the vendor's performance and ensuring that all the requirements of the procurement agreement (this is usually a contract) are met. When multiple vendors are providing goods and services to the project, Control Procurements entails coordinating the interfaces among all the vendors as well as administering each of the contracts or procurement agreements. If vendor A has a due date that will impact whether vendor B can perform their service, the management and coordination of the two vendors become important. Vendor A's contract and due dates must be monitored closely because failure to perform could affect another vendor's ability to perform, not to mention the project schedule. You can see how this situation could multiply quickly when you have six or seven or more vendors involved.

It's imperative that the project manager and project team are aware of any contract agreements that might impact the project so the team does not inadvertently take action that violates the terms of the contract.

Depending on the size of the organization, administering the contract or other procurement agreement might fall to someone in the procurement department. This doesn't mean you're off the hook as the project manager. It's still your responsibility to oversee the process and make sure the project objectives are being met, regardless of whether a vendor is performing the activities or your project team members are performing the activities. You'll be the one monitoring the performance of the vendor and informing them when and if performance is lacking. You'll also monitor the procurement agreement's financial conditions. For example, the seller should be paid in a timely manner when they've satisfactorily met the conditions of the agreement, and it will be up to you to let the procurement department know it's okay to pay the vendor. If administering the contract or procurement agreement is your responsibility, you might have to terminate the contract when the vendor violates the terms or doesn't meet the agreed-on deliverables. If the procurement department has this responsibility, you'll have to document the situation and provide this to the procurement department so that they can enforce or terminate the contract.

Control Procurements is closely linked with project management processes. You'll manage vendor relationships, monitor the progress of the contract, execute plans, track costs, measure outputs, approve changes, take corrective action, and report on status, just as you do for the project itself. According to the *PMBOK® Guide*, you must integrate and coordinate the Direct and Manage Project Work, Control Quality, Perform Integrated Change Control, and Control Risks processes during the Control Procurements process. I would personally add another one to this list: Control Communications.

Exam Spotlight

Buyers and sellers are equally responsible for monitoring the contract. Each has a vested interest in ensuring that the other party is living up to their contractual obligations and that their own legal rights are protected.

Controlling Procurements Inputs

Control Procurements has six inputs:

- Project management plan
- Procurement documents
- Agreements
- Approved change requests
- Work performance reports
- Work performance data

The project management plan, procurement documents, agreements, approved change requests, work performance reports, and work performance data are outputs from other processes. We'll look at approved change requests and some additional content for work performance reports as it pertains to this process next.

Approved Change Requests

Sometimes as you get into the work of the project, you'll discover that changes need to be made. This could entail changes to the contract as well. Approved change requests are used to process the project or contract changes and might include things such as modifications to deliverables, changes to the product or service of the project, changes in contract terms, or termination for poor performance.

Generally speaking, contracts end for three reasons: cause, convenience, or default. When a contract ends for cause, it's because one of the parties has violated the terms of the contract. A contract ends for convenience when one of the parties determines they no longer wish to participate in the contract. And contracts that end by default are those where one of the parties has failed to perform according to the terms of the contract.

Contracts can be amended at any time prior to contract completion, provided the changes are agreed to by all parties and conform to the change control processes outlined in the contract.

Exam Spotlight

Work performance data is an output of the Direct and Manage Project Work process. The results you gather in the Control Procurements process are actually collected as part of the Direct and Manage Project Work process output.

Work Performance Reports

Work performance reports include technical documentation that is developed by the seller according to the terms of the contract, as well as work performance information as it relates to the seller (or vendor).

Work performance information in the Control Procurements process concerns monitoring vendor work results and examining the vendor's deliverables. This includes monitoring their work results against the contract statement of work and making sure activities are performed correctly and in sequence. You'll need to determine which deliverables are complete and which ones have not been completed to date. You'll also need to consider the quality of the deliverables and the costs that have been incurred to date.

Vendors request payment for the goods or services delivered in the form of seller invoices. *Seller invoices* should describe the work that was completed or the materials that were delivered and should include any supporting documentation necessary to describe what was delivered. The contract should state what type of supporting documentation is needed with the invoice.

Controlling Procurements Tools and Techniques

The Control Procurements process has several tools and techniques:

- Contract change control system
- Procurement performance reviews
- Inspections and audits
- Performance reporting
- Payment systems
- Claims administration
- Records management system

You will look at each of these in the following sections.

Contract Change Control System

Much like the management plans found in the Planning processes, the *contract change control system* describes the processes needed to make contract changes. Because the contract is a legal document, changes to it require the agreement of all parties. A formal process must be established to process and authorize (or deny) changes. (Authorization levels are defined in the organizational policies.)

The purpose of the contract change control system is to establish a formal process for submitting change requests. It documents how to submit changes, establishes the approval process, and outlines authority levels. It includes a tracking system to number the change requests and record their status. The procedures for dispute resolution are spelled out in the contract change control system as well.

The change control system, along with all the management plan outputs, becomes part of the Perform Integrated Change Control process that I'll discuss later in this chapter.

Procurement Performance Reviews

Procurement performance reviews examine the seller's performance on the contract to date. These reviews can be conducted at the end of the contract or at intervals during the contract period. Procurement reviews examine the contract terms and seller performance for elements such as these:

- Meeting project scope
- Meeting project quality
- Staying within project budgets
- Meeting the project schedule

The performance reviews themselves might take the form of quality audits, inspections of documents as well as the work of the product itself, or as part of a status review. The point of the review is to determine where the seller is succeeding at meeting scope, quality, cost, and schedule issues, for example, or where they're not measuring up. If the seller is not in compliance, action must be taken to either get them back into compliance or terminate the contract. The yardstick you're using to measure their performance against is the contract SOW and the terms of the contract. When the RFP is included as part of the contract, you might also use it to determine contract compliance.

Inspections and Audits

I talked about quality audits as part of the Perform Quality Assurance process. The idea is the same here. The buyer, or some designated third party, will physically inspect the work of the seller and perform audits to determine whether there are any deficiencies in the seller's product or service.

Performance Reporting

Performance reporting is a large part of project management. This tool and technique entails providing your managers and stakeholders with information about the vendor's progress in meeting the contract objectives.

Payment Systems

Vendors submit seller invoices as an input to this process, and the *payment systems* tool and technique is used to issue payments. The organization might have a dedicated department, such as accounts payable, that handles vendor payments, or it might fall to the project manager. In either case, follow the policies and procedures the organization has established regarding vendor payments and make sure the payments themselves adhere to the contract terms.

Claims Administration

Claims administration involves documenting, monitoring, and managing contested changes to the contract. Changes that cannot be agreed on are called *contested changes*. Contested changes usually involve a disagreement about the compensation to the vendor for implementing the change. You might believe the change is not significant enough to justify additional compensation, whereas the vendor believes they'll lose money by implementing the change free of charge. Contested changes are also known as *disputes*, *claims*, or *appeals*. These can be settled directly between the parties themselves, through the court system, or by a process called arbitration. *Arbitration* involves bringing all parties to the table with a third, disinterested party who is not a participant in the contract to try to reach an agreement. The purpose of arbitration is to reach an agreement without having to go to court.

Exam Spotlight

According to the *PMBOK® Guide*, when the parties cannot reach an agreement themselves, they should use an alternative dispute resolution (ADR) process, like arbitration. Also note that the preferred method of settling disputes is negotiation.

Records Management System

It has been a while since I've talked about documentation, but discussing the *records management system* reminds me of the importance of having an organized system for contract documentation. A records management system involves not just documentation, but policies, control functions, and automated tools. These can all be considered part of the project management information system you use to manage project documents and should include your contract documents. Records management systems typically index documents for easy filing and retrieval.

Managing Control Procurements Outputs

The outputs to the Control Procurements process are as follows:

- Work performance information
- Change requests

- Project management plan updates
- Project documents updates
- Organizational process assets updates

These outputs relate to the tools and techniques just talked about and, in practice, work hand in hand with them. I've talked about work performance information and project management plan updates before, and I don't have anything new to add here. The remaining outputs have some additional information you need to know.

Change Requests

Requested contract changes are coordinated with the Direct and Manage Project Work and Perform Integrated Change Control processes so that any changes impacting the project are communicated to the project team and appropriate actions are put into place to realign the objectives. This might also mean you'll have to change the project management plan, the cost baseline, and/or the schedule baseline. That requires you to jump back to the Planning process group to bring the project management plan, or other documents, up-to-date. Once the plan is updated, the Direct and Manage Project Work process might require changes as well to get the work of the project in line with the new plan. Remember that project management is an iterative process, and it's not unusual to revisit the Planning or Executing processes, particularly as changes are made or corrective actions are put into place.

Contract changes will not always impact the project management plan, however. For example, late delivery of key equipment probably would impact the project management plan, but changes in the vendor payment schedule probably would not. It's important that you are kept abreast of any changes to the contract so that you can evaluate whether the project management plan needs adjusting.

Project Documents Updates

Here's your favorite topic again. This output includes (but isn't limited to) updating all of the following:

- Contract or other procurement documents
- Performance information
- Warranties
- Financial information (such as invoices and payment records)
- Inspection and audit results
- Supporting schedules
- Approved and unapproved changes

The records management system I talked about earlier is the perfect place to keep all these documents.

Organizational Process Assets Updates

Organizational process assets updates consist of organizational policies, procedures, and so on. Three elements of this output relate to contracts:

Correspondence   Correspondence is information that needs to be communicated in writing to either the seller or the buyer. Examples include changes to the contract, clarification of contract terms, results of buyer audits and inspections, and notification of performance issues. You'll use correspondence to inform the vendor if their performance is unsatisfactory. If they don't correct it, you'll use correspondence again to notify a vendor that you're terminating the contract because performance is below expectations and is not satisfying the requirements of the contract.

Payment Schedules and Requests   Many times, contracts are written such that payment is made based on a predefined performance schedule. For example, perhaps the first payment is made after 25 percent of the product or service is completed, or maybe the payment schedule is based on milestone completion. In any case, as the project manager, you will verify that the vendor's work (or delivery) meets expectations before the payment is authorized. It's almost always your responsibility as the project manager to verify that the terms of the contract to date have or have not been satisfied. Depending on your organizational policies, someone from the accounting or procurement department might request written notification from you that the vendor has completed a milestone or made a delivery. Monitoring the work of the vendor is as important as monitoring the work of your team members.

If the procurement department is responsible for paying the contractor, then that department manages the payment schedule (which is one of the terms of the contract). The seller submits a payment request, an inspection or review of their performance is conducted to make certain the terms of the contract were fulfilled, and the payment is made.

Seller Performance Evaluation   Seller performance evaluation is a written record of the seller's performance on the contract and is prepared by the buyer. It should include information about whether the seller successfully met contract dates, whether the seller fulfilled the requirements of the contract and/or contract statement of work, whether the work was satisfactory, and so on. Seller performance evaluations can be used as a basis for terminating the existing contract if performance is not satisfactory. It can also be used to determine penalty fees in the case of unsatisfactory performance or incentives that are due according to the terms of the contract. They should also indicate whether the vendor should be allowed to bid on future work. Seller performance evaluations can also be included as part of the qualified sellers lists.

Exam Spotlight

I recommend remembering the inputs, tools and techniques, and outputs of the contracting processes, including Plan Procurement Management, Conduct Procurements, and Control Procurements. Be certain you understand the purposes of these processes and don't simply memorize their components. Here's a brief recap:

- Plan Procurement Management: Preparing the SOW and procurement documents and determining source selection criteria

- Conduct Procurements: Obtaining bids and proposals from potential vendors, evaluating proposals against predetermined evaluation criteria, selecting vendors, and awarding the contract

- Control Procurements: Monitoring vendor performance to ensure that contract requirements are met

Controlling Communications

As mentioned, the Monitoring and Controlling process group concentrates on monitoring and measuring project performance to identify variances from the project plan. *Control Communications* is the process that monitors and controls communications throughout the life of the project. Control Communications is part of the Project Communications Management Knowledge Area. You will recall that this Knowledge Area is concerned with collecting, distributing, storing, archiving, and organizing project communications. Therefore, it plays a key role in collecting information regarding project progress and project accomplishments and reporting it to the stakeholders. This information might also be reported to project team members, the management team, and other interested parties through the Monitor and Control Project Work process. Reporting might include information concerning project quality, costs, scope, project schedules, procurement, and risk, and it can be presented in the form of status reports, progress measurements, or forecasts. As with other processes in the Monitoring and Controlling process group, Control Communications may produce changes that will require a trip back through Plan Communications Management and/or the Manage Communications processes.

Exam Spotlight

According to the *PMBOK® Guide*, this process is concerned with evaluating and controlling the impact messages may carry and delivering the right message to the right people at the right time.

Control Communications Inputs

You've examined most of the inputs to the Control Communications process previously, but we'll reexamine all of them briefly with the exception of work performance data which we've covered in previous chapters. They are as follows:

- Project management plan
- Project communications
- Issue log
- Work performance data
- Organizational process assets

Project Management Plan   The project management plan contains the project management baseline data (typically cost, schedule, and scope factors), which you'll use to monitor and compare results. Deviations from this data are reported to management.

Project Communications   Project communications includes information such as status, progress on performance, cost and budget information, schedule progress, and more. This information is used to make project decisions and take action where needed.

Issue Log   The issue log documents issues, assigns owners, tracks due dates, and more. The issue log is useful in status meetings and in the Control Communications process as a way to determine what issues remain that are potentially blocking progress and what's been resolved. I have found that reviewing issue logs at every status meeting helps to maintain stakeholder expectations and also holds them accountable for actions they are required to take to resolve the issue.

Organizational Process Assets   Several organizational process assets come into play in this process, including reporting templates, communication policies or standards, communication technologies, security issues surrounding data, communicating methods and mediums, and records retention policies.

Control Communications Tools and Techniques

The following are tools and techniques of this process:

- Information management systems
- Expert judgment
- Meetings

Let's look at each of these next.

Information Management Systems

Information management systems are used to record, store, and distribute information about the project, including cost, schedule progress, and performance information. According to the *PMBOK® Guide*, spreadsheet analysis, presentations, table reporting, and graphic capabilities are types of distribution formats.

Expert Judgment

In this process, experts from all areas—including the project team, consultants, stakeholders, industry groups, the PMO, and others as appropriate—are consulted to help interpret the information gathered during the Monitoring and Controlling processes and make decisions and take action where needed to align the work of the project with the project management plan. One of the obvious reasons you want to keep the work results on track with the plan is so that stakeholder expectations are realized.

Meetings

Meetings in this process include meetings involving the project team, vendors, functional managers, stakeholders, and others you will be working with on the project. Meetings may be formal, informal, in person, or online. The important point here is that you are meeting with all those involved in your project and exchanging information. Meetings with the project team are concerned with updating project performance information and communicating those updates to the appropriate parties, and working with stakeholders to provide them with requested project information.

One of the important meetings you will conduct throughout the life of the project is the *status review meeting*. Status meetings are a type of interactive communication and are important functions during the course of the project. The purpose of the status meeting is to provide updated information regarding the progress of the project. These are not show-and-tell meetings. If you have a prototype to demo, set up a different time to do that. Status meetings are meant to exchange information and provide project updates. They are a way to formally exchange project information. It's not unusual for projects to have three or four status meetings conducted for different audiences. They can occur between the project team and project manager, between the project manager and stakeholders, between the project manager and users or customers, between the project manager and the management team, and so on.

Notice that the project manager is always included in status review meetings. Take care that you don't overburden yourself with meetings that aren't necessary or meetings that could be combined with other meetings. Having any more than three or four status meetings per month is unwieldy.

Regular, timely status meetings prevent surprises down the road because you are keeping stakeholders and customers informed of what's happening. Team status meetings alert the project manager to potential risk events and provide the opportunity to discover and manage problems before they get to the uncontrollable stage.

The project manager is usually the expediter of the status meeting. As such, it's your job to use status meetings wisely. Don't waste your team's time or the stakeholders' time either. Notify attendees in writing of the meeting time and place. Publish an agenda prior to the meeting, and stick to the agenda during the meeting. Every so often, summarize what has been discussed during the meeting. Don't let side discussions lead you down rabbit trails, and keep irrelevant conversations to a minimum. It's also good to publish status meeting notes at the conclusion of the meeting, especially if any action items resulted from the meeting. This will give you a document trail and serve as a reminder to the meeting participants of what actions need to be resolved and who is responsible for each action item.

It's important that project team members are honest with the project manager and that the project manager is in turn honest about what they report. A few years ago, a department in my agency took on a project of gargantuan proportions and unfortunately didn't employ good project management techniques. One of the biggest problems with this project was that the project manager did not listen to the highly skilled project team members. The team members warned of problems and setbacks, but the project manager didn't want to hear about it. The project manager took their reports to be of the "Chicken Little" ilk and refused to believe the sky was falling. Unfortunately, the sky *was* falling! Because the project manager didn't believe the reports, she refused to report the true status of the project to the stakeholders and oversight committees. Millions of dollars were wasted on a project that was doomed for failure while the project manager continued to report that the project was on time and activities were completed when in fact they were not.

There are hundreds of project stories like this, and I'll bet you've got one or two from your experiences as well. Don't let your project become the next bad example. Above all, be honest in your reporting. No one likes bad news, but bad news delivered too late along with millions of dollars wasted is a guaranteed career showstopper.

Control Communications Outputs

The Control Communications process has several outputs:

- Work performance information
- Change requests
- Project management plan updates
- Project documents updates
- Organizational process assets updates

We'll look briefly at work performance information and change requests.

Work performance information includes information you've gathered and analyzed about the progress of the project to date. This information is typically documented in the work performance reports (an output of the Monitor and Control Project Work process we discussed earlier in this chapter) and is distributed to the stakeholders. Change requests come about as a result of actions taken to correct issues; to modify scope, schedule, or budget; or other items. These actions and decisions are made as a result of reviewing work performance information. Change requests are generated from this process (and others) but are processed through the Integrated Change Control process that we'll discuss in the next section of this chapter. As you'll see shortly, change requests may require updates to the project management plan, project documents, project baselines, and more.

Exam Spotlight

For the exam, remember that one of the purposes of the Monitoring and Controlling process group is to gather performance metrics, including work efforts, costs (both expended and remaining forecasted costs), milestone measures, and other work performance measures to determine project progress. The Control Communications process brings much of this information together into one format.

Exam Spotlight

Work performance data, work performance information, and work performance reports are all either inputs and/or outputs of various processes in the Executing and Monitoring and Controlling process groups. They are similar but do have differences. I recommend you understand the differences for the exam. Here is a recap of each for your study time. According to the *PMBOK® Guide*, the definitions are as follows:

Work Performance Data   This is the process of measuring and observing project activities. This may include data such as reporting on the percent of work complete, status of deliverables, technical performance measurements, the actual start and finish dates of schedule activities (schedule progress to date), the number of change requests or defects, costs incurred to date, etc. Work performance data is an input of the following processes:

- Validate Scope
- Control Scope
- Control Schedule
- Control Costs
- Control Quality
- Control Communications
- Control Risks
- Control Procurements
- Control Stakeholder Engagement

Work performance data is an output of the following processes:

- Direct and Manage Project Work

Work Performance Information   Work performance information is used in the Monitoring and Controlling processes to analyze information such as the status of deliverables, the status of change requests, and forecasts such as estimate to complete (i.e., the work performance data).

Work performance information is an input of the following processes:

- Monitor and Control Project Work

Work performance information is an output of the following processes:

- Validate Scope
- Control Scope
- Control Schedule
- Control Costs
- Control Quality
- Control Communications
- Control Risks
- Control Procurements
- Control Stakeholder Engagement

Work Performance Reports   Work performance reports are the physical manifestation of the work performance information you've gathered and analyzed using variance analysis, earned value calculations, or forecasts. Work performance reports may include status reports, memos, updates, and more. Work performance reports are intended to aid decision making and action plans.

Work performance reports are an input of the following processes:

- Manage Project Team
- Manage Communications
- Perform Integrated Change Control
- Control Risks
- Control Procurements

Work performance reports are an output of the following process:

- Monitor and Control Project Work

Managing Perform Integrated Change Control

The *Perform Integrated Change Control* process serves as an overseer, so to speak, of the Monitoring and Controlling processes. This is where you establish the project's change control process. Changes, which encompass corrective actions, preventive actions, and defect repair, are common outputs across all the Monitoring and Controlling processes. (Don't forget that change requests are also an output of the Direct and Manage Project Work process, which is an Executing process.) These processes can generate the change requests that are managed through the Perform Integrated Change Control process.

You're likely to see exam questions on several topics that involve change and the Perform Integrated Change Control process. Configuration management, for example, isn't listed as a tool and technique of this process, but you really can't perform the Perform Integrated Change Control process without it. I'll discuss this shortly. First, though, you'll look at change, what it is, and how it comes about.

Changes come about on projects for many reasons. It's the project manager's responsibility to manage these changes and see to it that organizational policies regarding changes are implemented. Changes don't necessarily mean negative consequences. Changes can produce positive results as well. It's important that you manage this process carefully, because too many changes—even one significant change—will impact cost, schedule, scope, and/or quality. Once a change request has been submitted, you have some decisions to make. Ask yourself questions such as these:

- Should the change be implemented?

- If so, what's the cost to the project in terms of project constraints: cost, time, scope, and quality?

- Will the benefits gained by making the change increase or decrease the chances of project completion?

Just because a change is requested doesn't mean you have to implement it. You'll always want to discover the reasons for the change to determine whether they're justifiable, and you'll want to know the cost of the change. Remember that cost can take the form of increased time. Let's say the change you're considering will result in a later schedule completion date. That means you'll need human resources longer than expected. If you've leased equipment or project resources for the team members to use during the course of the project, a later completion date means your team needs the leased equipment for a longer period of time. All this translates to increased costs. Time equals money, as the saying goes, so manage time changes wisely, and dig deep to find the impacts that time changes might make on the budget.

How Change Occurs

As the project progresses, the stakeholders or customers might request a change directly. Team members might also recommend changes as the project progresses. For example, once the project is under way, they might discover more efficient ways of performing tasks or producing the product of the project and recommend changes to accommodate the new efficiencies. Changes might also come about as a result of mistakes that were made earlier in the project in the Planning or Executing processes. (However, I hope you've applied all the great practices and techniques I've talked about to date and you didn't experience many of these.)

Changes to the project might occur indirectly as a result of contingency plans, other changes, or team members performing favors for the stakeholders by making that one little change without telling anyone about it. Many times, the project manager is the last to know about changes such as these. There's a fine line here because you don't want to discourage good working relationships between team members and stakeholders, yet at the same time, you want to ensure that all changes come through the change control process. If a dozen little changes slip through like this, your project scope suddenly exits stage left.

Change Control Concerns

Perform Integrated Change Control, according to the *PMBOK® Guide*, is primarily concerned with the following:

- Influencing the factors that cause change control processes to be circumvented
- Promptly reviewing and analyzing change requests
- Managing approved changes
- Maintaining the integrity of the project baselines (including scope, quality, schedule, cost, and performance measurement baseline) and incorporating approved changes into the project management plan and other project documents
- Promptly reviewing and analyzing corrective and preventive actions
- Coordinating and managing changes across the project
- Documenting requested changes and their impacts

Factors that might cause change include project constraints, stakeholder requests, team member recommendations, vendor issues, and many others. You'll want to understand the factors that are influencing or bringing about change and how a proposed change might impact the project if implemented. Performance measures and corrective actions might dictate that a project change is needed as well.

 Modifications to the project are submitted in the form of change requests and managed through the change control process. Obviously, you'll want to implement those changes that are most beneficial to the project. I'll talk more about change requests later in this chapter.

Managing changes might involve making changes to the project scope, schedule, or cost baseline, also known as the *performance measurement baseline*. This baseline might also involve quality or technical elements. The performance measurement baseline is the approved project management plan that describes the work of the project. This is used through Executing and Monitoring and Controlling to measure project performance and determine deviations from the plan. It's your responsibility to maintain the reliability of the performance measurement baselines. Changes that impact an existing or completed project management process will require updates to those processes, which might mean additional passes through the appropriate Planning and Executing processes.

The management plans created during the Planning process group should reflect the changes as well, which might require updates to the project management plan or the project scope statement. This requires a close eye on coordination among all the processes that are impacted. For example, changes might require updates to risk response alternatives, schedule, cost, resource requirements, or other elements. Changes that affect product scope always require an update to the project scope.

Exam Spotlight

Managing changes involves maintaining accurate and reliable performance measurement baselines; coordinating all processes impacted as a result of the change, including revisiting Planning and Executing processes where needed; and updating project scope to reflect any changes in product scope.

I caution you to not change baselines at the drop of a hat. Examine the changes, their justification, and their impacts thoroughly before making changes to the baselines. Make certain your project sponsor approves baseline changes and that the project sponsor understands why the change occurred and how it will impact the project. Be sure to keep a copy of the original baseline for comparison purposes and for lessons learned.

Configuration Control

Configuration control is concerned with changes to the specifications of the deliverables or project management processes. Configuration control is managed through the configuration management system. The *configuration management system* is a subsystem of the project management information system. It documents the procedures and authorized approval levels for managing and controlling changes to the physical characteristics of the deliverables.

Exam Spotlight

According to the *PMBOK® Guide*, change control involves changes to the deliverables, project baselines, and/or project documents. Configuration control, which is managed through the configuration management system, is concerned with changes to the specifications of the deliverables and/or the project management processes.

The following items are what the *PMBOK® Guide* notes as activities associated with configuration control in the Perform Integrated Change Control process:

Configuration Identification   Configuration identification describes the characteristics of the product, service, or result of the project. This description is the basis that's used to verify when changes are made and how they're managed. Configuration identification is also used to label products or documents, manage changes, and verify changes.

Configuration Status Accounting   This activity doesn't have to do with financials as you might guess from its title. It's about accounting for the status of the changes by documenting and storing the configuration information needed to effectively manage the product information. This includes the approved configuration identification, the status of proposed changes, and the status of changes currently being implemented.

Configuration Verification and Auditing   Verification and audits are performed to determine whether the configuration item is accurate and correct and to make sure the performance requirements have been met. It ensures that changes are registered in the configuration management system and that they are assessed, approved, tracked, and implemented correctly.

Change Control System

If you were to allow changes to occur to the project whenever requested, you would probably never complete the project. Stakeholders, the customer, and end users would continually change the project requirements if given the opportunity to do so. That's why careful planning and scope definition are important in the beginning of the project. It's your job as project manager to drive out all the compelling needs and requirements of the project during the Planning process so that important requirements aren't suddenly "remembered" halfway through the project. However, we're all human, and sometimes things are not known, weren't thought about, or simply weren't discovered until a certain point during the project. Stakeholders will probably start thinking in a direction they weren't considering during the Planning process, and new requirements will come to light. This is where the *change control system* comes into play.

Exam Spotlight

Understand for the exam that configuration management involves identifying the physical characteristics of the product, service, or result of the project (or its individual components); controlling changes to those characteristics; and documenting changes to verify that requirements are met. It also includes the change management system and documents the process for requesting, tracking, and determining whether change requests should be approved or denied.

The Purpose of the Change Control System

Change control systems are documented procedures that describe how the deliverables of the project and associated project documentation are controlled, changed, and approved. It also often describes how to submit change requests and how to manage change requests. They may include preprinted change request forms that provide a place to record general project information such as the name and project number, the date, and the details regarding the change request. Change control systems are usually subsystems of the configuration management system.

The change control system also tracks the status of change requests, including their approval status. Not all change requests will receive approval. Those changes that are not approved are also tracked, communicated to the appropriate stakeholders, and filed in the change control log for future reference.

The change control system might define the level of authority needed to approve changes, if it wasn't previously defined in the configuration management system. Some change requests could receive approval based on the project manager's decision; others might need to be reviewed and formally approved by the project sponsor, executive management, and so on.

The change control system is a subset of the project management system. It includes the processes for identifying the characteristics of the product, service, or result and includes the process for documenting, tracking, and approving changes.

Procedures that detail how emergency changes are approved should be defined as well. For example, you and your team might be putting in some weekend hours and be close to the completion of a deliverable when you discover that thing 1 will not talk to thing 2 no matter what you do. The team brainstorms and comes up with a brilliant solution that requires a change request. Do you stop work right then and wait until the change control board or committee can meet sometime next week and make a decision, or do you—the project manager—make the decision to go forward with this solution and explain the change to the appropriate parties later? That answer depends on the change procedures you have in place to handle situations like this and on the authority you have to make emergency changes as outlined in the change control system.

Many organizations have formal change control or change request systems in place. If that's the case, you can easily adopt those procedures and use the existing system to manage project change. But if no procedures exist, you'll have to define them.

There are three objectives you should know about for implementing and using configuration management systems and change control processes:

- Establish a method to consistently identify changes, request changes to project baselines, and analyze and determine the value and effectiveness of the changes.

- Continuously authenticate and improve project performance by evaluating the impact of each change.

- Communicate all change requests—whether approved, rejected, or delayed—to all the stakeholders.

But I Thought You Said...

Marcus was working on a web redesign project for a division of the marketing department in his organization. The project started out as a simple redesign of the look and feel of the site. Marcus made the mistake of not defining change control procedures for the project from the beginning because he reasoned that the project was small, the design changes were well understood by all, and the project could be finished in a matter of weeks.

After the work of the project started, Marcus's team showed the initial design results to the business lead, Kendra. Kendra asked for a few modifications that seemed minor, and Marcus was happy to accommodate. When his team finished the work and turned the site over for initial testing, Kendra created a list of changes that extended beyond the initial scope of the project. Marcus thought everyone had agreed that the project involved only an update to the look and feel of the site, but Kendra was requesting changes to the applications people used to order products from the website. Marcus knew that application changes need their own set of requirements and testing. Changing the look of the site was a lot different from changing the way an application worked and the results it produced. Kendra and Marcus were in disagreement over what the changes entailed. Kendra thought she had carte blanche to make changes until she was satisfied with the project. Marcus knew that the projects waiting in the queue were going to suffer because of the never-ending stream of changes to Kendra's project. The additional time her project was taking already had pushed the deliverable of the next project on their list by two weeks.

To resolve the dilemma, Marcus had to negotiate with Kendra on the list of changes she had requested. He agreed to all changes that required less than four hours to complete, and the remaining changes were moved to a new project request. Marcus also vowed to implement change control procedures for all projects from this point forward, no matter what the size or complexity of the project.

Requirements for Change

At the beginning of all projects, you should require two things regarding change. First, require that all change requests be submitted in writing. This is to clarify the change and make sure there's no confusion about what's requested. It also allows the project team to accurately estimate the time it will take to incorporate the change.

Second, require that all change requests must go through the formal change control system. Make sure no one is allowed to go directly to team members and request changes without the project manager knowing about them. Also make certain your stakeholders understand that going around the project manager can cause schedule delays, cost overruns, and sacrifices to quality and that it isn't good change management practice. From the beginning of the project, encourage the stakeholders to use the formal procedures laid out in the change control system to request changes.

It's good practice to require all change requests in writing. This should be a documented procedure outlined in your change control system. Beware! Stakeholders are notorious for asking for changes verbally even when there is a detailed process in place. If they don't want to follow the process, someone on the project team should have responsibility for documenting and logging the change requests for future reference.

Change Control Board

In some organizations, a *change control board (CCB)* is established to review all change requests. The board is officially chartered and given the authority to approve or deny change requests as defined by the organization. It's important that its authority is clearly defined and that separate procedures exist for emergency changes. The CCB might meet only once a week, once every other week, or even once a month, depending on the project. When emergencies arise, the established procedures allow the project manager to implement the change on the spot. This always requires follow-up with the CCB and completion of a formal change request, even though it's after the fact.

CCB members might include stakeholders, managers, project team members, and others who might not have any connection to the project at hand. Some organizations have permanent CCBs that are staffed by full-time employees dedicated to managing change for the entire organization, not just project change. You might want to consider establishing a CCB for your project if the organization does not have one.

Exam Spotlight

For purposes of the exam, note that the *PMBOK® Guide* states that the CCB is made up of a group of stakeholders who review and then approve, delay, or reject change requests.

Some organizations use other types of review boards that have the same responsibilities as the CCB. Some other names you might see are technical assessment board (TAB), technical review board (TRB), engineering review board (ERB), and configuration control board (CCB).

Perform Integrated Change Control Inputs, Tools and Techniques, and Outputs

The inputs for the Perform Integrated Change Control process are as follows:

- Project management plan
- Work performance reports
- Change requests
- Enterprise environmental factors
- Organizational process assets

Remember that the project management plan includes all the documents that make up that plan. According to the *PMBOK® Guide*, the documents included in the project management plan include at least the following:

- Scope management plan
- Requirements management plan
- Schedule management plan
- Cost management plan
- Quality management plan
- Process improvement plan
- Human resource management plan
- Communications management plan
- Risk management plan
- Procurement management plan
- Stakeholder management plan

As a reminder, the project baselines include at least the following:

- Schedule baseline
- Cost baseline
- Scope baseline

Pop Quiz: Do you remember what documents comprise the scope baseline? Turn back to Chapter 3 if you need a refresher.

Other documents (such as the issue log, quality checklists, statement of work, and many more) are considered project documents.

The tools and techniques for Perform Integrated Change Control include:

- Expert judgment
- Change control meetings
- Change control tools

Change control tools may include manual processes or software systems that assist in managing this process. It will track and record the change requests, record the decisions by the change control board, and help manage the distribution of the change request decisions and more.

The outputs of the Perform Integrated Change Control process are as follows:

- Approved change requests
- Change log
- Project management plan updates
- Project documents updates

Approved change requests are implemented during the Direct and Manage Project Work process. They are documented in the change log along with other items such as costs, risks associated with the changes, the timing of the change requests, and more. Project management plan updates are typically required as a result of an approved change or corrective action, especially those changes that impact a project baseline. It may sound obvious, but I'll tell you anyway: Changes made to baselines should reflect changes from the current point in time forward. You cannot change past performance. These changes are noted in the change control system or the configuration management system, and stakeholders are informed at the status meetings of the changes that have occurred, their impacts, and where the description of the changes can be found.

You should document all the actions taken in the Perform Integrated Change Control process (whether implemented or not) as part of the project document updates output. You should also record the reason for the change request. In other words, how did this particular change request come about? How did it change the original project management plan? Is this something you could or should have known about in the Planning processes? You should also note the corrective action taken and the justification for choosing that particular corrective action as part of lessons learned. You can use the information you capture here in your configuration management system as lessons learned for future projects. When you take on a new project, it's a good idea to review the lessons learned from similar projects so that you can plan appropriately and avoid, where possible, the variances that occurred in those projects.

Exam Spotlight

Remember that approved change requests are an output of the Perform Integrated Change Control process but they are implemented in the Direct and Manage Project Work process (an Executing process).

In the next chapter, you'll explore the individual change control processes (like Control Costs and Control Schedule) and the measurement tools you'll use to provide the variance measurements that are gathered and reported to the stakeholder via the Control Communications process that we discussed earlier in this chapter.

Controlling Stakeholder Engagement

The purpose of the *Control Stakeholder Engagement* process is to monitor your stakeholder relationships and ensure their continued engagement in the project. It's easy for stakeholders to become distracted on long projects. As more time goes by, the current project fades in importance and other issues can take their place. Keeping stakeholders engaged will help overall project success, it will help you efficiently manage the processes as the project progresses, and it will help your stakeholders stay up to date on issues and status as the project evolves so they can make informed decisions.

You have seen all of the inputs, tools and techniques, and outputs of this process before. For your reference they are listed next.

The inputs to the Control Stakeholder Engagement process are:

- Project management plan
- Issue log
- Work performance data
- Project documents

The tools and techniques of this process are:

- Information management systems
- Expert judgment
- Meetings

The outputs of this process are:

- Work performance information
- Change requests
- Project documents updates
- Organizational process assets updates

 Real World Scenario

Project Case Study: New Kitchen Heaven Retail Store

Your regularly scheduled status meeting is in progress. Let's see how it's progressing.

Your next agenda item is an update on change requests. Ricardo submitted a change request regarding the hardware installation at the new store site. A new, much anticipated operating system was just released, and Ricardo has plans to upgrade the entire company to the new operating system. Since he must purchase new equipment for this store anyway, he contends that it makes sense to go ahead and purchase the hardware with the newest operating system already loaded. His staff won't have to upgrade this store as part of the upgrade project because the store will already have the new operating system.

Ricardo's change request was submitted in writing through the change control system. A CCB was set up during the Planning stages of this project to handle change requests. At the CCB meeting, the following questions come up regarding Ricardo's request: Has the new operating system been tested with the existing system? Are there compatibility problems? If so, what risks are associated with getting the problems resolved and the equipment installed by opening day? Is the vendor ready to ship with the new operating system?

The CCB defers their decision for this request until Ricardo answers these questions.

During the next CCB meeting, the board reviews a change request from Jill. The gourmet food supplier she used went out of business, and Jill contracted with a new vendor. She received a sample shipment from the new vendor and was very unhappy with the results. Upon inspecting the products, she found broken containers and damaged packaging. Meanwhile, Jill found another vendor, who has sent her a sample shipment. She is very pleased with the new vendor's products and service. However, this vendor's prices are even higher than the first replacement vendor with whom she contracted. Jill submitted a cost change request to the CCB because of the increased cost of the gourmet food product shipment. The change in cost does not have a significant impact on the budget.

Jake reported that payments have been made to the vendor supplying the store's display cases and shelving and also gave an update on the vendor supplying the lighting for the store. Both vendors met or exceeded performance requirements and he's happy with their service.

You hold a seat on the CCB and are aware of the change requests and their impacts on the project. Ricardo satisfactorily answered all the questions the CCB had, so his request and Jill's request were both approved during the meeting.

You inform the group that you will be setting up some one-on-one meetings with each of the key stakeholders to check in with them on how the project is progressing from their viewpoint and to listen to their input and/or any issues they may have.

"Now I'd like to give a brief update on the project forecast," you tell the group. "Based on the preliminary data I've gathered, we are somewhat behind schedule but budget appears to be on track. I will have some forecast numbers for you at the next meeting."

Project Case Study Checklist

- Control Procurements
    - Monitor vendor performance
    - Document vendor performance
    - Monitor payments to seller
- Perform Integrated Change Control
    - Review and approve changes
    - Document changes in change log
- Configuration management systems
    - Configuration identification
    - Configuration status accounting

- Configuration verification and auditing
- Change control system
- Control Communications
  - Work performance information (status reports and meetings)
  - Forecasts
- Control Stakeholder Engagement
  - Meetings
  - Work performance information

Understanding How This Applies to Your Next Project

I've learned from experience the value of having a change control process in place for all projects. I've never managed a project that didn't encounter change—and there are hundreds of reasons that bring about change. One of the ways to help reduce the amount of change you might experience is to make certain you've documented the requirements of the project accurately and have obtained sign-off from the stakeholders. Beware! Just because the stakeholders have agreed to the requirements doesn't mean they won't want change. As you elaborate the deliverables and requirements, the product or end result becomes clearer, and that means some elements not previously known or at least not known in their entirety early in the planning process will require change.

If you don't already have a change control process in place, I recommend setting one up before you begin your next project. Document the procedures for requesting, tracking, and approving or denying changes. Make them one of the agenda items for discussion at your project kickoff meeting. It's easier to enforce change procedures (and deny changes that are out of scope) if the process is discussed with the stakeholders early in the project. You will likely want to include important stakeholders on the change control board, and that will give you another great opportunity to discuss and reinforce the process.

Administering contracts and procurements, as I mentioned earlier, may be managed by someone in your procurement department. In my experience, there is always someone from this department involved from the request process through contract administration. However, it will likely be up to you to monitor vendor performance, make sure deliverable dates are met, and verify time cards against the submitted invoice.

Keeping your stakeholders engaged throughout the entire project is key to its success. Don't let stakeholder interests drift. Make an effort to reach out to them and meet with them on a regular basis. Your enthusiasm for the project is contagious and will keep the stakeholders engaged.

Summary

This chapter examined several change control processes starting with the Monitor and Control Project Work process. This process is responsible for reviewing, tracking, and controlling project progress. It ensures that the performance objectives outlined in the project management plan are met.

The Control Procurements process is concerned with managing vendor relationships, monitoring performance, and implementing changes or corrections when necessary. Both buyer and seller are responsible for administering the contract (or other procurement vehicle) to ensure that contractual obligations are being met.

Perform Integrated Change Control is an important part of the project process. It's your responsibility as project manager to manage change and implement corrective action where needed to keep the project on track with the plan. Perform Integrated Change Control concerns influencing the things that cause change and managing the change once it has occurred. One or more of the project baselines may be affected when change occurs. Managing change might involve changes to the project plan, the project schedule, the project budget, project scope, and so on. Changes that impact processes you've already completed require updates to those processes. Corrective action is often a result of a change and ensures that the future performance of the project lines up with the project management plan.

Configuration management systems typically include change control systems that document the procedures to manage change and how change requests are implemented. Change requests might come in written or verbal forms, but ideally you should ask for all your change requests in writing. Change requests are processed through a formal change control system, and configuration control boards have the authority to approve or deny change requests.

Control Stakeholder Engagement concerns monitoring your relationships with the stakeholders and keeping them engaged throughout the project.

Exam Essentials

Name the outputs of the Monitor and Control Project Work process.   The outputs are change requests (which include corrective action, preventive action, and defect repair), work performance reports, project management plan updates, and project documents updates.

Name the processes that integrate with the Control Procurements process.   Direct and Manage Project Work, Control Communications, Control Quality, Perform Integrated Change Control, and Control Risks.

Describe the purpose of the Control Communications process.   Control Communications concerns monitoring and controlling communications throughout the life of the project.

Name the purpose of the Perform Integrated Change Control process.   Perform Integrated Change Control is performed throughout the life of the project and involves reviewing all the project change requests, establishing a configuration management and change control process, and approving or denying changes.

Be able to define the purpose of a configuration management system.   Configuration management systems are documented procedures that describe the process for submitting change requests, the processes for tracking changes and their disposition, and the processes for defining the approval levels for approving and denying changes. The configuration management system also includes a process for authorizing the changes. Change control systems are generally a subset of the configuration management system. Configuration management also describes the characteristics of the product of the project and ensures accuracy and completeness of the description.

Be able to describe a CCB.   The change control board (CCB) has the authority to approve or deny change requests. Their authority is defined and outlined by the organization. A CCB is made up of stakeholders.

Be able to describe the purpose for the Control Stakeholder Engagement process.   The purpose is to monitor stakeholder relationships and ensure their continued engagement in the project.

Key Terms

The processes introduced in this chapter give you the tools and techniques you need to keep your projects on track and to manage change. Know these processes by the PMI® terms if you want to be successful in obtaining your PMP® certification.

Control Communications

Control Procurements

Control Stakeholder Engagement

Monitor and Control Project Work

Perform Integrated Change Control

You've learned a lot of new key words in this chapter. PMI® has worked hard to develop and define standard project management terms that apply across industries. Here is a list of some of the terms you came across in this chapter:

arbitration	forecasting
change control board (CCB)	payment systems
change control system	performance measurement baseline
claims administration	records management system
configuration control	seller invoices
configuration management system	status review meeting
contested changes	work authorization system
contract change control system	work performance information

Review Questions

You can find the answers to the questions in Appendix A.

1. You are a project manager for an international marketing firm. You are ready to assign resources to your new project using a work authorization system. Which of the following statements is not true?

   A. Work authorization systems clarify and initiate the work for each work package.

   B. Work authorization systems are written procedures defined by the organization.

   C. Work authorization systems are used throughout the project Executing processes.

   D. Work authorization systems are a tool and technique of the Monitor and Control Project Work process.

2. You are working on a project and discover that one of the business users responsible for testing the product never completed this activity. She has written an email requesting that one of your team members drop everything to assist her with a problem that could have been avoided if she would have performed the test. This employee reports to a stakeholder, not to the project team. You estimate that the project might not be completed on time as a result of this missed activity. All of the following are true except for which one?

   A. You should recommend a corrective action to bring the expected future project performance back into line with the project management plan because of this employee's failure to perform this activity.

   B. You should recommend a preventive action to reduce the possibility of future project performance veering off track because of this employee's failure to perform this activity.

   C. You should recommend a change request, which is an output of the Monitor and Control Project Work process, to get the project performance back in alignment with the project management plan.

   D. You might have to request a change to the project schedule as a result of this missed activity.

3. Which one of the following is the most preferred method of settling claims and disputes according to the *PMBOK® Guide*?

   A. Arbitration

   B. Collaboration

   C. ADR

   D. Negotiation

4. Which option includes all of the tools and techniques of the Control Procurements process?

   A. Contract change control system, expert judgment, inspection and audits, performance reporting, payment systems, claims administration, and records management system.

   B. Contract change control system, procurement performance reviews, inspection and audits, performance reporting, payment systems, claims administration, configuration management system, and records management system.

    C. Contract change control system, expert judgment, inspection and audits, performance reporting, payment systems, claims administration, configuration management system, and records management system.

    D. Contract change control system, procurement performance reviews, inspection and audits, performance reporting, payment systems, claims administration, and records management system.

5. You are a project manager for an engineering company. Your company won the bid to add ramp-metering lights to several on-ramps along a stretch of highway at the south end of the city. You subcontracted a portion of the project to another company. The subcontractor's work involves digging the holes and setting the lamp poles in concrete. The subcontractor's performance to date does not meet the contract requirements. Which of the following is not a valid option?

    A. You document the poor performance in written form and send the correspondence to the subcontractor.

    B. You terminate the contract for cause and submit a change request through Control Procurements.

    C. You submit a change request through Control Procurements demanding that the subcontractor comply with the terms of the contract.

    D. You agree to meet with the subcontractor to see whether a satisfactory solution can be reached.

6. The Control Procurements process is closely integrated with all of the following processes except for which one?

    A. Direct and Manage Project Work

    B. Control Communications

    C. Perform Integrated Change Control

    D. Control Risks

7. You are holding a regularly scheduled status meeting for your project. You know all of the following are true regarding status meetings except which one?

    A. Status meetings are a type of communication method, which is a tool and technique of the Control Communications process.

    B. Status meetings are a type of interactive communication.

    C. Status meetings are a way to formally exchange information and update the stakeholders regarding project status.

    D. Status meetings should be held throughout the project and at regularly scheduled intervals.

8. You are performing actions such as collecting and reporting information regarding the progress of the project and ensuring that the right information is delivered to the right people at the right time. Which process are you performing?

    A. Control Communications

    B. Perform Integrated Change Control

    C. Monitor and Control Project Work

    D. Control Procurements

9. All of the following are tools and techniques of the Control Communications process except which one?

   A. Records management system

   B. Information management systems

   C. Expert judgment

   D. Meetings

10. The Delphi method, technology forecasting, and forecast by analogy are examples of what category of forecasting methods?

    A. Time series

    B. Judgmental

    C. Causal

    D. Econometric

11. Your project is progressing as planned. You are conducting a status meeting and are reviewing items that need resolution. You have asked the owners of these items to report their progress and are tracking the due dates for their resolution. Which input of the Control Communications process does this describe?

    A. Information management systems

    B. Issue log

    C. Meetings

    D. Work performance data

12. You are in the Conduct Procurements process. You and your vendor are in the midst of contested changes and cannot reach a resolution. Which of the following methods should be your first course of action to resolve this issue?

    A. Meet with the vendor until you resolve this on your own

    B. Use ADR techniques

    C. Take the vendor to court

    D. Terminate the contract

13. You are a project manager for Bluebird Technologies. Bluebird writes custom billing applications for several industries. A schedule change has been requested. From the perspective of the Perform Integrated Change Control, change is concerned with all of the following except which one?

    A. Influencing factors that circumvent the change control process

    B. Issuing change requests

    C. Reviewing change

    D. Maintaining the integrity of baselines

14. You are a project manager for Bluebird Technologies. Bluebird writes custom billing applications for several industries. One of your users verbally requests changes to one of the screen displays. You explain to her that the change needs to go through the change control system, which is a subset of the configuration management system. You explain that a change control system does all of the following except for which one?

    A. Documents procedures for change requests

    B. Tracks the status of change requests

    C. Describes the management impacts of change

    D. Determines whether changes are approved or denied

15. You are a project manager for Star Light Strings. Star Light manufactures strings of lights for outdoor displays. Its products range from simple light strings to elaborate lights with animal designs, bug designs, memorabilia, and so on. Your newest project requires a change. You have documented the characteristics of the product and its functionality using which of the following tools and techniques?

    A. Change control system

    B. Corrective action

    C. Configuration management

    D. Updates to the project management plan

16. You are a project manager for Star Light Strings. Star Light manufactures strings of lights for outdoor display. Its products range from simple light strings to elaborate lights with animal designs, bug designs, memorabilia, and so on. Your newest project requires a change. One of the business unit managers submitted a change through the change control system, which utilizes a CCB. Which of the following is true regarding the CCB?

    A. The CCB describes how change requests are managed.

    B. The CCB requires all change requests in writing.

    C. The CCB approves or denies change requests.

    D. The CCB requires updates to the appropriate management plan.

17. All of the following are activities of the configuration management system except for which one?

    A. Variance analysis

    B. Identification

    C. Status accounting

    D. Verification and auditing

18. According the *PMBOK® Guide*, this system centrally manages approved changes and baselines within a project:

    A. Records management system

    B. Change control system

    C. Work authorization system

    D. Configuration management system

19. You are performing the following activities: comparing actual performance against the project plan, assessing performance to determine if a corrective action is necessary, identifying new risks, providing forecasts to update current cost and schedule data, and monitoring implementation of approved changes. Which process are you in?

A. Perform Integrated Change Control

B. Control Communications

C. Monitor and Control Project Work

D. Control Stakeholder Engagement

20. All of the following are acronyms for other boards that fulfill the same responsibilities as a change control board except for which one?

A. TAB

B. TRB

C. ARB

D. ERB

Chapter

11

Controlling Work Results

THE PMP® EXAM CONTENT FROM THE MONITORING AND CONTROLLING THE PROJECT PERFORMANCE DOMAIN COVERED IN THIS CHAPTER INCLUDES THE FOLLOWING:

✓ Ensure that project deliverables conform to the quality standards established in the quality management plan.

✓ Prepare and communicate earned value measurements and forecasts.

✓ Update the risk register and risk response plan by identifying any new risks, assessing old risks, and determining and implementing appropriate response strategies in order to manage the impact of risks on the project.

✓ Assess corrective actions on the issue register and determine next steps for unresolved issues by using appropriate tools and techniques in order to minimize the impact on project schedule, cost, and resources.

✓ Communicate project status to stakeholders for their feedback in order to ensure the project aligns with business needs.

✓ Knowledge and Skills

  ▪ Performance measurement and tracking techniques (for example, EV, CPM, PERT)

  ▪ Project control limits (for example, thresholds, tolerance)

  ▪ Cost analysis techniques

  ▪ Variance and trend analysis techniques

  ▪ Project plan management techniques

  ▪ Change management techniques

  ▪ Integrated change control processes

You've almost made it to the homestretch. This chapter covers the last group of project processes in the Monitoring and Controlling group. A significant amount of information is packed into this chapter, and I recommend you memorize all the formulas presented here for the exam.

I'll cover the Control Risks, Control Costs, Control Schedule, Control Quality, Validate Scope, and Control Scope processes in this chapter.

The Control Risks process monitors the project for risks and monitors the risk response plans that have been or might need to be put into action. The Control Costs and Control Schedule processes are similar to Perform Integrated Change Control, which we discussed in the previous chapter. When you're reading these sections, remember that the information from the Perform Integrated Change Control process applies to these areas as well.

The Control Quality process involves several new tools and techniques that might show up on the exam. Take some time to understand these tools and techniques and know how to differentiate them from the tools and techniques associated with the Plan Quality Management and Perform Quality Assurance processes.

The Validate Scope process involves verifying and accepting work results. Control Scope is like the change control processes I discussed in Chapter 10, "Measuring and Controlling Project Performance," and is concerned with controlling changes to project scope.

The process names, inputs, tools and techniques, outputs, and descriptions of the project management process groups and related materials and figures in this chapter are based on content from *A Guide to the Project Management Body of Knowledge (PMBOK® Guide), Fifth Edition* (Sybex, 2010).

Monitoring and Controlling Risk

The *Control Risks* process involves implementing response plans, tracking and monitoring identified risks, and identifying and responding to new risks as they occur. You will examine performance information and use the tools and techniques of this process to analyze and implement other functions of this process, including the following:

- Evaluating risk response plans that are put into action as a result of risk events
- Monitoring the project for risk triggers

- Reexamining existing risks to determine if they have changed or should be closed out
- Monitoring residual risks
- Reassessing project assumptions and determining validity
- Ensuring that policies and procedures are followed
- Ensuring that risk response plans and contingency plans are put into action appropriately and are effective
- Ensuring that contingency reserves (for schedule and cost) are updated according to the updated risk assessment
- Evaluating the overall effectiveness of the Risk processes

Control Risks is a busy process. During the course of the project, risk responses, which were developed during the Planning process group, have been implemented and have reduced or averted the impact of risk events (or you hope they did).

Control Risks Inputs

This process has four inputs:

- Project management plan
- Risk register
- Work performance data
- Work performance reports

You'll recall that the risk register tracks and ranks individual risks, identifies the risk owner, describes risk triggers and residual risks, and lists the response plans and strategies you should implement if an actual risk event occurs. Keep in mind that some risk events identified in risk planning will happen and some will not. You will have to stay alert for risk event occurrences and be prepared to respond to them when they do occur. This means you should monitor the risk register regularly.

Work performance data includes information that may help you determine that a new risk event is about to occur, or it may assist you in monitoring previously identified risks. Remember that this entails elements such as the status of deliverables, costs to date, cost changes, schedule progress to date, schedule changes, and scope changes. Work performance reports (often in the form of a status report) is where you take this information and use variance analysis, forecasting, and earned value analysis to produce results (that are reported in the status report) that help aid in decision making, implementing risk responses, and taking corrective actions. This information should also be examined from the perspective of risks or risk response plans that might need close monitoring or changes to the response plans to coincide with the data in the work performance reports.

Additional risk response planning might be needed to deal with the new risks or with expected risks whose impact might be greater than expected. This might require repeating the Plan Risk Responses process to create new contingency plans or alternative plans to deal with the risk, or it might require modification to existing plans.

Control Risks Tools and Techniques

The tools and techniques of Control Risks are used to monitor risks throughout the life of the project. You should perform periodic reviews, audits, and new earned value analyses to check the pulse of risk activity and to make certain risk management is enacted effectively.

The tools and techniques of this process are as follows:

- Risk reassessment
- Risk audits
- Variance and trend analysis
- Technical performance measurement
- Reserve analysis
- Status meetings

You'll look at risk reassessment, risk audits, variance and trend analysis, and technical performance measurements next. You've examined all the other tools and techniques of this process in discussions of previous processes.

Risk Reassessment

Periodic, scheduled reviews of identified risks, risk responses, and risk priorities should occur during the project. The idea here is to monitor risks and their status and determine whether their consequences still have the same impact on the project objectives as when they were originally planned. If the risk is no longer viable, it should be closed. Every status meeting should have a time set aside to discuss and review risks and response plans.

Risk identification and monitoring is an ongoing process throughout the life of the project. Risks can change, and previously identified risks might have greater impacts than originally thought as more facts are discovered. Reassessment of risks should be a regular activity performed by everyone involved on the project. Monitor the risk register, including those risks that have low scores, and risk triggers. You should also monitor the risk responses that have been implemented for their effectiveness in dealing with risk. You might have to revisit the Perform Qualitative and Perform Quantitative Risk Analysis processes when new risk consequences are discovered or risk impacts are found to be greater than what was originally planned.

Risk Audits

Risk audits are carried out during the entire life of the project by risk auditors. Risk auditors are not typically project team members and are expertly trained in audit techniques and risk assessment. Risk audits are specifically interested in examining the implementation of response plans and their effectiveness at dealing with risks and their root causes. Risk audits may also examine the risk management process.

Variance and Trend Analysis

Variance analysis includes reviewing actual results and comparing them to what was planned to determine if there is a difference between the two. Variance analysis involves using performance information and earned value analysis to review overall project performance. If variance is detected, there is a potential for risks and therefore a potential for positive or negative consequences. Trend analysis involves observing trends as the project is performed and taking corrective action where needed or reassessing risk response strategies to take advantage of opportunities or lessen negative impacts.

Technical Performance Measurements

Technical performance measurements compares the technical accomplishments of project milestones completed during the Executing processes to the technical milestones defined in the project Planning processes. Variances might indicate that a project risk is looming, and you'll want to analyze and prepare a response to it if appropriate. For example, a technical milestone for a new computer software project might require that the forms printed from a particular module include a barcode at the bottom of the page. If the barcode functionality does not work once the module is coded, a technical deviation exists, which means you should reexamine project risks. In this particular example, project scope is likely at risk.

Control Risks Outputs

Control Risks should occur throughout the life of the project. Identified risks are monitored and plans are reexamined to determine whether they will adequately resolve the risk as it approaches during this process. Several outputs might come about as a result of monitoring risks:

- Work performance information
- Change requests (recommended corrective and preventive actions)
- Project management plan updates
- Project documents updates
- Organizational process assets updates

   I've discussed these outputs before, so I'll just bring to your attention the new points you need to know here about change requests and project documents updates.

Change Requests

Change requests must be processed through the Perform Integrated Change Control process. You might find that change requests take the form of corrective actions or preventive actions, and that implementing a contingency plan or a workaround may bring about the need for a change request. A *workaround* is an unplanned response to a negative risk event. It attempts to deal with the risk in a productive, efficient manner. If no risk response plan exists (this might be the case when you accept a risk event during the Planning process) or an unplanned risk occurs, workarounds are implemented to deal with the consequences of the risk.

Project Documents Updates

Some of the project documents that may require updating include the results of a risk audit or risk assessment, the outcomes or results of the project risks and risk responses, and updates to the risk register. The risk register is updated when a risk audit or risk reassessment concludes that some element of the original risk information has changed—for example, the impact or probability scores are updated to reflect new conditions, the priority of the risk has changed, the owner of the risk has changed, or the response plan has been updated. The risk register should also be updated when the risk is closed or when a risk event occurs. You'll want to note the results of the risk response. And don't forget that when new risks are identified throughout the project they should be added to the risk register.

Managing Cost Changes

The *Control Costs* process monitors the project budget and manages changes to the cost baseline. It's concerned with monitoring project costs to prevent unauthorized or incorrect costs from being included in the cost baseline. This means you'll also use Control Costs to ensure that the project budget isn't exceeded (resulting in cost overruns). If a change is implemented, you'll have to make certain the budget for the changed item stays within acceptable limits. All budget changes should be agreed to and approved by the project sponsor where applicable (the criteria for approvals should be outlined in the change control system documentation). Increases to the authorized budget should be submitted as change requests and approved through the Perform Integrated Change Control process. Stakeholders should be made aware of all budget changes.

The following list includes some of the activities you'll be involved in during this process:

- Monitoring changes to costs or the cost baseline and understanding variances from the baseline
- Monitoring change requests that affect cost and resolving them in a timely manner
- Informing stakeholders of approved changes and their costs
- Ensuring the project budget does not exceed acceptable limits by taking action when overruns are imminent
- Ensuring the project budget does not exceed the total funding authorized for the project or for the project phase

Control Costs Inputs

The Control Costs process includes the following inputs:

- Project management plan
- Project funding requirements
- Work performance data
- Organizational process assets

These inputs are examined using the tools and techniques of this process to determine whether revised cost estimates or budget updates are required. One thing you should note regarding the project management plan input is that it includes the cost baseline and the cost management plan. You'll use the cost baseline to compare actual expenditures to date on the project to the baseline. The cost management plan details how costs should be monitored and controlled throughout the life of the project. I've covered each of these inputs in previous chapters.

Control Costs Tools and Techniques

The tools and techniques of the Control Costs process are as follows:

- Earned value management (EVM)
- Forecasting
- To-complete performance index (TCPI)
- Performance reviews
- Project management software
- Reserve analysis

We'll look at each of these next, with the exception of project management software. This tool and technique has been discussed previously, but you should know that in this process it can help automate and calculate the formulas we're going to examine next. It can also display the results in graphical form for status reporting purposes.

Earned Value Management

You can accomplish performance measurement analysis using a technique called *earned value management (EVM)*. Simply stated, EVM compares what you've received or produced to what you've spent.

The EVM continuously monitors the planned value, earned value, and actual costs expended to produce the work of the project (I'll cover the definition of these terms shortly). When variances that result in cost changes are discovered (including schedule variances and cost variances), those changes are managed using the project change control system. The primary function of this analysis technique is to determine and document the cause of the variance, to determine the impact of the variance, and to determine whether a corrective action should be implemented as a result. We'll walk through various examples that illustrate how to determine these variances later in this section.

EVM looks at schedule, cost, scope, and resource measurements together and compares them to the actual work completed to date. You may recall that the schedule, cost, and scope baselines together make up the performance measurement baseline (PMB). The performance measurement baseline is determined using EVM and will be used throughout the project to measure the progress and performance of the project. Remember that it does not include management reserves but it does include contingencies.

EVM is the most often used performance measurement method. EVM is performed on the work packages and the control accounts of the WBS. To perform the EVM calculations, you need to first gather the three measurements mentioned earlier: the planned value (PV), actual cost (AC), and earned value (EV).

 If you do any research on your own regarding these values, you might come across acronyms that are different from what you see here. I've included their alternative names and acronyms at the end of each description. I recommend you memorize planned value (PV), actual cost (AC), and earned value (EV) and make certain you understand the meaning of each before you continue.

Let's take a look at some definitions of these key measurements before diving into the actual calculations:

Planned Value   The *planned value (PV)* is the cost of work that has been authorized and budgeted for a schedule activity or WBS component during a given time period or phase. These budgets are established during the Planning processes. For any given day, PV equals the planned cost of work that is scheduled to be completed on that day, whether or not the work is actually completed. PV is also called budgeted cost of work scheduled (BCWS).

Exam Spotlight

Remember to read exam questions carefully. PV might mean present value (as I talked about in Chapter 2, "Creating the Project Charter") or planned value, as defined here.

Actual Cost   *Actual cost (AC)* is the actual cost of completing the work component in a given time period. Actual costs might include direct and indirect costs but must correspond to what was budgeted for the activity. If the budgeted amount did not include indirect costs, do not include them here. Later you'll see how to compare this to PV to come up with variance calculation results. Actual costs include whatever is spent to complete the work regardless of what was budgeted. AC is also called actual cost of work performed (ACWP).

Earned Value   *Earned value (EV)* is the value of the work completed to date as it compares to the authorized budgeted amount assigned to the work component. EV is typically expressed as a percentage of the work completed compared to the budget. For example, if our budgeted amount is $1,000 and we have completed 30 percent of the work so far, our EV is $300. Therefore, EV cannot exceed the PV budget for the activity. EV is also called budgeted cost of work performed (BCWP).

Exam Spotlight

PV, AC, and EV are easy to mix up. In their simplest forms, here's what each means:

- *PV*—The approved budget assigned to work to be completed during a given time period

- *AC*—Money that's actually been expended during a given time period for completed work

- *EV*—The value of the work completed to date compared to the budget

---

According to the earlier definition, EV is the sum of the cumulative budgeted costs for completed work for all activities that have been accomplished as of the measurement date. For example, if your total budget is $1,000 and 50 percent of the work has been completed as of the measurement date, your EV would equal $500. You can plot all the PV, AC, and EV measurements graphically to show the variances between them. If there are no variances in the measurements, all the lines on the graph remain the same, which means the project is progressing as planned. Figure 11.1 shows an example that plots these three measurements.

FIGURE 11.1   Earned value

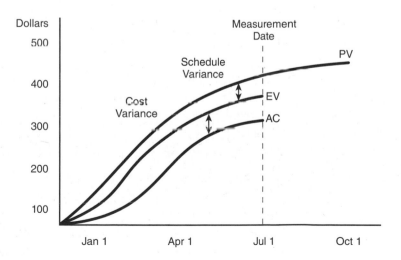

All of these measurements include a cost component. Costs are displayed in an S curve because spending is minimal in the beginning of the project, picks up steam toward the middle, and then tapers off at the end of the project. This means your earned value measurements will also take on the S curve shape.

Now you can calculate whether the project is progressing as planned or if variances exist in the approved baseline by using a variety of formulas discussed in the following sections. Use Figure 11.1 as your example for the formulas that follow. The Figure 11.1 totals are as follows:

$$PV = 400, EV = 375, AC = 325$$

Cost Variance

Cost variance is one of the most popular variances that project managers use. It's the difference between EV (where you are at this point) and AC (what you've spent). In other words, it tells you whether your actual costs are higher than expected (with a resulting negative number) or lower than expected (with a resulting positive number) at a certain point in time. It measures the actual performance to date (or during the period) against what's been spent.

The *cost variance (CV)* is calculated as follows:

$$CV = EV - AC$$

Let's calculate the CV using the numbers from Figure 11.1:

$$375 - 325 = 50$$

The CV is positive, which means you're spending less than what you planned for the work that you have completed as of July 1 (which Figure 11.1 shows because AC is less than EV).

If you come up with a negative number as the answer to this formula, it means that costs are higher than what you had planned for the work that was completed as of July 1 and these costs are usually not recoverable.

Schedule Variance

Schedule variance, another popular variance, tells you whether the schedule is ahead or behind what was planned for this period. It's the difference between where you are at this point (EV) and what was planned for this point (PV). This formula is most helpful when you've used the critical path methodology to build the project schedule. The *schedule variance (SV)* is calculated as follows:

$$SV = EV - PV$$

Let's plug in the numbers:

$$375 - 400 = -25$$

The resulting schedule variance is negative, which means you are behind schedule, or behind where you planned to be as of July 1.

Together, the CV and SV can be converted to *efficiency indicators* for the project and can be used to compare performance of all the projects in a portfolio.

Performance Indexes

Cost and schedule performance indexes are primarily used to calculate performance efficiencies, and they're often used to help predict future project performance.

The *cost performance index (CPI)* measures the cost efficiency of the work completed against actual cost. According to the *PMBOK® Guide*, it is the most critical of all the EVM measurements because it tells you the cost efficiency for the work completed to date, or at the completion of the project. If CPI is greater than 1, you're spending less than anticipated to date. If CPI is less than 1, you are spending more than anticipated for the work completed and have a cost overrun on your hands.

The cost performance index (CPI) is calculated this way:

$$CPI = EV / AC$$

Let's plug in the numbers and see where you stand:

$$375 / 325 = 1.15$$

This means cost performance is better than expected. You get an A+ on this assignment!

The *schedule performance index (SPI)* measures the efficiency of the project team to date in completing work tasks against the progress that was planned. This formula should be used in conjunction with an analysis of the critical path activities to determine if the project will finish ahead or behind schedule. If SPI is greater than 1, you are ahead of schedule and have completed more work than was planned. If SPI is less than 1, you are behind schedule and have not completed as much work as you planned to complete by the measurement date.

The schedule performance index (SPI) is calculated this way:

$$SPI = EV / PV$$

Again, let's see where you stand with this example:

$$375 / 400 = 0.94$$

Uh-oh, not so good. Schedule performance is not what you expected. Let's not grade this one.

There are two more indexes associated with cost and schedule that you should understand for the exam: cumulative CPI and cumulative SPI.

Cumulative CPI is a commonly used calculation to predict project costs at the completion of the project. It also represents the cumulative CPI of the project at the point the measurement is taken. First, you need to sum the earned value calculations taken to date, or cumulative EV, and the actual costs to date, or cumulative AC. The formula looks just like the CPI formula except that it uses the cumulative sums as follows:

$$Cumulative\ CPI = Cumulative\ EV / Cumulative\ AC$$

The difference between this and the CPI formula earlier is that the CPI formula is used for a single work period whereas the cumulative CPI is calculated using the sum of all the costs of every work component for the project. Additionally, you might also use cumulative CPI to calculate the total cost of a work component such as a deliverable, for example. Let's say you have a deliverable that has five work packages. You would total the EV and AC at the measurement date for all five work packages to determine the cost performance index for the deliverable.

Cumulative SPI predicts schedule performance at the completion of the project. Like cumulative CPI, it also represents the cumulative SPI of the project at the point the measurement is taken. The formula is as follows:

$$\text{Cumulative SPI} = \text{Cumulative EV} / \text{Cumulative PV}$$

Forecasting

Forecasting uses the information you've gathered to date and estimates the future conditions or future performance of the project based on what you know when the calculation is performed. Forecasts are based on work performance data (an output from the Executing process group) and your predictions of future performance.

The forecasting formulas you'll see later in this section are used to determine an *estimate at completion (EAC)* and an *estimate to complete (ETC)*. The EAC estimates (or forecasts) the expected total cost of a work component, a schedule activity, or the project at its completion by calculating the actual costs to date and then adding an estimate of what the remaining work will cost. The ETC is the anticipated cost estimate to finish the work of the project.

EAC is most often calculated by using actual costs incurred to date plus a bottom-up ETC estimate. The formula for the most typical EAC looks like this:

$$\text{EAC} = \text{AC} + \text{bottom-up ETC}$$

The bottom-up ETC estimate is usually provided by the members of the project team who are actually working on the project activities. They provide the project manager with an estimate of the amount of effort remaining (and, therefore, the cost of the effort) based on the activities they have completed to date and what they believe will occur in the future. Their estimates are summed to come up with a total ETC, also known as a bottom-up ETC.

There are three other EAC forecasting formulas outlined in the *PMBOK® Guide* that we'll look at next. A new term you'll need to know before we look at these formulas is *budget at completion (BAC)*. BAC is the total amount of PV (approved budgeted costs) for all of the work of a work component or all the work of the project. It is the sum of all the budgets established for all the work in the work package, control account, schedule activity, or project.

You may find that the EAC (estimate at completion) differs from the BAC (budget at completion). This could be due to changes in performance, risks, project changes, or any number of reasons. That means the BAC may no longer be a reasonable estimate given the changes in performance. When that occurs, use the EAC to project the cost of the project at completion.

The first EAC formula is called, "EAC forecast for ETC work performed at the budgeted rate." I know that's a mouthful. Here's what you should know. This formula calculates EAC based on the actual costs to date and the assumption that ETC work will be completed at the budgeted rate. The formula looks like this:

$$EAC = AC + (BAC - EV)$$

Let's assume your AC to date is $800, BAC is $1,200, and EV is $600. EAC, assuming work ETC will be completed at the budgeted rate, is as follows:

$$\$800 + (\$1,200 - \$600) = \$1,400$$

In English, you'll spend $1,400 to complete this work component, assuming the remaining work is performed at the budgeted rate. That is $200 more than what you have budgeted because your EV is less than the actual cost to date. I would recommend examining the quality of the work to date. You aren't getting what you're paying for.

The next EAC formula is called, "EAC forecast for ETC work performed at the present CPI." (I didn't make up these titles!) Here's what you need to know. This forecast assumes that future performance will be just like the past performance for the project. The formula looks like this:

$$EAC = BAC\ /\ CPI$$

For this example, let's assume that BAC is $2,200 and CPI is 1.2. The formula looks like this:

$$\$2,200\ /\ 1.2 = \$1,833.33$$

This result predicts you will spend less than the originally budgeted amount for the project. In this case, you are getting more work or goods for the dollars you're spending. Good for you.

The last formula is called, "EAC forecast for ETC work considering both SPI and CPI factors." This formula assumes two things: There is a negative cost performance to date and the project schedule dates must be met. The formula looks like this:

$$EAC = AC + [(BAC - EV)\ /\ (CPI \times SPI\ )]$$

Let's assume AC is $1,000, BAC is $1,500, EV is $900, CPI is 0.97, and SPI is 1.05. Here's the resulting EAC:

$$\$1,000 + [(\$1,500 - \$900)\ /\ (0.97 \times 1.05)] = \$1,589.10$$

Based on the assumption that cost performance to date is negative (AC is higher than EV) and we must meet the project schedule date, EAC is $1,589.10. We will have a slight cost overrun at the end of the project in order to meet the schedule date.

Exam Spotlight

For study purposes, the EAC formula and the three EAC calculations are shown here. Remember that if you monitor EAC regularly, you'll know if the project is within acceptable tolerances. The formulas are as follows:

The EAC formula

EAC = AC + bottom-up ETC using actual costs to date and assuming ETC uses budgeted rate:

$$EAC = AC + BAC - EV$$

EAC assuming future performance will behave like past performance:

$$EAC = BAC / CPI$$

EAC when cost performance is negative and schedule dates must be met:

$$EAC = AC + [(BAC - EV) / (CPI \times SPI)]$$

In addition to the bottom-up ETC provided by the project team, there are four other formulas for calculating ETC that you should be aware of for the exam. They are discussed next.

When you believe that the work will continue to proceed as planned, use this formula to calculate ETC:

$$ETC = EAC - AC$$

When you anticipate significant changes in the work and believe it will not continue as planned, you need to reestimate ETC from the bottom up. The formula, oddly enough, looks like this:

$$ETC = Reestimate$$

When you believe that future cost variances will be similar to the types of variances you've seen to date, you'll use this formula to calculate ETC:

$$ETC = (BAC - EV) / CPI$$

Assuming your earned value is 725, CPI is 1.12, and BAC is 1,000, plug in the numbers:

$$(1,000 - 725) / 1.12 = 245.54$$

Therefore, at the measurement date, you need $245.54 to complete all the remaining work of this work component (or project if you're using project totals), assuming variances in the future will be the same as they have been to date. That's a little less than the BAC, so this is good news.

When you believe that future cost variances will *not* be similar to the types of variances you've seen to date, you'll use this formula to calculate ETC:

$$ETC = (BAC - \text{cumulative EV})$$

Now calculate your value:

$$(1,000 - 725) = 275$$

In this case, you need $275 to complete all the remaining work of this work component, assuming variances in the future are different than they have been to date. In this case, your project is on track and won't need any measure to correct performance.

Exam Spotlight

For study purposes, the ETC formulas are shown here.

Bottom-up ETC

Manual summation of the costs of the remaining work based on estimates from the project team members working on these activities.

ETC when work is anticipated to proceed as planned:

$$ETC = EAC - AC$$

ETC when work is not anticipated to proceed as planned:

$$ETC = Reestimate$$

ETC when future cost variances will be similar to past variances:

$$ETC = (BAC - EV) / CPI$$

ETC when future cost variances are expected to be atypical:

$$ETC = (BAC - \text{cumulative EV})$$

To-Complete Performance Index

To-complete performance index (TCPI) is the projected cost performance the remaining work of the project must achieve in order to meet the BAC or EAC. It's calculated by dividing the work that's remaining by the funds that are remaining.

The formula for TCPI when using the BAC is as follows:

$$TCPI = (BAC - EV) / (BAC - AC)$$

Assume for this example that BAC is $1,000, EV is $700, and AC is $800.

$$($1,000 - $700) / ($1,000 - $800) = 1.5$$

This means you'll need to reach a CPI rate that's 1.5 times what you've experienced to date in order to meet the BAC goal. You will have to improve the level of performance in this scenario in order to bring costs back into alignment with the authorized budget. This may or may not be possible given other project factors such as risk, schedule, and other performance factors. If the result is less than 1, future work does not have to be performed as efficiently as past performance.

When the BAC is no longer attainable, the project manager should calculate a new EAC. This new estimate becomes the goal you'll work toward once it's approved by management. The TCPI formula when EAC is the goal you're aiming for is as follows:

$$TCPI = (BAC - EV) / (EAC - AC)$$

We'll use the same assumptions we used in the formula earlier and note that EAC is $1,200. The formula looks like this:

$$($1,000 - $700) / ($1,200 - $800) = 0.75$$

This result means that in order to complete the work within the EAC target, the project team needs to continue performing at an efficiency of 0.75. However, also remember that you revised the original BAC and are now using EAC as your estimate to complete so additional costs were incurred.

There is one last thing to note regarding these formulas: If cumulative CPI falls below 1, all future project work must be performed at the TCPI in order to stay within your authorized project budget (BAC). That may or may not be possible given the risks, resources, schedule, and other considerations. If it is not possible, you as the project manager should calculate a new EAC and use this as the new goal.

Performance Reviews

Performance reviews compare cost performance over time and the estimates of funds needed to complete the remaining work. Three types of analyses are associated with performance reviews: variance analysis, trend analysis, and earned value performance. We looked at earned value performance in the last section so let's move on to variance analysis and trend analysis next.

Variance Analysis

Variance analysis in the Control Costs process examines the difference between the baseline cost or baseline schedule against actual performance, and/or the variance at completion of the project. Variances in this process are usually due to cost or schedule impacts making cost and schedule the most commonly analyzed variances.

Cost variances are determined by subtracting AC from EV:

$$CV = (EV - AC)$$

If the cost variance is positive, your costs are under what was planned and you are doing better than expected. If they are negative, you are over what was planned.

Schedule variances are determined by subtracting PV from EV:

$$SV = (EV - PV)$$

If the schedule variance is positive, you are ahead of schedule; if it is negative, you are behind schedule.

Variance at completion (VAC) calculates the difference between the budget at completion and the estimate at completion. It looks like this:

$$VAC = BAC - EAC$$

If the result is a negative number, it means you're not doing as well with costs as you anticipated and that variance exists. If the result is positive, your costs are doing better than you planned. Assuming your project performance is improving, as the project progresses, variances will become smaller.

 You'll be given some scratch paper when you go into the exam. I recommend that you write these formulas down on a piece of your scratch paper either during the 15-minute tutorial time or right after you start the test but before you start answering questions. Keep your list handy. That way, the formulas are off your mind and you've got them in front of you to reference when you get to the portion of the exam where these questions appear. You might want to use this tip for other items you've memorized as well. If you write them down before you begin, you don't have to jog your memory on every question. If you forget something, leave a blank space where it goes and as soon as you remember it or see a question that reminds you what it is, fill in the blank.

Trend Analysis

According to the *PMBOK® Guide*, trend analysis determines whether project performance is improving or worsening over time by periodically analyzing project results. These results are measured with mathematical formulas that attempt to forecast project outcomes based on historical information and results. You can use several formulas to predict project trends, but it's outside the scope of this book to go into them. For the exam, you're expected to understand the concept behind trend analysis, not the formulas used to calculate it. You'll want to remember that you can use the results you've analyzed using trend analysis formulas to predict future project behavior or trends.

Reserve Analysis

Reserve analysis is used to monitor the project's contingency reserves and management reserves and determine if and when they are needed, how they will be applied, and if there is a change in the reserve amounts. Additional reserves may be needed in the case of risk events, risk mitigation, or other unforeseen events. If the reserves are no longer needed, you can give them up to be used on other projects.

Control Costs Outputs

The Control Costs process has six outputs:

- Work performance information
- Cost forecasts
- Change requests
- Project management plan updates
- Project documents updates
- Organizational process assets updates

I've discussed all of these outputs before. Keep in mind that the project management plan may need to be updated to reflect changes to the cost baseline or cost management plan and the project documents updates might include cost estimates or the basis of estimates.

Recap of Formulas

You have a lot of formulas to memorize. Keep in mind that you'll be given a calculator when you take the exam, so you don't have to do the math manually. Remember that variance and trend analysis are part of the project performance review's tool and technique. Here are the formulas I've covered in this chapter:

Performance indexes

Cost performance index: $CPI = EV / AC$

> Results > 1 are under planned cost
>
> Results < 1 are over planned cost

Cumulative cost performance index: cumulative CPI = cumulative EV / cumulative AC

> Results > 1 are under planned cost
>
> Results < 1 are over planned cost

Schedule performance index: $SPI = EV / PV$

> Results > 1 are ahead of schedule
>
> Results < 1 are behind schedule

Cumulative schedule performance index: cumulative SPI = cumulative EV / cumulative PV

> Results > 1 are ahead of schedule
>
> Results < 1 are behind schedule

Forecasting

EAC formula: EAC = AC + bottom-up ETC

EAC using actual costs to date and assuming ETC uses budgeted rate: EAC = AC + (BAC – EV)

EAC assuming future performance will behave like past performance: EAC = BAC / CPI

EAC when cost performance is negative and schedule dates must be met: EAC = AC + [(BAC – EV) / (CPI × SPI)]

Bottom-up ETC: Summation of the costs of the remaining work based on estimates from the project team members working on these activities

ETC when work is anticipated to proceed as planned: ETC = EAC – AC

ETC when work is not anticipated to proceed as planned: ETC = Reestimate

ETC when future cost variances will be similar to past variances: ETC = (BAC – EV) / CPI

ETC when future cost variances are expected to be atypical: ETC = (BAC – EV)

To complete performance index

TCPI using BAC: TCPI = (BAC – EV) / (BAC – AC)

Results > 1 are more difficult to complete

Results < 1 are easier to complete

TCPI using EAC: TCPI = (BAC – EV) / (EAC – AC)

Results > 1 are more difficult to complete

Results < 1 are easier to complete

Variance analysis

Cost variance. CV = EV – AC

Positive results means the costs are under what was planned

Negative results means the costs are over what was planned

Schedule variance: SV = EV – PV

Positive results mean the schedule is ahead of what was planned

Negative results mean the schedule is behind what was planned

Variance at completion: VAC = BAC – EAC

Problems with costs come about for many reasons, including incorrect estimating techniques, predetermined or fixed budgets with no flexibility, schedule overruns, inadequate WBS development, and so on. Good project management planning techniques during the Planning processes might prevent cost problems later in the project. At a minimum, proper planning will reduce the impact of these problems if they do occur.

Always inform appropriate stakeholders of revised budget or cost estimates and any changes of significant impact to the project. Keep them updated on changes, status, and risk conditions during regularly scheduled project meetings.

 Real World Scenario

Mustang Enterprise's New Accounting System

You are a stakeholder of the New Accounting System project for Mustang Enterprises. The existing accounting system resides on a mainframe, and some of the programs used to process data are more than 15 years old. Your company decided to hire a contract software services firm to write a thin-client, browser-based version of the accounting system so that the mainframe programs could be retired. You've also assigned a senior programmer to act as the project manager on behalf of your organization.

The project is in the Monitoring and Controlling process group, and the project manager keeps reporting that everything is okay and on schedule. When you asked him detailed questions and requested performance data, the project manager patted you on the back and said, "Don't worry, I've got everything under control."

You are a little worried because some of the key project team members have come to you confidentially to inform you of the progress of the project.

After further investigation, you discover that the project manager changed the database from SQL to Oracle midway through the project and didn't tell anyone except the project team. The project scope stated specifically that project development required a SQL database. The change in database products changed the project scope and product scope without letting the stakeholders know.

This change has caused schedule delays because the project team members have told you they need to be trained to use the new database development tools before they can proceed. Additionally, many of the programs have already been written to interface with SQL, not Oracle, and will have to be modified. To add insult to injury, the database switch will impact the project budget in two ways. First, purchasing the Oracle database involves substantially more money than purchasing the SQL database, and it requires the purchase of new development tools for the programming team. Second, several members of the programming staff will have to attend multiple training sessions on the new database product to fully integrate the programs and system. Training is currently running $2,200 per session per person.

Because you're a key stakeholder, you decide to bring this information out into the open at the next project status meeting. Additionally, you plan to meet with the project sponsor and the procurement department to determine what alternatives you have to request that the contracting firm realign the project to meet the original contractual requirements. However, you fear that because the project manager is the one who gave the orders to change the database, your organization might not have a lot of recourse. You will also make the project sponsor aware that the project manager doesn't have the skills needed to conduct this project and a new project manager should be hired as soon as possible. The project manager is invaluable to the organization as a programmer, but he doesn't have the project management experience needed to conduct a project of this size and complexity. This might cause further setback to the project, but the project management plan and project schedule will require updates anyway as a result of the existing project manager's decisions. You also determine to document all that has happened as a lesson learned and to set up a change control process to prevent this from happening in the future.

Monitoring and Controlling Schedule Changes

The *Control Schedule* process involves determining the status of the project schedule, determining whether changes have occurred or should occur, taking corrective or preventive action when needed, and influencing and managing schedule changes. In the following sections, you'll look at this process's inputs, tools and techniques, and outputs.

Control Schedule Inputs

Control Schedule inputs include the following:

- Project management plan
- Project schedule
- Work performance data
- Project calendars
- Schedule data
- Organizational process assets

I've covered each of these inputs previously. Keep in mind that the Control Schedule process works hand in hand with the Perform Integrated Change Control process we covered in Chapter 10 (as all the change control processes do) and that means any changes to the schedule baseline must be processed through Integrated Change Control.

Keeping the schedule on track means you're monitoring and controlling time—one of the classic triple constraints.

Control Schedule Tools and Techniques

The tools and techniques of the Control Schedule process are as follows:

- Performance reviews
- Project management software
- Resource optimization techniques
- Modeling techniques
- Leads and lags
- Schedule compression
- Scheduling tool

We've covered all of these tools and techniques previously. I'll give you a few new points you should know regarding performance reviews.

Performance reviews in this process examine elements such as actual start and end dates for schedule activities and the remaining time to finish uncompleted activities. There are several techniques you can use in this process, including trend analysis, critical path method, critical chain method, and earned value management. If you've taken earned value measurements, the SV and SPI will be helpful in determining the impact of the schedule variations and in determining whether corrective actions are necessary.

You will recall that the critical path is the longest path on the project schedule with zero or negative float. If there are variances in critical path tasks, your schedule is likely at risk. Examining critical path tasks, or those near a critical path task, can help alert you to schedule risk.

The *PMBOK® Guide* notes that if you're using the critical chain method to construct the schedule, you should compare the amount of buffer needed to the amount of buffer remaining to help determine if the schedule is on track. This will also indicate whether corrective actions are necessary to adjust the schedule.

In the Control Schedule process, because you're dealing with time issues, it's imperative that you act as quickly as possible to implement corrective actions so that the schedule is brought back in line with the plan and the least amount of schedule delay as possible is experienced.

Schedule changes might be potential hot buttons with certain stakeholders and can burn you if you don't handle them correctly. No one likes to hear that the project is going to take longer than originally planned. That doesn't mean you should withhold this information, however. Always report the truth. If you've been keeping your stakeholders abreast of project status, they should already know that the potential for schedule changes exists. Nevertheless, be prepared to justify the reason for the schedule change or start dusting off your résumé—maybe both, depending on the company.

Make sure to examine the float variance of the critical path activities when monitoring the schedule. Thinking back to the Develop Schedule process, you'll recall that float is the amount of time you can delay starting an activity without increasing the amount of time it takes to complete the project. Because the activities with the least amount of float have the potential to cause the biggest schedule delays, examine float variance in ascending order of critical activities.

Keep in mind that not all schedule variances will impact the schedule. For example, a delay to a noncritical path task will not delay the overall schedule and might not need corrective action. Use caution here, though—if a delay occurs on a noncritical path task or its duration is increased for some reason, that task can actually become part of the critical path. Delays to critical path tasks will *always* cause delays to the project completion date and require corrective action. Careful watch of the variances in schedule start and end dates will help you control the total time element of the project.

Control Schedule Outputs

The Control Schedule process has the following outputs:

- Work performance information
- Schedule forecasts
- Change requests
- Project management plan updates
- Project documents updates
- Organizational process assets updates

Project management plan updates include making updates to the schedule baseline, the schedule management plan, and/or the cost baseline. Changes to the cost baseline may be necessary when you've used a schedule compression or crashing technique. Changes to approved schedule start and end dates in the schedule baseline are called *revisions*. They generally occur as a result of a project scope change, or changes to activity estimates, and might result in a schedule baseline update. Schedule baseline updates occur when significant changes to the project schedule, such as the changes just mentioned, are made. This means a new schedule baseline is established that reflects the changed project activity dates.

Once the new baseline is established, it is used as the basis for future performance measurements. Never re-baseline a schedule without first having it approved by the project sponsor and archiving a copy of the original baseline and schedule.

> Take care when re-baselining a project schedule. Don't lose the original baseline information. Why do you care? Because the original baseline serves as historical information to reference for future projects. Make a backup copy of the original schedule so that you have a record of the original baseline as a reference. Even though some project management software allows you to save several baselines plus the original, it's still good practice to make a backup copy of the original.

Changes to the project schedule might or might not require updates to other elements of the project management plan as well. For example, extending a schedule activity involving a contractor might impact the costs associated with that activity.

The project documents updates output may require updates to the schedule data, project schedule, and/or the risk register. For example, project schedule network diagrams require updates as a result of schedule model data updates. Don't forget to document these changes and inform your stakeholders.

Exam Spotlight

For the exam, remember that when any changes are made to a project, as the project manager you must ensure that the team is working toward the revised project goals. Once the changes are accepted and agreed on by the stakeholders, the newly revised project goals—including new schedule dates, scope changes, and so on—are what you and the team should work toward. Project success will be measured against the revised goals, not the original goals.

Utilizing Control Quality Techniques

Plan Quality Management, Perform Quality Assurance, and Control Quality are part of the Project Quality Management Knowledge Area. These processes work together to define and monitor the work of the project and to make certain the quality activity results meet the quality requirements laid out in the plan.

Control Quality is specifically concerned with monitoring work results to see whether they comply with the standards set out in the quality management plan. You should practice Control Quality throughout the project to identify and remove the causes of unacceptable results. Remember that Control Quality is concerned with project results both from a management perspective, such as schedule and cost performance, and from a product perspective. In other words, the end product should conform to the requirements and product description defined during the Planning processes.

Control Quality Inputs

Control Quality includes the following inputs:

- Project management plan
- Quality metrics
- Quality checklists
- Work performance data
- Approved change requests
- Deliverables
- Project documents
- Organizational process assets

I've discussed each of these inputs previously, so I'll move on to tools and techniques.

Control Quality Tools and Techniques

The tools and techniques in the Control Quality process are as follows:

- Seven basic quality tools
- Statistical sampling
- Inspection
- Approved change requests review

The seven basic quality tools are cause-and-effect diagrams, control charts, flowcharts, checksheets, histograms, Pareto diagrams, and scatter diagrams. We talked about the fishbone diagram (a cause-and-effect diagram), also known as the Ishikawa diagram, in Chapter 6, "Risk Planning." Recall that the fishbone diagram is used to help determine root causes. Kaoru Ishikawa is known not only for the fishbone diagram; he was also a significant contributor in the realm of quality.

The primary purpose of each of the seven basic quality tools is to examine the product, service, or result as well as the project processes for conformity to standards. They are used with the plan-do-check-act cycle we talked about in Chapter 1, "What Is a Project?," to help identify and resolve problems related to quality defects. If the results fall within the tolerance range specified, the results are acceptable. Alternatively, if the results fall within the control limits set for the product (as defined by the various tools and techniques I'll discuss in the following sections), the process you are examining is said to be *in control*. Spend time understanding these tools and their individual uses because you might see exam questions about each of them.

I talked about cause-and-effect diagrams as a diagramming technique in the Identify Risks process in Chapter 6. This technique helps identify root causes. If you need a refresher, refer to Figure 6.2 in that chapter.

I also discussed flowcharts in the same section of Chapter 6. Flowcharts are diagrams that show the logical steps that must be performed in order to accomplish an objective. They can also show how the individual elements of a system interrelate. Flowcharting can help identify where quality problems might occur on the project and how problems happen. This is important because it gives the project team the opportunity to develop alternative approaches for dealing with anticipated quality problems identified with this tool and technique. Refer to Figure 6.3.

Histograms are typically bar charts that depict the distribution of variables over time. Chapter 7, "Planning Project Resources," contains an example of a histogram. In Control Quality, the histogram usually depicts the attributes of the problem or situation. (I'll discuss attributes shortly.)

We will look at the remaining seven basic quality tools and the other tools and techniques in more detail in the following sections.

Control Charts

Control charts measure the results of processes over time and display the results in graph form. Control charts are a way to measure variances to determine whether process variances are in control or out of control.

A control chart is based on sample variance measurements. From the samples chosen and measured, the mean and standard deviation are determined. Control Quality is usually maintained—or said to be in control—within plus or minus three standard deviations. In other words, Control Quality says that if the process is in control (that is, the measurements fall within the control limits), you know that 99.73 percent of the parts going through the process will fall within an acceptable range of the mean. If you discover a part outside of this range, you should investigate and determine whether corrective action is needed.

Figure 11.2 illustrates an example of a control chart.

Let's assume you've determined from your sample measurements that 5 mm is the mean in the example control chart. One standard deviation equals 0.02. Three standard deviations on either side of the mean become your upper and lower control points on this chart. Therefore, if all control points fall within plus or minus three standard deviations on either side of the mean, the process is in control. If points fall outside the acceptable limits, the process is not in control and corrective action is needed.

Differences in results will occur in processes because there is no such thing as a perfect process. When processes are considered in control, differences in results might occur because of common causes of variances or special-cause variances.

Common causes of variances come about as a result of circumstances or situations that are relatively common to the process you're using and are easily controlled at the operational level. *Special-cause variances* are variances that are not common to the process. For

FIGURE 11.2   Control chart

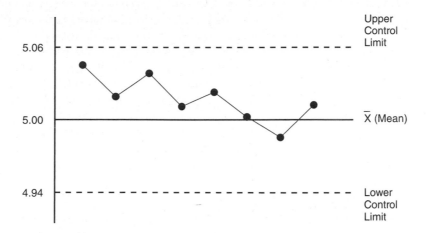

example, perhaps you have very detailed processes with specific procedures that must be followed in order to produce the output and a process gets missed. Or maybe your project requires the manufacturing of a certain part and a machine on the line has a problem and requires a special calibration. This is an easy set of terms to remember because their names logically imply their definitions.

For the exam, you should understand the three types of variances that make up common causes of variances:

Random Variances   Random variations might be normal, depending on the processes you're using to produce the product or service of the project, but they occur, as the name implies, at random.

Known or Predictable Variances   Known or predictable variances are variances that you know exist in the process because of particular characteristics of the product, service, or result you are processing. These are generally unique to a particular application.

Variances That Are Always Present in the Process   The process itself will have inherent variability that is perhaps caused by human mistakes, machine variations or malfunctions, the environment, and so on, which are known as variances always present in the process. These variances generally exist across all applications of the process.

Common cause variances that do not fall within the acceptable range are difficult to correct and usually require a reorganization of the process. This has the potential for significant impact, and decisions to change the process always require management approval.

Exam Spotlight

According to the *PMBOK® Guide*, when a process is in control, it should not be adjusted. When a process falls outside the acceptable limits, it should be adjusted.

The *Rule of 7* is another way for the project team to use control charts and determine if the process is in control. The Rule of 7 works like this. If seven consecutive points or more fall on one side of the mean, this may indicate there are factors influencing the result and should be investigated. So, while the overall results are within the control limits, the process may not necessarily be in control and those factors should be examined more closely.

Control charts are used most often in manufacturing settings where repetitive activities are easily monitored. For example, the process that produces widgets by the case lot must meet certain specifications and fall within certain variances to be considered in control. However, you aren't limited to using control charts only in the manufacturing industry. You can use them to monitor any output. You might consider using control charts to track and monitor project management processes. You could plot cost variances, schedule variances, frequency or number of scope changes, and so on to help monitor variances.

Pareto Diagrams

You have probably heard of the 80/20 rule. Vilfredo Pareto, an Italian economist and sociologist, is credited with discovering this rule. He observed that 80 percent of the wealth and land ownership in Italy was held by 20 percent of the population. Over the years, others have shown that the 80/20 rule applies across many disciplines and areas. As an example, generally speaking, 80 percent of the deposits of any given financial institution are held by 20 percent of its customer base. Let's hope that rule doesn't apply to project managers, though, with 20 percent of the project managers out there doing 80 percent of the work!

The 80/20 rule as it applies to quality says that a small number of causes (20 percent) create the majority of the problems (80 percent). Have you ever noticed this with your project or department staff? It always seems that just a few people cause the biggest headaches. But I'm getting off track.

Pareto diagrams, are displayed as histograms that rank-order the most important factors—such as delays, costs, and defects, for example—by their frequency over time. Pareto's theory is that you get the most benefit if you spend the majority of your time fixing the most important problems. The information shown in Table 11.1 is plotted on an example Pareto chart shown in Figure 11.3.

TABLE 11.1   Frequency of failures

Item	Defect frequency	Percent of defects	Cumulative percent
A	800	0.33	0.33
B	700	0.29	0.62
C	400	0.17	0.79
D	300	0.13	0.92
E	200	0.08	1.0

The problems are rank-ordered according to their frequency and percentage of defects. The defect frequencies in this figure appear as black bars, and the cumulative percentages of defects are plotted as circles. The rank-ordering of these problems shows you where corrective action should be taken first. You can see in Figure 11.3 that problem A should receive priority attention because the most benefit will come from fixing this problem.

FIGURE 11.3   Pareto chart

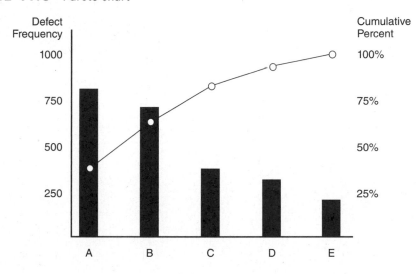

Checksheets

Checksheets, also known as tally sheets, are used to help organize data when performing inspections and gathering information on defects. They are similar to checklists. The frequencies or impacts of defects that are recorded on a checksheet can be displayed as a Pareto diagram.

Scatter Diagrams

Scatter diagrams use two variables: an *independent* variable, which is an input, and a *dependent* variable, which is an output. Scatter diagrams, also known as correlation charts, display the relationship between these two elements as points on a graph. This relationship is typically analyzed to prove or disprove cause-and-effect relationships. As an example, maybe your scatter diagram plots the ability of your employees to perform a certain task. The length of time (in months) they have performed this task is plotted as the independent variable on the x-axis, and the accuracy they achieve in performing this task, which is expressed as a score—the dependent variable—is plotted on the y-axis. The scatter diagram can help you determine whether cause-and-effect (in this case, increased experience over time versus accuracy) can be proved. Scatter diagrams can also help you look for and analyze root causes of problems.

The important point to remember about scatter diagrams is that they plot the dependent and independent variables, and the closer the points resemble a diagonal line, the closer these variables are related. Figure 11.4 shows a sample scatter diagram.

FIGURE 11.4 Scatter diagram

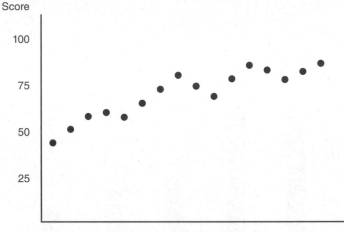

Statistical Sampling

Statistical sampling involves taking a sample number of parts from the whole population and examining them to determine whether they fall within acceptable variances. The formula for calculating the correct sample size is beyond the scope of this book. However, Creative Research Systems has an online calculator and an explanation of statistical sampling that you might find useful; visit www.surveysystem.com/sscalc.htm.

Perhaps you determine to statistically sample 25 parts out of a lot or run. The quality plan outlines that the lot will pass if four parts or fewer fall outside the allowable variance.

Statistical sampling might also involve determining the standard deviation for a process, as discussed in the control chart tool and technique. The quality management plan determines whether plus or minus two standard deviations—95.44 percent of the population—is adequate or whether plus or minus three standard deviations—99.73 percent—is adequate.

Inspection

Inspection involves physically looking at, measuring, or testing results to determine whether they conform to the requirements or quality standards. It's a tool used to gather information and improve results. Inspections might occur after the final product is produced or at intervals during the development of the product to examine individual components. Acceptance decisions are made when the work is inspected and the work is either accepted or rejected. When work is rejected, it might have to go back through the process for rework. According to the *PMBOK® Guide*, inspection is also known as *reviews*, *peer reviews, audits*, or *walkthroughs*.

Inspection might take actual measurements of components to determine whether they meet requirements. Maybe a component part for your product must be exactly 5 mm in length. To pass inspection, the parts are measured and must meet the 5 mm length requirement. If they measure 5 mm, they pass; if they do not, they fail.

Exam Spotlight

Don't confuse inspection with prevention; they're two different tools. Inspection keeps errors in the product from reaching the customer. *Prevention* keeps errors from occurring in the process. It always costs less to prevent problems in the first place than it does to fix problems built into the product after the fact. Rework, labor costs, material costs, and potential loss of customers are all factors to consider when weighing prevention costs versus the cost of rework. Philip Crosby developed the theory of Zero Defects, which deals with prevention costs. Loosely translated, Zero Defects means doing it right the first time.

Measurements can vary even if the variances are not noticeable. Machines wear down, people make mistakes, the environment might cause variances, and so on. Measurements that fall within a specified range are called *tolerable results*. So, instead of 5 mm exactly, maybe a range between 4.98 mm and 5.02 mm is an acceptable or tolerable measurement for the component. If the samples that are measured fall within the tolerable range, they pass; otherwise, they fail inspection.

One inspection technique uses measurements called *attributes*. The measurements taken during attribute sampling determine whether they meet one of two options, conforming or nonconforming. In other words, the measurements conform or meet the requirement or they do not conform. This can also be considered a pass/fail or go/no-go decision.

Attribute conformity and inspections are not necessarily performed on every component part or every end product that's produced. That's time-consuming and inefficient when you're producing numerous components. Inspection in cases like this is usually performed on a sampling of parts or products where every *x* number of parts is tested for conformity or measurement specifics.

Inspection will tell you where problems exist and will give you the opportunity to correct them, thereby leading to quality improvements. The other tools and techniques I'll talk about in these sections also lead to quality improvements in the product or process or in both.

Real World Scenario

An Ounce of Prevention

One of the main thoroughfares into your city requires a bridge replacement. You were appointed the project manager for the city and have managed this project since its initiation 15 months ago. The project entailed hiring a contractor to build the new bridge and manage the contract.

Approximately 28,000 vehicles travel across this bridge daily, carrying commuters and college students back and forth to the downtown area. One of the requirements was no more than three of the six lanes of traffic could be closed at one time during construction. Another requirement was that each piece of steel had to be painted with two coats before it was brought on-site. A third coat of paint was to be applied at the site after construction. The paint was to be guaranteed to last 25 to 30 years.

An on-site quality control inspection revealed that some of the paint was peeling. After further investigation, you discovered that the contractor did not allow the first coat of paint to cure properly, so when the second coat was applied, it peeled and flaked.

You informed the contractor that, according to the terms of the contract and the SOW specifications, they were required to apply three coats of paint to the bridge, and the paint was required to last 25 to 30 years. Paint that peeled before construction was completed did not comply with specifications. Corrective action was needed. As a result, the contract company decided to subcontract the painting work to another company while they finished their remaining tasks on the project.

Unfortunately, the subcontractor they hired was not up to the task and was unable to complete the paint job. Several months passed, and the original project completion date was missed. Obviously, revisions to the project schedule were required when it became clear that the subcontractor wasn't going to make the deadline to complete the painting task.

The original contractor found another subcontractor capable of completing the paint job. Because it was the middle of winter and temperatures were cold, the painting crew had to hang insulated tarps between the bays on the bridge and use heaters to warm up small areas of steel to the proper temperature to apply the paint. This process extended the completion date by more than three times its original estimate and ultimately delayed the completion of the project by two years. Additional costs were incurred to hire the subcontractor and rent the heaters.

Corrective action was taken as a result of the inspection, and eventually the project was completed, but not without schedule delays, schedule changes, scope changes, and rework—not to mention the increased cost to the original contractor. Because the contract was a fixed-price contract, the contractor's profit was eaten away paying for the painting job. The cost to correct the quality issue did not impact the city, but it did impact the contractor. This is a case where an ounce of prevention would have been worth several gallons of cure, as the old saying goes.

Approved Change Requests Review

We've talked about approved change requests a few times. The key in this process is to make certain you have reviewed the approved change requests and assure that they were implemented the way they were documented and approved.

Control Quality Outputs

Quality improvement, as mentioned in the Perform Quality Assurance process discussed in Chapter 9, "Conducting Procurements and Sharing Information," is a primary goal of the quality processes. Failure to meet quality requirements can have a significant impact on the project and the project team and might result in rework. *Rework* causes a project to take longer and cost more than originally planned because the project team has to repeat processes to correct the work. You should try to keep rework to a minimum so as not to impact the project schedule and budget. Rework has the potential to cause morale issues as well, especially if the team members thought they were doing a good job all along. Rework might require the project team to put in long hours, which in turn might cause more errors or other negative consequences. Monitor quality periodically so that rework is kept to a minimum.

Perform Quality Assurance is concerned with ensuring that the project is using the correct and most efficient processes to meet the project requirements; Control Quality is concerned with the accuracy of the project results.

Control Quality has several outputs:

- Quality control measurements
- Validated changes
- Verified deliverables
- Work performance information
- Change requests
- Project management plan updates
- Project documents updates
- Organizational process assets updates

I've already discussed many of these outputs, but I'll add a few quick notes here.

The results of changes, defect repairs, or variances that have been inspected and corrected are called validated changes. Validated changes, particularly corrective and preventive actions, can contribute to overall quality improvements and should be noted in the lessons learned documentation. Remember that processes that are in control should not be adjusted. Processes out of control might require adjusting, but this should occur only as a result of a management decision.

Verifying deliverables involves using the tools and techniques of this process to determine if the deliverable is correct and accurate and meets the user's needs. This output becomes an input to the next process we'll discuss, Validate Scope, which entails accepting the deliverables.

Completed checklists become part of the project's documentation and are included as part of the organizational process asset updates. Lessons learned should include the causes of variances found during this process and why the corrective actions were recommended.

Updates to the quality management plan and the process improvement plan may be required as part of the project management plan updates output of this process. Quality standards may also need to be updated as a result of this process, and they are included in the project document updates output.

Validating Project Scope

Managing and reporting on project progress make up the primary focus of the Monitoring and Controlling processes. The primary purpose of the *Validate Scope* process, which is one of those processes, is to formally accept completed deliverables and obtain sign-off that the deliverables are satisfactory and meet stakeholders' expectations and the documented requirements.

The inputs of the Validate Scope process are the project management plan, requirements documentation, requirements traceability matrix, verified deliverables, and work performance data. This process involves evaluating these inputs to determine whether the work is complete and whether it satisfies the project objectives. Evaluation is performed using inspection and group decision-making techniques, the only tools and techniques of this process. Even if the project is canceled, you should perform Validate Scope to document the degree to which the project was completed. This will serve as historical information, and if the project is ever started up again, you will have documentation that tells you what was completed and how far the project progressed.

Exam Spotlight

The most important fact you should know about the Validate Scope process is that Validate Scope formalizes the acceptance of the project scope and is primarily concerned with the acceptance of project deliverables. Don't confuse this process with the Control Quality process I just discussed.

You can remember the difference between Validate Scope and Control Quality this way:

- Control Quality = *checking* for correct work results and assuring that the quality requirements are met

- Validate Scope = *accepting* work results

The outputs of Validate Scope are accepted deliverables, change requests, work performance information, and project documents updates. Accepted deliverables are concerned with the formal acceptance of the work by the stakeholders. Remember that stakeholders include customers, the project sponsor, the project team, the management team, and so on. Document their acceptance with formal sign-off, and keep this with your project documents.

Controlling Scope

The Project Scope Management Knowledge Area includes Plan Scope Management, Collect Requirements, Define Scope, Create WBS, Validate Scope, and Control Scope. You'll recall that project scope describes the work required to produce the product, service, or result of the project. This broad statement usually includes the product scope statement and the product description, which describes the characteristics, features, and functionality of the product, service, or result. The *Control Scope* process involves monitoring the status of both the project and the product scope, monitoring changes to the project and product scope, and managing changes to the scope baseline. As with all the change processes change requests, and preventive and corrective actions that come about during this process are managed through the Perform Integrated Change Control process.

Any modification to the agreed-on WBS is considered a scope change. (It has been eons ago that you looked at this, so remember that the work breakdown structure is a deliverables-oriented hierarchy that defines the total work of the project.) This means the addition or deletion of activities or modifications to the existing activities on the WBS constitute a project scope change.

Changes in product scope require changes to the project scope as well. Let's say one of your project deliverables is the design of a piece of specialized equipment that's integrated into your final product. Now let's say that because of engineering setbacks and some miscalculations, the specialized equipment requires design modifications. The redesign of this equipment impacts the end product or product scope. Because changes to the product scope impact the project requirements, which are detailed in the scope document, changes to project scope are also required. This change, along with recommended corrective actions, should be processed through the Perform Integrated Change Control process.

Unapproved or undocumented changes that sometimes make their way into the project are referred to as *scope creep*. How often have you overheard a stakeholder speaking directly with a project team member and asking them to make "this one little change that doesn't impact anybody...really, no one will notice"? Make certain your project team members are well versed in the change control process and insist that they inform you of shenanigans like this. Scope creep can kill an otherwise viable project. Little changes add up and eventually impact budget, schedule, and quality.

Control Scope Inputs

The Control Scope process has five inputs, all of which you've seen before:

- Project management plan
- Requirements documentation
- Requirements traceability matrix
- Work performance data
- Organizational process assets

There is no new information you need to know about these inputs for this process, so let's move on to tools and techniques.

Control Scope Tools and Techniques

The Control Scope process has one tool and technique: variance analysis. Variance analysis includes reviewing project performance measurements to determine whether there are variances in project scope. It's also important to determine and document the cause and amount of variances and examine those against the scope baseline so that you can implement corrective or preventive actions if needed.

If you are using a configuration management system to control product scope, the change control system must also integrate with it. The configuration management system manages changes to product and project scope and ensures that these changes are reasonable and make sense before they're processed through the Perform Integrated Change Control process.

Control Scope Outputs

The outputs of the Control Scope process are as follows:

- Work performance information
- Change requests
- Project management plan updates
- Project documents updates
- Organizational process assets updates

Changes to scope will likely require that you repeat some of the project Planning processes and make any needed adjustments, including updating the project documents. Scope changes require an update to the project scope statement. This may require an update to the WBS and WBS dictionary as well. Here's a pop quiz: The project scope statement, WBS, and WBS dictionary are collectively known as what? The answer is the scope baseline. Scope baseline updates are part of the project management plan updates output of this process.

Scope changes include any changes to the project scope as defined by the agreed-on WBS. This in turn might require changes or updates to project objectives, costs, quality measures or controls, performance measurements baselines, or time in the form of schedule revisions. Scope changes almost always affect project costs and/or require schedule revisions.

Schedule revisions are almost always needed as a result of scope changes, but not all scope changes lengthen the project schedule. Some scope changes (a reduction in overall project requirements, for example) might reduce the number of hours needed to complete the project, which in turn might reduce the project budget. This most often occurs when the schedule is the primary constraint on the project and the start or end dates cannot be changed.

When scope changes are requested, all areas of the project should be investigated to determine what the changes will impact. The project team should perform estimates of the impact and of the amount of time needed to make the changes. Sometimes, however, the change request is so extensive that even the time to perform an estimate should be evaluated before proceeding. In other words, if the project team is busy working on estimates, they aren't working on the project. That means extensive change requests could impact the existing schedule because of the time and effort needed just to evaluate the change. Cases like these require you to make a determination or ask the change control board (CCB) to decide whether the change is important enough to allow the project team time to work on the estimates.

Always remember to update your stakeholders regarding the changes you're implementing and their impacts. They'll want to know how the changes affect the performance baselines, including the project costs, project schedule, project scope, and quality.

This process concludes the Monitoring and Controlling process groups. You'll look at the Closing processes in the next chapter.

 Real World Scenario

Project Case Study: New Kitchen Heaven Retail Store

Stakeholders have asked for an updated status on the project schedule as well as a remaining cost projection. You decide to provide several cost and schedule performance figures for the project on the status report.

"Build-out is behind schedule. They were scheduled to be completed by the 15th of January, but they aren't going to finish up until the 24th."

"What's that going to do to my schedule?" Jill asks. "I'm starting interviews for the store positions on the 16th. I hope to have that wrapped up by the 19th. As long as I have the majority of the staff hired by the 20th, we can have them stocking shelves starting the 22nd."

"Let's finish up the status of the other items, and I'll come back to that."

You've calculated some performance measurements, including earned value measures, and you show them to Jill and Dirk (all figures are in millions of dollars):

- BAC = 2; PV = 1.86; EV = 1.75; AC = 1.70

- Cumulative CPI is 1.03 (1.75 / 1.70)

- SPI is 0.94 (1.75 / 1.86)

- EAC is 1.94 (1.70 + ((2 − 1.75) / 1.03))

- ETC is 0.30 (2 − 1.70)

"What is all this telling us?" Dirk asks.

"The cost performance index tells us we're getting a good return for the money spent on the project so far. In other words, we've experienced a $1.03-value for every dollar spent to date," you respond.

"The schedule performance index isn't as cheery, but it's not dreadful news either. This performance indicator says that work is progressing at 94 percent of what we anticipated by this point.

"The estimate at completion tells us that based on what we know today, the total project will cost $1.94 million. That's coming in under the original $2 million we had budgeted for completion, so we're on track with the project budget. The last figure is the estimated cost of the remaining work."

"It looks like we're a little behind schedule based on what you have figured here," Dirk says.

"Yes, that's correct," you reply. "That brings us back to Jill's question. I have two alternatives to propose. One, we overlap the schedule and allow Gomez's crew to complete their work while Jill's staff starts stocking shelves."

Jill says, "I don't like this option. We'll be tripping over each other, and I don't want merchandise damaged by workers who are still dragging equipment around inside the store. What's your other option?"

"We could ask Gomez to increase the crew size so that they complete on time according to the contract. We have a provision in the contract that stipulates they add crew members if it looks as though they'll miss the scheduled completion date. I will instruct the contract management department to inform Gomez that we're requiring additional crew members."

"That will do the trick," Jill says. "We need the storefront to ourselves when stocking and preparing for opening. I'm glad you had that stipulation in the contract."

You report that sign-off has been obtained for the completed deliverables to date. Quality inspections and comparisons of the deliverables to the acceptance criteria were completed to Jill and Ricardo's satisfaction on the work performed to date.

Project Case Study Checklist

- Control Costs
    - Cost change control system
    - Performance measurement analysis
    - Forecasting
- Control Schedule
    - Schedule compression
- Validate Scope
    - Validated work results
- Control Quality
    - Assured quality requirements were met

Understanding How This Applies to Your Next Project

With the exception of the Perform Integrated Change Control process, we covered the meaty portion of the Monitoring and Controlling process group in this chapter. It's critical to monitor every process we discussed in order to keep the project in alignment with the objectives and to be able to take corrective action as soon as possible.

Controlling Risks is a process you'll perform once the work of the project begins and throughout the remainder of the project. Just like change, risk is something that will occur on most projects you undertake. I've never managed a project (except for projects that were started and finished within a matter of days) that didn't encounter risk. My experience has been that most risks are known-unknown, which makes contingency reserves (both time and money) essential on any project. Unknown-unknown risks are common also and require adequate management reserves. For example, during the writing of this book, we moved to a new home. I did the smart thing and got three estimates from three reputable moving companies in the area. The estimates were based on an hourly rate for a certain number of movers. Two estimates came back very close to each other, and the third was more than double the other estimates. I picked the company that said they could get us moved in two days rather than the three their competitor quoted. Fortunately, we don't move very often. Unfortunately, I didn't realize moving companies woefully underbid the amount of time it actually takes to pack you up, load the truck, and unload at the other end. By the third day, I had to insist they complete the job in four hours because we were at more than double the original quote at that point. It's a good thing I had a reserve tucked away for the unexpected, but this overrun wiped out the entire contingency fund! Taking on a project without knowing that risks will occur and without having some contingency set aside is a huge gamble because even the smallest projects have risks.

Earned value management is a tool you can't live without for measuring performance on your project, particularly the cost and schedule variance and the cost and schedule performance indexes. The size and complexity of the project will dictate how often you should run the performance measurements. The mantra of stakeholders everywhere is "on time and on budget." Therefore, controlling the project budget and the schedule will likely be two of your most time-consuming project management tasks. Use the tools we discussed in this chapter to keep yourself and your stakeholders informed of what's happening regarding these two important areas. If cost or schedule changes must occur, it's imperative you communicate what happened, why it happened, and if it's expected to happen again, and that you realign stakeholders' expectations with the new forecasted estimates.

Control Quality and Validate Scope work together to measure, inspect, and accept the project deliverables. Validating and accepting the work of the project shouldn't be a mind-boggling task at this point if you've been following the project management processes all along. For example, you should monitor and inspect deliverables as they're completed. At project's end, additional testing or inspection might be needed to verify that all the deliverables work together (if they're required to do so), but many issues or problems you've discovered regarding the deliverables should have been discovered already. However, I know that exceptions do exist. It isn't always possible to inspect the work of the project as it progresses because some projects aren't complete until the last piece of the puzzle is put into place. In that case, inspection, testing, and deliverables acceptance won't occur until the end of the project. However, if you've used sound Monitoring and Controlling tools and techniques to monitor the processes, ideally you won't encounter any big surprises at this stage.

Control Scope is absolutely essential for all projects. Time and again I've seen changes to scope end up pitting stakeholders against the project team because the requirements weren't defined adequately in the first place and because neither party clearly understood what was being requested. Scope changes can kill a project by significantly delaying the finish date or by so drastically modifying the original objective of the project that it no longer resembles what it set out to accomplish. I try to keep the questions regarding scope change simple, as in, "Do you absolutely have to have this to meet the objective of this project?" That isn't always easy for people to understand because we often confuse wants with needs. So, I might come up with an analogy they can relate to—something like this: "Let's say your one and only culinary skill is boiling water. Do you really need a designer stove with dual fuel options and a built-in warming oven to boil water? Wouldn't a simple store brand work in that case?"

Summary

We covered a lot of material in this chapter, and we also closed out the Monitoring and Controlling process group.

The Control Risks process responds to risks as they occur and implements workarounds for unplanned risk events. Some risk events planned for during the Plan Risk Responses process will occur, and some will not. Perhaps risk events that were previously identified do occur, and their impacts are much greater than anticipated during the Plan Risk Responses process. These will require updates to the risk management plan or workarounds.

Control Costs involves managing changes to project costs. It's also concerned with monitoring project budgets to prevent unauthorized or incorrect costs from getting included in the cost baseline. Control Costs uses tools and techniques such as earned value management (CV, SV, CPI, SPI), forecasting (ETC, EAC, and TCPI), and project performance reviews (variance analysis, trend analysis, and EVM) to monitor costs.

Control Schedule involves determining the status of the project schedule, determining whether changes have occurred or should occur, and influencing and managing schedule changes.

Control Quality monitors work results to see whether they fulfill the quality standards outlined in the quality management plan. Control Quality should occur throughout the life of the project. It uses many tools and techniques. Inspection measures results to determine whether the results conform to the quality standards. Attributes are measurements that either conform or do not conform. Control charts measure the results of processes over time, and Pareto charts are histograms that rank-order the most important quality factors by their frequency over time. You should not adjust processes that are in control; however, you can change these processes to realize improvements.

Validate Scope involves validating and accepting work results, while Control Scope is concerned with controlling changes to project scope.

Exam Essentials

Describe the purpose of Control Risks. Control Risks involves identifying and responding to new risks as they occur. Risk monitoring and reassessment should occur throughout the life of the project.

Name the purpose of the Control Costs process. The Control Costs process is concerned with monitoring project costs to prevent unauthorized or incorrect costs from being included in the cost baseline.

516 Chapter 11 · Controlling Work Results

Be able to describe earned value management techniques.   Earned value management (EVM) monitors the planned value (PV), earned value (EV), and actual costs (AC) expended to produce the work of the project. Cost variance (CV), schedule variance (SV), cost performance index (CPI), and schedule performance index (SPI) are the formulas used with the EVM technique.

Be able to name the tools and techniques of the Control Costs process.   The tools and techniques of the Control Costs process are earned value management, forecasting, to-complete performance index, performance reviews project management software, and reserve analysis.

Be able to name the purpose of the Control Quality process.   The purpose of the Control Quality process is to monitor work results to see whether they comply with the standards set out in the quality management plan.

Name the purpose of the Validate Scope process.   The purpose of Validate Scope is to determine whether the work is complete and whether it satisfies the project objectives.

Be able to describe product verification.   Product verification confirms that all the work of the project was completed accurately and to the satisfaction of the stakeholder.

Key Terms

I've discussed in detail the processes you'll use to monitor your project progress. You need to understand and use each of these processes to be an effective project manager. You'll need to know them by the names used in the *PMBOK® Guide* to be successful on the exam.

Control Costs

Control Risks

Control Schedule

Control Quality

Control Scope

Validate Scope

You've learned a lot of new key words in this chapter. PMI® has worked hard to develop and define standard project management terms that apply across industries. Here is a list of some of the terms you came across in this chapter:

actual cost (AC)	inspection
attributes	planned value (PV)
budget at completion (BAC)	prevention
common causes of variances	revisions
control charts	rework
cost performance index (CPI)	scatter diagrams
cost variance (CV)	Pareto diagrams
cumulative CPI	schedule performance index (SPI)
cumulative SPI	schedule variance (SV)
earned value (EV)	statistical sampling
earned value management (EVM)	technical performance measurements
efficiency indicator	tolerable results
estimate at completion (EAC)	variance at completion (VAC)
estimate to complete (ETC)	workaround

Review Questions

You can find the answers to the questions in Appendix A.

1. You are working on a project that was proceeding well until a manufacturing glitch occurred that requires corrective action. It turns out the glitch was an unintentional enhancement to the product, and the marketing people are absolutely crazy about its potential. The corrective action is canceled, and you continue to produce the product with the newly discovered enhancement. As the project manager, you know that a change has occurred to the product scope because the glitch changed the characteristics of the product. Which of the following statements is true?

   A. Changes to product scope should be reflected in the project scope.

   B. Changes to product scope should be documented in the scope management plan.

   C. Changes to product scope will result in cost changes.

   D. Changes to product scope are a result of corrective action.

2. You are working on a project that was proceeding well until a manufacturing glitch occurred that requires corrective action. It turns out the glitch was an unintentional enhancement to the product, and the marketing people are absolutely crazy about its potential. The corrective action is canceled, and you continue to produce the product with the newly discovered enhancement. As the project manager, you know that a variance has occurred. Which of the following is true?

   A. Common causes of variance, also known as special-cause variances, are situations that are unique and not easily controlled at the operational level.

   B. Random variances, known or predictable variances, and variances that are always present in the process are known as common causes of variance.

   C. Attribute inspection determines whether measurements fall within tolerable results.

   D. Scatter diagrams display the relationships between an independent and a dependent variable to show variations in the process over time.

3. Your project has experienced some changes to the agreed-on WBS elements. The changes were approved through the proper change control process. The WBS changes might in turn require which of the following?

   A. Scope changes

   B. Cost changes

   C. Schedule revisions

   D. Risk response changes

4. You are a project manager for Dakota Software Consulting Services. You're working with a major retailer that offers its products through mail-order catalogs. It is interested in knowing customer characteristics, the amounts of first-time orders, and similar information. The stakeholders have accepted the project scope. Work has begun on the project, and you're confirming some of the initial work results with the stakeholders. You've asked for acceptance of the work results. Which process are you performing?

    A. Control Risks

    B. Control Quality

    C. Validate Scope

    D. Control Scope

5. You are the project manager for a top-secret software project for an agency of the United States government. Getting top-secret clearances for contractors takes quite a bit of time, and waiting for clearances would jeopardize the implementation date. Your mission—should you choose to accept it—is to complete the project using internal resources. Your programmers are 80 percent of the way through the programming and testing work when your agency appoints a new executive director. Your programmers are siphoned off this project to work on the executive director's hot new project. Which of the following addresses the purpose of Validate Scope in this case?

    A. Validate Scope determines the correctness and completion of all the work.

    B. Validate Scope documents the level and degree of completion.

    C. Validate Scope determines whether the project results comply with quality standards.

    D. Validate Scope documents the correctness of the work according to stakeholders' expectations.

6. Which of the following statements is true regarding schedule variances?

    A. Schedule variances impact scope, which impacts the schedule.

    B. Schedule variances sometimes impact the schedule.

    C. Schedule variances always impact the schedule.

    D. Schedule variances never impact the schedule.

7. You are a project manager for Laurel's Theater Productions. Your new project is coming in over budget and requires a cost change through the cost change control system. You know all of the following statements are true regarding Control Costs except for which one?

    A. A description of how cost changes should be managed and controlled is found in the cost management plan.

    B. Approved cost changes are reflected in the cost baseline.

    C. EVM is used to determine the cost performance that must be realized for the remaining work of the project to meet the BAC goal.

    D. This equation, EAC = BAC / cumulative CPI, is used to forecast an estimate at completion assuming future project performance will be the same as past performance.

8. Which of the following might require re-baselining of the cost baseline?

    A. Corrective action

    B. Revised cost estimates

    C. Updates to the cost management plan

    D. Budget updates

9. What are the performance measurements for the Control Schedule process?

   A. SV = (EV – PV) and SPI = (EV / PV)

   B. SV = (EV – AC) and SPI = (EV / AC)

   C. SV = (EV – BAC) and SPI = (EV / BAC)

   D. SV = (PV – EV) and SPI = (PV / EV)

10. This measurement is the value of the work that has been completed to date compared to the budget.

    A. PV

    B. AC

    C. EV

    D. EAC

11. You are a contract project manager for a wholesale flower distribution company. Your project is to develop a website for the company that allows retailers to place their flower orders online. You will also provide a separate link for individual purchases that are ordered, packaged, and mailed to the consumer directly from the grower's site. This project involves coordinating the parent company, growers, and distributors. You are preparing a performance review and have the following measurements at hand: PV = 300, AC = 200, and EV = 250. What do you know about this project?

    A. The EAC is a positive number, which means the project will finish under budget.

    B. You do not have enough information to calculate CPI.

    C. The CV is a negative number in this case, which means you've spent less than you planned to spend as of the measurement date.

    D. The CV is a positive number in this case, which means you're under budget as of the measurement date.

12. A negative result from an SV calculation means which of the following?

    A. PV is higher than EV.

    B. PV equals 1.

    C. EV is higher than PV.

    D. EV is higher than AC.

13. You are a contract project manager for a wholesale flower distribution company. Your project is to develop a website for the company that allows retailers to place their flower orders online. You will also provide a separate link for individual purchases that are ordered, packaged, and mailed to the consumer directly from the grower's site. This project involves coordinating the parent company, growers, and distributors. You are preparing a performance review and have the following measurements at hand: PV = 300, AC = 200, and EV = 250. What is the CPI of this project?

A. 0.80

B. 1.25

C. 1.5

D. 0.83

14. You have accepted project performance to date and assume future work (ETC) will be performed at the budgeted rate. If BAC = 800, ETC = 275, PV = 300, AC = 200, EV = 250, and CPI = 1.25, what is the EAC?

A. 640

B. 750

C. 600

D. 550

15. You know that EAC = 375, PV = 300, AC = 200, and EV = 250. You expect the work of the project to continue as planned. What is the ETC?

A. 300

B. 125

C. 175

D. 50

16. You expect future project performance to be consistent with the project performance experienced to date for this work component. If BAC = 800, ETC = 275, PV = 300, AC = 200, EV = 250, and CPI = 1.25, what is the EAC?

A. 640

B. 750

C. 600

D. 550

17. You know that BAC = 500, PV = 325, AC = 275, CPI = 0.9, and EV = 250, and you are using actual costs to date and assuming ETC uses the budgeted rate. Variance at completion tells you which of the following?

A. 25

B. −52

C. 52

D. −25

18. You know that BAC = 2500, PV = 1250, AC = 1275, and EV = 1150, and that you are experiencing typical cost variances. What is ETC?

 A. 1467

 B. 2625

 C. 1500

 D. 2778

19. Your project progressed as planned until yesterday. Suddenly, an unexpected risk event occurred. You quickly devised a response to deal with this negative risk event using which of the following outputs of Control Risks?

 A. Risk management plan updates

 B. Workarounds

 C. Corrective action

 D. Additional risk identification

20. Which of the following is considered the most critical EVM metric?

 A. CPI

 B. CV

 C. SPI

 D. SP

Chapter 12

Closing the Project and Applying Professional Responsibility

THE PMP® EXAM CONTENT FROM THE CLOSING THE PROJECT PERFORMANCE DOMAIN COVERED IN THIS CHAPTER INCLUDES THE FOLLOWING:

✓ Obtain final acceptance of the project.

✓ Transfer the ownership of deliverables to the organization.

✓ Prepare administrative closure and index and file project records.

✓ Distribute the final project report, including all project closure-related information to all stakeholders.

✓ Document lessons learned and update the organization's knowledge base.

✓ Archive project documents.

✓ Measure customer satisfaction at the end of the project.

✓ Knowledge and Skills:

- Contract closure requirements
- Basic project accounting principles
- Close-out procedures
- Feedback techniques
- Project review techniques
- Archiving techniques and statutes
- Compliance (statute/organization)
- Transition planning techniques

Congratulations! You've made terrific progress, and after finishing this chapter you will be well equipped to take the Project Management Professional (PMP®) exam.

The Closing process group, which is the last process group we'll cover, has two processes: Close Project or Phase and Close Procurements. The Close Project or Phase process is concerned with verifying that the work of the project was completed correctly and to the stakeholders' satisfaction. Close Procurements supports the Close Project or Phase process and also verifies that the work of the project was completed correctly and the deliverables accepted.

Once you've obtained the PMP® designation, you have an obligation to maintain integrity, apply your subject matter and project management knowledge, and maintain the code of conduct published by the PMI®. You'll also be required to balance the interests and needs of stakeholders with the organization's needs. The exam might include questions on any of these topics.

As a project manager, you'll find yourself in many unique situations, different organizations, and possibly even different countries. Even if you never get involved in international project management, you will still come in contact with people from cultures and backgrounds different than yours. If you work as a contract project manager, you'll be exposed to many different organizations; each will have its own culture and ways of doing things. You should always strive to act in a professional, courteous manner in these situations.

I'll talk about each of these topics in this chapter.

The process names, inputs, tools and techniques, outputs, and descriptions of the project management process groups and related materials and figures in this chapter are based on content from *A Guide to the Project Management Body of Knowledge (PMBOK® Guide), Fifth Edition* (Sybex, 2010).

Formulating Project Closeout

All good projects must come to an end, as the saying goes. Ideally, you've practiced all the topics I've talked about that have led up to this point, and you've delivered a successful project to the stakeholders and customers. You've also put some of the vital tools of project management into play—planning, executing, controlling, and communicating—to help you reach that goal.

But how do you know when a project has ended successfully? Delivering the product or service of the project doesn't mean it has been completed satisfactorily. Remember back to the opening chapters, I said a project is completed successfully when it meets stakeholders' expectations and satisfies the goals of the project. During the Closing processes—Close Project or Phase and Close Procurements—you'll document the acceptance of the product of the project with a formal sign-off and file it with the project records for future reference. The formal sign-off is the way stakeholders indicate that the goals have been met and that the project meets their expectations so that the project ends.

Characteristics of Closing

A few characteristics are common to all projects during the Closing processes. One is that the probability of completing the project is highest during this process and risk is lowest. You've already completed the majority of the work of the project—if not all of the work—so the probability of not finishing the project is very low.

Stakeholders have the least amount of influence during the Closing processes, while project managers have the greatest amount of influence. Costs are significantly lower during this process because the majority of the project work and spending has already occurred. Remember those costly S curves we talked about in the Determine Budget process? This is where they taper off as project spending comes to an end.

One last common characteristic of projects during closing is that weak matrix organizations tend to experience the least amount of stress during the Closing processes. This is because, in a weak matrix organization, the functional manager assigns all tasks (project-related tasks as well) so the team members have a job to return to once the project is completed and there's no change in reporting structure.

All projects do eventually come to an end. You'll now examine a few of the reasons for project endings before getting into the Close Project or Phase and Close Procurements processes.

Project Endings

Projects come to an end for several reasons:

- They're completed successfully.
- They're canceled or killed prior to completion.
- They evolve into ongoing operations and no longer exist as projects.

Four formal types of project endings exist that you might need to know for the exam:

- Addition
- Starvation
- Integration
- Extinction

You'll look at each of these ending types in detail in the following sections.

Addition

Projects that evolve into ongoing operations are considered projects that end because of *addition*; in other words, they become their own ongoing business unit. An example of this is the installation of an enterprise resource planning system. These systems are business management systems that integrate all areas of a business, including marketing, planning, manufacturing, sales, financials, and human resources. After the installation of the software, these systems can develop into their own business unit because ongoing operations, maintenance, and monitoring of the software require full-time staff. These systems usually evolve into an arm of the business reporting system that no one can live without once it's installed.

A project is considered a project when it meets these criteria: It is unique, has a definite beginning and ending date, and is temporary in nature. When a project becomes an ongoing operation, it is no longer a project.

Starvation

When resources are cut off from the project or are no longer provided to the project, it's starved prior to completing all the requirements, and you're left with an unfinished project on your hands. *Starvation* can happen for any number of reasons:

- Other projects come about and take precedence over the current project, thereby cutting the funding or resources for your project.

- The customer curtails an order.

- The project budget is reduced.

- A key resource quits.

Resource starving can include cutting back or withholding human resources, equipment and supplies, or money. In any case, if you're not getting the people, equipment, or money you need to complete the project, it's going to starve and probably end abruptly.

In such cases, documentation becomes your best friend. Organizations tend to have short memories. As you move on to bigger and better projects, your memory regarding the specifics of the project will fade. Six months after the fact when someone important wonders why that project was never completed and begins the finger-pointing routine, the project documents will clearly outline the reasons the project ended early. That's one of the reasons project documentation is such an important function. I'll talk more about documenting project details shortly.

Integration

Integration occurs when the resources of the project—people, equipment, property, and supplies—are distributed to other areas in the organization or are assigned to other projects. Perhaps your organization begins to focus on other areas or other projects, and the next thing you know, functional managers come calling to retrieve their resources for other, more important things. Again, your project will come to an end due to lack of resources because they have been reassigned to other areas of the business or have been pulled from your project and assigned to another project.

The difference between starvation and integration is that starvation is the result of staffing, funding, or other resource cuts whereas integration is the result of reassignment or redeployment of the resources.

Again, good documentation describing the circumstances that brought about the end of a project because of integration should be archived with the project records for future reference.

Extinction

This is the best kind of project end because *extinction* means the project was completed and accepted by the stakeholders. As such, it no longer exists because it had a definite ending date, the goals of the project were achieved, and the project was closed out.

 Real World Scenario

Pied Piper

Jerome Reed is the project manager for Pied Piper's newest software project. His team is working on a program that will integrate the organization's human resource information, including payroll records, leave-time accruals, contact information, and so on. His top two programmers, Brett and Kathy, are heading up the coding team and are in charge of the programming and testing activities.

Pied Piper recently hired a new CIO who started working with the company just a few weeks ago. Jerome is concerned about his human resources project. It was the former CIO's pet project, but he's not sure where it falls on the new CIO's radar screen.

Jerome is in the computer room checking out the new hardware that just arrived for his project. Liz Horowitz, the director of network operations, approaches Jerome.

"That's a nice piece of hardware," Liz comments.

"It sure is. This baby is loaded. It's going to process and serve up data to the users so fast they'll be asking us to upgrade all the servers."

Liz replies, "You're right about that. I've asked Richard to burn it in and load the software."

"What software?" Jerome asks.

"You know, the new customer relationship management software. The CIO hired some vendor she has worked with before to come in and install their CRM system here. She said it was our top priority. I knew this new server was already on order, and it happens to be sized correctly for the new CRM system."

"I purchased this server for the human resources project. What am I supposed to use for that?"

Liz answers, "I've got a server over there on the bottom of the third rack that might work, or maybe you can order another one. But you should take this up with the CIO. All I know is she authorized me to use this server. She understood I was taking it from your project, so maybe she's thinking about going another direction with the human resources project.

"You probably should know I also asked to have Brett and Kathy assigned to the CRM project. Even though it's a vendor project, it still requires some of our coders. The CIO wanted the best, and they're the best we've got. It shouldn't take them long to make the changes I need, and then you can have them back for your project. In the meantime, they can give directions to your other programmers so they can keep working."

"I'm going to go see whether the CIO is in," Jerome replies.

This is a case where Jerome's project ends by integration because of the reassignment of resources. The new CIO came on board and changed the direction and focus of the project priorities, making her new project a higher priority than the previous project. As a result, Jerome's hardware and his top two resources were reassigned to the new project. Had the CIO cut the resources and equipment on the original project altogether, it would have ended because of starvation.

Closing Out the Project

The key activity of *Close Project or Phase* is concerned with completing all the activities associated with closing out the project management processes in order to officially close out the project or phase. In this process, you will review the scope baseline and other project documents to make certain the work reflected in the documents is complete and accurate. The work of the project was accepted and verified in the Validate Scope process. Remember that the project scope is measured against the project management plan so by this point in the project, the project management plan and associated project documents should be complete and up-to-date. For example, perhaps some scope change requests were implemented that changed some of the characteristics of the final product. The project information you're collecting during this process should reflect the characteristics and specifications of the final product. Don't forget to update your resource assignments as well. Some team members will have come and gone over the course of the project; you need to double-check that all the resources and their roles and responsibilities are noted.

Once the project outcomes are documented, you'll request formal acceptance from the stakeholders or the customer. They're also interested in knowing whether the product or service of the project meets the goals the project set out to accomplish. If your documentation is up-to-date, you'll have the project results at hand to share with them.

Remember that you obtained acceptance of the deliverables back in the Validate Scope process. In this process, you'll obtain final sign-off for the project or phase itself, verifying that all the exit criteria have been met.

The Close Project or Phase process is also concerned with analyzing the project management processes to determine their effectiveness and to document lessons learned concerning the project management processes. One of the other key functions of the Close Project or Phase process is to archive all project documents for historical reference and to perform administrative closure procedures for the project. This may include documenting the exit criteria for the project or phase, transferring the results of the phase or project to the operations area of the organization, and/or collecting project records and performing audits and lessons learned. You can probably guess that Close Project or Phase belongs to the Project Integration Management Knowledge Area since this process touches so many areas of the project.

Every project requires closure. According to the *PMBOK® Guide*, the completion of each project phase requires project closure as well. Before we dive into the inputs of this process, let's examine some of the administrative closure procedures you will perform as part of the project or phase closeout.

Exam Spotlight

Project closure occurs at the end of each phase of the project in order to properly document project information and keep it safe for future reference. You shouldn't wait until project completion to perform the Close Project or Phase process but rather perform it at the end of every phase, no matter whether the project phase was completed successfully or ended for some other reason.

Administrative Closure Procedures

Administrative closure procedures involve collecting all the records associated with the project, analyzing the project success (or failure), documenting and gathering lessons learned, and archiving project records. Keep in mind that when projects are performed under contract, the archiving of financial records is especially important. These records might need to be accessed if there are payment disputes, so you need to know where they are and how they were filed. Projects with large financial expenditures also require particular attention to the archiving of financial records for the same reasons. Financial information is especially useful when estimating future projects—so again, be sure to archive the information so it's easily accessible.

All of these documents should be indexed for reference and stored in a safe place. Don't forget to include electronic databases and electronic documents as part of your project archives as well. These records can be stored on a network drive or other data repository. When records are stored electronically, don't forget they are subject to your organization's retention policies and will be archived and eventually deleted according to the policy.

Administrative closure procedures also document the project team members' and stakeholders' roles and responsibilities in performing this process. According to the *PMBOK® Guide*, this should include the processes and methodologies for defining the following:

- Approval requirements of the stakeholders for project deliverables and changes to deliverables.

- Assuring and confirming that the project meets the requirements of the stakeholders, customers, and sponsor. This includes documenting necessary actions to verify that the deliverables have been accepted and exit criteria have been met.

- Assuring all activities associated with transferring the product, service, or result to the operations area (or next phase of the project) are complete.

- Assuring and confirming that the exit criteria for the project are satisfied.

Next, we'll look at the inputs of the Close Project or Phase process.

Close Project or Phase Inputs

The Close Project or Phase process gathers all the project records and verifies that they are up-to-date and accurate. According to the *PMBOK® Guide*, the overall purpose of this process is to finalize all the activities associated with all of the project management process groups in order to formally complete the project or project phase.

The project records must correctly identify the final specifications of the product or service the project set out to produce. Close Project or Phase is the place to ensure that this information accurately reflects the true results of the project.

The inputs to the Close Project or Phase process are as follows:

- Project management plan
- Accepted deliverables
- Organizational process assets

I've talked about all of these inputs previously.

Close Project or Phase Tools and Techniques

The three tools and techniques of Close Project or Phase are expert judgment, analytical techniques, and meetings. When you're conducting administrative closure activities, which we talked about earlier, the subject matter experts can help assure that the process is performed according to the organization's and to project management standards. Analytical techniques in this process might include regression analysis and/or trend analysis. Meetings in this process are used for final reviews, lessons learned, and closeout.

Close Project or Phase Outputs

Sometimes you'll work on projects where everything just clicks, your project team functions at the performing stage, the customers and stakeholders are happy, and things just fall into place according to plan. I often find it difficult to perform Close Project or Phases on projects that have progressed particularly well, just because I don't want them to end. Believe it or not, the majority of your projects can fall into this category if you practice good project management techniques and exercise those great communication skills.

The Close Project or Phase process has the following outputs:

- Final product, service, or result transition
- Organizational process assets updates

We'll take a brief look at each in the following sections.

Final Product, Service, or Result Transition

The name of this output is somewhat misleading. This actually refers to the turnover of the product, service, or result of the project to the organization. This usually requires a formal sign-off (I'll talk about that next), and in the case of a project performed on contract, it definitely requires a formal sign-off or receipt indicating acceptance of the project.

Formal acceptance includes distributing a notice of the acceptance of the product or service of the project by the stakeholders, customer, or project sponsor to stakeholders and customers. You should require formal sign-off indicating that those signing accept the product of the project.

The final product, service, or result is concerned with transitioning the final product, service, or result to the organization; organizational process assets updates involve documenting and archiving formal acceptance.

Organizational Process Assets Updates

The organizational process assets updates output is where the formal sign-off of the acceptance of the product is documented, collected, and archived for future reference. Documenting formal acceptance is important because it signals the official closure of the project, and it is your proof that the project was completed satisfactorily.

Another function of sign-off is that it kicks off the beginning of the warranty period. Sometimes project managers or vendors will warranty their work for a certain time period after completing a project. Projects that produce software programs, for example, might be warranted from bugs for a 30- or 60-day time frame from the date of implementation or acceptance. Typically in the case of software projects, bugs are fixed for free during the warranty period. Watch out, because users will try to squeeze new requirements into the "bug" category mold. If you offer a warranty, it's critical that the warranty spells out exactly what is covered and what is not.

This is also where the other project records and files are collected and archived. This includes the project planning documents (project scope statement, budget, schedule, risk responses, quality plan and baselines, and so on), change records and logs, issue logs, and so on.

Project or phase closure documents are included in this output. These include documentation showing that the project or phase is completed and that the transfer of the product of the project to the organization (or department responsible for ongoing maintenance and support) has occurred. In the case of a phase completion, the transfer would be the official hand-off to the next phase of the project rather than to an operations or maintenance group. If your project is canceled or ends prematurely, you should document the reasons for its premature end as well as the procedures for transferring the completed and uncompleted deliverables.

Exam Spotlight

According to the *PMBOK® Guide,* the project manager is responsible for reviewing documentation from prior phases of the project, reviewing and obtaining customer acceptance documentation (formal acceptance of the deliverables occurs in the Validate Scope process but you will collect and store the sign-off document during this process), and reviewing the contract if applicable to make certain all the requirements of the project are completed. If the requirements are not complete, you should not proceed with the Close Project or Phase project unless the project or phase has been terminated.

Historical information and lessons learned are used to document the successes and failures of the project. As an example, lessons learned document the reasons specific corrective actions were taken, their outcomes, the causes of performance variances, unplanned risks that occurred, mistakes that were made and could have been avoided, and so on.

Unfortunately, sometimes projects do fail. You can learn lessons from failed projects as well as from successful projects, and you should document this information for future reference. Most project managers, however, do not document lessons learned. The reason for this is that employees don't want to admit to making mistakes or learning from mistakes made during the project. They do not want their names associated with failed projects or even with mishaps on successful projects.

Lessons learned can include some of the most valuable information you'll take away from a project. We can all learn from our experiences, and what better way to have even more success on your next project than to review a similar past project's lessons learned document? However, lessons learned will be there only if you document them now. I strongly recommend you not skip this step.

You and your management team will have to work to create an atmosphere of trust and assurance that lessons learned are not reasons for reprimanding or dismissing employees but are learning opportunities that benefit all those associated with the project. Lessons learned allow you to carry knowledge gained on this project to other projects you'll work on going forward. They'll also prevent repeat mistakes in the future if you take the time to review the project documents and lessons learned prior to undertaking your new project.

Postimplementation audits aren't an official output, but they are a good idea. They go hand in hand with lessons learned because they examine the project from beginning to end and look at what went right and what went wrong. They evaluate the project goals and determine whether the product or service of the project satisfies the objectives. Postimplementation audits also examine the activities and project processes to determine whether improvements are possible on future projects.

Organizations might conduct postimplementation audits instead of lessons learned sessions. Documenting and gathering information during this procedure can serve the same function as lessons learned if you're honest and include all the good, the bad, and the ugly. Let's hope there's very little ugly.

 Real World Scenario

Cimarron Research Group

The Cimarron Research Group researches and develops organic pesticides for use on food crops. It is a medium-sized company and has established a project management office (PMO) to manage all aspects of project work. The PMO consists of project managers and administrative staff who assist with information handling, filing, and disbursement.

Terri Roberts is the project manager for a project that has just closed. Terri diligently filed all the pertinent project documents as the project progressed and has requested the research files and engineering notes from the director of engineering. All information regarding the research on this project should be included with the project archives because it's important that all the information about the project be in one place. The engineering department complies with her request but chooses to keep its own set of research records as well.

Terri's assistant has indexed all the project documents and recently sent notice of formal acceptance and approval of this project to the stakeholders, project sponsor, and management team. This notice officially closes the project. The next step is to archive the files and store them.

Closing Out the Procurements

Procurements have life cycles of their own—just like projects. I talked about the contract life cycles in Chapter 9, "Conducting Procurements and Sharing Information." As such, procurements and contracts come to a close just as projects come to a close. As you might guess, there is a process that deals with procurement closings; it's called Close Procurements.

The *Close Procurements* process is concerned with completing and settling the terms of the procurement. It supports the Close Project or Phase process because the Close Procurements process determines whether the work described in the procurement documentation or contract was completed accurately and satisfactorily. This is called *product verification*. Projects that have multiple deliverables may have procurements for some of the deliverables but not all. Obviously, this process applies only to those phases, deliverables, or portions of the project that were performed under some form of procurement.

Close Procurements is where you'll update records to document the final results of the contract or agreement, close out open claims, and archive the procurement information for future reference. These records detail the final results of the work of the project. I'll talk about the specifics of this when I cover the Close Procurements outputs.

Procurement documents might have specific terms or conditions for completion and closeout. You should be aware of these terms or conditions so that project closure isn't held up because you missed an important detail. If you are not administering the procurement yourself, be certain to ask your procurement department whether there are any special conditions that you should know about so that your project team doesn't inadvertently delay contract or project closure.

Close Project or Phase verifies and documents the project outcomes, just as the Close Procurements process does. Keep in mind that not all projects are performed under contract, so not all projects require Close Procurements. However, all projects do require the Close Project or Phase process. Because verification and documentation of the project outcomes occur in both of these processes, projects that are performed under contract need to have project results verified only one time.

Exam Spotlight

For the exam, remember that product verification, which determines whether all of the project work was completed correctly according to the contract or other procurement terms and is satisfactory according to stakeholder expectations, is performed during the Closing processes. Product documentation and deliverables are verified and accepted during the Validate Scope process. One more note: When projects end prematurely, the Validate Scope process is where the level of detail concerning the amount of work completed gets documented.

Close Procurements Inputs

The Close Procurements process has two inputs:

- Project management plan
- Procurement documents

I've discussed both these inputs before, but you should know a few more things about procurement documents for this process. Procurement documents include the contract itself (or other procurement documents) and all the supporting documents that go along with it. These might include things such as the WBS, the project schedule, change control documents, technical documents, financial and payment records, quality control inspection results, and so on. This information—along with all the other information gathered during the project—is indexed and filed once the project is closed out so that anyone considering a future project of similar scope can reference what was done.

Close Procurements Tools and Techniques

The Close Procurements process has three tools and techniques: procurement audits, procurement negotiations, and records management system. The records management system here serves the same function as the records management system I talked about in the discussion of the Control Procurements process in Chapter 9. *Procurement audits* are reviews of procurement processes to determine whether they are meeting the right needs and are being performed correctly and according to standards. The *PMBOK® Guide* says procurement audits are concerned with reviewing the procurement process, starting with the Plan Procurement Management process through Close Procurements.

The primary purpose of the procurement audit is to identify lessons learned during the procurement process. Procurement audits examine the procurement process to determine areas of improvement and to identify flawed processes or procedures. This allows you to reuse the successful processes on other procurement items for this project, on future projects, or elsewhere in the organization. It also alerts you to problems in the process so that you don't repeat them.

Procurement audits might be used by either the buyer or the vendor, or by both, as an opportunity for improvement. Documenting the lessons learned—including the successes and failures that occurred—allows you to improve other procurement processes currently underway on this project or other projects. It also gives you the opportunity to improve the process for future projects.

Procurement negotiations occur when using an alternative dispute resolution (ADR) technique due to disagreements about deliverables, payments, performance, and so on. Reaching a negotiated settlement through the aid of ADR techniques is the most favorable way to resolve the dispute.

Close Procurements Outputs

One of the purposes of the Close Procurements process is to provide formal notice to the seller—usually in written form—that the procurement is complete. The output of Close Procurements that deals with this is called closed procurements. This is a formal acceptance and closure of the procurement. It's your responsibility as project manager to document the formal acceptance of the procurement. Many times the provisions for formalizing acceptance and closing the procurement are spelled out in the procurement documents.

If you have a procurement department that handles contract administration, they will expect you to inform them when the procurement is completed and will in turn follow the formal procedures to let the seller know it's complete. However, you'll still note the procurement completion in your copy of the project records.

Depending on the terms of the procurement, early termination (whether by agreement, via default, or for cause) might result in additional charges to the buyer. Be certain to note the reasons for early termination in your procurement documentation.

The other output of Close Procurements is organizational process assets updates. This includes updating the procurement file, deliverables acceptance, and lessons learned. The *procurement file* is simply an indexed file of all the procurement records and supporting documents. These records should be indexed for easy reference and included as part of the project files in the Close Project or Phase process.

Exam Spotlight

The *PMBOK® Guide* does not state in which order these processes should be performed. In practice, you will likely close out the procurement before closing the project and archiving the project documents.

This process is your organization's way of formally accepting the product of the project from the vendor and closing out the procurement. The deliverable acceptance portion of the organizational process assets updates includes the formal written notice from the buyer that the deliverables are acceptable and satisfactory or have been rejected. If the product or service does not meet expectations, the vendor will need to correct the problems before you issue a formal acceptance notice. Ideally, quality audits have been performed during the course of the project, and the vendor was given the opportunity to make corrections earlier in the process than the closing stage. It's not a good idea to wait until the very end of the project and then spring all the problems and issues on the vendor at once. It's much more efficient to discuss problems with your vendor as the project progresses because it provides the opportunity for correction when the problems occur.

Lessons learned include information and documentation about what worked well and what didn't work well regarding the procurement processes. You can use this information on future projects to improve performance and prevent inefficiencies.

Celebrate!

I think it's a good idea to hold a celebration at the conclusion of a successfully completed project or a successfully completed phase on a large project. The project team should celebrate their accomplishment, and you should officially recognize their efforts and thank them for their participation. Any number of ideas come to mind here—a party, a trip to a ball game, pizza and sodas at lunchtime. This shouldn't be the only time you've recognized your team, as discussed during the Develop Project Team process, but now is the time to officially close the project and thank your team members. Even if no funds are available for a formal celebration, your heartfelt "thank you" can go a long way with the members of your team. It's tough for team members to remain disgruntled, and it's easier to revive them, when they know their efforts are appreciated.

A celebration helps team members formally recognize the project end and brings closure to the work they've done. It also encourages them to remember what they've learned and to start thinking about how their experiences will benefit them and the organization during the next project.

Releasing Project Team Members

Releasing project team members is not an official process. However, it should be noted that at the conclusion of the project, you will release your project team members, and they will go back to their functional managers or be assigned to a new project if you're working in a matrix type organization.

You will want to keep the functional managers or other project managers informed as you get closer to project completion so that they have time to adequately plan for the return of their employees. Start letting them know a few months ahead of time what the schedule looks like and how soon they can plan on using their employees on new projects. This gives the other managers the ability to start planning activities and scheduling activity dates.

In all the excitement of wrapping up the project, we shouldn't forget about our stakeholders. Let's take a look at balancing the stakeholders' interests and assuring we've met their expectations in the next section.

Balancing Stakeholders' Interests at Project Close

I know we discussed Managing Stakeholder Engagement in Chapter 9. Although stakeholder satisfaction is the key to project success and acceptance, I want to add some closing thoughts on this topic and discuss a few new concepts.

Projects are undertaken at the request of customers, project sponsors, executive managers, and others. You'll recall that stakeholders are those who have something to gain or lose by implementing the project. As such, stakeholders have different interests and needs, and one of your jobs is to balance the needs of the stakeholders.

Customer satisfaction is probably the primary goal you're striving for in any project. If your customer is satisfied, it means you've met their expectations and delivered the product or service they were expecting. You've got a winning combination when the customer is satisfied with the product, and you've also provided excellent customer service along the way. Satisfied customers tell others about your success and will most likely use your services in the future.

One of the key ways to ensure that customer satisfaction is achieved is to apply appropriate project management techniques to your project. This includes taking the time to discover all the requirements of the project and documenting them in the scope statement. You will find that stakeholders who have a clear understanding of the requirements and have signed off on them won't suffer from faulty memory or pull the ever-famous, "I thought that *was* included" technique. Take the time to define your requirements and get stakeholder sign-off. You can't forget or fudge what's written down.

In the following sections, I'll discuss how to juggle the competing needs of stakeholders, how to handle the issues and problems with stakeholders, and finally, how to balance project constraints against stakeholder needs.

Competing Needs

Stakeholders come from all areas of the organization and include your customer as well. Because stakeholders do not all work in the same areas, they have competing needs and interests. One stakeholder's concern on a typical IT project might take the form of system security issues, while another stakeholder is concerned about ease of use. As the project manager, you will have situations in which stakeholder needs compete with each other, and you'll have to decide between them and set priorities. Sometimes you'll be able to accommodate their needs, and sometimes you'll have to choose. You want to examine the needs against the project objectives and then use your negotiation and communication skills to convince the stakeholders of priorities.

Individual stakeholders might or might not have good working relationships with other stakeholders. Because of this, office politics come into play. I advise you to stay away from the politics game but get to know your stakeholders. You'll want to understand their business processes and needs in order to make decisions about stakeholder requirements.

Dealing with Issues and Problems

Problems will occur on your project—they're part of the process. Throughout this book, I've talked about how to deal with problems and risks and how to use conflict resolution techniques in handling problems. Balancing stakeholder needs comes into play here also.

You'll have to determine alternatives that will meet the key requirements of the project without jeopardizing the competing needs of stakeholders. Once you're into the Executing processes of the project and beyond, redefining scope becomes less and less of an option. So your responsibility is to resolve issues and determine alternative solutions to problems as they occur without changing the original objectives of the project. Enlist the help of your project team members and stakeholders during these times. Use some of the techniques I talked about in Chapter 6, "Risk Planning," such as brainstorming and the Delphi technique, to find solutions.

You might also have difficulty trying to make stakeholders understand your decision or the technical nature of a problem. Again, this is where communication skills help you immensely. Take the case of a technical problem that's cropped up on your project. You should not expect your stakeholder to understand the technical aspects of rocket science if they work in the finance department, for example. It's up to you to keep the explanation at a level they can understand without loading them down with technical jargon and specifications. Keep your explanations simple, yet don't skip important details they'll need to make decisions.

Balancing Constraints

Your toughest issues will almost always center on the triple constraints: time, cost, and scope. Because of the nature of the constraints, one of these is the primary driver, and one is the least important. Keep a close eye on stakeholders who want to switch the priority of the constraints for their own purposes. Let's say the project sponsor already told you that time is the primary constraint. Another stakeholder tells you that a requirement of the project is being overlooked and quality is suffering. Be careful that the stakeholder isn't trying to divert the primary constraint from time to quality to suit their own objectives.

 Real World Scenario

The Geographic Information System

Ryan Loveland is a project manager for a multinational company. He's working on a complex software project that involves rewriting the organization's mainframe accounting system to become a browser-based system running on thin-client architecture. A major problem with the existing system occurs when new accounts are entered into the system or account information changes. The accounts are tied to geographic areas, which are assigned to individual sales associates. Sales commissions are paid based on where the account resides. To date, the process of determining which territory an account belongs to has been done manually by looking at a map.

The project sponsor, Victor, requested a geographic information system (GIS) as part of the requirements of this project. The hope is that errors will be eliminated and commissions will be processed correctly. The sponsor hopes that Ryan's internal team can write the GIS that will tie to the accounting system. Let's drop in on Ryan and Victor's conversation.

"I just don't understand," Victor says. "I can go onto that Internet site and plug in an address and get directions and a map detailing those directions from my house to anywhere in the country. It seems easy enough to me. Why can't your team write code like that?"

"It isn't that we can't write a program to do that. But there are several issues surrounding this request that I'd like to explain to you. I'd like you to understand why I'm asking to purchase a software product from an external vendor that will take care of these functions for us."

"Let's hear it," Victor says.

"One of the first problems is that our sales force is multinational. It would take us months just to obtain address information to populate the program. The second issue is that our sales districts are not divided by any known boundaries. Most GIS systems work off of latitude and longitude or geographic boundaries such as county borders or ZIP code boundaries."

Victor interrupts, "Well, here's what we do. You give me a set of maps, I'll hand-draw in the sales districts, and then you can scan it into the system."

"Unfortunately, it's not that easy. Our sales district boundaries are not consistent with known boundaries, and our existing address database is not standardized. For example, some addresses use the word *Street* spelled out; some use the abbreviation *St.* All of the addresses need to be standardized, and then we'll have to figure out which addresses belong to which territory.

"This process could take a great deal of time. There are vendors specializing in GIS that could have us operational in a matter of weeks. I've already checked on a couple of the top vendors, and there aren't any problems interfacing with our new system. The time we'd save in the long run far outweighs the cost associated with purchasing this system from a vendor. And one last point: If I were to build this system internally, I'd have to take our top programming team off of existing project priorities to put them on this. GIS is extremely complicated. We're talking several months delay—if not a year or more—to get our programmers up to speed on GIS techniques and then write the programs."

Victor says, "If we're talking about a major delay in the schedule as you say, we can at least look at what these vendors have to offer. It's important that this system is accurate as well, and I think I hear you saying, 'Why reinvent the wheel?' Let's have a look at the costs."

We have officially closed out the project and hopefully satisfied our stakeholders' expectations. We have also completed our study of all of the project management processes from Initiating to Closing. But there's one more area you need to know about for the exam. We'll look at it next.

Professional Responsibility

As a certified Project Management Professional, you are required to adhere to the *PMI®
Code of Ethics and Professional Conduct*. You can find a copy of this code on the PMI®
website, `http://www.pmi.org/`.

You should read and understand this code because you will be agreeing to adhere to
its terms as part of the certification process. The *PMI® Code of Ethics and Professional
Conduct* outlines four areas of responsibility:

- Responsibility
- Respect
- Fairness
- Honesty

Exam Spotlight

Each of these areas is described in the code, along with sections called "Aspirational
Standards" and "Mandatory Standards" for each one. We will not cover every standard
in this chapter, so I recommend you read them and understand them for the exam. The
PMI® Code of Ethics and Professional Conduct notes that although it might be difficult to
measure the aspirational standards, they are something we should hold ourselves and
other practitioners accountable to and they are *not* optional.

There is no section on the exam that pertains solely to professional
responsibility. Instead, the exam incorporates professional responsibility
concepts into other questions throughout the exam. For example, you may
find that many of the questions in the Executing process group (and others)
pertain to Executing concepts and professional responsibility concepts
combined into one question. To make it easier to learn the principles in
the professional responsibility area, I've broken this topic out into its own
section in this chapter with questions based on these concepts.

You may find at least a few exam questions regarding professional responsibility on the
exam, so we'll look at each of these areas and a few others for good measure.

Responsibility

Responsibility is the act of making decisions that are for the good of the organization
rather than ourselves, admitting our mistakes, being responsible for the decisions we make

(or those we don't make) and the consequences that result, along with other actions. We'll look at several elements that fall within the responsibility arena.

Ensuring Integrity

As a project manager, one of your professional responsibilities is to ensure integrity of the project management process, the product, and your own personal conduct. I've spent the majority of this book discussing how to achieve project management integrity by following the project management processes.

 A product that has integrity is one that is complete and sound or fit for use.

Correctly applying the project management processes you've learned will ensure the integrity of the product. The effective execution of the Planning, Executing, and Monitoring and Controlling processes—including documenting scope, performing quality inspections, measuring performance, and taking corrective actions—will ensure that a quality product that satisfies the requirements of the stakeholders (and the project management plan) is produced. As you learned earlier, you will seek acceptance of the product from the stakeholders and customer during the Closing process group.

Accepting Assignments

This topic, as well as many of the others discussed in these sections, crosses two of the areas noted in the *PMI® Code of Ethics and Professional Conduct*—responsibility and honesty. You should always honestly report your qualifications, your experience, and your past performance of services to potential employers, customers, PMI®, and others. You should not knowingly accept assignments that are beyond your capabilities or experience.

Be honest about what you know and what you don't know as it relates to your experience. For example, the Quality Management processes as described in the *PMBOK® Guide* are used extensively in the manufacturing industry. However, the information technology field looks at quality issues in different ways. If you're a project manager in the information technology field, you've probably never used control charts and cause-and-effect diagramming techniques. Don't lead others to believe that you have used techniques you haven't used or that you have experience you don't have.

Emphasize the knowledge you do have and how you've used it in your specific industry, and don't try to fudge it with processes and techniques you've never used. Potential clients and employers would much rather work with you and provide training where you might need it than think they've got someone fully experienced with the project or industry techniques needed for a project when they don't.

If you're working on contract or you're self-employed, you have a responsibility to ensure that the estimates you provide potential customers are accurate and truthful. Clearly spell out what services you're providing and let the customer know the results they can expect at the end of the project. Accurately represent yourself, your qualifications, and your estimates in your advertising and in person.

Laws and Regulations Compliance

This might seem obvious, but as a professional, you're required to follow all applicable laws and rules and regulations that apply to your industry, organization, or project. This includes PMI® organizational rules and policies as well. You should also follow any ethical standards and principles that might govern your industry or the state or country in which you're working. Remember that rules or regulations you're used to in the United States might or might not apply to other countries, and vice versa.

Confidential Information

Many project managers work for consulting firms where their services are contracted out to organizations that need their expertise for particular projects. If you work in a situation like this, you will likely come across information that is sensitive or confidential. Again, this might seem obvious, but as part of the *PMI® Code of Ethics and Professional Conduct*, you agree not to disclose sensitive or confidential information or use it in any way for personal gain.

Often when you work under contract, you'll be required to sign a nondisclosure agreement. This agreement simply says that you will not share information regarding the project or the organization with anyone—including the organization's competitors—or use the information for your personal gain.

However, you don't have to work under contract to come into contact with sensitive or private information. You might work full-time for an organization or a government agency that deals with information regarding its customer base or citizens. For example, if you work for a bank, you might have access to personal account information. If you work for a government agency, you might have access to personal tax records or other sensitive material. It would be highly unethical and maybe even illegal to look up the account information of individuals not associated with the project at hand just to satisfy your own curiosity. In my organization, that is grounds for dismissal.

NOTE Don't compromise your ethics or your organization's reputation by sharing information that is confidential to the organization or would jeopardize an individual's privacy.

Company Data

Although it might seem obvious that you should not use personal information or an organization's trade secrets for personal gain, sometimes the organization has a legitimate need to share information with vendors, governmental agencies, or others. You need to understand which vendors or organizations are allowed to see sensitive company data. In some cases, you might even need to help determine which individuals can have access to the data. When in doubt, ask.

Here are some examples. Maybe the company you're working with has periodic mailings it sends to its customer base. If one of your project activities includes finding a new vendor to print the mailing labels, your organization might require the vendor to sign a nondisclosure agreement to guard the contents of the customer lists. Discovering just who should have access to this information might be tricky.

Another example involves data on citizens that is maintained by the government. You might think that because the data belongs to one agency of the government—say the Internal Revenue Service—any other agency of the government can have access to it. This isn't the case. Some agencies are refused access to the data even though they might have good reason to use it. Others might have restricted access, depending on the data and the agency policy regarding it. Don't assume that others should have access to data because it seems logical.

Most organizations require vendors or other organizations to sign nondisclosure agreements when the vendors or others will have access to sensitive company data. It's your responsibility to ensure that the proper nondisclosure agreements are signed prior to releasing the data. The procurement department often handles this function.

Intellectual Property

You are likely to come into contact with intellectual property during the course of your project management career. Intellectual property includes items developed by an organization that have commercial value but are not tangible and copyrighted material such as books (including this one), software, and artistic works. It might also include ideas or processes that are patented. Or it might involve an industrial process, business process, or manufacturing process that was developed by the organization for a specific purpose.

Intellectual property is owned by the business or person who created it. You might have to pay royalties or ask for written permission to use the property. Intellectual property should be treated just like sensitive or confidential data. It should not be used for personal gain or shared with others who should not have access to it.

Respect

Respect involves several areas as well, including the way we conduct ourselves, the way we treat others, listening to other viewpoints, conducting ourselves in a professional manner, and so on. We'll look at some of the elements of respect next.

Professional Demeanor

Acting in a professional manner is required of almost everyone who works in the business world. Although you are not responsible for the actions of others, you are responsible for your own actions and reactions. Part of acting professionally involves controlling yourself and your reactions in questionable situations. For example, a stakeholder or customer might lash out at you but have no basis for their outburst. You can't control what they said or did, but you can control how you respond. As a professional, your concern for the project and the organization should take precedence over your concern for your own feelings. Therefore, lashing out in return would be unprofessional. Maintain your professional demeanor, and don't succumb to shouting matches or ego competitions with others.

As project manager, you have a good deal of influence over your project team members. One of the items on the agenda at the project team kickoff meeting should be a discussion of where the team members can find a copy of organizational policies regarding conflict of interest, cultural diversity, standards and regulations, and customer service and standards of performance. Better yet, have copies with you that you can hand out at the meeting or have available the addresses of websites where they can find these documents.

When you see project team members acting out of turn or with less-than-desirable customer service attitudes, coach and influence those team members to conform to the standards of conduct expected by you and your organization. Your team members represent you and the project. As such, they should act professionally. It's your job as the project leader to ensure that they do.

Reporting Ethics Violations

When you hold the PMP® certification, one of the responsibilities that falls into this category is your responsibility to report violations of the PMP® code of conduct. To maintain integrity of the profession, everyone who holds the PMP® certification must adhere to the code of conduct that makes all of us accountable to each other.

When you know a violation has occurred and you've verified the facts, notify PMI®. Part of this process—and a requirement of the code of conduct—is that you'll verify that an ethics violation has occurred (in other words, don't report bogus or unsubstantiated reports) and will assist PMI® in the investigation by supplying information, confirming facts and dates, and so on. This includes anything listed as violations in the *PMI® Code of Ethics and Professional Conduct*, such as conflicts of interest, untruthful advertising, and false reporting of project management experience and credentials, appearances of impropriety, and so on. This one calls for some judgment on your part, but it's mostly based on common sense. For example, in most situations, a project manager with the PMP® designation should not have a family member working on the project team reporting to them (unless they own and run a family business).

Cultural Awareness

More and more companies compete in the global marketplace. As a result, project managers with multinational experience are increasingly in demand. This requires a heightened awareness of cultural influences and customary practices of the country where they're temporarily residing.

If you are used to working in the United States, for example, you know that the culture tends to value accomplishments and individualism. U.S. citizens tend to be informal and call each other by their first names, even if they've just met. In some European countries, people tend to be more formal, using surnames instead of first names in a business setting, even when they know each other well. Their communication style is more formal than in the United States, and although they tend to value individualism, they also value history, hierarchy, and loyalty. The Japanese, on the other hand, tend to communicate indirectly and consider themselves part of a group, not as individuals. The Japanese value hard work and success, as most of us do.

One thing I've witnessed when working in foreign countries is U.S. citizens trying to force their own culture or customs on those with whom they're visiting or working. That isn't recommended, and it generally offends those you're trying to impress. Don't expect others to conform to your way of doing things, especially when you're in their country. You know the saying, "When in Rome, do as the Romans do?" Although you might not want to take that literally, the intent is good. For example, a quick kiss on both cheeks is a customary greeting in many countries. If that is the case and it's how you're greeted, respond with the same.

Culture Shock

Working in a foreign country can bring about an experience called *culture shock*. When you've spent years acting certain ways and expecting normal, everyday events to follow a specific course of action, you might find yourself disoriented when things don't go as you expected.

One of the ways you can avoid culture shock is to read about the country you're going to work in before getting there. The Internet is a great resource for information such as this. Your local library is another place to research customs and acceptable practices in foreign countries.

When in doubt about a custom or what you should do in a given situation, ask your hosts or a trusted contact from the company you'll be working with to help you. People are people all over the world, and they love to talk about themselves and their cultures. They're also generally helpful, and they will respect you more for asking what's expected rather than acting as though you know what to do when you clearly do not.

Diversity Training

Sometimes you might find yourself working with teams of people from different countries or cultures. Some team members might be from one country and some from another. The best way to ensure that cultural or ethical differences do not hinder your project is to provide training for all team members.

Team-building activities are ways to build mutual trust and respect and bond team members with differing backgrounds. Choose activities that are inoffensive and ones in which everyone can participate.

Diversity training makes people aware of differences between cultures and ethnic groups, and it helps them to gain respect and trust for those on their team. Provide training regarding the project objectives and the company culture as well.

Remember that project objectives are why you are all together in the first place. Keeping the team focused on the objectives cuts across cultural boundaries and will help everyone concentrate on the project and tasks at hand rather than each other.

Respecting Your Neighbors

Americans tend to run their lives at high speed and get right down to business when working with vendors or customers. It isn't unusual for a businessperson to board a plane in the morning, show up at the client site and take care of business, and hop another flight to the next client site that night.

You'll find that this is not that common in many other countries. People in other countries will often expect you to take time to get to know them first, building an atmosphere of trust and respect. Some cultures build relationships first and then proceed to business. Don't expect to do that relationship building in a few hours. It could take several days, depending on the culture. They might even want you to meet their family and spend time getting to know them. Resist the urge to get right down to business if that's not customary in the culture because you'll likely spoil the deal or damage relationships past the point of repair.

Spend time building relationships with others. Once an atmosphere of mutual trust and cooperation is established, all aspects of project planning and management—including negotiating and problem solving—are much easier to navigate.

Perceiving Experiences

All of us see the world through our own experiences. Your experiences are not someone else's experiences; therefore, what you perceive about a situation might be very different from what others believe. Keep this in mind when it appears that a misunderstanding has occurred or that someone you're working with doesn't respond as you expect. This is especially true when you're working with someone from another country. Always give others the benefit of the doubt and ask for clarification if you think there is a problem. Put your feelings in check temporarily, and remember that what you think the other person means is not necessarily as it appears.

Fairness

Fairness includes avoiding favoritism and discrimination against others, avoiding and reporting conflict of interest situations, and maintaining impartiality in a decision-making process. We'll focus on conflict of interest in this section.

Conflict of Interest

The *PMI® Code of Ethics and Professional Conduct* discusses your responsibility to report to the stakeholders, customers, or others any actions or circumstances that could be construed as a *conflict of interest*.

A conflict of interest is when you put your personal interests above the interests of the project or when you use your influence to cause others to make decisions in your favor without regard for the project outcome. In other words, your personal interests take precedence over your professional obligations, and you make decisions that allow you to personally benefit regardless of the outcome of the project. Let's look at a few examples.

Associations and Affiliations

Conflicts of interest might include your associations or affiliations. For example, perhaps your brother-in-law owns his own construction company and you are the project manager who has just published an RFP. Your brother-in-law bids on the project and ends up winning the bid.

If you sit on the decision committee and don't tell anyone about your association with the winning bidder, that is clearly a conflict of interest. If you influence the bid decision so that it goes to your brother-in-law, he benefits from your position. Alternatively, if you are not so fond of your brother-in-law, you could influence the decision against him, in which case he loses the bid. Either way, this is a conflict of interest. You put your personal interests—or in this case the interests of your associations—above the project outcome. Even if you did not influence the decision in any way, when others on the project discover the winning bidder is your brother-in-law, they will assume a conflict of interest occurred. This could jeopardize the awarding of the bid and your own position as well.

The correct thing to do in this case would be to, first, inform the project sponsor and the decision committee that your brother-in-law intends to bid on the project. Second, refrain from participating on the award-decision committee so as not to unduly influence others in favor of your brother-in-law. Last, if you've done all these things and your brother-in-law still wins the bid, appoint someone else in your organization to administer the contract and make the payments for the work performed by him. Also, make certain you document the decisions you make regarding the activities performed by him and keep them with the project files. The more documentation you have, the less likely someone can make a conflict of interest accusation stick.

Vendor Gifts

Some professionals work in situations where they are not allowed to accept gifts in excess of certain dollar amounts. This might be driven by company policy, the department manager's policy, and so on. I have worked in organizations where it was considered a conflict of interest to accept anything from a vendor, including gifts (no matter how small), meals, or even a cup of coffee. Vendors and suppliers often provide their customers and potential customers with lunches, gifts, ball game tickets, and the like. It's your responsibility to know whether a policy exists that forbids you from accepting these gifts. It's also your responsibility to inform the vendor if they've gone over the limit and you are unable to accept the gift.

The same situation can occur here as with the brother-in-law example earlier. If you accept an expensive gift from a vendor and later award that vendor a contract or a piece of the project work, it looks like and probably is a conflict of interest. This violates PMI® guidelines and doesn't look good for you personally either.

Using the "I didn't know there was a policy" excuse probably won't save you when there's a question about conflict of interest. Make it your business to find out whether the organization has a conflict of interest policy and understand exactly what it says. Get a copy, and keep it with your files. Review it periodically. Put a note on your calendar every six months to reread the policy to keep it fresh in your mind. This is a case where not knowing what you don't know can hurt you.

Don't accept gifts that might be construed as conflicts of interest. If your organization does not have a policy regarding vendor gifts, set limits for yourself depending on the situation, the history of gift acceptance by the organization in the past, and the complexity of the project. It's always better to decline a gift you're unsure about than to accept it and later lose your credibility, your reputation, or your PMP® status because of bad judgment.

Stakeholder Influence

Another potential area for conflict of interest comes from stakeholders. Stakeholders are usually folks with a good deal of authority and important positions in the company. Make certain you do not put your own personal interests above the interests of the project when you're dealing with powerful stakeholders. They might have the ability to promote you or reward you in other ways. That's not a bad thing—but if you let that get in the way of the project or let a stakeholder twist your arm with promises of rewards, you're getting mighty close to a conflict of interest. Always weigh your decisions with the objectives of the project and the organization in mind—not your own personal gain.

Keep in mind that you might not always be on the receiving end of the spectrum. You should not offer inappropriate gifts or services or use confidential information you have at your disposal to assist others because this can also be considered a conflict of interest.

 Real World Scenario

The Golf Trip

Amanda Lewis is the project manager for a network upgrade project for her organization. This project will be outsourced to a vendor, and Amanda will manage the vendor's work. She also wrote the RFP and is a member of the selection committee.

The project consists of converting the organization's network from 100 MB Ethernet to Gigabit Ethernet. This will require replacing all of the routers and switches. Some of the cabling in the buildings will need to be replaced as well. The RFP requires that the vendor who wins the bid install all the new equipment and replace the network interface cards in each of the servers with Gigabit Ethernet cards. The grand total for this project is estimated at $1.2 million.

Steve James is a vendor with whom Amanda has worked in the past. Steve is very interested in winning this bid. He drops in on Amanda one day shortly after the RFP is posted.

"Amanda, it's good to see you," Steve says. "I was in the neighborhood and thought I'd stop in to see how things are going."

"I'm great," Amanda replies. "I'll bet you're here to talk to me about that RFP. You know I can't say anything until the whole process closes."

"You bet we bid on the project. I know you can't talk about the RFP, so I won't bring it up. I wanted to chat with you about something else. My company is sending 15 lucky contestants and one friend each to Scottsdale, Arizona, for a 'conference.' The conference includes the use of the Scottsdale Golf Club (green fees paid, of course), and all the hotel and meal expenses are on us for the length of the trip. I know Scottsdale is one of your favorite places to golf, so I thought of you. What do you say?"

Amanda sits forward in her chair and looks at Steve for a minute. "That sounds fabulous, and I do love Scottsdale. But you and I both know this isn't a conference. I wouldn't feel right about accepting it."

"Come on, Amanda. Don't look a gift horse in the mouth. It is a conference. I'll be there and so will the top brass from the company. We have some presentations and demonstrations we'd like to show you while you're there, no obligation of course, and then you're free to spend the rest of the time however you'd like."

"I appreciate the offer. Thanks for thinking of me, but no thanks. I'm on the selection committee for the RFP, and it would be a conflict of interest if I attended this conference. Besides, the value of the conference is over the $100 limit our company sets for vendor gifts and meals," Amanda says.

"Okay, we'll miss you. Maybe next time."

Honesty

Honesty can include a lot of topics: reporting the truth regarding project status, being honest about your own experience, not deceiving others, not making false statements, and so on.

One of the aspects of honesty includes your truthfulness about your PMP® application and certification, your qualifications, and the continuing reports you provide to PMI® to maintain your certification. Let's look at a few others.

Personal Gain

Honesty involves not only information regarding your own background and experience, but information regarding the project circumstances as well. For example, let's say you're a project manager working on contract. Part of your compensation consists of a bonus based on total project billing. Now, let's suppose your project is finishing sooner than anticipated, and this means your personal profit will decrease by $1,500. Should you stretch the work to meet the original contracted amount so that your personal bonus comes in at the full amount even though your project team is finished? I think you know the answer is of course not.

Your personal gain should never be a consideration when billing a customer or working on a project. Personal gain should never be a factor in any project decision. If the project finishes sooner than planned, you should bill the customer according to the terms of the procurement agreement. Compromising the project for the sake of your personal gain shows a lack of integrity, which could ultimately cost you your PMP® status and even your job.

Truthful Reporting

As a project manager, you are responsible for truthfully reporting all information in your possession to stakeholders, customers, the project sponsor, and the public when required. Always be up front regarding the project's progress.

Nothing good will come of telling stakeholders or customers that the project is on track and everything looks great when in fact the project is behind schedule or several unknown risk events have occurred that have thrown the project team a curveball. I've personally witnessed the demise of the careers of project managers who chose this route.

Tell the truth regarding project status, even when things don't look good. Stakeholders will likely go to great lengths to help you solve problems or brainstorm solutions. Sometimes, though, the call needs to be made to kill the project. This decision is usually made by the project sponsor or the stakeholders based on your recommendation and predictions of future project activities. Don't skew the reporting to prevent stakeholders from making this decision when it is the best solution based on the circumstances.

Truthful reporting is required when working with the public as well. When working in situations where the public is at risk, truthfully report the facts of the situation and what steps you're taking to counteract or reduce the threats. I recommend you get approval from the organization regarding public announcements prior to reporting the facts. Many organizations have public relations departments that will handle this situation for you.

You probably remember something your mother always told you: Actions speak louder than words. Always remember that you lead by example. Your team members are watching. If you are driven by high personal ethics and a strong desire for providing excellent customer service, those who work for you will likely follow your lead.

Role Delineation Study

In addition to the areas covered in the *PMI® Code of Ethics and Professional Conduct*, you should be aware of four other focus areas that PMI® discusses in its role delineation study. This study was published in PMI®'s publication *Project Management Professional (PMP®) Examination Specification*. The four focus areas are as follows:

- Ensure personal integrity and professionalism
- Contribute to the project management knowledge base
- Enhance personal professional competence
- Promote interaction among team members and other stakeholders

Throughout this chapter, I've covered most of the concepts surrounding these focus areas with the exception of contributing to the project management knowledge base. We'll look at that topic next.

Applying Professional Knowledge

Professional knowledge involves the knowledge of project management practices as well as specific industry or technical knowledge required to complete an assignment.

As a PMP® credential holder, you should apply project management knowledge to all your projects. Take the opportunity to educate others by keeping them up to date on project management practices, training your team members to use the correct techniques, informing stakeholders of the correct processes, and then sticking to those processes throughout the course of the project. This isn't always easy, especially when the organization doesn't have any formal processes in place. But once the stakeholders see the benefits of good project management practices, they'll never go back to the "old" way of performing their projects.

One way to apply professional knowledge is to become and remain knowledgeable in project management best practices techniques. I'll cover this topic next, along with how to become a PMI® education provider and the importance of having industry knowledge.

Project Management Knowledge

Project management is a growing field. Part of the responsibility when you hold the PMP® designation is to stay abreast of project management practices, theories, and techniques. You can do this in many ways, one of which includes joining a local PMI® chapter. There are hundreds of local chapters throughout the United States and in other countries as well. You can check the PMI® website to find a chapter near you.

Chapter meetings give you the opportunity to meet other project managers, find out what techniques they're using, and seek advice regarding your project. Usually, guest speakers appear at each chapter meeting and share their experiences and tips. Their stories are always interesting, and they give you the opportunity to learn from someone else's experiences and avoid making wrong turns on your next project. You might have a few stories of your own worth sharing with your local chapter. Volunteer to be a speaker at an upcoming meeting, and let others learn from your experiences.

One of the things you'll get when you join the PMI® organization and pay your yearly dues is its monthly magazine. This publication details real-life projects and the techniques and issues project managers have to deal with on those projects. Reading the magazine is a great way to learn new project management techniques or reinforce the information you already know. You might discover how to apply some of the knowledge you've already learned in more efficient ways as well.

PMI® offers educational courses through their local chapters and at the national level as well. These courses are yet another way for you to learn about project management and meet others in your field.

Education Providers

PMI® has a program that allows you or your organization to become a Registered Education Provider (REP). This enables you—once you're certified—to conduct PMI®-sanctioned project management training, seminars, and conferences. The best part is that your attendees are awarded professional development units (PDUs) for attending the training or seminar. As a PMP® credential holder, and especially as an REP, you have a responsibility to the profession and to PMI® to provide truthful information regarding the PMI® certification process, the exam applications, the PDU requirements, and so on. Keep up to date on the PMI®'s certification process by periodically checking the website.

Industry Knowledge

Contributing and applying professional knowledge goes beyond project management experience. You likely have specific industry or technical experience as well. Part of applying your professional knowledge includes gaining knowledge of your particular industry and keeping others informed of advances in these areas.

Information technology has grown exponentially over the past several years. It used to be that if you specialized in network operations, for example, it was possible to learn and become proficient in all things related to networks. Today that is no longer the case. Each specialized area within information technology has grown to become a knowledge area in and of itself. Many other fields have either always had individual specialties or just recently experienced this phenomenon, including the medical field, bioengineering, manufacturing, and pharmaceuticals, to name a few. You need to stay up to date regarding your industry so that you can apply that knowledge effectively. Today's fast-paced advances can leave you behind fairly quickly if you don't stay on top of things.

Earlier in the book, I mentioned that as a project manager you are not required to be a technical expert, and that still holds true. But it doesn't hurt to stay abreast of industry trends and knowledge in your field and have a general understanding of the specifics of your business. Again, you can join industry associations and take educational classes to stay on top of breaking trends and technology in your industry.

Real World Scenario

Project Case Study: New Kitchen Heaven Retail Store

Dirk strolls into your office maintaining his formal and dignified manners as always and then sits down in the chair beside your desk.

"I just want to congratulate you on a job well done," he says. "The grand opening was a success, and the store had a better-than-expected first week. I'm impressed you were able to pull this off and get the store opened prior to the Garden and Home Show. That was the key to the great opening week."

"Thank you, Dirk. Lots of people put in a lot of hard work and extra hours to get this job done. I'm glad you're happy with the results."

"I thought the banner with our logo, 'Great Gadgets for People Interested in Great Food,' was a wonderful touch."

"That was Jill's idea. She had some great ideas that made the festivities successful. As you know, though," you continue, "we did have some problems on this project. Fortunately, they weren't insurmountable, but I think we learned a thing or two during this project that we can carry forward to other projects."

"Like what?" Dirk asks.

"We should have contracted with Gomez Construction sooner so that we didn't have to pay overtime. We had a very generous budget, so the overtime expense didn't impact this project, but it might impact the next one. And we came fairly close to having a hardware disaster on our hands. Next time, we should order the equipment sooner, test it here at headquarters first, and then ship it out to the site after we know everything is working correctly."

"Good ideas. But that's old news." Dirks continues, "Now that this project is over, I'd like to get you started on the next project. We're going to introduce cooking classes in all of our retail stores. The focus is the home chef, and we might just call the classes the Home Chef Pro series. We'll offer basic classes all the way to professional series classes if the project is a hit. We'll bring in guest chefs from the local areas to give demos and teach some of the classes as well."

"I'm very interested in taking on this project and can't wait to get started. I'm thrilled that you want me to head this up. But I do have a few things here to wrap up before I start work on the new project," you reply.

Dirk says, "The project is over. The grand opening was a success. It's time to move on. Let Jill take over now; the retail stores are her responsibility."

"Jill has taken over the day-to-day operations. However, I've got to finish collecting the project information, close out the contract with Gomez, and make the final payment. Jake verified that all the work was completed correctly and to his satisfaction. Then I need to publish the formal acceptance notice to all of the stakeholders via email. I will also create a document that outlines the things I mentioned earlier that we should remember and reference during the next project; that document is called *lessons learned*. Then, after all those things are completed, all of the project records need to be indexed and archived. I can have all that done by the end of the week and will be free starting Monday to work on requirements-gathering and the charter document for the new project."

"This is just like the planning process discussion we got into with the tree, the breakdown structure thing, and all the planning, I suspect. I do have to admit all the planning paid off." As he gets up to leave, Dirk continues, "I'll give you until the end of the week to close out this project. Come see me Monday to get started on Home Chef Pro."

Jill Overstreet thought you did such a great job of managing this project that she has offered to buy you lunch at one of those upscale, white-tablecloth-type French restaurants. The iced teas have just been delivered, and you and Jill are chatting about business.

"I'm impressed with your project management skills," she remarks. "This store opening was the best on record. And you really kept Dirk in line—I admire that. He can be headstrong, but you had a way of convincing him what needed doing and then sticking to it."

"Thanks," you reply. "I've got several years of project management experience, so many of those lessons learned on previous projects helped me out with this project. I enjoy project management and read books and articles on the subject whenever I get the chance. It's nice when you can learn from others' mistakes and avoid making them yourself."

Jill takes a long drink of tea. She glances at you over the top of her glass and pauses before setting it down. "You know," she starts, "We almost didn't hire anyone for your position. Dirk wanted to do away with the project management role altogether. He had a real distaste for project management after our last project."

"Why is that?"

"The last project manager got involved in a conflict-of-interest situation. She was working on a project that involved updating and remodeling all the existing stores. Things like new fixtures, signs, shelving, display cases, and such were up for bid—and it was a very sizable bid. Not only did she accept an all-expenses-paid weekend visit to a resort town from one of the vendors bidding on the contract, she also revealed company secrets to them, some of which leaked to our competitors."

Your mouth drops open. "I can't believe she would accept gifts like that from a vendor. Revealing company secrets is even worse. Conflict of interest situations and not protecting intellectual property violate the code of professional conduct that we agree to when we gain PMP® certification. I can understand why Dirk didn't want to hire another project manager. Behavior like that makes all project managers look bad."

"I'm glad you kept things above board and won Dirk back over. The project management role is important to Kitchen Heaven, and I know your skills in this discipline are what made this project such a success."

"Jill, not only would I never compromise my own integrity through a conflict of interest situation, I would report the situation and the vendor to the project sponsor and to PMI® as an ethics violation. It's better to be honest and let the project sponsor or key stakeholders know what's happening than to hide the situation or, even worse, compromise your own integrity by getting involved in it in the first place. You have my word that I'll keep business interests above my own personal interests. I'll report anything that even looks like it would call my actions into question just to keep things honest and out in the open."

"That's good to hear," Jill replies. "Congratulations on your new assignment. Dirk and I were discussing the new Home Chef Pro project yesterday. We're venturing into new territory with this project, and I'm confident you'll do an excellent job heading it up. Dirk made a good choice."

Project Case Study Checklist

- Close Project or Phase
  - Product verification (work was correct and satisfactory)
  - Collecting project documents
  - Disseminating final acceptance notice
  - Documenting lessons learned
  - Archiving project records
- Close Procurements
  - Product verification (work was correct and satisfactory)
  - Formal acceptance and closure
- Adhering to the *PMI® Code of Ethics and Professional Conduct*
  - Ensuring personal and professional integrity
  - Not placing personal gain above business needs
  - Avoiding conflict of interest situations
  - Truthfully reporting questionable situations and maintaining honesty
  - Protecting intellectual property

Understanding How This Applies to Your Next Project

Closing out the project should always include a formal sign-off (from the project sponsor and key stakeholders at a minimum) that the work of the project is acceptable and complete. You've probably experienced, as I have, stakeholders with short-term memory lapses. For example, I'll get to the end of the project and find that a stakeholder has a list of additional requirements longer than their arm. Some of this goes back to ensuring that requirements are accurately defined during the Planning processes and that ongoing communication regarding project status, along with feedback from the stakeholders, is occurring on a regular basis. Another key here is making certain you are managing stakeholder expectations throughout the project. You might indeed have identified all the requirements and accurately documented the objective of the project. However, if the stakeholder had expectations that weren't captured or that took shape after the work of the project began, you could end up with a very unhappy stakeholder on your hands and, potentially, a failed project. In my experience, stakeholder expectations tend to stray midway through the project. That's because they are beginning to see nearly completed deliverables, and new possibilities for the product are developing that weren't thought of during the Planning stage. It's similar to buying a new house based on blueprints and then going on that first walk-through when the framing is finished. It's during walk-through that you think, "Gee, I thought that closet was bigger than this." Tune into what your stakeholders are saying and get at the basis of their questions (dig deep) so that there are no hidden expectations and you're able to manage any new expectations that pop up.

The professional responsibility section of this chapter can easily be boiled down to the Golden Rule: "Do unto others as you would have them do unto you." I wish I could tell you that everything I talked about here is practiced by all project managers everywhere. Unfortunately, you've likely read, as I have, the endless stories in the news about corporate execs acting in their own best interest rather than that of their organizations. Project managers make the news as well, especially when they're working on projects that involve public funds or charitable organizations. In my humble opinion, ignoring the practices and advice in this chapter isn't worth the damage it might cause to my organization, to the project, or to my career.

I'd also add that if your first thought on a new project is what a great résumé builder it's going to be for you and how you'll likely score that next big promotion after the project is complete, you've started off on the wrong foot. Although I'm the first to admit big projects (when they are executed well and satisfy the stakeholder expectations) *are* résumé builders, it's the wrong reason to take on a project. Consider your experience level and how and what you'll be able to contribute to the project to make it a success. It's okay if the project is a stretch for you—you can't grow your experience without taking on more complex projects as your career progresses. But also be wise enough to know when you might be in over your head.

There's no substitute for integrity and honesty when conducting your projects. Once you've tarnished your integrity, whether intentionally or not, it's almost impossible to regain the trust of your stakeholders and management staff. Because of this, I'm never afraid of telling anyone, "I don't know," but I always follow it up with, "But I'll find out." You're a project manager, not a miracle worker. No one expects you to have all the answers any more than they expect you to perform every single task on the project.

I had the unfortunate experience of being instructed to lie about project status and to purposely withhold project information from oversight boards. I spent a few sleepless nights worrying about where I'd find my next job because I immediately disobeyed those orders and reported the truth. I knew it would cost me my job. But I also knew it was better for me to lose the job than to compromise my integrity. As it turned out, I found a new job quickly. In retrospect, if I had not left the position when I did, my reputation would have taken a hit—not because of anything I had done but through association with the people on the project who compromised when they shouldn't have.

I hope you've found this study guide helpful both for your studies for the PMP® exam and for your next project. Thank you for spending some time with me in the pages of this book. I wish you the best of luck in your project management endeavors.

Summary

Project closure is the most often neglected process of all the project management processes. The two processes in the Closing process group are Close Project or Phase and Close Procurements. The four most important tasks of closure are as follows:

- Checking the work for completeness and accuracy
- Documenting formal acceptance
- Disseminating project closure information
- Archiving records and lessons learned

Close Project or Phase involves analyzing the project management processes to determine their effectiveness and to document lessons learned concerning the project management processes. It also involves archiving all project documents for historical reference and performing administrative closure procedures for the project. Documenting the formal acceptance of the project product is an important aspect of project closure as well as this ensures that the project scope, as compared to the project management plan, is complete and accurate and meets the exit criteria. Ultimately, you want to assure that the stakeholder or customer is satisfied with the work of the project and that it meets their needs.

Projects come to an end in one of four ways: addition, starvation, integration, or extinction. Addition is when projects evolve into their own business unit. Starvation happens because the project is starved of its resources. Integration occurs when resources are taken from the existing project and dispersed back into the organization or assigned to other projects. Extinction is the best ending because the project was completed, accepted, and closed.

Close Project or Phase is performed at the end of each phase of the project, as well as at the end of the project. Close Project or Phase involves documenting formal acceptance and disseminating notice of acceptance to the stakeholders, customer, and others. All documentation gathered during the project and collected during this process is archived and saved for reference purposes on future projects.

Close Procurements is concerned with settling the contract and completing the contract according to its terms. Its primary outputs include the contract file and formal acceptance and closure (both are components of the organizational process assets updates).

Lessons learned document the successes and failures of the project and of the procurement processes. Many times lessons learned are not documented because staff members do not want to assign their names to project errors or failures. You and your management team need to work together to assure employees that lessons learned are not exercises used for disciplinary purposes but benefit both the employee and the organization. Documenting what you've learned from past experiences lets you carry this forward to new projects so that the same errors are not repeated. It also allows you to incorporate new methods of performing activities that you learned on past projects.

Project management professionals are responsible for reporting truthful information about their PMP® status and project management experience to prospective customers, clients, employers and to PMI®. As a project manager, you're responsible for the integrity of the project management process and the product. In all situations, you are responsible for your own personal integrity.

Personal integrity means adhering to an ethical standard. As part of your PMP® designation, you'll be required to adhere to the *Code of Ethics and Professional Conduct* established by PMI®. Part of this code involves avoiding putting your own personal gain above the project objectives.

As a professional, you should strive to maintain honesty in project reporting. You're required to abide by laws, rules, and regulations regarding your industry and project management practices. You should also report any instance that might appear to be a conflict of interest. It's always better to inform others of an apparent conflict than to have it discovered by others and have your methods called into question after the fact.

You will likely come across confidential information or intellectual property during your project management experiences. Respect the use of this information and always verify who might have permission to access the information and when disclosures are required.

Stakeholders have competing needs and business issues and as such will sometimes cause conflict on your project. You will be required to balance the needs and interests of the stakeholders with the project objectives.

Many project managers today are working in a global environment. It's important to respect and understand the cultural differences that exist and not try to impose your cultural beliefs on others. Culture shock is an experience that occurs when you find yourself in an unfamiliar cultural environment. Training is a good way to provide project team members with relationship management techniques regarding cultural and ethnic differences.

Exam Essentials

Be able to name the primary activity of the Closing processes.   The key activity of this process is concerned with completing all the activities associated with closing out the project management processes in order to officially close out the project or phase.

Be able to describe when the Close Project or Phase process is performed.   Close Project or Phase is performed at the close of each project phase and at the close of the project.

Be able to define the purpose for lessons learned.   The purpose of lessons learned is to describe the project successes and failures and to use the information learned on future projects.

Be able to name the publication that describes the ethical standards to which PMP® credential holders are required to adhere.   The ethical standards PMP® credential holders are required to adhere to are described in the *PMI® Code of Ethics and Professional Conduct.*

Describe the areas in which PMP® credential holders must apply professional knowledge.   PMP® credential holders must apply professional knowledge in the areas of project management practices, industry practices, and technical areas.

Know the key activity that ensures customer satisfaction.   The key activity that ensures customer satisfaction is documenting project requirements and meeting them.

Define how multinational project managers must manage relationships.   Multinational project managers manage relationships by building relationships based on mutual trust and acceptance and by recognizing and respecting diverse cultures and ethnic beliefs.

Key Terms

We discussed two processes in this chapter that you need to understand for the exam.

Close Procurements

Close Project or Phase

Once again, you learned some new key words. PMI® has worked hard to develop and define standard project management terms that apply across industries. Here are the terms you came across in this chapter:

addition

conflict of interest

culture shock

extinction

integration

procurement audits

procurement file

product verification

starvation

Review Questions

You can find the answers to the questions in Appendix A.

1. You are the project manager for a top-secret software project for an agency of the United States government. Your mission—should you choose to accept it—is to complete the project using internal resources. Finding contractors with top-secret clearances takes quite a bit of time, and waiting for clearances would jeopardize the implementation date. Your programmers are 80 percent of the way through the programming and testing work when your agency appoints a new executive director. Slowly but surely your programmers are taken off this project and reassigned to the executive director's hot new project. Which of the following types of project-ending is this?

   A. Starvation

   B. Extinction

   C. Addition

   D. Integration

2. You are a project manager for Cinema Snicker Productions. Your company specializes in producing comedy films for the big screen. Your latest project has just been canceled because of budget cuts. Which of the following statements is true?

   A. This project ended due to starvation because the funding was cut off.

   B. This project ended due to integration because the resources were distributed elsewhere.

   C. This project ended due to starvation because the resources were distributed elsewhere.

   D. This project ended due to integration because the funding was cut off.

3. You are a project manager for Cinema Snicker Productions. Your company specializes in producing comedy films for the big screen. Your latest project has just been completed and accepted. You've been given your next project, which starts right away. Which of the following statements is true?

   A. This project ended due to extinction because it was completed and accepted.

   B. This project ended due to integration because it was completed and accepted and the project manager moved on to a new project.

   C. This project ended due to addition because it was completed, accepted, and archived into the company's catalog of available films.

   D. This project ended due to integration because it was completed and accepted.

4. You are a project manager for Dutch Harbor Consulting. Your latest project involves the upgrade of an organization's operating system on 236 servers. You performed this project under contract. You are in the Close Procurements process and know that you should document and file which of the following?

   A. Administrative closure procedures

   B. Close Procurements procedures

   C. Formal acceptance

   D. Product verification

5. You are a project manager for Dutch Harbor Consulting. Your latest project involves the upgrade of an organization's operating system on 236 servers. You performed this project under contract. You are in the Close Procurements process and have reviewed the contracting process to identify lessons learned. What is the name of the tool and technique you will use to perform this function?

   A. Procurement audits

   B. Performance reviews

   C. Performance audits

   D. Procurement reviews

6. Your project was just completed. Because of some unfortunate circumstances, the project was delayed, causing cost overruns at the end of the project. Which of the following statements is true?

   A. You should document the circumstances as lessons learned.

   B. You should pay particular attention to archiving the financial records for this project.

   C. Your project ended because of starvation because of the cost overruns.

   D. You should document the circumstances surrounding the project completion during the Scope Verification process.

7. Procurement audits review which of the following?

   A. The procurement processes from Plan Procurement Management through Close Procurements

   B. The procurement processes from Plan Procurement Management through Control Procurements

   C. The Plan Procurement Management and Conduct Procurements processes

   D. The procurement processes from Plan Procurement Management through Close Project or Phase process

8. As a project manager, you're responsible for maintaining and ensuring integrity for all of the following except which one?

   A. Personal integrity of others

   B. Project management process

   C. Personal integrity

   D. Product integrity

9. You are a project manager working on contract. You've performed earned value analysis and discovered that the project will be completed on time and under the original estimated amount. This means the profit to your company will decrease as will your personal bonus. Which of the following should you do?

    A. Add activities to the project to increase the cost enough to meet the original estimated amount.

    B. Tell the customer you're adding requirements to the project that were originally cut because of cost constraints.

    C. Upon completion, inform the customer the project has come in under budget.

    D. Bill the customer for the full amount of the contract because this was the original agreed-on price.

10. You are a project manager for a manufacturing firm that produces Civil War–era replicas and memorabilia. You discover a design error during a test production run on your latest project. Time is a critical constraint on this project. Which of the following is the most likely response to this problem?

    A. Reduce the technical requirements so that the error is no longer valid.

    B. Go forward with production and ignore the error.

    C. Go forward with production, but inform the customer of the problem.

    D. Develop alternative solutions to address the error.

11. You are a project manager for a telecommunications firm. You're working on a project that entails upgrading technical hardware and equipment. The estimated cost of the hardware and equipment is $1,725,000. You are reviewing products from three different vendors. One of the competing vendors invites you to lunch. What is the most appropriate response?

    A. Thank them, but let them know this could be a conflict of interest since you haven't made a decision about which vendor you're going to choose.

    B. Thank them, and decline. You know this could be considered personal gain, which could call your integrity into question.

    C. Thank them, and accept. You don't believe there is a conflict of interest or a personal integrity issue.

    D. Thank them, and decline. You believe this could be a conflict of interest on the part of the vendor, and you don't want to encourage that behavior.

12. You are a project manager for a telecommunications firm. You're working on a project that entails upgrading technical hardware and equipment. The estimated cost of the hardware and equipment is $1,725,000. You are reviewing products from three vendors. One of the vendors offers you and your family the use of the company yacht for the upcoming three-day weekend. What is the most appropriate response?

    A. Thank them, and accept. You don't believe there is a conflict of interest or an integrity issue at stake.

    B. Thank them, and decline. You know this could be considered personal gain, which could call your integrity into question.

    C. Thank them, and accept. Immediately report your actions to the project sponsor so that your motives are not called into question after the fact.

    D. Thank them, and decline. You know this could be considered an integrity issue on the part of the vendor.

13. You are a project manager working on contract with a company in a foreign country. At the project kickoff meeting, you are given an expensive-looking gift. The person who presented this to you said that it is customary in their country to give their business partners gifts. What is the most appropriate response?

    A. Thank them, and decline. Explain that this is considered personal gain, which is unacceptable in your country.

    B. Thank them, and accept. You don't believe there is a conflict of interest or an integrity issue at stake.

    C. Thank them, and decline. Explain that this is considered a conflict of interest, which is unacceptable in your country.

    D. Thank them, and accept because you know that it would be considered offensive to decline the gift in their culture. Immediately report the acceptance of the gift to the appropriate parties at your company so that your actions are not called into question later.

14. Life seems to be going very well for your close friend, a project manager, who like you has PMP® certification. She has taken a trip to France, purchased a new car, and stocked her wine cellar with a couple dozen expensive bottles of wine, all within the last six months. After a few cocktails one evening, she tells you her secret. The vendor she's working with on the $4 billion project she's managing has given her all of these items as gifts. Which scenario is the most appropriate?

    A. You tell your friend these gifts probably aren't appropriate and leave it at that.

    B. You and your friend have a long conversation about the gifts, and she decides to return them (with the exception of the trip) and not accept any more gifts in the future.

    C. You're happy for your friend and say nothing.

    D. Your friend doesn't see a problem with accepting these gifts at all. You know this is a conflict-of-interest situation and should be reported as an ethical violation.

15. As a project manager, you know that the most important activity to ensure customer and stakeholder satisfaction is which of the following?

    A. Documenting and meeting the requirements

    B. Documenting and meeting the performance measurements

    C. Reporting changes and updating the project plan and other project documents where appropriate

    D. Reporting project status regularly and in a timely manner

16. Your upcoming project includes project team members from a foreign country. To make certain that cultural differences don't interfere with team performance, thereby affecting the success of the project, your first course of action is to do which of the following?

    A. Provide diversity training to all the team members.

    B. Co-locate the project team.

    C. Perform team-building exercises.

    D. Inform the team members of the organization's rules and standards.

17. You are a contract project manager working with the State of Bliss. Your latest project involves rewriting the Department of Revenue's income tax system. One of the key stakeholders is a huge movie buff, and she has the power to promote you into a better position at the conclusion of this project. She has discovered that one of her favorite superstars lives in the State of Bliss and, therefore, must file income tax returns in that state. She asks you to look up the account of this movie star. What is the most appropriate response?

    A. Report her to the management team.

    B. Refuse to comply with the request, citing conflict of interest and violation of confidential company data.

    C. Look up the information she has requested. Because the data is considered part of the project, there is no conflict of interest.

    D. You believe that tax records are public information, so you comply with the request.

18. You are a contract project manager working with the State of Bliss. Your latest project involves rewriting the Department of Revenue's income tax system. As project manager, you have taken all the appropriate actions regarding confidentiality of data. One of the key stakeholders is a huge movie buff, and she has the power to promote you into a better position at the conclusion of this project. She's reviewing some report data that just happens to include confidential information regarding one of her favorite movie superstars. What is the most appropriate response?

    A. Report her to the management team.

    B. Request that she immediately return the information, citing conflict of interest and violation of confidential company data.

    C. Do nothing, because she has the proper level of access rights to the data and this information showed up unintentionally.

    D. Request that she immediately return the information until you can confirm that she has the proper level of access rights to the data.

19. You are a project manager with several years of experience in project management. You've accepted your first project in a foreign country. You've been in the country a week or two and are experiencing some disorientation. This is known as which of the following?

A. Co-location

B. Diversity shock

C. Global culturing

D. Culture shock

20. You are a project manager for a software manufacturing firm. The project you just finished created a new software product that is expected to become a number-one seller. All prerelease of software is handled through the marketing department. A friend of yours, who is a certified software instructor, asks you for a copy of the software prior to the beta release so they can become familiar with it. What is the most appropriate response?

A. Decline the request because the software is the intellectual property of the company.

B. Ask them to sign a nondisclosure agreement before releasing a copy of the software.

C. Decline the request because you stand to gain from this transaction by receiving free training.

D. Because your friend is certified to teach your company's brand of software, provide them with a copy of the software.

Appendix A

Answers to Review Questions

Chapter 1: What Is a Project?

1. C. The Project Management Institute (PMI®) is the industry-recognized standard for project management practices.

2. B. Projects exist to create a unique product, service, or result. The logon screen in this question is not a unique product. A minor change has been requested, indicating that this is an ongoing operations function. Some of the criteria for projects are that they are unique, temporary with definitive start and end dates, and considered complete when the project goals are achieved.

3. A. This is a project. The product line is new, which implies that this is a unique product—it hasn't been done before. You can discern a definite start and end date by the fact that the new appliances must be ready by the spring catalog release.

4. D. Progressive elaboration is the process of determining the characteristics and features of the product of the project. Progressive elaboration is carried out via steps in detailed fashion.

5. D. A project is considered successful when stakeholder needs and expectations are met.

6. B. Conflicts between stakeholders should always be resolved in favor of the customer. This question emphasizes the importance of identifying your stakeholders and their needs as early as possible in the project.

7. C. Project management brings together a set of tools and techniques to organize project activities. Project managers are the ones responsible for managing the project management processes.

8. B. Phase-end reviews can occur for all phase-to-phase relationships. Handoffs are typical of a sequentially phased project, not an overlapping phased project. Fast tracking occurs in an overlapping relationship.

9. D. Portfolios are collections of projects and/or programs. The projects or programs do not have to be directly related or interdependent to reside within the portfolio.

10. A. Negotiation and influencing skills are needed to convince Jack's boss and come to an agreement concerning his assignment.

11. A. The storyboard is a deliverable. Because the phases are performed sequentially, the deliverable must be approved before the next phase of the project can begin.

12. C. The best answer to this question according to the *PMBOK® Guide* is to negotiate with the functional manager to participate in the business analyst's annual performance review. D is an appropriate response but doesn't include the direction that the project manager should participate in the performance review.

13. B. The level of authority the project manager has is determined by the organizational structure, interactions with various management levels, and the project management maturity level of the organization.

14. A. Advantages for employees in a functional organization are that they have only one supervisor and a clear chain of command exists.

15. D. Employees in a balanced matrix often report to two or more managers. Functional managers and project managers share authority and responsibility for projects. There is a balance of power between the functional managers and project managers.

16. C. Projectized organizations are focused on the project itself. One issue with this type of structure is determining what to do with project team members when they are not actively involved in the project. One alternative is to release them when they are no longer needed.

17. D. Remember the acronym that that sounds like syrup of ipecac: IPECC (Initiating, Planning, Executing, Monitoring and Controlling, and Closing).

18. B. An overlapping phase-to-phase relationship allows you to begin the next phase before the phase you're working on is completed.

19. C. The Initiating process group is where stakeholders have the greatest ability to influence outcomes of the project. Risk is highest during this stage because of the high degree of unknown factors.

20. A. The three types of PMOs are supportive, controlling, and directive.

Chapter 2: Creating the Project Charter

1. A. The buyer provides the SOW when projects are performed under contract.

2. B. This came about because of an strategic opportunity/business need. Staff members were spending unproductive hours producing information for the management report that wasn't consistent or meaningful.

3. A. Develop Project Charter has five inputs, and they are project SOW, business case, agreements, enterprise environmental factors, and organizational process assets.

4. C. The most correct answer is to perform a feasibility study. Because this project is taking the company into a new, unknown market, there's lots of potential for error and failure. A feasibility study would help the stakeholders determine whether the project is viable and cost effective and whether it has a high potential for success.

5. D. Project Time Management involves the following processes: Plan Schedule Management, Define Activities, Sequence Activities, Estimate Activity Resources, Estimate Activity Durations, Develop Schedule, and Control Schedule.

6. B. The project SOW should contain the business need for the project and the product scope description and should support the organization's strategic plan.

7. B. Historical information on projects of a similar nature can be helpful when initiating new projects. They can help in formulating project deliverables and identifying constraints and assumptions and will be helpful later in the project Planning processes as well.

8. B. The Project Integration Management Knowledge Area consists of the following processes: Develop Project Charter, Develop Project Management Plan, Direct and Manage Project Work, Monitor and Control Project Work, Perform Integrated Change Control, and Close Project or Phase.

9. A. Benefit measurement methods include comparative methods, scoring models, and cash flow analysis. They are used as project selection tools to determine which project to proceed with or to determine which project among a list of projects should be undertaken.

10. B. Projects with NPV greater than 0 should be given an accept recommendation.

11. B. Projects with the highest IRR value are favored over projects with lower IRR values.

12. A. Net present value (NPV) assumes reinvestment is made at the cost of capital.

13. C. Year 1 and 2 inflows are each $100,000 for a total of $200,000. Year 3 inflows are an additional $300,000. Add one more quarter to this total, and the $575,000 is reached in three years and three months, or 39 months.

14. D. IRR assumes reinvestment at the IRR rate and is the discount rate when NPV is equal to 0.

15. C. The purpose of the business case is to understand the business need for the project and determine whether the investment in the project is worthwhile. This may include analysis using mathematical models and/or benefit measurement methods but that is not the primary purpose of the business case.

16. A. Stakeholder analysis involves three steps including: identifying stakeholders, analyzing potential impact, and assessing how stakeholders are likely to react to given situations.

17. B. Project B has a payback period of 21 months; $50,000 is received in the first 12 months, with another $75,000 coming in over each of the next three quarters, or nine months.

18. C. Payback period does not consider the time value of money and is, therefore, the least precise of all the cash flow analysis techniques.

19. C. The project should be kicked off with a project charter that authorizes the project to begin, assigns the project manager, and describes the project objectives and purpose for the project. Doing so ensures that everyone is working with the same purposes in mind.

20. D. According to the *PMBOK® Guide*, the project charter should be issued by the project sponsor or the project initiator.

Chapter 3: Developing the Project Scope Statement

1. A. The PMIS is one of the elements of the enterprise environmental factors, which is an input to the Develop Project Management Plan process.

2.   C. The project management plan describes the processes you'll use to perform the project and describes how the project will be executed, monitored, controlled and how the work of the project will be executed to meet the objectives.

3.   B. The scope management plan describes how project scope will be defined and verified, how the scope statement will be developed, how the WBS will be created and defined, and how project scope will be managed and controlled. Project scope is measured against the project management plan, whereas product scope is measured against the product requirements.

4.   D. These four decision-making techniques belong to the Collect Requirements process and are part of the group decision-making tool and technique in this process.

5.   B. The scope statement further elaborates the project deliverables and documents the constraints and assumptions for the project. It serves as a basis for future project decisions.

6.   D. The requirements traceability matrix links requirements to their origin and traces them throughout the project. Option A describes the requirements management plan, not the requirements document. Option B is partially true with the exception of the first statement. Requirements documents do not have to be formal or complex. Option C refers to the project scope statement, not the requirements.

7.   C. The scope baseline consists of the approved project scope statement, the WBS, and the WBS dictionary.

8.   D. Alternatives generation is a tool and technique of the Define Scope process that includes brainstorming and lateral thinking techniques.

9.   C. You could use each product as a level-one entry on the WBS so option A is correct, but you may choose to construct the WBS differently. Option C is not correct because rolling wave planning is the process of fully elaborating near term WBS work packages and elaborating others, like the third product in this question, at a later time when all information is known.

10. D. Option A might seem like a correct answer, but option D is more correct. There isn't enough information to determine whether stakeholders will require overtime. We do know that poor scope definition might lead to cost increases, rework, schedule delays, and poor morale.

11. D. Each element in the WBS is assigned a unique identifier. These are collectively known as the *code of accounts*. Typically, these codes are associated with a corporate chart of accounts and are used to track the costs of the individual work elements in the WBS.

12. A. The work package level is the lowest level in the WBS and facilitates resource assignment and cost and time estimates. In this question, the work package level contains four subprojects so it would not be used to create the activity list. The activity list will be created from the work package level for each WBS created for each subproject.

13. C. The primary constraint is time. Since the trade show demos depend on project completion and the trade show is in late September, the date cannot be moved. The budget is the secondary constraint in this example.

14.   A. Decomposition subdivides the major deliverables into smaller components. It is a tool and technique of the Create WBS process and is used to create a WBS. Level-two components might be deliverables, phases, subprojects, or some combination.

15.   B. Product analysis includes techniques such as value engineering, value analysis, systems analysis, systems engineering, product breakdown, and functional analysis.

16.   D. The primary constraint is quality. If you made the assumption as stated in options B and C, you assumed incorrectly. Clarify these assumptions with your stakeholders and project sponsors.

17.   C. This is an example of an assumption. You've used this vendor before and haven't had any problems. You're assuming there will be no problems with this delivery based on your past experience.

18.   B. Constraints restrict the actions of the project team.

19.   A. The project came about because of a business need. The phones have to be answered because that's the core business. Upgrading the system to handle more volume is a business need. An assumption has been made regarding vendor availability. Always validate your assumptions.

20.   B. The steps of decomposition include identify major deliverables, organize and determine the structure, identify lower-level components, assign identification codes, and verify correctness of decomposition.

Chapter 4: Creating the Project Schedule

1.   C. The tools and techniques for Estimate Activity Durations are expert judgment, analogous estimating, parametric estimating, three-point estimating, group decision-making techniques, and reserve analysis.

2.   B. The Sequence Activities process produces project schedule network diagrams and project documents updates, which may include updating activity attributes. The purpose of this process is to identify all activity dependencies.

3.   C. Reserve analysis takes schedule risk into consideration and adds a percentage of time or additional work periods to the estimate to prevent schedule delays.

4.   A. Parametric estimating uses an algorithm or formula that multiplies a known element—such as the quantity of materials needed—by the time it takes to install or complete one unit of materials. The result is a total estimate for the activity. In this case, 10 servers multiplied by 16 hours per server gives you a 160-hour total duration estimate.

5.   C. The activity list is a component of the project schedule, not the WBS. The activity list includes all the project activities, an identifier, and a description of the activity. The activity list is an output of the Define Activities process.

6.   D. This is an example of a mandatory dependency, also known as *hard logic*. Mandatory dependencies are inherent in the nature of the work. Discretionary dependencies, also called *preferred logic*, *preferential logic*, and *soft logic*, are defined by the project management team.

7.   A. The precedence diagramming method is also known as the activity on node (AON) diagramming method. GERT stands for Graphical Evaluation and Review Technique, a diagramming method that allows for conditions, branches, and loops.

8.   B. The arrow diagramming method uses only finish-to-start dependencies.

9.   D. Finish-to-start (FS) is the most commonly used logical relationship in PDM and the default relationship in most project management software packages.

10. C. CPM calculates a single early and late start date and a single early and late finish date for each activity. Once these dates are known, float time is calculated for each activity to determine the critical path. The other answers contain elements of PERT calculations.

11. B. The only information you have for this example is activity duration; therefore, the critical path is the path with the longest duration. Path A-D-E-H with a duration of 34 days is the critical path.

12. D. The only information you have for this example is activity duration, so you must calculate the critical path based on the durations given. The duration of A-B-C-E-H increased by 3 days, for a total of 35 days. The duration of A-F-G-H and A-F-G-E-H each increased by 3 days. A-F-G-E-H totals 36 days and becomes the new critical path.

13. D. You calculate the critical path by adding together the durations of all the tasks with zero or negative float. The critical path can be compressed using crashing techniques.

14. C. The calculation for PERT is the sum of optimistic time plus pessimistic time plus four times the most likely time divided by 6. The calculation for this example is as follows: $(48 + 72 + (4 \times 60)) / 6 = 60$.

15. D. You calculate the standard deviation by subtracting the optimistic time from the pessimistic time and dividing the result by 6. The calculation for this example is as follows: $(72 - 48) / 6 = 4$.

16. D. There is a 95 percent probability that the work will finish within plus or minus two standard deviations. The expected value is 500, and the standard deviation times 2 is 24, so the activity will take from 476 to 524 days.

17. B. A 68 percent probability is calculated using plus or minus one standard deviation, a 95 percent probability uses plus or minus two standard deviations, and a 99 percent probability uses plus or minus three standard deviations.

18. A. Crashing the schedule includes tasks such as adding resources to the critical path tasks or speeding up deliveries of materials and resources.

19. C. Resource leveling is used for overallocated resources and allows for changes to the schedule completion dates. Crashing and fast tracking are schedule compression techniques that shorten the schedule. Resource smoothing techniques will not allow for changes to the critical path or project end date, and since you are concerned about not overusing this resource, lengthening the schedule is a better option.

20. A. Project management software is a useful tool for the project manager, and it automates project scheduling, allowing for what-if analysis and easy changes. But if you focus too much on the tool and ignore the project, the tool becomes a hindrance.

Chapter 5: Developing the Project Budget and Communicating the Plan

1. A. Determining the cost of resources (not the amount) to complete all the activities for the project is the primary concern of the Project Cost Management Knowledge Area.

2. D. The cost management plan, an output of the Plan Cost Management process, is used to establish the criteria for planning, estimating, budgeting, and controlling costs.

3. D. Control thresholds are variance thresholds (typically stated as a percentage of deviation from the baseline) used for monitoring cost performance.

4. C. A control account can be placed at any level of the WBS and is used for earned value measurement calculations regarding project costs.

5. A. The inputs of Estimate Costs are cost management plan, human resource management plan, scope baseline, project schedule, risk register, enterprise environmental factors, and organizational process assets.

6. B. Three-point estimating can improve activity cost estimates because they factor in estimation uncertainty and risk.

7. A. Reserve analysis accounts for cost uncertainty by including a contingency reserve, usually expressed as a percentage of the estimated cost.

8. C. The expected activity cost using the three-point beta distribution formula (also known as PERT) is calculated this way: $((4 \times \text{most likely}) + \text{optimistic} + \text{pessimistic}) / 6$. Therefore, the answer is $((4 \times 42) + 35 + 54) / 6 = 43$.

9. C. Future period operating costs are considered ongoing costs and are not part of project costs.

10. B. Bottom-up techniques are the most time-consuming and generally the most accurate estimates you can use. With bottom-up estimating, each work item is estimated and rolled up to a project total.

11. A. Funding limit reconciliation concerns reconciling the funds to be spent on the project with funding limits placed on the funding commitments for the project.

12. B. The cost baseline is displayed as an S curve because of the way project spending occurs. Spending begins slowly, picks up speed until the spending peak is reached, and then tapers off as the project winds down.

13. D. Cost of quality is a tool and technique of Estimate Costs. The tools and techniques of Determine Budget are cost aggregation, reserve analysis, expert judgment, historical relationships, and funding limit reconciliation.

14. A. Analogous—or top-down—estimating techniques are a form of expert judgment. Because this project is similar to another recent project, you can use the cost estimates from the previous project to help you quickly determine estimates for the current project.

15. D. There are 36 channels of communication, yourself plus 8 stakeholders. The formula is 9 (9 – 1) / 2 = 36. Lines of communication are considered when using the communications requirements analysis tool and technique.

16. D. Communications requirements analysis, communication technology, communication models, communication methods, and meetings are the tools and techniques of the Plan Communications Management process.

17. C. Acknowledgment means the receiver has received the message but does not mean they agree with the message.

18. A. Push communication assures that information is distributed to specific recipients but does not certify that it was understood by the intended recipients.

19. B. This describes interactive communication. It is a communication method, which is a tool and technique of Plan Communications Management.

20. C. Reasons for the distribution of information belong in the communications management plan.

Chapter 6: Risk Planning

1. B. The cause-and-effect flowcharts—also called *fishbone diagrams* or *Ishikawa diagrams*—show the relationships between the causes and effects of problems.

2. C. The purpose of Perform Qualitative Risk Analysis is to determine what impact the identified risk events will have on the project and the probability they'll occur. It also puts risks in priority order according to their effects on the project objectives and assigns a risk score for the project.

3. B. The risk management plan details how risk management processes will be implemented, monitored, and controlled throughout the life of the project. The risk management plan does not include responses to risks or triggers. Responses to risks are documented in the risk register as part of the Plan Risk Responses process.

4. C. Distributions graphically display the probability of risk to the project objectives as well as the time or cost elements.

5. D. The information-gathering techniques in the Identify Risks process are brainstorming, the Delphi technique, interviewing, and root cause analysis.

6. C. Perform Quantitative Risk Analysis analyzes the probability of risks and their consequences using a numerical rating. Perform Qualitative Risk Analysis might use numeric ratings but can use a high-medium-low scale as well.

7. C. Probability of achieving time and cost estimates is an update that is produced from the Perform Quantitative Risk Analysis process.

8. B. This risk event has the potential to save money on project costs, so it's an opportunity, and the appropriate strategy to use in this case is the exploit strategy.

9. D. This risk event has the potential to save money on project costs. Sharing involves using a third party to help assure that the opportunity occurs.

10. A. The best answer is A. Triggers are warning signs of an impending risk event.

11. C. The probability and impact matrix multiplies the probability and impact to determine a risk score. Using this score and a predetermined matrix, you determine if the score is a high, medium, or low designation.

12. B. Monte Carlo analysis is a simulation technique that computes project costs many times in an iterative fashion.

13. C. Mitigation attempts to reduce the impact of a risk event should it occur. Making plans to arrange for the leased equipment reduces the consequences of the risk.

14. A. Risk appetite, risk tolerance, and risk threshold are the components of risk attitude.

15. A. This question describes risk tolerance levels of the stakeholders. Risk triggers are recorded in the risk register during the Plan Risk Responses process. The risk of buying a machine from a new supplier would pose a threat to the project, not an opportunity. Interviewing might have been used, but this question wasn't describing the Identify Risks process.

16. B. The question describes sensitivity analysis, which is a tool and technique of the Perform Quantitative Risk Analysis process. Tornado diagrams are often used to display sensitivity analysis data.

17. B. Decision tree diagrams are used during the Perform Quantitative Risk Analysis process. All the other options are diagramming techniques used in the Identify Risks process.

18. D. The RBS describes risk categories, and the lowest level can be used as a checklist to help identify risks. Risk owners are not assigned from the RBS but typically are assigned as soon as the risk is identified.

19. D. This is a response strategy known as *passive acceptance* because the team has decided to take no action and make no plans for the risk. This is a strategy that can be used for either positive or negative risks.

20. C. Perform Qualitative Risk Analysis is a fast and easy method of determining probability and impact.

Chapter 7: Planning Project Resources

1. D. Make-or-buy analysis is determining whether it's more cost effective to purchase the goods or services needed for the project or more cost effective for the organization to produce them internally.

2. C. Firm fixed-price contracts have the highest risk to the seller and the least amount of risk to the buyer. However, the price the vendor charges for the product or service will compensate for the amount of risk they're assuming.

3. B. Either the buyer or the seller can write the SOW. Sometimes the buyer will write the SOW and the seller might modify it and send it back to the buyer for verification and approval.

4. A. The cost plus incentive fee contract reimburses the seller for the seller's allowable costs and includes an incentive or bonus for exceeding the performance criteria laid out in the contract.

5. D. The RAM and RACI charts are tools and techniques of this process.

6. C. Source selection criteria can be based on price alone when there are many vendors who can readily supply the goods or services. The question states that only three vendors make the machine, which means source selection criteria should be based on more than price.

7. A. A constraint can be anything that limits the option of the project team. Organizational structures, collective bargaining agreements, and economic conditions are all constraints that you might encounter during this process.

8. B. Fixed-price contracts can include incentives for meeting performance criteria, but the question states the vendor helping with the programming task will be reimbursed for their costs and, depending on your satisfaction with their results, may receive an additional award. This describes a cost plus award fee contract.

9. A. RACI stands for responsible, accountable, consult, and inform.

10. B. Plan Procurement Management can directly influence the project schedule, and the project schedule can directly influence this process.

11. B. This is a cost-reimbursable contract that includes a fee as a percentage of allowable costs. This type of contract is known as a cost plus percentage of cost (CPPC) contract.

12. A. Design of experiments is a tool and technique of the Plan Quality Management process that provides statistical analysis for changing key product or process elements all at once (not one at a time) to optimize the process.

13. C. Philip Crosby devised the zero defects theory, meaning do it right the first time. Proper Plan Quality Management leads to less rework and higher productivity. Joseph Juran's fitness for use says that stakeholders' and customers' expectations are met or exceeded.

14. A. W. Edwards Deming conjectured that the cost of quality is a management problem 85 percent of the time and that once the problem trickles down to the workers, it is outside their control.

15. C. The benefits of meeting quality requirements are increased stakeholder satisfaction, lower costs, higher productivity, and less rework.

16. A. Internal failure costs are costs associated with not meeting the customer's expectations while you still had control over the product. This results in rework, scrapping, and downtime.

17. B. Quality metrics are an output of the Plan Quality Management process and not part of the quality management plan.

18. D. This is an example of design of experiments.

19. B. Six Sigma is a measurement-based strategy that focuses on process improvement and variation reduction by applying Six Sigma methodologies to the project.

20. C. Teaming agreements are not a named input of the Plan Procurement Management process, but they are an input to all of the Planning processes collectively.

Chapter 8: Developing the Project Team

1. B. Corrective action brings anticipated future project outcomes back into alignment with the project management plan. Because an important deadline that depends on a positive outcome of this test is looming, the equipment is exchanged so that the project plan and project schedule are not impacted.

2. A. The most difficult aspect of the Direct and Manage Project Work process is coordinating and integrating all the project elements. The clue to this question is in the next-to-last sentence.

3. A. The Executing process group and Monitoring and Controlling process group serve as inputs to each other.

4. B. This question describes the deliverable output. Deliverables can be intangibles, such as the completion of training.

5. D. Work performance data includes elements such as schedule status, the status of deliverables completion, lessons learned, and resource utilization.

6. C. The enterprise environmental factors input of the Acquire Project Team process considers elements such as prior experience, interest in working on the project, cost rates, and availability of potential team members.

7. A. This question describes a defect repair that was discovered and implemented. Defect repairs come about as a result of approved changes. Approved changes are implemented in the Direct and Manage Project Work process. The question implies that the change request was approved because the problem was corrected and the rest of the production run went smoothly.

8. B. Teams in the norming stage of team development exhibit affection and familiarity with one another and make joint decisions.

9. C. The introduction of a new team member will start the formation and development of the team all over again with the forming stage.

10. D. Delegating is a situational leadership style that is used when team members have performed the task before and need little to no input from the manager. The supporting style requires some input from the leader. An autocratic manager makes all the decisions with no input from the team, and the laissez-faire leader lets the team make all the decisions and has little involvement with the team. Neither the autocratic nor laissez-faire leadership style is a named style in the Blanchard Situational Leadership II Model.

11. B. The Expectancy Theory says that people are motivated by the expectation of good outcomes. The outcome must be reasonable and attainable.

12. B. Co-location would bring your team members together in the same location and allow them to function more efficiently as a team. At a minimum, meeting in a common room, such as a war room, for all team meetings would bring the team closer together.

13. B. Collaborate/problem solve is a problem-solving technique that seeks to determine the facts and find solutions based on the facts. It involves hearing multiple viewpoints and examining several perspectives. This results in a win-win resolution for all parties.

14. A. Referent power is power that is inferred on a leader by their subordinates as a result of the high level of respect for the leader.

15. B. Theory Y managers believe that people will perform their best if they're provided with the proper motivation and the right expectations.

16. A. Improving competencies, team interactions, and the team environment are characteristics of the Develop Project Team process, not the Manage Project Team process.

17. D. This technique is called *360-degree feedback*. It's part of the project performance appraisals tool and technique of the Manage Project Team process.

18. C. This question refers to preassignments, which are a tool and technique of the Acquire Project Team process. The other tools and techniques of this process are negotiation, acquisition, virtual teams, and multicriteria analysis.

19. B. Smoothing (also known as accommodating) and withdrawal (also known as avoidance) are both lose-lose techniques. Forcing is a win-lose technique. Compromise or reconcile is where neither side wins or loses.

20. D. Theory Z encourages employee loyalty because jobs are offered for life. This leads to increased productivity, morale, and high employee satisfaction.

Chapter 9: Conducting Procurements and Sharing Information

1.   D. Procurement documents include bids, quotations, RFIs, IFBs, RFPs, RFQs, and so on as you learned in the Plan Procurement Management process. They are an input of the Conduct Procurements process.

2.   C. Receivers filter information through cultural considerations, knowledge of the subject matter, language abilities, geographic location, emotions, and attitudes.

3.   A. Project reports describe project status and are an item that is distributed, not a distribution tool.

4.   B. Group sizes of 5 to 11 participants make the most accurate decisions.

5.   B. Lessons learned (which is what this question describes) are useful for activities and processes for the current project as well as future projects.

6.   A. Weighted systems are a type of proposal evaluation technique, which is one of the tools and techniques of this process used to evaluate vendors based on selection criteria defined by the organization.

7.   D. Bidder conferences are also known as vendor conferences, pre-bid conferences, and contractor conferences, according to the *PMBOK® Guide*.

8.   D. Qualified seller lists are a component of the organizational assets input of Conduct Procurements. Their purpose is to provide information about the sellers.

9.   C. Independent estimates, also called *should cost estimates*, are a way to check proposed pricing.

10.   C. Fait accompli is a tactic used during contract negotiations where one party convinces the other that the particular issue is no longer relevant or cannot be changed.

11.   B. Market research is a tool and technique of the Plan procurement Management process. The tools and techniques of Conduct Procurements are bidder conference, proposal evaluation techniques, independent estimates, expert judgment, advertising, analytical techniques, and procurement negotiations.

12.   B. The acceptance of work results happens later during the Validate Scope process, not during Perform Quality Assurance.

13.   A. The process analysis tool and technique in the Perform Quality Assurance process includes root cause analysis to analyze a problem and solution and to create preventive actions.

14.   C. Quality Management and Control Tools includes affinity diagrams, process decision program charts, interrelationship digraphs, tree diagrams, prioritization matrices, activity network diagrams, and matrix diagrams.

15. C. Face-to-face meetings are the most effective means for resolving stakeholder issues, provided these meetings are practical.

16. B. Status meetings are to report on the progress of the project. They are not for demos or show-and-tell. Option C is not correct because stakeholders are not concerned about the content of the technical documentation; they need to know that a qualified technician has reviewed the technical documentation and that the documentation task is accurate and complete.

17. D. The selected sellers output requires a negotiated contract.

18. A. The project manager alone is responsible for managing stakeholder expectations.

19. B. Procurement negotiations, a tool and technique of Conduct Procurements, can become its own process with inputs and outputs for large or complex projects.

20. C. The requirements phase is where the SOW is prepared. The fourth phase is where the contract is awarded. The solicitation phase is where bids and proposals are prepared. However, evaluation criteria is not applied and reviewed until the award phase. The requisition phase is where the RFP is prepared.

Chapter 10: Measuring and Controlling Project Performance

1. D. Work authorization systems are a tool used during Project Executing processes and are a subset of the project management information system considered part of the enterprise environmental factors input of the Monitor and Control Project Work process. They formally initiate the work of each work package and clarify the assignments.

2. B. You are in the Monitor and Control Project Work process and should recommend a change request that can take the form of a corrective action. Preventive actions reduce the possibility of negative impacts from risk events and do not apply to this situation.

3. D. Negotiation is the preferred method of settling claims or disputes in the Control Procurements process.

4. D. The tools and techniques of the Control Procurements process are contract change control system, procurement performance reviews, inspection and audits, performance reporting, payment systems, claims administration, and records management system.

5. C. The contract change control system describes the processes you'll use to make changes to the contract; it is not a means of communication. The changes might include contract term changes, date changes, and termination of a contract.

6. B. According to the *PMBOK® Guide*, the Control Procurements process is closely coordinated with the Direct and Manage Project Work, Control Quality, Perform Integrated Change Control, and Control Risks processes.

7. A. Communication methods are a tool and technique of the Manage Communications process.

8. A. This question describes the Control Communications process, which is concerned with collecting and reporting information regarding project progress and project accomplishments to the stakeholders.

9. A. The tools and techniques of the Control Communications process are information management systems, expert judgment, and meetings. Records management systems are a tool and technique of the Control Procurements and Close Procurements processes.

10. B. The Delphi method, technology forecasting, scenario building, and forecast by analogy are all in the judgmental methods category of forecasting.

11. B. This question describes the issue log input of the Control Communications process. It is used to track issues, assign owners, track due dates, and more. Options A and C are tools and techniques of this process, and Option D is an input.

12. B. When you are dealing with contested changes, the *PMBOK® Guide* says that ADR (alternative dispute resolution) is the technique you should use to try to reach resolution. The other options are alternatives after you've tried ADR.

13. B. Change requests are submitted through other processes like the Monitor and Control Project Work process, and they are reviewed, tracked, managed, analyzed, and documented in this process.

14. D. Change control systems are documented procedures that describe how to submit change requests. They track the status of the change requests, document the management impacts of change, track the change approval status, and define the level of authority needed to approve changes. Change control systems do not approve or deny the changes—that's the responsibility of the change control board (CCB).

15. C. The key to this question was that the characteristics of the product were documented with this tool. Configuration management documents the physical characteristics and the functionality of the product of the project.

16. C. Change control boards (CCBs) review change requests and have the authority to approve or deny them. Their authority is defined by the configuration control and change control process.

17. A. The three activities associated with configuration management are configuration identification, configuration status accounting, and configuration verification and auditing.

18. D. Configuration management systems are a way to manage approved changes and baselines.

19. C. These are elements with which the Monitor and Control Project Work process is concerned.

20. C. The other names for CCB's may include TAB, which stands for technical assessment board; TRB, which is a technical review board; and ERB, which is an engineering review board.

Chapter 11: Controlling Work Results

1. A. Changes to product scope should be reflected in the project scope.

2. D. Scatter diagrams display the relationship between an independent and dependent variable over time.

3. C. WBS element changes are scope changes. According to the *PMBOK® Guide*, schedule revisions are often required as a result of scope changes.

4. C. The Validate Scope process is concerned with the acceptance of work results. It also formalizes the acceptance of the project scope.

5. B. Validate Scope should document the level and degree of completion of the project given the circumstances in this question. If you come back at a later date and restart this project, Validate Scope will describe how far the project progressed and give you an idea of where to start.

6. B. Schedule variances will sometimes—but not always—impact the schedule. Changes to noncritical path tasks will not likely impact the schedule, but changes to critical path tasks will always impact the schedule.

7. C. To-complete performance index determines the cost performance that must be realized for the remaining work of the project to meet a goal such as BAC or EAC.

8. D. Budget updates might require cost re-baselining.

9. A. Schedule variance is (EV – PV) and schedule performance index is (EV / PV).

10. C. Earned value is referred to as the value of the work that's been completed to date compared to the budget.

11. D. The CV is a positive number and is calculated by subtracting AC from EV as follows: 250 – 200 = 50. A positive CV means the project is coming in under budget, meaning you've spent less than you planned as of the measurement date.

12. A. The SV calculation is EV – PV. If PV is a higher number than EV, you'll get a negative number as a result.

13. B. CPI is calculated as follows: EV / AC. In this case, 250 / 200 = 1.25.

14. B. When you accept project performance to date and assume future ETC work will be performed at the budgeted rate, EAC is calculated as follows: AC + (BAC – EV). Therefore, the calculation for this question looks like this: (200 + 800) – 250 = 750.

15. C. The correct formula for ETC for this question is as follows: EAC – AC. Therefore, ETC is as follows: 375 – 200 = 175.

16. A. When project performance is expected to behave like past performance, EAC is calculated as follows: EAC = BAC / CPI. Therefore, the calculation for this question looks like this: 800 / 1.25 = 640.

17. D. You first have to calculate EAC in order to calculate VAC. EAC for variances that are atypical is AC + (BAC – EV). So, our numbers are 275 + (500 – 250) = 525. VAC is calculated this way: BAC – EAC. Therefore, 500 – 525 = –25. Our costs are not doing as well as anticipated.

18. C. You must first calculate CPI in order to calculate ETC. CPI is EV / AC. We have 1150 / 1275 = 0.90. ETC with typical cost variances is (BAC –EV) / CPI. Our numbers are (2500 – 1150) / 0.90 = 1500.

19. B. Workarounds are unplanned responses. They deal with negative risk events as they occur. As the name implies, workarounds were not previously known to the project team. The risk event was unplanned, so no contingency plan existed to deal with the risk event, and thus it required a workaround.

20. A. CPI is considered the most critical EVM metric. It measures the cost efficiency of the project work completed at the measuring date.

Chapter 12: Closing the Project and Applying Professional Responsibility

1. D. Integration occurs when resources, equipment, or property are reassigned or redeployed back to the organization or to another project.

2. A. Starvation occurs because the project no longer receives the resources needed to continue. Resources include people, equipment, money, and the like.

3. A. Extinction is the best type of project end because it means the project was completed successfully and accepted by the sponsor or customer.

4. C. The project manager is responsible for documenting the formal acceptance of the work of the contract. This should be done during Close Procurements when projects are performed under contract or during Close Project or Phase if no work was performed under contract. In cases where part of the work was performed under contract and part with in-house staff, formal acceptance should occur in both of these processes.

5. A. Procurement audits are used to review the procurement process and identify and document any lessons learned during the procurement process for future reference.

6. A. Lessons learned document the experiences, successes, and failures that occurred during this project for future reference. There isn't enough information in the question to determine whether option B or D is correct. Option C is not correct because the project was completed.

7. A. According to the *PMBOK® Guide*, the procurement audit examines the procurement processes from Plan Procurement Management through Close Procurements.

8. A. You are not responsible for the personal integrity of others, but as project manager you do have influence over others, such as your project team members.

9. C. Integrity means you'll honestly report project outcomes and status. Your personal gain should not be placed above the satisfaction of the customer.

10. D. The best answer to this problem is to develop alternative solutions to address the design error. Reducing technical requirements might be an alternative solution, but it's not one you'd implement without looking at all the alternatives. Ignoring the error and going forward with production will result in an unsatisfactory product for the customer.

11. A. A luncheon date could be considered a conflict of interest prior to awarding a contract to a vendor. Consider what a competitor of this vendor would think if they spotted you having lunch together.

12. B. The best response to this situation is to thank the vendor and decline based on the fact that this could be considered personal gain on your part. Option D might seem correct, but remember, you're not responsible for the integrity of others. It's often common business practice for vendors to offer gifts to potential customers.

13. D. The best response in this case is to accept the gift because it would cause great offense to the other party if you were to decline. Report the gift and the circumstances as soon as possible to the appropriate parties at your company.

14. D. This is a conflict of interest situation, and you should report it as a violation of the *PMI®* *Code of Ethics and Professional Conduct.*

15. A. Documenting the requirements and meeting them is one of the key things you can do to ensure customer satisfaction. The requirements describe what the customer is looking for, and the final product is compared against them to determine whether all of the requirements were met.

16. A. The most correct response is to first provide training to your team members to educate them regarding how to respect and work with others from different cultures. Co-location might not be possible when you're working with team members from two different countries. Team-building exercises are a good idea as well but are not your first course of action.

17. B. The situation presented here requires you to put the interest of the company and the confidentiality of the data above your own personal interests or those of your stakeholders. Option D is not the most correct response because it says you believe the information is public. This implies you haven't verified whether the data is private or public. Until you know, treat the data as confidential. In this case, the information is confidential and should be shared only with those who have a valid reason for using it.

18. C. As project manager, it's your responsibility to make sure the people you will be sharing data with have the proper permissions to see the data; this question indicated that you did that. In this case, option D is not correct because it implies that you did not verify ahead of time that the stakeholder had the proper levels of approval to use the data.

19. D. Culture shock is the disoriented feeling that people might experience when working in a foreign country.

20. A. The most appropriate response is to deny the request. Software is considered intellectual property and should not be used for personal gain or given to others without prior consent from the organization. This question states that the release of the beta software is handled through the marketing department, so you should not give your friend a copy of the software outside of this process.

Appendix B

Process Inputs and Outputs

Throughout this book, I've discussed the inputs and outputs to the PMI® processes. In this appendix, you'll find the inputs, tools and techniques, outputs, and Knowledge Areas of the project management processes listed by process in the order they appear in the text. I think you'll appreciate the convenience of having all this information in one location. Enjoy!

Initiating Processes

Table B.1 lists the inputs, tools and techniques, outputs, and Knowledge Areas for the Initiating process group.

TABLE B.1 Initiating processes

Process name	Inputs	Tools and techniques	Outputs	Knowledge Area
Develop Project Charter	Project statement of work	Expert judgment	Project charter	Integration
	Business case	Facilitation techniques		
	Agreements			
	Enterprise environmental factors			
	Organizational process assets			
Identify Stakeholders	Project charter	Stakeholder analysis	Stakeholder register	Stakeholder
	Procurement documents	Expert judgment		
	Enterprise environmental factors	Meetings		
	Organizational process assets			

Planning Processes

Table B.2 lists the inputs, tools and techniques, outputs, and Knowledge Areas for the processes in the Planning process group.

TABLE B.2   Planning processes

Process name	Inputs	Tools and techniques	Outputs	Knowledge Area
Develop Project Management Plan	Project charter	Expert judgment	Project management plan	Integration
	Outputs from other processes	Facilitation techniques		
	Enterprise environmental factors			
	Organizational process assets			
Plan Scope Management	Project management plan	Expert judgment	Scope management plan	Scope
	Project charter	Meetings	Requirements management plan	
	Enterprise environmental factors			
	Organizational process assets			
				Scope
Collect Requirements	Scope management plan	Interviews	Requirements documentation	Scope
	Requirements management plan	Focus groups	Requirements traceability matrix	
	Stakeholder management plan	Facilitated workshops		

TABLE B.2   Planning processes *(continued)*

Process name	Inputs	Tools and techniques	Outputs	Knowledge Area
	Project charter	Group creativity techniques		
	Stakeholder register	Group decision-making techniques		
		Questionnaires and surveys		
		Observations		
		Prototypes		
		Benchmarking		
		Context diagrams		
		Document analysis		
Define Scope	Scope management plan	Expert judgment	Project scope statement	Scope
	Project charter	Product analysis	Project documents updates	
	Requirements documentation	Alternatives generation		
	Organizational process assets	Facilitated workshops		
Create WBS	Scope management plan	Decomposition	Scope baseline	Scope
	Project scope statement	Expert judgment	Project documents updates	
	Requirements documentation			
	Enterprise environmental factors			
	Organizational process assets			

Process name	Inputs	Tools and techniques	Outputs	Knowledge Area
Plan Schedule Management	Project management plan	Expert judgment	Schedule management plan	Time
	Project charter	Analytical techniques		
	Enterprise environmental factors	Meetings		
	Organizational process assets			
Define Activities	Schedule management plan	Decomposition	Activity list	Time
	Scope baseline	Rolling wave planning	Activity attributes	
	Enterprise environmental factors	Expert judgment	Milestone list	
	Organizational process assets			
Sequence Activities	Schedule management plan	Precedence diagramming method (PDM)	Project schedule network diagrams	Time
	Activity list	Dependency determination	Project documents updates	
	Activity attributes	Leads and lags		
	Milestone list			
	Project scope statement			
	Enterprise environmental factors			
	Organizational process assets			
Estimate Activity Resources	Schedule management plan	Expert judgment	Activity resource requirements	Time
	Activity list	Alternatives analysis	Resource breakdown structure	
	Activity attributes	Published estimating data	Project documents updates	
	Resource calendars	Bottom-up estimating		

TABLE B.2 Planning processes *(continued)*

Process name	Inputs	Tools and techniques	Outputs	Knowledge Area
	Risk register			
	Activity cost estimates			
	Enterprise environmental factors	Project management software		
	Organizational process assets			
Estimate Activity Durations	Schedule management plan	Expert judgment	Activity duration estimates	Time
	Activity list	Analogous estimating	Project documents updates	
	Activity attributes	Parametric estimating		
	Activity resource requirements	Three-point estimating		
	Resource calendars	Group-decision making techniques		
	Project scope statement	Reserve analysis		
	Risk register			
	Resource breakdown structure			
	Enterprise environmental factors			
	Organizational process assets			
Develop Schedule	Schedule management plan	Schedule network analysis	Schedule baseline	Time
	Activity list	Critical path method	Project schedule	
	Activity attributes	Critical chain method	Schedule data	

Process name	Inputs	Tools and techniques	Outputs	Knowledge Area
	Project schedule network diagrams	Resource optimization techniques	Project calendars	
	Activity resource requirements	Modeling techniques	Project management plan updates	
	Resource calendars	Leads and lags	Project documents updates	
	Activity duration estimates	Schedule compression		
	Project scope statement	Scheduling tool		
	Risk register			
	Project staff assignments			
	Resource breakdown structure			
	Enterprise environmental factors			
	Organizational process assets			
Plan Cost Management	Project management plan	Expert judgment	Cost management plan	Cost
	Project charter	Analytical techniques		
	Enterprise environmental factors	Meetings		
	Organizational process assets			
Estimate Costs	Cost management plan	Expert judgment	Activity cost estimates	Cost
	Human resource management plan	Analogous estimating	Basis of estimates	
	Scope baseline	Parametric estimating	Project documents updates	

TABLE B.2 Planning processes *(continued)*

Process name	Inputs	Tools and techniques	Outputs	Knowledge Area
	Project schedule	Bottom-up estimating		
	Risk register	Three-point estimating		
	Enterprise environmental factors	Reserve analysis		
	Organizational process assets	Cost of quality		
		Project management software		
		Vendor bid analysis		
		Group decision-making techniques		
Determine Budget	Cost management plan	Cost aggregation	Cost baseline	Cost
	Scope baseline	Reserve analysis	Project funding requirements	
	Activity cost estimates	Expert judgment	Project documents updates	
	Basis of estimates	Historical relationships		
	Project schedule	Funding limit reconciliation		
	Resource calendars			
	Risk register			
	Agreements			
	Organizational process assets			

Process name	Inputs	Tools and techniques	Outputs	Knowledge Area
Plan Quality Management	Project management plan	Cost–benefit analysis	Quality management plan	Quality
	Stakeholder register	Cost of quality	Process improvement plan	
	Risk register	Seven basic quality tools	Quality metrics	
	Requirements documentation	Benchmarking	Quality checklists	
	Enterprise environmental factors	Design of experiments	Project documents updates	
	Organizational process assets	Statistical sampling		
		Additional quality planning tools		
		Meetings		
Plan Human Resource Management	Project management plan	Organization charts and position descriptions	Human resource management plan	Human Resource
	Activity resource requirements	Networking		
	Enterprise environmental factors	Organizational theory		
	Organizational process assets	Expert judgment		
		Meetings		
Plan Communications Management	Project management plan	Communication requirements analysis	Communications management plan	Communications
	Stakeholder register	Communication technology	Project documents updates	
	Enterprise environmental factors	Communication models		
	Organizational process assets	Communication methods		

TABLE B.2 Planning processes *(continued)*

Process name	Inputs	Tools and techniques	Outputs	Knowledge Area
		Meetings		
Plan Risk Management	Project management plan	Analytical techniques		
	Project charter	Expert judgment	Risk management plan	Risk
	Stakeholder register	Meetings		
	Enterprise environmental factors			
	Organizational process assets			
Identify Risks	Risk management plan	Documentation reviews	Risk register	Risk
	Cost management plan	Information gathering techniques		
	Schedule management plan	Checklist analysis		
	Quality management plan	Assumptions analysis		
	Human resource management plan	Diagramming techniques		
	Scope baseline	SWOT analysis		
	Activity cost estimates	Expert judgment		
	Activity duration estimates			
	Stakeholder register			
	Project documents			

Process name	Inputs	Tools and techniques	Outputs	Knowledge Area
	Procurement documents			
	Enterprise environmental factors			
	Organizational process assets			
Perform Qualitative Risk Analysis	Risk management plan	Risk probability and impact assessment	Project documents updates	Risk
	Scope baseline	Probability and impact matrix		
	Risk register	Risk data quality assessment		
	Enterprise environmental factors	Risk categorization		
	Organizational process assets	Risk urgency assessment		
		Expert judgment		
Perform Quantitative Risk Analysis	Risk management plan	Data gathering and representation techniques	Project documents updates	
	Cost management plan	Quantitative risk analysis and modeling techniques		Risk
	Schedule management plan	Expert judgment		
	Risk register			
	Enterprise environmental factors			
	Organizational process assets			
Plan Risk Responses	Risk management plan	Strategies for negative risks or threats	Project management plan updates	Risk
	Risk register	Strategies for positive risks or opportunities	Project documents updates	

TABLE B.2 Planning processes *(continued)*

Process name	Inputs	Tools and techniques	Outputs	Knowledge Area
		Contingent response strategies		
		Expert judgment		
Plan Procurement Management	Project management plan	Make-or-buy analysis	Procurement management plan	
	Requirements documentation	Expert judgment	Procurement statement of work	Procurement
	Risk register	Market research	Procurement documents	
	Activity resource requirements	Meetings	Source selection criteria	
	Project schedule		Make-or-buy decisions	
	Activity cost estimates		Change requests	
	Stakeholder register		Project documents updates	
	Enterprise environmental factors			
	Organizational process assets			
Plan Stakeholder Management	Project management plan	Expert judgment	Stakeholder management plan	Stakeholder
	Stakeholder register	Meetings	Project documents updates	
	Enterprise environmental factors	Analytical techniques		
	Organizational process assets			

Executing Processes

Table B.3 lists the inputs, tools and techniques, outputs, and Knowledge Areas for the processes in the Executing process group.

TABLE B.3   Executing processes

Process name	Inputs	Tools and techniques	Outputs	Knowledge Area
Direct and Manage Project Work	Project management plan	Expert judgment	Deliverables	Integration
	Approved change requests	Project management information system	Work performance data	
	Enterprise environmental factors	Meetings	Change requests	
	Organizational process assets		Project management plan updates	
			Project documents updates	
Perform Quality Assurance	Quality management plan	Quality management and control tools	Change requests	Quality
	Process improvement plan	Quality audits	Project management plan updates	
	Quality metrics	Process analysis	Project documents updates	
	Quality control measurements		Organizational process assets updates	
	Project documents			
Acquire Project Team	Human resource management plan	Pre-assignment	Project staff assignments	Human Resource
	Enterprise environmental factors	Negotiation	Resource calendars	

TABLE B.3 Executing processes *(continued)*

Process name	Inputs	Tools and techniques	Outputs	Knowledge Area
	Organizational process assets	Acquisition	Project management plan updates	
		Virtual teams		
		Multicriteria decision analysis		
Develop Project Team	Human resource management plan	Interpersonal skills	Team performance assessments	Human Resource
	Project staff assignments	Training	Enterprise environmental factors updates	
	Resource calendars	Team-building activities		
		Ground rules		
		Co-location		
		Recognition and rewards		
		Personnel assessment tools		
Manage Project Team	Human resource management plan	Observation and conversation	Change requests	Human Resource
	Project staff assignments	Project performance appraisals	Project management plan updates	
	Team performance assessments	Conflict management	Project documents updates	
	Issue log	Interpersonal skills		
	Work performance reports		Enterprise environmental factors updates	

Process name	Inputs	Tools and techniques	Outputs	Knowledge Area
	Organizational process assets		Organizational process assets updates	
Manage Communications	Communications management plan	Communication technology	Project communications	Communi-cations
	Work perfor-mance reports	Communication models	Project documents updates	
	Enterprise environmental factors	Communication methods	Project management plan updates	
	Organizational process assets	Information management systems	Organizational process assets updates	
		Performance reporting		
Conduct Procurements	Procurement management plan	Bidder conference	Selected sellers	Procurement
	Procurement documents	Proposal evaluation techniques	Agreements	
	Source selection criteria	Independent estimates	Resource calendars	
	Seller proposals	Expert judgment	Change requests	
	Project docu-ments	Advertising	Project manage-ment plan updates	
	Make-or-buy decisions	Analytical techniques	Project documents updates	
	Procurement statement of work	Procurement negotiations		
	Organizational process assets			
Manage Stakeholder Engagement	Stakeholder man-agement plan	Communication methods	Issue log	Stakeholder
	Communications management plan	Interpersonal skills	Change requests	

TABLE B.3   Executing processes *(continued)*

Process name	Inputs	Tools and techniques	Outputs	Knowledge Area
	Change log	Management skills	Project management plan updates	
	Organizational process assets		Project documents updates	
			Organizational process assets updates	

Monitoring and Controlling Processes

Table B.4 lists the inputs, tools and techniques, outputs, and Knowledge Areas for the Monitoring and Controlling group processes.

TABLE B.4   Monitoring and Controlling processes

Process name	Inputs	Tools and techniques	Outputs	Knowledge Area
Monitor and Control Project Work	Project management plan	Expert judgment	Change requests	Integration
	Schedule forecasts	Analytical techniques	Work performance reports	
	Cost forecasts	Project management information system	Project management plan updates	
	Validated changes	Meetings	Project documents updates	
	Work performance information			
	Enterprise environmental factors			

Process name	Inputs	Tools and techniques	Outputs	Knowledge Area
	Organizational process assets			
Perform Integrated Change Control	Project management plan	Expert judgment	Approved change requests	Integration
	Work performance reports	Change control meetings	Change log	
	Change requests	Change control tools	Project management plan updates	
	Enterprise environmental factors		Project documents updates	
	Organizational process assets			
Validate Scope	Project management plan	Inspection	Accepted deliverables	Scope
	Requirements documentation	Group decision-making techniques	Change requests	
	Requirements traceability matrix		Work performance information	
	Verified deliverables		Project documents updates	
	Work performance data			
Control Scope	Project management plan	Variance analysis	Work performance information	Scope
	Requirements documentation		Change requests	
	Requirements traceability matrix		Project management plan updates	
	Work performance data		Project documents updates	

TABLE B.4   Monitoring and Controlling processes *(continued)*

Process name	Inputs	Tools and techniques	Outputs	Knowledge Area
	Organizational process assets		Organizational process assets updates	
Control Schedule	Project management plan	Performance reviews	Work performance information	Time
	Project schedule	Project management software	Schedule forecasts	
	Work performance data	Resource optimization techniques	Change requests	
	Project calendars	Modeling techniques	Project management plan updates	
	Schedule data	Leads and lags	Project documents updates	
	Organizational process assets	Schedule compression	Organizational process assets updates	
		Scheduling tool		
Control Costs	Project management plan	Earned value management	Work performance information	Cost
	Project funding requirements	Forecasting	Cost forecasts	
	Work performance data	To-complete performance index (TCPI)		
	Organizational process assets	Performance reviews	Change Requests	
		Project management software	Project management plan updates	
		Reserve analysis	Project documents updates	

Process name	Inputs	Tools and techniques	Outputs	Knowledge Area
			Organizational process assets updates	
Control Quality	Project management plan	Seven basic quality tools	Quality control measurements	Quality
	Quality metrics	Statistical sampling	Validated changes	
	Quality checklists	Inspection	Validated deliverables	
	Work performance data	Approved change requests review	Work performance information	
	Approved change requests		Change requests	
	Deliverables		Project management plan updates	
	Project documents		Project documents updates	
	Organizational process assets		Organizational process assets updates	
Control Communications	Project management plan	Information management systems	Work performance information	Communications
	Project communications	Expert judgment	Change requests	
	Issue log	Meetings	Project management plan updates	
	Work performance data		Project documents updates	
	Organizational process assets		Organizational process assets updates	

TABLE B.4   Monitoring and Controlling processes *(continued)*

Process name	Inputs	Tools and techniques	Outputs	Knowledge Area
Control Risks	Project management plan	Risk reassessment	Work performance information	Risk
	Risk register	Risk audits	Change requests	
	Work performance data	Variance and trend analysis	Project management plan updates	
	Work performance reports	Technical performance measurement	Project documents updates	
		Reserve analysis	Organizational process assets updates	
		Meetings		
Control Procurements	Project management plan	Contract change control system	Work performance information	Procurement
	Procurement documents	Procurement performance reviews	Change requests	
	Agreements	Inspections and audits	Project management plan updates	
	Approved change requests	Performance reporting	Project documents updates	
	Work performance reports	Payment systems	Organizational process assets updates	
	Work performance data	Claims administration		
		Records management system		
Control Stakeholder Engagement	Project management plan	Information management systems	Work performance information	Stakeholder

Process name	Inputs	Tools and techniques	Outputs	Knowledge Area
	Issue log	Expert judgment	Change requests	
	Work performance data	Meetings	Project management plan updates	
	Project documents		Project documents updates	
			Organizational process assets updates	

Closing Processes

Table B.5 lists the inputs, tools and techniques, outputs, and Knowledge Areas for the processes in the Closing process group.

TABLE B.5 Closing processes

Process name	Inputs	Tools and techniques	Outputs	Knowledge Area
Close Project or Phase	Project management plan	Expert judgment	Final product, service, or result transition	Integration
	Accepted deliverables	Analytical techniques	Organizational process assets updates	
	Organizational process assets	Meetings		
Close Procurements	Project management plan	Procurement audits	Closed procurements	Procurement
	Procurement documents	Procurement negotiations	Organizational process assets updates	
		Records management system		

Appendix
C

About the Additional Study Tools

IN THIS APPENDIX:

✓ Additional study tools

✓ System requirements

✓ Using the study tools

✓ Troubleshooting

Additional Study Tools

The following sections are arranged by category and summarize the software and other goodies you'll find at the companion website. If you need help with installing the items, refer to the installation instructions in the "Using the Study Tools" section of this appendix.

> The additional study tools can be found at www.sybex.com/go/pmpsg7e. Here, you will get instructions on how to download the files to your hard drive.

Sybex Test Engine

The files contain the Sybex test engine, which includes two bonus practice exams, as well as two bonus CAPM exams.

Electronic Flashcards

These handy electronic flashcards are just what they sound like. One side contains a question, and the other side shows the answer.

PDF of Glossary of Terms

We have included an electronic version of the glossary in PDF format. You can view the electronic version of the glossary with Adobe Reader.

Adobe Reader

We've also included a link to download a copy of Adobe Reader so you can view PDF files that accompany the book's content. For more information on Adobe Reader or to check for a newer version, visit Adobe's website at www.adobe.com/products/reader/.

Audio Files

Author Kim Heldman has provided audio review files in MP3 format. Download them to your MP3 player to get a last-minute review, in audio format.

System Requirements

Make sure your computer meets the minimum system requirements shown in the following list. If your computer doesn't match up to most of these requirements, you may have problems using the software and files. For the latest and greatest information, please refer to the ReadMe file located in the downloads.

- A PC running Microsoft Windows XP or later
- An Internet connection

Using the Study Tools

To install the items, follow these steps:

1. Download the zip file to your hard drive, and unzip to an appropriate location. Instructions on where to download this file can be found here: www.sybex.com/go/pmpsg7e.
2. Click the Start.exe file to open the study tools file.
3. Read the license agreement, and then click the Accept button if you want to use the study tools.

The main interface appears. The interface allows you to access the content with just one or two clicks.

Troubleshooting

Wiley has attempted to provide programs that work on most computers with the minimum system requirements. Alas, your computer may differ, and some programs may not work properly for some reason.

The likeliest problem is that either you don't have enough memory (RAM) for the programs you want to use or you have other programs running that are affecting installation or running of a program. If you get an error message such as "Not enough memory" or "Setup cannot continue," follow one or more of these suggestions and then try using the software again:

Turn off any antivirus software running on your computer.   Installation programs sometimes mimic virus activity and may make your computer incorrectly believe that it's being infected by a virus.

Close all running programs.   The more programs you have running, the less memory is available to other programs. Installation programs typically update files and programs, so if you keep other programs running, installation may not work properly.

Have your local computer store add more RAM to your computer.   Adding more memory can really help the speed of your computer and allow more programs to run at the same time.

Customer Care

If you have trouble with the book's companion study tools, please call the Wiley Product Technical Support phone number at (800) 762-2974, or email them at `http://sybex .custhelp.com/`.

Index

P

S

X

Z

ree Online Study Tools

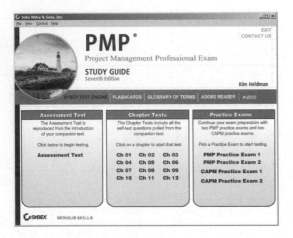

Go to www.sybex.com/go/pmpsg7e to register and gain access to this comprehensive study tool package.

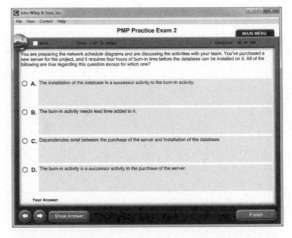

Comprehensive Study Tool Package Includes:

- **Assessment Test** to help you focus your study to specific objectives

- **Chapter Review Questions** for each chapter of the book

- **Two Full-Length PMP Practice Exams** to test your knowledge of the material **PLUS Two bonus CAPM exams**

- **Electronic Flashcards** to reinforce your learning and give you that last-minute test prep before the exam

- **Two Hours** of audio review from author Kim Heldman

- **Searchable Glossary** gives you instant access to the key terms you'll need to know for the exam

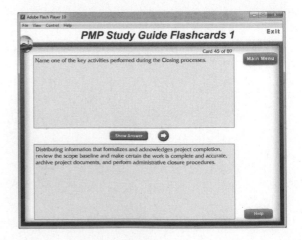